Immersive Technology for the Gig Economy:

Transformative Business Practices

Anna Masłoń-Orac
SGH Warsaw School of Economics, Poland

Pooja Kansra
Mittal School of Business, Lovely Professional University, Punjab, India

Sugandh Arora
Symbiosis School of Economics, Symbiosis International University, Pune, India

Sumit Oberoi
Indian Institute of Management Bangalore, India

IGI Global
Scientific Publishing
Publishing Tomorrow's Research Today

Vice President of Editorial Melissa Wagner
Director of Acquisitions Mikaela Felty
Director of Book Development Jocelynn Hessler
Production Manager Mike Brehm
Cover Design Jose Rosado

Published in the United States of America by
IGI Global Scientific Publishing
701 East Chocolate Avenue
Hershey, PA, 17033, USA
Tel: 717-533-8845
Fax: 717-533-7115
Website: https://www.igi-global.com E-mail: cust@igi-global.com

Library of Congress Cataloging-in-Publication Data

Names: MasÅ‚onÌ -Oracz, Anna, 1977- editor
Title: Immersive technology for the gig economy : transformative business practices / [edited by] Anna MasÅ‚onÌ -Oracz, Pooja Kansra, Sugandh Arora, Sumit Oberoi.
Description: Hershey, PA : IGI Global Scientific Publishing, [2025] | Includes bibliographical references and index. | Summary: "The book is intended for entrepreneurs and business managers interested in optimizing their business models across all areas of management"-- Provided by publisher.
Identifiers: LCCN 2025007587 (print) | LCCN 2025007588 (ebook) | ISBN 9798337312903 hardcover | ISBN 9798337312910 paperback | ISBN 9798337312927 ebook
Subjects: LCSH: Gig economy | Temporary employment | Personnel management | Virtual reality | Diffusion of innovations
Classification: LCC HD5109 .I46 2025 (print) | LCC HD5109 (ebook) | DDC 331.25/727--dc23/eng/20250508
LC record available at https://lccn.loc.gov/2025007587
LC ebook record available at https://lccn.loc.gov/2025007588

British Cataloguing in Publication Data
A Cataloguing in Publication record for this book is available from the British Library.

Table of Contents

Detailed Table of Contents

India's gig economy is reshaping the labor market, providing employment opportunities through platforms like Uber, Swiggy, and Amazon Flex. With the gig workforce in India projected to reach 59.28 million by 2035, this sector is emerging as crucial in fostering financial inclusion and regional economic decentralization. However, challenges such as wage volatility, job precarity, and inadequate social security disproportionately affect low-skilled workers, while high-skilled professionals benefit from greater stability. Gender disparities, algorithm-driven work allocation, and monopolistic practices further exacerbate inequalities. This study examines the economic contributions and structural vulnerabilities of the gig economy, advocating for legal recognition, fair wages, portable benefits, skill development programs, and stronger regulatory frameworks. A balanced approach, which ensures that workers are protected, without stifling innovation is essential to fostering an equitable and sustainable gig economy in India.

This paper examines the determinants of economic consequences in the gig economy through regression analyses of five key factors: platform design, regulatory environment, worker characteristics, market conditions, and technological infrastructure. Using convenience sampling, regression model explains 75.1% of the variance in economic outcomes, revealing a significant hierarchy of influence among these factors. Worker characteristics and market conditions emerged as the most potent predictors, challenging narratives that prioritize technological or regulatory factors. The findings suggest potential synergistic interactions among

accessibility and equity through innovations such as AI tutors, regional language resources, and low-cost e-reading devices. The study captures the global patterns with adoption before and after COVID-19 and evaluates various economic impacts- the creation of jobs and possible replacement for old positions-.

A country's exemplary financial structure provides an unquestionable foundation for sustainable development and economic progress. It makes banking services available to citizens at any level of the economy at convenient rates. The meaning of inclusive finance was further expanded to encompass other services financed, especially the fiduciary guardianship for savings and an extensive range of loan products for small businesses, as well as other financial mechanisms that reduce financing risk through a partition of investments and insurance mediation (Wang et al.2022). Inclusive finance calls for a solemn catalyst of all individuals' well-being and demystification by pulling down the bridge and teeming injustice. The world is a vastly different place today than it was a quarter of a century ago. A combination of civil unrest and technological evolution has reset the stage that people all over the globe have been living on. For some, this is tremendously positive news as for others this represents another step backwards for the progress made in the second half of the 20th century.

Sustainable finance has gained significant attention in recent years, fueled by the rise of the circular economy. It emphasizes evaluating investments with a focus on environmental, social, and governance (ESG) factors, aligning financial activities with sustainable development goals for long-term resilience in economic systems. This study aims to analyze co-authorship and co-citation trends in research on

"Sustainable Finance Management Systems (SFMS) and the Circular Economy," using data from 37,132 articles collected from Dimensions AI, and analyzed through VOSviewer software. The bibliometric analysis highlights growth patterns and trends in sustainable finance and circular economy research, illustrating valuable connections between authors, citations, and countries. It also identifies emerging research areas and sector-specific demands, providing insights for global collaboration and interdisciplinary partnerships in sustainable finance and the circular economy.

This chapter introduces the blockchain and other immersive technologies such as AI, cryptocurrency, RPA, De-Fi, virtual reality, and augmented reality. Followed by sufficient background information, it includes a literature review while identifying the research gap. Cases and real-world applications support the content to a larger extent. Challenges and hurdles during technological adoption by financial managers have evolved. Regulatory issues pertaining to cybersecurity and other technologies are inculcated. At last, conclusions and future recommendations are provided on ESG integration in digital finance and talent shortage in fintech. This chapter also explores the unique role of financial managers in assisting companies with their risk management. It presents a descriptive introduction of block-chain and other immersive technologies in the field of financial management. It also discusses how financial managers' core competencies add significant value in the growing digital era.

The current study focusses on how the independent variables financial attitude (FA), financial behaviour (FB), and financial knowledge (FK)) are related to the degree of digital financial literacy (DFL) among working people in Delhi NCR, India. This study investigates financial literacy among employed individuals in the Delhi-National Capital Region, using a sample of 354 participants from public and private enterprises. Data was gathered through a structured questionnaire. To analyze variable relationships and assess model validity, Structural Equation Modeling (SEM) was applied This study employs route analysis to examine the relationship among three independent variables for hypothesis testing. The findings reveal that digital financial literacy synergizes with financial behaviour and financial attitude, indicating that individuals with higher digital financial literacy have a propensity for responsible financial actions and positive perceptions toward financial management.

Khushi Jain, Sri Balaji University, Pune, India
B. Anjaly, SGI's Food and Agri Business School, India
Shiba Prasad Mohanty, Symbiosis International University, Pune, India
Santosh Gopalkrishnan, Symbiosis International University, Dubai, UAE

This study responds to how the macroeconomic variables, i.e., inflation and interest rate, influence personal finance. Specifically, the study explores the influence of macroeconomic indicators such as interest rates and inflation on financial behaviour in India. It also investigates the role of economic awareness, income, social factors, and financial attitude. This paper employs structural equation modelling (SEM) to examine how these aspects influence behavioural finance. The findings aim to shape the content of financial literacy and policy interventions by providing insights on how inflation and shifts in interest rates mean to perceptions of financial soundness for financial institutions and policymakers.

Ananya Pandey, Christ University, Bangalore, India

Over the past several years, blockchain technology has become more and more significant and widely accepted. Independent businesses that are actively involved in the upstream and downstream flows of goods, services, money and information from a source to a customer make a supply chain. Members of the supply chain must collaborate and exchange information in order to be managed effectively. Blockchain technology offers a platform for direct communication between supply chain participants to exchange reliable and unchangeable data, which has the potential to significantly enhance supply chain management and accomplish supply chain performance goals. Notwithstanding its potential, there are obstacles to the broad use of blockchain. Legal and regulatory issues are also very important for supply chain management in the future. Keeping in view the above, the chapter analyzes the role of blockchain in the industrial supply chain and explores the facet of transparency in supply chain management.

Blockchain technology has revolutionized Human Resource Management (HRM) practices. The study aims to unearth the role of blockchain in recruitment and selection, payroll management and managing the gig economy workers. The study is based on secondary sources of data. Blockchain in recruitment enhances trust via immutable candidate records, ensuring transparent and verified credentials. It streamlines verification processes, reduces fraud, and fosters efficient, secure candidate selection. Employing blockchain on payroll systems increases security, provides a transparent and immutable ledger for payroll records eliminating risk of fudging pay-roll. It also automates the process through smart contracts, thereby improving payroll processes, reducing wastage of time and administration charges. Blockchain manages gig workers by contract creation and identity verification, secure and verifiable recordkeeping, reducing fraud, dispute resolution, time and attendance tracking, payroll and performance management.

The gig economy offers flexibility and autonomy to workers but also presents significant challenges related to health and well-being, especially for delivery professionals who face irregular hours, physical strain, and limited access to healthcare. Immersive technologies, such as virtual reality (VR), augmented reality (AR), and artificial intelligence (AI), present innovative solutions to bridge these gaps. However, gig workers' adoption of these technologies remains underexplored. This paper applied the diffusion of innovation (DOI) theory to analyse the adoption patterns of immersive technologies within the gig economy and identified barriers, such as digital literacy and cost, alongside facilitators, like perceived usefulness and ease of integration. The paper provides insights into how these technologies can be effectively implemented in the gig workforce. The study highlights the role of platform policies and the broader regulatory landscape in shaping technology adoption, offering valuable recommendations for policymakers and technology developers.

In the rapidly evolving digital landscape, organizations face the dual challenge of adapting to technological advancements while fostering a workforce equipped with the skills necessary to thrive in this new paradigm. The chapter explores the pivotal role of Human Resources in cultivating digital dexterity defined as the ability of employees to adapt, learn, and innovate in a technology-driven environment. The chapter delves into the key components of digital dexterity, including technical proficiency and critical soft skills such as collaboration, creativity, and adaptability. It examines modern talent acquisition strategies, emphasizing the integration of digital competencies during recruitment and on boarding processes. The importance of upskilling and reskilling initiatives, powered by e-learning platforms and data-driven training programs, is highlighted as a cornerstone of HR's efforts. Furthermore, the use of cutting-edge technologies like artificial intelligence, virtual reality, and gamification in enhancing employee training and development are discussed.

Technological advancements have revolutionized Human Resource Development (HRD) and substituted traditional talent management. Organizations are operating in an AI-enabled, automated, big data, and digital learning environment. The chapter discusses digital transformation of HRD with focus on AI-driven hiring, digital learning, and performance tracking. The focus is on lifelong learning, upskilling, and reskilling to align with evolving industry needs. HR professionals must embrace digital enablers like Learning Management Systems (LMS), gamification, and microlearning. Remote work and the gig economy demand agile and inclusive talent solutions. Digitalization is advantageous but poses challenges in data protection, algorithmic bias, and technology resistance. The chapter, with case studies of MNCs and start-ups, provides best practices and ethical concerns in AI adoption. It finally provides strategic suggestions to HR leaders, academia, and business to align technology with people-first leadership to make HRD impactful in the digital era.

Preface

Esteemed Readers,

In an era marked by rapid technological advancements and shifting employment models, the intersection of immersive technology and the gig economy is pivotal to driving transformative change. The book, "Immersive Technology for the Gig Economy: Transformative Business Practices," is an outcome of a pressing desire to investigate the strategic, operational, and economic aspects of these changes as they transform the global corporate environment.

Immersive technologies, including blockchain, virtual reality (VR), and augmented reality (AR), are no longer confined to hypothetical futures or niche applications. They are actively shaping the methods that companies use to create experiences, optimize resources, and generate value. The gig economy, characterized by short-term, freelance, and flexible employment, has evolved from a trend into a vital aspect of modern workforce dynamics.

This book focuses on the convergence of these advancements, examining how digital tools and platforms affect organizational behavior, business structures, and value chains. The chapters provide a comprehensive analysis of emerging themes, including hybrid workplaces, virtual marketing, intelligent supply chains, and e-learning ecosystems, through the lenses of decentralized labor and immersive technology.

This edited volume brings together a diverse range of scholars and practitioners from around the world to explore the use of immersive technologies, including blockchain, AI, VR, and digital platforms, in addressing the complexities and opportunities of the labor economy. Each chapter examines a unique aspect, such as economic, technological, educational, or human-centric, highlighting the connections between agile work models and digital transformation.

The book is organized into four thematic clusters:

PART I: ECONOMIC AND STRUCTURAL FOUNDATIONS OF THE GIG ECONOMY

Chapter 1 delves into India's gig economy, analyzing its impact on productivity, inequality, and labor market structures, and proposing a framework for inclusive and balanced growth.

Chapter 2 investigates the key economic drivers and inhibitors of gig economy performance, using empirical models to challenge assumptions about platform work and regulation.

Chapters 3 and 4 examine the evolving role of education in a gig-driven world. While Chapter 3 focuses on curriculum and institutional adaptations in higher education, Chapter 4 showcases how e-learning and EdTech serve as catalysts for economic transformation in the digital age.

PART II: FINANCIAL INCLUSION, LITERACY, AND SUSTAINABLE FINANCE IN THE DIGITAL AGE

Chapter 5 analyzes the critical link between financial inclusion and broader economic development, calling attention to the role of digital finance in social equity.

Chapter 6 presents a bibliometric exploration of sustainable finance management and its relationship with the circular economy, highlighting trends in ESG-aligned investing.

Chapter 7 provides an in-depth look at immersive technologies—blockchain, AI, cryptocurrency—that are transforming financial management, while **Chapter 8** employs structural equation modeling to explore how digital financial literacy is influenced by financial attitudes and behaviors.

Chapter 9 continues this methodological thread, studying how inflation and interest rates influence financial behavior and policymaking.

PART III: BLOCKCHAIN, IMMERSIVE TECH, AND THE DIGITAL SUPPLY CHAIN

Chapter 10 focuses on how blockchain is driving transparency in industrial supply chains, highlighting its potential for real-time, secure, and efficient supply chain management.

Chapter 11 turns to human capital applications, showing how blockchain is revolutionizing HR functions—from recruitment to payroll and gig worker identity verification—via smart contracts and immutable records.

Chapter 12 explores immersive health technologies as solutions for gig worker wellness, offering frameworks to improve access and outcomes through AR/VR and AI innovations.

Part IV: Human Resource Management and Organizational Agility in the Gig Economy

Chapter 13 and **Chapter 14** examine how HR professionals can build digital dexterity and redefine human capital strategies to meet the fluid demands of gig and digital workforces.

Chapter 15 and **Chapter 16** address HR's evolving role in managing flexible labor. These chapters offer pragmatic insights into workforce agility, ethics, and performance management tailored to the gig paradigm.

When viewed collectively, the chapters in this book highlight a significant shift in the structure of modern business and employment. This volume not only charts the rise of gig work; it emphasizes how immersive technologies, when combined with strategic, ethical, and inclusive policies, can convert this new labor model into a sustainable and equitable force.

We hope this collection serves as a vital resource for researchers, educators, policymakers, platform designers, financial managers, and HR professionals navigating the intersections of digital transformation and the gig economy. As the world of work continues to evolve, these insights provide a way forward—one that is innovative, human-centered, and prepared for the future.

This endeavor would not have been possible without the dedication of our collaborators, whose academic rigor and diverse perspectives have significantly shaped this compilation. We express our deep gratitude to the reviewers, editors, and institutional supporters who enabled the successful completion of this volume.

We encourage you to recognize that immersive technology and gig-based business models are not distinct innovations; instead, they are integral components of a comprehensive transformation that requires strategic vision, ethical foresight, and agility as you move through the chapters.

This book serves as a source of inspiration and guidance as you navigate the challenges and opportunities of the digital economy.

We hope you enjoy the book and wish you much success.

Anna Maslon-Orac
SGH Warsaw School of Economics, Poland

Pooja Kansra
Mittal School of Business, Lovely Professional University, India

Sugandh Arora
Symbiosis School of Economics, Symbiosis International University, India

Sumit Oberoi
Indian Institute of Management Bangalore, India

Chapter 1
The Economic Impacts of India's Gig Economy: Navigating Productivity, Inequality, and Market Dynamics

Nikhat Khalid
https://orcid.org/0000-0002-3914-607X
Indian School of Business, Mohali, India

ABSTRACT

India's gig economy is reshaping the labor market, providing employment opportunities through platforms like Uber, Swiggy, and Amazon Flex. With the gig workforce in India projected to reach 59.28 million by 2035, this sector is emerging as crucial in fostering financial inclusion and regional economic decentralization. However, challenges such as wage volatility, job precarity, and inadequate social security disproportionately affect low-skilled workers, while high-skilled professionals benefit from greater stability. Gender disparities, algorithm-driven work allocation, and monopolistic practices further exacerbate inequalities. This study examines the economic contributions and structural vulnerabilities of the gig economy, advocating for legal recognition, fair wages, portable benefits, skill development programs, and stronger regulatory frameworks. A balanced approach, which ensures that workers are protected, without stifling innovation is essential to fostering an equitable and sustainable gig economy in India.

DOI: 10.4018/979-8-3373-1290-3.ch001

1. INTRODUCTION

The gig economy, which involves "*the exchange of labour for money between individuals or companies via digital platforms that actively facilitate matching between providers and customers, on a short-term and payment-by-task basis*" (Lepanjuuri et al., 2018), has rapidly expanded across the globe. The founding of Elance (now Upwork) in 1999 is recorded as one of the first instance of internet-mediated free-lance work, with the past decade as the period witnessing the most significant rise of app-based platforms (Oyer, 2020). Often described as one of the key components of the 'Future of Work,' the gig economy is classified as non-standard employment, deviating from conventional employment structures (Zeid et al., n.d.). It has provided millions of workers with flexible income opportunities while enabling businesses to access on-demand labour at reduced costs. The World Bank (2023) estimated that about 12 percent of the global labour market is accounted by the gig economy, and it is expected to grow rapidly, particularly in developing countries. Datta et al. (2023) found that the gig economy is has a marked presence in 186 countries, with 545 functioning gig work platforms, and it is only expected to rise in the times to come. Without a doubt, the rise of Gig economy can be classified as one of the 'creative innovation' of our times, one which has disrupted the traditional norms of employment, drawing from Schumpeter's (1942) concept of Creative Destruction[1]. From a macroeconomic perspective, gig economy has a significant impact on income, employment and aggregate demand, leading to an overall upliftment of the economy. However, the absence of traditional binding contracts with legal backing has raised concerns regarding job security, wage stability, social protections, and regulatory oversight. Often, the gig platforms have found themselves at crossroads with law with respect to a myriad of issues, such as worker classification and data privacy. Landmark cases such as the '*Uber BV v Aslam*' (United Kingdom Supreme Court, 2021) which held that Uber drivers are workers, therefore entitled to the national living wage and paid holidays, as well as '*Robo-Firing Case*' pertaining to firing and sacking of workers in Amsterdam court of appeal (Eurofound, n.d.) are examples where such platforms have found themselves answerable.

India, the fourth largest economy in the world has witnessed exponential growth in the gig economy over the past decade, fuelled by increasing smartphone usage, internet accessibility, digital payment solutions, and a vast labour force. As per NITI Aayog (2022), the gig economy workforce in India was estimated at 7.7 million in 2022 and is likely to expand to 23.5 million by 2029-30.

Although the gig economy provides new sources of work, it also contributes to income inequality. Highly skilled gig workers, especially in professional services and IT, receive competitive salaries, while less skilled workers like delivery people and ride-hailing drivers have volatile incomes. One of the critical concerns raised by gig work is the lack of legal framework in safeguarding gig workers against economic shocks and exploitation. As the gig workers are treated as independent contractors under India's Income Tax Act, their eligibility for financial and retiral benefits falls outside the ambit of formal employment linked schemes such as Employees' Provident Fund Organisation (EPFO) and Employees' State Insurance Scheme of India (ESI). With the exponential rise in gig platforms and their impact on employment, certain policy additions are being made, such as the addition of Section 194M under income tax laws which pertain to TDS on payment to resident contractors and professionals. In addition, the Code on Social Security, 2020 proposes the creation of a social security mechanism for gig workers, however the implementation of the code has remained nascent so far. The labour market structural transformation in India through gig work also has major regional economic decentralization implications.

Analysis in comparison of the worldwide gig economy refer to both gains and dangers entailed in work based on digital platforms. Global gig economy statistics show that according to McKinsey (2016) and European Commission (2021, 2025) while the gig economy raises the rates of workforce contribution and economic choice, it simultaneously promotes labour market polarization.

In view of the accelerated growth and changing dynamics of India's gig economy, this study seeks to conduct an overall assessment of its economic impact, sectoral distribution, and policy challenges. It analyses the contribution of the gig economy to GDP growth, employment creation, and financial inclusion while it identifies important structural challenges in terms of wage gaps, precarity of jobs, and regulatory deficits. The research also measures global best practices to suggest doable policy measures that guarantee fair and sustainable gig workforce development for India. This research addresses the above-mentioned crucial issues in order to continue the debate concerning the future of work, the protection of the labour force, and economic viability in platform-work models.

1.1 India's Key Economic Indicators and its Relevance for India's Gig Economy

India's key economic indicators in 2024 (Table 1) highlight both opportunities and challenges for the country's growing gig economy. With a nominal GDP of $3.9 trillion and a growth rate of 6.5%-7%, India is experiencing robust economic expansion, creating a favourable environment for digital and platform-based employment. However, a GDP per capita of $2,697 reflects persistent income disparities, which are evident in the gig sector, where high-skilled digital workers earn significantly more than low-skilled workers engaged in ride-hailing and delivery services. The sectoral composition of GDP and employment further emphasizes this imbalance—while services contribute 49.58% to GDP, they employ only 29.7% of the workforce, whereas agriculture engages 46.1% of workers but generates just 16% of GDP. This mismatch suggests that the gig economy could help transition surplus labour from agriculture into more productive roles, as was suggested by Lewis (1954).

India's high mobile (1.2 billion), internet penetration (850 million users), growth of digital payments, and with UPI transactions exceeding 12 billion per month (NPCI, 2024) provide a strong foundation for the expansion of platform-based work, enabling gig workers to access jobs across urban and semi-urban areas. Additionally, the 510 million Jan Dhan accounts underscore significant progress in financial inclusion, allowing gig workers, many of whom lack formal employment benefits, to participate in the digital economy (Ministry of Finance, 2024). Despite these positive developments, macroeconomic stability, reflected in forex reserves of over $600 billion, remains crucial for sustaining investor confidence in India's gig platforms (Ministry of Finance, 2024).

Table 1. Key economic indicators of India (2024)

Indicator	Value	Source
GDP (Nominal) in 2024	$3.9 trillion	Statista, 2024
GDP per capita in 2024	$2,697	Statista, 2024
GDP Growth Rate in 2024	6.5% - 7%	Economic Survey, 2024
Sectoral Composition of GDP in 2023	Agriculture:16% Industry:25.3% Services: 49.58%	Statista, 2023
Sectoral Composition of Employment in 2024	Agriculture:46.1% Industry:24.2% Services: 29.7%	Economic Survey, 2024
Internet Penetration in 2024	954 million users	PIB, 2024
Mobile Penetration in 2024	1.12 billion connections	Digital 2024: India Report
UPI Transactions (December 2024)	16,730.01 million (in volume); 23,24,699.91 crores (in value)	NPCI, 2024
Financial Inclusion (Jan Dhan Accounts)	54 crores	Ministry of Finance, 2024

Source: Author's collation from various sources specified above

1.2 Present Status of Gig Work in India and Projected Growth

India, in 2022 had 7.7 million gig workers, a number expected to rise to 9.9 million by 2023 and 23.5 million by 2029-30. The gig economy is witnessing significant growth, with companies expanding their operations. Sector-wise, 2.7 million gig workers are engaged in retail trade and sales, 2.5 million in e-commerce, 1.3 million in transportation, and 0.6 million each in manufacturing and finance & insurance services (NITI Aayog, 2022).

Figure 1. Radar chart on gig workers in India by sector (in millions)

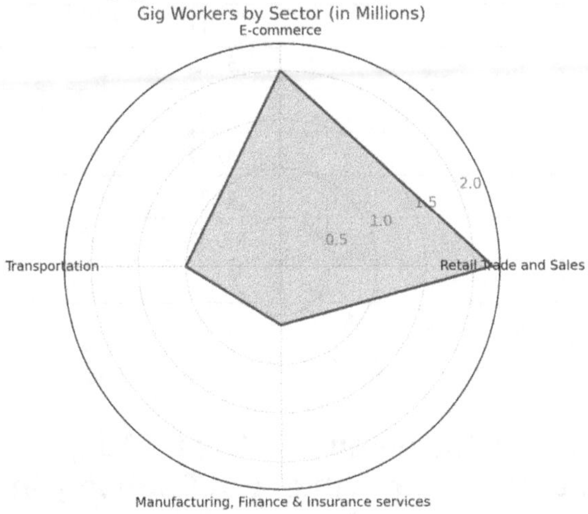

Source: Authors creation based on Niti Aayog (2022) data

Projected Growth of India's Gig Workforce (2022–2035)

As suggested by NITI Aayog (2022), and Business Standard (2024), the gig workforce is expected to grow at 17% CAGR annually. Table 2 depicts projected growth of India's gig workforce from 2023-35, highlighting a steady and significant increase over the years. In 2022, the gig workforce was estimated at 7.7 million, and this number is expected to rise consistently, reaching 59.28 million by 2035, indicating a growing reliance on gig employment.

Table 2. Projected growth of India's gig workforce

Year	Projected Gig Workforce (Million)
2022	7.7 (base year)
2023	9.01
2024	10.54
2025	12.33

continued on following page

Table 2. Continued

Year	Projected Gig Workforce (Million)
2026	14.43
2027	16.88
2028	19.75
2029	23.11
2030	27.04
2031	31.63
2032	37.01
2033	43.30
2034	50.67
2035	59.28

Source: Author's calculations

1.3 India's Financial Inclusion and Digital Adaption as Catalysts in Aiding the Growth of Gig Economy in India

India's financial inclusion and rapid digital adoption have been pivotal in driving the growth of the gig economy. The widespread implementation of the Jan Dhan-Aadhaar-Mobile (JAM) trinity has facilitated seamless financial transactions, with over 510 million Jan Dhan accounts opened as of December 2023, ensuring financial access for millions, including gig workers (Ministry of Finance, 2023). The rise of digital payment platforms has been significant, with Unified Payments Interface (UPI) transactions surpassing 12 billion in a single month (December 2023), reducing dependency on cash and fostering financial security among gig workers (NPCI, 2023). UPI has also contributed to a shift towards digital banking, with over 400 million users relying on instant and secure peer-to-peer and merchant transactions, directly benefiting gig workers by ensuring timely payments and access to credit facilities (NPCI, 2023).

Additionally, India's affordable smartphones and low-cost internet, driven by Digital India, have led to over 850 million internet users, making it easier for gig workers to connect with platforms. The integration of UPI-based payments within gig platforms like Swiggy, Zomato, Uber, and Ola has further streamlined earnings for workers, eliminating cash-based inefficiencies and enabling real-time payment settlements.

1.4 Comparative Analysis of the Gig Economy Across the World

The gig economy is expanding globally, with the global freelance market expected to grow at a compound annual rate of 15% and reach $12.01 billion by 2028 (DDIY, 2024). Table 3 compares gig economy regulations across countries. The study suggests that The United States, one of the most mature gig economies, primarily treats gig workers as independent contractors, offering limited protections, though some cities set wage floors. The European Union has taken a unified stance to reclassify many gig workers as employees, ensuring collective rights and social security through directives like the 2025 Platform Work Directive. India, still in early regulatory stages, has proposed social security through national and state-level laws, but enforcement remains limited. China and Mexico have introduced specific protections including minimum wages and platform contributions. Brazil, Australia, and South Africa show varied progress, with Australia moving toward employee recognition and others lagging on comprehensive reforms.

As noted in Table 3, comparing the global scenario of the gig economy with that of India's suggests that India's gig economy presents both economic opportunities and labour market vulnerabilities, as it is at an early, yet critical stage of development with limited database and policy directives.

Table 3. Comparative overview of gig economy regulatory frameworks across various countries

Country/ Region	Regulatory snapshot	Worker status	Protections	2021-25 actions
United States	Rules differ by state	Mostly contractors	Few mandated benefits	City wage floors (NYC, Seattle)
European Union	Bloc-wide directive	Often employees	Collective bargaining, social security	Platform Work Directive 2025; Spain "Rider Law"
India	Fast-growing, early stage	Contractors	Social Security Code (weak)	Rajasthan Act 2023; Karnataka Bill 2024
China	Proactive sector rules	Mixed	Minimum wage, insurance, relaxed deadlines	Delivery-worker protections 2021
Brazil	High but informal uptake	Mostly informal	Limited; reforms debated	Labour-court cases on platform duties
Mexico	Emerging framework	Hybrid	Platforms must pay into social security	Sector-specific regulations

continued on following page

Table 3. Continued

Country/ Region	Regulatory snapshot	Worker status	Protections	2021-25 actions
Australia	Strengthening rights	Moving to employee	Minimum wage, wider cover	Fair Work interventions 2024
South Africa	Growing, few rules	Contractors	Sparse	Policy talks under way

Source: Author's collation based on chapter content and international sources (European Commission, World Bank, national government reports)

2. REVIEW OF LITERATURE

The gig economy has emerged as a significant area of academic research. The literature found has been classified broadly into three sections, and the emerging research gap has been identified and elaborated towards the end of the section.

2.1. Ethical and Regulatory Challenges in the Gig Economy

The nature of gig work replicates 'dependant employment' and 'self-employment' (Zeid et al., n.d.), where workers are considered as 'partners', than 'employees'. Burke (2019) mentions that gig work includes in its purview more industries requiring lower-skill levels. Studies by Ravenelle (2017), Schor and Attwood Charles (2017) and Halliday (2019) found that such gig workers often experience insecurity lack of control, and precarity. Ruckelshaus (2008) noted that there is lack of regulatory clarity for gig work, allowing gig platforms to evade their legal and social responsibilities toward workers.

Tan et al., (2021) noted that gig economy has multifaceted ethical implications, while Oyer (2020) was of the view that even though non-traditional employment was an income opportunity for many, but it would not replace traditional employment. Van Doorn (2017) found that the gig economy disproportionately affects marginalized groups. Hickson (2023) remarked that we should seek to (re)build the rights and protections available to workers, rather than promote the further normalisation of under-regulated and precarious gig work. Similarly, Radhakrishnan and Roy (2023) remarked that considering the security of gig workers, whilst allowing gig platforms to flourish was essential.

Cherry and Aloisi (2016) study highlight that existing employment regulations are inadequate for addressing gig workers' concerns, necessitating new legal frameworks that balance flexibility with worker protections. On a similar note, De Stefano (2016) advocates for labour protection policies, that ensure minimum wage, job security, and legal protection for gig workers and Hickson (2023) proposed on building the rights and protections available to workers. A bibliometric analysis by Vadavi and Sharmiladevi (2024) also suggested streamlining of the several dimensions of the gig economy, including the definition and nature of gig work, its unorganised nature, income, and stability.

2.2 Multifaceted Impact of the Gig Economy

Studies by The Rockefeller Foundation (2013), World Bank (2015) and Easton-Calabria (2019) have found that the growth of gig platforms in low- and middle-income countries have the potential of reducing poverty. Joshi et al. (2024) in their study identified two major positive impacts if gig work, namely flexibility and job expansion. Fatima (2024) noted that in India while the gig economy has paved the way for more employment opportunities, but it has led to increased economic inequality and reduced labour rights.

Hwang (2024) studied the impact of gig economy on labour market and found that gig workers prioritised income and work-life balance, hence policy interventions must be required to ensure those. Chourasia (2024) found that the gig economy has led to job expansion, and contributed to income generation for families, particularly in periods of economic volatility. Similarly, a study by Huđek, I., & Širec (2023) advocated for fair working conditions, income stability, and ethical considerations to foster an inclusive and sustainable gig economy that benefits works and society.

2.3 Empirical Literature on Gig Economy in India

A study by Chaudhary and Mitra (2019) noted that the gig economy often leads to a disappearance of employer-employee relationship and is marked by a faster accumulation of capital of the aggregator. Yoganandham & Varalakshmi (2024) found that gig workers face the harsh reality of job insecurity, lack of social protections, and inconsistent income. While studying the impact of gig economy in India's economic growth trajectory, Saraswathi (2023) suggested that gig platforms have provided freelancers with a significant opportunity to enhance their income. Bekal et al (2023) suggested that as the sector continues to expand rapidly, the protection of gig workers is essential.

Another pertinent dimension of gig workers was studied by Joshi et al (2024) who noted a concerning trend of discrimination experienced by gig workers based on gender and race, particularly in less developed countries.

2.4 Research Gaps and Significance of the Study

The literature review reveals limited literature available on Gig economy in India. Additionally, there is lack of credible data available on Gig economy in India. The present study aims to fill in these critical gaps by provides a data-driven evaluation of the gig economy's contribution to GDP, employment, inequality and market dynamics, offering insights into policy reforms and social security frameworks. By addressing research gaps in worker classification, wage stability, and economic mobility, the study aims to inform policymakers, industry stakeholders, and researchers on strategies for fostering a more equitable and sustainable gig economy in India.

3. DATA AND METHODOLOGY

Data sources and research methodology form the core of a research argument. Based on secondary data sources, the study uses a mixed-method research approach, integrating quantitative and qualitative analysis from policy reports, industry assessments, and academic literature.

3.1 Data Sources

This research majorly relies on secondary data sources from government reports such as NITI Aayog (2022), industry analyses, academic literature, and workforce projections. Additionally, data from the Reserve Bank of India (RBI) and the Economic Survey (2024) provide insights into GDP contributions, employment trends, and financial inclusion. Industry and market reports also contribute to this study.

The study also incorporates a brief primary survey conducted by the author among Blinkit partners in Mohali (Punjab) during May 2025, to understand ground-level realities related to income, benefits, and job perceptions, which are presented as insights.

3.2 Research Methodology Techniques

Several analytical techniques are employed to interpret the data effectively. These techniques are mentioned below in detail.

3.2.1 Projections of Gig Workforce & GDP Contribution Using CAGR

The Compound Annual Growth Rate (CAGR) method is used to estimate the future expansion of India's gig workforce and its contribution to GDP. CAGR provides a smoothed annual growth rate over a given period, helping forecast long-term trends in gig employment and economic contribution. In terms of the application of this method in the present study, these projections based on CAGR is undertaken from 2022 to 2035.

$$\text{CAGR}=\left(\frac{Vf}{Vi}\right)^{\frac{1}{t}}-1$$

Where:
Vf= Final Value (Projected gig workforce or GDP contribution)
Vi= Initial Value (Current gig workforce or GDP contribution)
t= Number of years

3.3.2. Inequality Analysis Using Measures of Central Tendency

Income inequality within the gig economy is analysed using statistical measures of central tendency and dispersion. The inequality is studied at two levels, namely, inequality between high and low skilled gig workers, and inequality between male and female gig workers.

The study primarily uses Standard Deviation (σ) to assess income variability among gig workers.

$$\text{Standard Deviation }(\sigma) = \sqrt{\frac{\sum(x_i-\bar{x})^2}{N}}$$

Where:
x_i= Individual data point
$\bar{x}$= Mean
N= Number of data points in the population

3.3 Primary Field Insights Through Unstructured Questionnaire

To complement the secondary data analysis, the study incorporates qualitative insights gathered by the author through an unstructured questionnaire administered to Blinkit delivery partners in Mohali (Punjab) in April 2025. The objective was to explore the on-ground realities of gig work in last-mile delivery services. Workers were asked four open-ended questions regarding (i) earnings per order, (ii) access to health or life insurance, (iii) EPFO deduction from wages, and (iv) their suggestions for improving employment conditions in the sector.

3.4 Policy Gap Identification & Benchmarking

This study undertakes a comparative analysis of India's labour policies on gig work against global best practices. Through a benchmarking process, policies from the United States, the European Union, China, and Brazil are studied to identify regulatory gaps and potential areas for reform of gig economy in India. By analyzing these diverse policy frameworks, the study identifies gaps in India's gig labor laws and assesses their impact on worker rights and economic sustainability.

3.5 Research Limitations

One key challenge in research related to the gig economy in India is the lack of availability of credible published data. There are also inconsistencies in workforce classification, as the distinction between gig workers and the informal sector remains unclear in some reports.

4. DISCUSSION AND ANALYSIS

4.1 The Gig Economy's Contributions to GDP and Economic Growth

The gig economy's impact on the economy is multifaceted, with it becoming a key contributor to India's GDP growth and employment generation, spanning diverse sectors such as ride-hailing, food delivery, e-commerce logistics, and freelancing. According to NITI Aayog (2022), the gig workforce stood at 7.7 million in 2020-21 and is projected to reach 23.5 million by 2029-30, highlighting its increasing economic significance. Estimates suggest that the workforce could grow to 59 million by 2035 (Figure 2), accounting for 4.1% of India's total workforce (Staffing Industry, 2024). Additionally, the gig economy's contribution to GDP is expected to reach

1.25% by 2030 (Business Standard, 2024), driven by increasing digital adoption, technological advancements, and growing platform-based employment.

Figure 2 depicts a simple analysis through CAGR. The projections suggest that by 2035, the gig economy is expected to contribute about 2.55% to India's GDP, showing its increasing role in India's future economic expansion.

Figure 2. A graphical presentation of projected growth of gig workforce and GDP contribution (2022-2035)

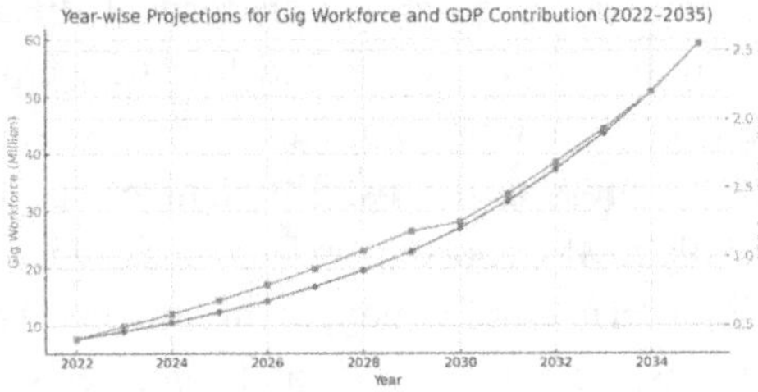

Source: Author's calculations

4.1.1 Macroeconomic Linkages: GDP Growth, Consumption, and Productivity

The gig economy's influence extends beyond employment to impact aggregate demand, consumption, labor productivity, and financial inclusion:

- **Aggregate Demand and GDP Growth**: The rise of gig work has led to an increase in household incomes, particularly among previously unemployed or underemployed workers. This increase in disposable income stimulates consumption spending, contributing to higher aggregate demand and economic growth. This aligns with Keynesian economic theory of multiplier (1936), which suggests that increased consumption expenditure has a multiplier effect in an economy as it serves as an injection, leading to higher aggregate demand, further driving economic expansion.
- **Consumption Patterns and Digital Economy Expansion:** The growing prevalence of digital payments has further amplified gig workers' contribution to the economy. Digital earnings have reduced reliance on cash-based informal transactions, bringing more workers into the formal economy. This comes at a time when the Indian Government has been pushing for financial inclusion in banking services through policies such as Pradhan Mantri Jan-

Dhan Yojana (PMJDY), thus enabling gig workers to access credit, insurance, and financial planning tools.

- **Labor Productivity and Efficiency Gains:** Gig platforms help reduce inefficiencies existing in the economy by optimizing labor allocation. This has led to a rise in productivity, particularly in logistics, last-mile delivery, and knowledge-based freelancing. For example, ride-hailing services like Ola and Uber have reduced idle time for drivers, increasing their earnings potential and improving overall transport efficiency in urban centers. From a Neoclassical economic perspective, gig platforms help achieve allocative efficiency by ensuring that labor is directed toward sectors where demand is highest, reducing friction in labor markets.
- **Business Competitiveness and Cost Efficiency:** The gig economy allows businesses, especially SMEs and startups, to access wider consumer base and markets without long-term employment commitments. This reduces overhead costs, improves profits, service delivery, and enhances scalability. Companies benefit from hiring gig workers for specialized tasks such as IT services, content creation, and customer support, lowering costs while maintaining operational flexibility. The Schumpeterian theory of creative destruction (1942) suggests that such flexible labor models drive innovation, forcing traditional businesses to adapt or be replaced by more efficient gig-based models.

4.2 Regional Development and Economic Decentralization

The gig economy is playing a pivotal role in India's regional economic development and decentralization. Employment opportunities provided by gig platforms are now not just restricted to tier 1 cities, but have expanded to more than 40 tier-2 and 3 cities. This is fostering regional development and strengthening local economies, as the satellite towns attached with tier 2 and 3 cities are also benefitting.

Traditionally, high-paying jobs have been concentrated in urban centers, but digital platforms, widespread internet access, and flexible gig opportunities are enabling workers from smaller towns and rural areas to integrate into the labor market. This shift is fostering inclusive economic growth, reducing migration pressures, and enhancing regional labor market efficiency.

Table 4. Gig platforms stepping up during times of crisis: Balancing regional development

Swiggy's Jumpstart Initiative: A Case on Gig Platforms promoting Regional Development
The covid pandemic completely tore down the restaurant/hospitality sector. Many restaurants which could not bear the fixed costs during lockdown had to take the harsh decision of shutting their doors forever.
In a classic case of gig platforms stepping up, Swiggy's "Jumpstart Initiative" (phase 1 and 2) in 2020 and 2021. In 2020, Swiggy aided over 50,000 restaurants partners in recovery and growth post the impact of Covid-19, while in phase 2, it extended a financial aid package of about 63 crores (Inc42, 2024). This is expected to have helped over 1 lakh delivery workers in tier-2 cities during the pandemic, highlighting the gig economy's positive role in regional employment generation, particularly during times of crisis.

Source: Author's collation

4.2.1 Key Factors Driving Regional Growth

Some of the key factors contributing to regional growth of the gig economy include increase in Digital Connectivity and Platform Expansion. As of 2024, India has over 936 million internet users and 650 million smartphone users (Drishti IAS, 2024), enabling more workers in semi-urban and rural areas to engage in digital and on-demand work. This increasing internet and mobile penetration, coupled with the rise in financial inclusion and digital payments has been instrumental in supporting gig economy expansion across regions. With the success of UPI transactions exceeding 12 billion per month (NPCI, 2024) and the proliferation of Jan Dhan accounts (510 million accounts, Ministry of Finance, 2024), gig workers in smaller towns now have access to seamless digital payments, microfinance, and formal financial services, enabling them to manage their earnings more effectively.

Platforms such as Amazon Flex, Ola, and Swiggy have also expanded their services to smaller cities, creating new income opportunities beyond traditional employment sectors. In addition, this trend is not only reducing overcrowding in metros but also fostering economic diversification in smaller cities.

4.2.2 Impact on Regional Employment and Migration Patterns

The expansion of gig economy to tier 2 and 3 cities has been creating Local Opportunities, reducing the pressure on urban centers. Swiggy and Zomato, for instance, have launched operations in smaller cities, providing thousands of local delivery jobs and curbing the need for workers to migrate to metros. In addition, Platforms such as Meesho and Etsy allow rural craftsmen and women entrepreneurs to sell their products directly to consumers nationwide, improving income levels and fostering economic independence in non-metro regions.

4.2.3 Challenges to Regional Gig Work Expansion

1. Digital Divide and Infrastructure Gaps

Despite progress, regional disparities in digital access remain a challenge. Many semi-urban and rural areas still suffer from patchy internet connectivity, lack of smartphone penetration, and digital illiteracy. These issues prevent potential gig workers from fully leveraging available opportunities.

2. Lack of Awareness and Skill Gaps

Many workers in smaller cities remain unaware of gig opportunities or lack the necessary digital skills to participate in higher-value work such as freelancing, data entry, or content creation. Government and private sector efforts are needed to train and upskill workers, ensuring that more individuals from diverse backgrounds can benefit from gig employment.

3. Regulatory Uncertainty and Worker Protections

Unlike traditional employment, gig work does not offer job security, fixed wages, or benefits such as insurance and pension schemes. State-level policies are yet to fully integrate gig workers into labor laws, leaving many at risk of income instability. Policymakers must ensure that gig work remains a sustainable employment avenue while providing fair labor protections.

4.3 Widening Income Disparities and Challenges in Equitable Wealth Distribution

The gig economy in India is a classic case of 'Dualism', wherein two starkly different systems coexist in the same economy. Inequality in the gig economy exists at two levels, namely the inequality between low skilled and high skilled workers, and inequality between male and female gig workers.

In terms of the inequality between high and low skilled workers, while professionals engaged in digital freelancing, IT consulting, and content creation earn competitive wages, low-skilled gig workers in food delivery and ride-hailing struggle with financial insecurity.

Additionally, gender and caste-based inequalities compound the challenges faced by marginalized groups in the gig economy. For instance, women gig workers earn significantly less than their male counterparts (ILO, 2022). Their representation in the gig economy also remains abysmal till date. A study by Singh (2024) highlights that currently, females comprise only 2% of Uber's driver base in India.

Table 5. Partners or Pawns? The Precarious Dual Nature of Gig Work

Jamshed, a 42-year-old man from Gujarat mentions to *Newslaundry* "They call us partners, but they don't treat us that way. We are slaves to them," "We aren't employees for them but labour, so they expect us to not raise our voices or ask questions. But with no job security, how do we survive?" (Sodhi, 2021).
Strikingly, a Freelance software engineer (Reddit user, 2024) comments that they "Make around 2.5-3 lakhs/ month these days through gig work".

Source: Author's collation

Inequality Analysis Based on Central Tendency Measures

With no credible dataset available on earnings of gig workers, data for gig workers has been stimulated and collated from secondary sources such as NITI Aayog (2022), Fairwork India (2022), and CMIE employment reports, and an analysis on inequality of two types has been undertaken (high skilled-low skilled and male-female).

Figure 3 suggests that the wage disparity between high-skilled and low-skilled gig workers is evident, with high-skilled workers earning a mean wage of 60,000, which is more than double the 25,000 earned by low-skilled workers. The greater standard deviation among high-skilled workers indicates higher income variability. A gender-based wage gap is also apparent, as female gig workers seemingly earn an average of 24,000, about 20% less than their male counterparts, who earn about 30,000. Additionally, the lower income variability among women suggests limited access to high-paying gig roles. The results are similar to those obtained by Kasliwal (2020) who observed that the gig economy's growth in India has yielded limited growth for females, as evidenced by low female labour force participation rate.

Figure 3. A graphical presentation of mean and standard deviation of gig workers by category

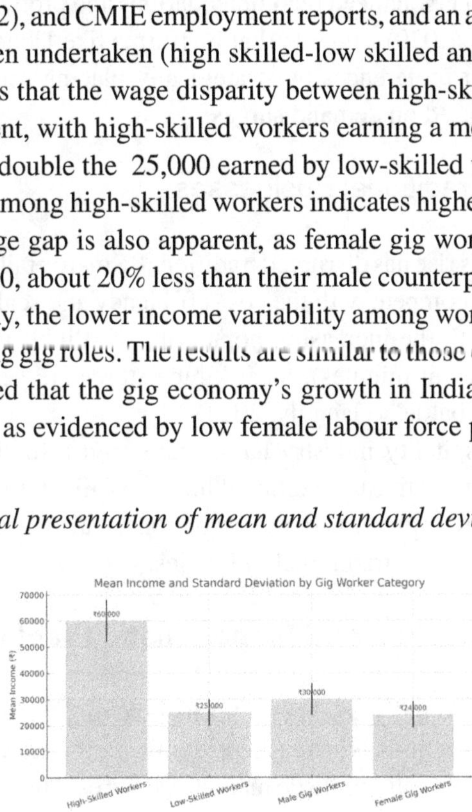

Source: Author's calculations

4.4 Implications for Consumer Behaviour

The rise of the gig economy has significantly transformed consumer behavior, fostering a landscape driven by convenience, affordability, and digital transactions. The increasing reliance on gig platforms has not only reshaped purchasing patterns but also altered consumer expectations. This is in sync with India's evolving market structure, driven by increased disposable incomes and the rise of Millennials and Gen Z as consumers, who are born surrounded by virtual world. This section explores key trends shaping consumer behavior, the economic and social consequences of these changes, and the broader policy implications.

4.4.1 Key Trends in Consumer Behavior

The gig economy has given rise to the 'On-Demand Culture', wherein consumers now expect instant service fulfilment across various sectors, from food delivery to ride-sharing and freelance work. People are now making algorithm-driven choices, with features such as personalized recommendations and promotional incentives. A study by Hagiu et al. (2020) suggests that platforms like UberEats and DoorDash manipulate consumer preferences by strategically placing sponsored listings and adjusting visibility based on demand surges.

4.4.2 Impact on Traditional Businesses

The gig economy's rise has disrupted traditional. Small retailers and local service providers struggle to compete with the cost-efficiency and scalability of gig-based models. Recently, with the increasing popularity of Blinkit in India (A platform that delivers groceries in minutes), local kirana stores are getting impacted, and evidently "losing the battle" (Ganguly, 2024).

Similarly, the hospitality industry has experienced a fundamental shift, with Airbnb offering an alternative to traditional hotels. While this competition benefits consumers through lower prices and diverse options, it also results in job losses and reduced job security within traditional industries.

4.5 Market Competition and Monopolistic Practices

The gig economy, initially celebrated for its potential to democratize work and create economic opportunities, is increasingly dominated by a few powerful platforms, leading to monopolistic or oligopolistic market structures. This market concentration has far-reaching implications for workers, consumers, and regulatory frameworks.

4.5.1 Consequences of Market Consolidation

Suppressed Worker Bargaining Power and Unionisation Efforts by Gig Workers in India

One of the most significant consequences of gig economy monopolization is the suppression of worker bargaining power. Large platforms unilaterally dictate pricing, commission rates, and algorithmic management policies, leaving gig workers with little leverage to negotiate fair compensation. Research by Rosenblat and Stark (2016) highlights how algorithmic control in ride-hailing services creates an asymmetry of power between drivers and platforms, reducing workers' autonomy and bargaining ability. A study by the Economic Policy Institute (EPI, 2022) found that gig workers often earn less than the minimum wage after accounting for expenses such as vehicle maintenance, insurance, and platform commission fees. In response, some workers have attempted to organize and advocate for better pay and conditions. However, due to their classification as independent contractors rather than employees, they are often excluded from traditional labor protections and collective bargaining rights (Cherry, 2016).

Although traditional trade unions have been slow to adapt to the platform economy, new forms of worker organization are emerging in India, signaling signal unionisation efforts. One of the most prominent examples is the Telangana Gig and Platform Workers Union (TGPWU), which was established in 2020 and is based in Hyderabad. The union has actively been advocating for the rights of app-based workers, pushing for inclusion in national social security schemes, accident insurance, and wage transparency. In addition, newer unions like the All-India Gig Workers Union (AIGWU),), have also gained visibility, particularly through legal advocacy. Similarly, the Indian Federation of App-Based Transport Workers (IFAT) has actively campaigned for better labour protections for drivers across Indian cities. These unions are not only organizing protests but also contributing to public discourse and policy consultations around labour codes and gig work regulation.

This suggests that although unionisation in the gig economy is still nascent and fragmented, these emerging efforts signal a critical shift wherein workers are increasingly asserting their rights through collective action, legal petitions, and engagement with state authorities. Strengthening union efforts and incorporating worker voices in policymaking will be crucial for achieving fair and inclusive growth in India's digital labor market.

Table 6. A Case Study on Exclusion of Platform Taxi Services: A Case of Goa

Goa is one of India's popular tourist destinations, with the year 2024 bringing in about 10 million tourists into the state. The state has a booming tourism economy, as result, the state has a large, but unorganised number of taxis and taxi operators. Till date, the taxi unions in Goa have not permitted platform taxi services like Uber and Ola to enter Goa, as they fear their incomes may drop significantly. In addition, their bargaining power would also be impacted. In 2014, Uber and Ola tried to start operations in Goa but met with huge protests from taxi operators leading to their ban. This is a classic case wherein the taxi unions in the state were so strong that they did not let platform taxi services to enter their area.

Source: Author's collation

Barriers for New Entrants and Regulatory Challenges

Market consolidation in the gig economy is further reinforced by network effects, wherein the value of a platform increases as more users and service providers join it. Established platforms have significant first-mover advantages, making it challenging for new entrants to compete. For instance, Uber's dominance in the ride-hailing industry is driven by its extensive driver network, consumer familiarity, and access to large pools of venture capital that enable aggressive pricing strategies, including predatory pricing to outcompete rivals (Schneider, 2017). Many of these companies operate under a "platform capitalism" model, where they function as intermediaries rather than direct service providers, allowing them to sidestep traditional labor and competition laws (Srnicek, 2017). Efforts to regulate gig economy monopolies have been inconsistent. For instance, the European Union has introduced measures to classify certain gig workers as employees, granting them access to labor rights (European Commission, 2021 and 2025).

Table 7. A Case Study on Workers Cooperatives in India and USA– NYC's Up & Go and Bengaluru's Rickshaw Union

Worker cooperatives have emerged as viable alternatives to corporate gig platforms, offering higher wages, job security, and greater worker autonomy. For example, New York's Up & Go allows workers to retain 95% of earnings, compared to 50–80% on typical platforms (OECD, 2023). Bengaluru's rickshaw union is another example of a worker-owned cooperative with strong bargaining power. Bunders et al. (2022) highlight that such co-ops can address many challenges of investor-owned platforms. Given their funding constraints, India can support these models through legal recognition and targeted financial aid (OECD, 2023).

Source: Author's collation

4.6 Balancing Productivity and Equity: Policy Recommendations

The gig economy has emerged as a significant driver of India's economic activity, providing flexible work opportunities, increased source of income and increasing productivity. However, concerns about job security, fair wages, and social protections for gig workers highlight the need for a comprehensive policy framework that balances economic growth with worker well-being. A report by ICRIER (n.d.) mentions that presently, India does not have any law or policy in place for gig workers. Although some progress has been made in the area, for example, recently the Union Budget 2025-26 announced that gig workers will receive identity cards, e-Shram registration, and healthcare coverage under the PM Jan Arogya Yojana. The report also noted that states like Rajasthan and Karnataka have taken steps in the positive direction, through Rajasthan Platform-Based Gig Workers (Registration and Welfare) Act, 2023 and Karnataka Platform-based Gig Workers (Social Security and Welfare) Bill, 2024 respectively. These legislations aim to provide social security and other benefits to platform-based gig workers. A study by Aggarwal (2023) suggested that adequate planning and state intervention is crucial for safeguarding the labour from disruptive forces of change in the gig economy's labour market. Comparing India's 2025 Directive with EU's 2025 Platform Regulation suggests that India's 2025 Platform Workers Directive proposes a national gig worker registry, minimum wages, and basic social protections like health insurance. However, it remains advisory, with limited enforcement. In contrast, the EU's 2025 Platform Work Directive presumes platform workers are employees, mandates algorithmic transparency, and grants collective bargaining rights.

With the growth of the platform economy, Indian states are introducing laws to protect gig workers. Rajasthan was the first to enact the Platform-Based Gig Workers Act, 2023, followed by Karnataka's draft Gig Workers Bill, 2024.

Table 8. Comparative Caselet of Rajasthan and Karnataka's Legislations for Gig Economy

Feature	Rajasthan Act, 2023	Karnataka Bill, 2024
Status	Enacted and implemented	Draft approved, pending implementation
Objective	Registration and welfare of gig workers	Social security and welfare provision
Registration	Mandatory via state portal	Mandatory via proposed registry
Welfare Board	Established	Proposed
Welfare Fund	1–2% platform fee + govt. grants	Platform fee (TBD) + CSR + govt. grants

continued on following page

Table 8. Continued

Feature	Rajasthan Act, 2023	Karnataka Bill, 2024
Social Security	Health, accident, pension, disability	Insurance, pension, maternity, skill training
Grievance Redressal	Online via Welfare Board	Proposed digital system
Platform Obligations	Data sharing; penalties	Disclosure on pay, terms, algorithms
Highlights	Auto-registration via app	Algorithmic transparency, skill dev.
Challenges	Platform pushback, low worker awareness	Implementation clarity pending

Source: Author's collation

Both laws reflect the growing push for gig worker protection and highlight the need for state-led action balancing worker welfare and platform sustainability.

The examples of Rajasthan and Karnataka suggest that some steps are being taken in the right direction, albeit a targeted approach and a dedicated policy in India is the need of the hour, which addresses issues such as labour laws, social security, competition regulations, skill development, and ethical platform governance. In addition, platforms providing gig work must also take up responsibility for the well-being of their partners. Khosrowshahi (2020) the C.E.O. of Uber mentioned that "*Gig Workers Deserve Better. Gig workers want both flexibility and benefits — we support laws that could make that possible*", reflecting upon the fact that gig platforms do recognise the need to improve the benefits extended to its workers. However, little progress has been made by platforms in upholding the rights of gig workers, particularly in developing countries. Government intervention will be crucial in determining the future trajectory of gig economy and workers in India.

Table 9. Insights from a Primary Survey of Blinkit Partners in Mohali (Punjab) India, May, 2025

In May 2025, the author conducted a brief survey of 10 Blinkit delivery partners in Mohali to assess their earnings and social protections. Most reported earning 20– 30 per order, with a 15 base fare plus surge pay. Income varied by order volume and incentives. None received health insurance, and no EPFO deductions were made, indicating a lack of retirement benefits. Workers recommended fixed minimum daily payouts, insurance coverage, and transparency in incentive structures. The findings underscore the precarious conditions of gig work and the urgent need for policy measures to ensure fair wages and basic protections for platform workers. These responses highlight the precarious nature of gig work, lack of social protection, and the need for regulatory intervention to ensure minimum income and benefits for platform-based workers.

Source: Author's field survey

For balancing productivity and equity as the gig economy develops, a mandatory national registration system for gig workers is essential, which would give regulators visibility across platforms and enable enforcement of labour rights and social protection. Re-classifying gig workers into a separate category, or creating a "dependent contractor" category—would align India with benchmarks such as California's AB5 and the EU draft directive, extending basic entitlements while preserving autonomy (European Commission, 2021; Forde et al., 2017). Platforms should be required to provide portable health, life-insurance and retirement accounts, modelled on Singapore's CPF and Dutch freelancer schemes, with employer-matched contributions (De Groen & Maselli, 2016; Tan, 2021). Complementary investments in vocational training and up-skilling can break the low-skill, low-wage trap that many full-time gig workers face (World Economic Forum, 2020).

In addition, platforms should disclose wage algorithms, commissions and tip policies, deterring hidden deductions and income volatility (Rosenblat & Stark, 2016). Worker councils, similar to Germany's works councils, could institutionalise voice in wage-setting and workplace governance (Forde et al., 2017). Statutory floor wages, algorithmic audits and universal portable benefits—covering health insurance, pensions and unemployment protection—would stabilise incomes and reduce gender pay gaps created by biased task allocation (Cherry, 2016; Forde et al., 2017).

Finally, curbing monopolistic practices through updated antitrust rules that target predatory pricing, data advantages and anti-competitive mergers is vital to restore bargaining power (Khan, 2017). Public financing and legal recognition for worker-owned cooperatives would diversify the market and ensure fairer revenue distribution (Scholz, 2016). Collectively, these measures offer a coherent roadmap for a fair, inclusive and competitive gig economy in India.

5. CONCLUSION

India is poised to become one of the world's largest gig economies, driven by rapid digitalization, expanding platform-based work, and a vast labour force. This growth has significantly reshaped the labour market by enhancing employment opportunities, improving service delivery, and promoting financial inclusion, especially in tier-2 and tier-3 cities. However, the unregulated and fragmented nature of India's gig economy has created significant challenges—marked by wage volatility, lack of social protection, and deepening income inequality.

The study finds that the gig economy in India is highly dualistic in nature: while high-skilled professionals in IT and digital freelancing earn competitive incomes, low-skilled workers in ride-hailing, delivery, and logistics face insecure earnings, algorithmic control, and limited bargaining power. Women and marginalized communities remain severely underrepresented, further exacerbating socio-economic disparities. Additionally, market consolidation among a few dominant platforms has stifled competition, limited worker mobility, and adversely impacted small businesses and traditional livelihoods.

Despite these issues, the gig economy has created a new avenue for earning income, facilitated economic decentralization and digital empowerment, creating new livelihood avenues outside urban centres. However, sustaining this growth equitably requires robust and inclusive policy intervention.

This study recommends the legal recognition of gig workers as a distinct employment category under a hybrid model that ensures both flexibility and protection. A national gig worker registry, portable social security benefits (including health insurance, pensions, and paid leave), and mandatory platform contributions are essential. In addition, the study proposes development of skills of low-skilled gig workers for achieving upward mobility. Promoting worker representation through unions and cooperatives, ensuring data portability, algorithmic transparency, and enforcing anti-monopoly regulations will help democratize the platform economy. Investments in digital skilling and government-backed reskilling initiatives will also enable upward mobility.

International best practices such as Spain's Rider Law, Singapore's Provident Fund and Southeast Asia's Grab—offer useful models. India must adapt such frameworks to its socio-economic context to build a gig economy that is not just productive, but also equitable and resilient.

REFERENCES

Aayog, N. I. T. I. (2022). *India's booming gig and platform economy: Perspectives and recommendations on the future of work.* Government of India.

Aggarwal, S. C. (2023, July). *'Gig' workers in India: An overview* [Preprint]. ResearchGate. DOI: 10.13140/RG.2.2.29650.32964

Anwar, M. A., & Graham, M. (2021). Hidden transcripts of the gig economy: Labour agency and the new art of resistance. *Review of International Political Economy, 28*(2), 309–331. DOI: 10.1080/09692290.2020.1737569

Bekal, S., Harish, A., Bhandari, K., Sachin, Y., Marda, K., & Bishnoi, Y. (2023). Review of Literature on the Topic of the Gig Economy in India. *International Journal of Innovative Science and Research Technology., 8*(4), 1049–1056.

Berg, J., Furrer, M., Harmon, E., Rani, U., & Silberman, M. S. (2018). *Digital labour platforms and the future of work: Towards decent work in the online world.* International Labour Organization. https://doi.org/DOI: 10.2139/ssrn.3197539

Bunders, D. J., Arets, M., Frenken, K., & De Moor, T. (2022). The feasibility of platform cooperatives in the gig economy. *Journal of Co-operative Organization and Management, 10*(1), 100167. DOI: 10.1016/j.jcom.2022.100167

Burke, A. E. (2019). *The freelance project and gig economies of the 21st century.* Centre for Research on Self-Employment (CRSE).

Business Standard. (2024). *India's gig economy may add 90 million jobs, contribute 1.25% to GDP.*https://www.business-standard.com

Chaudhary, R., & Mitra, S. (2019, November 22). *Labour practices in the emerging gig economy in India: A case study of Urban Clap* [Conference presentation]. Formalisation, Informalisation and the Labour Process Workshop, CeMIS, Goettingen.

Cherry, M. A., & Aloisi, A. (2017). 'Dependent contractors' in the gig economy: A comparative approach. *American University Law Review, 66*, 635. Saint Louis University Legal Studies Research Paper No. 2016-15. https://doi.org/DOI: 10.2139/ssrn.2847869

Datta, N., Rong, C., Singh, S., Stinshoff, C., Iacob, N., Nigatu, N. S., Nxumalo, M., & Klimaviciute, L. (2023). *Working without borders: The promise and peril of online gig work.* World Bank. DOI: 10.1596/40066

De Groen, W. P., & Maselli, I. (2016). *The Impact of the Collaborative Economy on the Labour Market.* CEPS.

De Stefano, V. (2016). The rise of the "just-in-time workforce": On-demand work, crowd work, and labor protection in the gig economy. *SSRN*, *37*(3), 471–504. DOI: 10.2139/ssrn.2682602

Department for Promotion of Industry and Internal Trade (DPIIT). (2024). *Foreign direct investment statistics.*https://www.dpiit.gov.in

Don't Do It Yourself (DDIY). (2024). *Freelance statistics: Facts, figures, and trends in the gig economy.* Retrieved from https://ddiy.co/freelance-statistics/

Drishti, I. A. S. (2024). *Impact of AI and Automation on India's Employment Landscape.*https://www.drishtiias.com

Easton-Calabria, E. (2019). *Digital livelihoods for people on the move.* UNDP. https://www.undp.org/content/dam/undp/library/prosperity/economic-recovery-mobility/MASTER%20-%20Migrant%20Union%20-%20Digital%20Livelihoods%20for%20People%20on%20the%20Move.pdf

Economic Policy Institute (EPI). (2022). *National survey of gig workers paints a picture of poor working conditions, low pay.* https://www.epi.org/publication/gig-worker-survey/

Electronic Frontier Foundation (EFF). (2016). *How Safe Is Your Data in the Gig Economy?*https://www.eff.org/press/releases/how-safe-your-data-gig-economy

Eurofound. (n.d.). *Amsterdam Court of Appeal decision in Uber case.* European Foundation for the Improvement of Living and Working Conditions. Retrieved March 12, 2025, from https://apps.eurofound.europa.eu/platformeconomydb/amsterdam-court-of-appeal-decision-in-uber-case-110150

European Commission. (2021). *Commission proposals to improve the working conditions of people working through digital labour platforms.*https://ec.europa.eu/commission/presscorner/detail/en/ip_21_6605

European Commission. (2025). *Improving the working conditions of platform workers.* https://www.europarl.europa.eu/thinktank/en/document/EPRS_BRI(2022)698923 Office.

Fairwork India. (2022). *Fairwork India ratings 2022: Labour standards in the platform economy.*https://fair.work/en/fw/publications

Fatima, A. (2024). Examining the Impact of Gig Economy on employment and poverty reduction in India. *International Journal of Legal Research and Applications*, *2*(7).

Forde, C., Stuart, M., Joyce, S., Oliver, L., Valizade, D., Alberti, G., & Hardy, K. (2017). *The social protection of workers in the platform economy.*https://www.europarl.europa.eu/RegData/etudes/STUD/2017/614184/IPOL_STU(2017)614184_EN.pdf

Ganguly, N. (2024, October 23). *Kirana stores are losing the battle against Zepto, Blinkit and Instamart.* Outlook Business. https://www.outlookbusiness.com/start-up/explainers/kirana-stores-are-losing-the-battle-against-zepto-blinkit-and-instamart

Government of Australia. (2023). *Fair Work Legislation Amendment (Protecting Worker Entitlements) Act 2023.*https://www.fairwork.gov.au

Government of India. (2020). *The Code on Social Security, 2020 (No. 36 of 2020).* Ministry of Law and Justice.

Graham, M., Hjorth, I., & Lehdonvirta, V. (2019). Decent work and the digital gig economy: A developing country perspective. SSRN *Electronic Journal.*https://doi.org/DOI: 10.2139/ssrn.3153436

Hagiu, A., Teh, T.-H., & Wright, J. (2020). Should platforms be allowed to sell on their own marketplaces? *RAND Journal of Economics.* Forthcoming. Available at *SSRN*: https://ssrn.com/abstract=3606055 DOI: 10.2139/ssrn.3606055

Halliday, D. (2019). Is there a moral problem with the gig economy? *Uehiro Oxford Institute.*https://podcasts.ox.ac.uk/there-moral-problem-gig-economy

Hickson, J. (2023). Freedom, domination and the gig economy. *New Political Economy*, *29*(2), 321–336. DOI: 10.1080/13563467.2023.2254712

Huđek, I., & Širec, K. (2023). Unveiling the impact of the gig economy on sustainable development. In V. Bevanda (Ed.), *ERAZ Conference – Knowledge-based sustainable development: Vol. 9. Selected papers* (pp. 125–133). Association of Economists and Managers of the Balkans. https://doi.org/DOI: 10.31410/ERAZ.S.P.2023.125

Hwang, J. (2024). The gig economy and its effects on the labor market. *International Journal of Science and Research Archive*, *13*(1), 3394–3404. DOI: 10.30574/ijsra.2024.13.1.1231

Inc42. (2024, March 11). *Swiggy extends financial aid package worth INR 63 Cr to its restaurant partners.* Inc42. https://inc42.com/buzz/swiggy-extends-financial-aid-package-worth-inr-63-cr

Indian Council for Research on International Economic Relations (ICRIER). (n.d.). *Regulation of gig workers.* Retrieved from https://icrier.org/policy_bank/regulation-of-gig-worker/

International Labour Organization (ILO). (2022). *The gender gap in employment: What's holding women back?*https://webapps.ilo.org/infostories/en-GB/Stories/Employment/barriers-women

Joshi, A., Jain, S., & Gupta, P. K. (2024). Challenges and impact of the gig economy. *Sustainable Economies*, *2*(2), 96. DOI: 10.62617/se.v2i2.96

Kasliwal, R. (2020, May). *Gender and the gig economy: A qualitative study of gig platforms for women workers* (ORF Issue Brief No. 359). Observer Research Foundation. https://www.orfonline.org/research/gender-and-the-gig-economy-65974/

Keynes, J. M. (1936). *The general theory of employment, interest, and money.* Macmillan. Retrieved from https://www.files.ethz.ch/isn/125515/1366_keynestheoryofemployment.pdf

Khan, L. (2017). Amazon's antitrust paradox. *The Yale Law Journal*, *126*(3). https://www.yalelawjournal.org/note/amazons-antitrust-paradox

Khosrowshahi, D. (2020, August 10). *I am the C.E.O. of Uber. Gig workers deserve better.* The New York Times. https://www.nytimes.com/2020/08/10/opinion/uber-ceo-dara-khosrowshahi-gig-workers-deserve-better.html

Lepanjuuri, K., Wishart, R., & Cornick, P. (2018). *The characteristics of those in the gig economy: Final report.* Department for Business, Energy & Industrial Strategy (BEIS).

Lewis, W. A. (1954). Economic development with unlimited supplies of labor. *Manchester School*, *22*(2), 139–191. DOI: 10.1111/j.1467-9957.1954.tb00021.x

McKinsey & Company. (2016). *Independent work: Choice, necessity, and the gig economy.*https://www.mckinsey.com

Ministry of Finance. (2023). *Jan Dhan accounts update: Financial inclusion progress.* Government of India.

Ministry of Finance. (2024). *Pradhan Mantri Jan Dhan Yojana progress report.* Government of India.

Ministry of Finance. (2024). Economic Survey 2023–24: Volume I & II. Department of Economic Affairs, Government of India. https://www.indiabudget.gov.in/economicsurvey/

National Payments Corporation of India (NPCI). (2023). *UPI transaction trends and digital payment adoption in India.*

National Payments Corporation of India (NPCI). (2024). *UPI transaction statistics.* https://www.npci.org.in

OECD. (2023). *Platform cooperatives and employment: An alternative for platform work.* OECD Local Economic and Employment Development (LEED). *Papers, 2023*(16). Advance online publication. DOI: 10.1787/20794797

Oyer, P. (2020). The gig economy. *IZA World of Labor: Evidence-Based Policy Making*. Advance online publication. DOI: 10.15185/izawol.471

Radhakrishnan, A., & Singha Roy, N. (2023). Gig economy workers' livelihood: A qualitative study of ride-hailing platforms in Bangalore City, India. *Artha Vijnana, 65*(2). Advance online publication. DOI: 10.21648/OPST6018

Ravenelle, A. J. (2017). Sharing economy workers: Selling, not sharing. *Cambridge Journal of Regions, Economy and Society, 10*(2), 281–295. DOI: 10.1093/cjres/rsw043

Reddit user. (2024, March). *What are some side income jobs/gigs that can make decent money in India?* [Online forum post]. Reddit. https://www.reddit.com/r/personalfinanceindia/comments/1hjwj9c/what_are_some_side_income_jobsgigs_that_can_make/

Reserve Bank of India (RBI). (2024). *Handbook of statistics on Indian economy.* https://www.rbi.org.in

Ruckelshaus, C. (2008). Labor's wage war. *The Fordham Urban Law Journal, 35*(2), 373.

Saraswathi, C. (2023). The role and challenges of gig work platforms in Indian economic development. *International Journal of Research and Analytical Reviews, 10*(2), 92–97.

Schneider, H. (2017). *Creative destruction and the sharing economy – Uber as disruptive innovation.* Edward Elgar Publishing., DOI: 10.4337/9781786433435

Scholz, T. (2016). *Platform Cooperativism Challenging the Corporate Sharing Economy.* Rosa Luxemburg Stiftung – New York Office. Retrieved from https://rosalux.nyc/wp-content/uploads/2020/11/RLS-NYC_platformcoop.pdf

Schor, J. B., & Attwood-Charles, W. (2017). The "sharing" economy: Labor, inequality, and social connection on for-profit platforms. *Sociology Compass, 11*(8), e12493. DOI: 10.1111/soc4.12493

Schumpeter, J. (1942). *Capitalism, socialism, and democracy*. Harper & Bros.

Singh, A. (2024, November 27). *Uber introduces new safety measures primarily focusing on female users.* Business Standard. Retrieved March 12, 2025, from https://www.business-standard.com/companies/news/uber-introduces-new-safety-measures-primarily-focusing-on-female-users-124112701083_1.html

Sodhi, T. (2021, August 14). *'We are slaves to them': Zomato, Swiggy delivery workers speak up against unfair practices.* Newslaundry. https://www.newslaundry.com/2021/08/14/we-are-slaves-to-them-zomato-swiggy-delivery-workers-speak-up-against-unfair-practices

Srnicek, N. (2017). The challenges of platform capitalism: Understanding the logic of a new business model. *Juncture*, *23*(4), 254–257. DOI: 10.1111/newe.12023

Staffing Industry Analysts. (2024). *India's gig economy projected to create 90 million jobs.* https://www.staffingindustry.com/news/global-daily-news/indias-gig-economy-projected-to-create-90-million-jobs

Tan, Z. M., Aggarwal, N., Cowls, J., Morley, J., Taddeo, M., & Floridi, L. (2021). The ethical debate about the gig economy: A review and critical analysis. *Technology in Society*, *65*, 101594. DOI: 10.1016/j.techsoc.2021.101594

The Rockefeller Foundation. (2013). *Digital jobs in Africa: Catalyzing inclusive opportunities for youth.* https://www.rockefellerfoundation.org/report/digital-jobs-in-africa-catalyzing-inclusive-opportunities-for-youth/

United Kingdom Supreme Court. (2021). *R (on the application of KBR, Inc) v Director of the Serious Fraud Office* (UKSC 5). British and Irish Legal Information Institute. Retrieved March 12, 2025, from https://www.bailii.org/uk/cases/UKSC/2021/5.html

Vadavi, S., & Sharmiladevi, J. C. (2024). Analysing the evolution and patterns of the gig economy: A bibliometric examination of growth and trends. *Cogent Business & Management*, *11*(1), 2424480. Advance online publication. DOI: 10.1080/23311975.2024.2424480

Van Doorn, N. (2017). Platform labor: On the gendered and racialized exploitation of low-income workers in the on-demand economy. *Information Communication and Society*, *20*(6), 898–914. DOI: 10.1080/1369118X.2017.1294194

World Bank. (2015). *Jobs without borders.* https://www.worldbank.org/en/news/feature/2015/06/02/jobs-without-borders

World Bank. (2023). *The gig economy in Latin America: Trends and challenges.* https://www.worldbank.org

World Economic Forum. (2020). The future of jobs report. WEF.

Yoganandham, G., & Varalakshmi, D. (2024). The gig economy in India: The rise of start-ups, infrastructure, and the organization of the informal workforce. *GIS Science Journal, 11*(2), 16–26.

Zeid, R., Alrayess, D., Ajwad, M. I., Soytas, M. A., & Rivera, N. (n.d.). *The gig economy and the future of work: Global trends and policy directions for non-standard forms of employment.*

Ziegler, A., Fischer, J., & Mertens, A. (2020). Psychosocial impacts of gig work: Stress, job satisfaction, and work-life balance. *Journal of Business Ethics, 167*(2), 225–240. DOI: 10.1007/s10551-019-04183-4

ENDNOTES

1 Creative Destruction refers to an economic theory by Joseph Schumpeter where new innovations disrupt and replace older industries, leading to economic transformation and progress.

Chapter 2
A Study on the Obstacles and Prospects of Economic Consequences of the Gig Economy

P. S. Venkateswaran
https://orcid.org/0000-0001-8958-103X
PSNA College of Engineering and Technology, Dindigul, India

R. S. Balasenthil
K.L.N. College of Engineering, India

Dhruv Relan
Agilityo Executive Education, Paris, France

Matthieu Gavois
Agilityo Executive Education, Paris, France

ABSTRACT

This paper examines the determinants of economic consequences in the gig economy through regression analyses of five key factors: platform design, regulatory environment, worker characteristics, market conditions, and technological infrastructure. Using convenience sampling, regression model explains 75.1% of the variance in economic outcomes, revealing a significant hierarchy of influence among these factors. Worker characteristics and market conditions emerged as the most potent predictors, challenging narratives that prioritize technological or regulatory factors. The findings suggest potential synergistic interactions among variables, where improvements in one area may enhance the effectiveness of others. The moderate

DOI: 10.4018/979-8-3373-1290-3.ch002

impact of regulatory environment indicates that regulatory approaches should support worker capabilities and adapt to market realities rather than imposing universal solutions. This paper provides strategic directions for platform companies, policymakers, educational institutions, and workers to optimize economic outcomes in the evolving gig economy landscape.

1. INTRODUCTION

The gig economy, characterized by temporary, flexible jobs mediated through digital platforms, has fundamentally transformed traditional employment paradigms in the 21st century. This shift from conventional employment structures to platform-based work arrangements has sparked intense academic discourse regarding its economic implications. While proponents argue that the gig economy fosters entrepreneurship and economic flexibility, critics contend that it may perpetuate income inequality and job insecurity. Understanding these contradictory perspectives has become increasingly crucial as digital labor platforms continue to proliferate globally, reshaping labor markets and economic systems (Venkateswaran et a.,2019).

Recent empirical evidence suggests that the gig economy's impact extends beyond individual workers to influence broader macroeconomic indicators, including labor force participation rates, wage structures, and social security systems. The intersection of technological advancement with labor market dynamics has created a complex ecosystem where traditional economic theories may require significant recalibration. This complexity is further amplified by regional variations in regulatory frameworks and socioeconomic conditions, which significantly influence the manifestation and consequences of gig work across different economies.

Table 1. Comparative key aspects of gig workers in the UK, US, India, and China

Aspect	UK	US	India	China
Legal Status	Worker status with limited rights; landmark Uber ruling	Independent contractors; limited legal protections	Mostly informal; lacks legal protection and benefits	Contractual/flexible work; government regulates platforms
Popular Platforms	Deliveroo, Uber, TaskRabbit	Uber, Lyft, DoorDash, TaskRabbit	Swiggy, Zomato, Ola, Urban Company	Didi, Meituan, JD Daojia
Average Income (monthly)	£1,500–£2,000 (varies by city and hours)	$2,000–$3,500 (based on full-time gig work)	12,000– 25,000 (city and task-dependent)	¥3,000–¥6,000 (urban areas, sector-dependent)
Technological Integration	App-based assignments, GPS tracking, digital payments	Highly automated platforms with AI-based scheduling	Basic apps, route maps, wallet integrations	Advanced AI for allocation, performance tracking

continued on following page

Table 1. Continued

Aspect	UK	US	India	China
Social Security Access	Partial access (pensions, sick leave) after court rulings	Rare unless self-subscribed (e.g., health insurance)	Minimal to no social security	Government initiatives to provide limited benefits
Government Regulation	Actively evolving; court judgments influencing policy	Fragmented; local/state-based regulations	Nascent regulation; Labour Codes under revision	Central regulation of platforms and digital economy laws
Challenges	Algorithmic control, unstable income, lack of benefits	Job insecurity, inconsistent protections, legal ambiguity	Low wages, long hours, lack of insurance	Harsh working conditions, strict surveillance

Source: Author compiled from various data sources

The research examines the multifaceted economic implications of the gig economy, focusing on both structural obstacles and future prospects. Through a comprehensive analysis of existing literature and empirical data, the study investigates how this emerging economic model affects labor market efficiency, income distribution, and social welfare systems. This analysis contributes to the growing body of literature by providing a nuanced understanding of the gig economy's role in shaping future economic landscapes.

The rapid expansion of digital platforms has catalyzed significant structural changes in labor markets worldwide, with estimates suggesting that approximately 36% of US workers participated in the gig economy during 2023. This transformation has created unprecedented challenges for policymakers and economic institutions, particularly in areas of worker classification, social protection mechanisms, and tax revenue systems. The traditional dichotomy between employees and independent contractors has become increasingly blurred, necessitating novel approaches to labor regulation and social security frameworks (Verma et al., 2025).

Machine learning and the analysis of big data allow researchers to find patterns in gig economy jobs; incomes and what consumers prefer. With these tools, you can see that job insecurity and fluctuating pay are big problems, but flexibility and running your own business are attractive opportunities. With the help of predictive models, businesses can recognize economic outcomes and upcoming business changes, so they can adjust plans and personalize their services. Thanks to data, companies can see how consumer behavior changes and how their workforce must adapt in the future (Venkateswaran and Sriramkumar, 2025).

According to Venkateswaran et al., (2025), Brand reputation during the gig economy is best evaluated by examining how people respond and talk about a brand online. Analysis through machine learning has noted that uneven service quality and worker unhappiness are among the main problems for the company. Alternatively, prospects come about when there is positive talk about being flexible and innovative. Following up on customer feedback helps organizations learn about public opinion, adjust their brand plans and build trust among their customers. With this method, brand reputation varies depending on the latest changes in the gig industry.

The gig economy's impact on market competition and business innovation warrants careful consideration. Platform companies have introduced disruptive business models that challenge established industry norms while simultaneously creating new markets and economic opportunities. This digital transformation has led to reduced transaction costs and increased market efficiency, though questions remain about the long-term sustainability of these models and their effects on traditional businesses and employment structures.

The intersection of technological advancement and labor market evolution has highlighted critical gaps in existing economic theories and policy frameworks. While digital platforms offer unprecedented flexibility and market access, they also raise concerns about data privacy, algorithmic management, and worker autonomy. These challenges are particularly salient in developing economies, where the gig economy often operates alongside informal sectors, creating unique regulatory and social protection challenges that demand innovative policy solutions.

Understanding the economic ramifications of the gig economy becomes increasingly vital for policymakers, businesses, and academic researchers as society progresses further into the digital age. This research aims to contribute to this understanding by examining both the obstacles that impede optimal functioning of the gig economy and the prospects that could enhance its positive impact on global economic systems. Through this analysis, the study seeks to inform policy discussions and provide insights for developing more equitable and sustainable economic frameworks in the platform economy era.

Technology plays a pivotal role in shaping the gig economy by enabling flexible, on-demand work through digital platforms. Mobile apps, AI algorithms, and GPS tracking systems connect gig workers with customers, streamline task allocation, and monitor performance in real time. These technologies enhance efficiency, reduce transaction costs, and expand employment opportunities. However, they also introduce challenges such as algorithmic control, surveillance, and job insecurity. Despite offering autonomy and convenience, the tech-driven nature of gig work often limits workers' bargaining power. Therefore, technology in the gig economy is both an enabler of flexibility and a source of structural vulnerabilities for workers.

2. REVIEW OF LITERATURE

The gig economy has emerged as a significant force in contemporary labor markets, characterized by flexible work arrangements facilitated by digital platforms. This transformation has profound economic consequences, presenting both opportunities and challenges for workers and businesses alike. The economic landscape shaped by the gig economy is marked by a shift from traditional employment models to more transient and adaptable work structures, which has implications for job security, income stability, and worker rights.

Key difficulties in the gig economy can be tackled and probabilities improved with the help of artificial intelligence and robotics (Venkateswaran et al.,2024). AI helps with distributing tasks, makes transactions clearer and guarantees proper salary for everyone based on data. Robotics helps in tough fields that require large amounts of work, making both work and safety better. They make possible better job protection and fewer examples of worker exploitation, supporting growth and making the business more consistent. They also contribute to personalized shopping, achieve better outcomes for the economy and influence trends in gig-based companies.

One of the primary advantages of the gig economy is the flexibility it affords workers. Gig workers can choose when and where to work, which can lead to improved work-life balance and increased job satisfaction. For instance, studies indicate that many gig workers appreciate the autonomy and control over their schedules, which can enhance their overall quality of life (Palhad, 2023; Itohan, 2023). The flexibility often comes at a cost, as gig workers frequently face income instability and lack of access to traditional employment benefits such as health insurance and retirement plans (Li, 2023; Oberoi, S., & Kansra, P, 2021)). This precarious nature of gig work can lead to significant financial stress, particularly during economic downturns or crises, as evidenced during the COVID-19 pandemic (Anwar et al., 2022; Joo & Shawl, 2021).

The gig economy has been linked to broader economic trends, including the rise of digital platforms that facilitate the matching of labor supply and demand. This platformization of work has transformed traditional employment relationships, often blurring the lines between independent contracting and employee status (Bucos, 2023). As a result, gig workers may find themselves in a legal gray area, lacking the protections afforded to traditional employees. This situation raises critical questions about labor rights and the need for regulatory frameworks that can adequately address the unique challenges posed by gig work (Hardy & McCrystal, 2022; Hwang, 2024).

The gig economy also contributes to economic inclusion by providing opportunities for marginalized groups, including women and youth, to participate in the labor market. In many regions, gig work has become a viable option for individuals who may struggle to find traditional employment due to various barriers (Ayon, 2023). Women gig workers often face additional obstacles, including gender discrimination and unequal pay, which can exacerbate existing inequalities in the labor market (Pangrazio et al., 2021). Furthermore, while gig work can offer entry points into the workforce, it may also perpetuate cycles of low pay and job insecurity, particularly for those in lower-skilled positions (Pal & Varanasi, 2021; Ayentimi et al., 2022).

Another significant aspect of the gig economy is its impact on small and medium enterprises (SMEs). Many SMEs leverage gig workers to reduce labor costs and increase operational flexibility. This trend can foster innovation and growth within these businesses, as they can quickly adapt to changing market conditions without the burden of maintaining a permanent workforce (Palhad, 2023; Malik et al., 2021). The reliance on gig labor can also lead to challenges in workforce management and employee engagement, as gig workers may feel disconnected from the organizational culture and goals of the companies they serve (Salmah, 2024; Unnikrishnan & Baral, 2023).

The economic implications of the gig economy extend to taxation and social security systems as well. Gig workers often operate as independent contractors, which complicates their tax obligations and access to social safety nets (Oyinkansola, 2024; Adelakun, 2023). Many gig workers are unaware of their responsibilities as small business operators, leading to issues of tax compliance and potential exploitation by platforms that do not provide adequate support or guidance (Bakar, 2024; Adelakun, 2023). This lack of clarity can hinder the ability of governments to effectively regulate the gig economy and ensure that workers are adequately protected.

Furthermore, the gig economy has been criticized for fostering a culture of overwork and burnout. Gig workers often face pressure to maximize their earnings by taking on multiple jobs, which can lead to long hours and insufficient rest (Mohamed, 2023). This relentless pursuit of income can have detrimental effects on mental and physical health, raising concerns about the sustainability of gig work as a long-term employment solution (Nimmagadda, 2024; Wu, 2023).

In light of these challenges, there is a growing recognition of the need for comprehensive policy responses to address the complexities of the gig economy. Policymakers are increasingly called upon to develop regulatory frameworks that protect gig workers while also fostering innovation and economic growth (Hardy & McCrystal, 2022; Hwang, 2024). This includes considerations for minimum wage laws, access to benefits, and protections against discrimination and exploitation (Tan et al., 2021; Hwang, 2024).

The integration of technology into the gig economy presents both opportunities and challenges. While advancements in digital platforms have facilitated the growth of gig work, they have also raised ethical concerns regarding data privacy, algorithmic bias, and worker surveillance (Kaushik, 2024; The Dilemma and Thinking of Gig Workers in the Digital Organization Environment, 2023). As the gig economy continues to evolve, it is essential for stakeholders to engage in ongoing dialogue about the implications of these technologies for worker rights and protections.

The modern workforce provides new opportunities for income generation, offers flexibility and enhanced work autonomy, facilitates skill formation, and ensures work-life balance; all these phenomena have created significant changes in the labour market (Banik & Padalkar, 2021; Bansal & Singh, 2020; Holland & Brewster, 2020; Sutherland & Jarrahi, 2018; van Doorn et al., 2022). As attention towards labour unions, wage differentials, and long-term employment prospects are getting diluted, it is time for labour economists to focus more on the emerging concept of the "Gig Economy," which is becoming more prominent and emerging as a transformative force in employment (Allon, Cohen, & Sinchaisri, 2023).

The current volatile employment scenario on the one side and individuals' desire to earn from their comfort zone on the other is instrumental in widening the scope of the gig economy (Batmunkh, Fekete-Farkas, & Lakner, 2022; Silva & Moreira, 2022). The future workforce prefers to engage in creative and entrepreneurial endeavors rather than monotonous, lifetime professions in one field (Jha et al., 2021; Netto & Tello-Gamarra, 2020). This exposure can increase job advancement and versatility as people gain diverse experiences and talents. Gig work's dynamic nature fosters adaptability and innovation, which are highly valued in today's market (Spreitzer et al., 2017).

The gig economy is proliferating due to technological improvements and societal shifts towards independence and flexibility in the workplace. The current generation has become very vocal about their preference for gig work over established job arrangements. 53% of gig employees between the ages of 18 and 34 rely on gig work as their primary source of income (Kolmar, 2023). This development highlights a more significant cultural shift in which people value autonomy and work-life balance. The gig economy is increasing fifteen times faster than the traditional labour market, demonstrating its substantial influence on employment (Li, 2023). As the gig economy continues to grow fast, it is taking shape as a significant part of the labour market (Wood et al., 2019). Gig workers are exposed to various projects and industries, promoting ongoing learning and skill development (Dominic et al.,2023; Silva & Moreira, 2022; Keswani., et al., 2022).

This exposure can increase job advancement and versatility as people gain diverse experiences and talents. Gig work's dynamic nature fosters adaptability and innovation, which are highly valued in today's market (Spreitzer et al., 2017). The gig economy has completely changed the nature of work by providing freedom and flexibility to employees. Working independently within the gig economy can provide individuals with independence and authority, freedom to select projects, clients, and collaborations, making them more responsible for their work (Flanagan, 2019). This arrangement is advantageous to all parties; employees benefit from the independence of freelance work, and corporations may access elite talent without being limited by geography and access to a skilled and diverse workforce. A significant motivating factor for employers is to engage people to complete specific jobs to save money on administrative and other compliance expenses associated with full-time employment (Ashford, Caza, & Reid, 2018; Taylor, 2018). Companies can save on their fixed cost, as gig workers usually bring their own equipment. As most gig employees are already trained, variable expenses on conducting training sessions are minimized. Additionally, firms are not required to offer benefits like paid time off, health insurance, or retirement plans, which saves money (Berg et al., 2018).

Gig workers have independence and autonomy, as they can choose their projects, work hours, and work surroundings. This independence can lead to higher job satisfaction and a healthier work–life balance. Customizing their schedules allows gig workers to pursue personal hobbies and family obligations, resulting in a more rewarding lifestyle (Graham et al., 2017). According to a Zippia survey, the gig economy increases workers' job happiness and provides flexibility. 84% of gig workers perceive their work favorably, and 97% say they are happier than their full-time peers (Kolmar, 2023).

The gig economy is often described as a subtype of precarious work, where employment insecurity is a defining characteristic (Montgomery & Baglioni, 2020). This precariousness is exacerbated by the lack of traditional employment benefits such as health insurance, retirement plans, and paid leave, which are typically associated with full-time employment (Janasz et al., 2020). The absence of these benefits can lead to a cycle of financial vulnerability, particularly for low-income workers who may rely on gig work as their primary source of income (Churchill & Craig, 2019).

The gig economy has been linked to a broader trend of casualization in the labor market, where traditional employment relationships are increasingly replaced by flexible, on-demand work arrangements (Wood et al., 2018). This shift not only affects the economic stability of workers but also raises questions about the long-term implications for labor rights and protections. As gig workers are often classified as independent contractors rather than employees, they are excluded from many labor protections that apply to traditional workers (Fusco, 2020). This classification can lead to exploitation, as companies may prioritize profit over the welfare of their workers, resulting in a labor market that favors flexibility at the expense of security (Duggan et al., 2019).

The gender dynamics within the gig economy further complicate its economic implications. Research indicates that women are disproportionately represented in gig work, often driven by the need for flexible employment that accommodates family responsibilities (Churchill & Craig, 2019). This reliance on gig work can perpetuate existing gender inequalities in the labor market, as women may face barriers to advancement and experience lower earnings compared to their male counterparts (Cook et al., 2020). The gig economy thus not only reflects but also reinforces systemic inequalities, raising concerns about its sustainability as a viable employment model for diverse populations.

Despite these challenges, the gig economy also presents opportunities for innovation and entrepreneurship. Many workers are drawn to gig work for its potential to provide autonomy and flexibility, allowing them to balance personal and professional commitments (Berger et al., 2019). This aspect of gig work can lead to increased job satisfaction for some individuals, as they can tailor their work schedules to fit their lifestyles (Zaman et al., 2020). Furthermore, the gig economy can serve as a stepping stone for individuals seeking to enter the workforce or transition between careers, providing access to income-generating opportunities that may not be available in traditional employment settings (Rao, 2019).

The economic prospects of the gig economy are also influenced by technological advancements and the rise of digital platforms that facilitate gig work. These platforms have revolutionized the way services are delivered, enabling workers to connect with consumers in real-time and expand their market reach (Deng et al., 2020). The technological reliance raises concerns about the implications of algorithmic management, where workers are subject to surveillance and control through digital means (Sutherland et al., 2019). The balance between leveraging technology for efficiency and ensuring fair treatment of workers remains a critical challenge for the gig economy.

The gig economy's impact on traditional labor markets cannot be overlooked. As gig work becomes more prevalent, it may contribute to the erosion of standard employment relationships, leading to a fragmented labor market characterized by a mix of gig and traditional jobs (Kaine & Josserand, 2019). This fragmentation can complicate efforts to regulate labor standards and protect workers' rights, as the gig economy operates outside the purview of conventional labor laws (Stefano, 2019). Policymakers face the challenge of adapting existing regulations to address the unique dynamics of gig work while ensuring that workers are afforded the protections they deserve.

The COVID-19 pandemic has further highlighted the vulnerabilities of gig workers, as many faced significant income losses due to lockdowns and reduced demand for services (Apouey et al., 2020). The pandemic has underscored the need for a more robust safety net for gig workers, who often lack access to unemployment benefits and other forms of financial support (Polkowska, 2020). As the gig economy continues to evolve, it is imperative that stakeholders—including governments, platform companies, and labor organizations—collaborate to develop policies that address the challenges faced by gig workers and promote equitable labor practices. From the literature review the following gaps were identified and addressed in this paper.

Research Gap

- There is a growing concern about the impact of algorithmic management on worker autonomy, privacy, and mental health. Research indicates that algorithmic controls can lead to increased work intensity and psychological stress among gig workers.
- The rapid evolution of technology, including AI and digital platforms, has transformed gig work. However, research is needed to understand how these advancements affect job quality, worker satisfaction, and employment stability.
- The gig economy often operates in legal grey areas, leaving workers without adequate protections. There is a need for research into effective regulatory approaches that balance flexibility with worker rights.

3. RESEARCH METHODS

Research Design

This study employed a descriptive research design to investigate the economic consequences of the gig economy, with particular focus on obstacles and prospects faced by platform-based service providers. A descriptive approach was selected as it provides a comprehensive framework for examining the current state of gig work and its economic implications within a specific regional context (Creswell & Creswell, 2018).

Population and Sampling

The target population comprised food delivery service providers working with major gig platforms (Swiggy and Zomato) operating in the Madurai region of Tamil Nadu, India. These platforms were selected due to their significant market presence and representative nature within the regional gig economy ecosystem. A convenience sampling technique was utilized to recruit participants, acknowledging the challenges in establishing a comprehensive sampling frame for this often-transient workforce. This non-probability sampling approach enabled efficient data collection while providing valuable insights into the economic experiences of gig workers within the defined geographical area (Etikan et al., 2016).

Instrument Development and Validation

A structured questionnaire was developed based on comprehensive literature review and adapted to the specific context of food delivery service providers. The instrument consisted of six primary sections corresponding to the key constructs identified in the conceptual framework: Platform Design & Structure, Regulatory Environment, Worker Characteristics, Market Conditions, Technological Infrastructure, and Economic Consequences. Each section contained multiple items measured on a five-point Likert scale ranging from "Strongly Disagree" (1) to "Strongly Agree" (5).

To ensure instrument validity, a rigorous validation process was implemented. Content validity was established through expert review by three academic researchers specializing in labor economics and two industry professionals with extensive experience in gig economy platforms. Based on their feedback, several items were revised for clarity and relevance. Subsequently, a pilot test was conducted with 25 gig workers not included in the final sample to assess the instrument's comprehensibility and functionality. Construct validity was confirmed through factor analysis, which demonstrated clear factor structures with strong loadings (ranging from .791 to .927) and minimal cross-loading. Reliability analysis using Cronbach's alpha revealed high internal consistency for all constructs ($\alpha > .80$).

Data Collection Procedure

Data collection was conducted between June and August 2023 using a multi-stage approach. Initially, the researchers established contact with local Swiggy and Zomato operational managers to gain permission for approaching service providers. Primary data collection sites included designated waiting areas near popular restaurants, delivery hubs, and platform-specific rest areas within the Madurai metropolitan region.

Trained research assistants approached potential participants during non-peak hours to minimize disruption to their work schedules. After explaining the research purpose and obtaining informed consent, participants were provided with physical questionnaires. The research team maintained strict confidentiality protocols, with all responses collected anonymously and personal identifiers removed during data processing.

Response Rate and Sample Characteristics

A total of 300 service providers were approached to participate in the study. The research team received 271 completed questionnaires, representing an initial response rate of 90.3%. During data screening, 17 questionnaires were excluded due to substantial missing data or response patterns indicating inattentive completion.

The final analysis included 254 valid responses, yielding an effective response rate of 84.7%.

The sample comprised predominantly male participants (91.3%) with a mean age of 27.4 years (SD = 5.2). Regarding education level, 42.5% had completed secondary education, 38.2% held undergraduate degrees, and 19.3% had graduate-level qualifications. The average tenure in gig work was 18.7 months (SD = 9.4), with 65.7% reporting gig work as their primary source of income.

Data Analysis

Data analysis was conducted using IBM SPSS Statistics version 26.0. The analytical procedure followed a systematic approach beginning with preliminary data screening to identify outliers, missing values, and verify assumptions for subsequent analyses. Descriptive statistics were computed for all variables to characterize the sample and examine response distributions.

Factor analysis was performed to confirm the underlying structure of the measurement instrument, employing Principal Component Analysis with varimax rotation. The Kaiser-Meyer-Olkin measure (.822) and Bartlett's Test of Sphericity ($\chi^2 = 10743.776$, df = 465, $p < .001$) confirmed the suitability of the data for factor analysis. Six distinct factors emerged, collectively explaining 76.09% of the total variance.

Multiple regression analysis was conducted to examine the relationships between the five predictor variables (Platform Design & Structure, Regulatory Environment, Worker Characteristics, Market Conditions, and Technological Infrastructure) and the outcome variable (Economic Consequences). This analysis revealed the relative influence of each factor and their collective impact on economic outcomes. Standardized coefficients were calculated to facilitate comparisons among predictors, while variance inflation factors were examined to ensure the absence of problematic multicollinearity. Throughout the analytical process, p-values less than .05 were considered statistically significant, and confidence intervals were calculated at the 95% level.

4. ANALYSIS

The KMO value of .822 indicates excellent sampling adequacy. The high KMO value in this analysis suggests that the patterns of correlations are relatively compact, making factor analysis yield reliable factors. This indicates that the sample size of 254 obtained through convenience sampling is adequate for the analysis being conducted.

Table 2. KMO and Bartlett's Test

KMO and Bartlett's Test		
Kaiser-Meyer-Olkin Measure of Sampling Adequacy.		.822
Bartlett's Test of Sphericity	Approx. Chi-Square	10743.776
	df	465
	Sig.	.000

Bartlett's Test examines whether the correlation matrix is an identity matrix, which would indicate that variables are unrelated and therefore unsuitable for structure detection. The significance value of .000 ($p < .001$) indicates that the null hypothesis of an identity correlation matrix is rejected. This confirms that there are significant relationships among the variables in the dataset.

Table 3. PCA Results

Total Variance Explained									
Component	**Initial Eigenvalues**			**Extraction Sums of Squared Loadings**			**Rotation Sums of Squared Loadings**		
	Total	**% of Variance**	**Cumulative %**	**Total**	**% of Variance**	**Cumulative %**	**Total**	**% of Variance**	**Cumulative %**
Platform Design & Structure	12.679	40.901	40.901	12.679	40.901	40.901	9.939	32.060	32.060
Regulatory Environment	4.076	13.149	54.050	4.076	13.149	54.050	4.677	15.086	47.146
Worker Characteristics	2.031	6.552	60.602	2.031	6.552	60.602	4.065	13.114	60.260
Market Conditions	1.921	6.197	66.799	1.921	6.197	66.799	1.965	6.338	66.598
Technological Infrastructure	1.541	4.970	71.769	1.541	4.970	71.769	1.500	4.839	71.437
Economic Consequences	1.339	4.319	76.087	1.339	4.319	76.087	1.442	4.650	76.087

Extraction Method: Principal Component Analysis.

The Principal Component Analysis (PCA) results presented in the Total Variance Explained table offer significant insights into the underlying factor structure of the gig economy data. The analysis identified six distinct components with eigenvalues exceeding 1.0, collectively accounting for 76.087% of the total variance in the dataset. Platform Design & Structure emerged as the dominant component, explaining 40.901% of variance with an initial eigenvalue of 12.679, suggesting its fundamental role in shaping gig economy dynamics.

The Regulatory Environment component accounts for an additional 13.149% of variance, bringing the cumulative explained variance to 54.050%. Worker Characteristics and Market Conditions contribute somewhat equally to the model (6.552% and 6.197% respectively), while Technological Infrastructure explains 4.970% of variance. The Economic Consequences component, which likely represents the outcome variable of interest, explains 4.319% of variance. The rotation sums of squared loadings reveal how the variance distribution was optimized through rotation, with Platform Design & Structure's contribution adjusted to 32.060% and other components' contributions proportionally redistributed.

This more balanced distribution following rotation indicates a more interpretable factor solution while maintaining the same cumulative explained variance. The high total explained variance (76.087%) validates the robustness of the six-component solution, suggesting that these dimensions comprehensively capture the complex interrelationships within the gig economy framework. This factor structure provides a solid empirical foundation for subsequent analyses examining the relationships between these components and their collective influence on economic outcomes in the gig economy ecosystem.

Table 4. Factor analysis

Component Matrix[a]						
	Component					
	1	2	3	4	5	6
Platform Design & Structure						
Gig platforms provide fair compensation relative to the skills and time required of workers.	.927					
Gig platforms offer transparent and accurate information about earning potential and working conditions.	.872					
Gig platforms provide adequate communication channels between workers and clients/customers.	.865					
Gig platforms design their algorithms to fairly distribute work opportunities.	.837					
Gig platforms provide adequate appeal processes for dispute resolution.	.816					

continued on following page

Table 4. Continued

Component Matrix[a]						
	Component					
	1	**2**	**3**	**4**	**5**	**6**
Regulatory Environment						
Current labor laws adequately protect gig workers' rights.		.874				
The classification of gig workers is appropriate for the work performed.		.858				
Tax policies for gig workers are fair and straightforward to navigate.		.852				
Local regulations support rather than hinder gig economy growth.		.833				
Benefits policies adequately address gig workers' needs.		.793				
Worker Characteristics						
Gig workers have sufficient access to skill development opportunities.			.914			
Gig workers possess adequate technology literacy to maximize platform opportunities.			.888			
Gig workers have adequate financial literacy to manage irregular income streams.			.855			
Gig workers have sufficient social networks to navigate entry and advancement in gig work.			.848			
Gig workers have adequate access to healthcare resources independent of traditional employment.			.824			
Market Conditions						
There is sufficient demand for gig services in the local economy.				.906		
Competition levels among gig workers are sustainable for maintaining adequate income.				.874		
The gig economy grows in response to gaps in traditional employment opportunities.				.840		
Urban density positively impacts the viability of gig economy participation.				.818		
Seasonal fluctuations in gig work demand are predictable and manageable for workers.				.792		
Technological Infrastructure						
Internet connectivity is sufficiently reliable and affordable for gig workers to operate effectively.					.888	
Digital payment systems are accessible and efficient for gig economy transactions.					.871	
Mobile device availability and affordability support inclusive gig economy participation.					.863	
Platform algorithms fairly match worker skills with appropriate opportunities.					.822	
Data privacy protections adequately safeguard gig workers' personal information.					.791	
Economic Consequences						

continued on following page

Table 4. Continued

Component Matrix[a]						
	Component					
	1	**2**	**3**	**4**	**5**	**6**
The gig economy has increased overall employment rates in my community.						.909
Gig work has led to improved financial stability for workers in my region.						.894
The proliferation of gig work has positively impacted wage levels across traditional employment sectors.						.886
The gig economy has contributed to a reduction in income inequality.						.868
The rise of gig work has strengthened local economic resilience during economic downturns.						.848
The gig economy has created sustainable long-term career paths for workers.						.837

Extraction Method: Principal Component Analysis.
a. 6 components extracted.

The component matrix presented in Table 4.1 provides comprehensive evidence of a well-defined six-factor structure underlying the gig economy framework. Each factor demonstrates excellent internal consistency with strong factor loadings, indicating robust construct validity. The Platform Design & Structure component exhibits the highest factor loadings ranging from .816 to .927, highlighting the critical importance of platform mechanics in shaping gig economy experiences. Items related to fair compensation, transparency, communication channels, algorithmic fairness, and dispute resolution processes all load strongly on this component, suggesting that platform architecture represents a foundational element of the gig economy ecosystem.

The Regulatory Environment component demonstrates similarly robust loadings (.793 to .874) across items addressing labor laws, worker classification, tax policies, local regulations, and benefits policies, underscoring the significant role that governance frameworks play in structuring gig economy outcomes.

The Worker Characteristics component reveals substantial loadings (.824 to .914) for items related to skill development, technological literacy, financial management capabilities, social capital, and healthcare access, confirming the importance of human capital dimensions in determining success within gig work arrangements.

Market Conditions emerge as a distinct factor with strong loadings (.792 to .906) for items measuring demand sufficiency, competition levels, relationship to traditional employment, geographic influences, and seasonal patterns, validating the contextual importance of economic environments.

The Technological Infrastructure component displays high loadings (.791 to .888) across items addressing internet connectivity, payment systems, device availability, algorithmic matching, and data privacy protections, confirming the enabling role of digital infrastructure.

The Economic Consequences component exhibits robust loadings (.837 to .909) for outcome measures related to employment rates, financial stability, wage impacts, income inequality, economic resilience, and career sustainability. The clean loading pattern with no significant cross-loadings provides strong empirical support for the conceptual framework proposed in this research, establishing a solid foundation for subsequent analyses examining the relationships between these components and their collective influence on economic outcomes in the gig economy.

Table 5. Impact of platform design & structure on economic consequences of the gig economy

ANOVA[a]						
Model		Sum of Squares	df	Mean Square	F	Sig.
1	Regression	96.253	1	96.253	190.455	.000[b]
	Residual	127.357	252	.505		
	Total	223.610	253			
R =.656		R Square = .430				
a. Dependent Variable: Economic Consequences						
b. Predictors: (Constant), Platform Design & Structure						

Coefficients[a]						
Model		Unstandardized Coefficients		Standardized Coefficients	t	Sig.
		B	Std. Error	Beta		
1	(Constant)	1.305	.190		6.869	.000
	Platform Design & Structure	.645	.047	.656	13.801	.000

a. Dependent Variable: Economic Consequences

Null Hypothesis H01: There is no significant relationship between gig platform design & structure and economic consequences of the gig economy.

The regression analysis examining the relationship between platform design & structure and economic consequences of the gig economy yielded statistically significant results ($F(1, 252) = 190.455$, $p < .001$). The null hypothesis (H01) positing no significant relationship between gig platform design & structure and economic consequences can be confidently rejected. The coefficient of determination (R^2 = .430) indicates that platform design & structure explains 43% of the variance in economic consequences, representing a substantial effect size in social science research.

The standardized coefficient (β = .656) demonstrates a strong positive relationship between platform design & structure and economic consequences. This indicates that improvements in platform design & structure are associated with more favorable economic outcomes in the gig economy. The unstandardized coefficient (B = .645) suggests that for each one-unit increase in platform design & structure ratings, economic consequences ratings increase by approximately 0.645 units. The t-statistic (t = 13.801, p < .001) confirms the statistical significance of this relationship, indicating that the observed association is highly unlikely to have occurred by chance.

Table 6. Regulatory environment as a determinant of economic consequences in the gig economy

ANOVA[a]						
Model		Sum of Squares	df	Mean Square	F	Sig.
1	Regression	123.575	1	123.575	311.299	.000[b]
	Residual	100.035	252	.397		
	Total	223.610	253			
R =.743		R Square = .533				
a. Dependent Variable: Economic Consequences						
b. Predictors: (Constant), Regulatory Environment						

Coefficients[a]						
Model		Unstandardized Coefficients		Standardized Coefficients	t	Sig.
		B	Std. Error	Beta		
1	(Constant)	1.088	.162		6.725	.000
	Regulatory Environment	.731	.041	.743	17.644	.000

a. Dependent Variable: Economic Consequences

Null Hypothesis H02: There is no significant relationship between the regulatory environment surrounding gig work and economic consequences of the gig economy.

The regression analysis examining the relationship between regulatory environment and economic consequences in the gig economy yielded highly significant results (F(1, 252) = 311.299, p < .001). The null hypothesis (H02) stating no significant relationship between regulatory environment and economic consequences can be decisively rejected. The model demonstrates considerable explanatory power, with a coefficient of determination ($R^2 = .553$) indicating that regulatory environment accounts for 55.3% of the variance in economic consequences, representing a robust effect size that exceeds typical standards in social science research.

The standardized coefficient ($\beta = .743$) reveals a strong positive relationship between regulatory environment and economic consequences, suggesting that more favorable regulatory conditions are associated with improved economic outcomes in the gig economy. The magnitude of this coefficient indicates that regulatory environment is a powerful predictor of economic consequences. The unstandardized coefficient ($B = .731$) demonstrates that for each one-unit improvement in regulatory environment ratings, economic consequences ratings increase by approximately 0.731 units. The t-statistic ($t = 17.644$, $p < .001$) confirms the statistical significance of this relationship with a high degree of confidence.

Table 7. The role of worker characteristics in determining economic consequences of the gig economy

ANOVA[a]						
Model		**Sum of Squares**	**df**	**Mean Square**	**F**	**Sig.**
1	Regression	138.636	1	138.636	411.143	.000[b]
	Residual	84.974	252	.337		
	Total	223.610	253			
R= .787		R Square = .620				
a. Dependent Variable: Economic Consequences						
b. Predictors: (Constant), Worker Characteristics						

Coefficients[a]						
Model		**Unstandardized Coefficients**		**Standardized Coefficients**	**t**	**Sig.**
		B	**Std. Error**	**Beta**		
1	(Constant)	.762	.157		4.864	.000
	Worker Characteristics	.808	.040	.787	20.277	.000

a. Dependent Variable: Economic Consequences

Null Hypothesis H03: There is no significant relationship between gig worker characteristics and economic consequences of the gig economy.

The regression analysis examining the relationship between worker characteristics and economic consequences in the gig economy produced exceptionally significant results ($F(1, 252) = 411.143$, $p < .001$). The null hypothesis (H03) positing no significant relationship between gig worker characteristics and economic consequences can be confidently rejected. The model demonstrates remarkable explanatory power, with a coefficient of determination ($R^2 = .620$) indicating that worker characteristics account for 62% of the variance in economic consequences of the gig economy, representing a substantial effect size that exceeds conventional thresholds in social science research.

The standardized coefficient ($\beta = .787$) reveals a strong positive relationship between worker characteristics and economic consequences, indicating that more favorable worker attributes and resources are associated with substantially improved economic outcomes in the gig economy. The magnitude of this coefficient suggests that worker characteristics constitute a critical determinant of economic consequences in this sector. The unstandardized coefficient ($B = .808$) demonstrates that for each one-unit improvement in worker characteristics ratings, economic consequences ratings increase by approximately 0.808 units. The t-statistic ($t = 20.277$, $p < .001$) confirms the statistical significance of this relationship with an exceptionally high degree of confidence.

Table 8. Market conditions as a predictor of economic consequences in the gig economy

ANOVA[a]						
Model		Sum of Squares	df	Mean Square	F	Sig.
1	Regression	138.311	1	138.311	408.610	.000[b]
	Residual	85.300	252	.338		
	Total	223.610	253			
R = .798		R Square = .637				
a. Dependent Variable: Economic Consequences						
b. Predictors: (Constant), Market Conditions						

Coefficients[a]						
Model		Unstandardized Coefficients		Standardized Coefficients	t	Sig.
		B	Std. Error	Beta		
1	(Constant)	.668	.162		4.125	.000
	Market Conditions	.816	.040	.798	20.214	.000

a. Dependent Variable: Economic Consequences

Null Hypothesis H04: There is no significant relationship between market conditions and economic consequences of the gig economy.

The regression analysis examining the relationship between market conditions and economic consequences in the gig economy produced highly significant results ($F(1, 252) = 408.610$, $p < .001$). The null hypothesis (H04) positing no significant relationship between market conditions and economic consequences can be decisively rejected. The model demonstrates exceptional explanatory power, with a coefficient of determination ($R^2 = .637$) indicating that market conditions account for 63.7% of the variance in economic consequences of the gig economy, representing a substantial effect size that considerably exceeds conventional benchmarks in social science research.

The standardized coefficient ($\beta = .798$) reveals a strong positive relationship between market conditions and economic consequences, indicating that more favorable market conditions are associated with substantially improved economic outcomes in the gig economy. This coefficient suggests that market conditions represent a critical determinant of economic consequences in this sector. The unstandardized coefficient ($B = .816$) demonstrates that for each one-unit improvement in market conditions ratings, economic consequences ratings increase by approximately 0.816 units. The t-statistic ($t = 20.214$, $p < .001$) confirms the statistical significance of this relationship with an exceptionally high degree of confidence.

Table 9. Technological infrastructure and economic consequences in the gig economy

ANOVA[a]						
Model		**Sum of Squares**	**df**	**Mean Square**	**F**	**Sig.**
1	Regression	108.458	1	108.458	237.352	.000[b]
	Residual	115.152	252	.457		
	Total	223.610	253			
R = .696		R Square = .485				
a. Dependent Variable: Economic Consequences						
b. Predictors: (Constant), Technological Infrastructure						
Coefficients[a]						
Model		**Unstandardized Coefficients**		**Standardized Coefficients**	**t**	**Sig.**
		B	**Std. Error**	**Beta**		

continued on following page

Table 9. Continued

1	(Constant)	.923	.195		4.735	.000
	Technological Infrastructure	.750	.049	.696	15.406	.000

a. Dependent Variable: Economic Consequences

Null Hypothesis H05: There is no significant relationship between technological infrastructure and economic consequences of the gig economy.

The regression analysis examining the relationship between technological infrastructure and economic consequences in the gig economy yielded statistically significant results ($F(1, 252) = 237.352$, $p < .001$). The null hypothesis (H05) positing no significant relationship between technological infrastructure and economic consequences can be confidently rejected. The coefficient of determination ($R^2 = .485$) indicates that technological infrastructure explains 48.5% of the variance in economic consequences, representing a substantial effect size that meets conventional thresholds for practical significance in social science research.

The standardized coefficient ($\beta = .696$) demonstrates a strong positive relationship between technological infrastructure and economic consequences, indicating that improvements in technological infrastructure are associated with enhanced economic outcomes in the gig economy. This coefficient suggests that technological infrastructure represents an important determinant of economic consequences in this sector. The unstandardized coefficient ($B = .750$) demonstrates that for each one-unit improvement in technological infrastructure ratings, economic consequences ratings increase by approximately 0.750 units. The t-statistic ($t = 15.406$, $p < .001$) confirms the statistical significance of this relationship with a high degree of confidence.

Table 10. Factors influencing economic consequences in the gig economy

ANOVA[a]						
Model		Sum of Squares	df	Mean Square	F	Sig.
1	Regression	168.029	5	33.606	149.946	.000[b]
	Residual	55.582	248	.224		
	Total	223.610	253			
	R = .867	R Square = .751				
a. Dependent Variable: Economic Consequences						
b. Predictors: (Constant), Technological Infrastructure, Platform Design & Structure, Regulatory Environment, Market Conditions, Worker Characteristics						

continued on following page

Table 10. Continued

Coefficients[a]						
Model		Unstandardized Coefficients		Standardized Coefficients	t	Sig.
		B	Std. Error	Beta		
1	(Constant)	-.143	.154		-.929	.354
	Platform Design & Structure	.181	.041	.184	4.409	.000
	Regulatory Environment	.136	.055	.138	2.481	.014
	Worker Characteristics	.285	.061	.278	4.659	.000
	Market Conditions	.284	.058	.274	4.885	.000
	Technological Infrastructure	.146	.052	.135	2.818	.005

a. Dependent Variable: Economic Consequences

Null Hypothesis H06: Platform design & structure, regulatory environment, worker characteristics, market conditions, and technological infrastructure have no significant impact on the economic consequences of the gig economy.

The multiple regression analysis examining the collective impact of platform design & structure, regulatory environment, worker characteristics, market conditions, and technological infrastructure on economic consequences in the gig economy yielded highly significant results ($F(5, 248) = 149.946$, $p < .001$). The null hypothesis (H06) asserting no significant impact of these factors on economic consequences can be definitively rejected. The model demonstrates exceptional explanatory power, with a coefficient of determination ($R^2 = .751$) indicating that these five predictors collectively account for 75.1% of the variance in economic consequences, representing a substantial effect size that far exceeds conventional thresholds in social science research.

Worker characteristics emerged as the strongest predictor ($\beta = .278$, $t = 4.659$, $p < .001$), indicating that worker-related factors such as skill development, technological literacy, and financial management capabilities have the most substantial influence on economic outcomes. Market conditions followed closely ($\beta = .274$, $t = 4.885$, $p < .001$), suggesting that factors such as service demand, competition levels, and geographic considerations play a nearly equally important role in determining economic consequences.

Platform design & structure demonstrated a moderate effect ($\beta = .184$, $t = 4.409$, $p < .001$), confirming that platform architecture, including compensation structures and communication channels, significantly impacts economic outcomes. Regulatory environment showed a smaller but still significant effect ($\beta = .138$, $t = 2.481$, $p =$

.014), indicating that labor laws, tax policies, and benefits frameworks contribute meaningfully to economic consequences. Technological infrastructure revealed the smallest but still significant effect (β = .135, t = 2.818, p = .005), confirming that technological foundations such as internet connectivity and payment systems influence economic outcomes.

5. DISCUSSION

The comprehensive regression analyses reveal the complex, multidimensional nature of economic consequences in the gig economy. Our findings demonstrate that each of the five investigated factors—platform design, regulatory environment, worker characteristics, market conditions, and technological infrastructure—independently exerts a significant influence on economic outcomes. When examined collectively in the multiple regression model, these factors explain an impressive 75.1% of the variance in economic consequences, providing a robust framework for understanding the determinants of economic success in the gig economy ecosystem.

The comparative analysis of standardized coefficients reveals a notable hierarchy in the influence of these factors. Worker characteristics and market conditions emerged as the most potent predictors, suggesting that the intersection of human capital and market dynamics plays a disproportionately important role in determining economic outcomes. These finding challenges the narratives that often emphasize technological or regulatory factors as primary drivers of gig economy success. Instead, our results indicate that the characteristics of the workers themselves—their skills, technological literacy, financial management capabilities, and access to resources—along with the market environment in which they operate, are the foremost determinants of economic consequences.

Figure 1. Shows the economic consequences in the gig economy

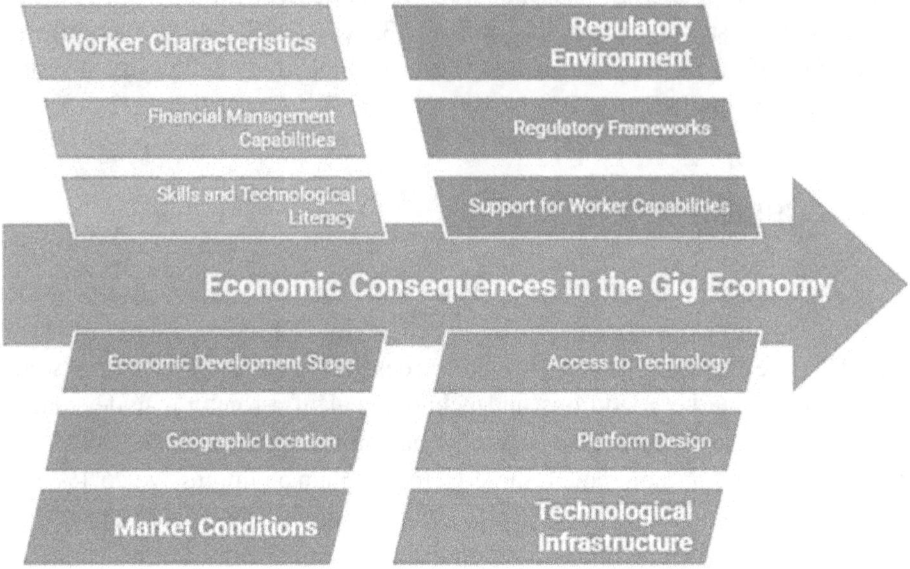

Figure 1 shows the economic consequences in the GIG economy

The multiple regression model's collective explanatory power ($R^2 = .751$) exceeds what might be expected from a simple additive combination of the individual models, suggesting potential synergistic interactions among the predictor variables. This indicates that improvements in one area may enhance the effectiveness of others. For instance, enhancements in technological infrastructure might amplify the benefits of strong worker characteristics, while favorable market conditions might increase the impact of well-designed platforms. These potential interaction effects merit further investigation to understand how these factors work in concert to shape economic outcomes.

The strong influence of market conditions ($\beta = .274$) underscores the importance of contextual factors in determining gig economy outcomes. This suggests that the economic consequences of gig work may vary significantly across different geographic locations, urban-rural divides, and economic development stages. The findings have important implications for the globalization of gig platforms, indicating that approaches successful in one market context may require substantial adaptation to achieve similar economic benefits in different environments.

The significant but comparatively moderate impact of regulatory environment ($\beta = .138$) presents an interesting contrast to often polarized public discourse around gig economy regulation. While regulatory frameworks clearly matter, their influence appears less pronounced than worker-centric and market factors. This suggests that regulatory approaches should be calibrated to support and enhance these more influential factors rather than being developed in isolation. The findings indicate that the most effective regulatory frameworks may be those that strengthen worker capabilities and adapt to market realities rather than imposing one-size-fits-all solutions.

Role of Technology for Gig Workers-a Case

In India, Swiggy, a leading food delivery platform, exemplifies the role of technology in supporting gig workers. Through its mobile application, Swiggy uses AI and geolocation to assign delivery tasks efficiently, track routes, and predict delivery times. For gig workers, this means a steady stream of orders, optimized travel routes, and digital payment systems that reduce cash handling. However, the app also uses performance metrics to rate workers, affecting their future opportunities. While the technology empowers workers with flexible schedules and earnings, it also enforces algorithmic control, making them dependent on opaque systems that often lack human intervention.

6. PRACTICAL IMPLICATIONS

Figure 2. Strategic framework of gig economy

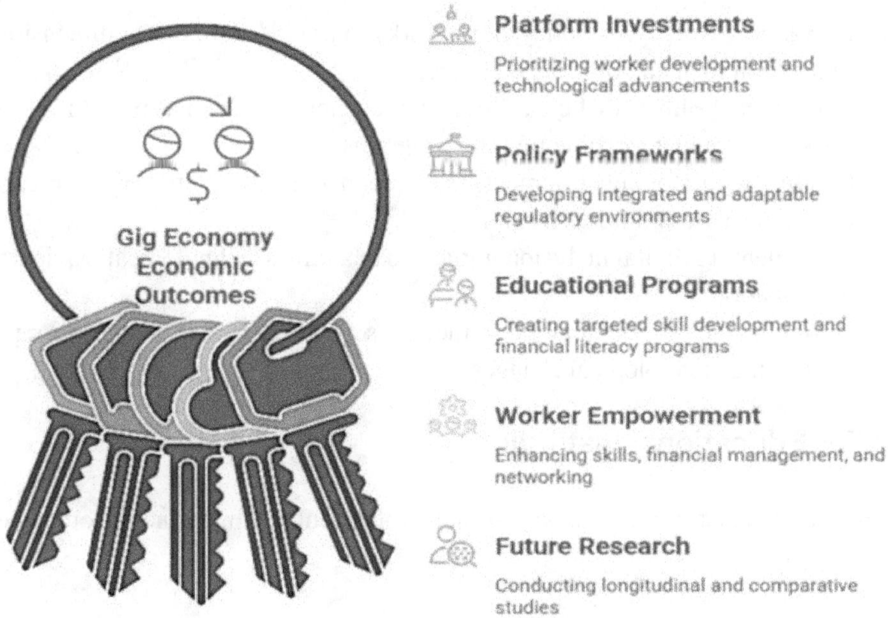

Figure 2 – Strategic framework of GIG economy

6.1 For Platform Companies

Platform companies should prioritize investments in worker development programs alongside technological improvements. The findings suggest that platforms could potentially achieve greater economic benefits by:

- Implementing comprehensive training programs to enhance worker skills and technological literacy
- Developing robust financial management tools tailored to gig workers' irregular income patterns
- Creating community structures that foster professional networking among workers
- Designing algorithms and matching systems that respond intelligently to local market conditions
- Ensuring platform features accommodate varying levels of technological access and literacy

6.2 For Policymakers

The findings suggest several strategic directions for policymakers seeking to optimize economic outcomes in the gig economy:

- Developing integrated policy frameworks that address multiple dimensions rather than focusing on isolated aspects
- Prioritizing policies that enhance worker capabilities, such as portable benefits systems and accessible training programs
- Creating regulatory environments that recognize and adapt to varying market conditions across different regions
- Implementing digital inclusion initiatives to address technological barriers to participation
- Designing flexible regulatory frameworks that can evolve alongside rapid market and technological changes

6.3 For Educational Institutions

Educational institutions can play a crucial role in enhancing economic outcomes in the gig economy by:

- Developing targeted skill development programs specifically designed for gig economy participation

- Creating curriculum elements focused on financial literacy for irregular income patterns
- Incorporating technological skills relevant to diverse gig platforms into vocational training
- Fostering entrepreneurial capabilities that enable workers to navigate complex market conditions
- Establishing continuing education programs that help workers adapt to evolving platform requirements

6.4 For Workers

Individual gig workers may benefit from these findings by:

- Prioritizing the development of platform-relevant skills and technological literacy
- Adopting sophisticated financial management practices suitable for irregular income
- Strategically selecting work opportunities based on local market conditions
- Building professional networks to enhance access to opportunities and information
- Advocating collectively for platform features and regulatory frameworks that enhance economic outcomes

6.5 For Future Research

This study identifies several promising directions for future research:

- Longitudinal studies examining how the influence of these factors evolves over time
- Investigation of potential interaction effects between the identified predictors
- Comparative analyses across different geographic contexts and regulatory regimes
- Qualitative exploration of the mechanisms through which worker characteristics influence economic outcomes
- Development of more nuanced measures of economic consequences beyond immediate financial metrics

7. CONCLUSION

The findings from this research underscore the complex and multifaceted nature of economic consequences in the gig economy. By explaining 75.1% of the variance through our multiple regression model, we have identified a clear hierarchy of influencing factors, with worker characteristics and market conditions emerging as predominant determinants. This challenges the techno-centric and regulatory-focused narratives often dominating discourse around gig economy outcomes.

The potential synergistic interactions between factors suggest that interventions should be coordinated across multiple dimensions rather than implemented in isolation. The moderate influence of regulatory frameworks indicates that policy approaches should be calibrated to enhance worker capabilities and respond to market conditions instead of imposing standardized solutions. Longitudinal studies examining how these relationships evolve over time and comparative analyses across different geographic and regulatory contexts would further enrich our understanding of gig economy dynamics.

For stakeholders across the ecosystem—platform companies, policymakers, educational institutions, and workers themselves—these findings provide actionable strategies to optimize economic outcomes. By acknowledging the primacy of human capital and market dynamics, interventions can be more effectively targeted to enhance the economic potential of participation in the gig economy while addressing its inherent challenges.

REFERENCES

Adelakun, B. O. (2023). Tax compliance in the gig economy: the need for transparency and accountability. Journal of Knowledge Learning and Science Technology ISSN: 2959-6386 (Online), 1(1), 191-198. DOI: 10.60087/jklst.vol1.n1.p219

Ahmad, K., Samad, K., Rahman, N., Daud, S., Marmaya, N., Nasution, Y., & Hamzah, R. (2024). Policies improving the well-being of gig workers in Malaysia. *Information Management and Business Review*, *16*(1(I)), 182–189. DOI: 10.22610/imbr.v16i1(I).3698

Allon, G., Cohen, M. C., & Sinchaisri, W. P. (2023). The impact of behavioral and economic drivers on gig economy workers. *Manufacturing & Service Operations Management*, *25*(4), 1376–1393. DOI: 10.1287/msom.2023.1191

Anan, K. (2024). The evolution of employment law in the gig economy. *Journal of Modern Law and Policy*, *4*(2), 29–41. DOI: 10.47941/jmlp.2160

Anwar, M. A., Otieno, E., & Stein, M. (2022). Locked in, logged out: Pandemic and ride-hailing in South Africa and Kenya. *The Journal of Modern African Studies*, *60*(4), 457–478. DOI: 10.1017/S0022278X22000234

Apouey, B. H., Roulet, A., Solal, I., & Stabile, M. (2020). Gig workers during the covid-19 crisis in France: financial precarity and mental well-being. SSRN Electronic Journal. DOI: 10.2139/ssrn.3688445

Arafin Ayon, S. M. M. (2023). Digital dreams, gendered realities: insights from Bangladesh's freelance sector... DOI: 10.31235/osf.io/95tsy

Asfahani, A., Alsobahi, G., & Dahlan, D. (2023). Navigating the Saudi gig economy: The role of human resource practices in enhancing job satisfaction and career sustainability. *Sustainability (Basel)*, *15*(23), 16406. DOI: 10.3390/su152316406

Ashford, S. J., Caza, B. B., & Reid, E. M. (2018). From surviving to thriving in the gig economy: A research agenda for individuals in the new world of work. *Research in Organizational Behavior*, *38*, 23–41. DOI: 10.1016/j.riob.2018.11.001

Auguste, D., Roll, S., & Despard, M. (2023). Democratizing the economy or introducing economic risk? gig work during the covid-19 pandemic. *Work and Occupations*, *51*(4), 550–606. DOI: 10.1177/07308884231202032

Ayentimi, D., Abadi, H., & Burgess, J. (2022). Decent gig work in sub-Sahara Africa? *The Journal of Industrial Relations*, *65*(1), 112–125. DOI: 10.1177/00221856221111693

Banik, N., & Padalkar, M. (2021). The spread of gig economy: Trends and effects. *Foresight and STI Governance, 15*(1), 19–29. DOI: 10.17323/2500-2597.2021.1.19.29

Bansal, R., & Singh, R. (2020). The emergence of gig economy in India: A paradigm shift. *Parishodh Journal, 9*(3), 123–134.

Batmunkh, A., Fekete-Farkas, M., & Lakner, Z. (2022). Bibliometric analysis of gig economy. *Administrative Sciences, 12*(2), 51. DOI: 10.3390/admsci12020051

Beatrice Oyinkansola, A. (2024). The gig economy: challenges for tax system. Journal of Knowledge Learning and Science Technology ISSN: 2959-6386 (Online), 3(3), 1-8. DOI: 10.60087/jklst.vol3.n3.p1-8

Berg, J., Furrer, M., Harmon, E., Rani, U., & Silberman, M. S. (2018). Digital labour platforms and the future of work – Towards decent work in the online world. International Labour Organization. https://doi.org/DOI: 10.2139/ssrn.3355364

Berger, T., Frey, C. B., Levin, G. I., & Danda, S. R. (2019). Uber happy? work and well-being in the 'gig economy'. *Economic Policy, 34*(99), 429–477. DOI: 10.1093/epolic/eiz007

Bucos, T. (2023). The gig economy – result of the labour market platformization. *Economica*, (2(124)), 25–42. DOI: 10.53486/econ.2023.124.025

Churchill, B., & Craig, L. (2019). Gender in the gig economy: Men and women using digital platforms to secure work in Australia. *Journal of Sociology (Melbourne, Vic.), 55*(4), 741–761. DOI: 10.1177/1440783319894060

Cook, C., Diamond, R., Hall, J. V., List, J. A., & Oyer, P. (2020). The gender earnings gap in the gig economy: Evidence from over a million rideshare drivers. *The Review of Economic Studies, 88*(5), 2210–2238. DOI: 10.1093/restud/rdaa081

Deng, X., Taylor, J., & Moussawi, S. (2020). Introduction to the minitrucks on crowdsourcing and digital workforce in the gig economy. *Proceedings of the Annual Hawaii International Conference on System Sciences*. DOI: 10.24251/HICSS.2020.488

Dominic, L. M., Sowmiya, S., & Venkateswaran, P. S. (2023). Study on the importance of entrepreneurship skill development programme (ESDP) for sustainable growth of MSMEs in India. *Proceedings on Engineering Sciences, 05*(3), 553–564. DOI: 10.24874/PES05.03.018

Duggan, J., Sherman, U., Carbery, R., & McDonnell, A. (2019). Algorithmic management and app-work in the gig economy: A research agenda for employment relations and hrm. *Human Resource Management Journal, 30*(1), 114–132. DOI: 10.1111/1748-8583.12258

Flanagan, F. (2019). Freedom or precarity? Freelancers and the future of the gig economy. *Work, Employment and Society*, *33*(3), 418–426. DOI: 10.1177/0950017018781870

Fusco, F. (2020). Rethinking the allocation criteria of the labour law rights and protections: A risk-based approach. *European Labour Law Journal*, *11*(2), 131–141. DOI: 10.1177/2031952520905152

Graham, M., Hjorth, I., & Lehdonvirta, V. (2017). Digital labour and development: Impacts of global digital labour platforms and the gig economy on worker livelihoods. *Transfer: European Review of Labour and Research*, *23*(2), 135–162. DOI: 10.1177/1024258916687250 PMID: 28781494

Hardy, T., & McCrystal, S. (2022). The importance of competition and consumer law in regulating gig work and beyond. *The Journal of Industrial Relations*, *64*(5), 785–800. DOI: 10.1177/00221856211068868

Holland, P., & Brewster, C. (2020). The gig economy: A threat to employment relations? *Human Resource Management Journal*, *30*(1), 90–101. DOI: 10.1111/1748-8583.12220

Hwang, J. (2024). The gig economy and its implications for labor laws and worker protections. *International Journal of Science and Research Archive*, *13*(1), 3405–3416. DOI: 10.30574/ijsra.2024.13.1.1714

Janasz, S. C., Kim, S. W., Schneer, J. A., Beutell, N. J., & Wong, C. M. (2020). Work-family integration and segmentation in the gig economy: Airbnb hosts' challenges and strategies. *Proceedings - Academy of Management*, *2020*(1), 20130. DOI: 10.5465/AMBPP.2020.20130abstract

Jha, S., Mehta, P., & Gupta, P. (2021). Millennials and the gig economy: Understanding the changing workplace preferences. *Journal of Management Research*, *21*(2), 122–138.

Joo, B. A. and Shawl, S. (2021). Covid-19 pandemic and the rising gig economy: an emerging perspective. Global Economics Science, 16-23. DOI: 10.37256/ges.232021917

Kaine, S., & Josserand, E. (2019). The organization and experience of work in the gig economy. *The Journal of Industrial Relations*, *61*(4), 479–501. DOI: 10.1177/0022185619865480

Kaushik, A. (2024). Comprehensive impact of on-demand platforms: Examining the gig economy\'s influence on specialized professionals, work-life balance, and gig workers\' perspectives. *International Journal for Research in Applied Science and Engineering Technology*, *12*(1), 552–559. DOI: 10.22214/ijraset.2024.58005

Keswani, S., Cavaliere, L. P. L., Venkateswaran, P. S., Muda, I., Raj, K. B., & Khanna, R. (2022). Economic practices and financial performances of pharmaceutical companies in rural areas. *Journal of Positive School Psychology*, *6*(3), 4091–4110. DOI: 10.1080/2168009X.2022.2123342

Khanal, S., & Khanal, M. (2024). Regulating gig economy in Nepal: How can Nepal benefitted from the gig platform? *J. Musikot Campus*, *2*(1), 173–192. DOI: 10.3126/jmc.v2i1.70844

Kolmar, C. (2023). 25 gig economy statistics [2023]: Facts, trends, and impacts. Zippia Research. Retrieved from https://www.zippia.com/advice/gig-economy-statistics/

Li, S. (2023). The gig economy and labour market dynamics. Advances in Economics. *Management and Political Sciences*, *61*(1), 275–281. DOI: 10.54254/2754-1169/61/20231285

Li, Y. (2023). Gig economy growth rate outpaces traditional employment: A comparative statistical analysis. *Labour Economics Review*, *28*(1), 44–57.

Malaysia, P., Uchiyama, Y., Nasrudin, M., & Akhir, M. (2022). Gig workers, social protection and labour market inequality: Lessons from Malaysia. *Jurnal Ekonomi Malaysia*, *56*(3). Advance online publication. DOI: 10.17576/JEM-2022-5603-09

Malik, R., Visvizi, A., & Skrzek-Lubasińska, M. (2021). The gig economy: Current issues, the debate, and the new avenues of research. *Sustainability (Basel)*, *13*(9), 5023. DOI: 10.3390/su13095023

Mohamed, S., & Mat, N. H. N. (2023). Gig work in post pandemic times: Does it an agile work structure? *Journal of Entrepreneurship and Business*, *11*(2), 56–68. DOI: 10.17687/jeb.v11i2.1014

Montgomery, T., & Baglioni, S. (2020). Defining the gig economy: Platform capitalism and the reinvention of precarious work. *The International Journal of Sociology and Social Policy*, *41*(9/10), 1012–1025. DOI: 10.1108/IJSSP-08-2020-0400

Mouazen, A., & Hernández-Lara, A. (2023). Entrepreneurial ecosystem, gig economy practices and women's entrepreneurship: The case of Lebanon. *International Journal of Gender and Entrepreneurship*, *15*(3), 249–274. DOI: 10.1108/IJGE-07-2022-0116

Netto, A. J., & Tello-Gamarra, J. (2020). The gig economy and human capital development: Empirical perspectives. *Global Journal of Human Resource Management, 8*(1), 12–25.

Nimmagadda, B., Vangaveti, Y., Aaluri, S., Mallikarjuna Rao, C., & Singh, B. (2024). An analytical study on navigating sustainability challenges and opportunities in the era of ai and the gig economy. MATEC Web of Conferences, 392, 01044. DOI: 10.1051/matecconf/202439201044

Oberoi, S., & Kansra, P. (2021). Motivating antecedents and consequences of blockchain technology in the insurance industry. In *Blockchain technology and applications for digital marketing* (pp. 276–285). IGI Global. DOI: 10.4018/978-1-7998-8081-3.ch017

Pal, B., & Varanasi, S. (2021). Rising popularity in gig economy: A case study from india. *International Journal of Religious and Cultural Studies, 3*(2). Advance online publication. DOI: 10.34199/ijracs.2021.09.08

Palhad, S., Onwubu, S., Singh, R., Thakur, R., Thakur, S., & Mkhize, G. (2023). The benefits and challenges of the gig economy: perspective of gig workers and small medium and micro enterprises (SMMES) in South Africa. African Journal of Inter/Multidisciplinary Studies, 5(1), 1-12. DOI: 10.51415/ajims.v5i1.1051

Pangrazio, L., Bishop, C., & Lee, F. (2021). Old media, new gigs: The discursive construction of the gig economy in Australian news media. *Work, Employment and Society, 37*(3), 606–624. DOI: 10.1177/09500170211034663

Polkowska, D. (2020). Platform work during the covid-19 pandemic: a case study of glove couriers in Poland. European Societies, 23(sup1), S321-S331. DOI: 10.1080/14616696.2020.1826554

Rao, R. (2019). Did gig economy change ways of work? evidence from American time use survey. *Proceedings of the International Academic Conference on Management and Economics*. DOI: 10.33422/conferenceme.2019.11.654

Salmah, E., Astuti, E., & Harsono, I. (2024). Employee engagement in the gig economy. [PRODUCTIVITY]. *Management Studies and Business Journal, 1*(1), 116–122. DOI: 10.62207/1e5dd842

Silva, M. F., & Moreira, A. C. (2022). The gig economy: A critical review of the literature and implications for human resource management. *International Journal of Human Resource Studies, 12*(1), 123–145. DOI: 10.5296/ijhrs.v12i1.19665

Sood, A., & Singh, R. (2023). The new emerging world of work: Growth story of India's gig economy. *International Journal of Management and Economics Invention, 09*(10). Advance online publication. DOI: 10.47191/ijmei/v9i10.03

Spreitzer, G. M., Cameron, L., & Garrett, L. (2017). Alternative work arrangements: Two images of the new world of work. *Annual Review of Organizational Psychology and Organizational Behavior, 4*(1), 473–499. DOI: 10.1146/annurev-orgpsych-032516-113332

Stefano, V. D. (2019). The gig economy and labour regulation: an international and comparative approach. Revista Direito Das Relações Sociais E Trabalhistas, 4(2), 68-79. DOI: 10.26843/mestradodireito.v4i2.158

Sutherland, W., & Jarrahi, M. H. (2018). The sharing economy and digital platforms: A review and research agenda. *International Journal of Information Management, 43*, 328–341. DOI: 10.1016/j.ijinfomgt.2018.07.004

Sutherland, W., Jarrahi, M. H., Dunn, M., & Nelson, S. (2019). Work precarity and gig literacies in online freelancing. *Work, Employment and Society, 34*(3), 457–475. DOI: 10.1177/0950017019886511

Tan, Z. M., Aggarwal, N., Cowls, J., Morley, J., Taddeo, M., & Floridi, L. (2021). The ethical debate about the gig economy: A review and critical analysis. *Technology in Society, 65*, 101594. DOI: 10.1016/j.techsoc.2021.101594

Taylor, M. (2018). Good work: The Taylor review of modern working practices. HM Government. Retrieved from https://www.gov.uk/government/publications/good-work-the-taylor-review-of-modern-working-practices

Unnikrishnan, P., & Baral, R. (2023). Reimagining hr practices to attract and engage gig talent: An organizational perspective. *NHRD Network Journal, 16*(3), 248–257. DOI: 10.1177/26314541231170433

Van Doorn, N., Ferrari, F., & Graham, M. (2022). Migration and digital labour: A relational perspective on platform work. Environment and Planning A. *Economy and Space, 54*(3), 491–510. DOI: 10.1177/0308518X211044853

Venkateswaran, P. S., Arun, B., Byloppilly, R., Rameshkkumar, S. R., & Reddy, M. S. (2025). *A Study on Evaluating Brand Reputation by Measuring Sentiment and Response Rates in the Digital Age. E-Commerce, Marketing, and Consumer Behavior in the AI Era*. IGI Global Publications.

Venkateswaran, P. S., Sabarirajan, A., Rajest, S. S., & Regin, R. (2019). The theory of postmodernism in consumerism, mass culture, and globalization. *Journal of Research on the Lepidoptera, 50*(4), 97–113. DOI: 10.36872/LEPI/V50I4/201075

Venkateswaran, P. S., & Sriramkumar, M. (2025). *Predictive Analytics: Utilizing Machine Learning and Big Data for Forecasting Future Trends in Business and Consumer Behavior. Strategic Brand Management in the Age of AI and Disruption*. IGI Global Publications., DOI: 10.4018/979-8-3693-9461-8.ch019

Venkateswaran, P. S., Sriramkumar, M., Vaddy, R. K., Kotagiri, A., Rajest, S. S., & Regin, R. (2024). Applications of artificial intelligence and robots in service industries. In *Advancing intelligent networks through distributed optimization* (pp. 61–80). IGI Global Publications., DOI: 10.4018/979-8-3693-3739-4.ch004

Verma, B., Bhardwaj, M., Arora, S., & Oberoi, S. (2025). Unveiling the impact of remittances on productive efficiencies: Investigating productivity growth of prominent remittance-receiving developing nations. *International Journal of Productivity and Performance Management, 74*(4), 1101–1124. DOI: 10.1108/IJPPM-05-2023-0213

Wood, A. J., Graham, M., Lehdonvirta, V., & Hjorth, I. (2018). Good gig, bad gig: Autonomy and algorithmic control in the global gig economy. *Work, Employment and Society, 33*(1), 56–75. DOI: 10.1177/0950017018785616 PMID: 30886460

Wu, H. (2023). The future of work: A comprehensive study of the gig economy beyond low labor-value added jobs. Advances in Economics. *Management and Political Sciences, 64*(1), 112–120. DOI: 10.54254/2754-1169/64/20231511

Zaman, U., Nawaz, S., Javed, A., & Rasul, T. (2020). Having a whale of a time: Linking self-determination theory (SDT), job characteristics model (JCM) and motivation to the joy of gig work. Cogent Business &Amp. *Cogent Business & Management, 7*(1), 1807707. DOI: 10.1080/23311975.2020.1807707

Chapter 3
Digital Transformation in Higher Education: Navigating the Gig Economy Revolution

Vladimir Radivojević
https://orcid.org/0000-0002-3928-0623
Faculty of Economics, University of Priština in Kosovska Mitrovica, Serbia

ABSTRACT

The rapid expansion of the gig economy is reshaping labor markets worldwide, driven by technological advancements and changing workforce dynamics. This paper explores the intersection of higher education and the gig economy, emphasizing the need for transformative changes in educational systems to address emerging challenges. The primary goal is to analyze how higher education institutions can adapt by incorporating innovative tools such as micro-credentials and massive open online courses to equip students with skills aligned with the demands of the digital economy. The methodology combines a comprehensive literature review and analysis of regional trends in gig work, focusing on the European Union and Western Balkans, alongside global perspectives. Key conclusions highlight the importance of aligning education with labor market needs, fostering lifelong learning, and addressing regional disparities through tailored strategies. The paper is valuable for policymakers, educators, and researchers aiming to modernize education and promote equitable and sustainable workforce development.

DOI: 10.4018/979-8-3373-1290-3.ch003

INTRODUCTION

The gig economy represents a profound shift in the global workforce, where traditional, long-term employment models are being replaced by flexible, independent work arrangements. Gone are the days when workers stayed with one company for decades, anticipating the long-term benefits and job security associated with permanent, full-time positions. Instead of remaining with a single employer for years, workers are increasingly piecing together their careers by engaging in various types of work, juggling multiple clients, and adopting roles that require a broader skill set. This includes becoming marketers, accountants, and business owners in addition to their primary profession. As noted by Horowitz (2011), this transition is as significant as the shift from an agricultural to an industrial economy, marking a transformation that is reshaping careers.

This massive transition in the workforce, however, has not been met with corresponding changes in higher education systems globally. As the demand for new knowledge and skills increases, driven by the growing gig economy and evolving labor market demands, higher education institutions (HEIs) have struggled to keep pace. The shift toward independent work requires workers to possess a diverse skill set, blending specialized expertise with entrepreneurial, digital, and problem-solving skills. Unfortunately, many higher education systems have not yet adapted to provide these essential competencies at scale. Consequently, there is a noticeable gap between the skills required by workers in the gig economy and those imparted by traditional educational institutions. This gap presents significant challenges, not only to individuals seeking to succeed in a rapidly changing labor market but also to economies striving for growth, sustainability, and more equitable wealth distribution.

For economies to thrive in this new landscape, it is crucial to align educational offerings with the evolving needs of the gig economy. Bridging this gap will be essential to ensure prosperity, a more equitable economic distribution, and sustainability in the face of ongoing global transformations. Without this shift, there is a risk that many workers will be left behind, unable to fully participate in the opportunities created by the digital economy.

In addition to global trends, the Western Balkan context introduces a set of region-specific challenges that deserve early attention. The region continues to grapple with persistent limitations in digital infrastructure, fragmented digital strategies, and underdeveloped workforce readiness. These challenges affect both the implementation of modern educational tools and the ability of graduates to engage in gig work, particularly in remote or digitally mediated roles. A clearer focus on these contextual elements underscores the urgency for targeted educational reforms and supports the paper's emphasis on localized solutions.

The primary aim of this paper is to explore how HEIs can better respond to the rise of the gig economy through curriculum reform, digital innovation, and strategic alignment with labor market needs – especially in under-researched regions such as the Western Balkans. The gig economy has rapidly grown into a significant global employment model, driven by digitalization and shifts in workforce dynamics. This paper delves into the role of HEIs in addressing the challenges posed by this transformation, including gaps in skills, digital competencies, and employability. Particular attention is given to the unique challenges faced by HEIs in the Western Balkans, where systemic obstacles such as resource constraints, fragmented strategies, and low awareness of digital tools hinder progress.

To achieve this goal, the paper employs a mixed-methods approach, incorporating a review of existing literature, case studies from leading universities and regions, and an analysis of quantitative data on gig work trends and educational adaptation. By synthesizing insights from global practices and specific examples, the study highlights innovative educational strategies such as micro-credentials and massive open online courses (MOOCs), which are increasingly recognized as essential tools in bridging the gap between traditional academia and the gig economy.

The findings of this paper contribute to the broader field of education and labor market studies by offering both theoretical and practical insights. On a theoretical level, the paper enriches understanding of how digital transformation influences the relationship between education and work. On a practical level, it provides a general roadmap for policymakers, university administrators, and industry leaders to design more adaptive, inclusive, and forward-thinking education policies and programs. This dual contribution underscores the significance of aligning educational frameworks with the realities of contemporary labor markets to foster sustainable economic growth and social equity.

The structure of the paper reflects this integrative approach. Following the introduction, the first section delves into the terminological diversity and conceptual challenges in defining the "gig economy", highlighting the inconsistent use of various terms across different contexts and regions. The next section examines the growing trend of gig work globally, providing a comparative analysis of the United States (US), the European Union (EU), and the Western Balkans. The subsequent section explores how HEIs can integrate innovative educational tools such as micro-credentials and MOOCs to prepare students for gig work. The paper then addresses the specific challenges facing HEIs in the Western Balkans, including financial limitations, insufficient infrastructure, and fragmented digital strategies. Finally, the conclusion summarizes key findings and proposes actionable recommendations for HEIs and policymakers to enhance their contributions to the gig economy.

By addressing these pressing issues, this paper aims to bridge the gap between academia and the rapidly transforming labor landscape, offering a comprehensive perspective on how HEIs can play a central role in shaping the workforce of the future.

DEFINING THE GIG ECONOMY

In existing literature and policy documents worldwide, there is considerable variation in the terminology used to describe the gig economy, reflecting the lack of a unified understanding of this rapidly growing sector. The terms "gig economy", "platform economy", "sharing economy", "crowd employment", and "on-demand economy" are frequently used across different countries and regions, but their meanings often overlap or differ depending on the context in which they are used (Eurofound, 2018). This lack of standardization can cause confusion in academic research, policy discussions, and regulatory frameworks, leading to inconsistent approaches when addressing the challenges and opportunities posed by the gig economy.

The "gig economy" is one of the most commonly used term and typically refers to short-term, freelance, or task-based work facilitated through digital platforms (Vadavi, Sharmiladevi, 2024). However, this term can encompass a broad range of work arrangements, from ridesharing to creative freelancing. In contrast, terms like "platform economy" and "platform work" tend to focus more specifically on work mediated by digital platforms, often involving paid labor for tasks that are broken down into discrete jobs and offered on-demand. "Sharing economy" is another frequently cited term, though it is somewhat broader and can refer to both paid and unpaid exchanges of goods or services between individuals, typically mediated by a digital platform. This broader definition includes non-remunerative exchanges such as lending or sharing goods, rather than strictly paid work.

The term "crowd employment" is also used to describe work arrangements where tasks are outsourced to a distributed network of workers, often through online platforms. "On-demand economy" focuses specifically on work that is requested and completed on demand, such as transportation or food delivery services. These different terms are sometimes used interchangeably but can refer to different facets of the gig economy, making it difficult to arrive at a clear, consistent definition that encompasses all forms of gig work. This lack of clarity complicates efforts to establish coherent labor policies and regulatory frameworks that ensure fair protections for gig workers across various sectors and countries.

Eurofound (2018) has conducted a comprehensive analysis of the alternative terms used to describe gig economy work in various EU member states, shedding light on the inconsistencies in terminology across the region (see Table 1). Their findings indicate that the lack of standardized definitions complicates the development of effective policies and regulations for platform workers. According to Eurofound's research, countries such as Latvia and Finland use a variety of terms, including "sharing economy", "on-demand economy", "collaborative economy", and "crowd sourcing", often interchangeably. This reflects a broad understanding of platform work that includes not only paid labor but also other forms of participation in digital platforms, such as non-monetary exchanges and collaborative consumption.

In contrast, countries like Denmark and Sweden have a more streamlined approach, primarily focusing on terms such as "sharing economy", "platform economy", or "gig economy". This more limited use of terms highlights a more specific focus on paid labor facilitated through digital platforms, and it may suggest a more targeted approach in defining and regulating platform work. The diversity in terminology across the EU member states, as shown in Eurofound's analysis, underscores the challenges in developing a unified regulatory framework for gig economy (gig work). The inconsistency in terms complicates the ability to draw consistent comparisons or implement uniform policies across countries, making it difficult to ensure that gig workers receive fair labor protections. The data presented in Table 1, which outlines the various terms used for gig economy in different EU countries, further highlights this issue, suggesting that a more standardized approach is necessary for the effective regulation and protection of gig workers in the EU.

Table 1. Alternative terms for gig economy used in selected EU Member States

Country	Sharing economy	Platform economy	Gig economy	Crowd employment	On-demand economy	Collaborative economy	Crowd sourcing	Peer-to-peer economy	Freelance
Austria		x	x	x			x		
Belgium	x	x						x	
Bulgaria			x	x					x
Croatia	x	x							
Denmark	x	x	x	x					
Estonia	x	x		x					
Finland	x	x	x		x	x	x	x	
France	x	x				x		x	x
Germany		x	x				x		
Ireland			x						
Italy	x	x	x		x	x			
Latvia	x	x		x	x	x	x		x
Netherl.	x	x	x		x				
Poland		x					x		x

continued on following page

Table 1. Continued

Country	Sharing economy	Platform economy	Gig economy	Crowd employment	On-demand economy	Collaborative economy	Crowd sourcing	Peer-to-peer economy	Freelance
Slovenia	x	x				x			
Spain	x	x			x	x			
Sweden	x	x	x			x			x
UK	x		x						

Source: Eurofound, 2018, p.10

The term "gig economy" was first coined during the financial crisis of 2009 when many individuals, unable to find full-time work, turned to multiple part-time jobs or "gigs" to make ends meet (Hook, 2015). Initially, gig work referred to short-term engagements, such as jazz musicians playing at clubs in the 1920s. However, in today's context, the gig economy has evolved significantly, largely due to the rise of digital platforms like *Uber* and *Airbnb*. These platforms have expanded gig work beyond traditional industries, enabling a broader range of people – such as retirees renting out rooms or office workers offering rides during their commutes – to participate (Hong, 2015). While the nature of gig work has changed, offering greater flexibility and access to a wider range of individuals, many of its core characteristics, such as the absence of benefits like healthcare, pensions, and paid leave, have remained consistent (Hook, 2015; Hong, 2015).

Following the discussion of the gig economy's evolution, it is essential to highlight how it is defined in contemporary research. McKinsey (2023) defines the gig economy as "the workforce of people engaged in freelance and side-hustle work", emphasizing its broad scope. Burtch et al. (2018) focus on the digital, on-demand nature of gig economy platforms, highlighting their role in enabling flexible work schedules and connecting workers with tasks in real-time. Eurofound (2018) focuses on platform work, a key component of the gig economy, defining it as "a form of employment that uses an online platform to enable organizations or individuals to access other organizations or individuals to solve problems or to provide services in exchange for payment" (p. 9). This definition emphasizes the intermediary role of online platforms in facilitating task-based, on-demand work arrangements. Minter (2017) further outlines the key labor practices of digital platform businesses, which typically exhibit the following characteristics:

(1) Work is divided into specific individual tasks or jobs, and workers are engaged on a task-by-task basis without any assurance of ongoing work
(2) Tasks are performed by individual workers but commissioned by end-users, which may include individual consumers or businesses

(3) Labor is facilitated by for-profit companies that charge users for services and pay workers for each task. These transactions are managed through digital platforms or web-based applications controlled by the company
(4) Workers are classified as independent contractors, meaning they lack standard employment benefits and protections, including sick leave, minimum wages, annual leave, and access to workers' compensation
(5) The price for each task is determined either by the platform company or by the commissioning customer. Payment is collected through the platform, which retains a portion of the fee before disbursing the remaining amount to the worker

The terminological diversity and varying definitions of the gig economy underscore its complexity and the challenges in capturing its full scope. While the evolution of the gig economy has been transformative, enabling flexibility and new forms of income generation, it has also highlighted the need for clear, standardized definitions to guide policy and regulation. The analysis of Eurofound's data on alternative terms across EU member states illustrates how fragmented the understanding of this concept remains, further complicating efforts to develop coherent labor policies. Ultimately, as the gig economy continues to evolve, achieving consensus on its terminology and definition will be critical to ensuring fair labor protections, fostering sustainable growth, and addressing the challenges faced by workers in this emerging labor model.

While the definitional ambiguity surrounding the gig economy highlights its conceptual complexity, it also sets the stage for examining the rapid and diverse growth of gig work across regions. Understanding how this evolving model manifests globally requires a closer look at regional trends, economic drivers, and digital platform dynamics, which are explored in the following section.

THE GROWING TREND OF GIG WORK ACROSS COUNTRIES

As digital platforms become increasingly embedded in the global economy, the gig workforce is expanding at a rapid pace, reshaping labor markets across the world. In developed economies such as the US and parts of Europe, more individuals are turning to gig work as either a primary or supplementary source of income. The rise of online platforms has lowered traditional barriers to entry by enabling workers to easily connect with clients and employers, fostering new opportunities in a labor market where long-term, stable employment is declining due to economic shifts, technological advancements, and evolving workforce dynamics (Srihita et al., 2025).

Despite its opportunities, the gig economy presents significant challenges. Income volatility, lack of benefits, job insecurity, and the absence of labor protections are pressing issues for gig workers. These individuals, often categorized as independent contractors rather than employees, lack access to essential protections such as health insurance, retirement plans, and minimum wage guarantees. Addressing these challenges requires coordinated efforts from governments, businesses, and educational institutions to adapt to the evolving labor landscape. Despite these insecurities, many individuals are either drawn to or compelled to enter gig work due to its flexibility, accessibility, or as a necessity in the face of limited traditional employment opportunities. This growing reliance on gig work highlights the need to explore the increasing number of gig workers worldwide and the factors driving this trend.

Globally, online gig work accounts for up to 12% of the labor force and serves as a vital source of income for millions (World Bank, 2024). According to the *Global Digital Platform Power Index 2023* (DinarStandard, 2023), the digital platform economy is experiencing unprecedented growth, with the top 370 platforms generating an estimated $1.87 trillion in annual revenue and attracting 371 billion average monthly users in 2022. US-based platforms dominate this market, comprising 48% of the total number of platforms and capturing 90% of the global user base. In contrast, China accounts for 12% of platforms but only 3% of global users, illustrating the concentration of platform power in the US.

This concentration has significant implications for global markets. The US, home to 178 of the leading platforms, outpaces all other countries, underscoring the global dominance of companies such as *Google*, *Facebook*, and *Amazon* (DinarStandard, 2023). While this leadership highlights the technological and economic influence of US platforms, it also raises concerns about data privacy, domestic market stability, and the ability of other countries to regulate these platforms effectively.

The report (DinarStandard, 2023) further identifies emerging economies that outperform their GDP rankings in platform development. For instance, China and India have climbed 50 and 46 positions, respectively, demonstrating the potential for lower-GDP countries to leverage strategic investment and infrastructure in the digital economy. Similarly, smaller nations like Singapore, Estonia, and Denmark have shown significant platform power, underscoring the potential of innovation and digital infrastructure to generate outsized returns, even with limited consumer bases.

The expanding gig economy's significance is further highlighted by the increasing number of freelancers in the US. Projections from 2017 to 2028 reveal rapid growth in freelance work, illustrating its rising importance within the broader economy (Statista, 2024).

Figure 1. Number of freelancers in the United States from 2017 to 2028 (in millions)

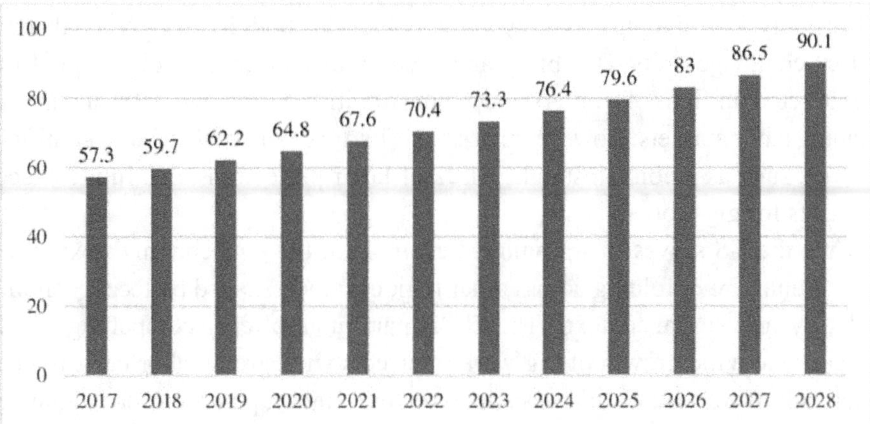

Source: Statista, 2024

As illustrated in Figure 1, the number of freelancers in the US has steadily increased from 57.3 million in 2017 to a projected 90.1 million by 2028 (Statista, 2024). This upward trajectory reflects a significant shift in the workforce, as more individuals opt for freelance or gig-based work instead of traditional, full-time employment. This growth highlights a broader global trend, where workers seek the flexibility, independence, and digital connectivity that the gig economy provides.

Breaking down the data year by year, the number of freelancers increased by 2.4 million from 2017 to 2018, a growth of approximately 4.2%. From 2018 to 2019, the number of freelancers grew by another 2.5 million, or 4.2%, continuing the upward trend. The period from 2019 to 2020 saw an even sharper increase, with freelancers rising by 2.6 million, or 4.2%. This spike can be attributed to the impact of the COVID-19 pandemic, which forced many individuals to seek alternative work arrangements as traditional job opportunities were disrupted.

From 2020 to 2021, the number of freelancers grew by 2.8 million, marking a 4.3% increase. The growth continued into 2022, with an additional 2.8 million freelancers entering the market. This steady increase reflects the resilience of the gig economy, even as traditional labor markets faced significant challenges during the pandemic. The continued rise in freelancing can be attributed to the increasing digitalization of work, the ease of accessing freelance platforms, and a broader cultural shift towards more flexible working arrangements.

Looking ahead, the number of freelancers is expected to increase consistently each year, with a projected 23.7 million more freelancers in 2028 compared to 2024. This steady growth reflects the ongoing demand for flexible labor in the US and suggests that platform work will continue to play a significant role in the future of work. The gig economy is likely to keep expanding as technological advancements, such as AI, automation, and remote work tools, create new opportunities for freelancing.

The analysis of the gig economy in the US reveals both its vast potential and its inherent challenges. The flexibility and accessibility offered by digital platforms have attracted millions of workers, redefining traditional employment structures and reshaping labor markets. However, these benefits are counterbalanced by significant concerns, such as income instability, lack of labor protections, and limited access to benefits for gig workers.

While the US serves as a prominent example of the gig economy's expansion, similar trends are unfolding across other regions, albeit shaped by local economic, regulatory, and digital contexts. The EU, in particular, offers a compelling case for analysis, where the growth of gig work intersects with strong labor laws, regional digitalization efforts, and diverse socio-economic landscapes. A closer examination of the EU's gig economy provides critical insights into how global trends manifest in unique ways across countries and regions.

THE DYNAMICS OF THE GIG ECONOMY IN THE EUROPEAN UNION

The gig economy in the European Union exemplifies a complex and evolving labor model, shaped by the interplay of robust labor laws, regional economic disparities, and the rapid pace of digital transformation. This unique dynamic provides valuable insights into the development of gig work and its broader implications for labor markets across the region. Understanding the trends, challenges, and opportunities within the EU's gig economy is essential for addressing its impact on economic and social systems.

The prominence of gig work in the EU has grown substantially in recent years, reflecting broader global trends. As of 2022, over 28 million individuals were engaged in digital platform work across member states, and this figure is projected to rise to 43 million by 2025 (European Council, 2024). This surge parallels the broader expansion of the gig economy, where revenues have grown substantially, increasing from approximately €3 billion in 2016 to €14 billion in 2020. These numbers reflect not only the growing prevalence of gig work but also its economic significance in the EU's evolving labor landscape. The study of Piasna et al. (2022) highlights significant country-level variations in platform work prevalence. Slovakia, Ireland, and Austria report the highest shares of platform workers, while Romania and Hungary have the lowest. Additionally, the intensity and type of platform work differ substantially. For instance, transport and delivery work dominate in Ireland and France, while remote professional tasks are more prevalent in Germany and Spain.

A 2022 pilot survey conducted by Eurostat (2023) provides further insights into the scale and nature of gig work in the EU. The survey found that 3% of individuals aged 15 to 64 participated in digital platform work for at least one hour in the previous year. While this proportion may seem modest, it underscores the growing importance of gig work as a flexible employment model, particularly in a rapidly digitalizing world. This trend highlights the role of gig work in providing opportunities for supplementary income and serving as a viable option for those seeking non-traditional forms of employment.

Despite these advancements, Europe lags behind global leaders like the US and Asia-Pacific in the gig economy. In 2023, Europe accounted for just 2.2% of the global gig economy, valued at $314.6 million, compared to the US, which holds over 80% of the market share with a value exceeding $11 billion (Hosseini, 2023). Asia-Pacific remains a critical player despite a slight decline, with countries like China and India hosting significant platforms. Europe's smaller market share highlights its struggle to compete on the global stage.

Key challenges for Europe's gig economy include regulatory complexities, fragmented digital markets, and slower adoption of digital innovation compared to the US and Asia-Pacific. These barriers limit scalability and competitiveness (Krstić et al., 2016), though Europe's emphasis on consumer protection and labor rights offers a balanced approach to the gig economy's challenges. Overall, the EU's gig economy reflects a significant labor market transformation, presenting both opportunities and challenges. While the region demonstrates steady growth, addressing regulatory barriers, fostering innovation, and investing in digital infrastructure will be essential to enhance its global competitiveness and ensure sustainable development for all stakeholders.

While much of the focus on gig work has been on EU countries with established digital economies, the gig economy is increasingly making its mark in Eastern and Southern Europe as well. In the Western Balkans, for example, the rise of gig work has become an increasingly important component of labor markets, shaped by advancements in digital platforms and the growing demand for flexible work arrangements. This region, which includes Albania, Bosnia and Herzegovina, Montenegro, North Macedonia, and Serbia, demonstrates a diverse landscape of gig work, influenced by varying levels of digital infrastructure, economic conditions, and workforce characteristics.

Figure 1 illustrated this growth trend in the US freelance market and should be interpreted in the context of broader platformization and labor flexibility. In contrast, Figure 2 highlights regional disparities in Southeastern Europe, offering insight into the uneven adoption of gig work driven by socio-economic and infrastructural differences. To provide a comparative perspective, Figure 2 illustrates the number of gig workers per 100,000 population in selected Southeastern European countries, including Bulgaria, Hungary, Croatia, and Romania, alongside the Western Balkan nations (Anđelković et al., 2024).

Figure 2. Number of gig workers per 100,000 population in selected Southeastern European countries

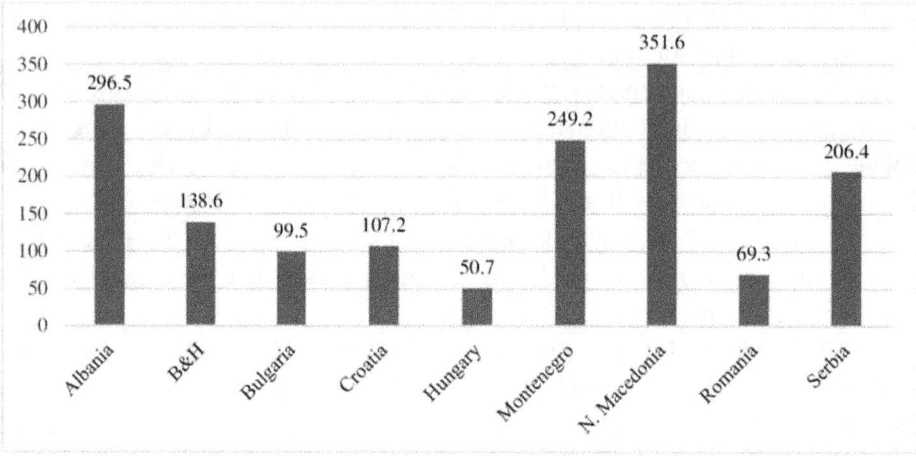

Source: Anđelković et al., 2024

The data presented in Figure 2 reveal significant variation in the prevalence of gig work across these countries. North Macedonia leads the Western Balkans with 351.6 gig workers per 100,000 inhabitants, followed by Albania (296.5) and Montenegro (249.2). Serbia, with 206.4 gig workers per 100,000, also demonstrates a substantial engagement in platform work, while Bosnia and Herzegovina lags behind with 138.6. These figures suggest that the gig economy is serving as a critical avenue for income generation and employment in the Western Balkans, where economic development remains limited, unemployment rates are high, and traditional job opportunities are scarce. Platforms like *Upwork*, *Freelancer*, and *Guru* dominate the region, collectively hosting approximately 100,000 active freelancers, underscoring the significant reliance on these platforms for connecting workers with global opportunities (Anđelković et al., 2024).

In contrast, neighboring countries that are members of the EU – such as Croatia (107.2), Bulgaria (99.5), Romania (69.3), and Hungary (50.7) – report significantly lower engagement in gig work. This disparity may stem from the broader range of economic opportunities available in these EU member states, where access to more secure and stable employment options reduces reliance on platform-based work. EU membership likely provides additional economic stability, better job prospects, and access to social benefits, making gig work less appealing compared to the Western

Balkans, where individuals are more driven to seek alternative income sources due to economic constraints.

The data underscores the economic divide between the Western Balkans and their EU neighbors. Citizens in the Western Balkans often turn to the gig economy out of necessity, leveraging platform work as a way to overcome economic challenges and access global labor markets. In countries like North Macedonia and Albania, the high engagement levels highlight how the gig economy can offer a lifeline for individuals facing limited traditional employment options.

Overall, the gig economy in the Western Balkans reflects both its potential as a growing labor market segment and the economic struggles that drive participation. The region's economic conditions –characterized by high unemployment and limited job opportunities – push individuals to embrace platform work as a viable alternative. Platforms like *Upwork*, *Freelancer*, and *Guru* play a central role in this ecosystem, connecting workers to international markets and enabling economic participation despite regional challenges. Addressing these issues requires targeted efforts to enhance digital infrastructure, reduce economic inequalities, and create pathways to more stable and diverse employment opportunities. Simultaneously, it offers an opportunity for Western Balkan countries to leverage their growing gig economy to build a competitive edge in the global digital labor market.

However, realizing the full potential of the gig economy in the Western Balkans also depends on addressing the legal and regulatory frameworks that shape platform work. Currently, labor protections for gig workers vary widely across countries – while some provide employment rights and social benefits, others apply more flexible or ambiguous classifications that leave workers without adequate protection. This regulatory uncertainty not only affects job quality and worker security but may also influence the attractiveness and sustainability of gig work in the region. A comparative overview of labor regulations – both within the Western Balkans and across other regions – would offer valuable insights into how different legal models impact platform accountability, social protection, and long-term workforce development.

ADAPTING HIGHER EDUCATION FOR THE GIG ECONOMY

The relationship between HEIs and the gig economy has become an increasingly prominent area of academic inquiry. As the gig economy reshapes labor markets globally, researchers are exploring how HEIs can adapt to better equip graduates with the skills and knowledge needed to thrive in this new landscape (Kurian, Bindu Madhavi, 2024; Pilatti et al., 2024). This growing body of research examines the evolving demands of digital work, the role of higher education in fostering entrepreneurship and adaptability, and the implications of gig work for lifelong learning.

These studies underscore the critical need for HEIs to align their curricula with the realities of a rapidly changing global workforce, ensuring that students are prepared for the opportunities and challenges presented by the gig economy.

The paper by Geng et al. (2023) explores how higher education and the digital economy interact in China, and how these sectors can align to promote sustainable development. Their study highlights the importance of coordination between the two, as well as the need for higher education to adapt to the demands of a rapidly changing digital landscape. The authors find that while the development of higher education is relatively stable, the digital economy is more dynamic, and the coordination between the two varies across different regions. Key findings indicate that higher education contributes to the digital economy by providing skilled labor and research, but that curricula are sometimes not aligned with the fast-evolving needs of the digital economy.

Moreover, the digital economy influences higher education by providing tools and platforms that enhance learning, though the rapid growth of digital sectors also presents challenges, such as increased competition for talent and concerns over data security (Shaya et al., 2025). Geng et al. (2023) suggest that policies should focus on improving the digital capabilities of higher education, fostering collaboration between universities and industries, and investing in infrastructure to ensure both sectors develop in tandem. This study underscores the importance of aligning higher education with the digital economy to ensure that graduates possess the skills necessary to thrive in the gig economy. By strengthening the connection between academia and industry, higher education can better prepare students for the demands of a digital workforce.

Similarly, the work of Wheelahan and Moodie (2022) examines the role of micro-credentials in the gig economy, offering an alternative to traditional degrees. Micro-credentials – short, competency-based certifications aligned with industry needs – have emerged as a critical tool for gig workers who need to acquire specific skills without the time or cost commitments of traditional education. The rise of micro-credentials reflects a broader shift toward more personalized, on-demand learning that is directly relevant to the gig economy. However, these authors also raise concerns about the potential for these credentials to contribute to the fragmentation of the labor market, arguing that while micro-credentials provide valuable industry-specific skills, they may fail to offer the broader, more holistic education required for long-term success in both the workforce and society. The authors emphasize that HEIs should strike a balance between providing specialized, practical training through micro-credentials and maintaining a broader educational foundation that fosters critical thinking and personal development. By embracing micro-credentials, higher education can support the dynamic needs of the gig economy while ensuring that students are also prepared for a broader, more meaningful role in society.

In parallel, Eveland and MacLennan (2019) explore the challenges faced by micro-entrepreneurs in the gig economy, particularly those running small businesses with minimal institutional support. Through an auto-ethnographical case study, the authors identify key challenges that micro-entrepreneurs face, such as formulating strategies, constructing value webs, utilizing mentors, and navigating ambiguity. The study underscores the need for HEIs to adapt their curricula to support micro-entrepreneurs by providing skills in entrepreneurship, strategy formulation, and network-building – areas often overlooked by traditional business programs. As the gig economy continues to expand, higher education must evolve to offer specialized programs that address the unique needs of gig workers, equipping students with the practical tools necessary to thrive in a rapidly changing labor market.

The emergence of the gig economy has fundamentally altered traditional labor market structures, challenging the well-established education-income paradigm. This shift is particularly notable in the online gig economy, where workers often offer services through digital platforms without the need for formal educational qualifications. This departure from traditional labor markets, where higher education is typically linked to higher income, raises critical questions about the role of formal education in the gig economy and the implications for HEIs.

Research has consistently supported the idea that higher educational attainment correlates with higher earnings in conventional labor markets. However, in the context of the gig economy, particularly online gig platforms, the relationship between education and income appears weaker. Studies show that, rather than educational credentials, factors such as a worker's reputation (measured through platform ratings) and work experience (both on and off the platform) play a more significant role in determining income levels. For example, Herrmann et al. (2023) and Herrmann (2023) found that for 1,607 gig workers across 14 Western economies, educational qualifications did not correlate with higher income (see Figure 3). Instead, positive platform reviews and relevant work experience were more influential in determining wage levels. This is especially true in high-skill tasks, such as programming or graphic design, where a worker's track record and skillset, developed through self-directed learning or on-the-job experience, are valued more than formal education (Herrmann, 2023). The qualitative insights from in-depth interviews conducted in these studies further explain this by highlighting how gig workers acquire the qualifications needed for their jobs, primarily through self-study, hands-on experience, and trial-and-error processes.

Figure 3. Average hourly income of online gig workers grouped by educational qualification

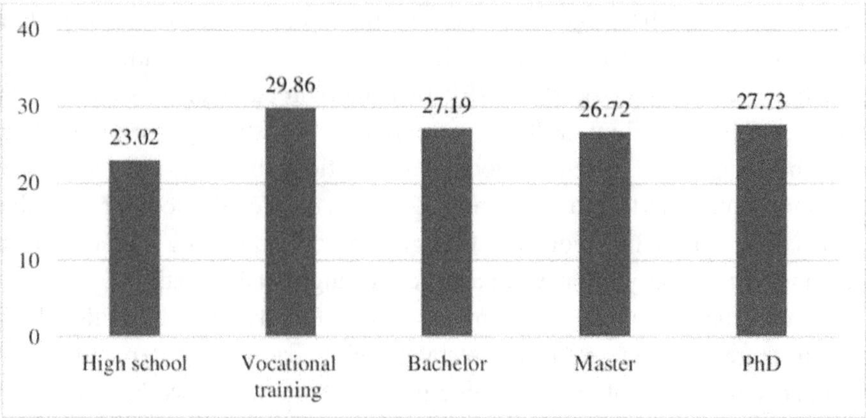

Source: Herrmann, 2023

Figure 3 illustrates the average hourly income of online gig workers, categorized by their educational qualifications (Herrmann, 2023). The data reveals that gig workers with vocational training tend to earn the highest average hourly income compared to those with other academic qualifications. Workers with a high school diploma or equivalent earn a slightly lower hourly wage, while those holding undergraduate degrees or master's degrees report similar income levels. Interestingly, workers with a PhD, the highest academic qualification, earn less on average than those with vocational training, highlighting a potential disconnect between formal education and income levels in the gig economy. This trend suggests that practical skills, possibly gained through vocational training or work experience, are more highly valued in the gig economy than advanced academic qualifications.

This disconnect between formal education and income is further explored by Herrmann et al. (2023), emphasizing that the gig economy demands workers to be entrepreneurial, self-reliant, and adaptable – skills often not nurtured in traditional academic settings. As digital platforms and remote work reshape industries, HEIs must recalibrate their offerings to focus more on real-world competencies rather than formal academic degrees. This shift toward skills-based education would better prepare students for the gig economy, providing them with the tools necessary to succeed in decentralized, flexible work environments. Higher education must move beyond conventional degree programs and embrace personalized, flexible learning opportunities that foster digital entrepreneurship, problem-solving, and the ability to navigate ambiguity (Scholkmann et al., 2024).

Taken together, these studies emphasize the urgent need for higher education to adapt to the demands of the gig economy. Traditional models focused on degree attainment are no longer sufficient to prepare students for the flexible, entrepreneurial nature of gig work. Institutions must prioritize skills-based, competency-driven learning and embrace digital transformation to offer personalized, flexible educational experiences that align with the needs of the gig economy. This shift will require a broad rethinking of how higher education prepares students, moving away from a rigid, degree-centered approach toward one that emphasizes practical, real-world competencies that can empower students to navigate the complexities of a digital and decentralized workforce. Higher education's ability to adapt to these changes will be critical in ensuring that future workers are equipped to succeed in an increasingly gig-oriented world.

While this chapter focuses primarily on institutional and systemic aspects of digital transformation in higher education, it acknowledges the limited representation of stakeholder perspectives – particularly those of students, faculty, and employers. This omission reflects a broader gap in the existing literature. For instance, few studies offer empirical insights into how students perceive their preparedness for gig-based work, how employers evaluate graduates entering platform-driven labor markets, or how faculty navigate the challenges of curriculum adaptation. Although this chapter does not provide direct empirical data on these perspectives, it highlights their importance and encourages future research to explore them through qualitative and survey-based methods. Including such voices would offer valuable context for shaping more inclusive and practice-oriented educational strategies.

In addition, much of the existing literature generalizes findings across countries without examining the distinctive dynamics of under-researched regions such as the Western Balkans. The present study aims to fill this gap by offering original insights into how local educational systems may adapt more effectively to the digital labor market.

Furthermore, attention to long-term career development remains limited. In a labor environment shaped by precarity and self-management, gig workers face ongoing challenges related to financial planning, mental health, and job security. HEIs can play a crucial role in equipping students with self-regulatory, psychological, and entrepreneurial skills necessary for sustainable success.

Finally, the ethical dimensions of gig work – such as data privacy, algorithmic control, and potential worker exploitation – are often overlooked in mainstream discussions. These issues raise critical questions about autonomy, labor fairness, and digital surveillance in gig-mediated employment. A more holistic educational response should integrate ethical reasoning, digital citizenship, and platform governance into the learning process.

MICRO-CREDENTIALS AND MOOCS: TRANSFORMING HIGHER EDUCATION FOR A DIGITAL WORLD

The accelerating pace of digital transformation and the rise of flexible learning platforms have prompted HEIs to rethink how they prepare students for modern labor markets. Among the most transformative tools in this evolving educational landscape are micro-credentials and MOOCs. These flexible, scalable, and learner-focused models provide tailored pathways for students and professionals to acquire job-relevant skills, bridging the gap between traditional academic frameworks and the fast-paced demands of modern labor markets. By integrating micro-credentials and MOOCs, HEIs can not only enhance the employability of graduates but also position themselves as drivers of lifelong learning, ensuring that education remains relevant in an era of rapid technological and economic change.

Micro-Credentials: Bridging Academia and Industry

Micro-credentials provide targeted educational opportunities, focusing on specific skills or competencies required in today's workforce. These short, modular courses cater to diverse learners, offering targeted skills and competencies that directly align with industry demands. These credentials enable learners to acquire specific, job-relevant abilities that enhance their employability, making them valuable assets for navigating the complexities of the modern workforce.

Prominent institutions such as the University of Texas System, Massachusetts Institute of Technology (MIT), and Stanford University have pioneered the integration of micro-credentials into their academic offerings, demonstrating the potential of these programs to bridge the gap between academia and industry. For instance, the University of Texas System, in collaboration with *Google* and *Coursera*, has launched *Google Career Certificates* embedded within undergraduate programs at no additional cost to students (Workcred & The University of Texas System, 2023). These certificates provide training in fields like data analytics, UX design, and digital marketing, addressing workforce demands in Texas, where over 60% of jobs are projected to require postsecondary credentials by 2030 (University of Texas System, 2022). By connecting students with major employers like *AT&T* and *Google*, this initiative exemplifies how micro-credentials can enhance job readiness while supporting regional economic growth.

Similarly, MIT's *MicroMasters* programs offer specialized, graduate-level courses in areas such as supply chain management, data science, and economics (MIT, n.d.). These modular programs serve dual purposes: they provide professional credentials recognized by numerous master's degree programs worldwide and enhance employability in high-demand fields. Stanford University's credentialing framework further underscores the potential of micro-credentials, offering tiered certifications that blend academic rigor with professional relevance. From *Graduate Certificates* that contribute to advanced degrees to *Professional Certificates* requiring over 150 hours of study, Stanford's approach caters to diverse learner needs while addressing labor market demands in sectors like technology and healthcare (Stanford online, n.d.).

In Europe, the role of micro-credentials is gaining traction as part of broader strategies to address skills gaps and promote lifelong learning (CIMEA, 2024). Initiatives such as Spain's *Plan Microcreds* and Portugal's *Adult Impulse Initiative* highlight the integration of modular learning pathways and collaboration between HEIs and industry. While countries like Ireland and Finland have developed centralized national portals to enhance transparency and access to micro-credentials, challenges persist across the European Higher Education Area (Casanova et al., 2024). These include establishing quality assurance mechanisms and ensuring cross-border recognition of micro-credentials.

By integrating micro-credentials into their educational frameworks, HEIs not only equip students with industry-relevant skills but also position themselves as hubs for lifelong learning. This alignment with labor market needs supports the digital transformation of education and empowers graduates to thrive in a rapidly evolving economy. However, the successful implementation of micro-credentials requires robust governance, consistent quality assurance, and strong collaboration between academia and industry. As the demand for flexible, skills-oriented education continues to grow, micro-credentials represent a transformative opportunity for HEIs to adapt and lead in the digital age.

MOOCs: Democratizing Access to Education

Massive open online courses (MOOCs) have emerged as a transformative force in higher education, offering accessible, scalable, and flexible learning opportunities to a global audience. Delivered through leading platforms such as *Coursera*, *edX*, and *FutureLearn*, MOOCs provide high-quality content developed by prestigious universities, spanning diverse disciplines like technology, business, arts, and social sciences (Top Universities, 2024). By addressing the needs of modern learners, MOOCs foster skill development and lifelong learning in an increasingly interconnected world.

One of the distinctive attributes of MOOCs is their integration with formal educational systems, providing pathways to recognized qualifications (Berde et al., 2024). Institutions like the University of London and the MIT allow students to complete MOOCs as part of accredited degrees or *MicroMasters* programs, bridging the divide between online and traditional learning. These initiatives enable students to acquire industry-relevant credentials, aligning academic goals with evolving workforce demands.

MOOCs also demonstrate their transformative potential through platforms like *edX*, which connects over 86 million learners globally with career-focused programs (edX, n.d.). Founded by Harvard and MIT to democratize access to high-quality education, *edX* now operates under *2U*, offering thousands of job-relevant courses in fields such as artificial intelligence, robotics, sustainability, and public health. This collaboration with universities and organizations at the forefront of their fields positions *edX* as a pivotal hub for professional progress.

Other institutions have followed suit, expanding the scope of MOOCs. For example, Stanford University provides courses designed to enhance professional skills in areas such as data science, artificial intelligence, and design thinking, delivering certifications highly regarded in global labor markets. Similarly, *FutureLearn* collaborates with universities like the University of Leeds and Monash University to offer programs that combine academic rigor with practical relevance, ensuring learners acquire skills applicable to real-world challenges.

By embedding MOOCs into their offerings, HEIs not only extend their global reach but also attract a broader, more diverse student base. These programs address the growing demand for flexible, skill-oriented education, especially in the context of the gig economy. The integration of MOOCs into degree curricula and professional development frameworks allows institutions to align their academic programs with the skills required in a rapidly transforming labor market. For instance, Serbia, which faces the challenge of modernizing its higher education system, could leverage MOOCs to improve teaching quality, expand access to education, and foster lifelong learning.

The increasing adoption of MOOCs underscores their potential to bridge the gap between academic learning and professional needs. They offer a flexible model for upskilling and reskilling, making them essential tools in preparing graduates for the digital economy. However, the strategic implementation of MOOCs, including tailoring content to regional needs and fostering partnerships between educational institutions and MOOC providers, will be crucial in maximizing their impact.

DIGITAL AND PEDAGOGICAL SHIFTS: THE WESTERN BALKAN HIGHER EDUCATION CONTEXT

The adoption and implementation of innovative learning methods, such as micro-credentials, MOOCs, and other digital tools, face significant challenges in the Western Balkans. Despite their potential to enhance education and align with contemporary labor market needs, the transition to these methods has been slow, reflecting broader systemic obstacles within HEIs in the region. While digital transformation is a strategic goal frequently highlighted in national and regional policies, its practical realization remains limited.

A central issue lies in the conceptualization of digital transformation as a purely technical task, often delegated to IT experts without a comprehensive institutional strategy. This narrow perspective overlooks the deeper, organization-wide shifts necessary for effective digital transformation. True transformation requires fostering innovation, collaboration, and a culture of continuous learning across teaching, administrative, and managerial domains. It also involves integrating digital tools into core processes, enhancing digital literacy, and leveraging data analytics for informed decision-making. As highlighted in recent research, the competitiveness of population skills, a critical driver of national economic growth and development, remains significantly lower in the Western Balkans compared to leading European countries, underscoring the urgent need for targeted reforms in higher education and workforce development (Krstić, Radivojević, 2022; Radivojević et al., 2019). However, many HEIs in the Western Balkans lack the strategic frameworks needed to implement these changes cohesively, resulting in fragmented and inefficient efforts.

Resource constraints further exacerbate these challenges. Public HEIs in the Western Balkans operate within tight financial limits, which restrict their ability to invest in digital infrastructure, professional development, and innovative learning methods. The region's economic conditions also mean that institutions often prioritize immediate operational needs over long-term transformative initiatives. As a result, many institutions struggle to provide adequate access to high-quality digital tools and training programs for both faculty and students.

The lack of awareness about the potential of digital learning methods further hinders progress (Alenzi, 2023; Graham et al., 2023). Many educators and students remain uninformed about the opportunities offered by micro-credentials and MOOCs. Even when awareness exists, cultural and contextual barriers – such as content primarily reflecting Western perspectives – reduce the perceived relevance and appeal of these tools. As Berde et al. (2024) emphasize, adapting these global solutions to local contexts is crucial to increasing their efficacy and adoption.

Given these constraints, a phased approach may be more realistic and impactful. Focusing initially on equipping professors with new methods and tools for teaching could provide a scalable and cost-effective solution. By investing in faculty development through tailored micro-credentials and MOOCs, HEIs can empower educators to adopt and adapt innovative methods that align with their institutional and regional contexts (Spirina et al., 2024). Professors who acquire advanced digital and pedagogical skills can then transfer their knowledge to students, creating a ripple effect that gradually modernizes the education system.

The digital transformation of HEIs in the Western Balkans must go beyond superficial adoption of technologies to embrace a holistic, strategic approach. This includes addressing financial barriers, building awareness, and fostering an inclusive digital culture that engages all stakeholders. By prioritizing professional development for faculty and focusing on long-term organizational change, HEIs can position themselves as leaders in modern education and contributors to regional development. These efforts, though challenging, are essential for bridging the gap between traditional education models and the demands of the digital era.

Another urgent concern is the issue of digital equity. Many institutions and individuals in the Western Balkans still face limited access to broadband internet, insufficient digital devices, and low levels of digital literacy. These inequalities hinder the effective adoption of online learning platforms and digital tools like MOOCs and micro-credentials. Without addressing these barriers, well-intentioned reforms risk deepening educational divides and failing to reach the most vulnerable student populations.

CONCLUSION

The rapid expansion of the gig economy has exposed a critical gap between traditional education systems and the skills required to navigate this evolving labor market. HEIs are uniquely positioned to bridge this gap, but doing so requires a transformation in educational design, delivery, and alignment with contemporary labor demands. This paper has explored the interplay between the gig economy and higher education, emphasizing the need for innovation, adaptability, and collaboration to prepare students for the realities of modern work.

The gig economy thrives on flexibility, digital connectivity, and self-reliance, demanding a workforce that is entrepreneurial and proficient in navigating digital platforms. To address these demands, HEIs must rethink their curricula to include skills such as digital literacy, entrepreneurship, project management, and financial planning. Initiatives like micro-credentials and modular learning pathways offer tailored, short-term training programs that equip students with specific skills in high demand. Case studies from the US, Europe, and beyond illustrate how universities can integrate such innovations into their offerings to better align with industry needs.

Moreover, the dynamic nature of the gig economy necessitates a shift toward lifelong learning frameworks. As technology and market demands evolve rapidly, graduates must be prepared to continuously update their skill sets. HEIs can facilitate this adaptability through partnerships with digital platforms and industry stakeholders, creating pathways for ongoing education and professional growth. This not only enhances employability but also positions universities as central agents of digital transformation in labor markets.

The Western Balkan context adds further complexity to this discourse. The digital transformation of HEIs in the region faces significant obstacles, including limited financial resources, fragmented strategies, and cultural barriers. These challenges highlight the need for a phased and localized approach, beginning with equipping educators with the tools and training required to embrace innovative teaching methods. As discussed in the paper, empowering faculty through micro-credentials and MOOCs can serve as a cost-effective starting point, fostering a gradual but sustainable modernization of higher education. By addressing systemic issues and emphasizing the importance of professional development, HEIs in the Western Balkans can overcome these barriers and align themselves with global trends in education and labor markets.

Higher education's role extends far beyond producing a qualified workforce. It is a rich cultural and scientific asset that fosters personal development, promotes innovation, and drives economic and social progress. Universities are places where knowledge is exchanged, research flourishes, and students are empowered to become critical thinkers and problem-solvers. While technological advancements like micro-credentials and MOOCs are valuable tools, their implementation should not overshadow the broader purpose of education: to cultivate informed, capable, and reflective individuals who contribute to society in meaningful ways.

As the gig economy reshapes the nature of work, education systems must evolve not only to prepare students for entry into this sector but also to support their long-term well-being and adaptability. This involves fostering digital and entrepreneurial skills, but also providing training in financial planning, stress management, and digital ethics. The gig economy presents both opportunity and risk, and HEIs are uniquely positioned to prepare students for both. Future-oriented strategies must address regional inequalities, institutional constraints, and regulatory ambiguities to build a more inclusive and sustainable higher education response.

The future of work demands an education system that not only prepares individuals for technical roles in platform-based environments but also nurtures critical thinking, ethical awareness, and the capacity for lifelong adaptation – values at the heart of both academic inquiry and societal progress.

ACKNOWLEDGEMENT

The author of this publication declares there are no competing interests.

Funding

This research received no specific grant from any funding agency in the public, commercial, or not-for-profit sectors. Funding for this research was covered by the author of the article.

REFERENCES

Alenezi, M. (2023). Digital Learning and Digital Institution in Higher Education. *Education Sciences*, *13*(1), 88. Advance online publication. DOI: 10.3390/educsci13010088

Anđelković, B., Jakobi, T., Ivanović, V., Kalinić, Z., & Radonjić, Lj. (2024). *Gigmetar Region*. Public Policy Research Center. http://gigmetar.publicpolicy.rs/en/region-en-2024-1

Berde, É., Mengesha, S. T., Mola, B. A., & Remsei, S. (2024). Massive Open Online Courses (MOOCs) for Ethiopian Educators: Evaluating MOOCs as a global development tool. *Research in Globalization*, *9*, 100263. DOI: 10.1016/j.resglo.2024.100263

Casanova, D., Bastos, G., & Antonaci, A. (2024). *Follow-up and analysis of national and EU policy developments on micro-credentials*. Research Report No. 6.1., Zenodo. https://doi.org/DOI: 10.5281/zenodo.13850890

CIMEA. (2024). *Micro-credentials for higher education institutions: Approaches developed in the EHEA using peer support*. https://www.cimea.it/Upload/Documenti/Micro-credentials%20in%20HE_1.pdf

DinarStandard. (2023). *Global Digital Platform Power Index 2023*. https://2feea378-8f71-46c9-9424-36229a900f86.usrfiles.com/ugd/2feea3_b69dbe6fa1ea49548d3768008b168446.pdf

edX. (n.d.). *About edX*. https://www.edx.org/about-us

Eurofound (2018). *Employment and working conditions of selected types of platform work*. Publications Office of the European Union, Luxembourg. https://www.eurofound.europa.eu/en/publications/2018/employment-and-working-conditions-selected-types-platform-work

Eurostat (2023). *Employment statistics - digital platform workers*. https://ec.europa.eu/eurostat/statistics-explained/index.php?title=Employment_statistics_-_digital_platform_workers

Eveland, T., & MacLennan, H. (2019). A micro-entrepreneur in the gig economy: Case study and implications for higher education. *Journal of Developmental Entrepreneurship*, *24*(3), 1950016. DOI: 10.1142/S108494671950016X

Friedman, G. (2014). Workers without employers: Shadow corporations and the rise of the gig economy. *Review of Keynesian Economics*, *2*(2), 171–188. DOI: 10.4337/roke.2014.02.03

Geng, Y., Chen, L., Li, J., & Iqbal, K. (2023). Higher education and digital Economy: Analysis of their coupling coordination with the Yangtze River economic Belt in China as the example. *Ecological Indicators*, *154*, 110510. DOI: 10.1016/j.ecolind.2023.110510

Graham, C., Danaa, G., Purevsuren, T., Martinez, A., Spricigo, C., Camilotti, B., & Batsukh, T. (2023). Digital Learning Transformation in Higher Education: International Cases of University Efforts to Evaluate and Improve Blended Teaching Readiness. *Education Sciences*, *13*(11), 1143. DOI: 10.3390/educsci13111143

Herrmann, A. M. (2023). How the Online Gig Economy Challenges the Education-Income Paradigm. *Entrepreneurship in Focus, 7*. https://www.ifm-bonn.org/fileadmin/data/redaktion/publikationen/policy_brief/dokumente/policybrief-07-23-EN.pdf

Herrmann, A. M., Zaal, P. M., Chappin, M. H., Schemmann, B., & Lühmann, B. (2023). "We don't need no (higher) education" - How the gig economy challenges the education-income paradigm. *Technological Forecasting and Social Change*, *186*, 122136. DOI: 10.1016/j.techfore.2022.122136

Hong, E. (2015, October 23). Making it work: A closer look at the gig economy. *Pacific Standard*. https://psmag.com/economics/making-it-work-a-closer-look-at-the-gig-economy/

Hook, L. (2015, December 29). Year in a word: gig economy. *Financial Times*. https://www.ft.com/content/b5a2b122-a41b-11e5-8218-6b8ff73aae15

Horowitz, S. (2011, September 1). The Freelance Surge is the Industrial Revolution of Our Time. *The Atlantic*. https://www.theatlantic.com/business/archive/2011/09/the-freelance-surge-is-the-industrial-revolution-of-our-time/244229/

Hosseini, H. (2023). Platform Economy 2023: U.S. leads; Europe lags. *Platform Economy*. https://www.platformeconomy.io/blog/platform-economy-2023-u-s-leads-europe-lags

Krstić, B., Stanišić, T., & Radivojević, V. (2016). The impact of innovativeness' factors on the EU countries competitiveness. *Industrija*, *44*(2), 101–116. DOI: 10.5937/industrija44-10674

Krstić, M., & Radivojević, V. (2022). Regional competitiveness: Theoretical and empirical aspects. In Akkuk, U. (Ed.), *Disruptive technologies and eco-innovation for sustainable development* (pp. 150–170). IGI Global. DOI: 10.4018/978-1-7998-8900-7.ch009

Kurian, J. S., & Bindu Madhavi, N. (2024). Navigating the gig economy: Exploring challenges and motivations for the wellbeing of Gen Y and Gen Z gig workers. *Cogent Psychology*, *11*(1), 2357458. Advance online publication. DOI: 10.1080/23311908.2024.2357458

Mc Kinsey & Company. (2023). *What is the gig economy?*https://www.mckinsey.com/featured-insights/mckinsey-explainers/what-is-the-gig-economy

Minter, K. (2017). Negotiating labour standards in the gig economy: Airtasker and Unions New South Wales. *Economic and Labour Relations Review*, *28*(3), 438–454. DOI: 10.1177/1035304617724305

MIT. (n.d.). *MITx MicroMasters Programs*. https://micromasters.mit.edu/

Piasna, A., Zwysen, W., & Drahokoupil, J. (2022). The platform economy in Europe: Results from the second ETUI Internet and Platform Work Survey. ETUI. https://www.etui.org/sites/default/files/2022-02/The%20platform%20economy%20in%20Europe_2022.pdf

Pilatti, G. R., Pinheiro, F. L., & Montini, A. A. (2024). Systematic Literature Review on Gig Economy: Power Dynamics, Worker Autonomy, and the Role of Social Networks. *Administrative Sciences*, *14*(10), 267. DOI: 10.3390/admsci14100267

Radivojević, V., Kahrović, E., & Krstić, M. (2019). Population skills as an indicator of European countries competitiveness in the modern economy. *Vojno delo, 71*(5), 105-116. https://doi.org/DOI: 10.5937/vojdelo1905105R

Scholkmann, A., Olsen, D., & Wollscheid, S. (2024). Perspectives on disruptive change in higher education. A critical review of digital transformation during COVID-19. *Higher Education Research & Development*, *43*(6), 1355–1369. DOI: 10.1080/07294360.2024.2325140

Shaya, N., Abukhait, R., Madani, R., & Ahmed, V. (2025). Conceptualizing blended learning models as a sustainable and inclusive educational approach: An organizational dynamics perspective. *International Journal of Sustainability in Higher Education, 26*(9), 90–111. DOI: 10.1108/IJSHE-03-2024-0167

Spirina, Y., Gorbunova, N., & Samoilova, I. (2024). Using MOOCs to organise problem-based learning in the professional training of IT students. *Obrazovanie i Nauka-Education and Science, 26*(10), 166–189. DOI: 10.17853/1994-5639-2024-10-166-189

Srihita, H. S., Goli, G., Rajyalaxmi, M., & Gobinath, R. (2025). Transformative dynamics of the gig economy: Technological impacts, worker well-being and global research trends. *International Journal of Engineering Business Management, 17*, 18479790241310362. Advance online publication. DOI: 10.1177/18479790241310362

Stanford online (n.d.). *Stanford Credentials.* https://online.stanford.edu/stanford-credentials

Statista (2024). *Number of freelancers in the United States from 2017 to 2028.* https://www.statista.com/statistics/921593/gig-economy-number-of-freelancers-us/

Top Universities. (n.d.). *MOOCs: The future of higher education.* https://www.topuniversities.com/student-info/distance-learning/moocs-future-higher-education

University of Texas System. (2022). *UT System and Google announce Google Career Certificates for up to 10,000 Texas university students.* https://www.utsystem.edu/news/2022/12/09/ut-system-and-google-announce-google-career-certificates-10000-texas-university-students

Vadavi, S., & Sharmiladevi, J. C. (2024). Analysing the evolution and patterns of the gig economy: A bibliometric examination of growth and trends. *Cogent Business & Management, 11*(1), 2424480. Advance online publication. DOI: 10.1080/23311975.2024.2424480

Wheelahan, L., & Moodie, G. (2022). Gig qualifications for the gig economy: Micro-credentials and the 'hungry mile'. *Higher Education, 83*(6), 1279–1295. DOI: 10.1007/s10734-021-00742-3 PMID: 34366441

Workcred & The University of Texas System. (2023). *Integrating Microcredentials into Undergraduate Experiences.* https://share.ansi.org/wc/Shared%20Documents/Workcred-Reports/Integrating-Microcredentials-into-Undergraduate-Experiences.pdf

World Bank. (2024). *Working Without Borders: The Promise and Peril of Online Gig Work.* https://www.worldbank.org/en/topic/jobsanddevelopment/publication/online-gig-work-enabled-by-digital-platforms

ADDITIONAL READING

Al-Adwan, A. (2020). Investigating the drivers and barriers to MOOCs adoption: The perspective of TAM. *Education and Information Technologies*, *25*(1), 5771–5795. DOI: 10.1007/s10639-020-10250-z

Burtch, G., Carnahan, S., & Greenwood, B. N. (2018). Can you gig it? An empirical examination of the gig economy and entrepreneurial activity. *Management Science*, *64*(12), 5497–5520. DOI: 10.1287/mnsc.2017.2916

Caza, B. B., Reid, E. M., Ashford, S. J., & Granger, S. (2021). Working on my own: Measuring the challenges of gig work. *Human Relations*, *75*(11), 2122–2159. DOI: 10.1177/00187267211030098

Kost, D., Fieseler, C., & Wong, S. I. (2020). Boundaryless careers in the gig economy: An oxymoron? *Human Resource Management Journal*, *30*(1), 100–113. DOI: 10.1111/1748-8583.12265

Olatokun, W. M., Oladokun, B. D., & Adetayo, A. J. (2024). Knowledge and use of MOOCs for teaching by library and information science educators in higher educational institutions in Nigeria. *Journal of Librarianship and Information Science*, 09610006241264826. Advance online publication. DOI: 10.1177/09610006241264826

Shi, Y., Haller, A., Reeson, A., & Li, X. (2024). Decoding the dynamics of knowledge pricing: An empirical investigation of MOOC platform edX's pricing structure and signaling effects. *International Journal of Information Management Data Insights*, *4*(1), 100220. DOI: 10.1016/j.jjimei.2024.100220

Zwettler, C., Straub, C., & Spurk, D. (2024). Kicking off a Gig Work Career: Unfolding a Career Learning Cycle of Gig Workers. *Journal of Career Assessment*, *32*(4), 650–677. DOI: 10.1177/10690727231212188 PMID: 39319276

KEY TERMS AND DEFINITIONS

Gig Economy: A labor market characterized by short-term, flexible, and task-based work arrangements, often mediated through digital platforms, where workers operate as independent contractors rather than traditional employees.

Platform Economy: An economic system based on digital platforms that facilitate exchanges between consumers, businesses, and workers. This model supports the gig economy by providing infrastructure for services such as ride-sharing, freelance work, and online marketplaces.

Higher Education Institutions (HEIs): Organizations that provide tertiary education, including universities, colleges, and specialized institutions, focused on delivering academic and professional qualifications, fostering research, and contributing to societal development.

Digital Transformation in Education: The integration of digital technologies and innovative methodologies into higher education systems to enhance teaching, learning, and administrative processes, addressing the evolving demands of the modern labor market.

Micro-Credentials: Short, focused qualifications that certify specific skills or competencies aligned with industry needs. These credentials are typically modular and can be stacked toward larger qualifications, enabling personalized and lifelong learning pathways.

Massive Open Online Courses (MOOCs): Online educational courses designed to provide accessible, scalable, and flexible learning opportunities to a global audience. MOOCs often involve high-quality content from leading universities and are offered through platforms like *Coursera* and *edX*.

Digital Literacy: The ability to effectively and critically navigate, evaluate, and create information using digital technologies. This skill is essential in modern education and the workforce, particularly within the context of the gig economy.

Lifelong Learning: A continuous process of acquiring skills and knowledge throughout an individual's life to adapt to changing personal, professional, and societal demands, often facilitated by micro-credentials, MOOCs, and other flexible learning tools.

Chapter 4
Education 4.0: E-Learning as an Economics Catalyst in the Digital Age

Neeru Sidana
https://orcid.org/0000-0003-1087-4214
Amity University, Noida, India

Mehek Singh
Amity University, Noida, India

Yash Bidhuri
https://orcid.org/0009-0005-1273-1817
Amity University, Noida, India

Poppy Febriana
Muhammadiyah Sidoarjo, Indonesia

ABSTRACT

Digital transformation and e-learning are making the educational landscape dramatically change, both economically and socially, around the world. With increased investments in the EdTech sector, innovative technologies like AI, AR, and VR are enhancing learning experiences and accessibility. These advancements are not only bridging educational gaps but also driving economic growth by creating new markets and job opportunities in the digital education ecosystem. This Chapter examines the evolution of the EdTech industry, putting a focus on AI-based solutions that enrich learning outcomes, interest, and individualization. It tackles the pertinent issues of accessibility and equity through innovations such as AI tutors, regional language resources, and low-cost e-reading devices. The study captures the global patterns with adoption before and after COVID-19 and evaluates various economic impacts-

DOI: 10.4018/979-8-3373-1290-3.ch004

the creation of jobs and possible replacement for old positions-.

1. INTRODUCTION

1.1 Background and Context

As of 2023, the global EdTech market has been estimated at around $142.37 billion and is projected to rise at a compound annual growth rate (CAGR) of 13.4% from 2024 to 2030 (Grand View Research, 2024). The forward momentum for this growth is provided by the digital transformation of education, in which modern innovations like artificial intelligence (AI), augmented reality (AR), virtual reality (VR), and adaptive learning systems are reshaping traditional learning paradigms (World Economic Forum, 2021). However, challenges like the digital divide, data protection, and content quality remain key concerns (World Economic Forum, 2021).

Currently, the Indian edtech market is said to be around $7.5 billion and will grow to nearly $29 billion by 2030 (Statista, 2024). The rise in smartphone usage and internet penetration has increased investments and the emergence of many unicorn startups (Business Standard, 2025). Over 17,000 EdTech startups from the K-12 segment, which include test prep, professional upskilling, and course catalogues in higher education, among many others (Tracxn, 2025).

Indian edtech is at $7.5 billion now value and is expected to multiply until the beginning of $29 billion by the year 2030 (Statista, 2024). Indian EdTech shines with bright prospects because it embraces innovation, personalizes learning, and equity of access to education. The growing demand for accessible, personalized, and scalable solutions for education offers an opportunity for education technology to usher in next-generation education. Research indicates there is much potential for the EdTech sector to create equal opportunity and quality education resources for each deserving child, mainly for those from marginalized communities or rural areas (Joy et al., 2022). Also, artificial intelligence university education technology may offer a radically shifting educational environment by supplying personalized learning experiences as well as closing gaps in education (Bulathwela et al., 2021).

1.2 Research Questions

RQ1. How do advancements in e-learning technologies, such as AI, contribute to economic growth by creating new markets, job opportunities, and innovation in the education sector?

RQ2. What are the financial advantages and disadvantages of e-learning for increasing accessibility, especially concerning affordability and closing the digital divide?

1.3 Research Objectives

1. To describe the role of advanced technologies, particularly AI, in enhancing the quality, accessibility, and personalisation of e-learning.
2. To review the economic impact of e-learning technologies, including job creation, market expansion, and the emergence of new business models in the EdTech sector.
3. To discuss the potential of e-learning technologies in reducing educational disparities and bridging the digital divide

1.4 Scope of the Study

The Chapter studies the impact AI-driven solutions have on the quality, accessibility and individualised study of e-learning. It focuses on adaptive learning systems, intelligent tutoring systems, and other AI-powered tools to improve quality education. It also discusses the economic impact of digital learning on the edtech sector by looking into job creation opportunities and market expansion and how this affects the traditional education industry.

Furthermore, the study explores the potential of AI and EdTech in bridging educational disparities. It evaluates how technology-based education can bridge the digital divide, and reviews policies and initiatives ensuring equitable access to digital learning resources. It also investigates the challenges and opportunities within the digital education ecosystem.

2. LITERATURE REVIEW

2.1 Early Development and Key Milestones

The evolution of digital learning and education technology has been a dynamic and transformative process for both teaching and learning. The earliest datable source of educational technology was the invention of the printing press by Johann Gutenberg in the 15th century. Industrialization led to the mass production of books, which democratized knowledge, allowing a wider access to materials for education, even outside the elite class (Eisenstein, 1979).

During the 1920s, radio was used for distance education, and by the 1950s, television was introduced in education with great success in BBC and other countries through the schools' broadcasts (Saettler, 2004). The early computerized educational system PLATO (Programmed Logic for Automated Teaching Operations), developed at the University of Illinois in 1960, included interactivity in the learning process (Murray, 1997). With the advent of Learning Management Systems (LMSs) such as Blackboard (1997) and Moodle (2002), institutions could run online courses thereby giving access to education (Watson & Watson, 2007). E-learning really took off, especially with the launch of Massive Open Online Courses (MOOCs) like Coursera and edX in the early 2010s that gave the world an opportunity toward better education (Yuan & Powell, 2013). With a particular focus on higher education, this study explores how technology advancements have changed university-level teaching and learning methodologies.

The integration of Artificial Intelligence (AI) into education technology has revolutionized learning personalization. AI-powered systems analyze student performance data and tailor content to individual needs, enhancing engagement and comprehension (Luckin et al., 2016). Intelligent tutoring systems such as Carnegie Learning's MATHia and AI-driven language learning apps like Duolingo have demonstrated the effectiveness of adaptive learning (Woolf, 2010). Moreover, AI-driven automation in grading, predictive analytics, and chatbots have streamlined administrative and instructional processes (Holmes et al., 2019).

2.2 The Role of Technology in Transforming Education

The most important technology personified in education concerns the innovativeness, access, and personalization of learning. From the age of digital classrooms to the dawn of artificial intelligence (AI) in tutoring, the role of technology has been tremendously improved in learning outcomes in the education itself (Selwyn, 2022). The platforms offer students flexible study time with different modes of course delivery and credentialed programs to make education richer (Means et al., 2021). LMSs like Moodle and Blackboard have enhanced the content delivery, communication, and assessment process among institutions of higher learning. Learning has been digitized and personalized with the help of AI-driven EdTech solutions that provide recommendations, adaptive assessments, and intelligent tutoring systems. AI tools like Carnegie Learning and Squirrel AI provide contents based on strengths and weaknesses of the students and ensures more personalized learning (Luckin et al., 2021). Machine-learning algorithms analyze student performance data to predict learning trajectories and to give targeted intervention to enhance the efficiency and engagement of learning experiences.

With great immersive learning experiences that accentuate comprehension and engagement, Virtual Reality (VR) and Augmented Reality (AR) have come on the educational scene. For instance, in a VR application, Google Expeditions and Engage are wonderful tools allowing students to take guided tours of historic sites, perform scientific experiments on a virtual set, and gain hands-on training in a simulated environment for medical practices (Bacca et al., 2018).An AR project builds digital content within the physical world to allow for the engagement of internal concepts in ways that are materialized and interactive (Dunleavy & Dede, 2014). Such gamification strategies have noticeably impacted student motivation and engagement by integrating varied elements including badges, leaderboards, and interactive challenges. Platforms like Kahoot! and Duolingo aims to engage their participants through competition while retaining knowledge via active participation in fun and entertaining learning experiences (Oberoi, Arora, Verma, & Roy, 2024).

Big data and learning analytics have allowed educators to make decisions on what they found by analyzing student performance matrices, engagement levels, and learning patterns. Predictive analytics enables risk-based identification of students while personalizing learning intervention and improving curriculum design (Daniel, 2015). On the flip side, while technology has changed education, it presents its challenges, such as digital divide, data privacy issues, or adaptability for its teachers. Moreover, ethical issues related to the collection of student data and AI biases require stringent regulations and transparent AI frameworks in education.

2.3 Pre- and Post-COVID-19 Adoption Patterns

In early 2020, the pandemic brought on by COVID-19 resulted in the shutdown of schools and learning facilities around the globe. By March 2020, as many as 180 countries had implemented school closures within certain cities of their countries. It is estimated that 90% of the world population was affected by these closures in one way or another throughout 2020 (Hale et al., 2020). As of November 2020, 24 countries had total school closure policies in place, this change resulted in approximately 224 million learners being affected (UNESCO, 2020a). Unfortunately, it remains unclear just how disruptive COVID-19 has been as many countries have started partial openings and lockdowns.

There's a view that the pandemic accelerated the digitalization of higher education and will likely stimulate profound and deep-seated changes. A great deal of respect is currently afforded to the EdTech sector as one of the industries that may receive a sustained boost as a result of the crisis (Krishnaraja & Schildhauer, 2020). The need for digital learning tools, content development, and AI-powered tailoring for education increased, which led to new jobs in technology, content development, as well as support services (HolonIQ, 2020). Yet some challenges such as the digital divide remained problems. In 2020, UNICEF indicated that one-third of the world's learners would have no access to remote education further aggravating the inequality created by the digital infrastructure (UNICEF, 2020). Nevertheless, these challenges did not prevent the rapid evolution of EdTech from changing the face of education as it is known today, where the means of teaching blend digital tools with traditional methods in a hybrid approach.

Like all other fields, the COVID-19 pandemic has brought unprecedented changes to the form and practice of education across all levels. Digital learning adoption skyrocketed as schools, universities, and training centres migrated to online platforms. Several shifts occurred in the EdTech market post-COVID-19. Educational closing impacted over 1.6 billion learners worldwide as a result, digital platforms became the primary provider of education (UNESCO, 2020). Firms operating in this sector such as Byju's, Coursera, and Google Classroom boomed. For instance, Byju's became the world's most-valued EdTech startup evaluated at $22 billion in 2021 (CB Insights, 2021). Governments also helped well enough by investing in the requisite digital infrastructure and e-learning support. In India, the Pradhan Mantri eVidya initiative was launched to commence initial level television and digital education for distant learners (Government of India, 2021). This change in the method of instruction led to new requirements for both the digital content and the teacher training programs.

3. METHODOLOGY

This research adopts a qualitative approach through an extensive review of secondary sources. Relevant academic articles, policy reports, market analyses, and data from international organizations such as UNESCO, the World Economic Forum, and Statista were examined. The selection focused on materials covering advancements in EdTech, Artificial Intelligence in education, and their economic implications. A thematic analysis was employed to identify patterns across key areas including personalization, accessibility, market growth, and policy responses.

4. RESULTS

4.1 Enhancing Learning Outcomes through AI

The education landscape is changing with new areas for improvement in the learning experience brought in by Artificial Intelligence (AI). In AI-driven adaptive learning systems, an analysis of student performance data produces customized learning paths whereby students are given content consistent with their own pace and level of understanding (Brown & Lee, 2022). It affords educators tools that help to carry their administrative load and strengthen instructional practices (Jones et al., 2020).AI tools may also assist in automating grade generation, the design of interactive lessons, and giving students real-time feedback (Doe & Taylor, 2021).

Also, AI is shifting the assessment process from a more traditional examination style to an evaluation method that draws better insights and interactions. AI-based assessments can instantly analyze students' responses and deliver time-sensitive feedback, indicating areas of student comprehension as well as their level of learning progress(Lee & Brown, 2022).AI streams can constitute an effective optimization procedure in those processes toward effective management styles of the educational institution(Rogers & Garcia, 2021).

Apart from the learners, AI also finds application in other educational management activities like timetabling, space management, and even admission of fresh students (Miller & Lee, 2021). Inevitably, the application of AI in education comes with some issues that need to be dealt with such as respect to privacy, bias in algorithms, and the setting of professional development for educators. Solving these issues will be very important if the goal of incorporating AI in education is to be achieved together with equal opportunities to quality education. Learning processes must be bolstered for students to be engaged, do well, and become excited about their learning (Williams, 2019).

4.2 Personalization and Individualized Learning

Among the top advantages AI-powered learning platforms offer is the creation of adaptive learning experiences that alter both content difficulty and learning pace through real-time assessments of student performance. This adaptive technology—which dynamically modifies materials based on individual learning needs—allowed pupils to progress through the content at their own pace while keeping up with their advanced peers, who were continuously presented with more difficult material to maintain their engagement (Baker & Siemens, 2014). To maximise engagement and success, DreamBox and Knewton have the added advantage of AI algorithms that determine the strengths and weaknesses of the learners and adjust the learning materials accordingly in real-time (Shute, 2008).

Alongside being able to personalize speed and content delivery, AI empowers an individualized approach to learning through targeted intervention based on data-informed insights. AI systems monitor students' behavior, evaluate their learning and comprehension instantaneously, and offer resources aimed precisely at disparities in what students know (Siemens, 2013). An application that beautifully captures this would be Socratic by Google; it gives personalized explanations and stepwise help on certain homework problems so that a learner gets support right when they need it (Baker et al. 2019).

In addition, AI facilitates personalization, considering not only academic performance but also factors such as emotional engagement and cognitive load. AI systems can employ powerful data analytics to detect signs of frustration or disengagement in students, dynamically changing their learning experiences to keep them engaged and focused (Pardo et al., 2019). Such high levels of personalized support are elemental for students with special educational needs as an AI-based platform may include assistive technology for the accommodation of students with disabilities. Integrating text-to-speech, adaptive font size, and visual aids into several AI platforms helps ensure that students with learning challenges receive the resources they need to succeed (Al-Azawei et al., 2017). When coupled with an AI model, personalization generates advantages both for learners and instructors on the back of strong data-driven insights about a learner's needs. This makes AI technologies a more scalable and sustainable alternative for personalized education in classrooms worldwide, thus moving away from traditional forms of teaching that may not provide for the diverse learning needs of students (Kulik & Kulik, 1991).

4.3 Regional Language Resources and Localization

Education 4.0—the fourth revolution in education characterized by technology integration, personalized learning experiences, and alignment with Industry 4.0's digital transformation needs—has raised the importance of localized e-learning solutions in multilingual contexts. This paradigm shift, which emphasizes AI-driven personalization, digital literacy, and preparing students for future workforce demands, has also magnified the importance of tailored e-learning solutions in multilingual and culturally diverse countries. Regional language resources are crucial to making the learning experience more inclusive, digitally accessible, and effective by teaching students in their native languages (Rao & Swaminathan 2022). In terms of economic merit, perhaps, it has enabled localizing digital learning material. All people should have this chance for skill enhancement and employability, which, according to Kumar (2023), rely on the language. So far, localization enhances student engagement which in turn serves retention and employability (UNESCO 2021).

Faster developments in AI and ML that have powered automatic translations ushered in real-time flexibility in content adaptation. EdTech companies are using text-to-speech and speech-to-text technologies to prepare interactive contextually relevant educational materials (Patel & Singh, 2022). With contextual accuracy and language knowledge for regional translations provided through OpenAI's GPT and Google's BERT, e-learning has become even more inclusive (Sharma, 2023). Yet localized operations deal with challenges that include different dialects of a language, expensive changes in content, and the need to have skilled language experts (Ranjan & Bose, 2022). Therefore, investments in digital infrastructures to create provisions for content developers must be put in place to create good regional language resources.

4.4 Economic Impacts of EdTech Advancements

The projection for the global EdTech market is to grow at a rate that will take it above $400 billion by 2025. The technological innovations have enhanced access to quality education, especially in developing areas by reducing the cost and increasing scalability of methodologies (Mishra & Koehler, 2021).

Directly affecting the economy, one major contribution of EdTech is improving the efficiency of labor markets. Personalized learning and skill-oriented training provide key tools with which EdTech platforms can throw a bridge across the chasm separating education and the arena of employability, thereby fostering adaptable workforce behaviour (Raut, Deshpande, Arora, Mittal, & Alandikar, 2022).

Opposite to the potential economic benefits, this very access limitation stands as the challenge to EdTech. Investment in digital infrastructure, teacher training, and data privacy regulations is a prerequisite for governments and policymakers to ensure a sustainable economic return from EdTech. Such an integration of EdTech will have to be well planned.

4.5 Job Creation in the Digital Education Ecosystem

From its genesis, the EdTech industry has been a source from which employment has been created in technical and non-technical areas. Some key job profiles include software programming, instructional designing, multimedia content creation, digital marketing, and AI professionals. Therefore, with an estimate of 3 million-plus job opportunities by 2030, the EdTech sector in India is poised to change the employment profile considerably. The demand for digital-educational solutions is propelling this growth (KPMG, 2022).

In addition to traditional models, EdTech platforms like Coursera, Udemy, and Skillshare enable freelance educators to reach global audiences. Courses on various topics have opened the door to allow decentralized education delivery, hence enabling people in remote areas to be part of the global workforce (PwC, 2021).

Rapid developments in artificial intelligence are changing the educational technology landscape almost overnight, creating new jobs while existing professionals now must reskill themselves to remain competitive. The rise of AI applications such as adaptive learning systems and virtual tutors has thus increased the need for expertise in AI integration and data analytics. The AI education market is projected to grow from 4.8 billion U.S. dollars in 2024 to 75.1 billion U.S. dollars by 2033, with a CAGR of 34.03% (8allocate, 2024). For this reason, continuing education and upskilling remain the order of the day for edtech practitioners who will engage AI smartly to keep pace with the evolving standards of their field (Oberoi & Kansra, 2022). As per the World Economic Forum, the development of sustainable lifelong learning opportunities and thus building the workforce of the future would depend on sound collaboration among employers, educators, and workers (World Economic Forum, 2025).

4.6 Displacement of Traditional Roles: Challenges and Opportunities

With the advent of AI and technology, the edtech sector is edging toward displacing age-old capabilities, overshadowing its prospects. Conventional tasks like tutoring, grading, or personalized learning are now being automated by AI-assisted tools. This raises questions about job security for educators and administrative support staff. Kerala now witnesses the unveiling of Iris, India's first AI teacher robot, by Maker Labs, other than creating new frontiers for education (The Hindu, 2023). This marks a significant milestone in India's EdTech journey, specifically the use of AI for personalized learning and efficient delivery of course content. As the AI fever catches up with schools, colleges, and universities in the foreseeable future, involvement in neighboring areas like teaching and tutoring must not be ruled out. Technology, such as AI, machine learning, gamification, or big data, could thus be one set of parameters for educational consideration where most advancement toward helping teachers and students is envisioned (Arora & Nabi, 2022). On one side, the increasing use of AI in education could lead to the replacement of certain teachers and tutor jobs.

On the other hand, tasks such as catering to the psychological and social needs of the students cannot be managed without direct human intervention, an area where AI and similar technologies cannot replicate human action. Currently, the fact holds true that AI does assist and enhance the overall teaching-learning process; however, AI cannot fully replace the human aspect involved in the teaching process. On the contrary, this kind of change is bringing forth new job titles to which professionals can transition, such as AI trainers, edtech consultants, and data analysts (Smith et al. 2024). Therefore, an important combination of strategies for upskilling and re-skilling professionals joined by strong partnerships between educational institutions and edtech providers shall be required to embrace these changes. Hence, the role of policymakers becomes paramount in ensuring the empowerment of any growth that will be inclusive through initiatives directed towards getting the workers ready for an ever-demanding environment in this sector (World Economic Forum, 2025).

4.7 Economic Growth through New Markets in EdTech

The introduction of AI tools, for example, allowed avenues for their advancement so that educators could integrate technology use into their teaching practices, requiring proficiency in pedagogical and technical skills (Williamson, 2023). Roles such as instructional designers, data scientists, software developers, digital content creators, and AI specialists are now critical to the building and maintaining of innovative EdTech platforms. Additionally, the emergence of EdTech companies has led to the creation of jobs in developing nations, where they hire local talent to create educational solutions that meet local needs. Such partnerships are creating a purple patch for strong ecosystem-building that democratizes access to quality education while also providing stimulation for economic activities.

Another effect of the opportunities generated by EdTech is indirect employment. The multiplier impact of EdTech investments propels expansion into other industries, including content creation, telecom services, and IT infrastructure (Udanoh & Zouria, 2023). Within the fold of expanding EdTech businesses, the need for cloud computing and cybersecurity services will further boost the digital economy. These initiatives are crucial for increasing worker productivity and lowering unemployment among marginalised populations, claims Rodriguez-Segura (2021).EdTech promises not only to prepare economies for the future workforce but also to reap the current rewards of job creation. As estimated by the World Economic Forum, the remaining $400 billion that the global digital learning sector is expected to contribute to the economy by 2030 will be mostly due to the creation of knowledge-intensive jobs (Williamson, 2023). Hence, while the EdTech industry now provides some remedy to continuing educational inequities, it also establishes a strong foothold for securing future economic viability.

4.8 E-Books vs. Print Books: A Comparative Analysis

4.8.1 Cost-Effectiveness and Accessibility

In the Indian edtech market e-books and online resources are emerging as money-saving and cost-efficient as compared to traditional textbooks. Physical textbooks for private school students cost between INR 2,000 and 10,000 annually. While e-books and subscriptions are available for INR 500 to 5,000 annually. They give good bargains even in subscription schemes by providing greater material and variations at cheaper rates, lessening the recurring cost (Kumar & Bhardwaj, 2023). As far as ebooks go, the digital divide still stands as one of the greatest challenges for the edtech industry. This challenge is more prominent in rural areas where inadequate internet connectivity is the major problem, which hinders the widespread adoption of e-books (Gupta & Basu, 2022). The digital divide is rather strong, with access to eBooks varying across geography and socio-economic status. The National Sample Survey (2017–18) noted that only 24 percent of Indian homes had internet connectivity, with the count being much less in the rural areas. Further, women on the Internet constitute just 33% in rural India, which means access to digital resources is also gender-specific (Internet and Mobile Association of India, 2020). Beyond that, an eBook is not even an affordable thing for poorer families, since the purchase of electronic devices that need to be used for accessing eBooks—computer, tablet, etc.—is well beyond their means. Some state governments put in place helpful measures to deal with these challenges. For instance, the Government of Uttar Pradesh launched a scheme in 2012 to distribute free laptops to high school graduates and students who passed intermediate examinations. Between 2012 and 2015, approximately 1.6 million laptops were distributed, making it one of the largest such schemes globally. However, such initiatives, while commendable, still face challenges in ensuring equitable access across gender and economic lines. Schools also save money by subscribing to platforms in some cases, giving students access to devices like tablets or laptops. Digital resources improve access for underprivileged communities through discounted or free services whereby they can access quality educational content (Brown, 2021).

4.8.2 Environmental Considerations

The strong shift from traditional books to e-books in India is thus reducing printing and distribution impacts that are environmentally hazardous. The manufacturing of physical books requires quite cumbersome resources. On the other hand, the digital platforms cut through these entire processes, thus working toward the development of a sustainable educational ecosystem. This paradigm shift is much more prominent in India since heavy-duty large-scale printing has reigned supreme for educational requirements (Sharma, 2023). The availability of e-learning for students in urban and rural areas through reasonably priced smartphones and tablets will, in turn, accelerate the acceptance of e-books (Patel & Kumar, 2021). The use of digital learning technologies in schools and colleges has tremendously witnessed an upsurge through Government programs, especially the Digital India initiative (Government of India, 2020). For instance, by 2023, over 12 lakh schools were connected to digital infrastructure under the DIKSHA (Digital Infrastructure for Knowledge Sharing) platform, and more than 4.5 crore students accessed e-learning content via this platform. Additionally, the SWAYAM portal recorded over 2 crore student enrollments for online courses in higher education by 2022. Government investment in EdTech also saw a significant boost — with 818 crore allocated to the PM eVIDYA initiative in 2021-22 alone, aiming to make multi-modal digital education accessible to all, especially in remote and rural areas

The enhanced use of e-books in the USA is part of a bigger thrust toward sustainable education. The digitization of textbooks lessens deforestation and the emission of carbon dioxide caused by the printing and distributing of such materials. Another way to offset the adverse environmental impact of education is to use digital materials encouraged by schools and publishers. Such partnerships become important in strengthening the ecosystems that promote economic activity and access to opportunities for high-quality education. EdTech investments, for example, promote economic growth and are expected to enhance employment opportunities in various sectors such as content development, telecommunications, and IT infrastructure (Udanoh & Zouria, 2023). Adopting EdTech in rural deployment helps support the upskilling and reskilling activities that would lead to increased productivity and, in turn, address unemployment at the grassroots level (Rodriguez-Segura, 2021).

The shift from printed textbooks to e-books significantly reduces the environmental burden traditionally associated with the production and distribution of educational materials. Physical books demand substantial resources — including wood for paper, water for processing, energy for printing, and fuel for transportation. Sharma (2023) points out that in India's government school systems, large-scale printing has historically led to 30–35% excess stock, much of which is discarded or underutilized. This growing awareness has prompted schools and publishers to opt for digitized learning materials to align with eco-conscious practices.

However, the sustainability of digital education also depends on the energy efficiency of the devices used. Older electronic devices contribute to energy consumption and e-waste, but the development of low-power, energy-efficient e-readers and tablets helps mitigate this. Smith et al. (2022) emphasize that the average energy consumption of a modern e-reader is less than 0.01 kWh per hour, making it a far more sustainable alternative to producing and recycling paper books.

4.8.3 Preferences and Adoption Patterns Among Users

In India, the printed book is regarded as a primary option especially by the government and other traditional schools, particularly in rural areas. E-books and online sources, however, are gradually gaining acceptance in urban centres/private supply schools. The preference of users for any digital material is determined by how convenient it is to access different resources and how interactive the digital platform is perceived to be. Yet, accessibility challenges and poor digital literacy remain detractors from the process of acceptance (Gupta & Basu, 2022). The existence of e-books and electronic gadgets in conjunction with the convenience and levels of interactivity offered by e-books have made them a choice for students and educators alike. Such trends seem to represent a much broader societal acceptance of enforcing technology in the learning environment (Brown,2021).

The trends in print and electronic book sales in the United States demonstrate that consumer interest has changed over the years. Sales rates for print books give a fluctuating picture from 2004 to 2022. For example, maximum sales were achieved in 2008 with 778 million sales whereas the lowest sales of 591 million were recorded in 2013 when the trend toward e-books accelerated. In 2021, while print seemed to recover to 843.1 million, a sense of renewed interest appeared to have resampled. The rise in e-book sales began steeply at first, from 69 million (2010) to 242 million (2013); after that, it began to trend downward in a steady line, falling between 168 million and 191 million during 2018 and 2020. Reader fatigue with digital media, the return to preference for physical books, and saturation in adoption with e-books substantiate the said decline.

Given the low availability of digital infrastructure in rural and government schools, print books reign supreme in these areas (Gupta & Basu, 2022). In contrast, urban and private schools are now preferring e-books for their accessibility and interactivity. E-books and online platforms have been widely accepted in the United States, especially for higher education purposes (Brown, 2021). On their part, declining e-book sales indicate a firm place for print books in deep reading and engagement. Hybrid approaches, combining digital and print methods, undergird key insights for EdTech and digital learning. The great digital divide still prevails as a major deterrent to e-book usage, especially in developing countries. With the advent of low-cost e-readers and the creation of AI-based learning solutions, EdTech has many opportunities.

5. DISCUSSION

5.1 Market Dynamics in the EdTech Sector

5.1.1 Opportunities for Start-Ups

Startups trying to monetize gaps and niches that have gone unattended by the big players hold promise for growth in the EdTech sector. By focusing on niche segments, start-ups can build solutions designed for the unique needs of those segments, particularly the undeserved ones: learners of regional languages and students with special educational needs (SEN). A growing trend for the importance of localized regional content can help, to some extent, bridge the gap for tier 2 and tier 3 cities where such localized education resources are far and between (Kumar, 2023). Start-ups also focus on providing a personalized learning experience denied to learners in large enterprises focusing solely on growth: i.e., using advanced analytics to understand customer learning styles (Siddiqui, 2022). This quality allows small firms to incorporate trends such as gamification and AI-enabled tutoring to achieve more profound engagement and learning impacts. As the costs become a factor, there has been increasing demand for solutions available to economically deprived communities, a section that has mostly been neglected by the big players (Singh and Verma, 2021).

5.1.2 Strategies of Tech Giants in EdTech

This world that witnesses the tech giants Google, Microsoft and Byju's at the forefront of a pack that employs scaling possibilities and resources like no other bear-proof is one where some companies mostly build and market massive solutions aimed to serve, for the most part, mainstream educational needs. Whereas these companies do efficiently deliver basic tools such as digital classrooms, cloud learning platforms and standard content (Patel, 2020), big investments are put in AI and machine learning to nurture adaptive systems that assess data for personalization on scale. Nonetheless, given scalability, these strategies largely tend to neglect the localized and niche markets (Sharma et al., 2023). Partnerships with governments and educational institutions confer further credence while acting as a propeller to larger adoption. The flip side, however, is that data privacy and the general notion of data security fears raised in the minds of parents and educators have made it hard (Rao & Gupta, 2021).

5.2. Addressing the Digital Divide

5.2.1 Barriers to Accessibility and Equity

Although, AI and digital technology have revolutionized the Education sector, the one area it lacks is accessibility and equity for all. Digital disparity is a critical issue faced especially in developing nations with inequality in terms of access to Internet connectivity, hardware and digital literacy. A lack of these amenities result in further widening the gap between urban and rural students. Less than half of the few schools in India with internet access have operational computers for students and around 34% have some measure to check the digital divide. Therefore, the fundamental digital infrastructure is blocking almost everyone from accessing AI applications for personalized learning. Students from disadvantaged backgrounds may find it especially tough because they have limited resources and unstable internet connections, whereas their teachers and family members may not have training in the digital literacy needed for effective use of learning by AI (UNESCO, 2024).

Inclusivity is another major concern since many of these EdTech platforms are standard designs that do not cater to different learning needs. For students with disabilities or from other linguistic and cultural backgrounds, this creates further challenges. For example, if educational content is not adapted for those who are visually or hearing-impaired, it may prove to be impossible to interact with; the same goes for online courses that set non-native speakers at a disadvantage due to language barriers (UNESCO, 2024). Students also face certain challenges with e-learning. Children from low-income families often lack access to devices and internet connectivity, while those pursuing practical subjects struggle due to the absence of hands-on experiences (UNICEF, 2022).For example, open-book tests emphasize problem-solving in preference to rote memorization, whereas gamification strategies bring about student involvement. However, children from disadvantaged backgrounds are at a very real risk of being denied a successful digital learning experience in the absence of proper resources, connectivity, and teacher training. A multifaceted strategy for ensuring equitable edtech access will have to integrate high-tech innovations with affordable solutions and be made to fit different learning needs (UNICEF, 2022).

5.2.2 Government Initiatives and Policies for Digital Inclusion

One of the main strategies by which improvement of internet connectivity is facilitated, especially in rural and remote locations, remains investment in digital infrastructure. For instance, the Universal Service Fund of India provides subsidies for internet infrastructure to improve internet access in unserved areas. The digital domain of India has witnessed reasonably large-scale changes, beginning with Universal Connectivity and Digital India from the year 2014 and culminating in 2024.This ensures affordable and accessible internet packages for both urban and rural India, especially tier-2, tier-3 cities and remote villages. By April 2024, these programs had greatly enhanced digital access and usage, thus bridging the gap and ensuring connectivity. Governments are also enacting policies for affordable technological access.

Furthermore, frameworks that favour inclusion are being set up to respond to the unique concerns of excluded communities. For example, the Indian National Policy on Persons with Disabilities attaches great significance to accessible educational technologies to ensure that students with disabilities have access to digital learning resources that address their unique requirements (Ministry of Social Justice and Empowerment, India, 2021). In creating inclusive environments, these policies support technologies that are flexible enough to address a range of disabilities, from screen readers for students with visual impairments to captioning for students with hearing impairments. Overall, government initiatives and legislation geared toward digital inclusion form a backbone for ensuring that no one is excluded in the Digital Age.

5.2.3 Potential Solutions to Close the Gap

In collaboration with private sector companies, governments could help fund the enhancement of broadband connectivity so that students in rural areas can access digital resources that students in urban areas can. Several avenues may be explored by governments in subsidizing digital education in the light of bringing down the purchase price of such technologies for certain families living at the margin. Brazil is one country out of many to have enacted some programs for students from public schools to receive laptops or tablets (Pereira et al., 2021). Also, programs to keep expenses for internet access low for low-income families can go a long way to ensuring effective access to online learning. Partnerships between governments and tech company firms can also produce cheap and durable digital devices customized for potential use in education (Vázquez & García, 2020).

Improving digital literacy is another major consideration. Both students and teachers need digital skills to take full advantage of using any sort of digital tool. Programs could prepare teachers for incorporating technology in their teaching along with taking care of the significant matter in teaching students' digital skills. In addition, students from disadvantaged backgrounds need to be part of digital literacy programs teaching them how to operate online learning environments, find information, and collaborate digitally (Brown & Green, 2021).Governments can make digital education more affordable by introducing subsidy programs that lower the cost of technology for low-income families. Additionally, policies that reduce internet expenses for financially struggling families can help ensure better access to online learning. Collaborations between governments and tech companies could also lead to the development of budget-friendly, durable digital devices designed specifically for education (Vázquez & García, 2020).

The design of educational technology tools must prioritize inclusivity. Edtech companies should develop products that accommodate learners with disabilities, ensuring that all students can benefit from digital learning. This includes providing tools that support text-to-speech, speech-to-text, sign language integration, and captions for video content (UNICEF, 2021). In addition, platforms should be designed in multiple languages to cater to diverse linguistic communities. These inclusivity features would make educational content accessible to a broader range of learners, ensuring that students from all backgrounds can engage in the digital learning experience (Arora & Nabi, 2022). Public-private partnerships (PPPs) can play a critical role in closing the gap by fostering innovation and pooling resources for large-scale educational projects. These collaborations can focus on developing and scaling technologies that are both affordable and accessible, such as open-source learning platforms or mobile-based education solutions. Additionally, PPPs can ensure that the benefits of these technologies reach marginalized communities by providing targeted funding and support (Glickman & Choi, 2022). Collaborative efforts can accelerate the development of new, effective solutions to promote equity in education.

While the digital divide presents significant challenges to the equitable distribution of educational opportunities, there are clear and actionable solutions that can help bridge this gap. By focusing on expanding digital infrastructure, subsidizing technology access, providing digital literacy training, and developing inclusive edtech tools, we can ensure that all learners, regardless of background or location, are empowered to succeed in the digital age. Furthermore, public-private partnerships and community engagement play a vital role in fostering collaboration and ensuring that marginalized groups are not left behind. The collective efforts of governments, educators, businesses, and communities are essential for creating a more inclusive and accessible education system, where technology serves as a tool for empowerment rather than exclusion. Through these strategic initiatives, we can build a future where the promise of digital education is realized for all students, contributing to a more equitable and sustainable global society.

5.3. Future Trends and Recommendations

AI shall be the growth engine for this sector, changing perceptions about education with improved engagement, accessibility, and personalized learning experience. AI-learning platforms evaluate a student's performance and proffer course materials to enhance the individual's learning experience per that evaluation (Baker & Siemens, 2022). In this context of adaptive learning, the intelligence recommendations adapt content material to flow with the student's learning speed and understanding. Khan Academy and Coursera are utilizing AI technologies to create customized learning pathways (Smith, 2021).

AI-powered language tools help develop educational material in regional languages that sort of bridge the digital divide (Sharma, 2023). Start-ups like Vedantu are now trying to invest in AI for vernacular education so that learning can be made available to students in smaller cities and even rural areas (Joshi, 2022). With competitive advantages such as the BERT model by Google and GPT-4 by OpenAI, multilingual translations of content for educational generation in a diverse range of languages are being made with fair ease (Gupta, 2023). The AI-focused blended learning model is thus the creation of digital classrooms, merging separate offline learning experiences (Brown, 2023). Gamification in the classroom is transforming the way students, in their engagement with course content, learn. AI enhances gamification by adaptively modifying the level of challenge according to student preferences and performance (Miller & Johnson, 2023). Virtual reality (VR)-augmented reality (AR) combination is expected to extend AI-based gamification in offering immersive experiences in education (Lee et al., 2023).

AI-based EdTech platforms offer targeted upskill and reskill courses across several highly sought-after areas: cybersecurity, data science, and AI (Wang & Li, 2023). While Udacity and LinkedIn Learning use AI to design targeted learning programs for a career (Rodriguez, 2022). Such platforms closely collaborate with professionals to keep up with the fast-changing labour market. AI is acting as a facilitator for enhancing an inclusive approach towards education. Assistive technology such as Natural Reader and Read & Write, in particular, would be enhancing reading experience for children who are having difficulties (Singh, 2022).

AI-related solutions may easily slip through the hands of the economically weaker sections. Government initiatives and freemium models could help narrow the gap. For example, in India, the DIKSHA platform helps offer free AI-based learning resources for children across all socioeconomic lines. In many ways, the combination of AI with regional language education, blended learning, and upskilling programs is set to redefine the very face of learning.

6. CONCLUSION

In conclusion, AI and digital learning technologies play significant roles in educational transformation for economic development. AI platforms allow personalization in instructional delivery, engaging students while enabling accessibility via adaptive systems and multilingual content. UNESCO has therefore affirmed that it is extremely important for governments to intervene via the creation of a digital infrastructure to address all these challenges and to engineering quality education for all (UNESCO, 2024). AI tools are expected to help learning and customize the instruction to lead to more involvement and quality learning for students in remote and underprivileged areas (Kumar, 2023). With the acceptance of AI, distance learning is expected to begin filling educational gaps by giving feedback to students for continuous improvement of skills on a session-by-session basis.

From the economic perspective, EdTech will continue to be in the high-growth area with investments directed toward growth and creating jobs. However, for the health of the industry to be sustained, it should be focused on policies and approaches that support human educators and mitigate the threats AI poses to jobs (Rodriguez-Segura, 2021). Investment in the training of teachers and digital literacy programs and policies specifically aiding start-ups within this domain are in favour of long-term growth.

The entrance of education into a digital world with the help of AI and EdTech heralds a new paradigm of the impartation and absorption of knowledge. Such developments offer an enormous chance to attain at different levels the accessibility of education for economic gain and conversely raise some pertinent questions about digital equity and AI ethics in education. Thus, cooperation among policymakers, educational institutions, and private entities shall be required to create an inclusive technology-driven learning ecosystem. A digital education ecosystem of transformation and sustainability is, therefore, envisaged in the tension between equitable access and responsible use of AI, with continued innovation.

REFERENCES

Al-Azawei, A., Serenelli, F., & Lundqvist, K. (2017). The effectiveness of adaptive learning technologies for students with learning disabilities: A systematic review. *Computers in Human Behavior*.

Al-Azawei, A., Serenelli, F., & Lundqvist, K. (2017). Universal design for learning.

Arora, S., & Nabi, T. (2022). Blockchain adoption in banking systems: A boon or bane.

Baker, R. S., & Siemens, G. (2014). Educational data mining and learning analytics. In Gilbert, S. J., & O'Brien, T. G. (Eds.), *Learning analytics: From research to practice*. DOI: 10.1007/978-1-4614-3305-7_4

Baker, R. S., & Siemens, G. (2014). Educational data mining and learning analytics.

Baker, R. S., & Siemens, G. (2022). The role of AI in personalized learning.

Brown, A., & Green, T. (2021). Digital literacy in the classroom: Bridging the gap..

Brown, P., & Lee, J. (2022). AI-driven personalized learning and its impact on academic success.

Brown, R. (2021). The shift to e-learning: The cost-effectiveness of e-books in the U.S.

Brown, T. (2021). Sustainable learning: The role of cloud-based education in reducing environmental impact.

Bulathwela, S., Perez-Ortiz, M., Yaneva, V., & Luckin, R. (2021). Towards an open data ecosystem for education: Addressing challenges of a machine learning pipeline for educational applications.

Daniel, B. (2015). Big Data and analytics in higher education: Opportunities and challenges.

Davis, J. (2020). The role of AI in providing academic support to students. *Learning and Individual Differences*.

Dunleavy, M., & Dede, C. (2014). Augmented reality teaching and learning.

Glickman, C., & Choi, A. (2022). The role of public-private partnerships in bridging the digital divide in education.

Grand View Research. (2024). Education technology market size & share report, 2030.

Gupta, A., & Basu, S. (2022). Challenges and opportunities in India's digital education transformation.

Gupta, S. (2023). AI and language learning: Implications for regional education.

Hale, T., Angrist, N., Goldszmidt, R., Kira, B., Petherick, A., Phillips, T., ... & Webster, S. (2020). Global assessment of COVID-19 school closures.

Hale, T., & Webster, S. (2020). Oxford COVID-19 government response tracker.

Holmes, W., Bialik, M., & Fadel, C. (2019). Artificial intelligence in education promises and implications for teaching and learning.

Holon, I. Q. (2020). *Global EdTech market trends and forecasts*. HolonIQ.

Johnson, R., & Lee, M. (2023). E-books and sustainability: Evaluating environmental benefits of digital learning. Journal of Educational Technology.

Joshi, A. (2022). The expansion of EdTech in rural India: AI-powered solutions.

KPMG. (2023). EdTech market trends and future projections. https://www.kpmg.com

Kulik, J. A., & Kulik, C.-L. C. (1991). Effectiveness of computer-based instruction: An updated analysis. *Computers in Human Behavior*, *7*(1-2), 75–94. DOI: 10.1016/0747-5632(91)90030-5

Kumar, P., & Bhardwaj, M. (2023). Comparative analysis of e-books and physical books in Indian education.

Kumar, S. (2023). Bridging the digital divide in Indian education: The role of regional language content.

Kumar, S. (2023). Digital inclusion through regional languages: The next frontier in Education 4.0.

Lee, J., Kim, H., & Park, S. (2023). VR and AR in education: AI-enhanced immersive learning.

Luckin, R., & Holmes, W. (2016). Intelligence unleashed: An argument for AI in education.

Miller, J., & Lee, P. (2021). AI in education: Managing administration and instructional efficiency. *Journal of Educational Technology & Society*.

Miller, T., & Johnson, K. (2023). AI-enhanced gamification in education.

Ministry of Social Justice and Empowerment. India. (2021). National Policy on Persons with Disabilities. https://socialjustice.nic.in

Mishra, S., Reddy, N., & Sharma, V. (2021). Mental Health and Online Learning: Addressing the Issues in EdTech.

Oberoi, S., Arora, S., Verma, B., & Roy, K. K. (2024). What do we know about artificial intelligence and blockchain technology integration in the healthcare industry.

Oberoi, S., & Kansra, P. (2021). Motivating antecedents and consequences of blockchain technology in the insurance industry.

Oberoi, S., & Kansra, P. (2022). Blockchain technology in the insurance industry.

Pardo, A., Han, F., & Kloos, C. D. (2019). Student engagement in personalized learning environments: The role of technology. *Computers in Human Behavior*.

Patel, A., & Singh, M. (2021). The role of NLP and AI in regional language inclusion in Indian EdTech.

Patel, A., & Singh, N. (2022). AI-driven localization in e-learning: Challenges and opportunities.

Patel, R. (2022). AI in blended learning environments.

Patel, S., & Kumar, R. (2021). E-learning in India: Trends and challenges in digital education. Indian Journal of Education and Technology.

Patel, S., & Singh, R. (2022). *AI-based translation for localizing digital education content*. Computers in Educatio.

Patel, V. (2020). Big tech's strategies in EdTech: A review of global trends.

Pereira, L., Santos, P., & Costa, D. (2021). Digital education programs in Latin America: Overcoming barriers to equity.

Ranjan, V., & Bose, S. (2022). Overcoming linguistic barriers in digital education: Policy interventions and future strategies.

Rao, M., & Swaminathan, K. (2022). Regional languages in digital learning: Impacts on student engagement and economic mobility.

Rao, P., & Gupta, M. (2021). Data privacy challenges in EdTech: The way forward.

Rao, P., & Swaminathan, S. (2022). Localized e-learning solutions: The role of AI in multilingual education. Indian Journal of Educational Technology.

Raut, R., Deshpande, A., Arora, S., Mittal, A., & Alandikar, R. (2022). An examination of the pricing of IPOs: The Indian perspective.

Renz, A., Krishnaraja, S., & Schildhauer, T. (2020, June). A new dynamic for EdTech in the age of pandemics.

Rodriguez, P. (2022). AI and lifelong learning: Upskilling for the future.

Rodriguez-Segura, D. (2022). EdTech in developing countries: A review of the evidence.

Selwyn, N. (2021). *Education and technology: Key issues and debates*. Bloomsbury Publishing.

Sharma, N. (2023). AI and digital education in India: Expanding reach and impact.

Sharma, P. (2023). *The impact of e-books on sustainable education in India*. Environmental Studies in Education.

Sharma, R. (2023). Economic implications of digital education resources in emerging economies.

Sharma, R. (2023). AI-powered translation tools in e-learning: Enhancing accessibility and efficiency.

Sharma, V., & Reddy, S. (2023). Barriers to regional language integration in Indian EdTech platforms.

Shute, V. J. (2008). Focus on formative feedback. *Review of Educational Research, 78*(1), 153–189. DOI: 10.3102/0034654307313795

Siddiqui, N. (2022). Adaptive learning technologies: Opportunities for innovation in EdTech start-ups.

Siemens, G. (2013). Learning analytics: The emergence of a discipline. *International Review of Research in Open and Distance Learning*.

Singh, R., & Verma, S. (2021). Affordable EdTech solutions for inclusive education: An Indian perspective.

Smith, A. (2021). Personalized learning and AI: Trends and impact..

Smith, J., Clark, P., & Lee, R. (2024). Adapting to the Future of Work in EdTech.

Smith, J., Green, L., & Carter, A. (2022). Digital textbooks and environmental sustainability: A comparative study.

Statista. (2024). Indian EdTech market projections: Growth from $7.5B to $29B by 2030.

Technavio. (2024). Edtech market growth analysis - size and forecast 2025-2029.

Udanoh, M. U., & Zouria, A. (2023). Impact of investment in EdTech: Government and entrepreneurial partnership venture in education in North and West Africa.

UNESCO. (2021). The importance of multilingual education in the digital era. https://unesdoc.unesco.org

UNESCO Institute of Statistics. (2020). UIS Statistics. https://data.uis.unesco.org/#

UNICEF. (2021). Inclusive education for children with disabilities: A guide to digital tools. https://www.unicef.org

Vázquez, D., & García, M. (2020). Innovating education through technology: Policies and practices in the digital age.

Watson, W. R., & Watson, S. L. (2007). An argument for clarity: What are learning management systems, what are they not, and what should they become?

Woolf, B. P. (2010). Building intelligent interactive tutors: Student-centered strategies for revolutionizing e-learning.

World Economic Forum. (2020). Reskilling Revolution. Initiatives.weforum.org. https://initiatives.weforum.org/reskilling-revolution/home

World Economic Forum. (2021). Education technologies are making learning more accessible.

Chapter 5
Deciphering the Link Between Financial Inclusion and Economic Growth: A Nexus Analysis

Ajay Khurana
https://orcid.org/0009-0007-3260-000X
University School of Business, Chandigarh University, Mohali, India

Shanul Gawshinde
https://orcid.org/0000-0002-6970-7237
Symbiosis Institute of Management Studies, Symbiosis International University, Pune, India

Harwinder Kaur
University School of Business, Chandigarh University, Mohali, India

ABSTRACT

A country's exemplary financial structure provides an unquestionable foundation for sustainable development and economic progress. It makes banking services available to citizens at any level of the economy at convenient rates. The meaning of inclusive finance was further expanded to encompass other services financed, especially the fiduciary guardianship for savings and an extensive range of loan products for small businesses, as well as other financial mechanisms that reduce financing risk through a partition of investments and insurance mediation (Wang et al.2022). Inclusive finance calls for a solemn catalyst of all individuals' well-being and demystification by pulling down the bridge and teeming injustice. The world is

DOI: 10.4018/979-8-3373-1290-3.ch005

a vastly different place today than it was a quarter of a century ago. A combination of civil unrest and technological evolution has reset the stage that people all over the globe have been living on. For some, this is tremendously positive news as for others this represents another step backwards for the progress made in the second half of the 20th century.

1. INTRODUCTION

The tripartite framework of Financial Inclusion, Financial Literacy, and Consumer Protection creates a fundamental foundation for an economy to survive. Financial Inclusion is the linchpin of this framework, as the mode of totalitarian framework through which financial services are widely provided to everyone in the society, focusing more on economically lesser endowed and less-income group members. This total gambit of inclusion goes beyond conventional financial instruments of merchandise to include insurance and offering equity asset classes.

In essence, Financial Inclusion hinges on the mainstreaming of each and every individual in the formal financial services milieu conducive to fostering robust financial infrastructure. The resilience of the financial structure will be the lifeblood of the economy wherein people become equipped with stepping through the many ways of dealing with financial services and be broader economic background where they can be part of. Financial inclusion (FI) is defined as comprehensive extent of access that all societal groups find enjoyable, comprising deposit, credit, insurance, and pensionary provisions, in accordance with the perspective articulated by CRISIL (2015) (Dahiya & Kumar, 2020).

The concept of "financial inclusion" was initially introduced by RBI in the annual proclamation of policy directives for the fiscal year 2005–2006. The financial institutions were encouraged to evaluate their endeavours in alignment with the overarching objective of fostering financial inclusion. This policy directive aimed to address disparity in access to banking services among various socio-economic strata. Notably, Mangalam, situated in the state of Tamil Nadu, emerged as a pioneering exemplar, achieving the distinction of becoming the inaugural village in India where each household attained ubiquitous access to formal banking services. (Sharma, 2016) Despite being classified as an emerging economy, India exhibits a poverty rate of 22%, surpassing the global average of 18%. This indicates that a significant proportion of India's population lives below the poverty line, highlighting a substantial socio-economic challenge within the country. Henceforth, poverty mitigation poses a formidable challenge for densely populated nations such as India. Financial inclusion emerges as a pivotal mechanism in addressing this issue by facilitating the widespread accessibility of financial services. The Indian Government is actively trying to build an overarching financial structure that promotes the development of all areas, which has led to the creation of a range of initiatives Arora, S.(2022). Some government schemes like Pradhan Mantri Jan Dhan Yojna (PMJDY), Pradhan Mantri Mudra Yojna (PMMY), Pradhan Mantri Jeevan Jyoti Bima Yojana (PMJJBY), Pradhan Mantri Suraksha Bima Yojana (PMSBY), Atal Pension Yojana (APY), and Stand-Up India Scheme were consolidated with the ide of allocating financial resources to all in a more equal manner for implementation after 2014.

The theoretical foundations of the relationship between financial inclusion (FI) and economic growth (EG) are laid out. FI is the dynamic process of ensuring broad and sustainable access to a full range of financial services, which leads to development that engenders improvements in resilience, equality, opportunity, and productivity. Four of its complementing components, access to financial services, affordability, quality and consumer protection, are frequently facilitated by digital technologies (Zhang et al., 2022). Of particular interest is FI that does not come at the expense of financial stability, is challenging in contexts prone to economic crises, and is a leverageable asset. In economic systems, households rely on financial systems to undertake saving, make payment transactions, and acquire liquid assets and planning instruments. The state of such systems, when robust, shapes the governance of economic trajectory. The effort is made to establish a first step in translating such principles into a compelling framework for understanding FI.

Effective financial inclusion refers to accessible financial services like savings, credit, payments, and insurance which acts as a sustainable economic development pillar. The World Bank (2023) states that having an account is one thing and using it to its full potential is another. Specifically, having access to financial services allows one to reduce poverty, improve social mobility, and increase entrepreneurship activities. Digital technologies, especially during the last decade, have improved access helping previously disregarded people and communities realize their full potential. Nonetheless, barriers based on income, gender, geography, and education level continue to be some of the persistent obstacles to fully attaining inclusive financial services (Sarma & Pais, 2019). This paper focuses on the relationship between financial inclusivity and economic growth while focusing on socio-economic disparities, fintech innovations, and their effects.

A nexus analysis of FI and EG lies at the interface of several theoretical perspectives. Endogenous growth theories hold that investment in knowledge and infrastructure catalyze positive externalities, which set in motion a virtuous cycle of faster productivity growth. Financial sector growth is a central ingredient of several mechanisms driving this kind of EG. The greater the FI, the greater the probability for talented individuals and firms to secure funding for high returns projects, increase education and training eventually translating into technological advances. This endogeneity, however, plays a potentially ambiguous role when mediated by the banking sector. On the one hand, more FI alleviates market imperfections and fosters an optimal allocation of resources, as severe informational asymmetries render the evaluation of the expected return of entrepreneurial initiatives harder. This generates a positive external effect of FI on EG and a profound impact on productivity growth. Finally, a more financially inclusive environment might spur innovation and new knowledge too risky for traditional banks. Klapper & Singer (2019) conducted a study documenting how digital financial services such as mobile money have been a major tool lifting households out of poverty in Sub-Saharan Africa, with the M-Pesa accounting for 98% of mobile money usage by adults in Kenya by 2022.

Still, and despite sustained policy maker effort, a very large group of people are still uninformed about and therefore still have no access to financial services (Dahiya & Kumar, 2020). The Reserve Bank of India (RBI) has developed the National Strategy for Financial Inclusion for India from 2019 to 2024. This was done in a very measured way through the guidance of the Advisory Committee on Financial Inclusion. The framework was developed collaboratively with the assistance of various components including the Indian Government, and other organs, agencies as the Securities and Exchange Board of India, Insurance Regulatory and Development Authority of India, and Pension Fund Regulatory and Development.

2. EVALUATING ADVANCEMENTS IN ACCESS TO FINANCIAL SERVICES

The Financial Inclusion Advisory Committee has been a guide to the making of the National Strategy for Financial Inclusion that has been developed by the Reserve Bank of India for the period 2019-2024. This framework has been borne out of a participatory process with various stakeholders, mainly involving the Indian government and regulators like the Securities Exchange Board of India (SEBI), Insurance Regulatory and Development Authority of India (IRDAI), and Pension Fund Regulatory and Development Authority of India (PFRDA). In addition, consultations with NABARD, NPCI, commercial banks, and corporate business correspondents further informed our understanding. The Reserve Bank of India (RBI) conducts detailed data collection on the moves of banking institutions on an array of elements of financial inclusion like implementation of FI Plans, credit allocation to the priority sector, lending to the disadvantaged members of the community, and status on important Government Schemes. Other than RBI, NABARD is involved in the collection of data from Rural Cooperatives and Regional Rural Banks.

Moreover, the financial sector regulatory authorities of India are engaged in the systematic collection of relevant data concerning the entities operating under their own regulatory purview. Moreover, the Ministry of Finance, Government of India, is actively involved in crafting an Index of Financial Inclusion, thereby enriching the intricate fabric of data resources in this domain. People examine advancements in financial inclusion by looking at three areas: access, use, and quality.

Figure 1. Areas of financial inclusion

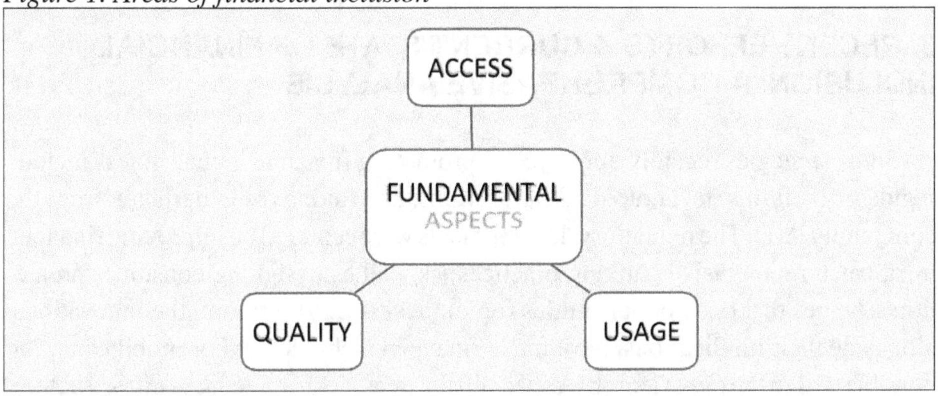

(Source: Reserve Bank of India)

- **Access** indicators shed light on the details of access points, including how banks are spread out. This covers PoS terminals, ATMs other business correspondent spots, and regular bank branches. These numbers are looked at in two ways: by area and by people. The first measures how many banking outlets there are per 1000 square kilometers, while the second looks at how many banks there are for every 100,000 adults. To get this info on access, we need to pull data from regulators or government bodies.
- **Usage** indicators show how people use financial products. To get this info, we use a mix of methods. We get numbers on accounts, product use, and similar things straight from the banks and other financial companies. But to understand how people act and what they like when it comes to financial products and services, we often use surveys or ask customers for feedback.
- **Quality** markers in financial inclusion outline the key elements needed to give clients the best service. At the heart of this idea is the belief that things like financial know-how and skill are must-haves helping customers to handle money matters with ease. But if financial companies don't provide good ser-

vice, it can lead to unhappy customers and make financial exclusion worse. Since judging quality is often a matter of opinion, it's crucial to create a thorough measure that can capture many aspects while adapting to different situations. Factors such as financial literacy and ability how well providers explain things and how satisfied customers are how easy it is to complain and get help, and how issues are solved all play a part in assessing quality in financial inclusion. (Source: RBI). The IMF (2022) discusses the role of fintech in widening access, especially during the pandemic, where digital transactions registered a rise of 35 percent globally.

3. RECENT EFFORTS & CURRENT STATE OF FINANCIAL INCLUSION: A COMPREHENSIVE ANALYSIS

Some strategies recently employed in promoting financial inclusiveness include regulatory reforms, technological innovations, and initiatives undertaken from the community level. The regulatory developments were centered on improving financial infrastructure; inclusive banking practices; as well as designing consumer protection schemes that open opportunities for fair access. Furthermore, the innovations, alongside their implications, have made financial technological or mobile banking possible within the given lengths, especially in areas lacking adequate infrastructure, thus creating availability in underserved locations. Community initiatives such as microfinance programs and financial literacy campaigns have specifically addressed local barriers to access, thus linking the marginalized groups with formal financial systems.

The World Bank's Findex database reveals that from 2014 to 2017, the uptake of financial services globally witnessed a remarkable increase, with nearly 515 million new adults being added as bank account holders. This increase stands as a concrete proof of the efforts made in the journey towards financial inclusion, with much propulsion from the widening outreach of formal banking services. The great change that the increase signified cannot leave out the proven effects of concert efforts aimed at broadening access to financial services worldwide. Concurrently, The GSMA's Report on the Current State of Mobile Money Industry is a clear indicator that mobile money accounts have proliferated exponentially, and this is marked in regions with scanty traditional banking provision. Sub-Saharan Africa seems to be the centre of this revolution, as registered mobile money accounts surpassed the remarkable threshold of 100 million by 2019. This statistic indicates a new dimension of access and usage of financial services in areas without traditional banking structures. Unfortunately, even as these advancements were made, the layers of financial inclusion also tended to separate gender. Many datasets have reflected this issue, including the Global Findex database and reputable reports from the World Bank and UN Women. An important finding from the Findex 2017 showed that in global terms, women were 9 percent less likely than men to hold a bank account. This gap has generally enlarged in some regions. It is necessary to redress these differences to enable equal access to financial services across all levels of the society. Furthermore, reports from major cybersecurity firms such as Symantec and Kaspersky highlight the increasing prevalence of cyber threats, both targeting financial institutions and normal users. For example, Symantec's Internet Security Threat Report shows an increasing number of phishing attacks targeting financial institutions, emphasizing the need for robust cybersecurity protocols to protect the digital finance ecosystem from such incursions. Increased vigilance and preemptive measures become necessary to safeguard integrity and security of financial systems in digital age. Besides technical inventions and regulatory changes, microfinance interventions have a major role in promoting financial inclusion. Research by well-known agencies like CGAP has given proof enough on how microfinance programs really change the face of financial inclusion. Evidence from CGAP primary research shows the importance of microfinance programs in increasing access to credit and financial services for poorer sections of the population, achieving real progress in poverty alleviation and empowerment. Although it will take some time to establish the overall framework for cash shortfall alleviation through microfinance for productive purposes among lower-income segments of the economy, these interventions are powerful engines for inclusive economic growth and social development. The knowledge bases feature elements promoting the significance of all-dimensional frameworks in establishing global relevance for financial inclusion agendas Arora, S (2022).

As a policy-makers country, India shows vehement cognizance into the facets of poverty, that is by poverty on economic balance but makes it always intensify efforts to combat such deprivation in all dimensions and ensure even distribution of the economic advancement within the socioeconomically marginalized people in India. India, thus, also puts serious pressure on such cooperative efforts with international partners and bodies particularly through the active participation in Global Partnership for Financial Inclusion (GPFI) and the Organization for Economic Co-operation and Development (OECD). .India, then, features substantially, alongside Indonesia and the United Kingdom, as co-chairpersons in the subset on Regulatory and Standardization Entities within the GPFI framework. Furthermore, India has contributed much in developing a wide-ranging research and policy frameworks in key areas of digitization, regulatory conditions, and financial inclusion that GPFI published. The RBI is also currently engaged in working groups categorized in four sectors in The Global Consortium for Financial Education (GCFE) formed under the OECD framework focusing on standards set, evaluation and implementation digital literacy with relevance to finance, financial literacy initiatives targeting small, micro and medium enterprises, and core competencies for financial literacy. Meanwhile, India has developed its National Strategy for Financial Inclusion (NSFI) gradually since June 2017, based on the guidance of Financial Inclusion Advisory Committee (FIAC). This strategy plan has been painstakingly constructed after debating on it with several significant parties, comprising the Department of Economic Affairs (DEA) and the Department of Financial Services (DFS) involved in the initiatives under the Ministry of Finance, RBI, SEBI, NABARD, IRDAI, PFRDA, and NPCI.

The essence of this program was to bring a fundamental set of financial services to every household that would help correct the inequities in access to banking, while utilizing the vast banking infrastructure in place and technological advances available (Sharma, 2016). The PMJDY was instrumental in the opening of 34.01 crore accounts in five years with the amount of total deposits as of January 30, 2019, being Rs. 89257 crores. It has also received accolades such as a place in the Guinness World Records for the greatest number of account openings in a week, attesting to the program's effectiveness and outreach. On top of this, PMJDY brought in a bouquet of financial products, that provided an overdraft facility, cover against unfortunate death and disability, term-life insurance, and schemes for pensions for the old, aimed at different needs of account holders. Furthermore, some of the complementary schemes include The Pradhan Mantri Suraksha Bima Yojana (PMSBY), Pradhan Mantri Jeevan Jyoti Bima Yojana (PMJJBY), and Atal Pension Yojana (APY) have been put in place to protect a varied age group of bank account holders from financial risk, further strengthening the base for longevity in financial stability. (Source: Reserve Bank of India).

In this subsection, financial inclusion is meticulously defined and explored. The concept of financial inclusion is embodied in various dimensions: accessibility of financial services, the availability of these services, and their usage. In an increasingly interconnected world, access to a bank account or any form of an inclusive financial system is necessary for individuals to save for, borrow capital, and spread risk (Arora, 2017). Financial inclusion emerges at the centre of the international development agenda as it plays a critical role in fostering economic participation. A growing body of research and evidence has demonstrated a positive correlation with various aspects of financial inclusion and countries' economic growth.

Over the last decades, financial inclusion has attracted the attention of scholars, international organisations, and policymakers. Consequently, a variety of indicators and metrics measuring financial inclusion have been created, capturing different facets of financial inclusion. A profound review of these indicators and metrics suggests that for the various regions and levels of development, it is pivotal to emphasize the wide range of the financial inclusion definition.

Emerging market economies, not as advanced in markets, focus more on the classic dimensions. At the same time, standard indicators such as total number of ATMs or commercial bank branches per 100,000 adults do not perfectly capture the financial inclusion concept. More advanced economies, however, put more emphasis on innovative aspects, reflecting rapidly growing digital financial inclusion. The introduction of mobile payment systems changes traditional payment practices, and countries that are developing these financial services are included in this sub-group 39. Oberoi, S; et.al: (2024). Moreover, it is essential to differentiate the financial inclusion concept from several closely related ones: financial literacy, financial capability, and consumer protection. Finally, there are several socioeconomic barriers to financial access, such as lower income, greater women's proportion in particular regions, higher distance to the nearest financial institutions, and lower education. Regulatory restrictions about currency exchange offices are substantial barriers. There are significantly positive and statistically significant effects of conditional cash programs and government-to-person transfer coverage on financial inclusion. Impact evaluations have shown impressive results about the success of conditional cash and government-to-person programs increasing formal financial services, as well as credit supply and individual incomes. Yet, another unconditional type of government-to-person program does not show any positive impact on financial inclusion. Considering the importance of commercial banks in the Turkish financial market and better-functioning agents for state-owned banks, several policy suggestions and recommendations are easily compatible with the existing infrastructure of the Turkish financial system. This subsection carefully outlines and defines various dimensions of the financial inclusion concept. Finally, the specified operational definition of these dimensions is necessary to analyze how the financial inclusion indicators intertwine with economic growth.

Theories of Economic Growth

Over the last five decades, a vast amount of research has been conducted into mechanisms of economic growth as economies strive to achieve sustainable development. This research is of interest to academics, policymakers, governments, corporations, and institutions. Classical growth theory elucidates the simple relationship between capital accumulation and population growth as a function of saving, investment, and technological progress, culminating in the famous Solow-Swan model. Neoclassical growth theory expands upon its forbear to explicitly incorporate savings, human capital, and innovation, thus accounting for long-term growth and the persistence of income differences among nations. Endogenous growth theory assigns innovation a central role in growth; its spillover effects are amplified through knowledge capital, such that the accumulation of this element crucially fuels development. Converging and diverging findings across these theories have been widely observed, the roots of which lie in diversified data samples, intricate mathematical formulations, and variable income levels among nations (A SHOBANDE & R LANRE, 2018).

Economic growth is a multifarious event, driven by an intricate combination of market and firm-level phenomena. Partly as a result, economies at diverse stages, sizes, and income levels tend to manifest dissimilar growth trends. The aspiration for a general theory of economic growth is correspondingly challenged. Furthermore, the macroeconomic theory of growth is innately linked to wider socio-economic features, such as political stability, factor endowments, fiscal strength, workable regulations, and powerful social institutions, all of which bear natural divergence around the globe. The task of this study is to scrutinize these theories concerning the nexus discovery, thereby informing policy and economic strategy; it is not to dispute the constant of any of the theories at their most elementary level. Indeed, the capacity of these theories to integrate broader socio-economic elements can be deemed a reservoir of their power. On the other hand, such adjacency highlights the importance of these externalities and internal dynamics for economic growth, situating them firmly as a topic of investigation in their own right.

The economic growth effects of financial inclusion marks its impact using a variety of models:

- Financial Intermediation Theory: Suggests that financial institutions aid in the mobilization of resources to increase efficiency as savings are set aside and funds are provided towards economically fruitful investments (Levine, 2005). Econometric analyses indicate that the greater the financial intermediation, the higher the economic growth rate (Dhaniya & Kumar, 2020).
- Technology Acceptance Model (TAM): Accounts for the adoption of fintech solutions by users as defined by the ease of use and usefulness, which are fundamental to digital financial inclusion (Venkatesh & Davis, 2000). The use of mobile banking is a striking example of this model.
- The Diffusion of Innovations Theory: Explains the spread of new technologies within one's society over a period of time and its effect on the adoption and level of inclusion (Rogers, 2003). The adoption of mobile money using M-Pesa in Kenya is a prime example of successful diffusion.

Role of Fintech and Technological Innovations

The Fintech has pushed the cause of financial inclusion by:

- Providing low-cost, accessible services through mobile applications.
- Facilitating instant payments, microloans, and insurance.

- Using blockchain technology for secure transactions.

Case Example: UPI System of India

UPI has been immensely popular since its launch in 2016 and is now witnessing more than 2.3 billion transactions per month, enabling digital payment modes for unbanked populations (NPCI, 2023). This was a major breakthrough in industry terms of banking penetration and lowering transaction costs.

According to IMF (2022), with fintech innovations, there is a reduction in operational costs and an expansion of outreach, especially in rural areas, but they also identified risks such as digital divides and cybersecurity threats.

3.1 Financial Inclusion (FI) Takes Different Forms in Different Demographic Cohorts

Indeed, active participation of marginalized groups in financially inclusive programmes is a way of enabling them. It acts as a type of social protection for them. Indeed, their inclusion facilitates the integration of various parts of society, thereby smoothing the transition into benefits across dimensions of all kinds. Dispensing micro credits through formal financial channels allows the poor to develop banking behavior, increase savings, stabilize consumption, and empower their nonrevenue capacity for necessary alternative investments in services such as health, educational facilities, and sanitation provisions. Research indicates that broadening financial inclusion can improve financial well-being and overall standard of life. As a result, it is essential to compute the extent of financial inclusion in India by evaluating the accessibility and effectiveness of financial services across a variety of demographic segments. Using the most recent Global Findex dataset, it is clear that there has been significant progress in achieving the fundamental criterion of FI, which is the possession of a bank account (Goel & Sharma, 2017). Yunus (2021) emphasizes that microfinance programs ensure reliable access to credit for rural entrepreneurs in Bangladesh, pointing to the need for tailor-made financial products.

Account ownership on a global scale surged from 51 percent to 76 percent between the years 2011 and 2021. Global account ownership has achieved a remarkable milestone, encompassing 76 percentof the global populace, with a substantial portion of 71 percent among individuals residing in developing regions (Fig 2.).

Figure 2. Over the decade spanning from 2011 to 2021, there was a notable escalation in the global prevalence of account ownership, surging from 51% to 76%

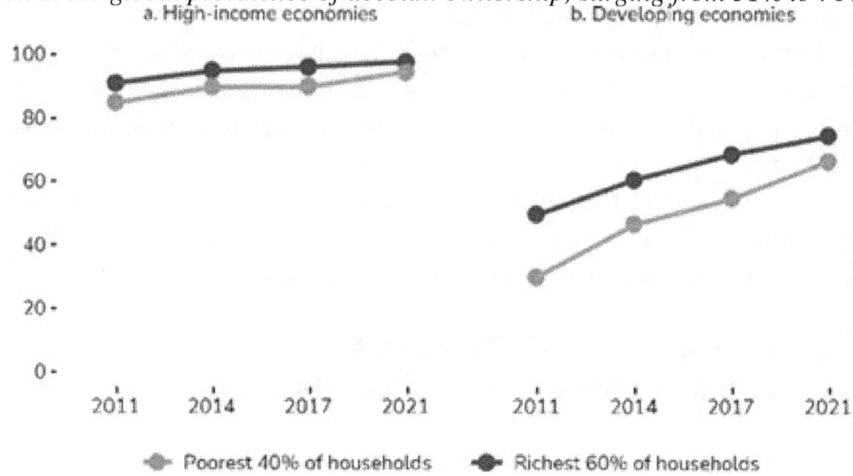

Source: Data Base of Global Findex 2021

Account ownership exhibits a distinct disparity between older adults, aged 25 and above, and young adults, aged 15 to 24, with the former cohort displaying higher ownership rates. Globally, the gap has narrowed slightly, decreasing by 4 percentage points from 17 points in 2011 to 14 points in 2021. Notably, in 2021, 79 percent of adults aged 25 and above had an account, whereas only 66 percent of individuals aged 15 to 24 possessed one. This trend holds true for both developed and emerging economies. However, the magnitude of the age gap varies considerably across developing economies. For instance, in the West Bank and Gaza, older adults exceed twice as their younger counterparts to have an account. Similarly, Algeria and Egypt, had the disparity in account ownership between age groups is nearly 25 percentage points. In Jordan, Morocco, and Tunisia, while the gap is not as pronounced, it remains in the double digits. Conversely, in economies such as Peru and the Philippines, the age gap is approximately 15 percentage points, mirroring the global trend. However, in China and Türkiye, there is negligible disparity in account ownership between age cohorts. Intriguingly, in Myanmar, younger adults exhibit an 11-percentage point advantage over older adults in terms of account ownership.(Barik & Sharma, 2019)

In Sub-Saharan Africa, mobile money accounts are helping younger women access finance more inclusively. As women get older, the gap between men and women having traditional bank accounts widens, but it stays small for those who only have mobile money accounts. Young men have a bank account prevalence rate 6 percentage points higher than young women but there's no difference in owning mobile money accounts. However, fewer older people have mobile money accounts, especially older women, who are 7 percentage points less likely to use them compared to younger women Raut, R (2022). This might be because older people might find it harder to use new technology or may prefer traditional ways of doing things.

Figure 3. In Sub-Saharan Africa, gender differences in access to mobile money accounts among young adults are minimal

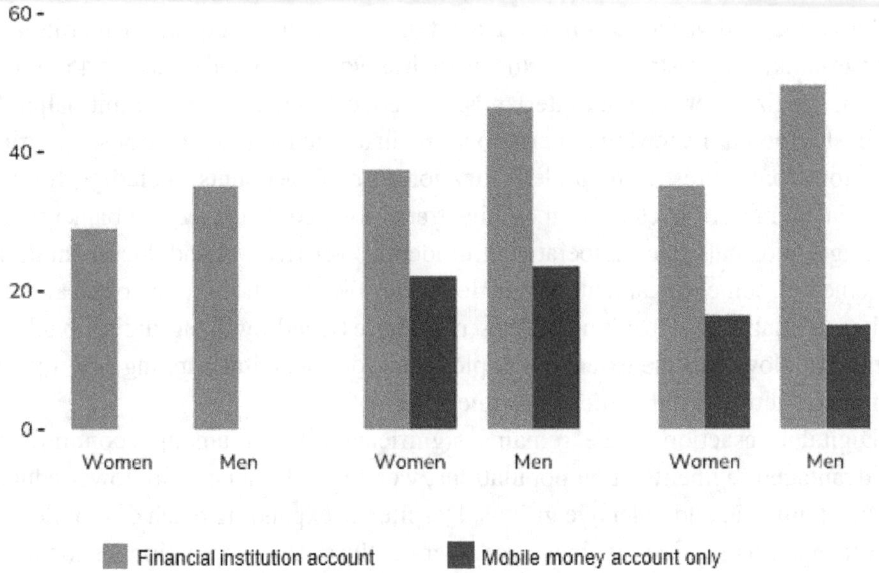

Source: Data Base of Global Findex 202r1

3.2 The Prospective Trajectory of Financial Inclusion

A meticulous examination of diverse datasets elucidates the commendable advancements in bolstering financial inclusion across India, juxtaposed against the formidable hurdles that impede the realization of comprehensive financial access. Despite notable strides, the journey towards universal financial inclusion remains protracted, marred by persistent challenges encompassing both accessibility and utilization facets. The substantive prevalence of dormant or underutilized accounts, particularly those catalysed by flagship initiatives such as the PMJDY, underscores the incongruity between account proliferation and effective utilization. Disparities persist in the proliferation of deposit, savings, and credit instruments, underscored by a paltry improvement in their active usage despite ostensible advancements in their establishment. A panoply of demand-side and supply-side determinants underscores the inertia afflicting bank accounts, including deficient financial literacy, constrained fiscal capacities, exorbitant transactional overheads, spatially constrained bank branch networks, identity validation exigencies, and procedural encumbrances. (Barik & Sharma, 2019)

The envisaged panacea in the form of digital banking encounters a labyrinth of challenges across heterogeneous demographic strata. Remarkably subdued digital transactional engagement characterizes economically marginalized cohorts, rural inhabitants, gender-diverse populations, individuals with rudimentary educational backgrounds, and geriatric cohorts. Despite the widening footprint of mobile and internet banking infrastructure, segments such as women beyond the age of 45, senior citizens, denizens of remote hinterlands, and educational novices exhibit palpably diminished proclivity towards smartphone-mediated financial interactions. A myriad of factors contributes to the underutilization of bank accounts, including limited financial literacy, restricted incomes, high transaction costs, inadequate bank branch coverage, and challenges associated with identity verification and documentation. Nonetheless, some fundamental obstacles issues like high transaction costs and the limited availability of banking offices may be lessened by using digital banking platforms, However, the extensive implementation of digital banking has diverse limitations across different demographic groups.

Digital transaction usage remains significantly lower among economically disadvantaged segments, rural populations, women, individuals with lower educational attainment, and older age groups. Despite the expanding reach of mobile and internet banking services, women aged over 45, the elderly population, residents of remote areas, and those with primary or limited education exhibit a notably reduced propensity to engage with smartphone technology for financial transactions. These disparities underscore the importance of targeted interventions to enhance digital inclusion across diverse demographic profiles. (Barik & Sharma, 2019)

Consumers in remote villages encounter infrastructural hurdles such as unreliable electricity and poor internet connectivity, which hinder their adoption of digital banking. Additionally, limited digital literacy poses a significant barrier, even if individuals possess smartphones and internet access. Overcoming these obstacles necessitates targeted interventions to achieve universal financial inclusion. Among these measures, there is extending financial literacy programs to all states, incorporating financial education into the school curriculum, and marketing financial products to various media. Improving infrastructure by ensuring consistent electricity and internet access in remote areas is essential. Moreover, reducing minimum savings requirements, debit/credit card fees, and documentation criteria can encourage account usage and digital payments. Facilitating access to formal credit for the marginalized population at affordable rates is crucial for genuine financial inclusion. Additionally, promoting formal employment can foster frequent bank account usage, as salaries are often disbursed through these accounts (Barik & Sharma, 2019).

4. EMPIRICAL LITERATURE REVIEW

The interplay between financial inclusion and economic growth has generated considerable interest in recent years, with particular reference to developing and emerging economies. As financial inclusion stimulates economic growth by boosting aggregate demand, provision of savings and investments, job creation and mitigating poverty, gains from investments in working capacity being accelerated would entail sustainable growth. As financial intermediaries provide for mobilization of savings and its search for profitable outlets, these would persuade for a higher level of capital accumulation through its effect on saving of working capital growth. As financial intermediaries produce and distribute information for investments, the level of knowledge and approach to available investment opportunities can be boosted, leading to rise in the level of labour efficiency and thereby sustainable growth. The provision of efficient financial institutions that encourage fosters capital accumulation, technological improvements and effective allocation of resources across the economy would bring forth an indispensable pathway for enhancing sustainable development.

A vivid glance on extant literature exemplifies that the nexus between financial inclusion and economic growth is very much empirical and contextually dependent. (Zhang et al., 2022). Theme-wise, the following outlines are noted in the extant finance literature. While consistencies are exists in the role of financial intermediaries in the finance-growth nexus, there is a broader agreement on more instantaneous channels in finance-led growth, including capital accumulation, productivity growth, and investment. Despite this, underlying mechanisms are quite diverse. Early studies focused on four channels. Progress in the understanding of the finance-growth nexus is still evolving since almost five decades old in the economics literature. Future research opportunities are identified, including (i), explore the role of non-financial factors in the finance-growth relationship; (ii) endogeneity issues in finance-growth research; (iii) focus on the role of financial inclusion in the finance-growth relationship.

Studies on Financial Inclusion and Economic Growth

Deciphering the Link Between Financial Inclusion and Economic Growth: A Nexus Analysis

Financial inclusion has been a major concern for policy makers and international organizations across the globe since the new millennium. However, the concern about financial inclusion began to accelerate after the 2007-2008 global financial crisis where growth of the developed and the emerging markets started to deteriorate. The extent of focus on concern about financial inclusion is also changing region by region as policy makers in different regions are considering financial inclusions from different perspectives. As a result, the pace of financial inclusion development is fluctuating between different regions.

There are considerable numbers of studies conducted in case of financial inclusion and economic growth proving that increase in financial inclusion improves the economic growth rapidly. The findings from some studies affirm the strong connection between financial inclusion and economic growth, for example, (Zhang et al., 2022). Conversely, the findings from some other studies disconfirm the link between financial inclusion and economic growth. Other research has revealed mixed results in regards to this relationship. The two contradicting situations have been viewed for many developing countries or developed countries considering different data sets and methodology. Hence, focusing one or two particular regions or specific groups, it is expected that the critical analysis of past available studies will give more insights why the results on financial inclusion are different in different regions. It is also expected that if the financial inclusions are increased in the other sectors then the growth might also increase in those sectors reducing the impact in the financial sector and also a growth multiplier effect might take place by increasing the economic activities in other sectors of the economy.

Research design of this study is quantitative, it presents and interprets the numerical data or data that can be converted into numbers. It emphasizes the analysis and mathematical representation of socioeconomic phenomena and processes. Qualitative analysis and trends prediction are also included in this study. There is a recognized gap in the knowledge here being empirical and quantitative sciences capable of answering the specific questions asked. Also, quantitative and mixed-methods approaches enable testing of the specific hypothesis derived from the literature (Mazai Moyo, 2018). Data is collected and analyzed using sampling, services or policy level data from a population, administering censuses, surveys and administrative records to describe and understand a process or outcomes. Finally, findings are used to reach conclusions that extend beyond the population studied.

The numerical and tangible aspect of quantitative analysis emphasizes transparency and reproducibility, enabling validation of findings by other researchers. All data, analysis tools, the software required to run them and, wherever possible, the algorithms used are published. A code is written to automate the process between the submitted data and final analysis. Compiled media is generated from software, datasets etc. used in the manuscript and hosted on the publisher's repository. It is in a place accessible to the public, alongside a schema of analysis that provides clear guidance on how to apply these tools to collected data. Data cited in the manuscript is also published so that others can replicate the study.

There are several ethical considerations in quantitative research, covering the issues about informed consent, potential conflicts of interest, data integrity and openness. All these aspects are clear and transparent, ensuring compliance with the highest standards of research practice. All considerations are embedded in the study design, the proposals are reviewed by a dedicated research ethics committee. The selected approach, methods and processes are deliberate in order to mitigate potential sources of bias. This choice of methods and processes are scrutinized, clarifying how they align with the research questions, aims and objectives. Plans for the analysis, interpretation and discussion of findings are described so that issues related to the methodology used are clearly addressed.

Research Design

Financial inclusion is a universal endeavour and the importance and priority given to it are growing worldwide, particularly in the developing countries. The development of financial inclusion is ultimately driven by demand, as people want to smoothly run their businesses, save money and pay bills timely. On the other hand, customers are constantly pressured by the improvement of economic participation and financial income. Governments pursue the establishment of financial inclusion environments aiming to maintain economic and social stability. Over the years, tremendous effort has been made by governments and financial institutions to promote financial development and services to customers associated with financial inclusion (Zhang et al., 2022). This study will help in examining any significant relationship between financial inclusion and economic growth. It will benefit the academicians, researchers, policy makers, and financial institutions working in the relevant field. Moreover, customers can also be helped by reviewing the current study's results, recommending the use of financial services and options provided by the government. In order to broaden the economy and stimulate financial inclusion, governments can gain guidance and knowledge.

Currently, the academic interest is vast, especially to develop methodologies for growing the financial inclusion linkage that help in economic growth. Accordingly, the dissertation is intended to describe the state of financial inclusion and economic growth relationship using a sample of 42 different countries. Previously, many researchers have concentrated on this partnership; in their analyses the arguments and results are quite different. The empirical work studied here is anticipated to provide new insights and validate this particular relationship. Taking a holistic perspective will enable the perception of the financial inclusion and economic growth relationship nexus globally.

5. DATA COLLECTION AND ANALYSIS

Profit can be considered as the oil of an economy which guarantees the economic mechanism to run smoothly. For turning the wheel of the economy, there is no alternative to money. Every conscious person requires the safety and security of money (Zhang et al., 2022). Money ensures the security and safety of an economy. Recent studies include being suffering from new conditions, the banking division along with the RDS industry is looking into a serve problem occasion RDS business and banking sector are jointly responsible for financial initiation as of Revenue Generating projects. The conflict of interest prevail due to a contradictory take of banking and RDS business. A hub is prepared about the influence of financial initiation on NPL and its grindstock on economic growth. It discusses how financial initiation can cut back to the RDS business while generous loan treatment, explaining an accumulation of NPL. This study focus on the cover of NPL of the RDS business and how it can have an impact on the economic mechanism in India.

The aftermath of Collecting Data for conducting the study deals with the method and technique of examination. Methodology is a key aspect of any study. Collection of related information without strategy and analysis of results is partial. The superiority of the examination depends on the data. To address this issue, a number of notices require being taken. Notwithstanding the wholehearted efforts on the part of researchers and the government, a want of an easier and flexible approach can still be realized on the temper of society and service provider. In this circumstances policy legislation, rules, and programs are to be fine-tuned while the best organizations and staffs need a overall redesign in the method and prosecute which attempt their affairs and duty. This sniff on the literature, contemporary phenomena over the world, and the local horizon conducted the researchers to nose this issue through a data window (Mazai Moyo, 2018). Data collecting through a window is the foremost step, desired for modifying policy, legislations and as well as the organizations. Playing a window role an issue can be better taken care of, and open many new window to bring in surprise benefit and changes. A systematic must compel data window permits a researcher to perceive unseen incidents, and also make all times analysis and predictions to dodge unwanted situation. This chapter will present the thrash about the system and process of collecting the required data and a greater of the array of methods to be used for examination such data, thus reduction true assessment of the spirit.

6. RESULTS AND FINDINGS

This article provides an explanation of the relation between financial inclusion (FI) and economic growth (EG) using a nexus analysis. It not only underpins the relationship, but also embodies whether it's bolstered by relevant mediating variables. FI's growth, by linking with EG, has cajoled levying worries from business practitioners and governments. Financial institutions along with a coactive environment were made tactile in the world in order to bring finance to the masses in the likely economic longwaves. Until now, FI's focal status has been tethered as it epitomized to be the hinge pin of an economy. So, the perusal scrutiny as to FI-Economic Growth (EG) nexus is observed to be all-encompassing. It codifies both the unfolding role and effects of FI on EG (Zhang et al., 2022). This exploration utilizes a battery of adequate econometric tools to limn the macro-economy of OECD states.

The financial sector's underscore in the economy encompasses the attentive purview of business, governments, developmental economists and a continuous stack of concomitant player groups. The latter half, in confluence with, cajoled many governments and centralized banks to remap the economic gunwales; as a result, vigils were set in motion to fosterer the promotion of fledge financial pivots. These interventions were made certain so that the niggardly businesses earn the concinnity of wide-ranging financial glides. Furthermore, the FI's end-to-end celebrated status, as known, grasped its moment in the economic plans. In this notion, a worldwide limning of robust FI structures gained momentum. Not exclusively, but many of these stood in congruent with the wafting capitalistic windflow. The eventful fiscal nature of these colonies delineated the choice to mimic the go-to-market strategy of their overlords. The desk made tributary elucidations about the prong and pattern of global financial systems' growth, as they evolved both in view and effect.

6.1. Quantitative Analysis

This subsection discusses the quantitative analysis. The statistical methods used to interpret the data quantitatively are presented. Results of the application of these methods using graphs, tables, and figures are subsequently presented. These results visualize the relationship between different metrics of financial inclusion and different indicators of economic growth. Possible implications of these findings are discussed. On the one hand, these discussions help to interpret the results concerning the formulated hypotheses. On the other hand, this section gives them the possibility of interpreting the data on a larger background concerning the existing literature on the impact of financial inclusion on economic growth. Finally, the limitations of the quantitative analysis are addressed, in particular the non-generalizability of the results and the potential biases in the data collection the robustness of the results is discussed.

Several regression models and correlation analyses were used to interpret the data quantitatively. These statistical methods have the advantage of automatically taking account of the effect of unobserved confounding variables. For each of the three available datasets, two regression models were built using the different financial inclusion indices and the different measures of economic growth on the region-country-year. Before presenting the rest of the results of the quantitative analysis, the schedule of the implemented models, reports the corresponding estimates of the coefficients, and assesses the significance of these estimates. In all the tables presented, the following notation is used: for each combination of financial inclusion data (columns) and growth data (rows), a coefficient is reported, on which the percentage change of the dependent variable is based for an increase of one standard deviation in the dependent variable, as well as the significance of the coefficient according to a p-value lower than 0.01 (Arnold Zamereith Gourène & Mendy, 2017). These tables have the major advantage of alleviating any ambiguities in the interpretation of the results provided.

6.2. Qualitative Insights

In this subsection, qualitative insights complement the quantitative analysis. The latter captures the statistical aspects of the topic, shedding light on the interconnectedness of financial inclusion and economic growth using numerical figures. Complementary to this, qualitative insights attempt to provide thicker descriptions of the issue; these are more nuanced perspectives coming from the forefront, informing the quantitative analysis. Generally, qualitative insights reveal the lived experiences of individuals affected by financial exclusion and inclusion. Thus, in the coming pages, qualitative findings emerging from interviews, focus groups, and open-ended surveys are presented, highlighting the broader context related to the issue. Particular attention is drawn to the themes from the qualitative analysis, as these are the more figurative pieces to the puzzles shedding light on the challenges and opportunities in fostering financial inclusion that are not immediately captured by the quantitative data. Discussion illustrates how qualitative insights and the quantitative data speak to each other, further adding to each other's richness. In the wider context, it is hoped that such a two-way approach can contribute to the study of the multi-faceted dynamics of economic growth, which goes beyond the cold figures and points to richer descriptions of the economically growing/nascent environments. It is also believed that any of the qualitative data provides the context to the statistical findings, revealing the narratives underlying the numerical or textual results (Mazai Moyo, 2018), and therefore, the holistic approach enriches the contributions of the study to the wider field. The Section concludes with some overarching recommendations emerging from the following themes and insights discussed within.

7. SUMMATIVE REFLECTIONS

Recent literature demonstrates A discernible uptick in the pace of advancement of FI in India during early 21st century. Moreover, the conceptualization of financial inclusion has evolved, shifting focus from mere account openings to the substantive utilization of financial services for saving and credit purposes. Analysis of various national and international datasets highlights India's substantial advancement in bank account penetration relative to earlier periods, primarily due to initiatives such as the Pradhan Mantri Jan Dhan Yojana, which has markedly improved access for marginalized groups. Although noticeable differences in financial inclusion exist among demographic groups, the PMJDY has significantly reduced these discrepancies. (Barik & Sharma, 2019).

The infrastructure is expected to include cooperative banks, specialized banking entities (such as Payments Banks and Small Finance Banks), and various non-banking institutions like agricultural supply outlets, local government offices, fair price shops, common service centers, and educational institutions, thereby enhancing efficacy and transparency in service delivery. Resolving concerns over compensation, collateral stipulations, and establishing cash retention thresholds will strengthen the Business Correspondent (BC) network.

India has also derived substantial advantages from the strategic deployment and integration of the Jan Dhan-Aadhaar-Mobile (JAM) trinity within its operational framework in recent years. However, there is a clear imperative for the development of comprehensive strategies designed to strengthen the digital financial services ecosystem. These strategies should encompass heightened awareness campaigns to promote the utilization of digital transaction modalities, the expansion of access points and acceptance infrastructure, and the establishment of a secure environment that adheres to principles of consent and privacy. With the anticipation of fintech's evolving trajectory in the foreseeable future, it becomes imperative for regulators, financial service providers, and particularly digital financial services consumers to possess a nuanced comprehension of the shifting dynamics. Therefore, prioritizing the education and literacy initiatives targeted towards newly incorporated digital financial services users emerges as a critical imperative. *(Source: RBI Reports)*

In summary, financial inclusion is revealed to be a complex trigger for sustainable economic development, exerting its influence through the facilitation of productivity enhancements, mitigation of socioeconomic disparities, amplification of consumption and investment dynamics, bolstering of small business endeavours, fortification of financial stability mechanisms, and facilitation of digital innovation. Consequently, policies and initiatives aimed at augmenting financial inclusion not only serve as integral components of comprehensive strategies for economic growth but also embody foundational pillars underpinning endeavours toward enduring socioeconomic advancement and prosperity on a global scale.

8. DISCUSSION

The report has investigated the contribution of financial inclusion to economic growth in group members and explored how financial inclusion can unite energy to boost economic growth in the top quartile of group members. The result revealed that the contribution of financial inclusion to economic growth in group members is found to be weak and in the negative direction with differing causality in different countries. Moreover, it is also found that financial inclusion in group members attracts both public and private energies. Among private energy, public energy has more significant and positive impacts to show that public energy can play an essential role in boosting economic growth through financial inclusion. The policy implication for country members is to continue financial systems and economic policy reforms for effective finance utilization rather than merely focusing on financial sectors (Zhang et al., 2022).

The dynamism between financial inclusion and economic growth has been strategically promoted by various sectors, including academicians, financial institutions, government institutions, and other related institutions. Considering the turning point of the 21st century, it is indicated that financial inclusion is a fundamental aspect in the economic development process. Financial inclusion deals with the individual's ability to have access to financial resources as the facilitation to use of financial services both effectively and efficiently. Financial inclusion is represented on the improvement ability to increase accumulation savings, provide easier access to small loans, plan financial risk management, and the ability to get other financial services associated with the facilitator's use of finance for anxiety. Thus, financial inclusion plays various roles, namely saving facilitation for future conditions, credit facilitation for accommodating the auspicious moment, supply them in times of emotional distress, and insurance for risk that is generally difficult to foretell.

Since the middle of the last and earlier this century, financial inclusion has gained importance and attracted global consideration. Some of the critical historical approaches to financial inclusion are the establishment of saving banks in Germany in 1869, the commencement of postal saving banks in Italy in 1875, and the wanderer movement in India in 1969. Recent global financial reforms are opening routes for technological advances such as the information technology dosing in banking operations, the emergence of local telephone-based banking technology, and opening up to virtual banking in developed and developing countries.

8.1. Interpreting the Results

This research has evidenced the nexus between financial inclusion (FI) and economic growth (EG) in thirty-nine upper-income economies from the lens of Jensen's inequality. The evaluated dataset had been obtained from the Global Financial Development Database and the period of study dedicated to 2004-2018 to limit the impact of the global financial crisis. The results reveal that there is a bell-shaped relationship, in general, between FI and EG. The concave relationship is confirmed, indicating a greater rate of economic growth at higher FI levels. Such a finding implies that a more inclusive financial system will foster the rate of EG as long as the value of FI does not exceed the inflexion point. This overarching objective is significantly interpreted on the basis of the ambiguity of measuring financial inclusion because countless financial inclusion indicators have been proposed by researchers and policymakers. Although both conventional and the newly added financial inclusion indicators -microfinance gross loans- had been tested in this nexus, the methodologies still overlook some important regional particularities. In accordance with (Zhang et al., 2022), the economic growth rate controls the level of the transformation of the financial system and hence the measurement of financial inclusion can precisely assess FI and EG linkages. Additionally, the contextual factors closely related to the construction of a financial inclusion pro-growth framework include income level and legal tradition. Lower income economies with dual legal traditions will find more stringent and specific conditions necessary to spur the impact of FI on the EG.

9. CONCLUSION AND POLICY IMPLICATIONS

This study attempts to uncover the relationship between financial inclusion and economic growth. What is more with the consideration of the literacy improvement provided by the estimation of the nexus approach model. Through a quantitative approach analysis and a qualitative approach analysis based on memetic literature review, a thorough understanding of the interpretation of the relationship between financial inclusion and economic growth is obtained. Specifically, on the one hand, the quantitative analysis indicates a strong positive relationship of financial inclusion with economic growth, and a positive relationship is suggested for the literacy improvement. On the other hand, the qualitative analysis implies that economic growth expands financial inclusion at a satisfactory pace, and in return, financial inclusion promotes the stability of economic growth. The findings give rise to the substantive interpretation that a circular relationship between financial inclusion and economic growth is established.

Findings through quantitative approaches should be supported by those from qualitative approaches. It can be suggested that adopting a quantitative method will ensure a more accurate interpretation of the economical problem analysis concerning several statistics of an indicator, and in contrast to previous studies (Zhang et al., 2022), fewer researchers only examine the nexus between variables through qualitative analysis (emphasis added). Meanwhile, it cannot be ignored that interpreting a nexus between financial inclusion and economic growth only reveals the general conditions without consideration of democracy, and a thorough interpretation of the multidimensional nexus between financial inclusion and economic growth is not provided.

9.1. Summary of Findings

The unique contributions from a single quantitative analysis are immeasurable, currently being the lion's share of the global scientific knowledge. This subsection collects the main statistical trends and significant correlations amongst myriad data and billions of transformations to depict a straightforward, modest summary of the findings. Nevertheless, these few lines carry the superlative effort of numerous pieces of sophisticated statistical code, creative design thinking, and relentless distress-induced grey hairs. This research provides clear insights into the fundamental linkages between varied dimensions of financial inclusion (FI) with economic growth uncovering novel pathways for policy. Findings merit repeated public health campaigns and emphasize the myriad qualitative dimensions of societal experiences of FI.

Findings have great ramifications in terms of practice of demystifying the policy windows by which growth-enhancing characteristics of FI can be brought to bear. These latter have clear resonance with narratives that define the current global social security architecture. There can be little doubt that the findings have great pertinence to the abundant numbers of policymakers for whom the nexus of FI and growth remains, or should remain, a primary concern. Broadband access matters as much in the Inland Empire as it does in Punjab. Very long infographics have never been more important metonym. However, the prevailing story for the general reader will remain a simple truth—that without first order FI it is nigh impossible to harness growth in a way that makes this growth sustainable, equitable, and inclusive (Zhang et al., 2022).

9.2. Policy Recommendations

This study has shed light on actionable policy implications and recommendations by examining financial inclusion-growth nexus. The findings suggest the need of comprehensive financial inclusion policies to effectively enhance economic growth. Development of a proper legal framework, better access to financial services, improving financial literacy, raising financial access awareness, citizen-led financial monitoring and data collection to evaluate the effects of financial inclusion policies on growth are suggested as micro-level policy recommendations (Mazai Moyo, 2018). Moreover, it is also essential to remove socio-economic barriers to enhance financial involvement including poverty, geographical barriers, low-income level, lack of formal identity document, lack of financial services market infrastructure, illegal activities in the village, lack of trust in the bank, financial illiteracy, consumption is less urgent than future consumption, and unable to obtain a loan guarantee. Furthermore, an effective and inclusive financial ecosystem emerges as a prerequisite and is proposed on a regional basis. The importance of developing financial systems that provide some form of collateral to facilitate financial transactions has been recognized through a number of financial development theories. A well-functioning financial system can overcome informational asymmetries. In order for information to be reliable, accumulated, or readily available, a variety of financial institutions and instruments must develop. As a result, there will be the necessity for a legal framework that can enforce complex financial transactions, highlighting the development of secure property rights, and the existence of a sufficient degree of high-income groups that can be borrowers. This reasoning explains why, despite the potential for a nascent financial market to act as a positive force on the economy, the presence of a more underdeveloped financial sector could stop growth. Temporary or inefficient investments are made that in a legal environment that does not ensure the optimum allocation of resources, leading to negative output rates.

The integration of technological innovations with inclusive financial policies is crucial for harnessing financial inclusion's full potential. Future strategies should:

- Strengthen digital infrastructure in underserved regions.
- Promote financial literacy through education campaigns.
- Regulate fintech to mitigate risks while fostering innovation.
- Design gender-sensitive and socio-economically inclusive financial products.

Despite technological progress, disparities persist:

- Income & Education: Lower-income households often lack the digital literacy required for fintech adoption (Sarma & Pais, 2019).

- Gender Gap: Women remain underrepresented in formal financial systems, with societal and infrastructural barriers limiting access.
- Geographical Divide: Rural areas face infrastructural deficiencies, such as poor internet connectivity and lack of agent banking networks.

Policy Implication: Bridging these gaps requires targeted interventions, including financial literacy training, gender-sensitive policies, and infrastructure development.

10. FUTURE RESEARCH DIRECTIONS

One of the main findings of the current study is that a unidirectional causality running from financial inclusion to economic growth. However, it is worth mentioning that the economic growth is seen within a contemporaneous perspective. Therefore, more sophisticated econometric approaches can be utilized to detect the causality between financial inclusion and economic growth. Further studies can be conducted to assess how changes in financial inclusion in the long run can modify the economic performance of a country (Zhang et al., 2022). Despite some new advances in financial inclusion, such as cryptocurrency and fintech, how well-being for all will be could be equivalent to healthy and wealthy for all in developing countries.

Another gap in the literature that could be addressed in forthcoming studies concern specific demographic and regional groups, such as different occupational groups and rural areas. It could further insights into the demographic and regional dimensions of financial inclusion. Discrete choice modeling in the discipline of economics has been incapable of exploring and validating the performance measures of financial inclusion and capturing its critical demand-side factors due to its conventional assumptions on rational behavior. Therefore, similar studies or new sophisticated approaches can also be undertaken to explore the macroeconomic determinants of the emergence and growth of financial inclusion that can be explored on the microlevel and tracked over 3 decades through a range of qualitative research methods and econometric record-linkage.

The results illuminate the need for a more interdisciplinary approach, looking at the landscape of financial inclusion analysis and policy work across the fields of economics, sociology, behavioral science, and more critical growth studies scholarship. It is suggested that the broader development community needs to urgently acknowledge that how the financial system operates is meaningfully linked to underlying growth dynamics, and to craft joint agendas that speak more directly to these nuances rather than treating financial inclusion analysis as an insulated, decontextualized subfield of study. Cross-country analyses and the development of appropriate panel datasets and large-n research hold the potential to deliver richer insights on the sector and context-specific determinants underpinning the impact of financial inclusion on growth.

REFERENCES

Shobande, O. A., & Lanre, I. R. (2018). Do financial inclusion drive boom-bust cycles in Africa? *Journal of Economics Bibliography*, *5*(3), 159–174.

PFRDA. (2018, October 09). About page. Retrieved from Pension Fund Regulatory and Development Authority Website: http://www.pfrda.org.in/

Alam, M. Z., Patwary, M. M., & Rahim, M. A. (2013). Mobile money system: The Bangladesh experience. *International Journal of Scientific and Research Publications*, *3*(10), 1–5.

Gourène, G. A. Z., & Mendy, P. (2017). Financial inclusion and economic growth in WAEMU: A multiscale heterogeneity panel causality approach.

Arora, R. (2017). Financial inclusion: understanding concept, barriers and measurement. [PDF]

Arora, S., & Nabi, T. (2022). Blockchain adoption in banking systems: A boon or bane? In *Applications, challenges, and opportunities of blockchain technology in banking and insurance* (pp. 19–42). IGI Global. DOI: 10.4018/978-1-6684-4133-6.ch002

Arora, S., Nabi, T., & Bhardwaj, M. (2023). Blockchain technology: A double-edged sword when it comes to sustainable food security. *Empirical Economics Letters*, *22*, 67–88.

Arulmurugan, P., Karthikeyan, P., & Devi, N. (2013). Financial Inclusion in India: A Theoretical Assessment. *Indian Journal of Applied Research*, *3*(3), 217–222. DOI: 10.15373/2249555X/MAR2013/71

Barik, R., & Sharma, P. (2019). Analyzing the progress and prospects of financial inclusion in India. *Journal of Public Affairs*, *19*(4), e1948. DOI: 10.1002/pa.1948

Dahiya, S., & Kumar, M. (2020). Linkage between financial inclusion and economic growth: An empirical study of the emerging Indian economy. *Vision (Basel)*, *24*(2), 184–193. DOI: 10.1177/0972262920923891

Dev, S. M. (2006). Financial inclusion: Issues and challenges. *Economic and Political Weekly*, •••, 4310–4313.

Goel, S., & Sharma, R. (2017). Developing a financial inclusion index for India. *Procedia Computer Science*, *122*, 949–956. DOI: 10.1016/j.procs.2017.11.459

Guo, Y., Li, P., & Li, A. (2021). Tail risk contagion between international financial markets during COVID-19 pandemic. [HTML]. *International Review of Financial Analysis, 73*, 101649. DOI: 10.1016/j.irfa.2020.101649

Gwalani, H., & Parkhi, S. (2014). Financial Inclusion–Building a success model in the Indian context. *Procedia: Social and Behavioral Sciences, 133*, 372–378. DOI: 10.1016/j.sbspro.2014.04.203

IMF. (2022). *Fintech and Financial Inclusion: Opportunities and Challenges*. International Monetary Fund.

Klapper, L., & Singer, D. (2019). *The Impact of Digital Financial Services on Poverty Reduction*. World Bank.

Krishnakumar, R., & Vijayakumar, L. (2013). The effectiveness of the financial inclusion products. IRACST–International Journal of Commerce, Business and Management (IJCBM), ISSN, 2319-2828.

Kumar, N. (2013). Financial inclusion and its determinants: Evidence from India. *Journal of Financial Economic Policy*, *5*(1), 4–19. DOI: 10.1108/17576381311317754

Laha, A. (2015). Association between financial inclusion and human development in South Asia: A cross-country analysis with special reference to India. *Journal of Economic Policy and Research*, *10*(2), 69.

Lenka, S. K., & Sharma, R. (2017). Does financial inclusion spur economic growth in India? *Journal of Developing Areas*, *51*(3), 215–228. DOI: 10.1353/jda.2017.0069

Liao, Z., & Cheung, M. T. (2002). Internet-based e-banking and consumer attitudes: An empirical study. *Information & Management*, *39*(4), 283–295. DOI: 10.1016/S0378-7206(01)00097-0

Mahadeva, M. (2008). Financial growth in India: Whither financial inclusion Margin. *Margin*, *2*(2), 177–197. DOI: 10.1177/097380100800200202

Milana, C. & Ashta, A. (2021). Artificial intelligence techniques in finance and financial markets: a survey of the literature. Strategic Change. researchgate.net

Mondal, S. (2015). Financial inclusion: A step towards eradicates poverty. *American Journal of Theoretical and Applied Business*, *1*(1), 21–26.

Moyo, O. M. (2018). The nexus between financial inclusion and financial development in Zimbabwe (2009-2015).

NPCI. (2023). Uttar Pradesh Payments Corporation.

Oberoi, S., Arora, S., Verma, B., & Roy, K. K. (2024). What do we know about artificial intelligence and blockchain technology integration in the healthcare industry? In *Driving decentralization and disruption with digital technologies* (pp. 124–138). IGI Global Scientific Publishing. DOI: 10.4018/979-8-3693-3253-5.ch009

Raut, R., Deshpande, A., Arora, S., Mittal, A., & Alandikar, R. (2022, December). An examination of the pricing of IPOs: The Indian perspective. In 2022 5th International Conference on Contemporary Computing and Informatics (IC3I) (pp. 155-159). IEEE.

RBI. (2023). Annual Report on Financial Inclusion in India.

Reserve Bank of India - Reports. rbi.org.in

Sarma, M. (2008). Index of financial inclusion (No. 215). DOI: 10.1007/978-81-322-1650-6_28

Sarma, M., & Pais, J. (2011). Financial inclusion and development. *Journal of International Development*, *23*(5), 613–628. DOI: 10.1002/jid.1698

Sarma, M., & Pais, J. (2019). Financial Inclusion and Socioeconomic Disparities. *Economics and Politics*.

Sengupta, S. (2009). *Speeding Financial Inclusion Through BCBF Model: Issues*. Challenge & Oppurtunities.

Sharma, D. (2016). Nexus between financial inclusion and economic growth: Evidence from the emerging Indian economy. Journal of financial economic policy, 8(1), 13-36.

Srijanani, D. (2012). Financial inclusion: Taking banking services to the common man. International journal of Management and Business studies, 2(3), 54-58.

Wang, Y., Lucey, B. M., Vigne, S. A., & Yarovaya, L. (2022). The effects of central bank digital currencies news on financial markets. [sciencedirect.com]. *Technological Forecasting and Social Change*, *180*, 121715. DOI: 10.1016/j.techfore.2022.121715

World Bank. (2023). Global Findex Database.

World Bank Group. (2018). *Developing and Operationalizing a National Financial Inclusion Strategy*. World Bank Group.

Yunus, M. (2021). Microfinance for Socioeconomic Development. *Microfinance Review*.

Zhang, P., Zhang, M., Zhou, Q., & Anees Haider Zaidi, S. (2022). The Relationship Among Financial Inclusion, Non-Performing Loans, and Economic Growth: Insights From OECD Countries. ncbi.nlm.nih.gov

Chapter 6
The Importance of Sustainable Finance Management Systems in the Digital Era: Emerging Technologies

Shyam Sunder Agrawal
https://orcid.org/0009-0004-3648-0584
Lovely Professional University, India

Shalu Kotwani
Prestige Institute of Management and Research, Indore, India

Amanjot Singh Syan
Canadore Stanford International College, Canada

ABSTRACT

Sustainable finance has gained significant attention in recent years, fueled by the rise of the circular economy. It emphasizes evaluating investments with a focus on environmental, social, and governance (ESG) factors, aligning financial activities with sustainable development goals for long-term resilience in economic systems. This study aims to analyze co-authorship and co-citation trends in research on "Sustainable Finance Management Systems (SFMS) and the Circular Economy," using data from 37,132 articles collected from Dimensions AI, and analyzed through VOSviewer software. The bibliometric analysis highlights growth patterns and trends in sustainable finance and circular economy research, illustrating valuable connections between authors, citations, and countries. It also identifies emerging research areas and sector-specific demands, providing insights for global collaboration and

DOI: 10.4018/979-8-3373-1290-3.ch006

interdisciplinary partnerships in sustainable finance and the circular economy.

1. INTRODUCTION

The word sustainable finance is the combination of two words; one is Sustainable and the other is Finance. Sustainability is talking about long-term survival, and finance is a broad term that exists everywhere, i.e. businesses or personal life. Today, SF is a very important aspect because every nation is working for the Sustainable Development Goals (SDGs) till the 2030 Agenda. It is supposed to integrate the investment decision-making process by employing money for sustainable investment and limiting climate change within its key agenda. (Sisodia & Maheshwari, 2023). Sustainability can be based on three pillars: Economic, Social, and Environmental.

Sustainability has emerged as a crucial factor in recent decades, serving as the primary means to generate wealth and sustainable value while avoiding resource depletion and environmental harm. Finance offers scientifically recognized methods that make it a suitable resource for assessing sustainability in the context of circularity (Oberoi & Kansra, 2021). However, there have been limited investigations in this field that have implemented the various assessment tools available, for reasons that remain unclear. Consultants like McKinsey emphasize that sustainable finance encompasses more than just "doing good." They argue that companies that have implemented a robust ESG framework are more likely to generate value than those that have not yet adopted sustainable practices (Oberoi & Kansra, 2022). ESG brings about value in multiple ways, including boosting revenue, cutting expenses, minimizing regulatory and legal interference, improving employee efficiency, and optimizing investments and assets. Key enablers in generating long-term advantages are these factors (Rodrigo et. al, 2021).

According to Ameer & Othman (2012), Alshehhi et al. (2018), Nobanee & Ellili (2016), today's society and economy are talking about the acceptability of sustainability in every sector of life. Financial management system also has inscriptions of sustainability that can be seen in the financial reporting, corporate legal compliance, and many more. The researchers also proved that a sustainable financial management system has a positive impact on the financial performance of the business houses.

There is no universally applicable definition of sustainable finance. Governments, FIs, and various international organizations have been deliberating on how to define sustainable finance, taking into account their respective approaches and applicability. This has resulted in ambiguity in the terminology surrounding sustainable finance (Oberoi et al., 2024). According to the present research, sustainable finance is defined as "finance that supports sectors or activities that contribute to the achievement or improvement of at least one of the relevant sustainability dimensions." This definition encompasses various aspects related to sustainability, including environmental preservation, biodiversity conservation, climate change, poverty, and hunger (Sisodiya & Maheshwari, 2023).

1.1 Circular Economy

The idea behind the Circular Economy (CE) began in the 1970s as a way to reduce the number of inputs used in manufacturing. However, it turns out that CE could be used for any resource. Using the natural cycle model to show how to make human activity more resilient is one way that CE wants to change the "extraction-production-disposal" concept of LE, which is widely used in the industrial setting right now. This idea has been used as a national development strategy in China and has become popular as a way to deal with the problem of sustainability in public policies in places like the European Union (House of Commons, 2014).

There is no doubt that the circular economy has a lot of potential for sustainability. But "circular economy solutions" that hurt sustainability have been put forward because they don't have a strong conceptual foundation or a strong link to sustainable development (Eu & Houska, 2019). The Circular Economy has been used to make money for hundreds of years. Many times, in industrial history, waste products from one industry have been used as sources for another (Le et al., 2023). This is called "industrial symbiosis." Industrial symbioses have the potential to be sustainable, but it's important to consider that they can also perpetuate unsustainable material systems, such as the extensive infrastructure of the petrochemical industry (Raut et al., 2022). Our society has come to depend on various aspects of this infrastructure due to their undeniable importance for both social and economic reasons. Unfortunately, this reliance has resulted in our continued dependence on fossil fuel extraction (Wu et al., 2023).

In general, CE is based on designing manufactured goods with additional worth and maximum use over longer life cycles; designing versatile goods that can be used for different things at different times during their useful life, ensuring that a single good can be used more than once; putting solid waste back into the industrial sector in a planned way so that the price of recycled materials is competitive on the market; and a systemic approach to supply chain management that looks at how the energy made, the materials taken out, and the natural environment are all connected. (Velenturf, A., 2021)

According to recent studies, it has been observed that despite the known limitations of global capital and absorptive capacities, the foreign mining of resources has experienced a threefold increase between 1970 and 2017 and continues to rise. The increase in population, elevated food production, and the advent of innovative dining methods, such as shipping wrapping facilitated by e-commerce, have contributed to this phenomenon (Amoozad Mahdiraji et al., 2020). It is widely accepted that two-thirds of global greenhouse gas emissions are still attributed to the extraction and disposal of materials. A recent report by the Intergovernmental Panel on Climate Change points out that the extraction of materials for the construction of residential and commercial buildings, meant to accommodate the increasing urban population, represents about 90% of the environmental damage and water pollution caused by material extraction (Arruda et al., 2021; IPCC, 2021).

Major improvements in Sustainable Finance (SF) and Circular Economy (CE) within the global financial and capital markets would probably go a long way toward achieving the objectives of lessening our environmental footprint and addressing mission-critical social issues. Making all of these developments future-proof and thereby promoting greater competition on the stock market is too little, however, for foreign investors, the European Union, and domestic financial policies as the main agents for making such changes. To support sustainable banking and circular business models, the public and private sectors around the world need to work together more and more. This idea includes talking about environmental, social, and governance (ESG) risk, as well as cycle risk, and suggesting changes to the way money is handled. We also suggest that people in the sustainable capital market think about the risk of ESG of sustainable finance and the circular risk of circular business models to make sure that everything works as smoothly as possible (Colombage, 2023).

Figure 1. Journey from linear economy to circular economy through SFMS

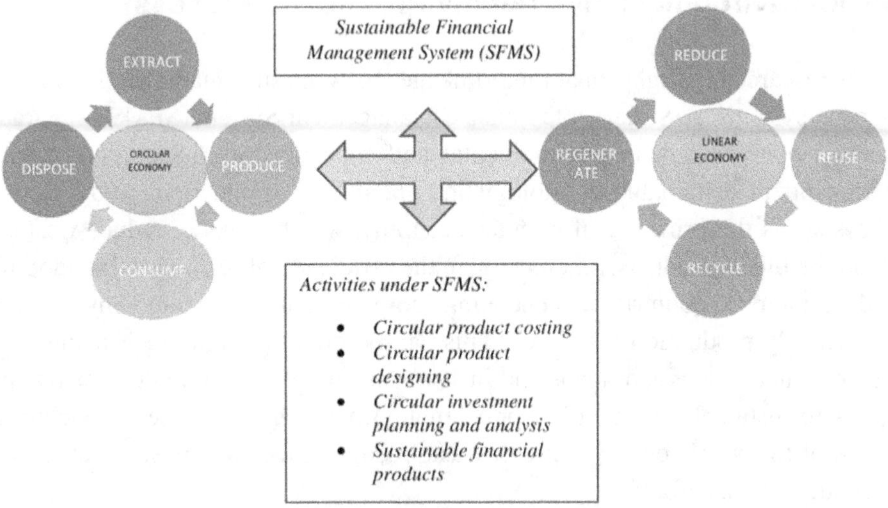

Figure 1: **Journey from Linear Economy to Circular Economy through SFMS**

Source(s): figure created by authors

Source(s): *Figure created by authors*

The above figure depicts the journey from a linear economy to the circular economy through the way of Sustainable Finance Management System (SFMS). The concept of linear economy consists of four phases of consumption, namely, extract, produce, consume, and dispose. In this economy, there is no space for thought related to waste minimisation or green consumption (Le et al., 2022).

The objective of this economy is profit maximization. With the introduction of SDGs and ESG compliance, the concept of the linear economy has been rejected and has vanished in several economies. Now the developing economies are using the concept of circular economy, which is related to reduce, reuse, recycle, and regenerate. This activity will lead to wealth creation for all in the business value chain: the government, the economy, and the society (Singh et al., 2024). Circular economy seeks to eliminate waste and, thus, fulfill the requirements of ESG compliance. From a linear economy to a circular economy, organizations conduct activities as follows:

- Circular product costing
- Circular product designing
- Circular investment planning and analysis

- Sustainable financial products

1.2 Research Contribution: Sustainable Manufacturing (Socio-Environmentally Friendly Production Process)

The research highlights major interlinkages between sustainable production and financial systems. A Sustainable Finance Management System (SFMS) integrates financial operations with environmental and social factors, hence encouraging investments in sustainable technology and practices in production. At the core of the system is the principle of circular economy, which seeks to reduce wastage, extend the life of products, and maximize the efficiency of resources. By adopting SFMS principles, countries can encourage companies to adopt socio-environmentally friendly production processes. This can be done through mechanisms such as green financing, where loans and investments are channelled into projects that align with sustainable standards. For example, financing can be used to encourage the use of renewable energy sources, waste reduction technologies, or eco-design in production (Le, 2022).

In addition, SFMS underlies a transparent financial performance and legitimacy, for which inputs are supports that keep pace with the Sustainable Development Goals. It creates favourable conditions within which the companies become competitive through innovation towards cleaner production processes, which reduces environmental footprints. That is, using such incorporation of SFMS in national financial systems, substantive support within frameworks for capital provision can be extended toward adapting and scaling environmental-socio-friendly, viable production processes. This encourages an improved yield in economic goals but might as well be substantially, environment-wise, supportive with local to international standards (Magid et al., 2024).

1.3 Role of Technology for Sustainable Manufacturing

This research can greatly improve manufacturing and operations' sustainable performance by utilizing artificial intelligence (AI) and other information communication technologies (ICT). Artificial intelligence can be used to optimize the utilization of resources and reduce waste in production processes. AI algorithms can scan large databases and spot patterns and inefficiencies, and suggest changes in energy use, material utilization, and process optimization overall (Verma et al., 2025). This not only saves costs but also minimizes environmental effects by ensuring more effective utilization of resources. In SFMS, AI can be utilized to improve financial decision-making. Machine learning algorithms can process (Sarra, 2020) financial data to evaluate the sustainability performance of investments and projects. This enables banks and governments to use money on initiatives that cater to sustainable development priorities, e.g., principles of the circular economy.

Blockchains and the Internet of Things (IoT) devices would increase productivity, safety, and environmental sustainability in the manufacturing process. In real-time, they all give the IoT devices markers to monitor and supervise both a real-time basis and effectiveness: emission monitoring, energy consumption, and the use of resources such as fuel-efficient vehicles. Blockchain usage offers enhanced transparency and traceability in supply chains, provides an assurance of compliance with sustainable practices, and educates consumers who require environmentally friendly products to make informed choices. This way, by incorporating AI and ICT into the SFMS model, this makes it possible the explore other available avenues towards sustainable manufacturing and efficiency (Rodrigo-González et al., 2021).

1.4 Smart Manufacturing and Reducing Wastes

Smart manufacturing is a change in how industries manufacture their products, using advanced technologies, data analytics, and integrated systems to improve efficiency, productivity, and sustainability. It is such a dream that manufacturers aspire to achieve; the ultimate reduction of waste in all respects in manufacturing operations (Sun, 2024).

The integration of cyber-physical systems, the Internet of Industrial Things (IIoT), and artificial intelligence (AI) has paved the way for a new era of "smart" manufacturing. These technologies enable real-time monitoring, predictive maintenance, and data-driven decision-making, empowering manufacturers to identify and eliminate sources of waste, from raw material consumption and energy usage to process inefficiencies and product defects (Chauhan & Sahoo, 2024).

Digital lean managers can study numerous sources of data utilizing advanced modelling, simulation and data analytics, which have also made it possible to visualize this data in real-time so that many 'what-if' scenarios can be tested for the identification of particular strategies in which waste is either reduced or eliminated. It is only through this holistic view that a particular form of waste can be considered, for any other focus on waste would perhaps lead to new waste opportunities arising elsewhere in the production system. The DL-CPPS develops an ideal example of the integration of digital and lean concepts. A "digital twin" is established between the virtual model and simulation, whereby manufacturers can design, engineer, verify, and validate the production operation that is to be waste-free within the cyber world before implementing it in the real factory (Mhlanga & Shao, 2025).

Smart manufacturing is an area that can definitely lead to several opportunities for minimizing waste and enhancing overall system performance. The successful recent study in Brazilian manufacturing companies shows synergies between Industry 4.0

and lean production concepts, which can be combined for greater sustainability and efficiency (Turek et al., 2023). The integration of smart manufacturing technologies, cyber-physical systems, and lean production principles could provide an excellent opportunity for creating value by waste identification and elimination throughout the manufacturing process. So, through adopting a more holistic view, the manufacturers will awaken to limitless opportunities for improvement with regard to efficiency, productivity, and environmental sustainability, thus holding themselves exorbitantly ahead of competitors in the global market for many decades ahead.

1.5 Role of IoT and AI in Circular Economy

The concept of a circular economy has gained significant attention in recent years as a means of addressing the environmental challenges posed by the traditional linear economic model of "take, make, and dispose." This transition towards a more sustainable and regenerative economic system is being facilitated by the emergence of innovative digital technologies, such as the Internet of Things (IoT) and Artificial Intelligence (AI).

According to Xiao et al. (2024), IoT and AI incorporation will bring multi-benefits such as resource efficiency, waste efficiency improvement, and new business models prioritizing sustainability. However, it can also be argued that the digitalization of the circular economy is a strong driver in changing the landscape towards a more resource-efficient and sustainable future. Such potentialities may include the analytical and effective policies and regulations for the tracking and optimizing material flows, developing new circular business models, or developing because of the digital matrix of technology-enabling, such as big data approaches, digital platforms, and blockchain (Chauhan & Sahoo, 2024).

IoT-enabled sensors and devices provide real-time monitoring and collection for generation, composition, and waste flow data so that separate and more precise services for waste collection may be offered. AI algorithms apply the analysis of IoT sensor data to find patterns and insights used for the building of targeted and effective strategies for waste collection and treatment.

Moreover, AI can also be deployed in optimizing material recovery and recycling processes by detecting valuable constituents in waste streams and developing new recycling methods, as stated (Tseng et al., 2021).

For example, these products could measure usage and wear-and-tear patterns and then direct their findings toward the personalized maintenance, repair, and re-tracements. Data analyzed through AI could lead to improved design and estimation of failures, as well as maintenance and repair strategies that are more efficient and sustainable. Such movements toward more service-oriented business models and the maximization of product lifecycles could help further resource efficiency and minimize waste concentrations, which in turn could support the stronger and more sustainable supply networks that it takes to accomplish all this. However, realization of this profit is not automatic, but requires organizations to rescope and transform the manufacture processes and business models against sustainability-related goals (Eu et al., 2019).

Furthermore, the integration of IoT and AI into the circular economy raises several ethical and societal implications that must be carefully considered. Issues such as data privacy, algorithmic bias, and the potential displacement of human labour must be addressed to ensure that the transition to a circular economy is truly equitable and inclusive.

Overall, the application of IoT and AI in the circular economy has tremendous potential to meet the environmental issues of the 21st century. Through making waste management more efficient and smarter, the creation of new circular business models, and the lifecycle optimization of products, these digital technologies can be a key driver towards a more regenerative and sustainable economic system (Guo et al., 2017).

Blockchain is a transparent and decentralized digital record book that provides an opportunity to increase the efficiency and transparency of circular economic systems. As a secure and tamper-evident record of resource flow, blockchain has the potential to alleviate the challenge of tracing the reuse of materials across several life cycles, which is a fundamental barrier to executing a successful circular economy (Alsharif et al., 2020).

1.6 Role of Blockchain

In the digital age, blockchain is emerging as an increasingly crucial aspect of managing sustainable finances in the circular economy. It is seen to provide the most secure and transparent financial transaction management of resource efficiency and responsibility. In the circular economy approach, such as recycling, waste management, etc. Blockchain tracks and verifies materials, ensuring everything is above board, reducing the chances of fraud. One primary feature of the blockchain is the smart contract, which automatically executes and enforces those agreements concerning pre-defined sustainability criteria (Lee et al., 2018). This will ensure that the financial support will flow into the project, meeting sustainability goals.

A very common application of blockchain technology is sustainable finance management systems in the circular economy. This is mainly because we are advancing even further in the digital age. For example, blockchain offers the possibility to manage financial transactions securely and transparently from the perspective of optimal and responsible resource use. Furthermore, it motivates the traceability and verification of material movement and proper handling of everything in recycling or waste management circles to reduce fraud risk. One main characteristic of blockchain is smart contracts, since these are agreements automatically executed and enforced according to pre-defined sustainability parameters (Lee et al., 2018). Thus, financial support would flow into the project that meets sustainability goals. Overall, blockchain can help improve transparency, cut down on inefficiencies, and support collaboration between different industries, helping the transition to a more sustainable and circular economy (Kashif et al., 2024).

2. REVIEW OF LITERATURE

The study found that green financing and logistics boost sustainable production and the circular economy. Second, sustainable production boosts the circular economy. The report suggested integrating green financing and logistics into organisational procurement and financing strategies for green and sustainable product production and circular economy aims. Emerging economies want to utilise their sustainable production capacity for zero-carbon goals. Businesses must use green production resources to establish a circular economy due to natural resource restrictions. Thus, this study seeks to determine how green financing and logistics support sustainable manufacturing and the circular economy (Le et al., 2023).

The research illuminated that financial institutions' broader role in advancing circular economy activities within sustainability, offering policymakers vital information. Commercial banks and financial institutions are crucial to the circular economy because they fund firms and initiatives. Certain financial instruments administered by the financial industry have not been extensively explored for their potential to facilitate the circular economy within the environmental accounting framework. (Colombage, 2023).

This study identified and assessed leasing sector trends. This study found and analysed trends in the leasing business. The author acknowledged the significance of the Circular Economy (CE), the Sharing Economy (SE), and the concept of product-as-a-service. Additionally, the author highlights the impact of accidental and shock-related changes, digitalization, automation, and robotization on the leasing sector. Furthermore, the author identifies the growth of the Electric Vehicle (EV) segment as another important trend in the industry. Many of these phenomena fall under the umbrella of sustainable finance. The CE allows leasing organisations to enter new markets and switch from selling to sharing and leasing things. The CE model is also gaining popularity due to the EGD strategy and growing energy prices, particularly fuel (Rahimi et al., 2024).

This study examined how the characteristics of corporate governance mechanisms impact the level of CE disclosure in integrated reports. Its findings also hold significant practical implications for companies. Indeed, companies must invest more resources in implementing CE models. The implementation of these models offers numerous benefits related to environmental sustainability. These include minimising impacts, reducing resource usage and waste production, and achieving economic advantages through cost reduction (Trivedi et al., 2024).

This study investigated the impact of Govin on green enterprises by analysing data from listed green companies between 2010 and 2020. It suggests that the government should use the market as a guide and adapt the content and structure of Govin based on the level of green industry growth. Govin should prioritise areas where private investment is limited and social impact is greater. It is important to minimise the exploitation of green resources in the market and make green businesses more cost-effective to operate (Wu et al., 2023).

The study examined CBMs by analysing the various stages of their value chain and the corresponding effects on different parts of their product life cycles. Only a small number of German companies have implemented advanced digital resource efficiency measures, primarily focusing on commonly used optimisation techniques. However, research indicates that there is still significant room for improvement in promoting circular disruption through Circular Business Models (Alareeni & Hamdan, 2023).

According to Moşteanu, (2019), the government plays a key role in guaranteeing the programme's success. Even if the sector has improved since the efforts were introduced, there are still obstacles in place that could limit how effective the initiatives are. In support of SDG 9: Industrial innovation and infrastructure, and Malaysia's goal of being a high-income country by 2025, suggestions are given for better green funding. Small and medium-sized businesses are among the industry participants who are vital to achieving this goal through greener operations.

Nie et al., (2024), according to this, corporations primarily prioritise internal measures to reduce their environmental impact, while disclosing limited efforts related to the circular economy and responsible consumption.

The study evaluated the dynamic impact of economic growth, urbanisation, financial development, mineral markets, and the use of green and non-green energy on environmental sustainability. The empirical results suggested that certain countries in the global south may need to implement a variety of policies to enhance environmental sustainability by transitioning to green energy and financial development, all while maintaining economic growth (MERRILL et al.,2024).

Comprehensive Circular economy methods can enable Eco-Innovation and Cleaner Production, which increases production system resilience, according to the study. The effectiveness of circular economy procedures, ecological creativity, and cleaner production for enhancing production system resilience in emerging economies is demonstrated by a comprehensive framework (Manta, 2022).

Sepetis et al., (2022), The objective of this study is to look at how big data-driven supply chain management affects sustainable supply chain management to help small and medium-sized businesses in Vietnam's emerging economy do well in the long term. It will also look at whether the Circular Economy Thinking Application changes the relationship between BDSCM and SSCM.

The study's findings provide insights into policy frameworks that effectively reconcile environmental sustainability, oil production, and financial inclusiveness. It is recommended to implement circular economy models, enhance energy efficiency, and promote investments in renewable energy sources as strategies to achieve balanced and sustainable development. The latest research findings have been utilised to propose various policy implications for the stakeholders affiliated with the organisation (Sun, 2024).

Xiao. et al., (2024), from 1995 to 2020, this study examined the effects of metal ore, coal mining efficiency, and education investment on the long-term growth of 10 Asian emerging and developing nations. Various models revealed that citizen’s education spending does not have a significant impact. However, it is worth noting that metal ore and coal efficiency play a crucial role in promoting sustainability. Among the two, coal mining efficiency has a greater influence due to its importance in producing and electricity generation.

Cities are currently dealing with a range of unique challenges and opportunities. The challenges encompass a range of pressing issues, from climate change to population growth. Additionally, there is a need to find effective ways to advance the European Union's goal of achieving climate neutrality through carbon emission reduction. It is crucially important to address these issues with a political-institutional approach. There is a wide range of interventions required in cities to achieve the objectives of the Green Deal. These interventions cover various areas such as energy, transportation, biodiversity and nature, agriculture and food, green finance, and the Circular Economy (Maglio & Monica, 2022).

A SLR identified such issues, researchers say the Fuzzy-Delphi approach was used to screen the retrieved difficulties. The second literature study revealed Game Theoretical Coordination Contracts (GTCCs). The SECA (Simultaneous Evaluation of Criteria and Alternatives) fuzzy version was created to concurrently assess the finalised challenge weights and GTCC (Global Technical Competitiveness Criteria) performance scores. The findings indicated that implementing the diamond category, which includes cost-tariff, profit-sharing, cost-sharing, and revenue-sharing-commission, would be the most effective approach to tackle inefficiencies in the core function of the Supply Chain (SC) (Xu et al., 2024).

Luo et al., (2022). This article summarises and analyses key power generation characteristics for Sustainable Development Goal 7. Eco-design and circular economy models are examined to discover answers for companies and legislators. The report also emphasises the importance of regulatory frameworks in encouraging eco-friendly behaviours.

Guo, et al., (2017), Lifestyle styles and behaviours are essential to attaining sustainable development. The findings demonstrated that although the public's awareness of sustainable development rose from 10.1% in 2008 to 57.5% in 2013, only 41% of respondents were familiar with the idea of circular economy, a sign of the public's poor comprehension of CE development. Furthermore, in 2013 only 58.5% of respondents believed that waste could be recycled, and citizens continued to struggle with uncertainty over accountability and ignorance regarding waste separation.

Pan, C., et al., (2022), The study indicated that stock returns are influenced by the pricing of carbon emissions. Thus, Researchers argue that investors will want additional pay in order to incorporate low-emitting companies in their portfolios, as an alternative to more polluting but dominating enterprises. Consequently, green enterprises experience an increased cost of financing. The authors suggested that introducing fiscal measures in the near to medium future could incentivize investors to adopt sustainable investment practices.

Le, T. et al., (2022), The study examined how Green Innovation and Green Supply Chain Management (GSCM) mediate the relationship between CSR & SME sustainability in an emerging country. This study highlighted the sustainability benefits of GSCM circular economies. Thus, it encourages SMEs to adopt strategic and operational changes with major environmental, social, and economic implications.

Zhong & Zhao, (2024). This study explored natural resource markets and ecological sustainability. It examines how mineral exploitation impacts Central Asian sustainability. Using the 2000–2022 two models - time series analysis and the autoregressive distributed lag model.

Blockchain, cash flow shortage, reverse factoring, risk assessment, and the triple bottom line are all significant factors in Sustainable Supply Chain Finance. Both a sophisticated local perspective and a cutting-edge global evaluation are employed to analyse the issues and disparities in various regions of the world. 35 countries and provinces are being put into five different geographical areas. The Caribbean, Africa, and Latin America are the only two of the five areas that need to improve their collaboration strategies and address financial crises. For improving sustainability, the effects of wars, natural disasters, and disease outbreaks that come from outside the system are seen as unavoidable (Tseng, 2021). Dey et al. (2022) The research showed that using the circular economy can improve environmental performance by lowering trash and making better use of resources.

This study has made significant contributions in terms of theory, management, and methodology. The initial contribution has been focused on eco-innovation and enhancing our comprehension of Resource Management Practice. The findings from the second contribution offer concise recommendations for companies to optimise resource allocation with greater efficiency and effectiveness. The third contribution incorporates fuzzy set theory to mitigate uncertainties and employs the fuzzy Delphi method to prioritise significant attributes, thereby enhancing the assessment's focus and efficiency while maintaining measurement consistency (Lee et al., 2018).

Wu et al., (2023), This study makes three significant contributions. first This study provides a well-structured interdependent hierarchical model with enough data to increase sustainable value chain understanding. Second The technique contribution manages diverse information in multiple ways to reduce judgement subjectivity. Reliable and valid aspects are commonly developed using EFA. Google Trends data is converted into grey entropy weights to compare organisations' self-perceptions and public expectations. Third Evaluations increase performance and meet public expectations even with limited resources.

2.1 Role of SFMS in Smart Manufacturing Practices

Sustainable Finance Management Systems support smart manufacturing practices. They help industries to prepare and invest in technology improvements that lead to higher efficiency, lower waste, and fewer use of natural resources for production. By managing financial resources wisely, companies can then adopt smart technologies such as automation, AI, and IoT (Internet of Things) in their factories to increase efficiency and increase the green nature of the manufacturing process. Sustainable financial systems therefore spur industrial investment mostly toward long-term value creation rather than short-term gain, thereby creating room for green and smart manufacturing shifts (Pan et al., 2022).

Sustainable financial management systems play an equal role in a circular economy. They direct firms to invest in projects that enhance recycling and reuse and diminish the use of materials along the product life cycle. Instead of adhering to the traditional “take-make-dispose” model, businesses imbued with sustainable finance can now design products worthy of repair and longer use, or those that can be disassembled and their materials reused upon death. By supporting projects financially, these systems drive industries toward a circular economy in which waste is reduced and resources are kept actively in use for as long as possible. This also heals the ecosystem while opening avenues for new business opportunities and promoting economic resilience (Rodrigo-González et al., 2021).

2.2 Role of Consumer and Market forces in Promoting the Circular Economy

The consumer and market forces play a vital role in fostering a circular economy. Consumers, through their purchase of products that are made for durability, reuse, and recyclability, can generate strong demand for sustainable products and services. If customers directly seek the different products manufactured with eco-friendly materials or in a circular economy (products that can be easily repaired, reused, and recycled), they influence the company in the direction of its production. Consumer behaviour is a strong force since companies tend to modify their strategies according to changing customer preferences. So, in this manner, demand for sustainable goods can compel organizations to redesign the way they produce, make, and dispose of their products (Velenturf & Purnell, 2021).

Market forces are also important, as they incentivize firms to embrace the circular economy values. Investors, as they continue to develop a growing interest in sustainability, are seeking to finance businesses that resonate with circular economy ambitions, for instance, in eliminating waste and protecting resources. Policy and regulatory actions that endorse green technologies, recycling infrastructure, and environmentally friendly standards also compel companies to switch towards circular processes. As consumer and market trends begin to move in the direction of sustainability, firms adopting circular economy principles not only enhance their environmental impact but also become competitive as they can respond to increasingly demanding consumers and regulators for more sustainable, cleaner products. It is this feedback loop between market forces and consumer behaviour that can help scale up the circular economy and make it a long-lasting success (Zhong & Zhao, 2024).

a. Research gap

Rationally, there is a long history of studies on the different dimensions of the current study. Some authors have highlighted the challenges faced by the business in achieving sustainable financial management along with a circular economy. Few researchers have proved the association between the green economy and financial management; likewise, different concepts have emerged on the same terms. Still, there are trivial bibliometric studies on the selective topic, so it becomes imperative to extract relevant conclusions from these studies based on the prominence of co-authorships, citations, and keywords.

b. Objectives of the study

- To explore the size and growth rate of research publications on the role of SFMS in the Circular Economy.

- To identify the most productive authors, institutions, and countries contributing to the field.

All the terms artificial intelligence, sustainable financial management, and circular economy are correlated and growing day by day. Already, thousands of studies have been published on the terms separately, this study is an attempt to track the evolution of associations and their impact on the other studies across the nation. As numerous authors worldwide have explored the terms mentioned above in their own way, it is essential to extract the most eminent study, author, institution, and country in the specific area of research.

c. Scope of work
    - The present study would assist in exploring the strategies used in the Sustainable finance management system in association with the circular economy. This would lead to detecting the limitations and developing better strategies for the future.
    - Co-authorship bibliometric analysis reveals the relationship of different studies based on disciplines and countries. This could be extended to accelerate the global collaboration of authors and countries.
    - To dive in depth into any country's specifications related to sustainable finance and circular economy, the present study can be further extended to the sector-wise bibliometric analysis of a specific country.

3. METHODOLOGY

A bibliometric analysis was performed in this research to systematically study the scholarly environment. Datasets were extracted from Dimensions AI, Scopus, Web of Science, and Google Scholar, a prolific multidisciplinary academic database. For the analysis, VOSviewer was a bibliometric mapping and network visualization software that visualizes and studies the relationship between authors, keywords, and publications (Donthu et al., 2021).

3.1 Search Strategy

The search strategy was designed to ensure a comprehensive retrieval of relevant studies. We employed a set of carefully selected keywords derived directly from the topic and related areas. The keywords included: "Sustainable finance," "Finance management systems," "Digital era," "Emerging technologies," "FinTech," "Green finance," "Digital finance," "Sustainable financial systems," "Smart Manufacturing,"

"AI in finance," and "ESG investing." To construct the search string, Boolean operators were applied: AND was used to combine different concepts (e.g., "Sustainable finance" AND "Digital era"), and OR was used to capture related or synonymous terms (e.g., "Emerging technologies" OR "FinTech" OR "Blockchain in finance"). Additional filters were set to narrow the results to publications from 2014 to 2024, written in English, and limited to peer-reviewed journal articles and conference papers. Initially, the data includes published chapters, articles, proceedings, edited books, monographs, and preprints from 2014 to 2024, and the number was 129,488. As the number was very large, it was decided to filter the publication type and concise on articles only to extract appropriate conclusions. The final number on which the bibliometric analysis was done was 37,132.

3.2 Inclusion and Exclusion Criteria

The inclusion criteria for this study required that articles be published between 2014 and 2024, written in English, and classified as peer-reviewed journal articles or conference papers. Additionally, only studies directly related to sustainable finance, finance management systems, digital finance systems, emerging technologies in finance, FinTech, blockchain applications in finance, AI in finance, or ESG investing were included. Publications were sourced exclusively from the Dimensions AI database. In contrast, the exclusion criteria ruled out articles published outside the specified time frame, non-English publications, document types such as editorials, letters, commentaries, book chapters, and non-peer-reviewed reports, as well as studies that did not align with the main research theme (Alsharif et al., 2020), table 1 explain the inclusion and exclusion criteria in quick view.

Table 1. Inclusion and exclusion criteria

Criteria	Inclusion	Exclusion
Publication Year	Publications between 2014 and 2024	Publications before 2014 or after 2024
Language	English-language publications	Non-English publications
Document Type	Peer-reviewed journal articles and conference papers	Editorials, letters, commentaries, book chapters, reports
Topic Relevance	Studies addressing sustainable finance, digital finance systems, emerging technologies in finance, FinTech, and ESG finance	Studies not related to sustainable finance or emerging technologies
Database	Articles sourced from Dimensions AI	Articles from other databases without cross-verification

Source: Self-Created

3.4 Data Extraction

Bibliographic information, such as article titles, abstracts, author names, affiliations, keywords, citation counts, and journal sources, was extracted for the data extraction and analysis. The cleaned and curated dataset was imported into VOSviewer for analysis. Different types of bibliometric mappings were conducted: co-authorship analysis to study collaboration patterns among researchers; co-citation analysis to identify influential studies and intellectual foundations; and keyword co-occurrence analysis to reveal major research themes, emerging hotspots, and underexplored areas within the field (Yang & Masron, 2022).

The use of bibliometric analysis was considered the most appropriate methodological choice for this research, as it provides a structured, objective, and quantitative overview of the academic landscape. By systematically identifying trends, key contributors, and research gaps, this method effectively highlights the areas that require further scholarly attention, thus justifying the need for deeper investigation into sustainable finance management systems in the digital age (Ellegaard & Wallin, 2015).

3.5 Assessment

Assessing research activity on the sustainable finance and circular economy helps in identifying the research gaps related to the theme, major contributions and association amongst them. The terms sustainable finance and circular economy share a very broad area of research, various concepts exist between them and it is not possible to extract crucial elements from them with the help of general research. Therefore, in the present study, the researchers have designated one important and explicit string that connects both the terms, namely, the role of sustainable finance in circular economy (Trivedi et al., 2024).

Although both the above-mentioned terms are relatively new, there is no count of the number of studies already done on the theme. Different qualitative and quantitative perspectives came from numerous researchers and their studies. Still, there is a lack of correlation among them. In the present study, the researchers, with the help of bibliometric analysis, have tried to explore the basis of the subject and their connections in different research fields (Turek et al., 2023).

Based on the above arguments and various previous studies referred to from different online research databases, the following primary research and sub-research questions are prepared-

Primary Research Question: What is the qualitative contribution to the review and development of the theoretical literature on the role of sustainable finance in the circular economy?

To answer the above question, it is very essential to explore the following sub-questions:

- What is the importance of bibliometric analysis in exploring the theoretical frameworks on the role of sustainable finance in Circular Economy (CE)?
- What structure is shaped by the publications and citations on the role of sustainable finance in Circular Economy (CE)?
- Who are the authors with the highest number of citations in the field of the role of sustainable finance in Circular Economy?

The role of sustainable finance in circular economy can be spotted in various ways. Through bibliometric analysis, the depth and trend pattern of the literature on the role of sustainable finance in circular economy can be explored and depicted. Moreover, it will also help researchers in discovering crucial research themes and exploring new areas on the theme. This study also includes extracting the most frequently occurring keywords, the most cited author and co-author, author coupling, and many more.

Block and Fisch stated that bibliometric analysis can "structure a field and detect links between disciplines, identify topic clusters, literature gaps and academic silos, and show the most impactful authors and their research." At the completion, it will give other scholars a blueprint or a path through which they can identify trends, research gaps, and associations with other related published research.

4. BIBLIOMETRIC ANALYSIS USING VOSVIEWER SOFTWARE

In VOSviewer software, numerous types of bibliometric analysis, namely, Co-citation analysis, Bibliographic coupling analysis, Citation analysis, Co-occurrence analysis, and Co-authorship analysis, can be done.

4.1 Co-Authorship Analysis

Co-authorship analysis helps in identifying and tracking the research networks over a specific period. It also shows the most active author/s, organisations, and countries who contribute in the selected field. It can be done on Full counting or the Fractional counting method. In this study, the full counting method is applied to represent the data network. The minimum number of documents and citations required for an author to be selected is set at 5 and the threshold is determined to be 38. The visualisation will only include authors who have co-authored a minimum of 5 papers. The largest set of collected items consists of 16 clusters, with a total link strength of 43. These findings were derived from the analysis of network visualisation, overlay visualisation, and density visualisation.

Figure 2. Co-authorship network visualisation

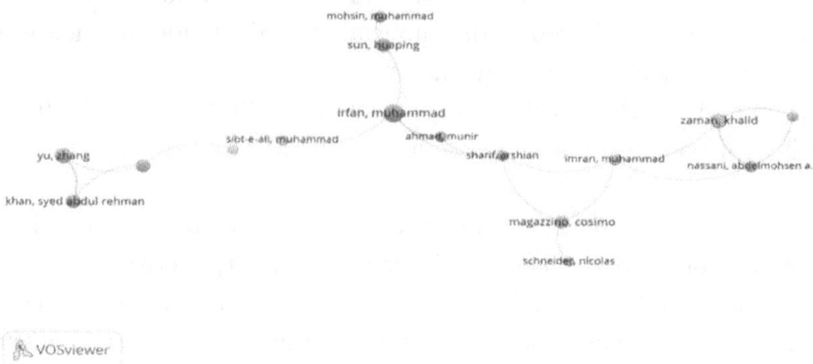

Figure 2: Co-authorship network visualisation

Figure 3. Co-authorship (Countries) Network Visualisation

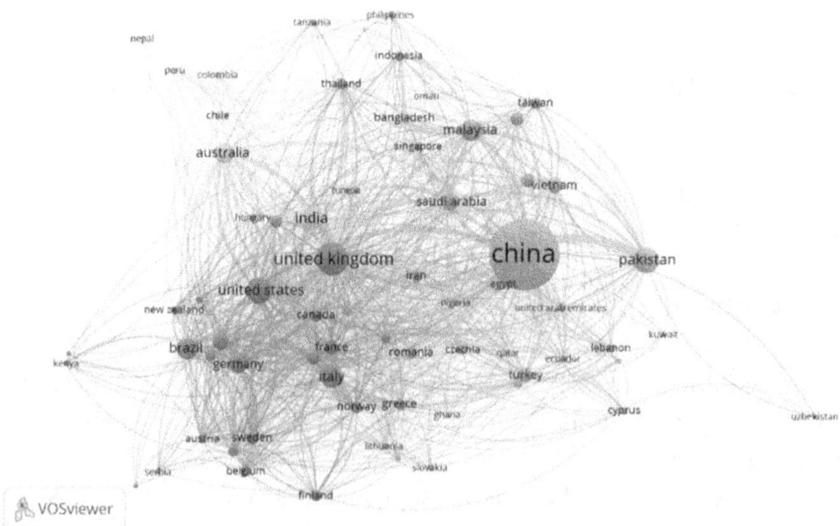

Figure 3: Co-authorship (Countries) Network Visualisation

Figure 4. Co-authorship overlay Visualisation

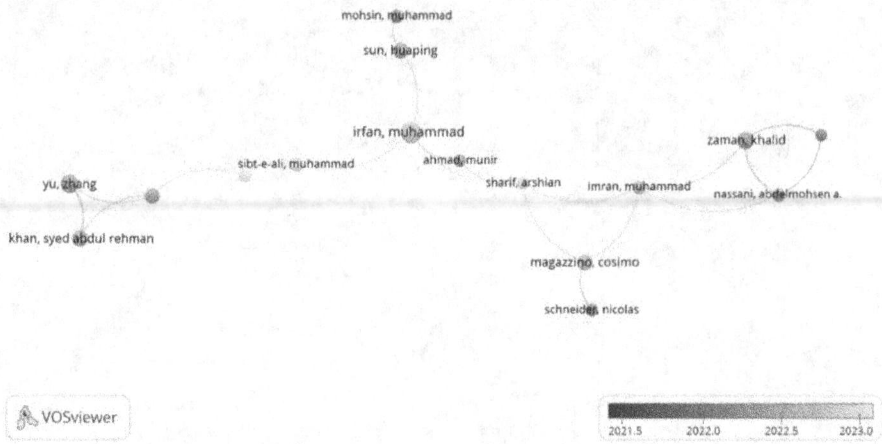

Figure 4: Co-authorship Overlay Visualisation

Figure 5. Co-authorship density visualisation

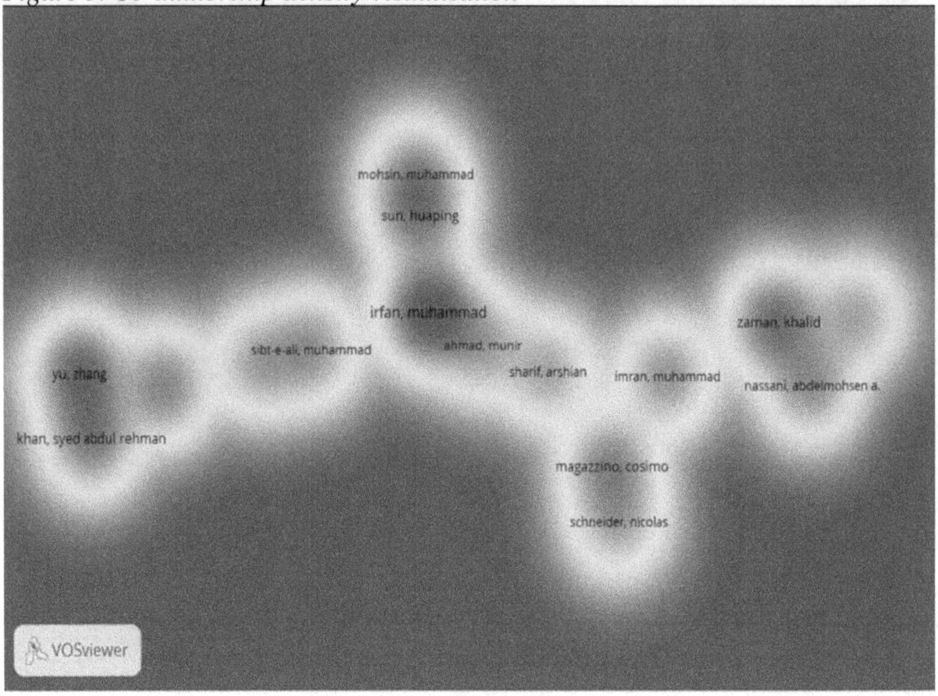

Figure 5: Co-authorship Density visualisation

Interpretation

The network visualisation above depicts the connections of co-authors in a network. The nodes in the network are sized based on the importance of the items, while the edges are thickened to represent the strength of the relationships between the objects. The overlay visualisation superimposes many data points and discerns links between them. The density visualisation illustrates the spatial arrangement of things inside a network, highlighting regions with a significant accumulation of items.

4.2 Citation Analysis

Citation analysis is used to ascertain the most notable papers in a particular topic and to monitor the influence of a study over time. Additionally, it showcases the publications, authors, organisations, and countries that have received the highest number of citations in a specific subject. It also allows for monitoring the changes and development of a topic over time. In the present study, the minimum number of citations was set as 10, which represents that only articles will be shown in the figure that have been cited at least 10 times; accordingly, 947 meet the threshold. The result shows 309 items and 32 clusters.

Figure 6. Citation (authors) network visualisation

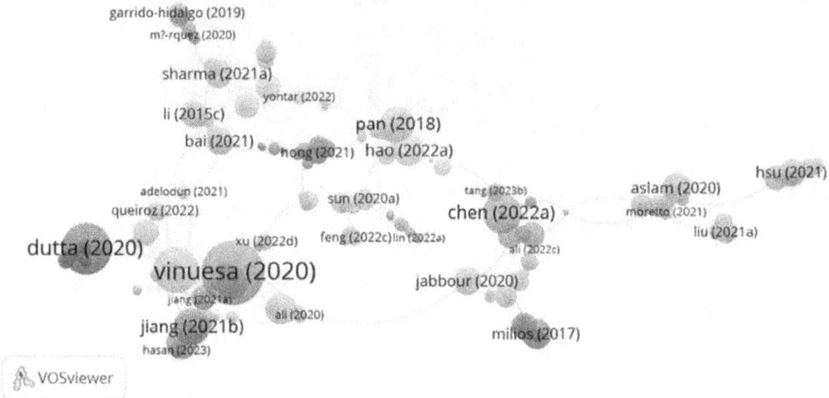

Figure 6: Citation (authors) Network Visualisation

4.3 Bibliographic Coupling Analysis

Bibliographic coupling analysis identifies related publications even if they do not share any common citation. It helps in tracking similar publications and emerging topics in the same research area. In the present study, the minimum number of citations is set as 10, accordingly, 947 documents meet the thresholds.

Figure 7. Bibliographic coupling analysis (documents) network visualization

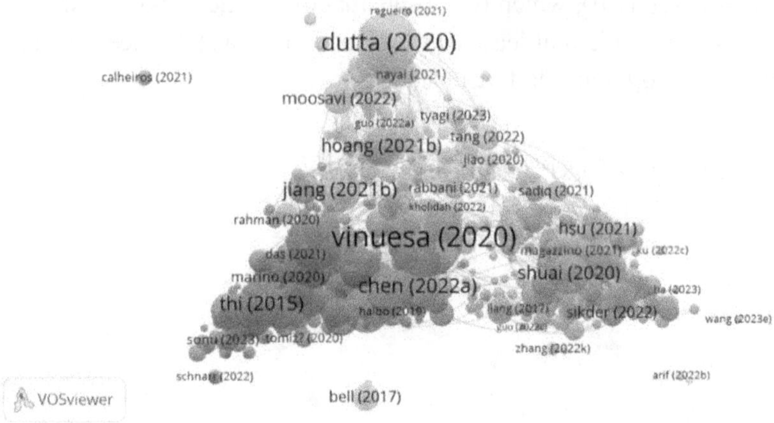

Figure 7: Bibliographic coupling analysis (documents) network visualization

4.4 Co-Citation Analysis

Co-citation analysis identifies related publications based on their content. It also shows the most persuasive research clusters in a specific area. In the present research, the minimum number of citations of a cited reference is set at 20, which meets 128 thresholds. The result comes with 4 clusters with 7247 total link strength.

Figure 8. Co-citation (cited reference) network visualisation

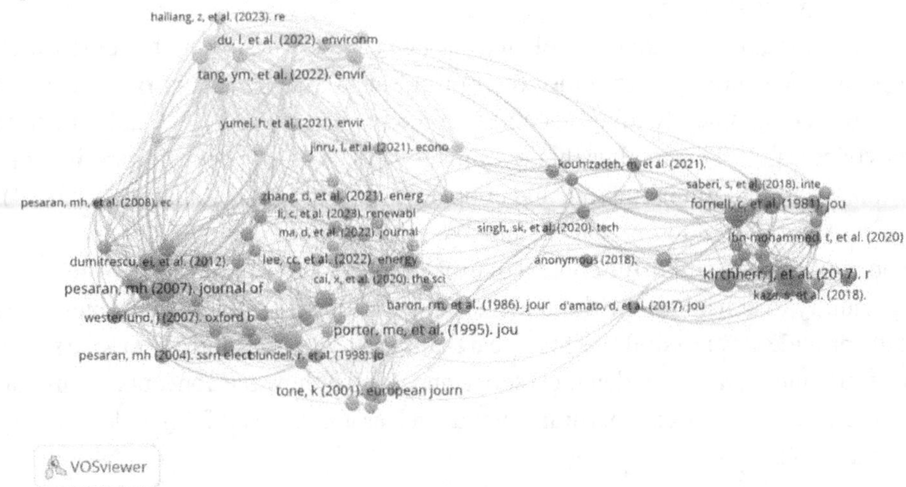

Figure 8: Co-citation (Cited reference) network visualisation

The current study demonstrates that the papers that were retrieved generated a substantial number of citations, indicating a significant level of interest among scholars in extracting the crucial aspects of sustainable finance's function in the circular economy. The reason for this is that both sustainable finance and circular economy are emerging concepts that hold the potential to drive the overall prosperity of a nation in the future (Kansra et al., 2024).

5. IMPLICATIONS OF THE STUDY

5.1 Implications for Academicians

This study provides valuable insights for academics by showing the current trends and gaps in research related to sustainable finance and the circular economy. The analysis helps researchers understand what areas are underexplored and need more attention. Identification of gaps draws researchers' attention to such topics, which could pave the way for future new and worthwhile studies. In this way, the present literature helps in keeping researchers well informed, along with making them choose research avenues that bear considerable scope for future research (Tanchangya et al. 2025).

In addition, the research is likely to assist researchers in making better research proposals. When researchers tailor their proposals to the gaps identified, they will receive funding since funding agencies are more interested in new and untapped areas of research. This implies that researchers will be able to convert gaps into opportunities for obtaining funding and cooperation for projects (Kansra et al., 2024).

One key observation is that sustainable finance and the circular economy are frequently debated within the context of urban economies, but there is a considerable opportunity to consider how these ideas can be used within rural economies. This would provide new possibilities for research that have not been entirely tapped so far, and academics can now widen their scope and think of how the concepts of circular economy can be beneficial for rural towns as well as urban areas (Taghizadeh-Hesary & Hyun, 2022).

5.2 Implications for Practitioners

For policymakers and finance professionals, the research provides useful advice. Policymakers can utilize the research to design and enact more effective policies to advance sustainable finance and the circular economy (Kansra et al., 2024). Through examination of what has been successful both in developed and developing nations, they can enhance the success rate of their plans. Knowing global best practice helps them develop strategies that are more likely to be successful in their nations (Kashif et al., 2024).

To financial professionals, the research illustrates the potential of applying cross-country studies to address real-world financial issues. With the implementation of sound case study findings, financial institutions can enhance their investment strategies and business models to incorporate sustainable and circular economy practices more effectively. This will not only ensure they make improved financial choices but also link them with global chains, enabling collaboration and learning from one another (Păun & Pinzaru, 2021).

5.3 Challenges Faced by Policymakers, Financial Institutions, and Policy Gaps

The study's findings are useful, but some challenges remain in applying them. Policymakers often grapple with incoherent and inconsistent regulations. In many instances, there are scarce clear laws to steer businesses in their implementation of circular economy practices. Without the necessary regulations, businesses cannot confidently proceed in its application, which retards the transition toward sustainability (Rahimi et al., 2022).

Financial institutions are also facing difficulties. There are a lot of risks associated with investing in a circular economy because the returns realized will mostly be termed as long-term, and the risks are quite hard to predict. Such uncertainty makes it quite complex for financial institutions to design models on how to fund such projects. Further, there's a lack of awareness among financial professionals about the benefits of these sustainable models, which makes it harder for them to promote and invest in such projects (Kansra et al., 2025).

There are also policy gaps that require attention. Most of the policies are related to urban areas, and little attention is given to rural areas, which are usually faced with different needs and opportunities. Specific industries have difficulties implementing circular economy practices because of existing infrastructure and market conditions; for instance, in manufacturing and agriculture. To remedy such challenges, policymakers need to design and craft more relevant policies in terms of specific industries and geographical regions, yet ensuring that all benefit from sustainable practices (Dzingirai & Mveku, 2023).

6. LIMITATIONS

While the researchers have made an effort to include all the essential visual analyses for the topic, certain limitations exist in the current study:

- **Database Limitation**: The study primarily relied on the Dimensions AI database for literature analysis. While Dimensions AI provides extensive coverage, there are other online databases that could offer additional perspectives and insights. Future research could incorporate these alternative databases to enrich and expand the scope of the study (Turek et al., 2023).
- **Geographical Scope**: The study includes data from multiple countries, which may influence the accuracy of the results due to regional differences in research trends and practices. To improve precision, future studies could focus on a single country, allowing for more detailed and context-specific findings (Xiao et al., 2024).
- **Bibliometric Analysis Tools**: **VOSviewer** is a powerful tool for bibliometric analysis, offering many options and dimensions for exploration. However, it was not possible to cover all aspects in this study. There is considerable potential to explore additional dimensions and functionalities of VOSviewer in future research to provide a more comprehensive analysis (Alsharif et al., 2020).

7. CONCLUSION

The current research provides a complete overview of the bibliometric studies of sustainable finance in the circular economy, along with some qualitative datasets from Dimensions AI, up to 2014-2024. It uses such extensive and good-quality data for examining theoretical, intellectual, and community structures within the subject (Arora & Nabi, 2022). The study has thus predominantly applied the VOSviewer application, which highlights a consistent upward trend in research showing that both sustainable finance and the circular economy are rapidly gaining grounds around the world, with a noticeable contribution from countries such as China, the UK, US, and India (Trivedi et al., 2024).

One of the most notable points brought forth by the study is emerging subjectivity concerning smart manufacturing and the circular economy framework. Advanced leading technologies such as AI, IoT, and automation, going to transform the industries towards more sustainable production processes, will significantly reduce waste and optimize resources (Arora et al., 2024). One of the main authors, Vinuesa, has brought legs and feet into the discussion of sustainable finance and how it can be applied in smart manufacturing systems. The study also points to possible cross and international collaborations since industries increasingly aim at embedding sustainable finance within their operations (Ahmad et al., 2025).

The rise in the gig economy is shaping the pace at which sustainable finance moves across sectors. Gig work, while bringing with it challenges, is providing some opportunities for harmonizing financial practices with labour market dynamics in sectors such as smart manufacturing. Here, flexible and decentralized labour is a focal point. These very changes demand a reconsideration of sustainable finance practice to guarantee economic resilience and inclusiveness (Wu et al., 2023).

The study sets directions for future studies into how nations and sectors could customize the sustainable finance strategy to address the growing demand for smart manufacturing while catering to the changing needs of the gig economy. It also calls upon the world to cooperate in developing systems to encourage sustainability in traditional sectors and recent emerging ones that propagate economic and environmental dividends in the long term (Nie et al., 2024).

REFERENCES

Ahmad, V., Arora, M., Sayal, A., Kumar, R., & Kumar, P. (2025). Exploring trends in e-business and sustainable finance: An integrated analytical approach. *Frontiers in Sustainable Cities*, *7*, 1549874. DOI: 10.3389/frsc.2025.1549874

Alareeni, B., & Hamdan, A. (2023). Sustainable Finance, Digitalization and the Role of Technology. In *Proceedings of the International Conference on Business and Technology (ICBT 2021)*. Springer International Publishing. DOI: 10.1007/978-3-031-08084-5

Alsharif, A. H., Salleh, N. O. R. Z. M. D., & Baharun, R. O. H. A. I. Z. A. T. (2020). Bibliometric analysis. *Journal of Theoretical and Applied Information Technology*, *98*(15), 2948–2962.

Alshehhi, A., Nobanee, H., & Khare, N. (2018). The Impact of Sustainability Practices on Corporate Financial Performance: Literature Trends and Future Research Potential. *Sustainability (Basel)*, *10*(2), 494–519. DOI: 10.3390/su10020494

Ameer, R., & Othman, R. (2012). Sustainability practices and corporate financial performance: A study based on the top global corporations. *Journal of Business Ethics*, *108*(1), 61–79. https://link.springer.com/article/10.1007/s10551-011-1063-y. DOI: 10.1007/s10551-011-1063-y

Amoozad Mahdiraji, H., Govindan, K., Yaftiyan, F., Garza-Reyes, J. A., & Razavi Hajiagha, S. H. (2023). Unveiling coordination contracts' roles considering circular economy and eco-innovation toward pharmaceutical supply chain resiliency: Evidence of an emerging economy. *Journal of Cleaner Production*, *382*, 135135. DOI: 10.1016/j.jclepro.2022.135135

Arora, S., & Nabi, T. (2022). Blockchain adoption in banking systems: A boon or bane? In *Applications, challenges, and opportunities of blockchain technology in banking and insurance* (pp. 19–42). IGI Global. DOI: 10.4018/978-1-6684-4133-6.ch002

Arora, S., Oberoi, S., Nabi, T., & Verma, B. (2024). How does blockchain impact sustainable food security? Insights from literature review. *International Journal of Information Management Data Insights*, *4*(2), 100276. DOI: 10.1016/j.jjimei.2024.100276

Arruda, E., Melatto, R., & Braga da Silva, N. (2021). Circular economy: A brief literature review (2015–2020). *Sustainable Operations and Computers.*, *2*, 79–86. Advance online publication. DOI: 10.1016/j.susoc.2021.05.001

Chauhan, M., & Sahoo, D. R. (2024). Towards a greener tomorrow: Exploring the potential of AI, blockchain, and IoT in sustainable development. *Nature Environment and Pollution Technology*, *23*(2), 1105–1113. DOI: 10.46488/NEPT.2024.v23i02.044

Colombage, S. (2023). Financial Technology (Fintech) and Sustainable Financing: A New Paradigm for Risk Management. *Journal of Risk and Financial Management*, *16*(12), 502. DOI: 10.3390/jrfm16120502

Dey, P. K., Malesios, C., Chowdhury, S., Saha, K., Budhwar, P., & De, D. (2022). Adoption of circular economy practices in small and medium-sized enterprises: Evidence from Europe. *International Journal of Production Economics*, *248*, 108496. Advance online publication. DOI: 10.1016/j.ijpe.2022.108496

Donthu, N., Kumar, S., Mukherjee, D., Pandey, N., & Lim, W. M. (2021). How to conduct a bibliometric analysis: An overview and guidelines. *Journal of Business Research*, *133*, 285–296. DOI: 10.1016/j.jbusres.2021.04.070

Dzingirai, M., & Mveku, B. (2023). The role of technology in sustainable finance towards the 5th industrial revolution: A dynamic capability view. *Business, Technology and Finance*, 1.

Ellegaard, O., & Wallin, J. A. (2015). The bibliometric analysis of scholarly production: How great is the impact? *Scientometrics*, *105*(3), 1809–1831. DOI: 10.1007/s11192-015-1645-z PMID: 26594073

Eu, J., & Houska, D. (2019). Sustainable Finance for a Circular Economy. . Report from Japan/EU Joint Workshop at the G20 Resource Efficiency Dialogue 2019 held on 10 October 2019 in Tokyo (Japan).DOI: 10.2779/171661

Guo, B., Geng, Y., Sterr, T., Zhu, Q., & Liu, Y. (2017). Investigating public awareness on circular economy in western China: A case of Urumqi Midong. *Journal of Cleaner Production*, *142*, 2177–2186. https://doi.org/https://doi.org/10.1016/j.jclepro.2016.11.063. DOI: 10.1016/j.jclepro.2016.11.063

Kansra, P., Kumar, P., & Paul, P. J. D. (2025). Sustainable Digitalisation: A Review of Literature and Indian Initiatives. *Digital Transformation for Business Sustainability and Growth in Emerging Markets*, 275-292.

Kansra, P., Oberoi, S., Gupta, S. L., & Singh, N. (2024). Factors limiting the application of consumer neuroscience: A systematic review. *Journal of Consumer Behaviour*, *23*(1), 31–42. DOI: 10.1002/cb.2131

Kansra, P., Oberoi, S., Singh, N., & Choi, H. (2024). Role of Innovation, Policy, Social Media, and Environmental Munificence for Sustainable Ecotourism Development in Punjab, India. *Sustainability (Basel)*, *16*(21), 9359. DOI: 10.3390/su16219359

Kansra, P., Singh, N., Verma, R., Gupta, S. L., & Bali, V. (2024). Guest editorial: Applications of blockchain technology for performance and reliability of business operations. *International Journal of Quality & Reliability Management*, *41*(8), 2001–2003. DOI: 10.1108/IJQRM-09-2024-456

Kashif, M., Pinglu, C., Ullah, S., & Zaman, M. (2024). Evaluating the influence of financial technology (FinTech) on sustainable finance: A comprehensive global analysis. *Financial Markets and Portfolio Management*, *38*(1), 123–155. DOI: 10.1007/s11408-023-00439-w

Le, T. T. (2022). Linking big data, sustainable supply chain management and corporate performance: The moderating role of circular economy thinking. *International Journal of Logistics Management*, *34*(3), 744–771. Advance online publication. DOI: 10.1108/IJLM-01-2022-0011

Le, T. T., Ferraris, A., & Dhar, B. K. (2023). The contribution of circular economy practices on the resilience of production systems: Eco-innovation and cleaner production's mediation role for sustainable development. *Journal of Cleaner Production*, *424*, 138806. https://doi.org/https://doi.org/10.1016/j.jclepro.2023.138806. DOI: 10.1016/j.jclepro.2023.138806

Le, T. T., Vo, X. V., & Venkatesh, V. G. (2022). Role of green innovation and supply chain management in driving sustainable corporate performance. *Journal of Cleaner Production*, *374*, 133875. https://doi.org/https://doi.org/10.1016/j.jclepro.2022.133875. DOI: 10.1016/j.jclepro.2022.133875

Lee, C. H., Wu, K. J., & Tseng, M. L. (2018). Resource management practice through eco-innovation toward sustainable development using qualitative information and quantitative data. *Journal of Cleaner Production*, *202*, 120–129. DOI: 10.1016/j.jclepro.2018.08.058

Luo, D., Luo, M., & Lv, J. (2022). Can digital finance contribute to the promotion of financial sustainability? A financial efficiency perspective. *Sustainability (Basel)*, *14*(7), 3979. DOI: 10.3390/su14073979

Luo, J., Pan, Z., & Zhang, S. (2024). Greening the economy: Techniques and regulations to promote natural resource efficiency. *Resources Policy*, *90*, 104686. https://doi.org/https://doi.org/10.1016/j.resourpol.2024.104686. DOI: 10.1016/j.resourpol.2024.104686

Magid, A. A., Hussainey, K., De Andrés, J., & Lorca, P. (2024). Powering the Future of Sustainable Finance: FinTech, Big Data Analytics, and the Evolving Investment Landscape in the Post-COVID-19 Era. In *Business Sustainability with Artificial Intelligence (AI): Challenges and Opportunities* (Vol. 1, pp. 215–225). Springer Nature Switzerland.

Maglio, Monica(2022). Visions of cities beyond the Green Deal: From imagination to reality, *Journal of Urban Regeneration & Renewal*, Volume 15 / Number 2 / Winter 2022, pp. 176-192(17).

Manta, O. (2022). Digital financial technologies and green finance, support tools for the sustainable development of the economy. In *Creşterea economică în condiţiile globalizării* (pp. 23-42). DOI: 10.36004/nier.cecg.III.2022.16.2

MERRILL, R. K., SCHILLEBEECKX, S. J., & BLAKSTAD, S. (2019). Sustainable digital finance in Asia: Creating environmental impact through bank transformation.

Mhlanga, D., & Shao, D. (2025). Blockchain Technology and Sustainable Supply Chain Finance: A Pathway to Environmental Responsibility and Profitability. In *Financial Inclusion and Sustainable Development in Sub-Saharan Africa* (pp. 215-230). Routledge.

Moşteanu, N. R. (2019, December). Green sustainable regional development and digital era. In *Green buildings and renewable energy: Med green forum 2019-part of world renewable energy congress and network* (pp. 181–197). Springer International Publishing.

Nie, P., Zhong, J., Ren, Z., & Huang, J. (2024). Sustainable financing solutions for the growth of resource-driven economies in the digital economy age. *Resources Policy*, *98*, 105350. DOI: 10.1016/j.resourpol.2024.105350

Nobanee, H., & Ellili, N. O. (2016). Corporate Sustainability Disclosure in Annual Reports: Evidence from UAE Banks: Islamic versus Conventional. *Renewable & Sustainable Energy Reviews*, *55*(March), 1336–1341. DOI: 10.1016/j.rser.2015.07.084

Oberoi, S., Arora, S., Verma, B., & Roy, K. K. (2024). What do we know about artificial intelligence and blockchain technology integration in the healthcare industry? In *Driving decentralization and disruption with digital technologies* (pp. 124–138). IGI Global Scientific Publishing. DOI: 10.4018/979-8-3693-3253-5.ch009

Oberoi, S., & Kansra, P. (2021). Motivating antecedents and consequences of blockchain technology in the insurance industry. In *Blockchain technology and applications for digital marketing* (pp. 276–285). IGI Global. DOI: 10.4018/978-1-7998-8081-3.ch017

Oberoi, S., & Kansra, P. (2022). Blockchain technology in the insurance industry. In *Applications, challenges, and opportunities of blockchain technology in banking and insurance* (pp. 160–172). IGI Global. DOI: 10.4018/978-1-6684-4133-6.ch009

Pan, C., Sun, T., Mirza, N., & Huang, Y. (2022). The pricing of low emission transitions: Evidence from stock returns of natural resource firms in the GCC. *Resources Policy*, *79*, 102986. https://doi.org/https://doi.org/10.1016/j.resourpol.2022.102986. DOI: 10.1016/j.resourpol.2022.102986

Păun, T., & Pinzaru, F. (2021). Advancing strategic management through sustainable finance. *Management Dynamics in the Knowledge Economy*, *9*(2), 279–291. DOI: 10.2478/mdke-2021-0019

Rahimi, M., Kumar, P., Moazzamigodarzi, M., & Mishra, A. R. (2022). Digital transformation challenges in sustainable financial service systems using novel interval-valued Pythagorean fuzzy double normalization-based multiple aggregation approach. *Environment, Development and Sustainability*, •••, 1–33. DOI: 10.1007/s10668-022-02719-3 PMID: 36373028

Raut, R., Deshpande, A., Arora, S., Mittal, A., & Alandikar, R. (2022, December). An examination of the pricing of IPOs: The Indian perspective. In *2022 5th International Conference on Contemporary Computing and Informatics (IC3I)* (pp. 155-159). IEEE.

Rodrigo-González, A., Grau-Grau, A., & Bel-Oms, I. (2021). Circular Economy and Value Creation: Sustainable Finance with a Real Options Approach. *Sustainability (Basel)*, *13*(14), 7973. DOI: 10.3390/su13147973

Sarra, Janis. (2020). Sustainable Finance and the Move to a Circular Economy .DOI: 10.1093/oso/9780198852308.003.0008

Sepetis, A., Pierrakos, G., & Schallmo, D. (2022). Sustainable Finance and the Digital Transformation in the Healthcare system. In *ISPIM Conference Proceedings* (pp. 1-21). The International Society for Professional Innovation Management (ISPIM).

Singh, N., Kansra, P., & Gupta, S. L. (Eds.). (2024). *Digital influence on consumer habits: marketing challenges and opportunities*. Emerald Publishing Limited. DOI: 10.1108/9781804553428

Sisodia, A., & Maheshwari, G. C. (2023). Exploring Sustainable Finance: A Review and Future Research Agenda. *Vision (Basel)*, *0*(0), 09722629231209177. Advance online publication. DOI: 10.1177/09722629231209177

Sun, T. (2024). Role of Inclusive Finance on oil Resource production targets: How Fiscal Pressures influence natural resources policy and green recovery in Gulf countries? *Resources Policy, 88*, 104337. https://doi.org/https://doi.org/10.1016/j.resourpol.2023.104337. DOI: 10.1016/j.resourpol.2023.104337

Taghizadeh-Hesary, F., & Hyun, S. (Eds.). (2022). *Green digital finance and sustainable development goals*. Springer. DOI: 10.1007/978-981-19-2662-4

Tanchangya, T., Islam, N., Naher, K., Mia, M. R., Chowdhury, S., Sarker, S. R., & Rashid, F. (2025). Financial technology-enabled sustainable finance for small-and medium-sized enterprises. *Environment. Innovation and Management, 1*, 2550006.

Trivedi, P., Ravisankar, A., Kumar, G. P., Krishnamoorthy, V., Shukla, S., & Boopathi, S. (2024). Finance and Technology-Integrated Digital Economy: Circular Age of a Sustainable Digital Revolution. In *Navigating the Circular Age of a Sustainable Digital Revolution* (pp. 91-120). IGI Global.

Tseng, M-L, Bui, T-D, Lim, M, Tsai, FM & Tan, RR (2021), 'Comparing world regional sustainable supply chain finance using big data analytics: A bibliometric analysis', *Industrial Management and Data Systems,* vol. (In-Press), pp. (In-Press). https://dx.doi.org/DOI: 10.1108/IMDS-09-2020-0521

Turek, J., Ocicka, B., Rogowski, W., & Jefmański, B. (2023). The role of Industry 4.0 technologies in driving the financial importance of sustainability risk management. *Equilibrium.Quarterly Journal of Economics and Economic Policy, 18*(4), 1009–1044.

Velenturf, A., & Purnell, P. (2021). Principles for a Sustainable Circular Economy. *Sustainable Production and Consumption, 27*, 1437–1457. DOI: 10.1016/j.spc.2021.02.018

Verma, B., Bhardwaj, M., Arora, S., & Oberoi, S. (2025). Unveiling the impact of remittances on productive efficiencies: Investigating productivity growth of prominent remittance-receiving developing nations. *International Journal of Productivity and Performance Management, 74*(4), 1101–1124. DOI: 10.1108/IJPPM-05-2023-0213

Wu, K. J., Tseng, M. L., Yang, W. H., Ali, M. H., & Chen, X. (2023). Re-shaping sustainable value chain model under post pandemic disruptions: A fast fashion supply chain analysis. *International Journal of Production Economics, 255*, 108704. Advance online publication. DOI: 10.1016/j.ijpe.2022.108704

Xiao, Z., Duritan, M. J. M., & Jia, R. (2024). Resourceful futures: Integrating responsible mining and green education for sustainable development in developing and emerging economies. *Resources Policy*, *88*, 104377. https://doi.org/https://doi.org/10.1016/j.resourpol.2023.104377. DOI: 10.1016/j.resourpol.2023.104377

Xu, T., Yang, G., & Chen, T. (2024). The role of green finance and digital inclusive finance in promoting economic sustainable development: A perspective from new quality productivity. *Journal of Environmental Management*, *370*, 122892. DOI: 10.1016/j.jenvman.2024.122892 PMID: 39447370

Yang, C., & Masron, T. A. (2022). Impact of digital finance on energy efficiency in the context of green sustainable development. *Sustainability (Basel)*, *14*(18), 11250. DOI: 10.3390/su141811250

Zhong, X., & Zhao, L. (2024). Alternative economic strategies for an ecological resurrection: The case of natural resource markets. *Resources Policy, 90*. DOI: 10.3390/su141811250

Chapter 7
Financial Management in the Digital Era:
Blockchain and Immersive Technologies

Aarti Gupta
https://orcid.org/0009-0006-3392-9459
Asian Business School, Noida, India

Swati Bhatia
https://orcid.org/0000-0003-3478-3640
Head IQAC, Asian Business School, Noida, India

ABSTRACT

This chapter introduces the blockchain and other immersive technologies such as AI, cryptocurrency, RPA, De-Fi, virtual reality, and augmented reality. Followed by sufficient background information, it includes a literature review while identifying the research gap. Cases and real-world applications support the content to a larger extent. Challenges and hurdles during technological adoption by financial managers have evolved. Regulatory issues pertaining to cybersecurity and other technologies are inculcated. At last, conclusions and future recommendations are provided on ESG integration in digital finance and talent shortage in fintech. This chapter also explores the unique role of financial managers in assisting companies with their risk management. It presents a descriptive introduction of block-chain and other immersive technologies in the field of financial management. It also discusses how financial managers' core competencies add significant value in the growing digital era.

DOI: 10.4018/979-8-3373-1290-3.ch007

1. INTRODUCTION

Financial management, the strategic planning, organizing, directing, and controlling of financial undertakings in an organization, has evolved substantially with technological advancement. Traditionally, financial management focused on manual bookkeeping, in-person transactions, and time-consuming audits. However, the digital era marked by the rise of the internet, mobile technologies, big data, artificial intelligence (AI), block-chain, and fin-tech innovations has revolutionized the field. Digitalization has transformed how companies manage financial information, make investment decisions, raise capital, assess risk, and ensure compliance. Financial data is now available in real-time, offering more precise insights and enabling faster decision-making. Moreover, financial operations are increasingly automated, reducing human error, improving efficiency, and allowing businesses to shift focus toward strategic growth.

This chapter is structured in various sections. It first introduces the block-chain and other immersive technologies such as AI, cryptocurrency, RPA, De-Fi, virtual reality and augmented reality. Followed by sufficient background information, it includes literature review while identifying the research gap. Cases and real world applications supports the content to the larger extent. Challenges and hurdles during technological adoption by financial managers are evolved. Regulatory issues pertaining to cybersecurity and other technologies are inculcated. At last, conclusion and future recommendations are provided on ESG integration in digital finance and talent shortage in fin-tech. This chapter also explores the unique role of financial managers in assisting companies with their risk management. Firstly, it presents a descriptive introduction of block-chain and other immersive technologies in the field of financial management. It also discusses how financial managers' core competencies add significant value in the growing digital era.

The COVID-19 pandemic further accelerated the digitalization trend, making remote financial management tools a necessity rather than a luxury. Companies across all sectors are now investing heavily in technologies such as cloud-based accounting, digital payment platforms, robotic process automation (RPA), machine learning for predictive analytics, and block-chain for secure transactions. In today's digital age, cybersecurity risks are a growing concern for organizations across the globe. As businesses increasingly store proprietary information, including customer and supplier data, in the Cloud and on digital networks. At the same time, the frequency of cyberattacks is also rising. According to the FBI, "There are only two types of companies: those that have been hacked, and those that will be" (Cowley 2012). The rapid rise of data breaches and cyber incidents, coupled with heightened concerns from stakeholders, has led companies to direct considerable resources toward strengthening their financial risk management efforts. Gopalkrishnan, S., Mohanty, S. P., & Jaiwani, M. (2023).

Arora & Nabi (2022) explored that Blockchain is being explored for applications beyond traditional banking, including trade finance, digital supply chains, and smart contract-based insurance processing. Institutions such as JP Morgan Chase (Quorum division) and Bank of America are developing Blockchain-based solutions. Blockchain's ability to ensure data security, transparency, and cost-efficiency positions it as a key enabler for future financial systems.

Gopalkrishnan, Mohanty & Jaiwani (2023) revealed that Data Envelopment Analysis (DEA) has been extensively applied to measure the performance of banks in India and globally. Studies by Das and Ghosh (2006), Kumar and Gulati (2008), Kaur and Gupta (2015), and Gulati and Kumar (2017) explored efficiency among public and private sector banks by considering inputs like branch networks, NPA levels, and profitability. Notably, Gulati and Kumar's (2017) two-stage DEA approach highlighted that public sector banks struggled with generating income, and bank size positively influenced intermediation efficiency. Research also expanded to insurance firms and stock markets. Ilyas and Rajasekaran (2019) and Sinha (2015) studied the Indian non-life insurance sector using DEA, finding moderate technical efficiency and highlighting areas for operational improvement. Internationally, DEA has been used to assess banking efficiency, especially post the Global Financial Crisis (GFC), to study cost optimization, regulatory impacts, and performance. Researchers such as Avkiran (2006), Drake and Hall (2003), and Sufian (2008, 2011) provided evidence from different country contexts.

2. BLOCKCHAIN AND IMMERSIVE TECHNOLOGIES

Blockchain technology has the potential to address these challenges. A Blockchain is a distributed, decentralized ledger system in which transactions (or records) are verified, stored, and made publicly accessible across a network of peers. Each "block" in the chain contains a series of transactions, and once added to the chain, it cannot be altered or deleted—this creates an immutable, tamper-proof record. Blockchain operates without the need for a central authority, which is one of its primary advantages. Instead, it relies on a decentralized network of nodes, where each node (or participant) has a copy of the entire Blockchain and contributes to validating transactions. This makes Blockchain particularly well-suited for applications requiring transparency, trust, and data integrity—such as tracking misconduct in the finance profession. Blockchain technology initially gained traction through Bitcoin and cryptocurrencies but has expanded beyond financial transactions to offer broader applications in data storage, decentralized governance, and operations management (Swan, 2015; Tapscott & Tapscott, 2017).

Arora & Nabi (2022) revealed that The convergence of emerging technologies such as the Internet of Things, big data analytics, and cloud manufacturing has created fertile ground for innovations like Blockchain technology, which is increasingly seen as a transformative force across various industries, particularly banking. Block chain's key features—immutability, decentralization, and real-time data sharing—can be harnessed to create a solution for aggregating and sharing instances of finance misconduct. By leveraging Blockchain, the finance profession could overcome current issues of data fragmentation and enable a more proactive and transparent approach to misconduct monitoring.

2.1. Artificial Intelligence (AI)

The finance profession has witnessed a significant transformation with the advent of artificial intelligence (AI). Firms are making substantial investments in AI technologies, recognizing their potential to streamline financial management processes, improve efficiency, and enhance the objectivity and credibility of their work. A pivotal challenge that firms face is balancing the desire to build strong, favourable relationships with clients while maintaining independence, objectivity, and trust in the financial management process. This chapter explores a ground-breaking study by Libby and Witz (2024), which investigates how AI can mitigate the legal risks financial managers face when their independence is questioned, particularly in the context of juror assessments of negligence.

2.1.1. AI Mitigating Financial Managers' Liability

Libby and Witz (2024) present a novel perspective on how AI can be used to address the long-standing dilemma of financial manager independence. Their study demonstrates that the use of AI in financial management procedures, particularly in performing analytical procedures, can significantly reduce the appearance of financial manager bias and mitigate the legal liability associated with such concerns.

The researchers conducted an experiment with mock jurors who evaluated a hypothetical financial management litigation case involving a financial management firm and a client. In the case, the financial management firm had either a close relationship with the client or maintained a formal, professional relationship. Participants were informed that the financial management firm had relied on either human financial managers or an AI system to perform analytical procedures during the financial management.

The results of the experiment were striking. When independence concerns were higher—due to the close relationship between the financial manager and the client—jurors were less likely to find the financial management firm negligent when AI was used to perform analytical procedures. In fact, jurors were 14% less likely to assess the financial management firm as negligent when AI was involved compared to when human financial managers performed the procedures. Additionally, jurors awarded significantly lower damages in the AI condition, underscoring the value of AI in reducing perceived bias.

2.1.2. AI's Influence on Perceived Objectivity and Trust

The results of the study also suggest that the use of AI helps reinforce the perception of objectivity in the financial management process. When jurors were asked to evaluate the perceived objectivity of the financial managers, they rated AI as more objective than human financial managers, especially in cases where independence concerns were prominent. This perception of objectivity plays a critical role in reducing jurors' assessments of negligence and, in turn, mitigating legal liability for financial managers.

By incorporating AI into financial management processes, financial managers can create a clearer distinction between their judgment and the technology's analysis, effectively shifting the focus away from potential biases that may arise from human relationships. This increased perception of objectivity builds greater trust in the financial management process, which is essential for defending against claims of negligence and bias.

2.2. Cryptocurrencies

Cryptocurrency transactions have introduced a novel set of challenges for financial managers, raising concerns regarding competence, resource allocation, risk management, and the absence of official guidance. This chapter explores the unique challenges of financial management cryptocurrencies, emphasizing their implications for client acceptance, retention, financial management planning, and evidence gathering. The rise of cryptocurrencies has significantly altered the landscape of financial transactions. However, the lack of clear and consistent regulatory guidance poses a major challenge for financial managers. The Public Company Finance Oversight Board (PCAOB) has expressed concern about digital assets and their impact on financial management processes. Although cryptocurrencies, including Bitcoin and Ethereum, have gained wide acceptance, they remain under-regulated in comparison to traditional financial assets. Without clear standards, financial managers are left navigating emerging risks without a comprehensive framework.

The inherent volatility, anonymity, and lack of centralized control in cryptocurrency transactions create additional risks when conducting financial statement financial managements. Financial management firms are required to consider these factors during client acceptance and retention and in planning financial management procedures. A key aspect of this process is understanding the client's use of cryptocurrencies and its alignment with the business purpose and strategy. Further complicating matters is the lack of consistent, authoritative guidance from regulators like the Financial Finance Standards Board (FASB) and the International Financial Reporting Standards (IFRS). As a result, financial managers must rely on principle-based finance, guidance from specialized publications, and their own developing expertise.

The advent of Robotic Process Automation (RPA) has sparked a transformative change in the way businesses manage their operations. With its ability to automate repetitive and rule-based tasks, RPA has unlocked significant efficiencies across various industries, including finance and finance. By mimicking human interactions with digital systems, RPA streamlines workflows, reduces errors, and accelerates task completion.

However, the integration of RPA into finance functions may have unintended consequences, particularly regarding the practices of earnings management (EM). EM refers to the manipulation of financial records, either through accruals-based methods (AM) or real activities manipulation (RM), to meet specific earnings targets. This chapter delves into the relationship between RPA adoption and EM in finance, exploring both its potential benefits and the risks it introduces.

2.3. Robotic Process Automation in Finance

RPA is a cutting-edge technology that enables businesses to automate highly repetitive tasks such as data entry, report generation, and transaction processing. Unlike traditional automation methods, RPA does not require deep integration with existing systems, making it a versatile and adaptable solution. The technology mimics human actions by interacting with digital interfaces, performing tasks such as keystrokes, navigating systems, and extracting data from various platforms. The result is faster, more accurate processes that significantly enhance operational efficiency.

In finance, RPA is particularly beneficial due to the rule-based nature of many financial tasks. For instance, reconciling accounts, processing invoices, and generating financial reports are all processes that lend themselves well to automation. RPA can handle these tasks more efficiently and accurately than human employees, thereby reducing the potential for human error. Furthermore, RPA's ability to provide real-time insights into financial data has the potential to improve decision-making and promote better financial reporting.

Despite these advantages, the widespread adoption of RPA in finance raises concerns regarding the potential for increased earnings management. As companies become more adept at using automated tools to manipulate financial data, there is a risk that they may exploit these technologies to artificially enhance earnings or meet performance targets. This chapter investigates how RPA adoption impacts both accruals-based EM and real activities manipulation, offering insights into the broader implications for financial reporting practices.

2.3.1. RPA in Earnings Management

The introduction of RPA into finance functions has the potential to reshape the landscape of earnings management. While RPA enhances operational efficiency and decision-making, it may also create new opportunities for managers to engage in both accrual-based and real activities-based earnings management. The technology's capacity to automate and standardize financial processes offers a double-edged sword—while it can improve accuracy and transparency, it also provides managers with powerful tools to manipulate financial outcomes.

2.3.2. Impact on Accrual-Based Earnings Management

RPA's ability to automate complex financial processes may inadvertently encourage accrual-based earnings management. By providing managers with real-time access to financial data and sophisticated reporting tools, RPA can facilitate the manipulation of financial statements. For example, managers may adjust estimates for bad debts or alter revenue recognition practices to meet earnings targets. While RPA can increase the speed and accuracy of these processes, it can also provide managers with greater opportunities to exercise discretion in finance choices, which can lead to the manipulation of earnings.

Moreover, RPA systems often operate based on predefined rules and algorithms. If these rules are not properly designed or monitored, there is a risk that the system could inadvertently reinforce earnings management practices. As companies adopt RPA without robust control mechanisms, the technology's potential for unintended consequences increases, particularly in the realm of accruals-based earnings management.

2.3.3. Impact on Real Activities Manipulation

RPA's ability to streamline operational tasks and provide real-time data also has the potential to influence real activities manipulation. Managers may use the technology to alter the timing of transactions, such as accelerating sales or delaying expenses, to meet short-term earnings targets. By automating data collection and analysis, RPA makes it easier for managers to identify areas where they can influence reported earnings through operational decisions.

Furthermore, RPA's efficiency and speed may create new opportunities for real activities manipulation. For instance, the automation of inventory management and production processes could encourage managers to overproduce goods or delay maintenance activities in order to reduce reported costs and inflate reported profits. While RPA can enhance operational performance, it may also enable managers to manipulate key financial indicators that reflect the company's true economic activities.

2.4. Cybersecurity & Financial Risk Management

In response to the increasing need for robust cybersecurity practices, the American Institute of Certified Public Financial analysts (AICPA), in partnership with the Financial Management Standards Board, has issued a voluntary cybersecurity reporting and assurance framework. This framework provides a set of guidelines that companies can follow to disclose their cybersecurity risk management efforts to external stakeholders. In this chapter, we integrate general concepts from enterprise risk management with AICPA's cybersecurity guidance, forming the foundation for a model of effective cybersecurity risk management.

This model outlines five stages:

A. Risk Identification and Prioritization
B. Control System Design
C. Testing the Operating Effectiveness of Cybersecurity Controls
D. External Cybersecurity Reporting
E. Assurance on External Cybersecurity Reporting

While the stages are presented sequentially, they should be viewed as a continuous and iterative process, with organizations revisiting each stage as new risks arise.

A. Risk Identification and Prioritization

The first step in effective cybersecurity risk management is identifying and prioritizing potential risks and vulnerabilities. This is crucial because failing to identify the right risks or giving them insufficient attention can result in significant security breaches. Finance firms can play a pivotal role here, as they have strong expertise in risk assessment. Many have been trained in financial management and internal controls, allowing them to apply these skills to cybersecurity risk assessment.

Financial analysists can employ sophisticated technologies, such as vulnerability scanning tools (e.g., Nessus, OpenVAS), to identify potential weaknesses in the company's network or systems. By conducting risk assessments and vulnerability scans, they can pinpoint where cybersecurity efforts should be focused. For example, in the Target breach, hackers exploited vulnerabilities in point-of-sale systems, which Target had failed to prioritize based on specific cybersecurity threats. A more comprehensive risk identification process could have helped prevent or mitigate the attack.

B. Control System Design

Once risks have been identified, organizations must design and implement controls to mitigate these risks. Financial analysts are uniquely positioned to assist in this stage due to their expertise in internal controls, including IT controls. While most cybersecurity controls are not explicitly required by Sarbanes-Oxley (SOX) regulations, financial analysts bring significant experience in evaluating internal controls that affect financial reporting, including IT-related controls.

Finance firms are also highly proficient in leveraging new technologies to design and implement cybersecurity controls. They stay up to date with innovations like Blockchain, advanced authentication methods, and cloud security, which are crucial in modern cybersecurity systems. By combining their knowledge of internal controls with their ability to evaluate and integrate cutting-edge technology, financial analysts can help design robust cybersecurity control systems.

The Home Depot breach, where hackers exploited vendor credentials and a vulnerability in Windows, highlights the importance of designing effective controls. Multifactor authentication for vendors, standardized remote access procedures, and more granular network segmentation could have significantly reduced the likelihood of this breach. Financial analysts, with their understanding of both IT systems and internal controls, could have identified and implemented these types of preventive measures.

C. Testing the Operating Effectiveness of Cybersecurity Controls

After cybersecurity controls are put in place, they must be tested regularly to ensure they are working effectively. Financial analysts, particularly those with IT financial management experience, are skilled in testing the operating effectiveness of controls. These professionals can develop and execute financial management programs to verify that cybersecurity controls are operating as intended and mitigating identified risks.

Finance firms also possess advanced technologies to test controls, such as tools that simulate cybersecurity attacks or analyse large datasets (e.g., suspicious login attempts, unusual data flows). These tools help assess the resilience of cybersecurity controls in real-world conditions.

The Anthem breach, which compromised personal information for millions of individuals, underscores the importance of effective testing. Insufficient monitoring of data outflows and unencrypted data allowed hackers to extract sensitive information over an extended period. If Anthem had regularly tested the operating effectiveness of their monitoring and encryption controls, the breach could have been detected sooner or prevented entirely.

D. External Cybersecurity Reporting

In response to growing demand from investors, customers, and other stakeholders, companies are increasingly required to disclose information about their cybersecurity practices. The AICPA's framework provides guidelines for companies to voluntarily report their cybersecurity risk management efforts. Financial analysts are ideally suited to assist in this stage, thanks to their expertise in preparing and presenting accurate external reports.

The reporting process includes a narrative description of the company's cybersecurity risk management program and management's assertions regarding its compliance with established guidelines. While financial analysts cannot independently assess the accuracy of these reports, their skills in external reporting can enhance the quality of the disclosures.

Financial analysts can also assist in evaluating the effectiveness of cybersecurity controls for management's assertions, as discussed in the Home Depot and Target breaches. External reporting can help companies restore trust and confidence with stakeholders, especially after a cybersecurity incident. Research suggests that well-executed external cybersecurity reporting can reduce the negative impact of data breaches on investor sentiment (Frank et al. 2019).

E. Assurance on External Cybersecurity Reporting

Independent assurance adds credibility to external cybersecurity reporting, especially after a company has experienced a cybersecurity incident. The AICPA's attestation guide for cybersecurity reports provides an independent assessment of the organization's cybersecurity risk management efforts. Financial analysts are skilled in assurance engagements and can evaluate the effectiveness of a company's cybersecurity program and the accuracy of their external reports.

Assurance services are especially valuable for companies that have experienced breaches, as research indicates that independent verification of cybersecurity disclosures helps restore investor confidence (Frank et al. 2019). For example, independent assurance over the cybersecurity risk management report of Target or Home Depot could have bolstered stakeholder confidence following their respective breaches.

2.5. Augmented Reality (AR) and Virtual Reality (VR)

The rapid evolution of financial services over the past few decades has been propelled by technological advancements, most notably through the integration of Augmented Reality (AR) and Virtual Reality (VR). These technologies are redefining customer engagement, service delivery, and education within the financial sector. The historical progression from traditional banking models to fintech solutions has paved the way for the adoption of immersive technologies. Researchers like Aggarwal and Karwasra (2023) and Meena (2023) have underscored how globalization and the proliferation of smart devices contributed to the digital economy's emergence, creating fertile ground for AR and VR applications.

2.5.1. Foundations and Distinctions Between AR and VR

The foundational concepts of AR and VR date back to the 1960s (Cipresso et al., 2018), with a clear differentiation. AR overlays digital content onto the real world, while VR creates a fully immersive digital environment. Scholars such as Enyedy and Yoon (2021) emphasize their educational potential, enriching environments and increasing engagement. Meanwhile, others like Soccini (2016) and Christensen et al. (2018) highlight the artistic and commercial potentials, projecting AR/VR as the next technological milestone. User experience (UX) is crucial in AR/VR success. Studies by Ghazwani and Smith (2020) and Chandana et al. (2023) stress challenges such as motion sickness and cognitive overload, pushing for more intuitive, human-centric designs.

2.5.2. Technological Advancements and Industrial Adoption

Technological developments, particularly in healthcare, retail, and industrial applications, have shown significant promise. Kitaria and Mwadulo (2022) detail AR/VR's transformative impact in healthcare, despite cost and security challenges. Similarly, McLean and Wilson (2019) and SikLanyi and Withers (2020) discuss how AR/VR enhances consumer experiences and industrial productivity, respectively.

2.5.3. Applications Across Sectors

Beyond healthcare, AR and VR have revolutionized architecture, engineering, tourism, and education (Tan et al., 2022; Siddiqui et al., 2022). These applications demonstrate AR/VR's ability to provide immersive, accessible experiences, though challenges like technological infrastructure and authenticity persist.

2.5.4. Theoretical Framework for Financial Services

Drawing parallels from other sectors, Goyal et al. (2023) propose a framework for AR/VR integration into finance, emphasizing customer-centric experiences, personalization, and ethical considerations. Saudagar et al. (2023) further stress customization, accessibility, and privacy as crucial pillars.

2.5.5. Enhancing Customer Experience

The ability of AR/VR to personalize and demystify financial services is a key benefit. Authors such as Soni et al. (2022) and Rane (2023) demonstrate that immersive technologies can improve customer satisfaction, loyalty, and financial literacy. Malik et al. (2020) suggest that customer relationship management could be revolutionized via AR/VR, facilitating more meaningful client interactions.

2.5.6. Regulatory and Security Considerations

The integration of these technologies is not without risks. Goyal et al. (2023) and Nnamonu et al. (2023) highlight cybersecurity threats, data privacy concerns, and the pressing need for robust regulatory frameworks to safeguard consumers.

3. FINANCIAL MANAGEMENT IN DIGITAL ERA: CASE STUDIES & REAL WORLD APPLICATIONS

The integration of Blockchain and Artificial Intelligence (AI) into financial management is reshaping the way organizations handle transactions, investments, compliance, and risk. These technologies offer enhanced security, transparency, automation, and predictive capabilities that address longstanding inefficiencies in financial systems. Indian banks, including the State Bank of India, are experimenting with Blockchain in areas such as vendor financing, syndicated loans, KYC (Know Your Customer), anti-money laundering (AML), and customer loyalty programs. Globally, financial institutions use Blockchain for secure transactions, smart contracts, data storage, and remittance services, reducing transaction fees significantly compared to traditional systems (Guo & Liang, 2016; Hassani et al., 2018).

Blockchain, known for its decentralized and immutable ledger system, is playing a transformative role in cross-border payments. For example, Ripple's Ripple Net enables real-time international money transfers by allowing financial institutions like Santander and PNC Bank to settle transactions instantly and at significantly lower costs. This has helped reduce reliance on intermediaries, speeding up transactions and enhancing transparency.

Another key application of Blockchain lies in smart contracts, particularly within Decentralized Finance (DeFi). Platforms such as Aave and Compound allow users to lend and borrow cryptocurrencies without involving traditional financial intermediaries. Smart contracts automate these processes, embedding loan terms directly into code and executing transactions once conditions are met. This approach minimizes credit risk and streamlines lending while offering users full control over their assets.

Blockchain also enhances auditing and regulatory compliance. For instance, PwC's Halo audit tool leverages Blockchain to perform real-time verification of cryptocurrency transactions and balances. This capability ensures transparency, minimizes fraud, and improves the efficiency of audit processes by providing a reliable, tamper-proof trail of financial activity.

On the other hand, AI contributes significantly to fraud detection, investment management, and credit assessment. Mastercard's Decision Intelligence system employs AI to monitor and analyse patterns in transaction data. By learning from past behaviour, the system can detect fraudulent transactions with a high degree of accuracy in real time, reducing both losses and customer inconvenience caused by false positives.

AI also powers Robo-advisors like Betterment and Wealth front, which provide automated, personalized investment services. These platforms use algorithms to assess an individual's financial goals and risk tolerance, creating tailored portfolios and offering features like tax-loss harvesting and automatic rebalancing. This democratizes access to quality investment management, making it more affordable and scalable.

In the realm of lending, AI-driven credit scoring platforms such as Zest AI have revolutionized underwriting. By analysing hundreds of data points, including alternative credit indicators, these systems provide more inclusive and accurate assessments of borrower risk. As a result, lenders can offer loans to individuals who may have been overlooked by traditional credit models while maintaining low default rates.

A particularly powerful development emerges from the combination of Blockchain and AI. In trade finance, IBM and Maersk's Trade Lens platform utilizes Blockchain to maintain a transparent and immutable ledger of shipping and trade documents. Simultaneously, AI analyses this data to identify bottlenecks and predict potential risks. This integration significantly improves supply chain visibility, reduces paperwork, and optimizes trade operations.

Another innovative collaboration is seen in the work of Singularity NET and Ocean Protocol, which merge decentralized AI with Blockchain-secured data sharing. This model allows organizations to analyse financial data while preserving data privacy and control. Blockchain ensures secure and traceable data access, while AI provides advanced financial forecasting and decision-making capabilities.

In summary, the synergy of Blockchain and artificial intelligence is delivering tangible benefits in financial management. From fraud prevention and automated investing to cross-border payments and decentralized lending, these technologies are not only enhancing operational efficiency but also enabling more inclusive, transparent, and intelligent financial ecosystems.

4. CHALLENGES AND LIMITATIONS OF BLOCKCHAIN AND ARTIFICIAL INTELLIGENCE IN FINANCIAL MANAGEMENT

While Blockchain and artificial intelligence offer transformative potential in financial management, their adoption is not without significant challenges and limitations. One of the primary concerns with Blockchain technology is scalability. Most public Blockchain, such as Bitcoin and Ethereum, struggle with high transaction volumes, often leading to network congestion, slower processing times, and increased fees. Although newer consensus mechanisms like proof-of-stake aim to address these issues, they are still under scrutiny in terms of security and decentralization. Another limitation is the lack of regulatory clarity. In many jurisdictions, regulatory frameworks for Blockchain and cryptocurrencies remain ambiguous, creating legal uncertainties for financial institutions that wish to integrate Blockchain-based systems. Furthermore, the immutability of Blockchain, while beneficial for security, becomes a liability in cases of errors or fraud, as reversing or altering transactions is nearly impossible once recorded.

In the case of AI, data dependency is a critical barrier. The effectiveness of AI models in financial applications hinges on the availability of vast, high-quality datasets. However, financial data is often sensitive and subject to strict privacy regulations like GDPR and CCPA, which can limit its accessibility. Moreover, AI systems are susceptible to algorithmic bias—models trained on biased historical data may perpetuate existing inequities, particularly in areas like credit scoring or loan approval. Another concern is the lack of explain ability in many AI systems. Financial decisions made by AI, such as credit denial or investment recommendations, often cannot be fully explained to customers or regulators due to the "black box" nature of deep learning algorithms, raising questions about transparency and accountability.

Both technologies also face integration challenges within legacy financial infrastructure. Many financial institutions still operate on decades-old systems that are not readily compatible with decentralized platforms or AI-driven analytics, requiring costly and time-consuming overhauls. Additionally, there is a shortage of skilled professionals with expertise in both emerging technologies and financial systems, which hampers implementation and innovation. Finally, there are cybersecurity and ethical concerns, especially when combining AI and Blockchain. While Blockchain is often praised for its security, smart contracts and decentralized applications (dApps) are not immune to code vulnerabilities. Similarly, AI systems can be targeted through adversarial attacks or data poisoning, leading to flawed or dangerous outcomes in financial decision-making.

In summary, while Blockchain and AI are revolutionizing financial management, their implementation is constrained by technical, regulatory, ethical, and organizational challenges. A balanced approach that includes stronger regulatory frameworks, better data governance, ethical AI practices, and robust infrastructure modernization is essential to unlock their full potential responsibly. Several operational challenges hinder the seamless adoption of AR/VR in finance. High costs, technological immaturity, and a steep learning curve are recurring barriers (Dinh et al., 2023; Marín-Rodriguez et al., 2023). Organizational readiness and alignment with business goals also play a critical role (Papanastasiou et al., 2018).

4.1. The Challenge of Financial Managers' Independence

Independence is a core principle of financial management, as financial managers are expected to remain unbiased and objective when conducting financial managements for clients. However, maintaining independence in practice is fraught with challenges. Financial management firms often develop close relationships with their clients in order to secure cooperation and long-term business relationships. This dynamic, while beneficial for business growth, may lead to the perception that the financial manager's objectivity is compromised, especially in cases where financial managers have greater financial dependence on the client or provide non-financial management services that could create conflicts of interest.

Research has shown that such perceived independence concerns can lead to increased legal liability for financial managers. For instance, in litigation involving financial managers, plaintiff attorneys frequently leverage the perception of bias to sway jurors' emotions, making it difficult for financial managers to defend themselves against claims of negligence. Moreover, factors like the financial manager-client relationship and the financial manager's role in decision-making can amplify these concerns, exposing financial management firms to greater litigation risk.

4.2. Client Acceptance and Retention: A Risk-Based Approach

Client acceptance and retention decisions are critical components of any financial management engagement. Under the PCAOB's quality control standards, financial management firms must ensure they have the requisite competence and resources to perform a financial manager. When dealing with clients involved in cryptocurrency transactions, financial managers face a unique challenge: the absence of experience and understanding in digital asset transactions can influence resource estimation and risk assessment.

A model developed for cryptocurrency client acceptance and retention assesses risks across four quadrants based on the firm's competence, access to resources, and the client's competency in cryptocurrency management. High-risk clients—where either the firm or the client lacks the required expertise—demand careful consideration and a resource-intensive approach. Financial managers must address the increased complexity and assess whether their existing internal controls and expertise are sufficient for handling cryptocurrency transactions.

5. CONCLUSION: IMPLICATIONS FOR THE FUTURE OF FINANCIAL REPORTING

As financial management firms continue to integrate AI into their practices, they are not only improving the efficiency and accuracy of their financial managements but also addressing critical issues related to financial manager independence and perceived bias. The use of AI, as demonstrated by Libby and Witz (2024), offers financial management firms a valuable tool to mitigate legal risks, enhance perceived objectivity, and ultimately reinforce trust in the financial management process. The future of financial management may well lie in the strategic use of AI, enabling firms to maintain strong client relationships while preserving their independence and credibility in the eyes of regulators, litigants, and the public. The fragmented reporting of misconduct in the finance profession presents a serious challenge to maintaining trust and integrity in the industry. The proposed Financial Blockchain offers a transformative solution that could aggregate misconduct data in real time, ensuring transparency and fairness across the profession. While the road to implementation is fraught with technical, logistical, and financial challenges, the potential benefits are profound: increased trust, more timely information, and a stronger finance profession overall.

The future of the finance profession may well hinge on the adoption of such innovative technologies, helping to safeguard the integrity of the profession for years to come. Financial management firms are investing heavily in artificial intelligence (AI) to enhance the efficiency and effectiveness of financial management processes, as well as to improve perceived objectivity and trust. A recent study by Libby and Witz (2024) highlights that AI can help mitigate legal liability in situations where financial manager independence is questioned, particularly by reducing the negative impact of perceived conflicts of interest on juror negligence assessments.

The study suggests that AI's role in analytical procedures can help financial managers defend themselves against accusations of bias, especially when relationships with financial management clients are perceived as too friendly. The chapter specifies when financial managers used AI instead of humans for analytical procedures, jurors were less likely to find the financial management firm negligent and awarded lower damages, especially when there were concerns about financial manager independence. AI helped reinforce the perception of objectivity and reduced the likelihood of financial managers being seen as biased, which is crucial in mitigating legal risks associated with financial management work.

This chapter provides financial management firms with a potential solution to the long-standing dilemma of balancing favourable client relationships with the need to maintain an unbiased and independent financial management process. The use of AI could thus become an essential tool in managing the risks associated with financial manager independence concerns. Furthermore, the study suggests that AI's objectivity-enhancing capabilities could influence defence strategies in litigation, encouraging attorneys to focus on AI's role in reducing bias.

In practical terms, financial management firms should consider integrating AI across various stages of the financial management process to benefit from its perceived objectivity. This could help manage legal liability risks while ensuring the financial management process remains high-quality and trustworthy. However, the deployment of AI must be done consistently and with proper training to ensure its effectiveness and the reliability of the data it processes.

6. RECOMMENDATIONS FOR FINANCIAL MANAGERS

The growing prominence of cryptocurrency transactions poses a significant challenge to the financial management profession. The absence of standardized guidance and the complexities involved in verifying, valuing, and ensuring the accuracy of cryptocurrency transactions increase the risk of material misstatement. Consequently, financial managers must continually enhance their knowledge and skills regarding cryptocurrencies, build internal expertise, and invest in specialized software tools to address these challenges.

Financial management firms should prioritize training their staff, hiring specialists with digital asset expertise, and fostering a culture of cryptocurrency awareness within the organization. In addition, during the planning stage, financial managers must pay careful attention to the client's internal controls and consider implementing compensating controls where weaknesses are identified. As the cryptocurrency landscape continues to evolve rapidly, financial managers must remain flexible, stay informed about industry developments, and adapt their financial management procedures to mitigate emerging risks. Looking ahead, AR and VR are poised to drive Financial Services 4.0, emphasizing mixed reality experiences, blockchain integration, and smarter educational tools (Narayanan et al., 2021; Ashta and Hermann, 2021). Zhao et al. (2023) predict these technologies will shape the next generation of financial literacy and decision-making frameworks.

This chapter offers a foundational framework to assist financial managers in navigating the complexities of cryptocurrency financial managements, but it is important to recognize that new risks may emerge as the cryptocurrency ecosystem evolves. Financial managers must continue to update their approaches, ensuring that they meet the evolving standards and best practices in the field of cryptocurrency financial management. The chapter proposes the establishment of a Council of Blockchain Technology to regulate, promote, and standardize block chain adoption in banking. Legislative updates, particularly to the Information Technology Act, 2000, are recommended to accommodate block chain's decentralized nature. Emphasis is placed on cross-industry collaboration, education and awareness campaigns, and pilot projects to demonstrate block chain's economic value and foster broader acceptance.

6.1. The Proposed Blockchain Model

To implement Blockchain in the context of finance misconduct, a new Blockchain-based system could be established, which we will call the Financial Blockchain. The idea is to create a platform in which key stakeholders—state boards, CPA societies, regulatory bodies (e.g. IRS, SEC, PCAOB), and the AICPA—can contribute and access information regarding misconduct in real time.

A. Identifying Practitioners

One of the first steps in building this system is to uniquely identify each CPA. Rather than using personal details, which could raise privacy concerns, each CPA could be assigned a unique digital address or account on the Blockchain. This account would serve as the practitioner's identifier within the system. Upon passing the CPA exam, a practitioner could receive a digital endorsement from the AICPA, indicating that they have met the necessary professional qualification standards. Similarly, each state board of finance could issue an endorsement for practitioners who are licensed within their state.

B. Reporting and Sharing Misconduct

The key feature of this Blockchain is its ability to facilitate the reporting and sharing of misconduct. Any of the key participants (state boards, CPA societies, regulatory agencies, etc.) could have the authority to report misconduct incidents (e.g., fraud, license suspension) by adding them as transactions on the Blockchain. Each transaction would be immutable, ensuring that once misconduct is recorded, it cannot be altered or erased. For example, if the SEC identifies a CPA engaging in fraudulent activities, the SEC could record the misconduct on the financial Blockchain. This would be available to all other participants, such as state boards, the AICPA, and potential employers, who could view the practitioner's history of sanctions and decide whether to engage with them.

C. Transparency and Trust

Since the Blockchain is public, all interested parties can view the misconduct data in real time. Importantly, no single entity controls the Blockchain, ensuring transparency and trust. The decentralized nature of the Blockchain ensures that no party can manipulate or withhold information, promoting fairness and accountability across the profession. By having a collective of trusted parties maintaining the Blockchain, the system ensures that misconduct records are accurate, up-to-date, and complete. Practitioners' records would reflect their qualifications, any sanctions or violations, and the history of their professional behaviour—helping employers, regulators, and clients make informed decisions about who to trust with important finance tasks.

REFERENCES

Aggarwal, V., & Karwasra, N. (2023). A bibliometric analysis on trade openness and economic growth: Current dynamics and future direction. *Competitiveness Review*. Advance online publication. DOI: 10.1108/CR-11-2022-0177

Arora, S., & Nabi, T. (2022). Blockchain adoption in banking systems: A boon or bane? In *Applications, challenges, and opportunities of blockchain technology in banking and insurance* (pp. 19–42). IGI Global. DOI: 10.4018/978-1-6684-4133-6.ch002

Arora, S., Nabi, T., & Bhardwaj, M. Blockchain technology: A double-edged sword when it comes to sustainable food security. *Empirical Economics Letters, 22*, 67-88.

Arora, S., Oberoi, S., Nabi, T., & Verma, B. (2024). How does blockchain impact sustainable food security? Insights from literature review. *International Journal of Information Management Data Insights*, *4*(2), 100276. DOI: 10.1016/j.jjimei.2024.100276

Ashta, A., & Herrmann, H. (2021). Artificial intelligence and fintech: An overview of opportunities and risks for banking, investments, and microfinance. *Strategic Change*, *30*(3), 211–222. DOI: 10.1002/jsc.2404

Avkiran, N. K. (2006). Developing foreign bank efficiency models for DEA grounded in finance theory. *Socio-Economic Planning Sciences*, *40*(4), 275–296. DOI: 10.1016/j.seps.2004.10.006

Banker, R. D., Charnes, A., & Cooper, W. W. (1984). Some models for estimating technical and scale inefficiencies in data envelopment analysis. *Management Science*, *30*(9), 1078–1092. DOI: 10.1287/mnsc.30.9.1078

Chandana, B. H., Shaik, N., & Chitralingappa, P. (2023). Exploring the Frontiers of User Experience Design: VR, AR, and the Future of Interaction. In *2023 International Conference on Computer Science and Emerging Technologies (CSET)* (pp. 1-6). IEEE. DOI: DOI: 10.1109/CSET58993.2023.10346724

Charnes, A., Cooper, W. W., & Rhodes, E. (1978). Measuring the efficiency of decision-making units. European Journal of Operational Research, 2(6), 429–444. https://doi.org/ 90229-7.DOI: 10.1016/0377-2217(79)

Christensen, C. M., McDonald, R., Altman, E. J., & Palmer, J. E. (2018). Disruptive innovation: An intellectual history and directions for future research. *Journal of Management Studies*, *55*(7), 1043–1078. DOI: 10.1111/joms.12349

Cipresso, P., Giglioli, I. A. C., Raya, M. A., & Riva, G. (2018). The past, present, and future of virtual and augmented reality research: a network and cluster analysis of the literature. Frontiers in psychology, p.2086. https://doi.org/DOI: 10.3389/fpsyg.2018.02086

Cowley, S. (2012). FBI Director: Cybercrime Will Eclipse Terrorism. Available at: https://money.cnn.com/2012/03/02/technology/fbi_cybersecurity/

Das, A., & Ghosh, S. (2006). Financial deregulation and efficiency: An empirical analysis of Indian banks during the post-reform period. Review of Financial Economics, 15(3), 193–221. https://doi.org/. rfe.2005.06.002DOI: 10.1016/j

Dinh, A., Tseng, E., Yin, A. L., Estrin, D., Greenwald, P., & Fortenko, A. (2023). Perceptions About Augmented Reality in Remote Medical Care: Interview Study of Emergency Telemedicine Providers. *JMIR Formative Research*, *7*, e45211. DOI: 10.2196/45211 PMID: 36976628

Drake, L., & Hall, M. J. (2003). Efficiency in Japanese banking: An empirical analysis. *Journal of Banking & Finance*, *27*(5), 891–917. DOI: 10.1016/S0378-4266(02)00240-6

Eaton, T. V., Grenier, J. H., & Layman, D. (2019). Accounting and Cybersecurity Risk Management. *Current Issues in Auditing*, *13*(2), C1–C9. https://publications.aaahq.org/cia/article/13/2/C1/7123/Accounting-and-Cybersecurity-Risk-Management. DOI: 10.2308/ciia-52419

Enyedy, N., & Yoon, S. (2021). Immersive environments: Learning in augmented+ virtual reality. International handbook of computer-supported collaborative learning, pp.389-405. DOI: 10.1007/978 3 030 65291 3_21

Frank, M. L., Grenier, J. H., & Pyzoha, J. S. (2019). How disclosing a prior cyberattack influences the efficacy of cybersecurity risk management reporting and independent assurance. *Journal of Information Systems*, *33*(3), 183–200. Advance online publication. DOI: 10.2308/isys-52374

Ghazwani, Y., & Smith, S. (2020). Interaction in augmented reality: Challenges to enhance user experience. In *Proceedings of the 2020 4th International Conference on Virtual and Augmented Reality Simulations* (pp. 39- 44). https://doi.org/DOI: 10.1145/3385378.3385384

Gopalkrishnan, S., Mohanty, S. P., & Jaiwani, M. (2023). Do efficiencies really matter? Analysing the housing finance sector and deriving insights through data envelopment analysis. *Cogent Economics & Finance*, *11*(2), 2285158. DOI: 10.1080/23322039.2023.2285158

Goyal, N., Chauhan, S. S., Pandey, S., Singh, R., Kumar, A., & Joshi, K. (2023) Financial Services 4.0-Future Perspective based on Mixed Reality. In 2023 IEEE International Conference on Contemporary Computing and Communications (InC4) (Vol. 1, pp. 1-4). IEEE. DOI: DOI: 10.1109/InC457730.2023.10263246

Gulati, R., & Kumar, S. (2017). Analysing banks' intermediation and operating efficiencies using the two-stage network DEA model. *International Journal of Productivity and Performance Management*, *66*(4), 500–516. DOI: 10.1108/IJPPM-03-2016-0055

Guo, Y., & Liang, C. (2016). Blockchain application and outlook in the banking industry. *Financial Innovation*, *2*(1), 1–12. DOI: 10.1186/s40854-016-0034-9

Hassani, H., Huang, X., & Silva, E. (2018). Banking with blockchain-ed big data. *Journal of Management Analytics*, *5*(4), 256–275. DOI: 10.1080/23270012.2018.1528900

Ilyas, A. M., & Rajasekaran, S. (2019). An empirical investigation of efficiency and productivity in the Indian non-life insurance market. *Benchmarking*, *26*(7), 2343–2371. DOI: 10.1108/BIJ-01-2019-0039

Information Systems Research. Journal of Information Systems. Volume XX, Number XX, pp.1-46. https://publications.aaahq.org/jis/article/doi/10.2308/ISYS-2023-061/13339/Neuroaccounting-Integrating-Neurophysiological

Kaur, S., & Gupta, P. K. (2015). Productive efficiency mapping of the Indian banking system using data envelopment analysis. *Procedia Economics and Finance*, *25*, 227–238. DOI: 10.1016/S2212-5671(15)00733-9

Kitaria, D., & Mwadulo, M. (2022). Adoption of Augmented Reality (AR) and Virtual Reality (VR) in healthcare systems. African Journal of Science, Technology. *Innovation and Sustainability*, *1*(1). Advance online publication. DOI: 10.58506/ajstss.v1i1.70

Kumar, S., & Gulati, R. (2008). An examination of technical, pure technical, and scale efficiencies in Indian public sector banks using data envelopment analysis. *Eurasian Journal of Business and Economics*, *1*(2), 33–69.

Lai, H. K., & Hsieh, S. F. (2024). Evaluating the Impact of Robotic Process Automation on Earnings Management. *Journal of Information Systems*, *XX*(XX), 1–31. https://publications.aaahq.org/jis/article/doi/10.2 08/ISYS-2024-032/13273/Evaluating-the-Impact-of-Robotic-Process

Libby, R., & Witz, P. D. (2024). Can artificial intelligence reduce the effect of independence conflicts on audit firm liability? *Contemporary Accounting Research*, *41*(2), 1346–1375. DOI: 10.1111/1911-3846.12941

Libby, R., & Witz, P. D. (2024). Artificial Intelligence in Auditing: How Auditor AI Use Can Mitigate Legal Liability. *Current Issues in Auditing, XX*(XX), 1–11. https://www.researchgate.net/publication/378512804_Can_artificial_intelligence_reduce_the_effect_of_independence_conflicts_on_audit_firm_liability. DOI: 10.2308/CIIA-2024-029

Liu, M., Wu, K., & Xu, J. (2019). How Will Blockchain Technology Impact Auditing and Accounting: Permission less Versus Permissioned Blockchain. *Current Issues in Auditing, 13*(2), A19–A29. https://publications.aaahq.org/cia/article/13/2/A19/7134/How-Will-Blockchain-Technology-Impact-Auditing-and. DOI: 10.2308/ciia-52540

Malik, H. R., Nawaz, N. A., & Al-Zghoul, M. B. (2020). Impact of Augmented Reality and Virtual Reality in the Transformation of Virtual Customer Relationship Management Sector. In 2020 IEEE 7th International Conference on Engineering Technologies and Applied Sciences (ICETAS) (pp. 1-5). IEEE. DOI: DOI: 10.1109/ICETAS51660.2020.9484306

McLean, G., & Wilson, A. (2019). Shopping in the digital world: Examining customer engagement through augmented reality mobile applications. *Computers in Human Behavior, 101*, 210–224. DOI: 10.1016/j.chb.2019.07.002

Meena, R. (2023). The Impact of Financial technology on Financial Services: A Comprehensive Analysis. *Research Review International Journal of Multidisciplinary, 8*(3), 185–192. DOI: 10.31305/rrijm.2023.v08.n03.022

Mohanty, S. P., Gopalkrishnan, S., & Mahendra, A. (2021). The intertwined relationship of shadow banking and commercial banks' deposit growth: Evidence from India. *International Journal of Innovation Science, 14*(3/4), 570–587. DOI: 10.1108/IJIS-01-2021-0022

Nagrjuna, B., Gawande, N. M., Bhandari, D., Roy, M. S., & Adhav, S. (2012). Marketing Effectiveness and Business Performance of Housing Finance Institutions.

Nnamonu, O., Hammoudeh, M., & Dargahi, T. (2023). Metaverse Cybersecurity Threats and Risks Analysis: The case of Virtual Reality Towards Security Testing and Guidance Framework. In *2023 IEEE International Conference on Metaverse Computing, Networking and Applications (MetaCom)* (pp. 94-98). IEEE. DOI: DOI: 10.1109/MetaCom57706.2023.00028

Oberoi, S., Arora, S., Verma, B., & Roy, K. K. (2024). What do we know about artificial intelligence and blockchain technology integration in the healthcare industry? In *Driving decentralization and disruption with digital technologies* (pp. 124–138). IGI Global Scientific Publishing. DOI: 10.4018/979-8-3693-3253-5.ch009

Oberoi, S., & Kansra, P. (2021). Motivating antecedents and consequences of blockchain technology in the insurance industry. In *Blockchain technology and applications for digital marketing* (pp. 276–285). IGI Global. DOI: 10.4018/978-1-7998-8081-3.ch017

Oberoi, S., & Kansra, P. (2022). Blockchain technology in the insurance industry. In *Applications, challenges, and opportunities of blockchain technology in banking and insurance* (pp. 160–172). IGI Global. DOI: 10.4018/978-1-6684-4133-6.ch009

Oyewole, A. T., Adeoye, O. B., Addy, W. A., Okoye, C. C., Ofodile, O. C., & Ugochukwu, C. E.Adedoyin Tolulope OyewoleOmotayo Bukola AdeoyeWilhelmina Afua AddyChinwe Chinazo OkoyeOnyeka Chrisanctus OfodileChinonye Esther Ugochukwu. (2024). Augmented and virtual reality in financial services: A review of emerging applications. *World Journal of Advanced Research and Reviews.*, *21*(03), 551–567. DOI: 10.30574/wjarr.2024.21.3.0623

Papanastasiou, G. P., Drigas, A., Skianis, C., Lytras, M. D., & Papanastasiou, E. (2018). Virtual and augmented reality effects on K-12, higher and tertiary education students' twenty-first century skills. *Virtual Reality (Waltham Cross)*, *23*(4), 425–436. DOI: 10.1007/s10055-018-0363-2

Rane, N. (2023). Enhancing customer loyalty through Artificial Intelligence (AI), Internet of Things (IoT), and Big Data technologies: improving customer satisfaction, engagement, relationship, and experience. Internet of Things (IoT), and Big Data Technologies: Improving Customer Satisfaction, Engagement, Relationship, and Experience. DOI: 10.2139/ssrn.4616051

Raut, R., Deshpande, A., Arora, S., Mittal, A., & Alandikar, R. (2022, December). An examination of the pricing of IPOs: The Indian perspective. In *2022 5th International Conference on Contemporary Computing and Informatics (IC3I)* (pp. 155-159). IEEE.

Rotaru, K., Rose, J. M., Ganbold, O., Anna, M. R., Loveridge, J., & Stamatelatos, A. (2024). Neuroaccounting. *Integrating Neurophysiological Techniques into Accounting and Accounting*, *13*(3), 21582440231190821. DOI: 10.1177/21582440231190821

Saudagar, A. K. J., Kumar, A., & Khan, M. B. (2023). MediverseBeyond Boundaries: A Comprehensive Analysis of AR and VR Integration in Medical Education for Diverse Abilities. *Journal of Digital Research.*, *3*(1), 20230066. DOI: 10.57197/JDR-2023-0066

Sheldon, M. D. (2018). Using Blockchain to Aggregate and Share Misconduct Issues across the Accounting Profession. *Current Issues in Auditing*, *12*(2), A27–A35. https://publications.aaahq.org/cia/article/12/2/A27/6992/Using-Blockchain-to-Aggregate-and-Share-Misconduct. DOI: 10.2308/ciia-52184

Sik Lanyi, C., & Withers, J. D. A.SikLanyi. (2020). Striving for a Safer and More Ergonomic Workplace: Acceptability and Human Factors Related to the Adoption of AR/VR Glasses in Industry 4.0. *Smart Cities*, *3*(2), 289–307. DOI: 10.3390/smartcities3020016

Soccini, A. M. (2016). Virtual and Augmented Reality in the Art of Lucio Fontana. In *EVA'16 Proceedings of the conference on Electronic Visualisation and the Arts* (pp. 144-149). British Computer Society. http://dx.doi.org/DOI: 10.14236/ewic/EVA2016.30

Soni, S., Yadav, U., & Soni, A. (2022). Virtual Reality & Augmented Reality: A way to Digital Transformation of Customer Engagement. In *2022 International Conference on Machine Learning, Big Data, Cloud and Parallel Computing (COM-IT-CON)* (Vol. 1, pp. 573-577). IEEE. DOI: DOI: 10.1109/COM-IT-CON54601.2022.9850954

Sufian, F. (2008). Revenue shift and the non-bank institutions' productivity: Empirical evidence from Malaysia. *Studies in Economics and Finance*, *25*(2), 75–92. DOI: 10.1108/10867370810879410

Sufian, F. (2011). Benchmarking the efficiency of the Korean banking sector: A DEA approach. *Benchmarking*, *18*(1), 107–127. DOI: 10.1108/14635771111109841

Swan, M. (2015). Blockchain: Blueprint for a new economy. O'Reilly Media, Inc.
Tapscott, D., & Tapscott, A. (2017). How blockchain will change organizations. *MIT Sloan Management Review*, *58*(2), 10–13.

Tan, Y., Xu, W., Li, S., & Chen, K. (2022). Augmented and Virtual Reality (AR/VR) for Education and Training in the AEC Industry: A Systematic Review of Research and Applications. *Buildings (Basel, Switzerland)*, *12*(10), 1529. DOI: 10.3390/buildings12101529

Verma, B., Bhardwaj, M., Arora, S., & Oberoi, S. (2025). Unveiling the impact of remittances on productive efficiencies: Investigating productivity growth of prominent remittance-receiving developing nations. *International Journal of Productivity and Performance Management*, *74*(4), 1101–1124. DOI: 10.1108/IJPPM-05-2023-0213

Vincent, N. E., & Wilkins, A. M. (2020). Challenges when Auditing Cryptocurrencies. *Current Issues in Auditing*, *14*(1), A46–A58. https://publications.aaahq.org/cia/article/14/1/A46/7049/Challenges-when-Auditing-Cryptocurrencies. DOI: 10.2308/ciia-52675

Zhao, Q., Tsai, P. H., & Wang, J. L. (2019). Improving financial service innovation strategies for enhancing china's banking industry competitive advantage during the fintech revolution: A Hybrid MCDM model. *Sustainability (Basel)*, *11*(5), 1419. DOI: 10.3390/su11051419

Zhao, X., Ren, Y. and Cheah, K.S. (2023). Leading Virtual Reality (VR) and Augmented Reality (AR) in Education: Bibliometric and Content Analysis from the Web of Science (2018–2022). SAGE Open

Chapter 8
A Structural Equation Modelling Approach to the Linkage of Financial Attitude, Financial Behavior, and Financial Knowledge Towards Digital Financial Literacy

Mansi Yadav
https://orcid.org/0000-0003-3045-0902
K.R. Mangalam University, India

Akanksha Kathuria
https://orcid.org/0000-0001-7887-5710
K.R. Mangalam University, India

Firdous Ahmad Malik
https://orcid.org/0000-0002-7815-0143
University of People, USA

ABSTRACT

The current study focusses on how the independent variables financial attitude (FA), financial behaviour (FB), and financial knowledge (FK)) are related to the degree of digital financial literacy (DFL) among working people in Delhi NCR, India. This study investigates financial literacy among employed individuals in the Delhi-National

DOI: 10.4018/979-8-3373-1290-3.ch008

Capital Region, using a sample of 354 participants from public and private enterprises. Data was gathered through a structured questionnaire. To analyze variable relationships and assess model validity, Structural Equation Modeling (SEM) was applied This study employs route analysis to examine the relationship among three independent variables for hypothesis testing. The findings reveal that digital financial literacy synergizes with financial behaviour and financial attitude, indicating that individuals with higher digital financial literacy have a propensity for responsible financial actions and positive perceptions toward financial management.

1. INTRODUCTION

The constant digital revolution continues to define various aspects of everyday life, with the financial sector being particularly highly affected. In the last several decades, there has been a significant trend towards the utilisation of digital financial products. Digital Financial Services (DFS) have seen worldwide popularity as one of the major contributors to financial inclusion, having substantially increased access to financial capital (Lyons, Kass-Hanna, & Greenlee, 2020). DFS have grown significantly in India at a fast pace, promoting innovative services consistent with the vision of the government for a digitally empowered economy. DFS is defined as the capability to access and use financial services via digital channels at any point in time. These services now bear significant importance in the economy, unveiling instruments such as virtual banking, APIs, digital lending, and alternative credit scoring (OECD, 2013; Arora & Nabi, 2022). Since they have been largely adopted, the need to improve public awareness of financial well-being to have a secure financial future (Zhang, 2021) thus highlights the increasing need to raise digital financial literacy levels among people.

FL is currently the biggest issue faced by all nations worldwide. Knowing about, being skilled at, and having a positive attitude about money are all components of financial literacy. It facilitates sound decision-making and fosters personal growth (Thomas & Gupta, 2021). The purpose of the role that financial services companies like banks, brokerage, investments, and insurance play in the lives of their investors is to empower people with financial well-being rather than to influence them with the return, risk, or financing of their demands (Goyal et al. 2021).

"Financial behaviour spans a wide spectrum of four disciplines, namely, saving, spending, borrowing and investment." Individuals have distinct habits, and these behaviours are impacted by a complex interplay of factors, including family counsel, financial knowledge, social connections, advertisements, economic standing, relationship status, outlook on the future, and income levels, among others. Even if the investment portfolio is quite huge these days, locals still favour a few tried-

and-true methods and strategies. The goal of the government authorities and other administrative entities is to inform the populace about the value of making wise financial decisions and acting responsibly (Goyal et al. 2021). It appears that over the past several years, educators, community organisations, corporations, governmental organisations, and policymakers have begun to place a higher priority on the subject of FL. Well-informed individuals should be able to make better decisions for their families that will improve their financial security and general well-being (Yadav & Banerji, 2024). Family stability improves a family's capacity to contribute to a vibrant community, which in turn supports local economic growth. As a result, FL is crucial for communities as well as for each household and family.

The suggestion of education is a frequent remedy for this lack of financial awareness, based on the common presumption that more information would lead to more wise financial decisions. According to some data, the connection between knowledge and behaviour is more complex than previously thought because greater knowledge does not always translate into better behaviour (Taylor & Noë, 2021). Chujan, Ngoc, and Faizi (2022) highlighted that psychological elements like locus of control may operate as a mediating component in the effect of financial information on behaviour. The available evidence implies that financial literacy is crucial, but there are still uncertainties regarding the precise nature of knowledge's influence on overall financial well-being.

Digital financial literacy (DFL) is increasing due to the Fintech revolution and the prevalence of mobile phones among over 67 per cent of the global population. Digital finance provides a promising approach to improving financial inclusion (Yadav & Banerji, 2024). The recent World Bank call for Universal financial access (UFA) by 2020 reflects the global significance of financial inclusion. This study discloses the important function of both financial and digital literacy in enhancing financial resilience and financial inclusion (Kass-Hanna, Lyons). While Yadav and Banerji (2024) presented several features of DFL, no consensus definition has yet been reached. In the digitalised age, DFL is the cornerstone for using digital financial services, and DFL is a necessary element of study in this new digital era (Morgan et al., 2020). DFL can be described as the digital alternative to core Financial literacy (2018; Setiawan et al., 2020). Kumar et al. (2019) emphasise the financial inclusion of adolescents and prefer virtual banking tools as an ideal method for promoting. Financial inclusion is improved via DFL. Security concerns with digital technologies in financial transactions are always a hurdle that prevents individuals from adopting them completely.

The existing literature revealed that because of the immense potential of Digital financial literacy in the era of digitalisation more works need to be done to unfold its aspects that benefit in economic growth (Alliance for Financial Inclusion, 2021). There is a strong urge to measure and analyze Digital financial literacy that helps in shaping financial inclusion (Morgan et al., 2019). There is a clear need for robust global research to comprehend the impact of the increasing digitization of the financial services sector (Seldal & Nyhus, 2022; Kass-Hanna, Lyons, & Liu, 2022). This highlights the growing importance of evaluating financial literacy in today's digital landscape. According to Tian (2022), individuals should take initiative in enhancing their digital financial literacy, as it plays a crucial role in reducing household debt levels and minimising systemic financial risks. In spite of this applicability, hitherto there has not been any study that has brought forth a psychometrically tested scale to assess the DFL. To participate meaningfully in the digital economy, one needs not only the essential financial knowledge and competence but also technical proficiency to operate digital devices like smartphones, tablets, and mobile phones (Carlin et al., 2019). Parallelly, it is important to regularly assess people's digital financial literacy as well as the numerous factors that affect it so that proper digital financial education programs can be designed and modified accordingly. So, governments, schools, and financial institutions must make digital financial education a priority and encourage it in every walk of life. This will help policymakers and stakeholders to determine existing deficiencies and take necessary action to correct them.

DFL is outlined by the OECD as "an integration of awareness, digital knowledge, skill, attitude, and behaviour necessary to make well-versed financial decisions on digital platforms and progressively targets in the attainment of financial goals." Financially aware people have a greater tendency for appropriate financial judgments and are comparatively less vulnerable to being misled about their financial situation. Tian (2022) previous research revealed that FL is extremely low on a global scale. To increase financial literacy, governments, institutions, and organisations are putting various efforts into practice, such as financial education programmes. For people to benefit the most from financial education programmes, they must be built around the numerous facets of FL, such as financial attitude, behaviour, and knowledge. A thorough evaluation of FL has been made available by the OECD. FA, FB, and FK are all combined to make up financial literacy, according to the OECD. Therefore, the emphasis is not only on financial awareness and knowledge but also on financial attitude and behaviour assessment to raise the degree of financial literacy among individuals.

The majority of the nation is struggling with the challenge of financial literacy. In order for an individual and their family to thrive financially, they must have a sufficient level of FK. Sound money management can influence consumer behaviour such that they are more prone to a financial crisis. Financial literacy education is now imperative as it can minimise the probability that a person would get cheated while making an investment decision (Asyik et al.,2022). In India, numerous digital financial services have been developed and implemented, and these are used by the customers, owing to the visionary mindset of the customers and the facilitating initiatives of the government bodies of India.

"Unified Payment Interface", "Bharat Interface for Money", Bharat Quick Response code, National Automated Clearing House, Rupay cards, National Electronic Toll Assortment, and Aadhaar Enabled Payment Administrations are a few of the digital financial services schemes that are extremely popular and readily accepted by all. Digital financial services have revolutionised the way people, institutions, and families make payments, borrow funds, settle bills, purchase monetary products, invest, and make remittances (Yang et al., 2020).

2. LITERATURE REVIEW

2.1 Financial Literacy

Financial literacy has been extensively researched using various methods worldwide, with many surveys employing objective instruments to measure general financial knowledge (Zulaihati et al., 2020). While some research only examines basic numeracy, others measure wider domains of personal finance (Goyal et al., 2021). Financial literacy, according to the OECD (2013), is critical to the growth and stability of the economy but lacks a common definition (Remund, 2010). The OECD has defined it as a combination of knowledge, behaviour, attitude, and awareness that allows an individual to make sound financial choices. Financial Attitude (FA), Financial Behaviour (FB), and Financial Knowledge (FK) are the most essential variables to determine financial literacy. Huston (2010) and Atkinson & Messy (2012) emphasise that, along with education and information, the ability to analyse and manage personal finances is important.

2.2 Attitude Towards Money

Attitude towards Money is the perception of an individual towards money and influences long-term savings and investment. Bhushan and Medury (2014) identify a good attitude for long-term benefit in future generations. Ibrahim and Alqaydi (2013) identify that financial knowledge promotes wise habits, like limiting the usage of credit. Research shows that attitude is closely related to financial behaviour, which further decides the general financial condition. Positive attitudes towards money among young people are linked with improved habits and improved financial literacy (Heuberger et al., 2018; Gill et al., 2018). Utkarsh et al. (2020) also observed a positive relationship between financial attitude and financial literacy.

2.3 Financial Behaviour

Financial behaviour encompasses how people handle money—e.g., saving, budgeting, investing, and paying bills on time. These behaviours are indicative of financial prudence and are essential in the evaluation of literacy (Bhushan & Medury, 2014; Kalekye & Memba, 2015). Financial behaviour is an important aspect of financial literacy, as reported by the OECD (2013). Atkinson and Messy (2012) emphasise that good money habits promote financial well-being, while bad habits, such as bad debt, can cause damage. Hasler and Lusardi (2017) identified that people less at ease with financial risk have difficulty with money management. Gender differences also emerge—women, even though more risk-averse, tend to have lower financial literacy, influencing their financial conduct and retirement saving (OECD, 2013; Hasler & Lusardi, 2017).

2.4 Financial Knowledge

Financial knowledge is the comprehension of some core financial concepts needed for successful money management (Sanderson, 2015). Incorporating financial education in schools will establish such knowledge at an early stage (Amagir et al., 2018). Hasler and Lusardi (2017) quantified financial literacy through simple questions regarding interest, inflation, and risk. People who possess better financial knowledge better manage their finances and are better prepared for retirement. The OECD (2013) emphasises the significance of financial knowledge in personal financial decision-making.

Even with education, most working-class individuals continue to face financial independence. There is limited literature on the subject in the Delhi NCR. This study hence endeavours to investigate financial literacy beliefs among working-class individuals in this area.

2.5 Financial Literacy to Digital Financial Literacy

As the digital era unfolds, the transition from traditional financial literacy to digital financial literacy has become increasingly important. With the ongoing evolution of digital technologies in the financial sector, skills and knowledge related to digital platforms and tools need to be acquired (Yadav & Banerji, 2023). Financial literacy digital is about understanding various things such as online banking, digital payments, budgeting apps, online investments, cybersecurity, and taking ethical financial behaviours in the digital environment (Asyik et al., 2022).

Financial literacy prevents individuals from facing potential financial issues (Cude, 2021). Financial literacy allows one to make intelligent and effective financial decisions (Shen et al., 2018). In the prevailing digital era, digital financial literacy is becoming a highly significant aspect of knowledge (Yadav & Banerji, 2024). Digital and financial literacy are hence highly essential to enhance (Stephen, 2022). The widespread use of internet platforms—accessible on computers, smartphones, laptops, and other electronic gadgets—has contributed immensely to the way customers engage with and acquire knowledge about financial concepts (Tiwari et al., 2020).

Research has consistently proven that financially literate individuals are more likely to adopt and utilise digital financial services (Panos & Wilson, 2020; Jain, 2022). Financial literacy in the digital age allows individuals to make better financial planning, gain access to diversified financial tools, and be involved in the digital financial world confidently (Meoli et al., 2022; Morgan & Trinh, 2019).

In today's digital age, security concerns around data are closely linked to the increasing importance of Digital Financial Literacy (DFL) (Yadav & Banerji, 2023). As more financial dealings are done through digital platforms, DFL involves the capacity to employ digital tools securely and understand the risks involved, such as identity theft, phishing, and data breaches. Since a deficiency of DFL increases one's vulnerability to these internet risks, the security of data is a critical part of money education (Lyons & Kass-Hanna, 2021).

2.6 A Conceptual Framework for Digital Financial Literacy

Lyons and Kass-Hanna (2021) first proposed a conceptual framework that demonstrates the interconnectedness of digital literacy, financial literacy, and digital financial literacy. Their framework encompasses five fundamental dimensions that are relevant to all three literacies, and also marks out the specific competencies for each. The five dimensions are: (1) fundamental knowledge and key skills; (2) knowledge of financial and digital products and services available; (3) adequate use of and access to these products; (4) decision-making, attitudes and money behaviour; and (5) consumer protection, including consumer rights and protection of personal data.

This model is important not just in outlining the elements of each of these literatures but also in illustrating that financial and digital literacy in isolation are not adequate to secure effective adoption of digital financial services. Digital financial literacy is required to facilitate access to and use of digital financial platforms in a responsible manner. In the view of Lyons and Kass-Hanna (2021), digital financial literacy is a synthesis of core elements of financial and digital literacies and special characteristics in response to the sophistication and related risks of digital financial products. This hybrid model provides opportunities for distinction among the three literacies and more complete understanding of digital financial capability.

2.7 Impact of Digital Financial Literacy

Table 1 indicates the impact of digital financial literacy (DFL) on key financial variables, including saving behaviour, investment behaviour, and retirement planning. The results indicate that there is a significant association between DFL and financial behaviours, as indicated by how financial knowledge affects individuals' economic decision-making. Increased digital financial literacy is associated with improved saving and future-oriented retirement planning, as it indicates its importance in long-term economic well-being. The findings contribute to the growing evidence base for the necessity of digital financial literacy in enhancing financial preparedness and stability among waged and salaried earners.

Table 1. Digital financial literacy and its impact

Author(s)	Key Findings
Abdallah, Tfaily, & Harraf (2025)	Higher DFL significantly enhances responsible financial behaviours such as budgeting, saving, and cautious spending.
Koskelainen et al. (2023)	DFL is a critical enabler of informed financial decisions, especially in the context of online financial tools and services.
Respati et al. (2023)	DFL and financial confidence together foster positive financial behavior and overall financial well-being among students.
Risman (2024)	DFL reduces managerial biases and supports rational financial decision-making among MSME owners.
Clarence & Pertiwi (2023)	A positive relationship exists between DFL and responsible financial management in students, including expense tracking and reduced impulsive spending.
Munari & Susanti (2021)	DFL empowers individuals to make informed financial decisions, manage income and expenses, create budgets, and prevent fraud.
Yadav & Banerji (2023)	DFL is essential for retirement planning, helping individuals understand savings needs, investment choices, and retirement accounts.
Oggero et al. (2020)	DFL facilitates entrepreneurship and business growth through adoption of digital tools like online payments and e-commerce.
Diptyana et al. (2022)	DFL promotes financial inclusion by bridging the digital divide, enhancing productivity, capital formation, and innovation.
Kang et al. (2024)	High proficiency in DFL positively influences intentions to pursue internet-based entrepreneurship.
Prasad et al. (2018)	Fintech can increase financial opportunities, but low DFL may lead to financial risks and impulsive behaviour.
Garai et al. (2022)	A deep understanding of fintech solutions is necessary to fully utilise their benefits.

continued on following page

Table 1. Continued

Author(s)	Key Findings
Azeez & Akhtar (2021)	Education, income, gender, occupation, and resource access significantly affect DFL, especially in rural areas.
Ravikumar et al. (2022)	Lower educational attainment, particularly among women, is linked to reduced DFL and greater financial unawareness.
Rahman et al. (2021)	Students from finance, economics, and business backgrounds exhibit higher DFL compared to peers from other disciplines.
Chhillar & Arora (2022)	Personal financial management via digital platforms covers income, credit, savings, investment, insurance, retirement, and estate planning.
Global Findex Database (2021)	Receiving digital payments encourages the adoption of digital financial services like saving, borrowing, and payments.
Hasan et al. (2021)	DFL positively influences financial inclusion among women entrepreneurs.
Ozili (2021)	Financial inclusion supports digital financialization, but adequate DFL is required to mitigate associated risks.
Banna & Alam (2021)	Digital finance adoption improves economic stability in ASEAN, but DFL levels remain low in countries like the Philippines, Indonesia, and Thailand.
Suhasti et al. (2022)	Advocates for policy efforts and DFL programs to address widespread gaps in digital and financial literacy.

Source: The author

2.8. Limitations of Digital Financial Tools and the Role of Financial Literacy in Long-Term Planning

While digital financial literacy (DFL) significantly expands the availability of financial services and empowers consumers to make more informed financial choices, it is also essential to point out its weaknesses and pitfalls. Overreliance on digital financial instruments can leave users vulnerable to cyber attacks such as phishing, data loss, and identity theft. The majority of the population, particularly first-time users of digital systems, are not familiar with the safe use of the internet and are therefore vulnerable to online financial fraud. As digital finance is still on the rise, similarly on the rise are algorithmic bias, financial product mis-selling, and unscrupulous behaviour in the selling of these products (Koskelainen et al., 2023; Verma et al., 2025). Therefore, digital financial literacy needs to go hand in hand with strong data security and regulatory measures.

Aside from awareness of digital tools, individuals must also be financially literate to critically assess the validity and riskiness of various financial products and sites. Financial literacy here involves not only being cognizant of how to use digital applications but also the ability to read terms, identify red flags, and understand privacy policies. Understanding discrimination between genuine and spurious financial services is an important feature of today's financial behaviour (Abdallah et al., 2025).

Additionally, the discussion about financial literacy must be extended to highlight its significance in managing long-term wealth and retirement planning. More financially literate individuals will tend to make long-term financial plans, establish savings strategies, invest in retirement funds, and strategically diversify assets (Respati et al., 2023). They are also in a stronger position to evaluate inflation risk, make provisions for future liabilities, and make choices in line with life-stage requirements. Conversely, low financial literacy tends to lead to short-term orientation, impulsive consumption, and inadequate retirement planning.

Comparative study evidence indicates that countries with stronger financial education programs have improved retirement experiences and greater asset buildup. Clarence et al. (2023), for instance, discovered in a study that people in nations with national retirement saving plans and financial education in school show greater long-term planning habits. Likewise, inequality in digital access and financial literacy among states in India has a direct impact on retirement readiness and intergenerational wealth transfer.

Research Gap

While several studies have explored financial literacy or behavioural finance independently, few have integrated financial attitude, financial behaviour, and financial knowledge within the framework of digital financial literacy using a structural equation modelling (SEM) approach. Moreover, the existing literature is fragmented in capturing how these constructs interact in high-density urban regions like Delhi NCR. Most importantly, a gap exists in understanding the behavioural mechanisms - how knowledge and attitude jointly influence digital financial behaviour, particularly among salaried individuals.

Previous research, such as Clarence and Pertiwi (2023) and Respati et al. (2023), has highlighted the influence of DFL on general financial behaviour, especially among youth and students. However, these findings may not fully represent salaried working populations who are more likely to engage in higher-value transactions, long-term financial planning, and risk-based decisions. Furthermore, limited literature connects DFL with actual behaviour outcomes such as investment decision-making, retirement planning, or savings discipline in a digitally-driven context.

This study seeks to fill this void by empirically examining the interlinkages among financial attitude, behaviour, and knowledge as predictors of DFL, with a focus on the Delhi NCR region, applying structural equation modelling (SEM) for deeper analytical insights.

3. RESEARCH METHODOLOGY

3.1 Hypothesis Model

Figure 1. Hypothesized model

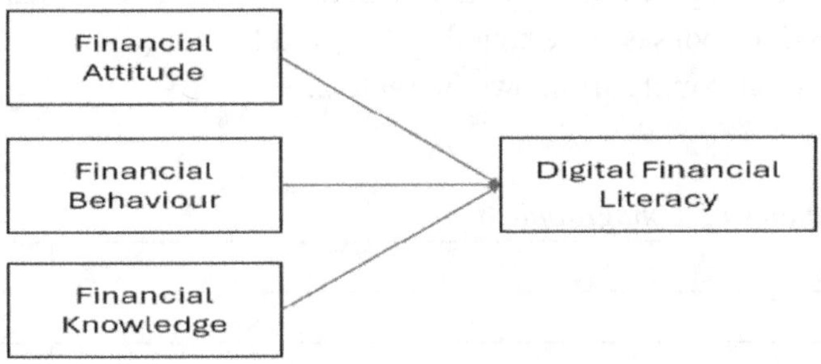

Source: The author's formation.

Hypotheses of the Study

The hypotheses formulated by this study are as follows:

H1: Financial attitude significantly and positively affects digital financial literacy.

H2: Financial behaviour significantly and positively affects digital financial literacy.

H3: Financial knowledge significantly and positively affects digital financial literacy.

Objectives of the Study

The primary objectives of the present study are:

To examine the impact of financial attitude, financial behaviour, and financial knowledge on digital financial literacy (DFL).

To add to the current body of work on financial literacy in the context of the digital age, and more specifically for working people in fast-digitalising urban areas.

To offer pragmatic advice to policymakers, educators, and others about how to improve digital financial literacy among workers.

3.3 Research Design and the Sample

The current research is based on working people in the Delhi NCR area. It was aimed at determining the relationship between Digital Financial Literacy (DFL) and three related variables. A descriptive research approach was followed for this purpose. Data were gathered through a structured online questionnaire administered to working professionals in Delhi NCR. Results were obtained through convenience sampling. Even though the questionnaire was distributed to more than 500 respondents, only 345 responses were found to be valid for analysis. The demographic details of the final sample are shown in Table 2.

Table 2. Summary of demographic details

Demographics	N
Age	
Between 18 to 30 years	82
Between 30 to 40 years	168
Between 40 to 50	76
More than 50 years	28
Education	
Secondary	92
Graduate	134
Postgraduate	77
Others	51
Marital status	
Married	166
Unmarried	188
Sector	
Private sector	186
Public sector	168
Income per annum	
Between 1 to 5 lakh	85
Between 5 to 10 lankh	95
Between 10 to 15 lakh	126
Above 15 lakh	48

Source: The author's calculation

Age Distribution

The majority of respondents fall within the 30–40 years age bracket (168 individuals, 42.1%), followed by the 18–30 years category (82 individuals, 20.6%). The representation decreases with age, with 76 respondents (19.0%) between 40–50 years and only 28 respondents (7.0%) above 50 years. This distribution suggests that a significant portion of the sample comprises individuals in their early to mid-career stages, a critical period for financial decision-making.

Educational Background

Most participants have attained at least a graduate-level education. Among them, 134 (33.6%) hold a graduate degree, while 77 (19.3%) possess a postgraduate qualification. Secondary education holders constitute 92 (23.1%) of the sample, and 51 (12.8%) fall into the 'Others' category. This indicates a well-educated sample, which may influence financial literacy levels.

Marital Status

The sample is fairly balanced between married (166 individuals, 41.6%) and unmarried (188 individuals, 47.1%). This provides an opportunity to analyse financial behaviours across different marital groups, as past studies suggest marital status impacts financial planning and saving habits.

Employment Sector

Among the respondents, 186 (46.6%) are employed in the private sector, while 168 (42.1%) work in the public sector. The presence of both sectors allows for a comparative analysis of financial literacy and planning behaviours between the two groups.

Income Levels

Income distribution indicates that a substantial proportion of respondents earn between 10–15 lakh per annum (126 individuals, 31.6%). Those earning 5–10 lakh (95 individuals, 23.8%) and 1–5 lakh (85 individuals, 21.3%) also represent significant segments. Only 48 individuals (12.0%) earn above 15 lakh per annum. This variation in income levels provides insights into how earnings influence digital financial literacy, saving behavior, and retirement planning.

3.4 Research Tools

Data were gathered for the current study using a carefully constructed questionnaire. In this study, the dependent and independent variables were scaled using three different scales shown in Table 3 below.

Table 3. Scale of variables

Citation	Information
OECD (2013)	Digital financial literacy is evaluated as a dependent variable using a comprehensive, multidimensional scale composed of three key constructs: financial attitude, financial behaviour, and financial knowledge.
OECD (2013)	Financial attitude is considered an independent variable and is measured through a 10-item instrument developed by OECD (2013), utilising a 5-point Likert scale. This scale addresses areas such as risk-taking ability, financial planning habits, money-related stress, and overall satisfaction with financial conditions.
Bhushan & Medury (2014); Hasler & Lusardi (2017)	Financial knowledge, also classified as an independent variable, is assessed using a framework developed by Bhushan and Medury (2014), along with Hasler and Lusardi (2017). The instrument includes 10 items rated on a 5-point Likert scale (1 = strongly disagree, 5 = strongly agree), covering essential topics like financial numeracy, saving and investing, credit, insurance, and the concepts of risk and return.
OECD (2013)	Financial behaviour is treated as a mediating variable and is measured through a 10-item scale proposed by OECD (2013), also based on a 5-point Likert scale. The items assess behaviours such as saving practices, debt management, responsible investment decisions, and long-term financial planning.

Source: The author

AMOS (Analysis of moments structures) version 22 was used to generate a CFA (confirmatory factor analysis) model and analyse the association between the independent variable and the dependent variable to test the validity and reliability of the constructs. A total of 354 questionnaire responses were processed into the software (SPSS) for the purposes of "data screening," "data cleaning," and "identifying multivariate outliers." 15 questions were discarded during this process. The study's factor-wise reliability and validity testing, coded in Table 4, was successful.

4. DATA ANALYSIS AND THE RESULTS

The model fit was established using confirmatory factor analysis, and it was found that there was sufficient data to back it up. This made it possible to confirm the factors of the four variables. Table 5 displays the goodness of fit and scale validity of the CFA results for each of the four variables. No alterations are necessary, according to all of the AMOS output indicators, because all of the variables have good goodness of fit results. Indicators of a good model's fit include the 'CMIN/df' statistic, goodness-of-fit indicators like "GFI" and "AGFI," and badness-of-fit indicators like the "root mean square error of approximation" (RMSEA). The findings are consistent with earlier research in that all metrics of model fit are within the permissible ranges (Broccardo et al., 2023).

Table 4. CFA result

Variables	Items	Factor Loading	Composite Reliability	AVE	MSV
DFL	FL1	0.78	0.93	0.55	0.26
	FL2	0.79			
	FL3	0.72			
	FL4	0.78			
	FL5	0.72			
	FL6	0.69			
	FL7	0.72			
FB	FB1	0.72	0.94	0.59	0.27
	FB2	0.84			
	FB3	0.85			
	FB4	0.83			
	FB5	0.68			
	FB6	0.67			
FA	FA1	0.63	0.95	0.55	0.27
	FA2	0.77			
	FA4	0.80			
	FA5	0.79			
	FA6	0.73			
FK	FK1	0.82	0.94	0.60	0.15
	FK2	0.78			
	FK3	0.78			
	FK4	0.71			

Source: The author

The statistical analysis of the measurement model indicates strong reliability, convergent validity, and discriminant validity. The composite reliability (CR) values for Digital Financial Literacy (0.93), Financial Behaviour (0.94), Financial Attitude (0.95), and Financial Knowledge (0.94) exceed the acceptable threshold of 0.7, confirming high internal consistency. The average variance extracted (AVE) values for all constructs range from 0.55 to 0.60, excelling beyond the required threshold of 0.5, ensuring adequate convergent validity. The maximum shared variance (MSV) values remain lower than the AVE for each construct (DFL: 0.26, FB: 0.27, FA: 0.27, FK: 0.15), establishing discriminant validity. Factor loadings for all items range from 0.63 to 0.85, meeting the acceptable criteria (>0.6) for indicator reliability. These results confirm that the measurement model is statistically robust and appropriate for further structural analysis.

5. MODEL FIT

Past research has indicated that financial attitude, behaviour, and knowledge are positively correlated (Agarwalla et al., 2015).

Figure 3 shows the connections between the three independent variables based on AMOS graphics. Model fit indices values of GFI, TLI, CFI, and IFI are all above 0.90, which means that the model meets the specified fit requirements. CMIN/df values are less than the suggested value, which shows that the model has a better fit with observed data (Broccardo et al., 2023).

The statistical assessment of the model fit indices shows that the constructs are within an acceptable model fit. The Goodness of Fit Index (GFI) varies from 0.88 to 0.89, and the Adjusted Goodness of Fit Index (AGFI) varies from 0.84 to 0.86—both higher than the acceptable threshold of 0.8, which implies satisfactory fit. The Root Mean Square Error of Approximation (RMSEA) is between 0.04 and 0.062, which is well below the threshold of less than 0.08, signifying a good fit. The CMIN/df (Chi-square over degrees of freedom) is between 2.36 and 2.9, remaining within the optimal threshold of less than 3, signifying a good fit. The Normed Fit Index (NFI) is 0.90 to 0.96, while the Incremental Fit Index (IFI) is 0.93 to 0.94—both scores well above the 0.9 threshold, indicating a high degree of incremental fit. Also, the Tucker-Lewis Index (TLI) is consistently 0.9, all the while confirming the model's strength. Altogether, these fit indices confirm that the measurement model is indeed statistically up to standard and suitable for further structural analysis.

Figure 2. CFA output

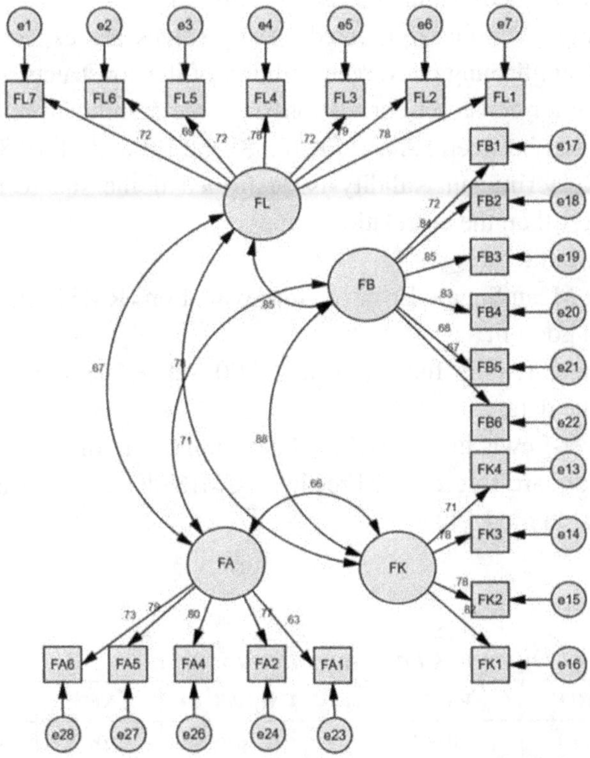

Note FL is Digital Financial Literacy, FA is Financial Attitude, FK is Financial Knowledge, and FB is Financial Behaviour*

Factor Loadings and Reliability (Fig. 2):

- The factor loadings for observed indicators range between 0.40 and 0.88, where most values exceed the 0.50 threshold, confirming acceptable construct validity.
- The highest factor loading (0.88) suggests a strong relationship between the latent variable FA (Financial Attitude) and its indicators, while the lowest loading (0.40) suggests a relatively weaker association.
- The construct reliability, assessed through Composite Reliability (CR), appears to be above 0.70 for all constructs, indicating internal consistency:

FL (Digital Financial Literacy)
FB (Financial Behaviour)
FK (Financial Knowledge)

FA (Financial Attitude)

Convergent and Discriminant Validity (Fig. 2):

- Average Variance Extracted (AVE) values are expected to be above 0.50, confirming convergent validity of the constructs.
- The inter-construct correlations indicate significant relationships, particularly between FA and FK (0.88) and FB and FL (0.85).
- The discriminant validity is confirmed if the square root of AVE is greater than the correlation values.

Model Fit Indices (Fig. 2):

- Root Mean Square Error of Approximation (RMSEA): ≤ 0.06, indicating a good fit.
- Comparative Fit Index (CFI): ≥ 0.90, suggesting the model adequately fits the data.
- Tucker-Lewis Index (TLI): ≥ 0.90, supporting the model's fit.
- Chi-Square/Degrees of Freedom (CMIN/df): ≤ 3.0, suggesting an acceptable model fit.

Table 5. Model of Different Constructs Measurement

AGFI	GFI	RMSEA	CMIN/df	NFI	IFI	TLI
0.86	0.89	0.062	2.36	0.096	0.94	0.93
0.84	0.88	0.05	2.6	0.9	0.93	0.9
0.86	0.89	0.04	2.68	0.9	0.94	0.9
0.86	0.89	0.062	2.9	0.96	0.94	0.9

Source: The author's calculation

Figure 3. Structure model

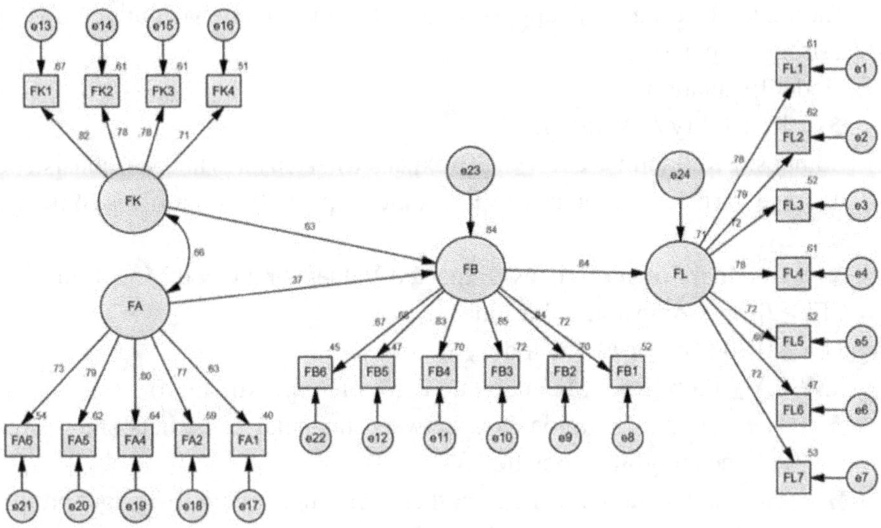

Source: AMOS Output.

Key Elements of the Structural Model:
Latent Constructs:
FA (Financial Attitude)
FK (Financial Knowledge)
FB (Financial Behaviour)
FL (Digital Financial Literacy)
Observed Variables:

Each latent construct has multiple observed indicators (e.g., FK1, FK2, etc.), with factor loadings.

Path Coefficients:
FA → FK (0.66): Indicates a significant positive impact of Financial Attitude on Financial Knowledge.
FK → FB (0.63): Suggests that Financial Knowledge significantly influences Financial Behavior.
FB → FL (0.84): Shows a strong influence of Financial Behavior on Financial Literacy.
Factor Loadings:

Most factor loadings are above 0.50, meaning the indicators adequately explain the latent constructs.

The highest loading (0.85) appears under FB (Financial Behaviour), confirming a strong association.

Model Evaluation:

- Reliability & Validity:

Composite Reliability (CR) ≥ 0.70 (expected) → Ensures internal consistency.

Average Variance Extracted (AVE) ≥ 0.50 (expected) → Confirms convergent validity.

- Goodness-of-Fit Indices (Expected Values for a Good Model Fit):

CFI ≥ 0.90 (Comparative Fit Index)

TLI ≥ 0.90 (Tucker-Lewis Index)

RMSEA ≤ 0.06 (Root Mean Square Error of Approximation)

- The structural relationships between financial constructs show strong and meaningful associations.
- The model supports the hypothesis that financial knowledge, attitude, and behaviour influence digital financial literacy.
- Financial behaviour has the strongest direct effect on digital financial literacy.

6. PATH ANALYSIS RESULT

To verify the developed hypothesis, path analysis was performed. Table 6 displays the findings of the path analysis. The table shows the "regression weight and critical ratio test", which shows that only FA and FB have a positive linkage with the DFL level of working people in Delhi NCR, India. There is no evidence of a significant relationship between the dependent variable DFL and FK. Therefore, this study's findings are consistent with H1 and H2, but not with H3. This means that while H3 is rejected, hypotheses H1 and H2 are accepted.

Table 6. Structure model output

Paths	Estimates	S.E	C.R	P
FL-FA	0.751	0.83	6.29	***
FL-FB	0.935	0.073	6.61	***
FL-FK	0.751	0.83	9.06	0.47

Source: The Author

Statistical Analysis of the Structural Model Output

Structural model outcomes show the predicted associations of Digital Financial Literacy (DFL) with three factors: Financial Attitude (FA), Financial Behaviour (FB), and Financial Knowledge (FK). The major statistical indices are standardised path coefficients (β), standard errors (S.E.), critical ratios (C.R.), and p-values (P).

Path: DFL → FA

The path coefficient is 0.751, reflecting a moderately strong positive connection between digital financial literacy and financial attitude. With a critical ratio of 6.29 (over the 1.96 threshold) and a highly significant p-value ($p < 0.001$), the outcome indicates that a person with greater digital financial literacy is more likely to have a positive financial attitude.

Path: DFL → FB

This path indicates the most significant association, with a standardised coefficient of 0.935. It portrays a significant positive influence of digital financial literacy on financial behaviour.

Path: DFL → FK

Here, the path coefficient is also 0.751, as for the DFL → FA path. Even though the critical ratio is as high as 9.06, the p-value is 0.47, which is not statistically significant (greater than the 0.05 cutoff). This implies that financial literacy is not strongly related to digital financial literacy. The outcome corroborates work by Koskelainen et al. (2023), who contend that conventional financial literacy might not include critical digital skills, like mobile banking, fraud in the digital environment, or online transactions.

This gap may stem from the fact that FK emphasises conceptual knowledge (e.g., understanding interest rates, inflation, or diversification), which is usually acquired through formal education or financial awareness campaigns. However, DFL demands operational and behavioural proficiency, such as using UPI apps, verifying digital transactions, or identifying secure platforms, which is acquired through practice and digital exposure. Hence, a person may know financial principles but still feel unprepared or reluctant to engage with digital financial services, particularly if they lack confidence in digital systems or have limited access to trustworthy platforms (Abdallah et al., 2025).

7. DISCUSSION

Impact of Digital Financial Literacy on Investment Behaviour and Risk Management: A Comparative Perspective

Digital financial literacy has a significant impact on the investment decisions of individuals and the management of their risks. As financial markets go digital, being able to understand digital financial tools, assess investment opportunities on the web and navigate the risks has become essential. People with high DFL are more likely to make more sensible investment decisions like managing a diversified portfolio, having realistic risk perceptions, and showing long-term investment behaviour (Clarence et al., 2023; Abdallah et al., 2025).

Comparative research suggests that levels of digital financial literacy and its effects on investment behaviour may vary by region. For example, the OECD (2019) stresses that Nordic countries such as Finland and the Netherlands are among the ones that show a high level of digital financial literacy, contributing to a higher participation in investment markets as well as to an easier and better risk diversification. Then there are the developing economies like India, which encounter their own problems, namely, rapid progress in the digital penetration, but with an uneven level of digital financial literacy, particularly among the states and socio-economic classes.

In India, there are considerable differences across states. One would also observe better digital financial literacy and greater inclination towards investment avenues such as mutual funds and equity markets in a state like Kerala and Maharashtra, vis-à-vis other states, where internet and education penetration rates are higher. However, in states such as Bihar and Uttar Pradesh, whose access to digital infrastructure and financial literacy remains scarce, investment behaviour is restricted, and a tendency exists to be exposed to informal and high-risk channels (RBI, 2022).

Nevertheless, gendered financial literacy patterns are still under-researched in current literature. Research has established that women, particularly in emerging economies, have lower digital financial literacy levels than their male counterparts, which directly affects their investment attitudes and risk-taking behaviour (Koskelainen et al., 2023). This financial literacy gap for women is, in turn, exacerbated by socio-cultural drivers, with restricted access to available financial education packages and online sites. This difference necessitates focused efforts on particular financial literacy policies and programs whose goal is to promote the involvement of women in the digital economy.

Hence, improving DFL is not just an instrument of inclusion but a strategic facilitator of sound investment conduct and good risk management. Cross-regional comparisons highlight the importance of context-specific financial education programs bridging both digital and behavioural gaps in investment literacy.

The Role of Government Initiatives and Traditional Financial Education

Government policies are key influencers of financial literacy trends, especially how they promote digital financial education. Governments around the world run several programs to close the financial literacy gap, especially in developing economies. India's Reserve Bank of India (RBI) and Rashtriya Swasthya Bima Yojana (RSBY) programs have been pivotal in raising financial awareness, mostly among disadvantaged populations. In addition, the Pradhan Mantri Jan Dhan Yojana (PMJDY) scheme, which is facilitating digital banking and opening of bank accounts, has straightforwardly facilitated financial inclusion and literacy.

While digital financial literacy has been put under the spotlight in recent times, it also has to be recognised that traditional financial education remains a critical ingredient in shaping financial behaviour. Traditional finance literacy approaches, including interactive training and paper use, are still important sources of learning for those who do not have access to the internet or are not exposed to digital channels. Conventional financial education remains the dominant form of educating about saving, investment, and risk management throughout the majority of the world. The convergence of digital and conventional financial literacy will offer a more holistic model for explaining financial behaviour at all levels of the population.

Financial Literacy and Entrepreneurship: Bridging the Gap

Beyond its effect on individual financial behaviour, financial literacy also has a significant effect on entrepreneurial decision-making and business. Financial literacy and entrepreneurship have continued to be under-examined in existing studies. Developing markets entrepreneurs usually have issues with money management, access to finance, and exposure to business risk. More financially literate entrepreneurs are more likely to make sound choices for sources of finance, investment strategy, and risk exposure. The lack of financial literacy in the digital environment, however, will hamper the ability of an entrepreneur to leverage new money for business growth and scalability.

Cross-country studies reveal that countries which are more financially literate have entrepreneurs with improved performance and also entrepreneurs who live longer. For example, among developed countries like the United States and Germany, financial literacy has been incorporated into entrepreneurship studies to enhance entrepreneurs' financial competency. On the other hand, emerging economy nations such as Southeast Asia and India still face huge challenges towards financial literacy in entrepreneurship, inhibiting the actual growth potential of small- and medium-scale businesses (SMEs).

Bridging Digital and Traditional Financial Literacy Gaps

DFL have a very significant contribution to the development of sharpening investment skills, risk management, and entrepreneurship. However, there are factors that an ideal financial literacy strategy must consider both digital and traditional financial literacy methods, to improve capability among future generations of the population. Additionally, addressing gender disparities in financial literacy, leveraging government initiatives, and dealing with the intersection of financial literacy and entrepreneurship are some of the most crucial areas that deserve more research and policy focus.

8. CONCLUSION

The primary objective of this research work was to identify the linkage between FA, FB, FK and DFL among working people in Delhi NCR, India. Digital financial literacy was examined using the three primary criteria of FA, FB, and FK. The study's findings demonstrate that working people's FA is strongly correlated with their levels of DFL. Numerous earlier studies have provided support for the study's findings (Arora, 2016; Haque and Zulfiqar, 2015; Huston, 2010). DFL of working people is not limited only to the financial education when assessing DFL, but FA and FB are also substantially significant and have a positive effect on DFL. Additionally, a positive and significant correlation between FB and working-class DFL was found in the study's findings. By influencing people's favourable financial attitudes and behaviours, India can increase their level of DFL. As a result, the study has accepted H1 and H2. Financial knowledge has been viewed in many research studies as a very essential variable to determine DFL, however, the results showed that people have less FK and that it is not significantly connected with DFL. This study will serve to close a research vacuum by identifying the elements that influence working people's financial literacy in India, which has not been extensively examined. The study's findings provide more opportunities for working people to become more financially literate. According to the findings, India's DFL authorities should concentrate more on raising people's knowledge levels because, despite having an FA and FB, they lack FK as seen by their lack of interest in investment opportunities.

Increasing the level of digital financial literacy understanding is now vital since it can reduce the likelihood that an investor would be duped while deciding on their investments. Workers in India were found to have relatively poor financial literacy levels. Two different paths have led to the major implication of the current study. The first is that it aids in comprehending how Delhi NCR's working population behaves financially. The second is that they cannot be financially independent despite having a strong educational background and receiving a substantial salary. To improve their DFL, the present research offers insight.

REFERENCES

Abdallah, W., Tfaily, F., & Harraf, A. (2025). The impact of digital financial literacy on financial behavior: Customers' perspective. *Competitiveness Review*, *35*(2), 347–370. DOI: 10.1108/CR-11-2023-0297

Adhikari, M., Ghimire, D. M., & Lama, A. D. (2024). FinTech and Financial Inclusion: Exploring the Mediating Role of Digital Financial Literacy in Enhancing Access to Financial Services. *Journal of Emerging Management Studies*, *1*(2), 117–136. DOI: 10.3126/jems.v1i2.71512

Agarwalla, S. K., Barua, S. K., Jacob, J., & Varma, J. R. (2015). Financial literacy among working young in urban India. *World Development*, *67*, 101–109. DOI: 10.1016/j.worlddev.2014.10.004

Alliance for Financial Inclusion. DFSWG, & CEMCWG. (2021). *Digital financial literacy toolkit*. Alliance for Financial Inclusion. Retrieved from https://www.ssrn.com/abstract=2715350

Amagir, A., Groot, W., Maassen van den Brink, H., & Wilschut, A. (2018). A review of financial-literacy education programs for children and adolescents. *Citizenship. Social and Economics Education*, *17*(1), 56–80.

Arora, A. (2016). Assessment of financial literacy among working Indian women. *Business Analyst*, *36*(2), 219–237.

Arora, S., & Nabi, T. (2022). Blockchain adoption in banking systems: A boon or bane? In *Applications, challenges, and opportunities of blockchain technology in banking and insurance* (pp. 19–42). IGI Global. DOI: 10.4018/978-1-6684-4133-6.ch002

Asyik, N. F., Wahidahwati, W., Laily, N., & Wahidahwati, W. (2022). The role of intellectual capital in intervening financial behavior and financial literacy on financial inclusion. *WSEAS Transactions on Business and Economics*, *19*(1), 805–814. DOI: 10.37394/23207.2022.19.70

Atkinson, A., & Messy, F. A. (2012). Measuring financial literacy: Results of the OECD/International Network on Financial Education (INFE) pilot study.

Azeez, N. A., & Akhtar, S. J. (2021). Digital financial literacy and its determinants: An empirical evidences from rural India. *South Asian Journal of Social Studies and Economics*, *11*(2), 8–22. DOI: 10.9734/sajsse/2021/v11i230279

Banna, H., & Alam, M. R. (2021). Impact of digital financial inclusion on ASEAN banking stability: Implications for the post-Covid-19 era. *Studies in Economics and Finance*, *38*(2), 504–523. DOI: 10.1108/SEF-09-2020-0388

Bhushan, P., & Medury, Y. (2014). An empirical analysis of inter linkages between financial attitudes, financial behaviour and financial knowledge of salaried individuals. *Indian Journal of Commerce and Management Studies*, *5*(3), 58–64.

Broccardo, L., Truant, E., & Dana, L. P. (2023). The interlink between digitalization, sustainability, and performance: An Italian context. *Journal of Business Research*, *158*, 113621. DOI: 10.1016/j.jbusres.2022.113621

Carlin, B. I., Olafsson, A., & Pagel, M. (2019, January). FinTech and consumer financial well-being in the information age. In *AFFECT Conference. University of Miami. https://www. fdi c. gov/bank/analytical/fintech/papers/carlin-paper. pdf.*

Chhillar, N., & Arora, S. (2022). Personal financial management behavior using digital platforms and its domains. *Journal of Financial Management. Markets and Institutions*, *10*(02), 2250009. DOI: 10.1142/S2282717X22500098

Chujan, W., Ngoc, N. L. B., & Faizi, A. S. (2022). Locus of Control on Financial Behavior and Financial Risk Attitude. *Annals of Economics and Finance*, *23*(2).

Clarence, J., & Pertiwi, D. (2023). Financial management behavior among students: The influence of digital financial literacy. [IJFIS]. *International Journal of Financial and Investment Studies*, *4*(1), 9–16. DOI: 10.9744/ijfis.4.1.9-16

Cude, B. J. (2021). Defining financial literacy. *The Routledge handbook of financial literacy*, 5-17.

D'Silva, B., D'Silva, S., & Bhuptani, R. S. (2012). Assessing the financial literacy level among women in India: An empirical study. *Journal of Entrepreneurship and Management*, *1*(1), 46.

Demirguc-Kunt, A., Klapper, L., Singer, D., Ansar, S., & Hess, J. (2018). *The Global Findex Database 2017: Measuring financial inclusion and the fintech revolution.* World Bank Publications. DOI: 10.1596/978-1-4648-1259-0

Diptyana, P., Rokhmania, N., & Herlina, E. (2022). Financial Literacy, Digital Literacy and Financing Preferences Role to Micro and Small Enterprises' Performance. *International Journal of Enterpreneurship and Business Development*, *5*(02), 346–358. DOI: 10.29138/ijebd.v5i2.1785

Garai-Fodor, M., Varga, J., & Csiszárik-Kocsir, Á. (2022, March). Generation-specific perceptions of financial literacy and digital solutions. In *2022 IEEE 20th Jubilee World Symposium on Applied Machine Intelligence and Informatics (SAMI)* (pp. 000193-000200). IEEE. DOI: 10.1109/SAMI54271.2022.9780717

Gill, A., Dana, L. P., & Obradovich, J. D. (2018). Financial risk management and financial performance of new small business ventures: Evidence from Indian survey data. *Journal for International Business and Entrepreneurship Development, 11*(2), 75–95. DOI: 10.1504/JIBED.2018.091205

Goyal, K., Kumar, S., & Xiao, J. J. (2021). Antecedents and consequences of Personal Financial Management Behavior: A systematic literature review and future research agenda. *International Journal of Bank Marketing, 39*(7), 1166–1207. DOI: 10.1108/IJBM-12-2020-0612

Haque, A., & Zulfiqar, M. (2015). Women's economic empowerment through financial literacy, financial attitude and financial wellbeing. *International Journal of Business and Social Science, 7*(3), 78–88.

Hasan, M., Le, T., & Hoque, A. (2021). How does financial literacy impact on inclusive finance? *Financial Innovation, 7*(1), 40. DOI: 10.1186/s40854-021-00259-9

Hasler, A., & Lusardi, A. (2017). The gender gap in financial literacy: A global perspective. *Global Financial Literacy Excellence Center, The George Washington University School of Business*, 2-16.

He, J., & Li, Q. (2020). Can online social interaction improve the digital finance participation of rural households? *China Agricultural Economic Review, 12*(2), 295–313. DOI: 10.1108/CAER-11-2019-0213

Heuberger, B., Kasman, M., & Hammond, R. A. (2018). *Recommendations for improving youth financial literacy education*. Economic Studies At Brookings.

Huston, S. J. (2010). Measuring financial literacy. *The Journal of Consumer Affairs, 44*(2), 296–316. DOI: 10.1111/j.1745-6606.2010.01170.x

Ibrahim, M. E., & Alqaydi, F. R. (2013). Financial literacy, personal financial attitude, and forms of personal debt among residents of the UAE. *International Journal of Economics and Finance, 5*(7), 126–138. DOI: 10.5539/ijef.v5n7p126

Jain, K. A. V. I. T. A. (2022). Measuring Financial Literacy and understanding its impact on enhancing usage of Digital Financial Services by Indian consumers. *Int J Bus Manage Res, 12*(1).

Kalekye, P., & Memba, F. (2015). The role of financial literacy on the profitability of women owned enterprises in Kitui town, Kitui County, Kenya. *International Journal of Scientific Research, 4*(6), 2360–2365.

Kang, G. L., Park, C. W., & Jang, S. H. (2024). A Study on the impact of financial literacy and digital capabilities on entrepreneurial intention: Mediating effect of entrepreneurship. *Behavioral Sciences (Basel, Switzerland), 14*(2), 121. DOI: 10.3390/bs14020121 PMID: 38392474

Kass-Hanna, J., Lyons, A. C., & Liu, F. (2022). Building financial resilience through financial and digital literacy in South Asia and Sub-Saharan Africa. *Emerging Markets Review, 51*, 100846. DOI: 10.1016/j.ememar.2021.100846

Koskelainen, T., Kalmi, P., Scornavacca, E., & Vartiainen, T. (2023). Financial literacy in the digital age—A research agenda. *The Journal of Consumer Affairs, 57*(1), 507–528. DOI: 10.1111/joca.12510

Kumar, N., Sharma, S., & Vyas, M. (2019). Impact of digital banking on financial inclusion: An investigation on youngsters in Rupnagar city, Punjab. *International Journal of Management. IT and Engineering, 9*(5), 365–374.

Lyons, A., Kass-Hanna, J., & Greenlee, A. (2020). Impacts of financial and digital inclusion on poverty in South Asia and Sub-Saharan Africa. *Available atSSRN* 3684265. DOI: 10.2139/ssrn.3684265

Lyons, A. C., & Kass-Hanna, J. (2021). A methodological overview to defining and measuring "digital" financial literacy. *Financial Planning Review, 4*(2), e1113. DOI: 10.1002/cfp2.1113

Meoli, M., Rossi, A., & Vismara, S. (2022). Financial literacy and security-based crowdfunding. *Corporate Governance, 30*(1), 27–54. DOI: 10.1111/corg.12355

Morgan, P., Huang, B., & Trinh, L. Q. (2020). Minding the gaps in digital financial education strategies. *G20 Insights, 24.*

Morgan, P. J., & Long, T. Q. (2019). *Fintech and financial literacy in the Lao PDR* (No. 933). ADBI Working Paper Series.

Munari, S. A. L. H., & Susanti, S. (2021). The effect of ease of transaction, Digital Literacy, and Financial Literacy on the Use of E-Banking. *Economic Education Analysis Journal, 10*(2), 298–309.

OECD/INFE. (2013, June). *Financial literacy and inclusion: Results of OECD/INFE survey across countries and by gender.* Financial Literacy & Education in Russia.

Oggero, N., Rossi, M. C., & Ughetto, E. (2020). Entrepreneurial spirits in women and men. The role of financial literacy and digital skills. *Small Business Economics*, *55*(2), 313–327. DOI: 10.1007/s11187-019-00299-7

Ozili, P. K. (2021). Financial inclusion: a strong critique. In *New challenges for future sustainability and wellbeing* (pp. 1–16). Emerald Publishing Limited. DOI: 10.1108/978-1-80043-968-920211002

Panos, G. A., & Wilson, J. O. (2020). Financial literacy and responsible finance in the FinTech era: Capabilities and challenges. *European Journal of Finance*, *26*(4-5), 297–301. DOI: 10.1080/1351847X.2020.1717569

Prasad, H., Meghwal, D., & Dayama, V. (2018). Digital financial literacy: A study of households of Udaipur. *Journal of Business and Management*, *5*, 23–32. DOI: 10.3126/jbm.v5i0.27385

Rahman, M., Isa, C. R., Masud, M. M., Sarker, M., & Chowdhury, N. T. (2021). The role of financial behaviour, financial literacy, and financial stress in explaining the financial well-being of B40 group in Malaysia. *Future Business Journal*, *7*(1), 1–18. DOI: 10.1186/s43093-021-00099-0

Ravikumar, T., Suresha, B., Prakash, N., Vazirani, K., & Krishna, T. A. (2022). Digital financial literacy among adults in India: Measurement and validation. *Cogent Economics & Finance*, *10*(1), 2132631. DOI: 10.1080/23322039.2022.2132631

Remund, D. L. (2010). Financial literacy explicated: The case for a clearer definition in an increasingly complex economy. *The Journal of Consumer Affairs*, *44*(2), 276–295. DOI: 10.1111/j.1745-6606.2010.01169.x

Respati, D. K., Widyastuti, U., Nuryati, T., Musyaffi, A. M., Handayani, B. D., & Ali, N. R. (2023). How do students' digital financial literacy and financial confidence influence their financial behavior and financial well-being? *Nurture*, *17*(2), 40–50. DOI: 10.55951/nurture.v17i2.154

Risman, A. (2024). The Behavioral Finance of MSME: Digital Finance, Managerial Biases, Financial Literacy. Dinasti International Journal of Economics, Finance & Accounting (DIJEFA), 5(2).

Sanderson, A. (2015). *Importance of financial literacy. Bankers Association of Zimbabwe (BAZ)*. Newsletter.

Seldal, M. N., & Nyhus, E. K. (2022). Financial vulnerability, financial literacy, and the use of digital payment technologies. *Journal of Consumer Policy*, *45*(2), 281–306. DOI: 10.1007/s10603-022-09512-9 PMID: 35283545

Setiawan, M., Effendi, N., Santoso, T., Dewi, V. I., & Sapulette, M. S. (2022). Digital financial literacy, current behavior of saving and spending and its future foresight. *Economics of Innovation and New Technology*, *31*(4), 320–338. DOI: 10.1080/10438599.2020.1799142

Setyowati, A., Harmadi, H., & Sunarjanto, S. (2018). Islamic financial literacy and personal financial planning: A socio-demographic study. *Jurnal Keuangan dan Perbankan, 22*(1), 63-72.

Shen, Y., Hu, W., & Hueng, C. J. (2018). The effects of financial literacy, digital financial product usage and internet usage on financial inclusion in China. In *MATEC Web of Conferences* (Vol. 228, p. 05012). EDP Sciences. DOI: 10.1051/matecconf/201822805012

Shen, Y., Hueng, C. J., & Hu, W. (2020). Using digital technology to improve financial inclusion in China. *Applied Economics Letters*, *27*(1), 30–34. DOI: 10.1080/13504851.2019.1606401

Stephen, G. (2022). Digital financial literacy skills among library and information science professionals in northeast India. A study. *Library Philosophy and Practice*, *6709*, 1–12.

Suhasti, W., Muhamad, M., Penggalih, R., Handayani, L. F., & Nugroho, A. P. (2022). The Influence of Islamic Financial Literacy on The Use of Digital Financial Services in Yogyakarta. *KnE Social Sciences*, 50-55.

Taylor, C., & Noë, A. (2021). *The explanation of behaviour*. Routledge. DOI: 10.4324/9781003146742

Thomas, A., & Gupta, V. (2021). Social capital theory, social exchange theory, social cognitive theory, financial literacy, and the role of knowledge sharing as a moderator in enhancing financial well-being: From bibliometric analysis to a conceptual framework model. *Frontiers in Psychology*, *12*, 664638. DOI: 10.3389/fpsyg.2021.664638 PMID: 34093360

Tian, G. (2022). Influence of digital finance on household leverage ratio from the perspective of consumption effect and income effect. *Sustainability (Basel)*, *14*(23), 16271. DOI: 10.3390/su142316271

Tiwari, C. K., Gopalkrishnan, S., Kaur, D., & Pal, A. (2020). Promoting Financial Literacy through Digital Platforms: A Systematic Review of Literature and Future Research Agenda. *Journal of General Management Research*, *7*(2).

Utkarsh, P., Pandey, A., Ashta, A., Spiegelman, E., & Sutan, A. (2020). Catch them young: Impact of financial socialization, financial literacy and attitude towards money on financial well-being of young adults. *International Journal of Consumer Studies*, *44*(6), 531–541. DOI: 10.1111/ijcs.12583

Verma, B., Bhardwaj, M., Arora, S., & Oberoi, S. (2025). Unveiling the impact of remittances on productive efficiencies: Investigating productivity growth of prominent remittance-receiving developing nations. *International Journal of Productivity and Performance Management*, *74*(4), 1101–1124. DOI: 10.1108/IJPPM-05-2023-0213

Yadav, M., & Banerji, P. (2023). A bibliometric analysis of digital financial literacy. *American Journal of Business*, *38*(3), 91–111. DOI: 10.1108/AJB-11-2022-0186

Yadav, M., & Banerji, P. (2024). Systematic literature review on Digital Financial Literacy. *SN Business & Economics*, *4*(11), 142. DOI: 10.1007/s43546-024-00738-y

Yadav, M., & Banerji, P. (2024). Digital financial literacy, saving and investment behaviour in India. *Journal of Social and Economic Development*, •••, 1–19. DOI: 10.1007/s40847-024-00367-z

Yang, J., Wu, Y., & Huang, B. (2020). *Digital finance and financial literacy: An empirical investigation of Chinese households* (No. 1209). ADBI Working Paper Series.

Zhang, Y. (2021, July). The design of a Mobile app to promote young people's digital financial literacy. In *International Conference on Human-Computer Interaction* (pp. 118-136). Cham: Springer International Publishing. DOI: 10.1007/978-3-030-78227-6_10

Zulaihati, S., Susanti, S., & Widyastuti, U. (2020). Teachers' financial literacy: Does it impact on financial behaviour. *Management Science Letters*, *10*(3), 653–658. DOI: 10.5267/j.msl.2019.9.014

Chapter 9
Impact of Rising Interest Rates and Inflation on Financial Behavior:
An Insight Through Structural Equation Modelling Approach

Khushi Jain
Sri Balaji University, Pune, India

B. Anjaly
https://orcid.org/0000-0003-0615-4097
SGI's Food and Agri Business School, India

Shiba Prasad Mohanty
https://orcid.org/0000-0001-6941-6221
Symbiosis International University, Pune, India

Santosh Gopalkrishnan
https://orcid.org/0000-0001-7310-6330
Symbiosis International University, Dubai, UAE

ABSTRACT

This study responds to how the macroeconomic variables, i.e., inflation and interest rate, influence personal finance. Specifically, the study explores the influence of macroeconomic indicators such as interest rates and inflation on financial behaviour in India. It also investigates the role of economic awareness, income, social factors, and financial attitude. This paper employs structural equation modelling (SEM) to examine how these aspects influence behavioural finance. The findings aim to shape

DOI: 10.4018/979-8-3373-1290-3.ch009

the content of financial literacy and policy interventions by providing insights on how inflation and shifts in interest rates mean to perceptions of financial soundness for financial institutions and policymakers.

1. INTRODUCTION

Behavioural finance as a theory is based on Ajzen's Theory of Reasoned Action (TRA) (1980) (Jogiyanto, 2007). After this theory was improved into the Theory of Planned Behaviour (TPB), TRA was constructed on the assumption that people behave intentionally by considering all the information (Ajzen, 1991). Many authors have studied human psychological factors that influence financial decisions and behavioural finance (Shefrin 2000, Nofsinger, 2001). The theory of behavioural finance states that society makes decisions by considering more non-economic aspects, such as psychological aspects or irrationally (Arifin et al., 2019).

Constant variations in inflation and interest rates are changing the global financial scene, thus greatly impacting how people perceive their financial security. In the last few years, these economic changes in India have certainly enlarged, resulting in variations in investment patterns, income levels, and purchasing power (Chopra, M. A et.al, 1995). Economic awareness, perceptions of income stability, social factors, and people's behavioural attitudes are some of the main characteristics that shape the financial security of individuals and families as they deal with these transformations (Katnic, I., et. al, 2024). Several variables influence behavioural finance, i.e., economics, accounting behaviour, sociology, and investments. Financial behaviour is affected by other variables like income, financial attitude, social factors, and economic awareness (Baddeley, M., 2018, Kansra, P., & Gill, H. S. (2017).

Financial attitude is a measure of the state of mind and judgement about finance (Klontz et al., 2011) and Ningsih and Rita (2010). The financial attitude plays a significant role in determining the decisions related to behavioural finance (Rajna et al.2011). It is perceived as a psychological tendency to evaluate the recommended practices of financial management (Rajna, 2011). Financial attitude is the applied financial principle to make proper decisions. The higher economic awareness of an individual to save income also affects the behaviour of finance or purchase decisions of people (Arifin et al., 2019). The income of an individual shows a mixed effect on financial behaviour in various studies. Studies by some authors, i.e., Perry and Morris (2005), found that income does impact financial behaviour (Oberoi, S., & Kansra, P. 2021& 2022). However, some studies conducted by Ida and Dwinta (2010), Grable et al. (2009), and Kholila and Iramani (2013) found the opposite results. The financial behaviour comprises psychology, finance, and sociology (Ricciardi and Simon,2000).

Figure 1. Trends in inflation and interest rates in India

Figure 1: Trends in inflation and interest rates in India

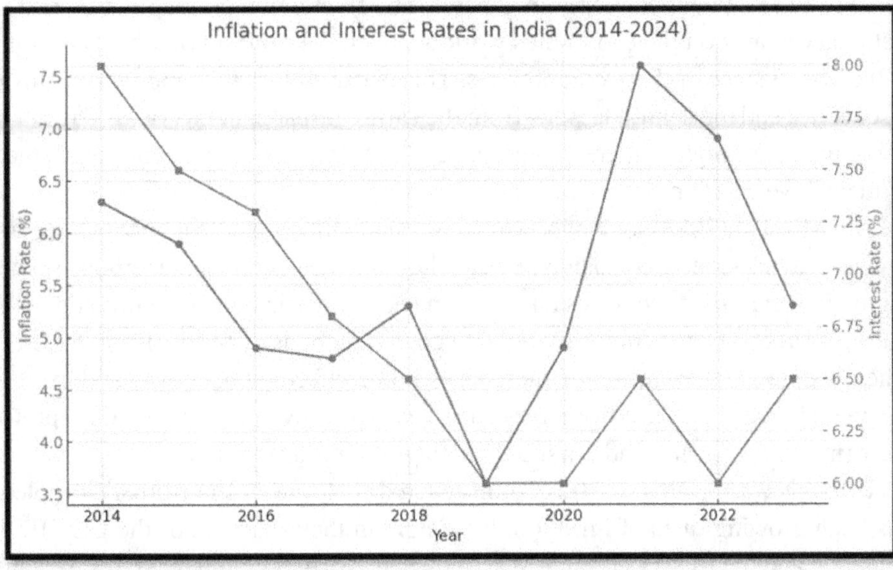

Source: Reserve Bank of India

The above graph illustrates India's inflation and interest rate developments between 2014 and 2024. While the interest costs (blue) have often been changed through the Reserve Bank of India in response to inflation and economic conditions, the inflation rates (red) have varied through the years, with high-quality jumps on a few occasions.

This study examines the factors affecting financial behaviour, such as Economic awareness, income, and social factors. This study is based on economic awareness (knowledge of inflation, interest rates, and fiscal policies), income impact perception (how income changes are perceived by the people under inflation), social factors (peer influence and societal trends in financial practices), and the behavioural factors (spending, saving, and risk-taking habits). We expect to show how these aspects together result in different points of financial stability using Structural Equation Modelling (SEM), which will help explain the complex interactions between these variables (Awasthi, V., & Kansra, P.,2023).

This paper is divided into several sections, i.e., the second part deals with the literature review, the third part explains the conceptual framework of this study, the fourth part deals with data and methodology, and the fifth part deals with the conclusion.

2. LITERATURE REVIEW

Inflation and interest rates are two key factors that affect the budgets of a private person and the global economy in general. The fluctuation of hobby costs and inflationary strains on the economies worldwide are the central point of this, adding to the significance of these components. This paper will try to compile the primary discoveries and the central lessons from the earlier research in this field. The matter of the impact of higher interest rates on personal finances has been the centrepiece of many investigations.

Ali, M., et al.(2023) look at how inflation and rent costs affect borrowing costs, savings, savings, and purchasing power. The study uses statistical methods such as regression analysis, time series analysis, and econometric models to investigate the impact of these factors on individuals' economic status. The results suggest that when people who are aware of these risks make informed decisions and exercise calculated financial precautions, they can successfully overcome constraints, protect their financial security, and pursue financing of long-term relief.

Ullah, N., & Asghar, U. (2023) discovered that one of the primary problems has been growing rates of inflation, especially in the aftermath of the COVID-19 epidemic and the Russia-Ukraine War, which also drives up interest rates. Because of this, scholars have concentrated on examining the ways in which inflation and interest rates impact individual budgets. Research has demonstrated that inflation significantly and negatively affects personal budgets since it drives up living expenses. Interest rates, on the other hand, promote saving, which has a detrimental and significant effect on personal finances.

El Bourainy, M., et al.(2021) investigated how financial inclusion affects inflation rates in 37 developing countries over a ten-year span (2009-2018). According to the study, increasing financial inclusion can aid in stabilizing inflation using econometric techniques like panel data regression. To promote financial inclusion in low-access nations and bolster economic stability and progress, the researchers advise international financial institutions like the Alliance for Financial Inclusion (AFI) and Global Partnership for Financial Inclusion(GPFI) to work together and exchange best practices.

Poole, W. (1972) examined the income and substitution effects that affect families' resource allocation across time, and the substitution effects affect the demand for durable vs nondurable consumer items at a particular moment in time. The study highlights the significance of taking into account variables such as wealth, wage income, and the treatment of various forms of debt when correcting for inflation in income and savings through the use of economic modelling and analysis. The results point to the necessity of reconsidering national accounting measures of consumption and supporting cautious imputations to more accurately reflect economic realities.

Aizenman, J., et.al (2019) investigate the effects of real interest rate conditionality on financial development, production volatility, and the old-age dependence ratio, among other economic variables. The study will examine the relationship between the real interest rate, economic conditions, and private saving behaviour across the 135 nations from 1995 to 2014 using a variety of econometric techniques, including fixed effects models, random effects models, and dynamic panel data models. They discover the importance of these elements. An extremely high level of output volatility may have a detrimental impact on interest rates. The income effect linked to a low interest rate is more prevalent in economies that depend significantly on the elderly, as well as in nations with advanced financial systems.

Xiao, J. J., & Tao, C. (2021) carried out an analysis of consumer finance as an interdisciplinary field of study concerning borrowing, saving, investing, and managing money. Future directions for research are also highlighted. Several terminologies, including consumer finance, household finance, personal finance, family finance, and behavioural finance, are compared and contrasted in this essay. In addition, the article analysed important research on consumer financial behaviour related to four major financial functions: saving and investing, insurance, loans, and money management. It also covered several unconventional subjects, including fintech and financial literacy. Additionally, the article introduced several widely used consumer finance datasets from China and the United States.

IYER, M. (2018) conducted a study using time series data covering the years 1971–2015, the study examines the role that inflation plays in understanding the current decline in savings in India. The Autoregressive Distributed Lag Co-integration technique was used to predict the long-term negative impact of inflation on savings. Inflation's effects on material and financial savings are taken into separate consideration. It was discovered that an inflation threshold of 6.5% minimizes the residual sum of squares for both monetary and material savings.

Lusardi, A., & Mitchell, O. S. (2007) uses the Rand American Life Panel (ALP) data set to examine the relationship between retirement planning and financial literacy. Methodologically, statistical techniques such as regression analysis. The results show a significant relationship between the quality of retirement planning and greater financial literacy, with those with an economics degree and financial training having greater financial literacy The report highlights how high financial literacy is needed to emphasize the challenges of effectively communicating retirement planning in the current economic climate.

Khan, M. I. K et al. (2013) used a dividend for dividend strategy, the study aims to investigate how consumer purchasing power, as revealed by the Comprehensive Consumer Price Index (CPI), influences firms' payment policy. In this study, the author employed Two-Stage Least Squares (2SLS) regression analysis. The findings of the study show that inflation has a negative and magnitude-related effect on capital gains. There is clearly a correlation between market development and inflation, with a comparable pattern observed in the growing numbers of growth in the sector.

Davcev, L., et al. (2018) investigates how inflation and interest rates influence GDP growth in Romania, Bulgaria, and Yugoslav Republic of Macedonia from 2000 to 2014. It examines differences in these effects across the three nations, emphasizing FYROM's EU aspirations and differing monetary policies in Bulgaria and Romania, both EU countries outside the Eurozone. Using unit root tests, Granger causality, and cointegration analyses, the study reveals small negative correlations between inflation, interest rates, and GDP in Bulgaria, larger negative correlations in Romania, and weak correlations in FYROM.

Were, M., & Wambua, J. (2013) on their study investigated the factors that influence interest rate spreads in Kenya's banking industry. It makes use of panel data analysis methodologies and regression analysis to examine the roles played by macroeconomic variables and bank-specific factors. Research results demonstrate that bank-specific characteristics have a substantial impact on interest rate spreads, although macroeconomic variables such as real GDP growth and inflation rate do not exhibit a significant impact.

Manasseh, C. O et al. (2018) used a modified consumer spending model, this study examines how interest and inflation rates affect consumer spending in Nigeria. Granger causality tests are used to assess the causal relationship between consumer expenditure, interest rates, and inflation rates. The data analyzed spans the years 1981 to 2011. The results show that interest rates, inflation, savings, per capita income, and indirect taxes can explain 93.38% of the volatility in consumer expenditure. The report suggests enacting expansionary fiscal and monetary policies, such as higher government spending, lower tax and interest rates, to encourage economic development and stability.

Ousman Jallow (2020) aims to examine how interest rates and inflation affected The Gambia's exchange rate from January 2007 to December 2018. The study uses dynamic models such as Fully Modified Ordinary Least Squares,(FMOLS), Dynamic Ordinary Least Squares(DOLS), and Canonical Cointegrating Regression(CCR) to reveal a positive correlation between inflation and exchange rates. This suggests that higher inflation causes the Gambian Dalasi to appreciate relative to the US dollar. On the other hand, there is a negative correlation between interest rates and exchange rates, indicating that higher interest rates lead to a depreciation of the Dalasi. A feedback loop between interest rates and exchange rates, as well as a unidirectional causal relationship from inflation to exchange rates, is confirmed by EG-Causality analysis.

Existing literature has extensively investigated the direct financial effects of inflation and interest rates on individual finances(Ali, M. et al,2023); however, few studies have been conducted to assess how these economic factors alter people's perceptions of the financial stability of an individual or behavioural finance. Specifically, there is a vacuum in knowing how economic awareness, income, social variables, and financial stability perception influence the individual's behavioral finance views on personal income, especially during economic uncertainty, such as the post-COVID-19 setting and global instability(Yazdanparast, A., & Alhenawi, Y., 2022). This study tries to address this vacuum by looking at these aspects together, providing insights into how people manage their finances in the face of changing economic situations. This study aims to inform policies that support individuals' financial resilience during times of rising inflation and interest rates by investigating the roles of economic awareness, income impact perception, social influences, and behavioural factors in shaping perceptions of financial stability.

3. OBJECTIVES OF THE STUDY

1. To evaluate the influence of economic awareness on financial behaviour.
2. To assess the impact of income perception on financial behaviour.
3. To analyse the role of social factors in shaping financial behaviour.
4. To examine the effect of financial stability perception on financial behaviour.

4. CONCEPTUAL FRAMEWORK

Figure 2. Conceptual framework

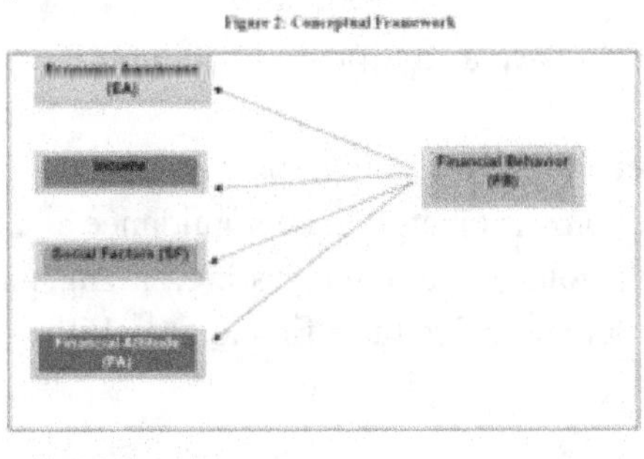

Conceptual Framework Overview

The framework focuses on how a number of social factors, income, economic literacy, and economic considerations, affect people's behavior. The main objective of this framework is to understand how these independent variables influence people's behavior in the face of rising interest rates and inflation.

Economic Awareness (EA):
EA: Economic literacy does have a significant impact on economic behavior.

EA describes an individual's understanding of economic concepts, including inflation, interest rates, and monetary policy. EA affects people's ability to understand economic fluctuations, helping them recognize the impact on their income and change their spending behaviour. People with high levels of EA anticipate the financial consequences of their financial well-being and make appropriate decisions.

Impact of Income:
II: Income does have a significant impact on economic behavior.

This stage looks at how people interpret changes in their incomes caused by economic changes such as inflation and interest rates. People's overall sense of financial security is influenced by their perceived decline in purchasing power or income, which in turn affects their sense of financial security.

Social Factors:
SF: Social factors do have a significant impact on Financial behaviour.

Family and social networks have a big impact on how people behave financially, especially when the economy is changing. Peer guidance and support networks can promote wiser financial habits, including investing, saving, and frugal spending, all of which affect how people perceive their financial stability.

Financial Attitude:
FA: Financial Attitude does have a significant impact on Financial behaviour.

The ultimate goal of this measure is to assess people's perceptions of their financial security in the face of changing market conditions. Perceptions of financial intentions refer to how well a person feels in control of their money and how well prepared they are for changes in the economy, including inflation and interest rates.

Financial Behaviour (Dependent variable): Behavioural factors encompass financial attitudes and behaviours like spending patterns, risk tolerance, and saving habits. Economic Awareness and social factors have an impact on behavioural elements, which serve as mediators in determining how people react to changes in the economy, particularly when it comes to risk management and financial planning.

5. DATA AND METHODOLOGY

The study has gathered 357 samples by using a structured questionnaire to collect the responses. Convenient sampling has been used in this study for data analysis. In this study, the authors employed Structural Equation Modelling (SEM). Structural Equation Modeling is a broad-ranging methodology in the formulation and testing of hypotheses concerning relationships between latent variables and their indicators. It describes the essential constituents of the SEM technique and explains, without delving into sophisticated statistics, the SEM approach to researchers and students who possess foundational knowledge of inferential statistics. SEM model invokes various concepts from conventional social and behavioral science frameworks such as associational regression, multivariate correlation, and ANOVA.(Hoyle, R. H. 1995)

SEM Application in the Framework

The investigation of direct and indirect influences on the perception of financial stability will be made possible via structural equation modelling SEM. By establishing connections between independent and dependent variables. SEM allows us to examine how each component influences financial impressions.

Direct Paths: We can create direct paths from each of the independent variables—EA, Income Impact, Social Factors, Financial Attitude and—to the dependent variable, Financial Behaviour, using SEM.
Indirect Paths: SEM will also record how behavioural factors influence people's financial attitude. Economic Awareness, for instance, may have an indirect effect on the formation of financial attitudes through behavioural factors, emphasizing the role that prudent financial practices play in promoting stability.

By examining how well each variable predicts shifts in Financial Stability Perception, we may use Structural Equation Modelling to validate each hypothesis. Because it takes into consideration the intricate linkages and dependencies between numerous factors, SEM is especially helpful for this framework. It offers insights into the direction and strength of these relationships.

Empirical Methodology and Discussion

The reliability analysis shows a strong internal consistency, indicated by a Cronbach's Alpha of 0.858 for 15 items. All 357 responses were valid, with no missing data, ensuring a comprehensive dataset for the analysis. These findings confirm that the survey instrument is dependable for assessing factors like economic awareness, income, social influences, financial attitude and financial behaviour.

Structural Equation Modelling (SEM) Analysis

The study consists of two steps: These steps include:

1) Determining the measurement model, which includes the procedure of confirmatory factor analysis,
2) Describing the estimated model coefficients through the structural Equation model.

Table 1. Confirmatory factor analysis (CFA) model fit indices

Fit Indices	Recommended	Observed	Result
Chi-Square test	Insignificant Chi-square test($\chi 2$)	$\chi 2$=240.977 D f = 80 p-value = .000	Significant Chi-square test
CMIN	Less than 5	3.012	Good fit
CFI (Comparative fit index)	More than 0.9 good fit 0.8-0.9 borderline fit	0.887	Acceptable fit
TLI	More than 0.9 good fit 0.8-0.9 borderline fit	0.852	Acceptable fit
RMESEA (Root mean square error of approximation)	Less than 0.08 for adequate fit 0.08-0.1 for acceptable fit	0.080	Acceptable fit

Source: Author's own estimation

The results of the Confirmatory Factor Analysis (CFA) indicate that the model demonstrates an acceptable fit overall. The Chi-Square test yielded a significant result ($\chi 2$\chi^2$\chi 2$ = 240.977, df = 80, p-value = .000), which is expected due to the test's sensitivity to sample size. The CMIN value of 3.012 is below the recommended threshold of 5, indicating a good fit. The Comparative Fit Index (CFI) stands at 0.887, which, while slightly below the ideal threshold of 0.9, is within the acceptable range for borderline fit. Similarly, the Tucker-Lewis Index (TLI) at 0.852 suggests an acceptable fit, though it falls short of the optimal range. Lastly, the Root

Mean Square Error of Approximation (RMSEA) is 0.080, meeting the threshold for adequate fit. These indices collectively suggest that the model is reasonably well-specified, with minor areas for improvement in achieving a perfect fit.

Figure 3. Confirmatory factor analysis model

Figure 3: Confirmatory Factor Analysis Model

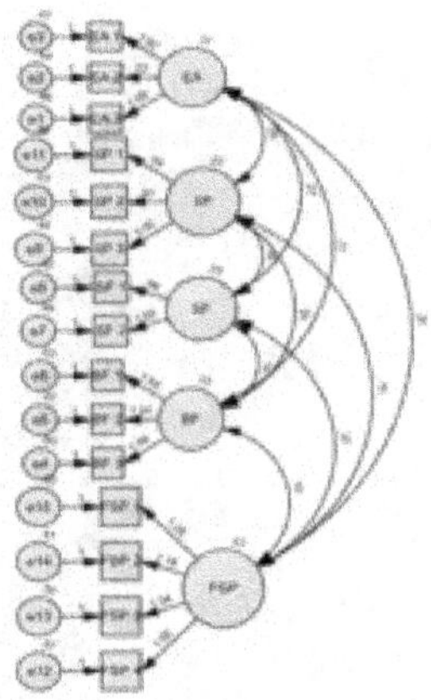

Source: Author's own compilation

Figure 4. Structural equation modelling (SEM analysis)

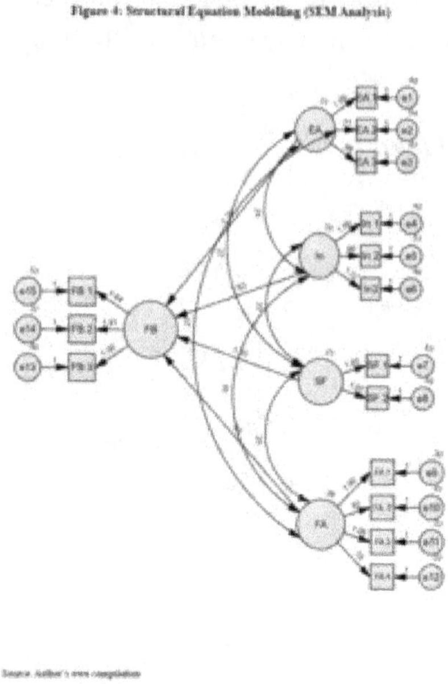

The structural equation model represents the relationships among five constructs: Financial Attitude (FA), Economic Awareness (EA), Social Factors (SF), Income Impact (II), and Financial Behavioural (FB). Each construct is measured using multiple observed indicators, such as FA1 to FA4 for Financial Attitude. Financial Behavioural Factors have the most significant influence on FA, with a path coefficient of 1.64. Income Impact and Economic Awareness also impact FA, with coefficients of 1.07 and 0.98, respectively. Social Factors have a smaller but noteworthy impact on FA, indicated by a path coefficient of 0.38. This model emphasizes that Financial Behavioural Factors play a critical role in determining financial behaviour, with other factors contributing in varying proportions.

Table 2. Hypothesis analysis

Hypothesis	path	Standardized Coefficient	C.R	P- Value	Result
H1	Economic awareness/ Behavioural factors	0.721	7.329	<.001	Supported
H2	Income impact perception/ Behavioural factors	0.908	7.612	<.001	Supported
H3	Social factors/Behavioural factors	0.991	8.006	<.001	Supported
H4	Financial stability perception/ Behavioural factors	1.281	9.989	<.001	Supported

Source: Author's own estimation

The analysis reveals significant relationships between behavioural factors and four key predictors: economic awareness, income impact, social factors, and financial attitude.

H1: Economic Awareness → Financial Behavioural

Economic awareness moderately impacts behavioural factors with a standardized coefficient of 0.721. The critical ratio (C.R.) of 7.329 and a p-value < 0.001 confirm the relationship is statistically significant, indicating that greater economic awareness positively influences behavioural patterns.

H2: Income Impact → Financial Behavioural

Income impact perception demonstrates a strong influence on behavioural factors, with a standardized coefficient of 0.908. The high C.R. value of 7.612 and a p-value < 0.001 validate the significance of this relationship, highlighting that perceptions of income strongly shape behaviour.

H3: Social Factors → Financial Behavioural

Social factors exhibit a very strong effect on behavioural factors, reflected in a coefficient of 0.991. The critical ratio of 8.006 and a p-value < 0.001 confirm this is a statistically significant relationship, emphasizing the substantial role of social factors in behavioural outcomes.

H4: Financial Attitude → Financial Behavioural

Financial stability perception emerges as the most impactful variable, with a standardized coefficient of 1.281. A C.R. value of 9.989 and a p-value < 0.001 further affirm this strong and statistically significant relationship. This suggests that perceptions of financial stability have the greatest influence on behavioural factors.

All four hypotheses are supported, indicating that behavioural factors are significantly influenced by economic awareness, income impact perception, social factors, and financial stability perception. Among these, financial stability perception has the strongest effect, followed by income impact perception, social factors, and economic awareness. These findings underscore the importance of enhancing financial stability perception and economic awareness to positively shape behavioural patterns, particularly in decision-making contexts.

Findings

The findings indicate that financial behavioural factors play an essential role in financial choice when interest rates are high and inflation is rising. Thus, economic awareness, having a strong connection with the behavioural responses brought about, underscores the importance of financial literacy to help people better understand such daunting economic environments. People who have better information about economic trends and conditions are usually more thoughtful in their financial choices. In addition, notions of how income would change would meaningfully contribute to driving behaviour, much of it by being sensitive to stable vs. changeable income stability and its implications in financial planning and behaviour under uncertainty. Social factors also play a meaningful role, and this could mean that societal influences-culture and peer group behaviour influence the way people manage their finances. Finally, it is found that financial behavioural factors themselves have strong effects on perception of financial stability, and, thus, after embracing disciplined financial habits, only then can they experience safety in an economically stressful period.

6. CONCLUSION

The conclusion of this study emphasize that high interest rates and inflation pose significant challenges to personal finance, affecting personal investment behavior and decision-making processes with high levels of financial literacy. Individuals are prepared well enough to navigate inflation and interest rate fluctuations, as such they are more likely to make informed financial decisions in line with their long-term goals and also, socio-economic factors hear as household income, social networks and external economic pressures, in response to changing macroeconomic conditions. The study has found how people change their spending strategies. It is known that inflation and interest rates tend to increase consumer spending is reduced, increased debt burden and increased financial pressures, especially for lower income groups. Consequently financial institutions and policy makers should pay attention improving financial education skills to empower individuals in the face of economic uncertainty. This study finds a strong link to monetary provides a comprehensive analysis of the relationship between macro and personal investment decisions. Future research in this area opens up avenues for determining how millennials and retirees respond to currently experienced changes and trends in economic changes, such as rising interest rates and inflation. The study will be helpful for policymakers to understand the relationship between the public financial behaviour in uncertain economic conditions.

REFERENCES

Aizenman, J., Cheung, Y. W., & Ito, H. (2019). The interest rate effect on private saving: Alternative perspectives. *Journal of International Commerce. Economic Policy*, *10*(01), 1950002.

Al Kholilah, N., & Iramani, R. (2013). Studi financial management behavior pada masyarakat surabaya. *Journal of Business & Banking*, *3*(1), 69–80. DOI: 10.14414/jbb.v3i1.255

Ali, M., Naqi, S. M. A., & Habib, M. (2023). The study "Unravelling the Impact: Assessing the Impacts of Rising Rates of Interest and Inflation on Individual Finances". sjesr, 6(2), 56-62.

Awasthi, V., & Kansra, P. (2023). Blockchain in the healthcare industry: process and applications. In *Advanced machine learning algorithms for complex financial applications* (pp. 81–93). IGI Global. DOI: 10.4018/978-1-6684-4483-2.ch006

Baddeley, M. (2018). *Behavioural Economics and Finance*. Routledge. DOI: 10.4324/9781315211879

Chopra, M. A., Collyns, M. C., Hemming, M. R., Parker, M. K. E., Chu, W., & Fratzscher, M. O. (1995). *India: economic reform and growth*. International Monetary Fund.

Davcev, L., Hourvouliades, N., & Komic, J. (2018). Impact of interest rate and inflation on GDP in Bulgaria, Romania and FYROM. *Journal of Balkan & Near Eastern Studies*, *20*(2), 131–147. DOI: 10.1080/19448953.2018.1379746

El Bourainy, M., Salah, A., & El Sherif, M. (2021). Assessing the impact of financial inclusion on inflation rate in developing countries. *Open Journal of Social Sciences*, *9*(01), 397–424. DOI: 10.4236/jss.2021.91030

Friedman, B. M., & Kuttner, K. N. (2010). Implementation of monetary policy: How do central banks set interest rates? In *Handbook of Monetary Economics* (Vol. 3), 1345-1438.

Garcia, M. J. R. (2013). Financial education and behavioral finance: New insights into the role of information in financial decisions. *Journal of Economic Surveys*, *27*(2), 297–315. DOI: 10.1111/j.1467-6419.2011.00705.x

Gevorkyan, A. V., & Kvangraven, I. H. (2016). Assessing recent determinants of borrowing costs in sub-Saharan Africa. *Review of Development Economics*, *20*(4), 721–738. DOI: 10.1111/rode.12195

Grable, J. E., Park, J. Y., & Joo, S. H. (2009). Explaining financial management behavior for Koreans living in the United States. *The Journal of Consumer Affairs, 43*(1), 80–107. DOI: 10.1111/j.1745-6606.2008.01128.x

Hartono, J. (2022). Teori portofolio dan analisis investasi.

Hoyle, R. H. (1995). The structural equation modeling approach: Basic concepts and fundamental issues. In Hoyle, R. H. (Ed.), *Structural equation modeling: Concepts, issues, and applications* (pp. 1–15).

Ida, I. D. A., & Dwinta, C. Y. (2010). Pengaruh Locus Of Control, financial knowledge, income terhadap financial management behavior. *Jurnal Bisnis dan Akuntansi, 12*(3), 131-144.

IYER, M. (2018). Nature of Relationship Between Inflation and Savings: Evidence from India. *NMIMS Journal of Economics and Public Policy*, 46-60.

Joof, F., & Jallow, O. (2020). The impact of interest rate and inflation on the exchange rate of the Gambia. *International Journal of Economics, Commerce and Management,, 8*.

Kansra, P., & Gill, H. S. (2017). Role of perceptions in health insurance buying behaviour of workers employed in informal sector of India. *Global Business Review, 18*(1), 250–266. DOI: 10.1177/0972150916666992

Katnic, I., Katnic, M., Orlandic, M., Radunovic, M., & Mugosa, I. (2024). Understanding the Role of Financial Literacy in Enhancing Economic Stability and Resilience in Montenegro: A Data-Driven Approach. *Sustainability (Basel), 16*(24), 11065. DOI: 10.3390/su162411065

Khan, M. I. K., Meher, M. A. K. M., & Syed, S. M. K. (2013). Impact of inflation on dividend policy: Synchronization of capital gain and interest rate. *Pensee Journal, 75*, 389–393.

Klontz, B., Britt, S. L., Mentzer, J., & Klontz, T. (2011). Money beliefs and financial behaviors: Development of the Klontz Money Script Inventory. *Journal of Financial Therapy*, *2*(1), 1. DOI: 10.4148/jft.v2i1.451

Lusardi, A., & Mitchell, O. S. (2007). Baby boomer retirement security: The roles of planning, financial literacy, and housing wealth. *Journal of Monetary Economics, 54*(1), 205–224. DOI: 10.1016/j.jmoneco.2006.12.001

Lusardi, A., & Mitchell, O. S. (2007). Financial literacy and retirement planning: New evidence from the Rand American Life Panel. Michigan Retirement Research Centre Research Paper No. WP 2007-157.

Manasseh, C. O., Abada, F. C., Ogbuabor, J. E., Onwumere, J. U. J., Urama, C. E., & Okoro, O. E. (2018). The effects of interest and inflation rates on consumption expenditure: Application of consumer spending model. *International Journal of Economics and Financial Issues*, *8*(4), 32–38.

Ningsih, R. U., & Rita, M. R. (2010). Financial Attitudes dan Komunikasi Keluarga Tentang Pengeluaran Uang Saku: Ditinjau dari Perbedaan Gender. *Informatics & Business Institute Darmajaya*, *8*(2), 206–219.

Oberoi, S., & Kansra, P. (2021). Motivating antecedents and consequences of blockchain technology in the insurance industry. In *Blockchain technology and applications for digital marketing* (pp. 276–285). IGI Global. DOI: 10.4018/978-1-7998-8081-3.ch017

Oberoi, S., & Kansra, P. (2022). Blockchain technology in the insurance industry. In *Applications, challenges, and opportunities of blockchain technology in banking and insurance* (pp. 160–172). IGI Global. DOI: 10.4018/978-1-6684-4133-6.ch009

Perry, V. G., & Morris, M. D. (2005). Who is in control? The role of self-perception, knowledge, and income in explaining consumer financial behavior. *The Journal of Consumer Affairs*, *39*(2), 299–313. DOI: 10.1111/j.1745-6606.2005.00016.x

Poole, W. (1972). The role of interest rates and inflation in the consumption function. *Brookings Papers on Economic Activity*, *1972*(1), 211–220. DOI: 10.2307/2534122

Rajna, A., Ezat, W. S., Al Junid, S., & Moshiri, H. (2011). Financial management attitude and practice among the medical practitioners in public and private medical service in Malaysia. *International Journal of Business and Management*, *6*(8), 105.

Rashid, A., & Khalid, S. (2020). Exploring the impacts of inflation, interest rates, and their uncertainty on deposits and advances of conventional and Islamic Banks of Pakistan. *Journal of Economic Cooperation & Development*, *41*(3), 117–150.

Ricciardi, V., & Simon, H. K. (2000). What is behavioral finance? *Business. Education & Technology Journal*, *2*(2), 1–9.

Ullah, N., & Asghar, U. (2023). The effect of an increase in the interest rate and inflation on personal finances in Islamic Republic of Pakistan. Al-Qamar, 81-94.

Were, M., & Wambua, J. (2013). Assessing the determinants of interest rate spread of commercial banks in Kenya: An empirical investigation (No. 4). KBA Centre for Research on Financial Markets and Policy Working Paper Series.

Xiao, J. J., & Tao, C. (2021). Consumer finance/household finance: The definition and scope. *China Finance Review International*, *11*(1), 1–25. DOI: 10.1108/CFRI-04-2020-0032

Yazdanparast, A., & Alhenawi, Y. (2022). Impact of COVID-19 pandemic on household financial decisions: A consumer vulnerability perspective. *Journal of Consumer Behaviour*, *21*(4), 806–827. DOI: 10.1002/cb.2038 PMID: 37519436

Chapter 10
Blockchain in Industrial Supply Chains:
Tracing the Transparency

Ananya Pandey
https://orcid.org/0000-0002-2419-6314
Christ University, Bangalore, India

ABSTRACT

Over the past several years, blockchain technology has become more and more significant and widely accepted. Independent businesses that are actively involved in the upstream and downstream flows of goods, services, money and information from a source to a customer make a supply chain. Members of the supply chain must collaborate and exchange information in order to be managed effectively. Blockchain technology offers a platform for direct communication between supply chain participants to exchange reliable and unchangeable data, which has the potential to significantly enhance supply chain management and accomplish supply chain performance goals. Notwithstanding its potential, there are obstacles to the broad use of blockchain. Legal and regulatory issues are also very important for supply chain management in the future. Keeping in view the above, the chapter analyzes the role of blockchain in the industrial supply chain and explores the facet of transparency in supply chain management.

INTRODUCTION

The network of all the people, businesses, assets, processes, and technology used in the production and marketing of a product is known as a supply chain (Seuring et al., 2008). Everything from the transfer of raw materials from the supplier to the

DOI: 10.4018/979-8-3373-1290-3.ch010

producer to the final delivery to the customer is included in a supply chain. The distribution channel is the part of the supply chain that handles moving the final product from the producer to the customer. The coordination and administration of a complicated web of operations involved in getting a product from suppliers of raw materials to the customer is known as supply chain management (Strauss & Frost, 2014). For organizations to guarantee that products are delivered on schedule, within budget, and in good shape, effective supply chain management is essential. It entails a number of procedures, such as manufacturing, distribution, logistics, and procurement, all of which need to be carefully managed to attain maximum effectiveness and client satisfaction (Croxton et al., 2001). The absence of traceability and transparency is one of the main issues in supply chain management. Conventional supply chains frequently have several middlemen, each of whom keeps their own records. This disjointed strategy may result in inconsistencies, hold-ups, and higher expenses (Grant & Startz, 2022). Furthermore, it becomes challenging to track down the products' origins, which is especially troublesome in sectors like food and medicines where authenticity and safety are crucial.

Many of these issues can be resolved by blockchain technology, which offers an unchangeable and transparent record of each supply chain transaction. Blockchain makes it possible for all supply chain participants to access a single, shared ledger, guaranteeing that everyone is aware of the same data (Zelbst et al., 2020). Supply chains can become more efficient and economical by reducing fraud, mistakes, and inefficiencies as a result of this transparency. In essence, blockchain technology is a distributed ledger system that makes it possible for numerous parties to securely, openly, and impenetrably record transactions (Benton et al., 2018). A blockchain is managed by a network of nodes, each of which has a copy of the complete ledger, in contrast to conventional centralized databases. By preventing any one party from controlling the entire system, this decentralized structure lowers the possibility of fraud and manipulation. A list of transactions is contained in each of the blocks that make up a blockchain (Tripathi et al., 2023). A chain is created by cryptographically connecting these blocks to one another. The ledger is immutable once a block is added to the chain because it cannot be changed without also altering all blocks that come after it (Sun, 2020). The immutability of blockchain is one of its primary characteristics. Another essential element of blockchain technology is smart contracts. The terms of these self-executing contracts are encoded directly into the code. When certain criteria are satisfied, they automatically execute and enforce the terms of the contract, doing away with the need for middlemen and lowering the likelihood of disagreements. Increased transparency is another benefit of blockchain technology (Abdelhamid & Hassan, 2019). All network users can see every transaction that is recorded on the blockchain, making it a single source of truth. In sectors like finance, healthcare, and supply chain management where confidence and verification are essential, this transparency can be very helpful (Xu et al., 2021).

In light of the above perspective, this chapter explores the role of blockchain in industrial supply chain management. Further it analyzes the innovations, challenges and pathways in determining transparency in the supply chain with the help of blockchain technology.

EVOLUTION OF BLOCKCHAIN IN SUPPLY CHAIN: A BRIEF OVERVIEW

The early 1990s saw the establishment of a large portion of the blockchain's foundation. While working for the US software business Bellcore, Stuart Haber and Scott Stornetta met and recognized a problem that the world relied too much on records that weren't independently verified, which undermined confidence in their effectiveness (Popper, 2015). The two decided to start developing a solution. Haber and Stornetta wrote the algorithm that would be known as the blockchain within a year after presenting their concept. The phrase itself comes from the way information is bundled into blocks and connected like a chain, including transaction records and their unique hashes (Popovski et al., 2018). The chain gets stronger as more blocks are added. By the late 1990s, computer scientist Nick Szabo had tried one of the earliest uses of this new "decentralized" system, putting forward "bit gold," which was a precursor to the now-famous bitcoin. It would take another ten years before someone would expand on Haber and Stornetta's efforts to introduce decentralized money, and Bit Gold was never put into use (Larrier, 2021). By publishing a white paper under the pseudonym Satoshi Nakamoto, a developer or group of developers conceptualizes the cryptocurrency bitcoin and establishes the blockchain as its public transaction record (Saraji, 2023). The cryptocurrency market would soar during the ensuing ten years as a result of this. Vitalik Buterin, an early bitcoin fan, developed Ethereum five years after the white paper was released. When he failed to get the bitcoin community to agree, he created his own blockchain-based platform because he believed that Bitcoin needed a scripting language for application development (Sheldon, 2021). For instance, it is the foundation upon which NFTs are constructed and makes use of smart contracts. Supply chain experts start utilizing blockchain technology. Supply chain blockchains "tokenize" a range of transaction-related data in place of currency, giving purchase orders, inventory units, and bills of lading distinct and easily verifiable identifiers (Higgins, 2022). Tokens going along the chain are "signed" using the individual digital signatures of each chain participant.

FUNDAMENTALS OF BLOCKCHAIN FOR SUPPLY CHAIN

Blockchain is projected to help procurement organizations across all industries in reducing costs and improving performance while creating more value for their businesses (Chang & Chen, 2020). This includes enhanced security and visibility as well as the capacity to track intricate variables connected to sustainability and ethical sourcing. Some of the fundamentals of blockchain in enhancing traceability and transparency in the supply chain are classified below.

Smart Contracts

Digital agreements that are maintained on a blockchain and are automatically carried out when specific terms and circumstances are fulfilled are known as smart contracts. Usually, smart contracts are used to automate the implementation of an agreement so that everyone involved can know the result right away, without the need for a middleman or wasting time (Levy, 2017). They can also automate a workflow, so that when certain conditions are satisfied, the next step is triggered. Simple "if/when…then…" words that are encoded into code on a blockchain are the basis for how smart contracts operate (IBM, n.d.). When certain requirements are satisfied and confirmed, a network of computers carries out the actions. These could be sending alerts, registering a car, issuing a ticket, or releasing payments to the right people. After the transaction is finished, the blockchain is updated (Macrinici et al., 2018). This implies that the transaction cannot be altered and that the outcomes are only visible to those who have been given authorization. A smart contract can contain as many conditions as necessary to reassure participants that the activity will be finished to their satisfaction (Javaid et al., 2022). Participants must decide how transactions and their data are represented on the blockchain, decide on the "if/when...then…" rules that control those transactions, look into any potential exceptions, and design a dispute resolution procedure in order to set the conditions (IBM, n.d.). A developer can then program the smart contract, though more and more companies using blockchain technology for business are offering templates, web interfaces, and other online tools to make the process of creating smart contracts easier (Taherdoost, 2023).

Distributed Ledgers

The core component of Distributed Ledger Technology (DLT) is an encoded, dispersed database that houses transaction records. A distributed ledger is a database that is accessible by numerous users worldwide and dispersed among numerous computers, nodes, organizations, or nations (Deshpande et al., 2017). In distributed ledgers, transactions are recorded, shared, and synchronized in their individual electronic ledgers by independent nodes rather than being stored on a single centralized server. Blockchain applications are made possible by a number of technologies, including distributed ledger technology, digital signatures, distributed networks, and encryption/decryption techniques (Collomb & Sok, 2016). Blockchain is one of the DLT kinds where transactions are recorded using a hash, which is an immutable cryptographic signature. Distributed ledgers are frequently referred to as blockchains for this reason. Since anyone may see all transaction records, distributed ledgers offer a high degree of transparency. Nodes must verify the addition of data using a variety of consensus techniques (Panwar & Bhatnagar, 2020). Additionally, any attempt to modify or update data in the ledger is instantly mirrored on all network nodes, preventing illegitimate transactions. Errors at the central authority level can cause a single point of failure in a centralized network, which can disrupt the entire system (Ganne, 2018). However, a single point of failure is not a possibility with distributed networks. Participating nodes' trust factor rises as a result of the decentralized structure. Transaction costs are decreased by the decentralized structure of validation (Zarrin et al., 2021).

Consensus Mechanism

The programming and procedure used in blockchain systems to reach distributed agreement over the status of a data set or the ledger is known as a consensus mechanism. The usage of distributed ledgers, blockchains, and cryptocurrencies is advantageous because consensus processes take the place of much slower, occasionally erroneous, or unreliable human auditors and verifiers (Zhang et al., 2020). After comparing the request with its records, nodes that have entered data from a pending transaction report back with an approval or disapproval status. An immutable ledger, for instance, would readily reject a user's request to conduct a transaction using previously spent coins that have already been accounted for, as evidenced by a majority disapproval (Lashkari & Musilek, 2021). Networks frequently ban users who don't follow consensus. A node would need to request a network-wide recall in order to contest the record. The transaction is verified, dispersed, and permanently recorded in the blockchain if more than two-thirds of their peer nodes concur (Memon et al., 2018). Since consensus mechanisms gained popularity, researchers have been experimenting with them in an effort to figure out how to safely scale blockchains without sacrificing their decentralized nature (Bashir, 2022). In order to achieve this, a number of consensus techniques are in use, the majority of which fall short of simultaneously improving security, scalability, and decentralization. Instead, even on the blockchains that say they have "solved" this trilemma, one of these elements is typically sacrificed to improve one or two of the others (Komalavalli et al., 2020).

APPLICATIONS OF BLOCKCHAIN IN INDUSTRIAL SUPPLY CHAIN

The decentralized structure of modern blockchain technology is the best remedy for these pressing issues facing the supply chain sector. The distributed ledger concept is the foundation of blockchain technology (Tripathi et al., 2023). Blockchain technology entails building a transparent, decentralized network for transaction recording and verification. The verified transactions are now organized into blocks, which are subsequently sequentially added to the current chain of blocks (Islam, 2023). Every block in the chain has a distinct digital signature known as a hash that connects to the block before it. Some of the significant applications of blockchain in the industrial supply chain are as follows.

Traceability and Provenance

Blockchain-based traceability is becoming more and more popular as a means of correctly identifying fraud and counterfeiting, swiftly proving the validity and origin of items, and securely sharing asset provenance data among supply chain participants (Ahmed & MacCarthy, 2023). With blockchain for provenance and traceability, sensitive corporate data is better protected, asset-related data and transactions are fully visible, and product source data can be traced back in seconds as opposed to days (Mann et al., 2018). After being verified and encrypted, data and transactions are kept in time-stamped blocks connected chronologically inside the blockchain network for provenance and traceability. The blocks come together to create an immutable distributed ledger, which functions as a database that is accessible to numerous authorized users and offers a single source of truth for confirming the origin of inventories and assets (Raja Santhy & Muthuswamy, 2022). Through role-specific web applications, network users engage with the distributed ledger to conduct transactions and track data (Frankenfield, 2023). For instance, food traceability is crucial for a number of reasons, including maintaining product safety, reducing the risk of foodborne illness, confirming ingredient claims, and enabling prompt response to contamination issues (Pal & Kant, 2019). The food supply chain methods in place today are largely antiquated, have contributed to numerous global outbreaks of foodborne illness, are rife with supply chain fraud, and frequently lack data openness amongst supply chain participants (Chaturvedi et al., 2014). Blockchain food traceability systems offer numerous advantages, such as assisting in the efficient containment of contamination outbreaks, allowing product tracing in seconds rather than weeks, producing an auditable trail of precise data in a manner that is impenetrable to tampering, and drastically reducing expenses (Feng et al., 2020).

Smart Contracts for Automation

Smart contracts are automatically activated when certain conditions are met. Automation and operational efficiency are fueled by this. A supply chain manager might, for instance, establish a contract with precise terms for a given order and deposit the money into a holding account (Lamb, 2018). After the designated task is finished, the money will automatically leave the holding account without any human involvement. When distributed ledger technology and the internet of things (IoT) are combined, the capability of smart contracts increases dramatically (Uddin et al., 2021). GPS enabled by the Internet of Things can improve the company's ability to monitor and trace products across the supply chain. When certain predetermined criteria are satisfied, data from RFID sensors can be used as an automatic trigger for a smart contract (Oladele, 2024). Due to the Internet of Things, RFID, temperature sensors, mobile devices, DLT, and Bluetooth, collaborative smart contracts have seen significant progress. For instance, Shipchain makes it possible to follow shipments from the manufacturer to the final delivery, and Modum's smart contracts include a patented temperature logger to measure the environmental conditions of the shipments (Zheng et al., 2020). Its Ethereum network powers its smart contracts, which side chains can copy and employ to save money. Next is TE-Foods, which unifies all food partners to trace food from farm to table and combat fraud and unreliable supply chains (Duan et al., 2024).

Sustainability and Ethical Sourcing

By offering a common, real-time platform for information sharing, blockchain encourages cooperation among supply chain actors. Throughout the whole supply chain network, this cooperative approach makes it easier to establish and oversee ethical sourcing standards (Agarwal et al., 2021). One such sector that needs traceability implementation to address the issues of low visibility and information asymmetry is the textile and apparel industry (Kumar et al., 2017). Consumers have trouble accessing product information that can guarantee product authenticity or encourage ethical purchasing practices (Alves et al., 2014). Furthermore, in an unsafe setting when there is a chance of data manipulation and a fear of losing information advantage, it is difficult for stakeholders to exchange important information. One potential remedy for these supply chain problems is the implementation of supply chain traceability (Mandolla et al., 2019). By establishing an information trail and guaranteeing security and data immutability, blockchain has surfaced as a potential way to implement traceability (Wang et al., 2019). Secure information exchange, real-time data collection, supply chain transparency and visibility, product quality monitoring and control, and operation monitoring and control are all made possible by blockchain-based traceability (Agarwal et al., 2021).

Combating Counterfeit and Fraudulent Activities

Businesses and consumers alike are seriously threatened by fake products in the supply chain. The proliferation of fake goods frequently leads to a number of problems, such as monetary losses, legal ramifications, and harm to one's reputation (Ghadge et al., 2021). Another common problem in the supply chain sector is product misrepresentation. Giving misleading information regarding the items and goods can lead to safety risks, legal ramifications, and harm to one's reputation. Manufacturers can add actual product serial numbers to the ledgers with the use of blockchain technology (Visciano & Schirone, 2021). It is impossible to tamper with the serial number that is kept in the ledger. Customers can verify a product's legitimacy before purchasing it by using the saved serial number (Saraswathi et al., 2024). Customers can also post reviews of the goods they buy to confirm the legitimacy of a manufacturer or seller. A new strategy for improving transparency and trust in the verification process is provided by the system's deeper integration of customer reviews (Yi et al., 2022). Blockchain technology may offer a workable way to stop counterfeiting and supply chain fraud. This distributed ledger technology makes transactions safe, transparent, and impenetrable. Blockchain technology facilitates a safe, transparent record of each transaction in the supply chain that is accessible to all participants, giving them full insight into the process (Sunny et al., 2020).

ADVANTAGES OF BLOCKCHAIN IN SUPPLY CHAIN

Blockchain is being proposed as a distributed record organization system using a consensus mechanism in the industry 4.0 era (Fernández-Caramés et al., 2019). Its qualities—transparency, authenticity, trust, and security—as well as its ability to cut costs, disintermediate, operate efficiently, and produce less waste—have the potential to revolutionize supply chain management (Gao et al., 2018; Philipp et al., 2019; Dutta et al., 2020). Additionally, every transaction made possible by blockchain is more transparent, safe, economical, and efficient. Therefore, it is widely accepted that blockchain's distributed nature helps reduce risks in the supply chain related to piracy, hacking, vulnerability, costly government regulation compliance, and contract disputes (Queiroz et al., 2020). With the use of smart contracts, blockchain also makes it easier to automate manufacturing processes and settle orders in real time (Min, 2019). Additionally, blockchain guarantees that the disruption brought on by shifting paradigms is minimized in the supply chain (Sheel & Nath, 2019; Ivanov et al., 2019). The foundations of supply chain reengineering—traceability, privacy, and data management—are all made possible by blockchains, which also improve supply chain's transparency and visibility, automate processes, remove middlemen, and allow real-time tracking (Chang et al., 2019). Information tracking across all business domains can be synchronized with a well-reengineered supply chain (Zhihong et al., 2019). Additionally, using smart contracts can help save time and money, which will aid supply chain reengineering even more (Dolgui et al, 2020). Data and resource provenance, integrity assurance, privacy and access control, secrecy, and authentication are all made possible by blockchain in the services it offers (Fu & Zhu, 2019). Additionally, it makes it possible to develop a risk control analytics framework for researching the relationship between engineering, business, and information, as well as to collect an analytics viewpoint on digitization in supply chain. Since blockchain can scale up according to needs, it can offer strong risk control even in large production enterprises (Kshetri, 2017). Due to its improved cybersecurity and performance, blockchain is far more secure than conventional IoT systems or security services (Agarwal et al., 2021). Through its integration with supply chains, blockchain enhances cycle time, productivity, and quality; it also creates new business prospects and allows for product differentiation. Numerous studies have been conducted on the effective use of blockchain technology for price management and product elimination (Yoo & Won, 2018). The conventional price tracking system does not display end-to-end price fluctuation across the supply chain and was created in an opaque manner (Gao et al., 2018). During transactions, it only displays the item's final price to the customer immediately. Blockchain can provide all the information to the public and give customers access to the precise prices of suppliers, distributors, and raw materials. All parties involved will disseminate truthful information as a result, guaranteeing price transparency (Agarwal et al., 2021).

CHALLENGES OF BLOCKCHAIN IN SUPPLY CHAIN

One of the most important technological advancements that has already captured the interest of several major industries is the blockchain. The last few years have seen an exponential increase in the use of blockchain technology (Levis et al., 2021). Although most marketers claim that blockchain technology is revolutionary, there is still more work to be done. The blockchain sector continues to face the difficulty of managing a high number of users simultaneously. A single transaction is processed by a number of intricate algorithms using blockchain technology (Sarmah, 2018). The average transaction has also increased significantly as more and more individuals become accustomed to it. It significantly impacted the transaction processing performance because more users mean more computers writing and accessing the network, making the system more clumsy overall (Conte de Leon et al., 2017). The absence of governmental control in the blockchain industry creates a volatile atmosphere and makes it a prime target for market manipulation. For example, the well-known One Coin fraud, in which numerous investors lost money after believing it to be the next big digital currency, turned out to be a Ponzi scheme swindle (Agarwal et al., 2021). No matter how well one understands cryptocurrencies, there's always a danger that the authorities will restrict online wallet or hack it because of some dubious activities. The intricacies of blockchain technology make it difficult for the average person to grasp its advantages (Luchkin et al., 2020). One must read this ground-breaking application and comprehend distributed ledger and encryption concepts before beginning. The fact that financial institutions can offer safe payment gateways and other services at reasonable pricing in comparison to the expenses associated with blockchain is another factor that hinders the adoption of blockchain (Gad et al., 2022). Blockchain is an open ledger that is accessible to all users. Although it is often a necessary component, using it in a delicate setting makes it a liability. Blockchain technology still has a long way to go before it is widely used. It is necessary to redesign the ledger so that only those with permission can access it and that access is restricted. Blockchain is typically used to reduce the costs associated with the third parties and middlemen that are engaged in value transfers (Javaid et al., 2021). Despite its many advantages, blockchain technology is still in its infancy and is difficult to incorporate into established systems. It prevents both the government and commercial companies from adopting it because it is an expensive issue overall (Javaid et al., 2022). The blockchain technology, its advantages, and how it is changing the infrastructure of new technologies like InsurTech and others have market analysts giddy. It will take some time before blockchain becomes a crucial component of every industry, nevertheless, as the aforementioned difficulties are still difficult to overcome (Tripathi et al., 2023).

FUTURE DIRECTIONS

Blockchain offers a non-centralized method of protecting Internet of Things devices, which are vulnerable to cyberattacks using this control system technique. Using a blockchain system to rationalize device administration solves the issue of all devices being connected to a single system (Gad et al., 2022). Blockchain-based smart contracts can manage transactions between Internet of Things devices and preserve the relative states of the data without the need for a mediator. This is particularly advantageous in regions with autonomous cars, smart cities, and agriculture (Hewa et al., 2021). IoT devices with blockchain support are able to transport products automatically and instantly while monitoring proper product programming. One may be certain that the information is accurate, the location is kept the same, and the goods are accepted safely everywhere it goes (Javaid et al., 2021). Governments and regulatory agencies are paying more and more attention to blockchain technology, particularly in the fields of financial regulation and central bank digital currencies (CBDCs) (Karam, 2023). CBDCs are state-issued digital money that conducts safe, transparent transactions via blockchain technology. While other nations including the United States, the European Union, and India are in the process of establishing their own CBDCs, China's digital currency, known as e-CNY, is now leading the way (Sethaput & Innet, 2023). The regulatory evaluation rises in tandem with the growing blockchain uses in banking. The focus is on regulatory compliance regarding digital tax issues, client identification (KYC), and money laundering (AML) (Mekpor, 2019). Blockchain technology is still developing quickly, and new developments are changing a variety of sectors, including supply chain management, gaming, banking, and more (Javaid et al., 2022). Blockchain is getting closer to being widely used as scalability solutions, DeFi expansion, NFTs, and environmental projects gain traction (Far et al., 2023). In the meantime, blockchain is becoming an increasingly important technology in the global digital economy because of its integration with IoT, enterprise adoption, and regulatory changes. Blockchain technology has a bright future ahead of it, and companies and individuals hoping to take use of it will need to keep ahead of these new developments (Uddin et al., 2021).

CONCLUSION

Blockchain technology holds transformative potential for enhancing transparency in industrial supply chains. By offering an immutable, decentralized ledger, blockchain ensures real-time tracking and verification of goods at every stage, mitigating inefficiencies and fostering trust among stakeholders. This technology empowers businesses to combat fraud, reduce delays, and enhance traceability, which are critical for industries like pharmaceuticals, agriculture, and manufacturing, where accountability and quality control are paramount (Nwariaku et al., 2024). The integration of blockchain in supply chains also strengthens sustainability efforts. By enabling detailed tracking of materials and their origins, companies can ensure compliance with environmental regulations and ethical sourcing practices, appealing to increasingly eco-conscious consumers. Furthermore, smart contracts—self-executing agreements coded within the blockchain—automate transactions and eliminate intermediaries, reducing operational costs and enhancing efficiency (Lamb, 2018). Despite its advantages, challenges remain. The high implementation costs, scalability issues, and the need for industry-wide standardization can hinder widespread adoption. Moreover, the transition requires significant investment in infrastructure and training to bridge the knowledge gap. Data privacy and security concerns, especially in sensitive industries, also demand robust solutions. Nevertheless, as technology matures, the potential benefits outweigh these obstacles. Collaborations among industry leaders, policymakers, and tech innovators are crucial to addressing these challenges and ensuring blockchain's seamless integration into global supply chains. In conclusion, blockchain technology has the power to revolutionize industrial supply chains by providing unmatched transparency, efficiency, and accountability. Its adoption will not only streamline operations but also redefine industry standards, making supply chains more resilient, ethical, and future-ready in an increasingly interconnected world. Supply chains can be made much better in terms of coordination, finance, end-to-end traceability, and product delivery speed. The time has come for supply chain managers who have been watching from the sidelines to evaluate how blockchain technology might benefit their companies. They must work together to create new regulations, test new technology, run trials on multiple blockchain platforms, and create an ecosystem with other businesses. In fact, resources will need to be committed, but the investment should yield a respectable return.

REFERENCES

Abdelhamid, M., & Hassan, G. (2019, April). Blockchain and smart contracts. In *Proceedings of the 8th International Conference on Software and Information Engineering* (pp. 91-95).

Agarwal, J. D., Agarwal, M., Agarwal, A., & Agarwal, Y. (2021). Economics of cryptocurrencies: Artificial intelligence, blockchain, and digital currency. In *Information for efficient decision making: big data, blockchain and relevance* (pp. 331-430).

Agrawal, T. K., Kumar, V., Pal, R., Wang, L., & Chen, Y. (2021). Blockchain-based framework for supply chain traceability: A case example of the textile and clothing industry. *Computers & Industrial Engineering*, *154*, 107130. DOI: 10.1016/j.cie.2021.107130

Ahmed, W. A., & MacCarthy, B. L. (2023). Blockchain-enabled supply chain traceability–How wide? How deep? *International Journal of Production Economics*, *263*, 108963. DOI: 10.1016/j.ijpe.2023.108963

Alves, B., Schumacher, M., Cretton, F., Calvé, A. L., Cherix, G., Werlen, D., . . . Cloux, P. (2014). Fairtrace: applying semantic web tools and techniques to the textile traceability. In *Enterprise Information Systems: 15h International Conference, ICEIS 2013, Angers, France, July 4-7, 2013, Revised Selected Papers 15* (pp. 68-84). Springer International Publishing. DOI: 10.1007/978-3-319-09492-2_5

Bashir, I. (2022). Blockchain consensus. In *Blockchain Consensus: An Introduction to Classical, Blockchain, and Quantum Consensus Protocols* (pp. 207–257). Apress. DOI: 10.1007/978-1-4842-8179-6_5

Benton, M. C., Radziwill, N. M., Purritano, A. W., & Gerhart, C. J. (2018). Blockchain for Supply Chain: Improving Transparency and Efficiency Simultaneously. *Software Quality Professional, 20*(3).

Chang, S. E., & Chen, Y. (2020). When blockchain meets supply chain: A systematic literature review on current development and potential applications. *IEEE Access : Practical Innovations, Open Solutions*, *8*, 62478–62494. DOI: 10.1109/ACCESS.2020.2983601

Chang, S. E., Chen, Y. C., & Lu, M. F. (2019). Supply chain re-engineering using blockchain technology: A case of smart contract-based tracking process. *Technological Forecasting and Social Change*, *144*, 1–11. DOI: 10.1016/j.techfore.2019.03.015

Chaturvedi, A., Armstrong, B., & Chaturvedi, R. (2014). Securing the food supply chain: Understanding complex interdependence through agent-based simulation. *Health and Technology*, *4*(2), 159–169. DOI: 10.1007/s12553-014-0086-7 PMID: 32219055

Collomb, A., & Sok, K. (2016). Blockchain/distributed ledger technology (DLT): What impact on the financial sector? *Digiworld Economic Journal*, (103).

Conte de Leon, D., Stalick, A. Q., Jillepalli, A. A., Haney, M. A., & Sheldon, F. T. (2017). Blockchain: Properties and misconceptions. *Asia Pacific Journal of Innovation and Entrepreneurship*, *11*(3), 286–300. DOI: 10.1108/APJIE-12-2017-034

Croxton, K. L., Garcia-Dastugue, S. J., Lambert, D. M., & Rogers, D. S. (2001). The supply chain management processes. *International Journal of Logistics Management*, *12*(2), 13–36. DOI: 10.1108/09574090110806271

Deshpande, A., Stewart, K., Lepetit, L., & Gunashekar, S. (2017). Distributed Ledger Technologies/Blockchain: Challenges, opportunities and the prospects for standards. *Overview report The British Standards Institution (BSI), 40*(40), 1-34.

Dolgui, A., Ivanov, D., Potryasaev, S., Sokolov, B., Ivanova, M., & Werner, F. (2020). Blockchain-oriented dynamic modelling of smart contract design and execution in the supply chain. *International Journal of Production Research*, *58*(7), 2184–2199. DOI: 10.1080/00207543.2019.1627439

Duan, K., Onyeaka, H., & Pang, G. (2024). Leveraging blockchain to tackle food fraud: Innovations and obstacles. *Journal of Agriculture and Food Research*, *18*, 101429. DOI: 10.1016/j.jafr.2024.101429

Dutta, P., Choi, T. M., Somani, S., & Butala, R. (2020). Blockchain technology in supply chain operations: Applications, challenges and research opportunities. *Transportation research part e: Logistics and transportation review*, *142*, 102067.

Far, S. B., Rad, A. I., & Asaar, M. R. (2023). Blockchain and its derived technologies shape the future generation of digital businesses: A focus on decentralized finance and the Metaverse. *Data Science and Management*, *6*(3), 183–197. DOI: 10.1016/j.dsm.2023.06.002

Feng, H., Wang, X., Duan, Y., Zhang, J., & Zhang, X. (2020). Applying blockchain technology to improve agri-food traceability: A review of development methods, benefits and challenges. *Journal of Cleaner Production*, *260*, 121031. DOI: 10.1016/j.jclepro.2020.121031

Fernández-Caramés, T. M., Blanco-Novoa, O., Froiz-Míguez, I., & Fraga-Lamas, P. (2019). Towards an autonomous industry 4.0 warehouse: A UAV and blockchain-based system for inventory and traceability applications in big data-driven supply chain management. *Sensors (Basel), 19*(10), 2394. DOI: 10.3390/s19102394 PMID: 31130644

Frankenfield, J. (2023). Distributed Ledger Technology (DLT): Definition and How It Works. *Investopedia.Retrieved*, (February), 26.

Fu, Y., & Zhu, J. (2019). Big production enterprise supply chain endogenous risk management based on blockchain. *IEEE Access : Practical Innovations, Open Solutions*, *7*, 15310–15319. DOI: 10.1109/ACCESS.2019.2895327

Gad, A. G., Mosa, D. T., Abualigah, L., & Abohany, A. A. (2022). Emerging trends in blockchain technology and applications: A review and outlook. *Journal of King Saud University. Computer and Information Sciences*, *34*(9), 6719–6742. DOI: 10.1016/j.jksuci.2022.03.007

Ganne, E. (2018). *Can Blockchain revolutionize international trade?* World Trade Organization.

Gao, Z., Xu, L., Chen, L., Zhao, X., Lu, Y., & Shi, W. (2018). CoC: A unified distributed ledger based supply chain management system. *Journal of Computer Science and Technology*, *33*(2), 237–248. DOI: 10.1007/s11390-018-1816-5

Ghadge, A., Duck, A., Er, M., & Caldwell, N. (2021, April). Deceptive counterfeit risk in global supply chains. In *Supply Chain Forum* []. Taylor & Francis.]. *International Journal (Toronto, Ont.)*, *22*(2), 87–99.

Grant, M., & Startz, M. (2022). *Cutting out the middleman: The structure of chains of intermediation* (No. w30109). National Bureau of Economic Research.

Hewa, T., Ylianttila, M., & Liyanage, M. (2021). Survey on blockchain based smart contracts: Applications, opportunities and challenges. *Journal of Network and Computer Applications*, *177*, 102857. DOI: 10.1016/j.jnca.2020.102857

Higgins, M. (2022, April). Blockchain in Supply Chain. *Forbes*.https://www.forbes.com/councils/forbestechcouncil/2021/11/08/blockchain-in-supply-chain/

IBM. (n.d.). What are Smart Contracts? *IBM*. https://www.ibm.com/topics/smart-contracts

Islam, M. D. (2023). A survey on the use of blockchains to achieve supply chain security. *Information Systems*, *117*, 102232. DOI: 10.1016/j.is.2023.102232

Ivanov, D., Dolgui, A., & Sokolov, B. (2019). The impact of digital technology and Industry 4.0 on the ripple effect and supply chain risk analytics. *International Journal of Production Research*, *57*(3), 829–846. DOI: 10.1080/00207543.2018.1488086

Javaid, M., Haleem, A., Singh, R. P., Khan, S., & Suman, R. (2021). Blockchain technology applications for Industry 4.0: A literature-based review. *Blockchain: Research and Applications*, *2*(4), 100027.

Javaid, M., Haleem, A., Singh, R. P., Suman, R., & Khan, S. (2022). A review of Blockchain Technology applications for financial services. *BenchCouncil Transactions on Benchmarks. Standards and Evaluations*, *2*(3), 100073.

Karam, A. A. (2023). Central Bank Digital Currency (CBDC) and blockchain enable the future of payments. *Retrieved*, (September), 13.

Komalavalli, C., Saxena, D., & Laroiya, C. (2020). Overview of blockchain technology concepts. In *Handbook of research on blockchain technology* (pp. 349–371). Academic Press. DOI: 10.1016/B978-0-12-819816-2.00014-9

Kshetri, N. (2017). Blockchain's roles in strengthening cybersecurity and protecting privacy. *Telecommunications Policy*, *41*(10), 1027–1038. DOI: 10.1016/j.telpol.2017.09.003

Kumar, V., Hallqvist, C., & Ekwall, D. (2017). Developing a framework for traceability implementation in the textile supply chain. *Systems*, *5*(2), 33. DOI: 10.3390/systems5020033

Lamb, K. (2018). Blockchain and Smart Contracts: What the AEC sector needs to know.

Larrier, J. H. (2021). A brief history of blockchain. *Transforming Scholarly Publishing With Blockchain Technologies and AI*, 85-100.

Lashkari, B., & Musilek, P. (2021). A comprehensive review of blockchain consensus mechanisms. *IEEE Access : Practical Innovations, Open Solutions*, *9*, 43620–43652. DOI: 10.1109/ACCESS.2021.3065880

Levis, D., Fontana, F., & Ughetto, E. (2021). A look into the future of blockchain technology. *PLoS One*, *16*(11), e0258995. DOI: 10.1371/journal.pone.0258995 PMID: 34788307

Levy, K. E. (2017). Book-smart, not street-smart: Blockchain-based smart contracts and the social workings of law. *Engaging Science, Technology, and Society*, *3*, 1–15. DOI: 10.17351/ests2017.107

Luchkin, A. G., Lukasheva, O. L., Novikova, N. E., Melnikov, V. A., Zyatkova, A. V., & Yarotskaya, E. V. (2020, August). Cryptocurrencies in the global financial system: problems and ways to overcome them. In *Russian Conference on Digital Economy and Knowledge Management (RuDEcK 2020)* (pp. 423-430). Atlantis Press. DOI: 10.2991/aebmr.k.200730.077

Macrinici, D., Cartofeanu, C., & Gao, S. (2018). Smart contract applications within blockchain technology: A systematic mapping study. *Telematics and Informatics*, *35*(8), 2337–2354. DOI: 10.1016/j.tele.2018.10.004

Mandolla, C., Petruzzelli, A. M., Percoco, G., & Urbinati, A. (2019). Building a digital twin for additive manufacturing through the exploitation of blockchain: A case analysis of the aircraft industry. *Computers in Industry*, *109*, 134–152. DOI: 10.1016/j.compind.2019.04.011

Mann, S., Potdar, V., Gajavilli, R. S., & Chandan, A. (2018, December). Blockchain technology for supply chain traceability, transparency and data provenance. In *Proceedings of the 2018 international conference on blockchain technology and application* (pp. 22-26). DOI: 10.1145/3301403.3301408

Mekpor, E. S. (2019). Anti-money laundering and combating the financing of terrorism compliance: Are FATF member states just scratching the surface? *Journal of Money Laundering Control*, *22*(3), 451–471. DOI: 10.1108/JMLC-09-2018-0057

Memon, M., Bajwa, U. A., Ikhlas, A., Memon, Y., Memon, S., & Malani, M. (2018, November). Blockchain beyond Bitcoin: block maturity level consensus protocol. In *2018 IEEE 5th International Conference on Engineering Technologies and Applied Sciences (ICETAS)* (pp. 1-5). IEEE. DOI: 10.1109/ICETAS.2018.8629232

Min, H. (2019). Blockchain technology for enhancing supply chain resilience. *Business Horizons*, *62*(1), 35–45. DOI: 10.1016/j.bushor.2018.08.012

Nwariaku, H., Fadojutimi, B., Lawson, L. G. L., Agbelusi, J., Adigun, O. A., Udom, J. A., & Olajide, T. D. (2024). Blockchain technology as an enabler of transparency and efficiency in sustainable supply chains. *International Journal of Science and Research Archive*, *12*(2), 1779–1789. DOI: 10.30574/ijsra.2024.12.2.1454

Oladele, O. K. (2024). Internet of Things (IoT) in Logistics: Transforming Supply Chains with Connected Devices and Data Analytics.

Pal, A., & Kant, K. (2019). Using blockchain for provenance and traceability in internet of things-integrated food logistics. *Computer*, *52*(12), 94–98. DOI: 10.1109/MC.2019.2942111

Panwar, A., & Bhatnagar, V. (2020, February). Distributed ledger technology (DLT): The beginning of a technological revolution for blockchain. In the 2nd *International Conference on Data, Engineering and Applications (IDEA)* (pp. 1-5). IEEE.

Philipp, R., Prause, G., & Gerlitz, L. (2019). Blockchain and smart contracts for entrepreneurial collaboration in maritime supply chains. *Transport and Telecommunication Journal, 20*(4), 365–378. DOI: 10.2478/ttj-2019-0030

Popovski, L., Soussou, G., & Webb, P. B. (2018). A brief history of blockchain. *Legaltech news, 2018*, 3.

Popper, N. (2015). *Digital gold: The untold story of Bitcoin.* Penguin UK.

Queiroz, M. M., Telles, R., & Bonilla, S. H. (2020). Blockchain and supply chain management integration: A systematic review of the literature. *Supply Chain Management, 25*(2), 241–254. DOI: 10.1108/SCM-03-2018-0143

Raja Santhi, A., & Muthuswamy, P. (2022). Influence of blockchain technology in manufacturing supply chain and logistics. *Logistics (Basel), 6*(1), 15. DOI: 10.3390/logistics6010015

Saraji, S. (2023). Introduction to Blockchain. In *Sustainable Oil and Gas Using Blockchain* (pp. 57–74). Springer International Publishing. DOI: 10.1007/978-3-031-30697-6_3

Saraswathi, S., Suresh, J., & Gandhi, D. M. (2024). Combating Counterfeit Products with Blockchain Technology to Enhance Trust and Authenticity in Consumer Markets. *Indian Journal of Science and Technology, 17*(34), 3512–3521. DOI: 10.17485/IJST/v17i34.1449

Sarmah, S. S. (2018). Understanding blockchain technology. *Computing in Science & Engineering, 8*(2), 23–29.

Sethaput, V., & Innet, S. (2023). Blockchain application for central bank digital currencies (CBDC). *Cluster Computing, 26*(4), 2183–2197. DOI: 10.1007/s10586-022-03962-z PMID: 36686339

Seuring, S., Sarkis, J., Müller, M., & Rao, P. (2008). Sustainability and supply chain management–an introduction to the special issue. *Journal of Cleaner Production, 16*(15), 1545–1551. DOI: 10.1016/j.jclepro.2008.02.002

Sheel, A., & Nath, V. (2019). Effect of blockchain technology adoption on supply chain adaptability, agility, alignment and performance. *Management Research Review, 42*(12), 1353–1374. DOI: 10.1108/MRR-12-2018-0490

Sheldon, R. (2021). A timeline and history of blockchain technology. *URL:*https://www. techtarget. com/whatis/feature/A-timeline-and-history-of-blockchain-technology

Strauss, J., & Frost, R. (2014). *E-marketing*. Pearson.

Sun, L. (2020, September). Service Chaining Security Based on Blockchain. []. IOP Publishing.]. *Journal of Physics: Conference Series*, *1634*(1), 012031. DOI: 10.1088/1742-6596/1634/1/012031

Sunny, J., Undralla, N., & Pillai, V. M. (2020). Supply chain transparency through blockchain-based traceability: An overview with demonstration. *Computers & Industrial Engineering*, *150*, 106895. DOI: 10.1016/j.cie.2020.106895

Taherdoost, H. (2023). Smart contracts in blockchain technology: A critical review. *Information (Basel)*, *14*(2), 117. DOI: 10.3390/info14020117

Tripathi, G., Ahad, M. A., & Casalino, G. (2023). A comprehensive review of blockchain technology: Underlying principles and historical background with future challenges. *Decision Analytics Journal*, 100344.

Uddin, M. A., Stranieri, A., Gondal, I., & Balasubramanian, V. (2021). A survey on the adoption of blockchain in iot: Challenges and solutions. *Blockchain: Research and Applications*, *2*(2), 100006.

Visciano, P., & Schirone, M. (2021). Food frauds: Global incidents and misleading situations. *Trends in Food Science & Technology*, *114*, 424–442. DOI: 10.1016/j.tifs.2021.06.010

Wang, Y., Singgih, M., Wang, J., & Rit, M. (2019). Making sense of blockchain technology: How will it transform supply chains? *International Journal of Production Economics*, *211*, 221–236. DOI: 10.1016/j.ijpe.2019.02.002

Xu, P., Lee, J., Barth, J. R., & Richey, R. G. (2021). Blockchain as supply chain technology: Considering transparency and security. *International Journal of Physical Distribution & Logistics Management*, *51*(3), 305–324. DOI: 10.1108/IJPDLM-08-2019-0234

Yi, Z., Yu, M., & Cheung, K. L. (2022). Impacts of counterfeiting on a global supply chain. *Manufacturing & Service Operations Management*, *24*(1), 159–178. DOI: 10.1287/msom.2020.0912

Yoo, M., & Won, Y. (2018). A study on the transparent price tracing system in supply chain management based on blockchain. *Sustainability (Basel)*, *10*(11), 4037. DOI: 10.3390/su10114037

Zarrin, J., Wen Phang, H., Babu Saheer, L., & Zarrin, B. (2021). Blockchain for decentralization of the internet: Prospects, trends, and challenges. *Cluster Computing*, *24*(4), 2841–2866. DOI: 10.1007/s10586-021-03301-8 PMID: 34025209

Zelbst, P. J., Green, K. W., Sower, V. E., & Bond, P. L. (2020). The impact of RFID, IIoT, and Blockchain technologies on supply chain transparency. *Journal of Manufacturing Technology Management*, *31*(3), 441–457. DOI: 10.1108/JMTM-03-2019-0118

Zhang, C., Wu, C., & Wang, X. (2020, May). Overview of blockchain consensus mechanism. In *Proceedings of the 2020 2nd International Conference on Big Data Engineering* (pp. 7-12).

Zheng, Z., Xie, S., Dai, H. N., Chen, W., Chen, X., Weng, J., & Imran, M. (2020). An overview on smart contracts: Challenges, advances and platforms. *Future Generation Computer Systems*, *105*, 475–491. DOI: 10.1016/j.future.2019.12.019

Zhihong, L., Yuxiang, H., Zechun, C., Tiancheng, L., & Yuehua, W. (2019). Creativity in trusted data: Research on application of blockchain in supply chain. *International Journal of Performability Engineering*, *15*(2), 526.

KEY TERMS AND DEFINITIONS

Blockchain: A blockchain is a shared, immutable ledger that records transactions and tracks assets across a network. It's a distributed database, meaning it's stored across multiple computers, making it resistant to tampering and central control. Essentially, it's a digital, public record of transactions linked together in blocks, each verified by the network.

Cybersecurity: Cybersecurity is the practice of defending computers, servers, mobile devices, electronic systems, networks, and data from malicious attacks. It's also known as information technology security or electronic information security. The term “cybersecurity” applies in a variety of contexts, from business to mobile computing, and can be divided into a few common categories.

Data Governance: Data governance is a principled approach to managing data during its life cycle, from acquisition to use to disposal. Every organization needs data governance. As businesses throughout all industries proceed on their digital-transformation journeys, data has quickly become the most valuable asset they possess.

Smart Contracts: A smart contract is a self-executing computer program stored on a blockchain that automatically executes the terms of an agreement when predetermined conditions are met. Essentially, it's a digital contract where the conditions of the agreement are encoded as computer code and run automatically, eliminating the need for a third-party intermediary.

Supply Chain: A supply chain is a network of all activities, resources, and organizations involved in creating a product or service and delivering it to the end user. This includes everything from sourcing raw materials to distributing the finished product. It encompasses various entities like suppliers, manufacturers, distributors, retailers, and supporting entities such as warehouses and logistics providers.

Sustainability: In 1987, the United Nations Brundtland Commission_defined sustainability as "meeting the needs of the present without compromising the ability of future generations to meet their own needs".

Sustainable Development: Sustainable development is development that meets the needs of the present without compromising the ability of future generations to meet their own needs' (defined by the Brundtland Commission and multilaterally agreed by the UN Conference on Environment and Development – Rio 1992). The question of how to translate this generic ideal into practice has been answered over the years in different ways. The 2002 World Summit on Sustainable Development (Johannesburg, South Africa) introduced the notion of the three pillars of sustainable development, that is the environmental, the social and the economic, considered as "interdependent and mutually reinforcing". To ensure policy coherence with the 2030 Agenda, this draft policy has adopted the three dimensions of sustainable development from the conceptual framework adopted at the wider UN level, complemented by peace and security (paragraphs 2 and 35 of the 2030 Agenda).

Transparency: Transparency is a condition where the material facts of an enterprise are made available in a timely, and preferably reusable, manner. Material facts encompass reliable information critical to the decision making of both internal and external stakeholders.

Chapter 11
Role of Blockchain Technology in Recruitment, Payroll Management, and Managing Gig Economy Workers: Recent Trends and Research Agenda

Akansha Mer
https://orcid.org/0000-0001-9974-8278
Banasthali Vidyapith, Tonk, India

Avantika Srivastava
Big 4 Accounting Firm, Bengaluru, India

Farha Khan
Graphic Era Hill University, Bhimtal Campus, India

ABSTRACT

Blockchain technology has revolutionized Human Resource Management (HRM) practices. The study aims to unearth the role of blockchain in recruitment and selection, payroll management and managing the gig economy workers. The study is based on secondary sources of data. Blockchain in recruitment enhances trust via immutable candidate records, ensuring transparent and verified credentials.

DOI: 10.4018/979-8-3373-1290-3.ch011

It streamlines verification processes, reduces fraud, and fosters efficient, secure candidate selection. Employing blockchain on payroll systems increases security, provides a transparent and immutable ledger for payroll records eliminating risk of fudging pay-roll. It also automates the process through smart contracts, thereby improving payroll processes, reducing wastage of time and administration charges. Blockchain manages gig workers by contract creation and identity verification, secure and verifiable recordkeeping, reducing fraud, dispute resolution, time and attendance tracking, payroll and performance management.

INTRODUCTION

The first cryptocurrency i.e. Bitcoin was the first application of Blockchain Technology, introduced by Nakamoto in 2008, as the first decentralized digital currency that allowed for currency exchange between peers without any central intermediary (Krishnan et al., 2020). Blockchain is shorthand for decentralised digital ledger technology, which is the basis for many applications. Thus, distributed ledger technology is an umbrella term encapsulating Blockchain technology and other distributed ledgers (Oberoi et al., 2024). Its key feature is decentralisation itself: data is stored distributed across a peer-to-peer network of nodes, and there is no single point of control. Smart contracts on the blockchain are enhanced through combining the capabilities of smart contracts (to self-execute) with those of the blockchain to alter the landscape of the contract management forever (Verma et al., 2025).

There are multiple benefits of using blockchain technology such as transparency -and immutability (Arora & Nabi, 2022). Transparency arises from the fact that it is open and publicly verifiable, such that the status of a blockchain is visible to all participants (Arora et al., 2024). Together with decentralisation and transparency comes immutability: once data has been saved on the ledger, it cannot be changed or erased without consensus from the network (Khan et al., 2024).

Although the first application of Blockchain technology was in financial sector, it made its way in several other domains such as human resource management, marketing etc. Blockchain technology has emerged as a transformative tool with the potential to revolutionize Human Resource Management (HRM) practices (Mathew et al., 2025). As blockchain technology continues to evolve, it holds the potential to further enhance HRM practices. The proliferation of interoperable blockchain networks could collectively amplify the utility of blockchain-enabled smart contracts (Oberoi & Kansra, 2022), fostering even more secure, scalable, and efficient solutions for HRM. Blockchain's inherent features, including decentralization, transparency, and immutability, can be harnessed to develop smart contracts that automate and optimize the management of human resource in organizations. The benefits of integrating technology into HRM are undeniably substantial in this data-driven narrative (Mer & Virdi, 2022). Data-driven advantages like reduced administrative costs, decreased disputes, and faster payments emerge as key highlights of blockchain technology in HRM (Mathew et al., 2025). Blockchain technology has made its presence in almost all the functions of HRM such as recruitment and selection, training and development, performance management, payroll management, managing gig economy workers, employee engagement, data protection of employees, etc.

With limited studies on blockchain technology on managing human resources, the objective of the study is to uncover blockchain's role in recruitment and selection, payroll management, and the management of gig economy workers. The study addresses the research gap as it is pioneer study in investigating the role of blockchain in managing gig economy workers.

The chapter is divided into six parts. The first part is introduction, followed by theoretical framework of the study, research methodology, role of blockchain technology in three aspects of human resource management (blockchain in recruitment, payroll management and blockchain in managing gig economy workers). The fifth part is future research and the sixth part is the conclusion.

STUDIES ON BLOCKCHAIN IN HRM

Mishra and Venkatesan (2021) conducted an empirical study on blockchain technology in HRM in organizations. The study revealed that blockchain in HRM helps in maintaining human resource records "to update and validate the candidate credentials to prevent fraud and incorrect information. It will increase overall profitability of business. Blockchain can lead to time and cost savings in HR function".

Chillakuri and Attili (2021) study on the "Role of blockchain in HR's response to new normal" revealed that it helps in "certificates verification, skill mapping, payroll processing, data protection and performance management".

Kisi (2022) conducted an exploratory study "on the use of Blockchain Technology in Recruitment". The study divulged that before the advent of blockchain, there were problems such as reduced efficiency, increased cost, fraud risks, and time consuming procedures in the process of finding and hiring the right talent for companies." The study revealed that blockchain overcomes these challenges and leads to efficiency, saves time and decreases cost, leads to transparency. Besides it helps in the verification of candidates during Talent acquisition.

Khan et al. (2024) indicated that "Blockchain-based decentralized identity management empowers the users to have greater control over their digital identity and also gives them more security and privacy. Blockchain ensures and validates authentication by cryptography tools like digital signatures and public-private key pairs. It also eliminates older identity authentication methods that are vulnerable to theft and hacking. Decentralized identity management will transform the user experience in the digital space and help build trust, privacy and control in digital spaces".

Mathew et al. (2025) in their study divulged a huge role of blockchain technology in human resource management in various aspects such as recruitment and selection in context of transparency, fairness and trust, ensuring hiring right person for right job. The study also elucidated the role of blockchain technology in promoting diversity, equity and inclusion through transparent data management and decision-making for diversity and inclusion. Also, blockchain technology helps in promoting employee engagement and employee retention.

Research findings demonstrate blockchain technology's expanding influence on human resource management. Recruitment processes benefited from blockchain integration as Sharma and Bansal (2021) found a 35% decrease in time-to-hire and a 25% improvement in quality-of-hire due to verified credentialing. A multinational pilot project demonstrated that blockchain-enabled payroll systems from Accenture (2022) decreased administrative processing time by 40%.

THEORETICAL FRAMEWORK OF THE STUDY

The theoretical framework of the study is resource-based view theory, according to which an organization comprises of a collection of human as well as physical resources and organizational resources. These resources are rare, valuable and difficult to replicate, thereby making them drivers of organization's competitive advantage (Barney, 1991). As per resource based view theory, organization's resources are heterogeneous across organizations. Thus, blockchain technology in HRM can act as a resource for the organizations that provide competitive advantage to them.

RESEARCH METHODOLOGY

Search Strategy

The literature was searched from working, published papers, book chapters, e-newspapers, reports of renowned organizations and magazines. The study is based on secondary sources of data. Data were sourced from reports of renowned organizations such as PwC, Wipro and IBM. Magazines included McKinsey Quarterly and Forbes Magazine. E-newspapers included economic times and financial express.

Keywords Selection

Keywords search algorithm used to search the relevant data on blockchain were "blockchain technology" OR "smart contracts". On the other hand, keywords search algorithm used to search the relevant data related to human resource management were "recruitment & selection" OR "payroll management" OR "salary" "payroll" OR "compensation management" OR "managing gig economy workers" OR "human resource management" OR "HRM".

Next, the authors combined the Boolean operator "AND" with the chosen search terms for each theme, which are blockchain technology and HRM. Thus, the search encapsulated ("blockchain technology" OR "smart contracts") AND ("recruitment & selection" OR "payroll management" OR "salary" "payroll" OR "compensation management" OR "managing gig economy workers" OR "human resource management" OR "HRM").

Inclusion and Exclusion Criteria

In compliance with Tranfield, Denyer, and Smart (2003) and Crossan and Apaydin (2010), a thorough literature review was carried out to find research themes and ways to carry out studies on blockchain technology in HRM. A clear and repeatable technique was used in a systematic manner to improve the overall quality of the evaluation (Crossan & Apaydin, 2010). The primary topics were identified, and the current research was critically examined, synthesized, and mapped as part of a comprehensive literature review process. All publications published until March 2025 for systematic review papers were considered. Results were restricted to English language. Peer reviewed journals were part of the study and non-peer reviewed journals and conference papers were not part of the study.

Total 103 articles were retrieved through title, abstract and keywords search. This number encapsulated duplicate articles also. Duplicate articles were later removed. This led to 90 articles. Out of 90 articles, 61 articles were further removed as these articles were not related to block chain in recruitment, payroll managing and managing gig economy workers. This led to total 29 articles for the current paper.

BLOCKCHAIN IN RECRUITMENT

A standard textbook definition of recruitment is "identifying, sourcing, screening, shortlisting, and interviewing candidates for jobs (either permanent or temporary) within an organization."

As important as hiring the right talent is, the biggest challenge for recruiters is weeding out inconsistent candidates' resumes. A study conducted by Resume Lab found that of 1051 Americans, at least 93% had lied on their resumes (Turczynski, 2023). It is therefore important to have robust tools and technologies to ensure that every hiring decision is correct.

Thus, an organization's need to rely on a tool that not only supports them to identify genuine candidates but also helps protect data while maintaining transparency is crucial. One such technology widely gaining popularity in the recruitment process is blockchain. Blockchain is a distributed ledger technology that helps manage data transparently (Archana et al., 2023).

As per people matters, a prominent talent consulting provider, blockchain technology can help organizations seamlessly validate the candidate's entire employment and education history. It can also help in eliminating the issues associated with manually sourcing of recruitment information resulting in cost optimization and a recruitment process that is not only lean but also robust (Kapoor, 2019).

Role of Blockchain in Recruitment Process

HRM traditionally used centralized systems alongside manual processes to handle essential tasks (Mer & Virdi, 2023; Mer & Srivastava, 2023) including recruitment. The establishment of trust in candidates depended on manual background checks together with reference calls and credential verification which presented time-consuming challenges and was susceptible to human error and fraudulent documentation (Choudhury & Pattnaik, 2022). An analysis of traditional recruitment practices shows that they depend heavily on manual operations and personal decision-making. Traditional recruitment methods included advertising job openings in newspapers and internal noticeboards alongside basic job portals and then manually reviewing resumes before conducting personal interviews (Nguyen et al., 2021).

Blockchain technology, has contributed in the following aspects of the recruitment process is revolutionized.

i) ***Identifying***: As a decentralized digital ledger, blockchain technology records transactions in a secure and transparent way. Every block in the chain contains multiple transaction records, which are then cryptographically linked to the previous block. This, in turn, creates an interlinked chain of blocks that can neither be altered nor deleted.

In an identity verification process based on the blockchain technology the historical information about the candidate including identity, educational qualifications, and work experience is recorded and verified on a blockchain. This record is highly secure and cannot be altered making it highly accurate. The hiring organizations can readily access this record during the recruitment, ensuring that the candidates are identified to continue in the process, have provided accurate information, and meet the job criteria (Seth, 2023).

ii) ***Sourcing***: Organizations and staffing agencies keep their staffing ledgers that maintains talent pools, human resource documentation and other records of the candidates. A blockchain architecture can update all the shared records through peer to peer records every time a transaction occurs. Here every user is both a producer and a consumer so the data is always synchronized every time users send or receive transactions from other users. In short it helps keep everything up to date and even the slightest change is shared among the peer network. As per Bass (2021), the blockchain direct sourcing process would be as follows:

a) New hiring position is created in an organization; b) The hiring manager creates a job description. This triggers a smart contract- a set of digital rules that will form the base of the entire process i.e., the criteria fulfilment for hiring c) All the other providers in the shared ecosystem and privileges will be able to view, the requisition once it's released. This allows them to start with the sourcing process from the talent pool available with them; d) The entities in the ecosystem can range from universities\colleges, recruitment agencies, alumni network, talent exchange etc who have a steady access to talent and candidate databases; e) The hiring manager can view the talent inventory. The transactions involving the sourcing and submitting candidate profiles are immutably recorded stamped and visible. All the information around the educational qualification, work experience, references of the candidate are visible in the candidate profile. When the hiring manager extends the offer the smart contract is first validated and then executed f) The prospective candidates looking for opportunities can also view the opening in the system and apply. g) Once the hiring decision is finalized, the blockchain also generates the electronic forms needed for executing arrangement; h) The hiring process runs till the defined termination point. i.e., superannuation, assignment roll off, layoff, termination, business closure, no new positions.

iii) ***Screening*:** Using blockchain, organizations are able to access candidate data that is verified much faster. This helps minimize manual verification and the delays that come with it. It also streamlines the process of selecting a candidate, thereby enabling HR professionals to focus more on evaluating the other aspects of the candidate profile (Sharma, 2023).

The screening process can be done using the credentialing technology based on blockchain. The credentialing technology of verifiable functions is a decentralized way which involves creating the trust action between the following parties or users:

a) Credential issuer: The entity that issues authentic and verifiable credentials is called the "issuer"; b) Credential holder: The entity for which the credentials are issued is called a "holder" it can be an individual or an organization. The holder is the sole owner of the issued credentials against their name and can control is use and verification c) Verifier of the credentials: Any entity that requests the digital certificates from the holder is the "verifier". This entity cross verifies credentials (data, validity, etc.) issued by institutions or organisations with authority to do so.

This technology consolidates credentials from multiple issuers for a candidate in one place. This provides the recruiters the ability to easily verify and review credentials. It avoids issues like self-attestation, or reliance on candidates for their employment records, roles, skillsets and educational qualification. In short, it removes dependency on the resumes to authenticate information (BC Diploma, 2023),

Using the credentialing technology all the recruiter now has to do is review the candidate's digital locker. Since all of the information is already in the blockchain credential locker they are not required, to contact the previous employers or individual universities to gather the candidate's employment information (Zielinski, 2021).

The product called Credentials by WorkDay is a good example of blockchain-powered credentialing technology. This product is designed to help the organizations issue, manage and verify the user's digital credentials (Ruggiero, 2019).

iv) ***Shortlisting*:** The blockchain technology securely stores valid and authorized proofs for identifying signatures and documents related to verifiable credentials. It is a decentralized database that is permanent and tamper-proof nature. It ensures that anything that it incorporated in it cannot disappear get updated over time, thus making it possible to establish trust between its users (Issuers, Holders, Verifiers) (BC Diploma, 2023). Thus, moving forward, the recruiter can shortlist candidates with valid credentials to suit the job requirement for the interview (Sine, 2018).

v) ***Onboarding*:** The onboarding of an employee is a time-consuming manual process. Right from inputting the candidate information till the background screenings. However, if a technology like Blockchain was integrated in the recruitment process, it would mean that a candidate's credentials and other information were already validated. Thus, saving the time of HR professionals spent on these activities. A recruitment process based on blockchain could reduce the risk of fraud as the information available is more authentic and verifiable (Sharma, 2023).

Advantages of Using Blockchain in Recruitment

***Streamlined screening*:** Blockchain technology allows organizations to access authentic, verified data at a faster pace. It reduces significant delays associated with the manual screening process during candidate selection, allowing HR professionals to shift gears and focus on other aspects of the candidate's profile.

***Increased transparency and authenticity*:** The data entered in the blockchain ecosystem can neither be tampered with nor be deleted. This provides a higher degree of authenticity and reliability to the data. This makes the process smoother and more transparent for both the candidate and the organization

***Accurate and reliable data*:** The blockchain stores dates across multiple nodes. This significantly reduces the risk of data manipulation and errors, leading to more accurate and reliable results during the verification process. This, in turn, enables organizations to make better hiring decisions.

***Quicker onboarding*:** Since all of the candidate data has already been verified for its authenticity prior to onboarding, it does not have to be done again. This speeds up the onboarding process, as the recruiter does not have to go over the manual process to gather, verify, and analyse candidate information. This allows the organizations to close open positions faster, improving productivity and reducing costs associated with open positions.

***Privacy*:** Blockchain provides safety and privacy for candidate data. It gives candidates full control over who can access their information and for what purpose. This helps in data protection and ensures that sensitive data is in the right hands.

Challenges with Implementing Blockchain in Recruitment

Operating performance: Blockchain is slower in terms of functionality compared to traditional databases. This is because every transaction in a blockchain environment carries more operations, such as signature authentication and consensus mechanisms. Also, there is a lot of redundancy in the blockchain ecosystem. This is because each node in the network stores the same information and is validated when verifying a transaction.

High cost of implementation: Compared to the traditional database the blockchain is much costlier to implement, also it needs a lot of planning and execution to integrate blockchain to the recruitment process.
Data modification**:** In case of an error, it is not easy to modify a record. This is because the data, once entered, is stored in all the nodes. The code will have to be rewritten to rectify that error and modify the record.
Complex technology**:** Implementing and maintaining blockchain requires a high level of technical expertise. At any time, a technical challenge can hamper the adoption of blockchain technology by discouraging potential stakeholders from engaging with it. The high level of complexity associated with blockchain also causes implementation errors and inefficiencies.
Interoperability**:** Compatibility between the different blockchain networks is also a challenge. Several blockchain platforms have their protocols and operating standards, leading to compatibility issues between each other. The lack of interoperability between the blockchains can lead to higher inefficiencies, as to get information, the organization may be required to interact with different networks.
Energy Consumption**:** A lot of computing power is used to validate transactions on a blockchain network. Concerns surround the carbon footprint and the overall impact of blockchain technology on the environment (Marr, 2023).
Inherent Privacy Risks of Blockchain: HR data stores personally identifiable information (PII) which encompasses educational background and employment history along with biometric data, health records, performance evaluations and recruitment assessments. The immutable nature of blockchain prevents records from being changed or removed once they are documented. This becomes ethically challenging in cases of the presence of mistakes or obsolete details in staff files or hiring assessments.

Cases

Wipro's Blockchain-Powered Background Verification: Wipro, an Indian IT services leader, established a blockchain system for background verification with educational institutions and recruitment firms. The system achieved a reduction in verification duration to fewer than 3 days from an initial period of 15–20 days by utilizing shared and immutable ledgers for educational and employment information (Wipro, 2022).

IBM implemented blockchain technology for talent credentialing which stored employee certifications together with recruitment histories and performance records on a permanent ledger. IBM's system allowed businesses to reallocate talent quickly during internal transitions and performance-based staffing needs as well as during recruitment processes (IBM, 2021).

BLOCKCHAIN IN PAYROLL MANAGEMENT

Payroll management is streamlining and automating various processes involved in executing the payroll administration within an organization. This involves managing employees' financial records, including employee salaries, job benefits, taxes, and other deductions. Managing an organization's payroll is an exhaustive task. Organizations usually apply a payroll management system to automate the payroll process to minimize the time and errors associated with a manual process. A payroll management system actively calculates employees' wages, makes wage payments, keeps payroll records up to date, and collects applicable tax forms. HR is crucial in managing payroll as it involves ensuring accurate and on-time compensation payments to employees while adhering to all legal requirements and company policies.

Role of Blockchain Technology in Payroll Management

The traditional management of payroll encapsulates several issues:

Administrative burden: Several businesses, especially the smaller ones, continue to rely on the manual in-house payroll process. Such a process brings in a lot of paper work. It creates an administrative burden on the company's resources. Data entry errors are frequent and can create payment issues.
Organizational Issues: Keeping all the information around employee records and payroll organized is daunting. It could also be a workflow challenge which involves keeping all the files and related documents at a centralized place for a uniform file processing.
Tracking Employee Absence: Time sheets and paper time cards are often prone to misuse and errors. In addition to payroll, keeping track of the employee's absence reason is critical to effective planning and maximizing productivity.
Compliance: The business must remain compliant and updated to all the norms and regulations to avoid complaints and government investigations that could prove to be costly to the organization not only in terms of money but also reputation (Ruhland, 2015)

With all the challenges that come as a part of the traditional payroll process, the blockchain technology can potentially change the payroll management systems. When we talk of the blockchain technology in the context of payroll management, it simply means that sensitive and confidential information like the employee data, financial information, and contractual agreements are securely stored on the blockchain network, this greatly minimizes the risk of data breaches and ensures that records are reliable and tamperproof (Bello & Daniel, 2022).

Some of the important roles of blockchain technology in payroll management are:

- ***Making instant payments*:** The payroll within an organization is an amalgamation of a lot of parameters such as employee performance, eligible benefits, employee trainings and certifications etc. Blockchain technology can store all these parameters securely, enabling smart contracts that sit within the blockchain. The smart contract is enabled automatically and instant payment is done once the parameters are met. For instance, the contractors who have been hired for set number of hours are payed automatically once they fulfil that requirement. The hours worked in this case will activate the smart contract and the payment will be initiated without any manual intervention (Cloudpay, 2021).
- ***Tracking Employee Attendance:*** Blockchain technology has a huge potential in tracking employee attendance as it can create secure and tamper-proof records. A blockchain Hyperledger framework can be used to track employee attendance. The Hyperledger is a permissioned blockchain framework that can perform validation mechanisms within a short period that is much shorter than the current blockchain consensus. A hyper ledge is also equipped with a smart contract system known as the chain-code which is a function that will be executed only after several conditions are met. Thus, it is an appropriate tool to store attendance data for the employee and ensure its integrity thus providing a reliable source of employee attendance for payroll and other compliance checks (Hanggoro, Windiatmaja, Sari, 2022).
- ***Seamless cross border payments:*** Traditional payroll management involved several intermediaries, "such as banks and payment processors, which delayed payments and added extra fees. Blockchain technology cuts out these middlemen by enabling direct, peer-to-peer transactions. This makes payroll faster and more efficient—an advantage that is particularly important for multinational companies managing complex cross-border payments" (OPS, 2025).
- ***Alternative payment options*:** Blockchain provides an alternative payment option for employees that have relocated internationally and who do not have a bank account. In their case the payments can be redirected to family members based overseas with little to no cost incurred in terms of remittance fees.
- ***Real-time processing:*** Unlike traditional payroll system, blockchain technology enables real-time processing of transactions. Consequently, payments such as salary, bonus, overtime can be made instantly. This facilitates timely payment (OPS, 2025).

Real-time tax calculation and collection: Block chain allows the calculation and collection of tax in real time accurate to per minute or hour real time payments. Such positive impacts on processing payroll can revolutionize the global payroll processes (Sandner, 2022).

Payroll Dispute resolution: Since all the contractual interactions that take place between parties are recorded in the traceable, tamper-proof, ledger-based system, therefore it lays the ground for resolving disputes.

Advantages of Using Blockchain in Payroll Management

Eliminating intermediaries: Organizations these days work on a global scale. Payments made in the home country are straightforward; however, international payments are usually more complex, as they can take days to settle, and there is a conversion fee proportional to the amount sent.

The other big challenge with the contractors and "gig economy" workers who are often hired lack bank accounts, which is usually required for automatic deposits to happen from a payroll system. Local regulations and IT security schemes can often stop the traditional electronic payments. The blockchain can overcome this hurdle as blockchain removes the banks from the payment process and ensures that the transaction authenticity is validated (Sandner, 2022).

Reducing fraud: Fake paystubs are common within the traditional payroll system. They not only hamper the organization's financial stability but also put employee morale and trust in jeopardy. These fake paystubs generate fraudulent records of an individual's income and employment status, which could lead to serious consequences like tax evasion and improper loan approvals from the banks.

Blockchain technology can easily counter this fraud as it stores an immutable record for all transactions that can be audited transparently. Thus, creating fake paystubs and data tampering becomes impossible. The blockchain system is designed to track and verify each transaction that occurs within the chain structure, so it is not possible to tamper with the entries. Thus, blockchain keeps the database safe from fraud and adds credibility to the business (Jones, 2023).

Cost reduction and efficiency: Conventional payroll systems are time consuming and costly because of the intricate processes like, tax calculation, measuring overtime, and benefits calculation etc. that come as a part of payroll management. Adopting the blockchain technology in the payroll system can help reduce these complexities drastically. As the blockchain network uses smart contract to execute transactions automatically these payroll processes can be executed as soon as the conditions of a smart contract are met, making the payroll system faster, more accurate and cheaper.

The efficiency and accuracy brought by blockchain give the organization more time to focus on the larger picture and achieve strategic goals rather than consuming resources in routine admin tasks.

Challenges With Implementing Blockchain Technology in Payroll Management

Impact on performance speed: Blockchain is slower than the traditional database as it executes more operations. Signature verification involves signing a transaction cryptographically, and the consensus mechanism relies on validating transactions. Processes like payroll require systems to be quick and agile, so slowing down payroll processes in an organization could create operational challenges.

Integration with existing systems: Block chain is very costly and time consuming to implement and needs proper planning from the business leadership. So, the upgrade of the systems can never be done immediately and if the requirement is to upgrade the payroll systems immediately and there has been no planning behind it in terms of time and cost, a block chain solution cannot be implemented

Data modification: As the data that has once been entered in the blockchain sequence is shared across its nodes, modification is a very difficult task once the information is recorded and would require rewriting code for all the blocks to update that information. So, at any time if there has been a wrong entry made to the payroll system rectifying it will be tedious, time consuming and expensive (Budhi, 2022).

Legal and ethical issues along with integration challenges: The adoption of blockchain in HRM by organizations makes legal and regulatory compliance an essential issue to address. Blockchain technology's unchangeable and distributed design poses compliance challenges with data protection regulations like the EU's GDPR and new privacy laws such as India's Digital Personal Data Protection Act, 2023. The GDPR grants individuals the "right to be forgotten" which gives them the power to demand their personal data be erased according to Article 17. The core feature of blockchain which is immutability creates a significant challenge to erase data after it has been entered on-chain (Finck,

2021). The methods suggested to handle data on blockchain by using off-chain storage and hashing personal data remain ambiguous in terms of compliance because metadata or hash pointers might still expose confidential information indirectly (Zavolokina et al., 2021).

The Indian DPDPA requires user consent and data minimization but faces challenges with blockchain systems because data distribution across network nodes transcends jurisdictional boundaries. Decentralized HRM systems store sensitive employee data across global nodes which violates local data localization regulations according to Ghosh (2023). To maintain compliance with legal standards organizations need to implement permissioned blockchain networks that include established data governance protocols and access controls based on user roles. The storage of performance appraisal data on blockchain results in permanent records of subjective assessments which pose challenges for correcting unfair evaluations and adapting to employee growth (Levitin, 2019).

High Implementation Costs: Blockchain adoption requires substantial initial investment despite future savings from decreased fraud and improved administrative efficiency.

- Infrastructure development (blockchain nodes, data storage),
- Smart contract creation and auditing,
- Regulatory compliance expenses.

Blockchain adoption for SMEs creates an unfavorable cost–benefit balance that only improves when they participate in consortium-based approaches or government-backed initiatives (Tapscott & Tapscott, 2022).

Privacy in Performance Appraisal Data: The use of blockchain for storing performance evaluations establishes permanent professional records that raise ethical questions about fairness and employee development opportunities. If performance evaluations become universally accessible poor appraisal outcomes will follow employees to new employers which poses a risk of long-term reputational damage (Zwitter & Boisse-Despiaux, 2020).

Ethical Issues in Data Protection: The integration of blockchain technology into HR systems has the potential to transform existing power structures within human resources departments. Universal verification of permanent candidate histories may produce unexpected discrimination and reputational damage. Ethical dilemmas include:

Organizations need to determine if historical data such as contract termination information should be accessible to users.

On the whole the application of blockchain in the payroll management processes increases the overall security by providing a tamper proof and transparent ledger. It helps maintain accurate and immutable records, thereby reducing fraud and risks.

BLOCKCHAIN IN MANAGING GIG ECONOMY WORKERS

In essence, gig employment consists of relatively short jobs, or gigs, for which workers are typically classified as independent contractors rather than employees. Because of this, companies operating in the gig economy do not employ employees; rather, they serve as an intermediary between clients and workers, allocating tasks and managing associated processes through algorithms.

A gig economy illustrates a free and international market where independent contractors and clients connect for a brief professional working relationship that allows for great flexibility and minimal commitment from all parties. Put another way, it's a labor market where all jobs are temporary and performed by independent contractors or freelancers. These gigs or employment are typically mediated by digital platforms that pair the requester or client with someone who works independently as a service provider rather than an employee. The gig worker is often paid upon completion of each activity, with the intermediary platform company typically earning a fixed-rate percentage from each gig (McDonnell, Carbery, Burgess & Sherman, 2021).

Role of Blockchain Technology in Managing Gig Economy Workers

Traditional HR systems lacked the necessary capabilities to efficiently handle freelance workers together with contract-based staff and part-time employees in the gig economy. Gig workers encounter inconsistent onboarding procedures and unclear contracts while dealing with irregular payment schedules and absent structured performance evaluations in contrast to permanent employees (Gupta & Arora, 2021).

Smart contracts are data-powered contracts, in which the if part of if/then triggers the then, depending on what the data attached to the if is. Taking a standard employment contract in one particular field, which is typically fixed for the duration of the contract, and converting it into a simple smart contract exposes all the businesses in that sector to the potential of data automation – people who are hired temporarily and paid based on a 'gig'.

Yet temporary workers represent a new kind of contract: they are always temporary, which creates a gap between their contracts, their pay and hours worked. Current contract management, based on approval slips and centralised record-keeping, isn't properly designed to handle these exceptions.

This is where blockchain comes in. The distributed and tamper-proof ledger that underpins blockchain technology can be employed to overcome the problems associated with traditional approaches to contract management, and improve the quality of contracts while eliminating disputes about information disparities.

As such, transactions on what is called a chain of blocks cannot be altered or modified in any way. The blockchain renders the transaction history permanent, effectively giving a transparent record of all transactions, which is especially important in the gig economy for the prompt and successful completion of all agreements, project milestones and related financial transactions (Javaid et al., 2022). Thus, blockchain technology plays a major role in the following:

> ***Time and attendance tracking:*** Smart contracts offer a secure, transparent, and automated solution that caters to the unique needs of freelancers and independent contractors (Chain, 2023). Traditional time and attendance tracking in the gig economy faces challenges due to manual processes, causing disputes over compensation and project timelines, and introducing uncertainty and potential inefficiencies in payment processing (Mer et al., 2024). Blockchain-based smart contracts automate time tracking for gig economy workers, encoding terms and conditions, and triggering triggers for project completion, transforming how freelancers manage their time (Gridlex, n.d.).

Gig workers can focus on tasks, ensuring accurate working hours through a transparent, decentralized system. Blockchain technology ensures tamper-proof time records, providing a transparent history of work hours, a crucial feature in the gig economy, preventing disputes over time and attendance (Malik, Visvizi & Skrzek-Lubasińska, 2021).

Blockchain's integration with decentralized identity verification systems enhances time tracking reliability by ensuring smart contracts associate time entries with verified gig workers, reducing identity fraud and confirming actual work performed (Agarwal, 2021).

> ***Payroll Management for gig economy workers*:** In the gig economy, timely and accurate payments are critical. Blockchain-enabled smart contracts can automate the payment process, ensuring workers are remunerated immediately upon fulfilling the agreed-upon conditions. This eliminates payment delays and enhances worker satisfaction and financial stability. Traditional payroll

systems struggle to adapt to the gig economy's dynamic nature, causing financial uncertainty and administrative delays, while relying on intermediaries can introduce complexities (Emmanuel, 2023).

Smart contracts or self-executing contracts are programmed to automatically make a payment as soon as the project or task is completed, or a milestone has been reached or a deliverable validated. This yields quite a few advantages. First, using blockchain technology means that payments disburse much more rapidly than conventional methods. Rather than giving people the money upfront, then leaving them to chase the agency for it only to find it might be a long wait and that it hasn't been properly processed and the agency needs some reminding, smart contracts have automated the process by removing its central control. Money is instantly paid out as soon as a project is completed or the milestones are hit or a deliverable declared whole and satisfactory. Second, it dispenses entirely with the core agency being able to delay payments, thus ensuring that your money from one project arrives before you have completed that project (Webcom Systems Pvt Ltd, 2023). Smart contracts can help workers to be paid as soon work is assigned (thus reducing stress and increasing productivity), and can encourage trust between employers and employees, as issues like transparency and payment automation become standardised.

The gig economy is transforming payroll management with smart contracts and blockchain technology, automating payments, ensuring transparency, and providing a tamper-proof record (McKinsey & Company, 2016). "Not only is the middle party eliminated with the blockchain-based ad network, but micropayments are enabled and are automatic. Every impression is an impression paid" (Nunn, 2019).

Smart contracts are digital contracts stored on a Blockchain that are automatically fulfilled after the contract conditions are met. The participants involved are certain of the outcome post completion (like the terms and payment) without the involvement of a middleman, intermediary, or third party. This feature of Blockchain can be applied for streamlining, hiring, and finally paying contract workers (PWC Report, 2017). This technology helps in seamless cross border payment.

Performance Management for gig economy workers: Smart contracts and blockchain technology are revolutionizing performance management for gig economy workers, providing transparency, objectivity, and efficiency in the dynamic and decentralized gig economy. Traditional performance management for gig workers faces challenges due to its fluid nature, lack of alignment with project cycles, and subjectivity, which can lead to biases and discrepancies in evaluations (Zhang & Liu, 2020).

Self-executing 'smart contracts', based on the blockchain provide automated and highly transparent metrics for the continuous, agile tracking of gig economy performance. They assess potential gig workers against clearly defined criteria before engaging them, and during the relationship report in real time on relevant achievements, enhancing the transparency and relevance of recognition and aligning it with concrete successes. Moreover, open, decentralised ledger technology allows gig workers and clients to securely and transparently access performance data at any time. All performance metrics, client feedback or milestones are stored in the ledger, rendering them auditable. This reduces conflict and misinterpretation, thus creating a more productive, cooperative and accountable working relationship.

Integrating blockchain with decentralised identity verification systems also improves the trustworthiness of performance evaluation. The smart contract associates the evaluation of performance metrics to the verified identity of the worker, and hence reduces the identity fraud. It adds value to the worker's reputation score, thereby benefitting gig workers, helping their clients to identify projects, and ultimately building trust in the gig economy ecosystem. A smart contract can be associated with impartial performance assessment, which can help to make the analytics streamlined.

> Offboarding and Termination: By using smart contracts and blockchain technology, offboarding and termination processes for platform work are being simplified to ensure the quality, security and fairness of the processes – all issues that hinder the current approach. Firstly, freelancers operating on gig economy platforms are more mobile than regular employees. The move from one platform to another creates issues for contract termination, as many of these freelancers do not have a fixed residence for important notifications. Hence, finalising a contract on termination can involve difficulties as well as disputes over payment.

Programmable self-executing contracts, called smart contracts, are built into the offboarding process to execute tasks in the gig economy on the blockchain. Upon completing a project or after a date delay, smart contracts execute assigned offboarding quests. This automation reduces the risk of error in performing offboarding tasks and creates conditions of certainty for gig workers and their clients. Standardisation and transparency – in view of what was initially agreed upon – is part of all blockchain-based offboarding. Because computers execute smart contracts, the process is as indisputable and creditworthy as the technology on which it sends and confirms orders.

Blockchain brings security to termination records since tamper-proof ledgers greatly reduce the chances of dispute and provide a detailed audit trail. Its security measures are important since they protect sensitive information such as respectively final payments, contractual obligations and confidential details from unauthorised access or data leakage (Pradeep, Yiu, Zou and Amor, 2021).

Smart contracts help gig professionals to offboard and terminate contracts with all stakeholders in a fair and consistent way by automating highly time-critical and controversial steps and executing actions without any subjective bias and delivering a pleasant experience to the gig workers.

Advantages of Blockchain Technology in Managing Gig Economy Workers

Enhances efficiency and transparency: Integrating smart contracts and blockchain technology in gig economy time and attendance tracking enhances efficiency, transparency, and security, fostering a reliable relationship between workers and clients, and could become a cornerstone in the evolving gig economy (Salisu, 2023).

Mitigates fraud and security risks: Blockchain technology mitigates fraud and security risks related to temporary worker contracts by employing encryption and consensus mechanisms, which avoid data modification in the ledger. For example, cryptographic mechanisms protect information such as personal data, authentication information, employment information and wages in the distributed ledgers. This prevents bad actors from gaining access to the temporary worker agreement (Huynh-The et al., 2023).

Simplified offboarding & termination: Blockchain technology simplifies offboarding and termination

Challenges with implementing blockchain in managing gig economy workers

Ethical and Privacy Concerns in Blockchain-Driven HRM

Conflicts with Privacy Laws like GDPR: The European Union's General Data Protection Regulation (GDPR) stands as one of the most referenced legal frameworks because it imposes stringent guidelines for collecting, processing, and deleting personal data (Khan & Mer, 2023). The General Data Protection Regulation includes several provisions that create obstacles to blockchain suitability.

- Right to be forgotten (Article 17): When employees or job applicants ask to delete their personal information it stands in opposition to blockchain's permanent nature.
- Data minimization (Article 5): Blockchain systems duplicate data throughout multiple nodes which can breach the data minimization principle.
- Purpose limitation and consent (Articles 6 & 7): The transparent and distributed nature of blockchain architecture allows data to be reused or accessed without obtaining new consent (Finck & Moscon, 2019).

The Digital Personal Data Protection Act of 2023 in India requires data erasure requirements alongside consent-based processing but encounters issues with blockchain technology because of its rigid structure regarding data localization and grievance redressal mechanisms according to Ghosh's 2023 study.

Data sharing across borders via blockchain in recruitment and gig economy platforms creates jurisdictional conflicts when gig workers' personal data resides in nodes located in multiple countries and triggers localization and sovereignty challenges (Papadopoulos, 2019).

Ethical Dilemmas In Transparency Vs. Confidentiality

The ability of blockchain to ensure transparency becomes problematic in HR contexts because complete openness can breach employee privacy rights. For instance:, making performance ratings public through blockchain systems could lead to biased assessments and discrimination among peers along with causing emotional distress.

Because disciplinary records on blockchain remain unchangeable they can negatively impact future job opportunities which contradicts the idea of giving people a second chance.

Blockchain technology receives support in the gig economy for its ability to maintain decentralized work records along with reputation systems. Immutable negative feedback or dispute records have the potential to irreversibly harm gig workers' professional opportunities preventing them from obtaining future employment despite any subsequent improvements or resolved issues (Scholz, 2017).

Thus, one should develop blockchain systems that are ethically guided to ensure transparency while protecting confidentiality for vulnerable gig workers and marginalized job.

Cases

Walmart explored blockchain technology for handling freelance contract agreements and payment transactions. The smart contract implementation achieved reduced payroll disputes but experienced interoperability issues with existing Oracle HR systems and required middleware solutions to function properly (Walmart Blockchain Report, 2022).

PwC tested a smart contract payroll system for a multinational company with a workforce of employees and gig workers operating across different jurisdictions. The smart contract system managed payroll by automatically processing payments and taxes before executing transfers which led to faster payroll processing and increased audit readiness (PwC, 2021).

Table 1. Summary of role of BT in recruitment, payroll management and managing gig economy workers

Role of BT in Recruitment	Role of BT in Payroll Management	Role of BT in managing gig economy workers
Verification of candidate credentials	Making instant payments	Time & attendance tracking
Decentralised candidate profiles	Payroll dispute resolution	Transparency in payment
Digital identity and immutable records	Seamless cross border payment	Micro Payment for gig workers
Transparency and trust in hiring process	Payroll and taxation automation	Seamless cross border payment
Cheaper transaction cost of hiring	Faster payments & reduced delays	Simplified offboarding & termination
Quicker onboarding	Facilitates alternative payment action	Mitigates fraud and security risk
	Tracking employee attendance	
	Real-time payroll processing	
	Real time tax calculation & collection	
	Privacy & trust in performance appraisal data	

Source: Authors

FUTURE RESEARCH

More future research could explore other dimensions of HRM in which the role of blockchain is in its early stages of evolution, such as blockchain in the empowerment of workers, in creating decentralised work environments, blockchain in the career of individuals, on succession planning and organisation change and management. Future research and development should focus on Hybrid solutions that integrate blockchain technology with existing databases provide improved compliance and operational flexibility. Studies can be conducted on a blend of artificial intelligence (AI), machine learning (ML) with blockchain technology (Arora et al., 2025) to advance decision-making capabilities and secure predictive analytics.

Future research can also be done on AI-Blockchain Synergy in Performance Appraisal: Smart contracts can connect with AI-based performance evaluation systems to automatically initiate actions such as promotions or training interventions based on verified blockchain data (Rouhani & Deters, 2021).

CONCLUSION

Overall, the conclusion on the function of blockchain in the recruitment process, payroll management and managing the gifts economy workers highlight its uniqueness of improving all these domains.

In first aspect, blockchain can help improving the security and transparency of candidate credentials during recruitment process, hence organisational reputation. In second aspect, blockchain can increase the trust in the payroll process, minimize the possibility of bad payroll and guaranteed income, by creating an immutable record of the payroll. Finally, in third aspect, blockchain, due to its construction deleting all intermediaries involved in transaction, can improve hiring and firing process among all talents participating in gifts economy, hence reducing the cost of management based on employees contract, and achieving transfer of payment particularly during the working period.

There are still several issues such as scalability, regulatory issues for taxation and adoption by corporations and industry. In my perspective, the gifts of blockchain looks promising as long as innovation continue, and broad engagement from the all, with its efficiency, trust and reliability enhancing process of these HR domains.

REFERENCES

Abu Mizar, Y. S. M. (2021). Decentralized Project Management for the Gig Economy Using Blockchain to Ensure Trust and Reliable Ranking (Bachelor's thesis). Retrieved from https://opus4.kobv.de/opus4-haw/files/1087/I000992830Thesis.pdf

Archana K, Hanis Sultana A, Vishnu Priya V, Prabakaran V, Krishnaveni P, Swarnam S, Senthil Kumar S and Shamini SD. (2023). Blockchain Technology As A Tool For Effective Recruitment: A Design Thinking Approach. 1603-1604.

Arora, S., & Nabi, T. (2022). Blockchain adoption in banking systems: A boon or bane? In *Applications, challenges, and opportunities of blockchain technology in banking and insurance* (pp. 19–42). IGI Global.

Arora, S., Oberoi, S., Nabi, T., & Verma, B. (2024). How does blockchain impact sustainable food security? Insights from literature review. *International Journal of Information Management Data Insights*, *4*(2), 100276. DOI: 10.1016/j.jjimei.2024.100276

Arora, S., Pawar, M., Joshi, M., Pargaien, S., Mer, A., & Misra, A. (2025). Handshake between humans and artificial intelligence: A review. *Challenges in Information, Communication and Computing Technology*, 693-697.

Barney, J. (1991). Firm resources and sustained competitive advantage. *Journal of Management*, *17*(1), 99–120. DOI: 10.1177/014920639101700108

Bass, B. (2021). How Blockchain Could Work for Staffing: Hint, Direct Sourcing and Diversity. Retrieved from https://www.olooptech.com/post/how-blockchain-could-work-for-staffing-hint-direct-sourcing-and-diversity#:~:text=The%20Blockchain%20Direct%20Sourcing%20Process%201%20A%20client,the%20requisition%20once%20it%E2%80%99s%20released.%20...%20More%20items)

Bello, M. I., & Daniel, T. R. (2022). Potentials of Blockchain Technology for Payroll Systems. Potentials of Blockchain Technology for Payroll Systems" (2022). *SAIS 2022 Proceedings*. 20.https://aisel.aisnet.org/sais2022/20

Budhi, V. (2022). Advantages And Di. (Behera, B. (2022). Should you start accepting salary in Bitcoin? Retrieved from, https://economictimes.indiatimes.com/markets/cryptocurrency/should-you-start-accepting-a-salary-in-bitcoin/articleshow/90455216.cms

Chain. (2023, August 26). Chain Insights — Redefining the Post-Pandemic Freelance Economy with Web3. Retrieved from https://medium.com/@chaininc/chain-insights-redefining-the-post-pandemic-freelance-economy-with-web3-1ea280b27dd1

Chillakuri, B., & Attili, V. P. (2022). Role of blockchain in HR's response to new-normal. *The International Journal of Organizational Analysis*, *30*(6), 1359–1378. DOI: 10.1108/IJOA-08-2020-2363

Cloudpay (2021). Three Essential Uses for Blockchain in Payroll and HR. retrieved from, https://www.cloudpay.com/resources/three-essential-uses-for-blockchain-in-payroll-and-hr)

Diploma, B. C. (2023). Blockchain: how do "verifiable credentials" work? Retrieved from https://www.bcdiploma.com/en/blog/blockchain-verifiable-credentials

Eliaçık, E. (2022, August 12). Is HR ready for blockchain? Dataconomy. Retrieved from https://dataconomy.com/2022/06/22/blockchain-in-hr/#:~:text=IBM%20Garage%20created%20a%20private,employers%20or%20across%20the%20network

Emmanuel, C. (2023, October 10). Revolutionizing HR and Finance: Chrono.tech's Path to a Seamless Future. Medium. https://medium.com/@clemzyemmanuel/revolutionizing-hr-and-finance-chrono-techs-path-to-a-seamless-future-af972b71eed3

Finck, M. (2021). *Blockchain and the General Data Protection Regulation: Reconciling immutable ledgers with data privacy rights*. Oxford Internet Institute.

Hanggoro, D., Windiatmaja, J. H., & Sari, R. F. (2022, July). Blockchain-based Attendance Management and Payroll System using Hyperledger Composer Framework. In *2022 IEEE Region 10 Symposium (TENSYMP)* (pp. 1-6). IEEE. DOI: 10.1109/TENSYMP54529.2022.9864383

Huynh-The, T., Gadekallu, T. R., Wang, W., Yenduri, G., Ranaweera, P., Pham, Q.-V., da Costa, D. B., & Liyanage, M. (2023). Blockchain for the metaverse: A review. *Future Generation Computer Systems*, *143*, 401–419. DOI: 10.1016/j.future.2023.02.008

IBM. (2021). *IBM-AT&T blockchain talent platform: A case study*. IBM Reports.

Jones, R. (2023). The Future of Payroll Powered by Blockchain Technology. Retrieved from, https://chainbulletin.com/the-future-of-payroll-powered-by-blockchain-technology

Khan, F., Khati, K., Pargaien, S., Mer, A., Arora, S., & Gangola, S. (2024). Harnessing Artificial Intelligence and Blockchain: Advancing Cybersecurity and Identity Protection. *Available atSSRN* 5091178.

Khan, F., & Mer, A. (2023). Embracing Artificial Intelligence Technology: Legal Implications with Special Reference to European Union Initiatives of Data Protection. In *Digital Transformation, Strategic Resilience, Cyber Security and Risk Management* (pp. 119-141). Emerald Publishing Limited.

Khan, S. N., Loukil, F., Ghedira-Guegan, C., Benkhelifa, E., & Bani-Hani, A. (2021). Blockchain smart contracts: Applications, challenges, and future trends. *Peer-to-Peer Networking and Applications, 14*(5), 2901–2925. DOI: 10.1007/s12083-021-01127-0 PMID: 33897937

Kişi, N. (2022). Exploratory research on the use of blockchain technology in recruitment. *Sustainability (Basel), 14*(16), 10098. DOI: 10.3390/su141610098

Li, X., Jiang, P., Chen, T., Luo, X., & Wen, Q. (2020). A Survey on the Security of Blockchain Systems. *Future Generation Computer Systems, 107*, 841–853. DOI: 10.1016/j.future.2017.08.020

Malik, R., Visvizi, A., & Skrzek-Lubasińska, M. (2021). The Gig Economy: Current Issues, the Debate, and the New Avenues of Research. *Sustainability (Basel), 13*(9), 5023. DOI: 10.3390/su13095023

Marr, B. (2023). The 5 Biggest Problems With Blockchain Technology Everyone Must Know About. Retrieved from https://www.forbes.com/sites/bernardmarr/2023/04/14/the-5-biggest-problems-with-blockchain-technology-everyone-must-know-about/?sh=78079bf855d2

Mathew, J., Mer, A. & Khan, F. (2025). 5 Blockchain Smart. *Digital HR: Technologies for HR Transformation and Performance Improvement*, 64.

McDonnell, A., Carbery, R., Burgess, J., & Sherman, U. (2021). Technologically mediated human resource management in the gig economy. *International Journal of Human Resource Management, 32*(19), 3995–4015. DOI: 10.1080/09585192.2021.1986109

Mer, A., Mathew, J., & Arora, S. (2024). Managing Gig Economy Workers Through Artificial Intelligence: Applications and Challenges. *Fostering Industry-Academia Partnerships for Innovation-Driven Trade*, 17-30.

Mer, A., & Srivastava, A. (2023). Employee engagement in the new normal: Artificial intelligence as a buzzword or a game changer? In *The adoption and effect of artificial intelligence on human resources management, Part A* (pp. 15-46). Emerald Publishing Limited.

Mer, A., & Virdi, A. S. (2022). Artificial intelligence disruption on the brink of revolutionizing HR and marketing functions. In *Impact of artificial intelligence on organizational transformation* (pp. 1–19). Wiley. DOI: 10.1002/9781119710301.ch1

Mer, A., & Virdi, A. S. (2023). Navigating the paradigm shift in HRM practices through the lens of artificial intelligence: A post-pandemic perspective. *The Adoption and Effect of Artificial Intelligence on Human Resources Management, Part A*, 123-154.

Mishra, H., & Venkatesan, M. (2021). Blockchain in human resource management of organizations: An empirical assessment to gauge HR and non-HR perspective. *Journal of Organizational Change Management, 34*(2), 525–542. DOI: 10.1108/JOCM-08-2020-0261

Nunn, J. (2019). Bitcoin's Emerging Gig Economy. Retrieved from https://www.forbes.com/sites/jeffersonnunn/2019/02/19/bitcoins-emerging-gig-economy/

Oberoi, S., & Kansra, P. (2022). Blockchain technology in the insurance industry. In *Applications, challenges, and opportunities of blockchain technology in banking and insurance* (pp. 160–172). IGI Global.

Oberoi, S., Arora, S., Verma, B., & Roy, K. K. (2024). What do we know about artificial intelligence and blockchain technology integration in the healthcare industry? In *Driving decentralization and disruption with digital technologies* (pp. 124–138). IGI Global Scientific Publishing.

OPS. (2025). How Blockchain Technology is Transforming Payroll. Retrirved from https://ops.ae/how-blockchain-technology-is-transforming-payroll/

Papadopoulos, G. (2019). Blockchain and the law: Resolving data protection conflicts across jurisdictions. *Computer Law & Security Review, 35*(4), 105344.

Pradeep, A. S. E., Yiu, T. W., Zou, Y., & Amor, R. (2021). Blockchain-aided information exchange records for design liability control and improved security. *Automation in Construction, 126*, 103667. DOI: 10.1016/j.autcon.2021.103667

Report, P. W. C. (2017). *How will blockchain technology impact HR and the world of work.*, Retrieved from https://www.pwc.co.uk/issues/futuretax/assets/blockchain-can%20impact-hr.pdf

Ruhland, T. (2015), 5 Common Problems With Payroll Management. Retrieved from, https://blog.accuchex.com/5-common-problems-with-payroll-management

Sandner, P. (2022). Three Ways How Blockchain Technology Is Already Changing The Lives Of Thousands Of Workers In Emerging Countries. Retrieved by, https://www.forbes.com/sites/philippsandner/2022/08/31/three-ways-how-blockchain-technology-is-already-changing-the-lives-of-thousands-of-workers-in-emerging-countries/?sh=5af53afb4f3f

Scholz, T. (2017). *Uberworked and underpaid: How workers are disrupting the digital economy*. Polity Press.

Seth, H. (2023). Blockchain-based identity verification: A solution to the growing problem of job candidate fraud. Retrieved from https://www.financialexpress.com/business/blockchain-blockchain-based-identity-verification-a-solution-to-the-growing-problem-of-job-candidate-fraud-3084923/

Sharma, S. (2023). Unleashing the Potential of Blockchain-Based Background Verification. Retrieved from https://www.forbes.com/sites/forbeshumanresourcescouncil/2023/05/12/unleashing-the-potential-of-blockchain-based-background-verification/?sh=2fbdac065a9c)

Sine, R. (2018). How The Blockchain Will Change Recruiting. Retrieved from, https://www.forbes.com/sites/adp/2018/03/21/how-the-blockchain-will-change-recruiting/?sh=152778a45f32)

Turczynski, B. (2023). Lying on a Resume (2022 Study). Retrieved from https://resumelab.com/resume/lying#:~:text=When%20we%20broke%20down%20the%20data%20by%20industry%2C,lying%20on%20a%20resume%20based%20on%20education%20level.

Verma, B., Bhardwaj, M., Arora, S., & Oberoi, S. (2025). Unveiling the impact of remittances on productive efficiencies: Investigating productivity growth of prominent remittance-receiving developing nations. *International Journal of Productivity and Performance Management*, *74*(4), 1101–1124. DOI: 10.1108/IJPPM-05-2023-0213

Webcom Systems Pvt Ltd. (2023, July 20). Smart Contracts: Revolutionizing Transactions through Impeccable Automation. LinkedIn. https://www.linkedin.com/pulse/smart-contracts-revolutionizing-transactions-through/

Zhang, Y.-D., & Liu, M.-J. (2020). Analysis of the Influencing Factors of Enterprise Management on Employee Loyalty in Gig Economy. In *2020 International Conference on Wireless Communications and Smart Grid (ICWCSG)*, Qingdao, China (pp. 331-334). DOI: 10.1109/ICWCSG50807.2020.00076

Zielinski, D. (2021). How Blockchain Benefits Recruiters, Job Candidates. Retrieved from, https://workplacetechcommunity.shrm.org/s/articles/a2D1T000005sbksUAA/how-blockchain-benefits-recruiters-job-candidates)

Chapter 12
Driving Better Health Outcomes for Gig Workers Through Strategic Health Initiatives

Pooja Kalbalia
https://orcid.org/0000-0002-3739-3165
Christ University, India

Kailash Koushik
Christ University, India

ABSTRACT

The gig economy offers flexibility and autonomy to workers but also presents significant challenges related to health and well-being, especially for delivery professionals who face irregular hours, physical strain, and limited access to healthcare. Immersive technologies, such as virtual reality (VR), augmented reality (AR), and artificial intelligence (AI), present innovative solutions to bridge these gaps. However, gig workers' adoption of these technologies remains underexplored. This paper applied the diffusion of innovation (DOI) theory to analyse the adoption patterns of immersive technologies within the gig economy and identified barriers, such as digital literacy and cost, alongside facilitators, like perceived usefulness and ease of integration. The paper provides insights into how these technologies can be effectively implemented in the gig workforce. The study highlights the role of platform policies and the broader regulatory landscape in shaping technology adoption, offering valuable recommendations for policymakers and technology developers.

DOI: 10.4018/979-8-3373-1290-3.ch012

INTRODUCTION

The rapid expansion of the gig economy has significantly reshaped global labour markets, particularly in sectors like transportation, food delivery, and freelance services (Kalbalia et al., 2024). Digital platforms have played an important role in this transformation by connecting workers with customers in real time, offering flexible work arrangements that appeal to a wide range of individuals seeking autonomy and income opportunities (Katsnelson & Oberholzer-Gee, 2021). While this model has undeniably broadened access to employment, it also raises concerns about the working conditions and health security of gig workers, especially those in physically intensive roles like delivery services (Kumar, 2023). Delivery professionals often work long, irregular hours under demanding physical conditions, frequently without the protections or benefits associated with traditional employment (Graham et al., 2017; Koohang et al., 2023).

The absence of employer-provided health insurance, paid sick leave, and structured wellness programs forces many to rely on out-of-pocket healthcare or digital health tools, which increases their vulnerability and deepens health inequities (Friedland & Balkin, 2023). These structural gaps reflect a broader issue within platform-based work. While flexibility is a key selling point, it often masks a lack of job security, income stability, and occupational safeguards (Randolph, 2019). As gig workers continue to operate in hazardous environments, the need for innovative, technology-driven interventions becomes urgent (Kalbalia & Koushik, 2025). Solutions must go beyond convenience and connectivity, addressing the systemic absence of health protections and support mechanisms within the platform economy (Lester et al., 2021).

Immersive technologies like virtual reality (VR), augmented reality (AR), and AI-driven health applications have emerged as potential tools to transform how gig workers manage health, access training, and navigate daily tasks (Behar et al., 2020; Devagiri et al., 2022). These tools can support remote consultations, real-time monitoring, and skill development (Albahri, Albahri, et al., 2018; Albahri, Zaidan, et al., 2018). But even with their promise, adoption by delivery workers remains limited, and the reasons why are not well understood. We need a structured way to explore how and why certain innovations catch on. That's where Diffusion of Innovation (DOI) Theory helps.

This study applies the Diffusion of Innovation (DOI) Theory to understand how immersive health technologies spread among gig delivery workers (Akir, 2003). Originally proposed by Everett Rogers, the DOI provides a framework for analysing how new technologies spread across populations (Curtis, 2020; Pereira et al., 2022). The theory describes five key stages: knowledge, persuasion, decision, implementation, and confirmation, through which individuals become aware of, evaluate, and ultimately adopt or reject a new innovation (Bhattacharya, 2015; Seligman,

2006). For gig workers, this process involves becoming aware of innovations like VR-based training or AI health tools, evaluating their usefulness and ease of use, and deciding whether to adopt them, often under the influence of peers, platform cues, and individual attitudes (Ling et al., 2021). Continued use depends on user experience and tangible outcomes.

However, DOI is not enough; Platform algorithms, digital literacy gaps, and financial stress also influence whether a worker can or will adopt new tools (Barrette, 2015). Most gig workers are in low-income settings, where affordability and simplicity are key (Zhu et al., 2024). Platforms also act as gatekeepers, deciding which tools are introduced and shaping usage patterns, often reinforcing power imbalances through algorithmic control and data surveillance. DOI does not fully account for these structural and political dynamics, nor the risks of technologies being repurposed for productivity tracking rather than genuine worker support.

To account for these complexities, the Technology Acceptance Model (TAM) offers valuable insights. TAM focuses on perceived usefulness and ease of use, key factors for time and resource-constrained gig workers (Du Toit, 2017; Lee et al., 2025; Rahimi & Oh, 2024). By blending DOI and TAM, this study bridges the social diffusion of technology with individual user perceptions, offering a more holistic view of adoption in precarious labour markets. This dual framework unpacks both systemic barriers and personal motivations, revealing the real-life conditions under which immersive tech can support gig workers or fall short.

This study focuses specifically on delivery professionals, a prominent segment of the gig workforce, whose health risks and dependence on digital platforms make them a critical group for studying technology adoption. By analysing how immersive technologies are received, resisted, or embraced, the research identifies key factors influencing adoption decisions. These insights aim to guide platform operators, policymakers, and technology developers in designing tools that are accessible, supportive, and aligned with workers' lived realities. While immersive technologies hold the promise to improve gig work, their broader adoption is hindered by barriers like low digital literacy, limited accessibility, and scepticism toward unfamiliar tools. These challenges disproportionately affect low-income workers who dominate the gig workforce. This paper explores how DOI and TAM, when applied together, can illuminate pathways for overcoming these barriers and promote more inclusive, health-supportive technologies for gig workers.

OBJECTIVE

1. To explore how delivery workers engage with immersive health technologies using the DOI and TAM frameworks.

2. To identify challenges and drivers shaping adoption, and suggest ways to boost access and support.

LITERATURE REVIEW

1. Gig Economy, Health Risks, and the Promise of Immersive Tech

The gig economy has become a defining feature of modern labour, offering flexibility but also implanting deep insecurity. Delivery workers, in particular, face harsh conditions, long hours, exposure to accidents, and no safety nets like health insurance or paid leave (Koohang et al., 2023). These vulnerabilities are compounded by platform governance mechanisms like algorithmic nudges and impervious rating systems that drive precariousness under the guise of digital efficiency (Ravenelle et al., 2021). Technological advancements have reshaped modern work environments, with the gig economy emerging as a significant area of transformation (Albahri, Albahri, et al., 2018). The gig economy encompasses short-term, flexible employment facilitated by digital platforms that connect workers with consumers (Katsnelson & Oberholzer-Gee, 2021).

While this model provides autonomy and income opportunities, it also exposes workers to various challenges, including inconsistent pay, lack of social security, and limited access to healthcare (Myhill et al., 2021). Delivery professionals, a major subset of gig workers, experience these vulnerabilities acutely due to the physical demands of their work and the absence of employer-sponsored health benefits (Kovács et al., 2023). As digital solutions evolve, immersive technologies present new possibilities for addressing these issues. Virtual reality (VR), augmented reality (AR), and artificial intelligence (AI) can facilitate remote healthcare access, improve occupational training, and enhance worker safety. However, understanding the factors that drive or hinder the adoption of these technologies requires a theoretical lens that captures both individual behaviour and broader socio-economic influences.

2. Theoretical Framework: DOI, Its Fit, and Its Limits

The Diffusion of Innovation (DOI) Theory offers a structured framework to analyse how new technologies spread and become integrated into daily practices, making it a suitable approach for examining immersive technology adoption among gig workers (Akir, 2003). DOI Theory, developed by Rogers, outlines how innovations diffuse through populations over time (Hornik, 2004). The process unfolds in five stages: knowledge, persuasion, decision, implementation, and confirmation

(Mcgrath & Zell, 2001). In the knowledge stage, individuals become aware of the technology, followed by the persuasion stage, where attitudes toward its perceived benefits and risks form. The decision stage involves choosing whether to adopt or reject the innovation. If adopted, the implementation stage represents the practical use of the technology, while the confirmation stage reflects the reinforcement or discontinuation of its use based on experience and outcomes. Rogers emphasises that the rate of diffusion depends on five key attributes: relative advantage, compatibility, complexity, trialability, and observability (Akir, 2003). For gig workers, these attributes are apparent through practical considerations such as whether immersive technologies reduce work-related risks, align with their existing routines, and are easy to adopt.

3. Limitations of DOI in Platform Context

Studies applying DOI Theory to digital adoption suggest that user perceptions of utility and ease of use significantly influence technology uptake. In gig work contexts, these perceptions are shaped by economic pressures, digital literacy, and the structural constraints of platform-mediated labour. In gig work, DOI helps surface individual adoption patterns, for example, whether a VR safety module feels usable or relevant to a rider's daily experience. Studies like (K. T. Huang et al., 2019) show that immersive tools can increase task efficiency and reduce errors in logistics-based roles. But DOI is not neutral. It often assumes Western-centric access to infrastructure and privileges individual agency without grappling with platform-imposed constraints or coerced adoption. Gig workers might "choose" to adopt AI monitoring tools, but that choice often happens under economic duress or a policy vacuum. To address these blind spots, we need to layer DOI with alternative models, like the Technology Acceptance Model (TAM), which foregrounds user perceptions of usefulness and ease of use, or Platform Cooperativism, which emphasises collective ownership and control over tech deployment (Lee et al., 2025; Rahimi & Oh, 2024).

4. Opportunities and Challenges in Tech Adoption in the Gig Economy

Existing research on technology adoption in the gig economy highlights both opportunities and challenges in integrating advanced digital tools. Huang et al. (2019) examine how immersive technologies improve task efficiency and training outcomes, finding that VR-based simulations enhance learning retention and reduce operational errors. For delivery professionals, this translates to safer work practices and better preparedness for unpredictable conditions. Abdulmalek et al. (2022)

explore AI-driven health monitoring systems, demonstrating that personalised wellness interventions mitigate the physical strains of gig work. However, these studies also point to barriers such as technological complexity, cost, and apprehension toward new systems. Robinson et al. (2020) emphasise that digital inequalities persist within gig workforces, as low-income workers often face limited access to advanced tools. This digital divide raises concerns about the equitable distribution of technological benefits. Furthermore, gig workers' autonomy and lack of formal employment protections worsen vulnerabilities, making it difficult to implement long-term technological solutions without external support. A critical gap in the literature concerns how immersive technologies specifically influence the health and well-being of gig workers through the adoption process. While several studies address technology use in formal employment, research on the gig economy remains fragmented. For instance, Wood et al. (2019) examine algorithmic management and its psychological effects on gig workers, but do not explore how digital tools could alleviate these pressures. Similarly, (Babalola et al., 2023) analyse platform governance but overlook how immersive technologies might empower workers to manage occupational health risks.

Studies on the adoption of health-related technologies provide additional context for analysing immersive tools in the gig economy. (Whitehead et al., 2023) find that trust in digital health platforms is a key determinant of adoption. For gig workers, who often lack consistent healthcare access, trust may be influenced by the perceived reliability and accuracy of virtual health consultations. Similarly, (Cornet et al., 2020) argue that user-centred design improves adoption rates by aligning technology features with users' practical needs. This insight is relevant to immersive technologies, as complex or unintuitive interfaces may deter gig workers from regular use. In delivery work, where time efficiency is supreme, technologies must integrate seamlessly into workflows without increasing cognitive or physical burdens.

5. Platform Governance and Structural Power Dynamics

Research on digital labour highlights the structural factors shaping technology adoption. Ravenelle et al. (2021) argue that gig work's precarious nature affects how workers engage with technology, as those in insecure employment situations lack the resources to invest in new tools. This structural vulnerability intersects with the digital divide, limiting access to advanced technologies among marginalised groups. Furthermore, Huang. (2023) emphasise that platform policies directly influence how technology is adopted, as algorithmic management systems often dictate work processes. In the case of immersive technologies, adoption depends not only on individual decisions but also on how platform governance structures shape the availability and use of these tools. Adding to this, platform governance builds in power imbalances that limit how much say workers actually have in tech use. The platforms usually control everything, from which tools get introduced to how they are used, so workers often end up just adapting to systems they had no hand in shaping. With immersive technologies, this could mean that VR training or AR-based health tracking gets rolled out in ways that prioritise efficiency or data collection over actual worker well-being. Without worker involvement in these decisions, immersive tools could easily become about surveillance and control than support and empowerment. Such dynamics underscore the need for a structured lens to map these tensions, which this study captures through the conceptual dimensions outlined in Table 1.1.

Table 1. Details of the papers

Year	Study	Focus Area	Key Findings
2025	Lee, J., Park, Y., & Kim, S. (2025)	Technology Acceptance Model in gig platforms	Showed that perceived usefulness and ease of use predict adoption of platform tools
2024	Rahimi, M., & Oh, L. (2024)	Platform cooperativism	Argued for collective ownership to offset platform exploitation
2023	Huang, H. (2023)	Algorithmic management in delivery platforms	Ethnography reveals algorithmic control structures that shape labour
2023	Whitehead, M., & Smith, K. (2023)	Trust in digital health tools	Trustworthiness is central to users' engagement with e-health
2023	Koohang, A., Sierpinska, B., & Rongo, T. (2023)	Health risks in gig delivery	Highlighted high stress, injury risk, and lack of safety nets
2023	Kovács, G., Nagy, A., & Molnár, P. (2023)	Healthcare access among gig workers	Systematic review finds major barriers to utilising services
2022	Abdulmalek, F., Hasan, Z., & Lee, S. (2022)	AI-driven health monitoring	Wearables plus AI can pre-emptively flag health issues
2021	Katsnelson, R., & Oberholzer-Gee, F. (2021)	Gig work flexibility	Drivers highly value autonomy but face income instability
2021	Myhill, W., Pande, A., & Becker, G. (2021)	Healthcare utilisation in gig work	Documented erratic pay and insurance gaps
2021	Ravenelle, A., Barnhart, J., & Spreitzer, G. (2021)	Algorithmic surveillance	Showed how nudges and ratings deepen insecurity
2020	Cornet, V., & Holden, R. (2020)	User-centred design in mHealth	Intuitive UCD boosts adoption of mobile health apps
2019	Wood, A., Lehdonvirta, V., & Graham, M. (2019)	Algorithmic management stress	Algorithms act as "invisible cages," increasing burnout
2019	Huang, M., Zhao, X., & Chen, L. (2019)	VR training in logistics	VR simulations cut errors and boost safety training retention

continued on following page

Table 1. Continued

Year	Study	Focus Area	Key Findings
2018	Albahri, A., Albahri, O., Hashim, S., & Alwan, J. K. (2018)	Gig economy emergence	Mapped how platforms reshape labour markets
2004	Hornik, R. (2004)	Diffusion of innovations	Reflected on Rogers's stages of diffusion in health communications
2003	Akir, D. (2003)	DOI attributes in adoption	Highlighted traits like compatibility and observability
2001	McGrath, R. G., & Zell, D. (2001)	Innovation adoption stages	Defined knowledge confirmation lifecycle

METHODOLOGY

This study adopts a qualitative research design, relying on a narrative literature review to examine the adoption of immersive technologies by delivery professionals in the gig economy. Since tools like virtual reality, augmented reality, and AI-driven health solutions are constantly evolving, a literature-based method helps provide a detailed overview of what has been studied so far and what gaps still exist. This design aligns with the study's objective to explore adoption trends and barriers through the lens of the Diffusion of Innovation Theory. A narrative literature review is well suited for this study as it enables a broad examination of relevant scholarly works while allowing for thematic synthesis (Khan et al., 2021). The focus is on constructing a cohesive argument by drawing from prior research, highlighting key debates, and identifying emerging themes. This method also allows for a historical and conceptual exploration of how immersive technologies have been introduced, evaluated, and integrated into digital labour markets (Eager et al., 2022).

The review encompasses academic literature published in high-impact journals, conference proceedings, and industry reports over the past two decades. Given the rapid evolution of digital labour platforms, priority is given to recently published studies, reflecting the period when platform-based gig work and immersive technologies began to gain prominence (Cropanzano et al., 2022; Kadolkar et al., 2024). The review includes empirical studies, theoretical papers, and policy reports that address technology adoption among gig workers, digital workplace transformations, and the application of immersive tools in professional settings. Sources are identified through academic databases such as Scopus, Web of Science, IEEE Xplore, ScienceDirect, and Google Scholar, using search terms including "immersive technologies in gig work," "Diffusion of Innovation in digital labour," "virtual reality for workforce training," and "augmented reality in last-mile delivery."

Only studies directly focused on immersive technology adoption in gig settings or closely connected sectors such as online freelancing, remote work, or other forms of platform-mediated labour were selected. Special attention was paid to research applying the Diffusion of Innovation Theory to tech adoption, as this is the primary conceptual framework of the paper. In addition to scholarly work, reports from global organisations, including the International Labour Organisation and the World Economic Forum, were consulted to expand the perspective on platform design, regulatory changes, and policy challenges.

The analysis is structured around the five stages of the Diffusion of Innovation Theory. The knowledge stage looks at how delivery workers first encounter immersive technologies, including exposure through app features, digital onboarding, or peer sharing. This part also draws on research exploring inequalities in digital access and literacy that can affect who gets to participate in tech-enhanced work. The persuasion stage focuses on how workers form attitudes toward these technologies, especially in terms of usability, trust, and relevance. The decision stage deals with what influences the actual choice to adopt or reject these tools. The implementation stage covers how immersive tech is used in real-time work tasks such as navigation, telehealth consults, or training. Finally, the confirmation stage brings in findings related to sustained use, satisfaction, and whether or not these tools become part of workers' routines.

All sources were critically appraised for quality, focusing on methodological rigour, theoretical contribution, and empirical clarity. Conceptual works were examined for how they added to the theoretical foundation, while empirical studies were categorised by research design, including qualitative interviews, case studies, and surveys. Longitudinal studies were highlighted for their value in tracking adoption over time. Where available, cross-country comparisons were included to understand how national context affects the pace and style of tech integration. There are a few limitations to this method. Since the study relies only on published literature, there is no direct field interaction with delivery workers. That makes it difficult to capture the most recent behavioural shifts that might not yet be documented in peer-reviewed research.

Another challenge is that gig platforms vary widely in their business models and technological approaches, making broad generalisations difficult. Lastly, the pace of change in immersive technology is rapid, so some earlier studies may already be outdated even though they laid foundational insights. Despite these limitations, the narrative literature review provides a strong and theory-driven structure for understanding how immersive technologies are entering and reshaping platform work. Through this approach, the study offers a grounded understanding of adoption dynamics, the structural issues gig workers face, and the broader social and policy implications of integrating immersive tools into precarious forms of labour.

FINDINGS AND DISCUSSION

The findings synthesise key insights from the literature on immersive technology adoption in the gig economy, focusing on delivery professionals and their interaction with virtual reality (VR), augmented reality (AR), and artificial intelligence (AI)-driven tools. Anchored in the Diffusion of Innovation (DOI) framework and supported by the Technology Acceptance Model (TAM), the findings are structured around five stages of adoption: knowledge, persuasion, decision, implementation, and confirmation. The discussion also integrates structural barriers and enablers that shape adoption at both individual and systemic levels.

The knowledge stage is a crucial first step in adoption, as gig workers must become aware of immersive technologies and their potential applications. Existing research suggests that knowledge diffusion in gig work settings is largely mediated by platform-driven exposure, peer networks, and targeted training initiatives(Dean & Spoehr, 2018). Studies indicate that digital labour platforms significantly shape technology awareness, often introducing new tools through app updates, notifications, or mandatory onboarding modules(Dijck, 2018). However, research also highlights significant disparities in digital literacy among gig workers, which affects how they perceive and engage with technological innovations(Sutherland et al., 2020) Gig workers who lack exposure to advanced digital tools may struggle to navigate immersive platforms, limiting their ability to access AI-powered health consultations or AR-based navigation assistance (Jabagi et al., 2019). Furthermore, studies on digital inclusion in the gig economy emphasise that language barriers, educational backgrounds, and economic constraints shape workers' ability to acquire knowledge about emerging technologies (Graham et al., 2017).

In the persuasion stage, workers form attitudes toward immersive technologies based on perceived benefits, usability, and risks. The Technology Acceptance Model proposes that perceived usefulness and perceived ease of use directly shape users' intention to adopt new systems, highlighting how these beliefs influence initial attitudes. Literature on technology acceptance suggests that gig workers' adoption decisions are influenced by trust in digital systems, perceived ease of use, and expected work-related advantages (Jabagi et al., 2019) Studies on AI-driven telehealth solutions reveal that workers are more likely to embrace remote healthcare tools if they perceive them as accessible, accurate, and responsive to their needs (Burrell, 2023). However, questioning algorithmic decision-making remains a key barrier, with concerns about data privacy, surveillance, and potential biases in AI recommendations. Similarly, studies on AR-based navigation and training tools indicate that while these technologies can improve route efficiency and skill acquisition, some workers view them as intrusive or overly complex, leading to reluctance to adopt them (Tallat et al., 2024). Additionally, financial considerations play a significant role if immersive technologies require an upfront investment in hardware or data costs, and adoption rates decline among low-income gig workers.

In the decision stage, the Technology Acceptance Model reminds us that a user's intention to adopt a system is shaped by perceived usefulness and ease of use, directly predicting whether they move forward with it. Gig workers' actual commitment to using immersive technologies often hinges on peer influence, platform incentives, and hands-on trial experiences (Zhang et al., 2023). Platforms nudge adoption through bonuses, optimised earnings algorithms, or mandatory feature rollouts, so workers who see colleagues gaining better ratings or higher pay are more likely to take the plunge (Tandon et al., 2022). Many remain sceptical, questioning whether VR training or AI health checks genuinely improve their working conditions or simply serve the platform's bottom line (A. J. Nair et al., 2024).

During the implementation stage, workers begin integrating immersive technologies into their daily routines, and research reveals varied usage patterns based on work demands, infrastructure support, and digital adaptability (Kumar, 2023). Studies on AI-powered health monitoring tools suggest that some gig workers actively use these technologies to track fatigue, monitor exertion levels, and schedule breaks, improving overall well-being (Chatterjee & Sujatha, 2024). However, barriers to sustained implementation include platform control over technology access, lack of technical support, and unstable connectivity. Research on AR-based navigation and logistics highlights that while real-time assistance can enhance delivery efficiency, workers in regions with poor digital infrastructure or unreliable internet access often face difficulties maintaining continuous engagement with such tools (Chang et al., 2020). Additionally, findings indicate that gig workers with higher digital adaptability, those accustomed to using mobile apps and algorithm-driven systems, are more likely to incorporate immersive technologies into their routines.

The confirmation stage involves the reinforcement or rejection of immersive technology use over time, and literature suggests that long-term adoption is contingent on perceived usefulness, work-related outcomes, and evolving platform policies (Radu, 2014). Studies on technology acceptance in gig work emphasise that workers continue using digital tools when they experience tangible benefits, such as reduced physical strain, increased earnings, or greater work autonomy (Bajwa et al., 2018). However, research also indicates that platform-imposed technology mandates can lead to worker pushback if they perceive adoption as being forced rather than beneficial (Diener & Seligman, 2004). For instance, studies on AI-based performance monitoring systems suggest that gig workers often engage with these tools out of necessity rather than preference, leading to passive compliance rather than active adoption. Similarly, findings on VR-based training programs reveal that while some workers appreciate the interactive learning experience, others abandon these tools due to time constraints, discomfort, or technical difficulties (Huang et al., 2021).

Beyond the DOI framework, existing research also sheds light on structural and policy-related factors influencing immersive technology adoption in the gig economy. Studies on digital labour rights highlight that adoption is shaped by individual choices and broader systemic conditions, such as regulatory frameworks, labour protections, and platform governance (Alanzi, 2021). Research from labour studies indicates that gig workers in jurisdictions with stronger digital rights policies and worker protections are more likely to engage with technology to benefit their well-being (Friedland & Balkin, 2023). In contrast, workers in unregulated environments often face exploitative technology use. Additionally, findings suggest that the commercial interests of platform companies influence technology diffusion, with adoption being driven by corporate profit motives rather than worker-centric innovation (Barrette, 2015).

The literature also identifies socioeconomic disparities in immersive technology access, emphasising that low-income gig workers, women, and workers from marginalised communities often face greater barriers to adoption due to cost concerns, digital access gaps, and exclusionary design practices (Mehta, 2022; Nair et al., 2023). Research on algorithmic inequality and digital divide issues underscores the need for inclusive technology policies to address these disparities, ensuring that immersive tools benefit all workers rather than reinforce existing inequities (López Barreda et al., 2019).

The literature reveals a complex and uneven landscape of immersive technology adoption among gig workers, shaped by factors spanning individual perceptions, platform influences, infrastructural limitations, and policy environments (Nair et al., 2023). While immersive technologies can improve health and work practices, widespread adoption is hindered by digital literacy challenges, economic constraints, apprehension toward technology control, and structural inequities in the gig economy. These findings underscore the importance of worker-centred design approaches, regulatory oversight, and equitable access initiatives to ensure that immersive technologies serve as enablers of well-being rather than exploitation tools.

Delivery professionals' journey with immersive technologies is anything but linear. While DOI maps the stages of awareness to routine use, TAM sharpens our understanding of the beliefs that drive each transition. True, these tools hold promise for improving health, safety, and efficiency, but only if they are accessible, trustworthy, and optional. Platforms must move beyond one-size-fits-all rollouts and embed worker feedback in every stage of design, deployment, and governance. Likewise, policymakers have a critical role in ensuring that tech serves worker well-being, not just platform profitability. Only through this combined focus on personal perceptions and structural safeguards can immersive technologies fulfil their potential as genuine enablers of gig workers' health and empowerment.

THEORETICAL AND PRACTICAL CONTRIBUTIONS

This study extends Everett Rogers' Diffusion of Innovation (DOI) framework into the realm of platform-mediated labor, revealing how power asymmetries and governance structures reshape the typical diffusion curve. By layering the Technology Acceptance Model (TAM) onto DOI, it demonstrates that gig worker adoption is driven not only by individual perceptions of usefulness and ease of use but also by platform incentives, algorithmic nudges, and policy environments. The practical recommendations that follow draw directly from these insights, outlining concrete steps for designers, operators, and regulators to ensure that immersive technologies empower rather than exploit gig workers.

Theoretical Contributions

This research challenges the assumption that innovation diffusion in the workplace is a neutral, voluntary process. Traditional DOI posits that adopters move through awareness, persuasion, decision, implementation, and confirmation based primarily on personal evaluations and peer networks (Akir, 2003). In contrast, our analysis shows that platform algorithms dictate when and how workers encounter immersive tools, skewing the awareness stage toward corporate interest. Second, while DOI's five attributes (relative advantage, compatibility, complexity, trialability, observability) remain useful, they must be reconsidered in light of digital labour policies and platform governance. For example, "trialability" often comes wrapped in mandatory feature rollouts that workers cannot truly refuse. Finally, integrating TAM reveals that workers' behavioural intentions depend heavily on trust and perceived control, factors underplayed in DOI alone. When gig workers view immersive solutions as surveillance tools rather than support systems, perceived usefulness and ease of use plummet, stalling adoption.

Practical Recommendations

1. Enshrine Voluntary Adoption

Platforms must decouple immersive tech from punitive performance metrics. Adoption should be optional, with no negative impact on work allocation, ratings, or deactivation risk. This respects worker autonomy and aligns with TAM's emphasis on voluntary use.

2. Co-Design with Workers

AR, VR, and AI-driven health applications should be developed alongside delivery professionals. Engaging workers in design workshops, usability tests, and feedback loops ensures tools meet real needs and build trust, key drivers in both the DOI's persuasion stage and TAM's perceived ease of use

3. Strengthen Regulatory Safeguards

Policymakers should mandate transparency around data collection, algorithmic logic, and decision criteria for immersive tools. Legislation akin to the EU's Digital Services Act can require platforms to disclose and justify any tech-linked incentives or penalties, preventing covert coercion.

4. Bridge the Digital Divide

Targeted subsidies for hardware and data plans can level the playing field for low-income, migrant, and marginalised gig workers. Public private partnerships, modelled on New York's Black Car Fund, could offer free digital literacy programs and device loans, ensuring equitable access to immersive solutions

5. Promote Platform Cooperativism

Supporting alternative, worker-owned platforms can create environments where immersive technologies genuinely serve user interests. Platform cooperatives, which give workers ownership stakes and decision-making power, demonstrate higher trust and long-term engagement with tech innovations. By embedding these recommendations into platform design and policy, immersive technologies can transition from coerced novelties to genuine tools for worker health, safety, and empowerment, fulfilling the promise illuminated by our combined DOI-TAM analysis.

LIMITATIONS

The study's reliance on a narrative literature review means it synthesises existing work without new field data. As with most narrative reviews, this approach offers breadth but sacrifices the depth and specificity of primary research; it cannot capture real-time shifts in gig workers' attitudes or usage patterns that only direct interviews or surveys would reveal. Moreover, because immersive technologies in gig work are still emerging, many insights come from pilot studies or proprietary reports that may lack peer-reviewed rigour and can quickly become outdated as platforms update features and business models. The diversity of gig platforms with varying policies, technical infrastructures, and worker populations also limits generalizability: what holds for delivery riders in one city may not apply to freelancers or rideshare drivers elsewhere.

The theoretical framing around Diffusion of Innovation and the Technology Acceptance Model provides a structured lens on individual and social factors, but underplays broader systemic and cultural dynamics. DOI's emphasis on individual decision-making can overlook how local labour laws, union presence, or cultural attitudes toward technology shape adoption in different regions. Similarly, TAM focuses on perceived usefulness and ease of use but does not fully address power imbalances or algorithmic governance that coerce rather than persuade gig workers. Finally, by centring primarily on health and well-being outcomes, the paper may miss other critical dimensions such as income volatility, job security, or career development, which immersive tools could also influence. Addressing these gaps will require mixed-methods fieldwork, cross-sector comparisons, and the integration of political-economy or human-computer interaction perspectives in future research.

CONCLUSION

The adoption of immersive technologies in the gig economy presents a complex interplay of technological, economic, and social factors that shape how delivery professionals engage with digital tools. This study, grounded in the Diffusion of Innovation (DOI) Theory, has examined the factors influencing adoption, the barriers that hinder diffusion, and the broader implications of these technologies for gig workers' health and work practices. The findings indicate that while immersive technologies offer potential benefits, their adoption remains uneven, constrained by issues of accessibility, platform control, economic precarity, and worker agency.

A key insight from this research is that technology adoption in the gig economy is not merely an individual choice but is strongly shaped by platform governance structures. Unlike traditional DOI applications, where individuals independently evaluate innovations, gig workers encounter a mediated diffusion process controlled by platform algorithms, nudges, and digital infrastructure. Platforms act as gatekeepers, deciding when and how immersive technologies are introduced. This results in a non-linear diffusion process, where some gig workers must adopt immersive technologies as part of platform policies. In contrast, others remain excluded due to cost barriers, digital illiteracy, or infrastructural constraints. This raises an important question: Does technology diffusion in the gig economy serve the interests of workers, or does it primarily function as a tool for platform control?

Findings suggest that gig workers' engagement with immersive technologies follows patterns of selective adoption, where those with stable digital access, strong social networks, and supportive learning environments are more likely to integrate these tools into their work. Conversely, marginalised groups such as low-income gig workers, migrant labourers, and those in underdeveloped regions face systemic barriers to adoption. These disparities are consistent with research on digital labour markets, where algorithmic decision-making often reinforces existing inequalities rather than addressing them. The study argues that the digital divide in the gig economy is not simply a matter of technological access but a structural issue embedded in labour precarity and platform governance.

The persuasion stage in the DOI theory reveals that gig workers' attitudes toward immersive technologies are shaped by perceived utility, trust, and financial incentives. One recurring concern is the lack of trust in AI-driven health and navigation tools, a finding supported by studies on algorithmic opacity and worker surveillance. Many gig workers express concerns over data privacy, algorithmic bias, and the risk of increased control by platforms, leading to selective engagement with immersive technologies. Prior research on platform surveillance and algorithmic governance suggests that digital tools often serve dual functions, ostensibly enhancing efficiency while simultaneously reinforcing managerial control. This study confirms that gig workers are acutely aware of this duality, often resisting full adoption unless platforms provide clear data usage and worker rights transparency.

One of the most significant findings pertains to coerced versus voluntary adoption. Gig workers are often nudged or indirectly forced into using immersive technologies through platform-driven incentives, rating systems, or work allocation algorithms. This contradicts traditional DOI assumptions, which assume rational decision-making by adopters based on perceived benefits. In reality, gig workers often face limited agency in deciding whether to engage with these technologies, as refusal may lead to fewer work opportunities, lower visibility on the platform, or even deactivation. This study thus contributes to critical scholarship on digital labor by demonstrating that technological adoption in the gig economy is often shaped by coercive mechanisms rather than voluntary innovation diffusion.

Beyond individual adoption patterns, findings highlight macro-level structural challenges that impede sustained engagement with immersive technologies. Digital infrastructure, financial constraints, and labour policies all play a decisive role in shaping gig workers' ability to integrate these tools into their daily work. Research on platform capitalism suggests that technology adoption is often dictated by the business models of platform operators rather than worker needs. Even when immersive technologies are introduced with ostensible benefits for gig workers, they may primarily serve platform interests, such as route optimisation, customer engagement, or data collection for algorithmic training. This finding raises critical ethical questions: to what extent do immersive technologies genuinely enhance worker well-being, and to what extent do they serve as instruments of digital labour control?

The confirmation stage in DOI theory further illustrates that the long-term adoption of immersive technologies depends on sustained worker benefits. While some gig workers report improved navigation, enhanced customer interactions, and reduced cognitive load through augmented reality (AR) interfaces and AI-driven work management tools, others express frustration with usability issues, lack of adequate training, and the unintended consequences of excessive technology dependence. Research on automation in digital labour environments suggests that gig workers often experience a paradoxical relationship with technology, benefiting from efficiency gains while simultaneously losing control over work autonomy. This aligns with findings from studies on human-AI interaction in labour markets, which highlight that worker satisfaction with technology adoption is contingent on whether they perceive themselves as empowered users rather than passive subjects of algorithmic management.

REFERENCES

Abdulmalek, S., Nasir, A., Jabbar, W. A., Almuhaya, M. A. M., Bairagi, A. K., Khan, M. A. M., & Kee, S. H. (2022). IoT-Based Healthcare-Monitoring System towards Improving Quality of Life: A Review. *Healthcare (Basel)*, *10*(10), 1993. DOI: 10.3390/healthcare10101993 PMID: 36292441

Akir, Z. (2003). Diffusion of innovations. In *Education and Technology: An Encyclopedia* (Vol. 1–2, pp. 205–210). Routledge., DOI: 10.4337/9781800883284.diffusion.of.innovations

Alanzi, T. M. (2021). Gig health vs ehealth: Future prospects in saudi arabian health-care system. *Journal of Multidisciplinary Healthcare*, *14*, 1945–1953. DOI: 10.2147/JMDH.S304690 PMID: 34326645

Albahri, O. S., Albahri, A. S., Mohammed, K. I., Zaidan, A. A., Zaidan, B. B., Hashim, M., & Salman, O. H. (2018). Systematic Review of Real-time Remote Health Monitoring System in Triage and Priority-Based Sensor Technology: Taxonomy, Open Challenges, Motivation and Recommendations. In *Journal of Medical Systems* (Vol. 42, Issue 5, pp. 1–27). Springer. DOI: 10.1007/s10916-018-0943-4

Albahri, O. S., Zaidan, A. A., Zaidan, B. B., Hashim, M., Albahri, A. S., & Alsalem, M. A. (2018). Real-Time Remote Health-Monitoring Systems in a Medical Centre: A Review of the Provision of Healthcare Services-Based Body Sensor Information, Open Challenges and Methodological Aspects. In *Journal of Medical Systems* (Vol. 42, Issue 9, pp. 1–47). Springer. DOI: 10.1007/s10916-018-1006-6

Babalola, A., Manu, P., Cheung, C., Yunusa-Kaltungo, A., & Bartolo, P. (2023). Applications of immersive technologies for occupational safety and health training and education: A systematic review. In *Safety Science* (Vol. 166, p. 106214). Elsevier., DOI: 10.1016/j.ssci.2023.106214

Bajwa, U., Gastaldo, D., Di Ruggiero, E., & Knorr, L. (2018). The health of workers in the global gig economy. In *Globalization and Health* (Vol. 14, Issue 1). BioMed Central Ltd. DOI: 10.1186/s12992-018-0444-8

Barrette, C. M. (2015). Usefulness of technology adoption research in introducing an online workbook. *System*, *49*, 133–144. DOI: 10.1016/j.system.2015.01.005

Behar, J. A., Liu, C., Kotzen, K., Tsutsui, K., Corino, V. D. A., Singh, J., Pimentel, M. A. F., Warrick, P., Zaunseder, S., Andreotti, F., Sebag, D., Kopanitsa, G., McSharry, P. E., Karlen, W., Karmakar, C., & Clifford, G. D. (2020). Remote health diagnosis and monitoring in the time of COVID-19. In *Physiological Measurement* (Vol. 41, Issue 10, p. 10TR01). IOP Publishing. DOI: 10.1088/1361-6579/abba0a

Bhattacharya, M. (2015). A conceptual framework of RFID adoption in retail using Rogers stage model. *Business Process Management Journal, 21*(3), 517–540. DOI: 10.1108/BPMJ-06-2014-0047

Burrell, D. N. (2023). Dynamic Evaluation Approaches to Telehealth Technologies and Artificial Intelligence (AI) Telemedicine Applications in Healthcare and Biotechnology Organizations. *Merits, 3*(4), 700–721. DOI: 10.3390/merits3040042

Chang, S. C., Hsu, T. C., Chen, Y. N., & Jong, M. S. (2020). The effects of spherical video-based virtual reality implementation on students' natural science learning effectiveness. *Interactive Learning Environments, 28*(7), 915–929. DOI: 10.1080/10494820.2018.1548490

Chatterjee, J. M., & Sujatha, R. (2024). *Transforming Healthcare: The Synergy of Telemedicine, Telehealth, and Artificial Intelligence*. Springer., DOI: 10.1007/978-981-97-2938-8_1

Cornet, V. P., Toscos, T., Bolchini, D., Ghahari, R. R., Ahmed, R., Daley, C., Mirro, M. J., & Holden, R. J. (2020). Untold stories in user-centered design of mobile health: Practical challenges and strategies learned from the design and evaluation of an app for older adults with heart failure. *JMIR mHealth and uHealth, 8*(7), e17703. DOI: 10.2196/17703 PMID: 32706745

Cropanzano, R., Keplinger, K., Lambert, B. K., Caza, B., & Ashford, S. J. (2022). The Organizational Psychology of Gig Work: An Integrative Conceptual Review. *The Journal of Applied Psychology, 108*(3), 492–519. DOI: 10.1037/apl0001029 PMID: 36222635

Curtis, M. (2020). Toward Understanding Secondary Teachers' Decisions to Adopt Geospatial Technologies: An Examination of Everett Rogers' Diffusion of Innovation Framework. *The Journal of Geography, 119*(5), 147–158. DOI: 10.1080/00221341.2020.1784252

Dean, M., & Spoehr, J. (2018). The fourth industrial revolution and the future of manufacturing work in Australia: Challenges and opportunities. *Labour & Industry, 28*(3), 166–181. DOI: 10.1080/10301763.2018.1502644

Devagiri, J. S., Paheding, S., Niyaz, Q., Yang, X., & Smith, S. (2022). Augmented Reality and Artificial Intelligence in industry: Trends, tools, and future challenges. In *Expert Systems with Applications* (Vol. 207, p. 118002). Pergamon., DOI: 10.1016/j.eswa.2022.118002

Diener, E., & Seligman, M. E. P. (2004). Beyond Money: Toward an Economy of Well-Being. *Psychological Science in the Public Interest, 5*(1), 1–31. DOI: 10.1111/j.0963-7214.2004.00501001.x PMID: 26158992

Du Toit, I. (2017). Copyright and Citation Considerations for This Thesis/ Dissertation. In *Ujcontent.Uj.Ac.Za*. https://ujcontent.uj.ac.za/vital/access/manager/Index?site_name=Research Output

Eager, B., Maritz, A., & Millemann, J. (2022). The silver economy on wheels: A narrative review of the mature-aged, hypermobile gig worker phenomena. *Small Enterprise Research, 29*(1), 68–85. DOI: 10.1080/13215906.2022.2032295

Friedland, J., & Balkin, D. B. (2023). When gig workers become essential: Leveraging customer moral self-awareness beyond COVID-19. *Business Horizons, 66*(2), 181–190. DOI: 10.1016/j.bushor.2022.05.003 PMID: 35601275

Graham, M., Hjorth, I., & Lehdonvirta, V. (2017). Digital labour and development: Impacts of global digital labour platforms and the gig economy on worker livelihoods. *Transfer: European Review of Labour and Research, 23*(2), 135–162. DOI: 10.1177/1024258916687250 PMID: 28781494

Hornik, R. (2004). Some reflections on diffusion theory and the role of everett rogers. In *Journal of Health Communication* (Vol. 9, Issue S1, pp. 143–148). Taylor & Francis Group. DOI: 10.1080/10810730490271610

Huang, H. (2023). Algorithmic management in food-delivery platform economy in China. *New Technology, Work and Employment, 38*(2), 185–205. DOI: 10.1111/ntwe.12228

Huang, K. T., Ball, C., Francis, J., Ratan, R., Boumis, J., & Fordham, J. (2019). Augmented versus virtual reality in education: An exploratory study examining science knowledge retention when using augmented reality/virtual reality mobile applications. *Cyberpsychology, Behavior, and Social Networking, 22*(2), 105–110. DOI: 10.1089/cyber.2018.0150 PMID: 30657334

Huang, X., Zou, D., Cheng, G., & Xie, H. (2021). A systematic review of AR and VR enhanced language learning. In *Sustainability (Switzerland)* (Vol. 13, Issue 9, p. 4639). Multidisciplinary Digital Publishing Institute. DOI: 10.3390/su13094639

Jabagi, N., Croteau, A. M., Audebrand, L. K., & Marsan, J. (2019). Gig-workers' motivation: Thinking beyond carrots and sticks. *Journal of Managerial Psychology, 34*(4), 192–213. DOI: 10.1108/JMP-06-2018-0255

Kadolkar, I., Kepes, S., & Subramony, M. (2024). Algorithmic management in the gig economy: A systematic review and research integration. *Journal of Organizational Behavior*, job.2831. Advance online publication. DOI: 10.1002/job.2831

Kalbalia, P., & Koushik, K. (2025). Regulating the gig economy: Addressing worker rights in India's quick commerce sector. In *Sustainability and Adaptability of Gig Economies in Global Business* (pp. 85–105). IGI Global., DOI: 10.4018/979-8-3693-9385-7.ch004

Kalbalia, P., Nath, N. J., & Haneefa, K. V. (2024). Utilisation and Accessibility of Healthcare Services Among Gig Workers: A Systematic Review. *Population. Environmental Disease*, •••, 77–95. DOI: 10.1007/978-3-031-67624-6_5

Katsnelson, L., & Oberholzer-Gee, F. (2021). *Being the Boss: Gig Workers' Value of Flexible Work*. Harvard Business School.

Khan, T. H., MacEachen, E., Hopwood, P., & Goyal, J. (2021). Self-employment, work and health: A critical narrative review. *Work (Reading, Mass.)*, *70*(3), 945–957. DOI: 10.3233/WOR-213614 PMID: 34744041

Koohang, A., Nord, J. H., Ooi, K.-B., Tan, G. W.-H., Al-Emran, M., Aw, E. C.-X., Baabdullah, A. M., Buhalis, D., Cham, T.-H., Dennis, C., Dutot, V., Dwivedi, Y. K., Hughes, L., Mogaji, E., Pandey, N., Phau, I., Raman, R., Sharma, A., Sigala, M., & Wong, L.-W. (2023). Shaping the Metaverse into Reality: A Holistic Multidisciplinary Understanding of Opportunities, Challenges, and Avenues for Future Investigation. *Journal of Computer Information Systems*, *63*(3), 735–765. DOI: 10.1080/08874417.2023.2165197

Kovács, M., Muity, G., Szapáry, Á., Nemeskéri, Z., Váradi, I., Kapus, K., Tibold, A., Zalayné, N. M., Horvath, L., & Fehér, G. (2023). The prevalence and risk factors of burnout and its association with mental issues and quality of life among hungarian postal workers: A cross-sectional study. *BMC Public Health*, *23*(1), 75. Advance online publication. DOI: 10.1186/s12889-023-15002-5 PMID: 36627594

Kumar, P. (2023). *Gig Workers in Chhattisgarh: Emerging Opportunities in the New Economy*. http://www.centralasianstudies.org

Lee, A. T., Ramasamy, R. K., & Subbarao, A. (2025). Understanding Psychosocial Barriers to Healthcare Technology Adoption: A Review of TAM Technology Acceptance Model and Unified Theory of Acceptance and Use of Technology and UTAUT Frameworks. In *Healthcare (Switzerland)* (Vol. 13, Issue 3, p. 250). Multidisciplinary Digital Publishing Institute. DOI: 10.3390/healthcare13030250

Lester, G. V., Brock Baskin, M. E., & Clinton, M. S. (2021). Employer-Sponsored Benefits in the United States: The Past, Present, and Future. *Compensation and Benefits Review*, *53*(1), 24–42. DOI: 10.1177/0886368720947609 PMID: 34955602

Ling, E. C., Tussyadiah, I., Tuomi, A., Stienmetz, J., & Ioannou, A. (2021). Factors influencing users' adoption and use of conversational agents: A systematic review. *Psychology and Marketing*, *38*(7), 1031–1051. DOI: 10.1002/mar.21491

López Barreda, R., Robertson-Preidler, J., & Bedregal García, P. (2019). Health assessment and the capability approach. *Global Bioethics = Problemi di Bioetica*, *30*(1), 19–27. DOI: 10.1080/11287462.2019.1673028 PMID: 31632214

Mcgrath, C., & Zell, D. (2001). The Future of Innovation Diffusion Research and its Implications for Management: A Conversation with Everett Rogers. *Journal of Management Inquiry*, *10*(4), 386–391. DOI: 10.1177/1056492601104012

Mehta, A. (2022). Analyse The Challenges Faced By Gig Workers During The Covid Pandemic In India-Case Study Of OLA Drivers. *Public Policy and Research International*.

Myhill, K., Richards, J., & Sang, K. (2021). Job quality, fair work and gig work: The lived experience of gig workers. *International Journal of Human Resource Management*, *32*(19), 4110–4135. DOI: 10.1080/09585192.2020.1867612

Nair, A. J., Manohar, S., Mittal, A., & Chaudhry, R. (2024). Unleashing Digital Frontiers: Bridging Realities of Augmented Reality, Virtual Reality, and the Metaverse. *The Metaverse Dilemma: Challenges and Opportunities for Business and Society*, 85–112. DOI: 10.1108/978-1-83797-524-220241006

Nair, M. R., Kumar, S. S., Babu, S. S., Chandru, B. A., Kunjumon, K. S., Divya, C. S., & Varma, R. P. (2023). Health inequities around gender, disability and internal migration: Are local governments doing enough? *Public Health Action*, *13*(1), 6–11. DOI: 10.5588/pha.22.0032 PMID: 36949745

Pereira, V., Behl, A., Jayawardena, N., Laker, B., Dwivedi, Y. K., & Bhardwaj, S. (2022). The art of gamifying digital gig workers: A theoretical assessment of evaluating engagement and motivation. *Production Planning and Control*. Advance online publication. DOI: 10.1080/09537287.2022.2083524

Radu, I. (2014). Augmented reality in education: A meta-review and cross-media analysis. *Personal and Ubiquitous Computing*, *18*(6), 1533–1543. DOI: 10.1007/s00779-013-0747-y

Rahimi, R. A., & Oh, G. S. (2024). Beyond theory: a systematic review of strengths and limitations in technology acceptance models through an entrepreneurial lens. *Journal of Marketing Analytics*, 1–24. DOI: 10.1057/s41270-024-00318-x

Randolph, S. A. (2019). Gig Workers. *Workplace Health & Safety*, *67*(8), 439–440. DOI: 10.1177/2165079919860545 PMID: 31313647

Ravenelle, A. J., Kowalski, K. C., & Janko, E. (2021). The Side Hustle Safety Net: Precarious Workers and Gig Work during COVID-19. *Sociological Perspectives*, *64*(5), 898–919. DOI: 10.1177/07311214211005489

Robinson, L., Schulz, J., Dunn, H. S., Casilli, A. A., Tubaro, P., Carvath, R., Chen, W., Wiest, J. B., Dodel, M., Stern, M. J., Ball, C., Huang, K.-T., Blank, G., Ragnedda, M., Ono, H., Hogan, B., Mesch, G. S., Cotten, S. R., Kretchmer, S. B., & Khilnani, A. (2020). Digital inequalities 3.0: Emergent inequalities in the information age. *First Monday*. Advance online publication. DOI: 10.5210/fm.v25i7.10844

Seligman, L. (2006). Sensemaking throughout adoption and the innovation-decision process. *European Journal of Innovation Management*, *9*(1), 108–120. DOI: 10.1108/14601060610640050

Sutherland, W., Jarrahi, M. H., Dunn, M., & Nelson, S. B. (2020). Work Precarity and Gig Literacies in Online Freelancing. *Work, Employment and Society*, *34*(3), 457–475. DOI: 10.1177/0950017019886511

Tallat, R., Hawbani, A., Wang, X., Al-Dubai, A., Zhao, L., Liu, Z., Min, G., Zomaya, A. Y., & Hamood Alsamhi, S. (2024). Navigating Industry 5.0: A Survey of Key Enabling Technologies, Trends, Challenges, and Opportunities. *IEEE Communications Surveys and Tutorials*, *26*(2), 1080 1126. DOI: 10.1109/COMST.2023.3329172

Tandon, N., Basu, P., Krishnan, O., & Bhavani, R. V. (2022). Emerging work trends in Urban India: COVID-19 and beyond. *Emerging Work Trends in Urban India: COVID-19 and Beyond*, 1–208. DOI: 10.4324/9781003264194

van Dijck, J. (2018). The platform society : public values in a connective world / José van Dijck, Thomas Poell, Martijn de Waal. In *Platform Society*. https://books.google.co.in/books?hl=en&lr=&id=xLhwDwAAQBAJ&oi=fnd&pg=PT8&dq=Existing+research+suggests+that+knowledge+diffusion+in+gig+work+settings+is+largely+mediated+by+platform-driven+exposure,+peer+networks,+and+targeted+training+initiatives&ots=AUv1

Whitehead, L., Talevski, J., Fatehi, F., & Beauchamp, A. (2023). Barriers to and Facilitators of Digital Health Among Culturally and Linguistically Diverse Populations: Qualitative Systematic Review. In *Journal of Medical Internet Research* (Vol. 25, Issue 1, p. e42719). JMIR Publications Inc. DOI: 10.2196/42719

Wood, A. J., Graham, M., Lehdonvirta, V., & Hjorth, I. (2019). Good Gig, Bad Gig: Autonomy and Algorithmic Control in the Global Gig Economy. *Work, Employment and Society*, *33*(1), 56–75. DOI: 10.1177/0950017018785616 PMID: 30886460

Zhang, Y., Lee, E. W. J., & Teo, W. P. (2023). Health-Seeking Behavior and Its Associated Technology Use: Interview Study among Community-Dwelling Older Adults. *JMIR Aging*, *6*, e43709. Advance online publication. DOI: 10.2196/43709 PMID: 36996003

Zhu, G., Huang, J., Lu, J., Luo, Y., & Zhu, T. (2024). Gig to the left, algorithms to the right: A case study of the dark sides in the gig economy. *Technological Forecasting and Social Change*, *199*, 123018. DOI: 10.1016/j.techfore.2023.123018

Chapter 13
Building Digital Dexterity: HR's Role in Talent and Skill Development

Mukesh Sehrawat
https://orcid.org/0009-0008-7928-1568
IAMR Group of Institutions, India

Anand Nandwani
Management Education and Research Institute, India

Jyoti Tyagi
https://orcid.org/0009-0006-1206-9437
IAMR Group of Institutions, India

Vishal Jain
https://orcid.org/0000-0003-1126-7424
Sharda University, India

ABSTRACT

In the rapidly evolving digital landscape, organizations face the dual challenge of adapting to technological advancements while fostering a workforce equipped with the skills necessary to thrive in this new paradigm. The chapter explores the pivotal role of Human Resources in cultivating digital dexterity defined as the ability of employees to adapt, learn, and innovate in a technology-driven environment. The chapter delves into the key components of digital dexterity, including technical proficiency and critical soft skills such as collaboration, creativity, and adaptability. It examines modern talent acquisition strategies, emphasizing the integration of digital competencies during recruitment and on boarding processes. The importance of upskilling and reskilling initiatives, powered by e-learning platforms and data-driven training programs, is highlighted as a cornerstone of HR's efforts. Furthermore,

DOI: 10.4018/979-8-3373-1290-3.ch013

the use of cutting-edge technologies like artificial intelligence, virtual reality, and gamification in enhancing employee training and development are discussed.

1. INTRODUCTION

The workplace is experiencing a profound change, facilitated by rapid changes in digital technology. AI, automation, and data analytics are evolving industries, modifying work tasks and transforming whom and what we consider "talent" to build the next generation of capacity to navigate complexity and change. The digital age has radically different paradigms since the introduction of microprocessors and is also rapidly producing technological convergence and information overload (Martin Hilbert and O. Cairó 2008). This uprising does not stop at business, it is also reshaping culture through heritage preservation (Feng et al., 2019), arbitrating basic education and knowledge economies and redistricting conventional professions like auditing in which data assets generate efficiencies alongside new issues (Tahir, 2024).

Amid these tectonic shifts, organizations face dual forces: to move with the pace of technological change and to develop a workforce that will be successful in meeting that change. The answer is digital dexterity; a multi-dimensional skill that requires leveraging technical competence with adaptive soft skills that include creativity, collaboration, and critical thinking. While it does not come naturally, it must be developed as a mindset and a skill. This chapter, which examine how Human Resources (HR) can take the lead role on empowering employees' agility and adaptability needed for the digital age. The chapter provides an overall description of the impact of digital transformation in the workplace, based on best practices and recent research and also presents the strategic value of developing digital readiness. The chapter mentions high-performance HR practices that support learners, boost adaptability and instil continuous skills building. The chapter also explores current learning environments; for instance, tailored training, microlearning, and e-learning platforms that encourage self-directed learning and stimulate lifelong learning. This chapter also investigates how emerging technologies–including AI, VR, gamification, and even blockchain–can be used to increase training effectiveness and ease of engagement. In looking forward to what work will look like going ahead, we argue that HR should function as both catalyst and steward of digital dexterity. By considering skills likely to be in demand in the future and developing a culture of innovation, HR will position organizations to not just survive, but thrive in a world veering ahead towards more digital.

1.1 Overview of Digital Transformation and Its Impact on the Workplace

Digital transformation (DT) is when an organization's use of information and communications technologies facilitates change based on a collective customer need (Pihir et al., 2018). It enables innovative and entirely new business and operational models, along with evidence-based decision-making. Digital transformation is enabled by several megatrends such as social media, the internet of things (IoT), big data, cloud computing, and artificial intelligence (AI) (Tang, 2021). In fact, DT programs have been associated with delivering greater organizational growth and associated cost savings than other transformational initiatives which is why managers connect strategies and objectives to digital innovations (Ries et al., 2018; Tang, 2021). DT creates new varieties of organizational structures and employee roles and introduces opportunities and challenges as well. Change means employees will need to change Search Engines, tools, and processes and will need to overcome resistance as well as knowledge gaps (Xiao, 2024). While ambidextrous forms might allow for innovation, they may also introduce constraints which may signal tension and need for adaptive actions (Smith & Beretta, 2020),

Organizational Change involves less hierarchy, more decentralized decision-making, and increased teamwork (Mirković et al., 2019; Kretschmer & Khashabi, 2020). In order to ensure the transition involves continued momentum, organizations must invest through cascading training programs, leadership buy-in, and overall cultural positivity (Xiao, 2024). Overall, DT is multifaceted, long term, and organizations must change and grow structures and systems to remain a competitive best practice. Digital transformation is a complex, long-term process that involves an ongoing process of balancing flexible and structural to help their organization succeed in navigating the digital world they now must operate. The success of digital efforts will ultimately depend on the organization's employees' agility and adaptability to changes.

1.2 The Need for Agility and Adaptability in Employees

Recent studies underscore the significance of employee agility in the fast-changing business world of today. Agility includes adaptive as well as proactive aspects, where employees can respond to organizational changes and create innovations (Vliet, 2017). High-performance work practices have a substantial effect on employee agility, with satisfaction and commitment mediating between them (Mian & Mian, 2018). Agile workers were described as problem-solving, innovative, and dynamic, allowing them to respond appropriately to complex situations and organizational outcomes. Organizations must encourage a culture that allows workers to adapt to technological disruptions and current trends in industry (Deshpande, 2021). Following are the key enablers of agility and adaptability:

***Learning Agility*:** Learning agility is an ability to learn from experience and apply that learning to new situations. It is imperative for employees facing the challenge of adapting themselves in changing environments and roles. A validated measure assessing individual differences in learning agility can help organizations to measure, cultivate, and develop this quality across different organizational cultures (Milani R, et. al. 2024).

***High-Performance Human Resource Practices*:** HR practices like continuous feedback, performance-based incentives, and career development planning create environments that allow for agile thinking and innovative practices from employees. Employee learning agility (ELA) is an important precursor to high-performance HR practices (HPHRP) because it will help employees with their ability to adopt and integrate new knowledge and then optimize organizational practices (Kumar, et al., 2023).

***Digital Transformation*:** Agility is a necessity for workforce performance during digital transformations as it is built upon employees' agile attitudes, skills, and behaviors in collaboration, innovation, and adaptability. The digital transformation is fuelled by risk-taking and knowledge-sharing agile behaviors that nurture continuous learning and adaptation within the organization (Muduli & Choudhury, 2024).

***Adaptability and Change Support*:** Genuine support for change requires leader involvement, communication, and sense of psychological safety; so that employees can cope with transitions more freely and effectively. Leaders play a major role in enabling successful organizational change and facilitating employee creativity. Authentic leadership was discovered to cultivate psychological safety, which partially mediated the relationship between leadership and employees' change readiness. Inclusive leadership represented by openness, accessibility, and responsiveness facilitates an environment for psychological safety, thereby facilitating employee participation in creative and adaptive endeavours (Carmeli, A. et. al, 2010).

***Practical Implementation*:** Strategies such as personalized learning platforms, rotational assignments, and real-time digital capability assessments, not only impart skills to employees but also cultivate a cognitive mindset for workplace success in a dynamic and evolving reality. This supports a culture of continuous learning and operational agility, which is important for workplace success in uncertain contexts (Westover, 2024).

While these adaptive competencies, or "meta-competencies" are critical to addressing a digital transformation, Human Resources plays an important part in developing and implementing strategies that facilitate ongoing skills development and a digital ready workforce.

1.3 Role of Human Resources (HR) in Driving Skill Development and Digital Readiness

In rapidly changing online environments, the roles of human resource management (HRM) are well positioned to extend beyond previous roles to offer organizational digital readiness as a catalyst. Today, HR leaders have the additional responsibility for establishing these human resources in a way that can face the demands of people resulting from digital transformation when establishing desired competencies in recognition of both the interests of developing employees and the organization. This strategic alignment means not only are skills development programs aligned to support the employability of workers, but it also means a more nuanced level of institutional achievement.

***Developmental HR Leadership/Digital Competencies*:** HR leadership is formative in aligning the skillsets of employees with the digital competencies which are required for competitive, resilient organizations (Zervas & Stiakakis, 2024). Strategic HR best practices play a formative role in reducing the skills gap and weaving digital proficiency into all aspects of organizational talent management (Khatri et al., 2024). By developing HR leadership competencies that assist in building strategic partnerships and transformational leadership, HR professionals can help organizations negotiate the challenges posed by digital transformation while simultaneously articulating a compelling organization vision for the future (Zhang et al., 2024).

***HR Leadership and Digital Skills Development*:** The digital transformation of HR functions—recruitment, training, and employee engagement—has led to facilitation technologies that promote instant feedback loops and data-driven decision-making (Shivaraj, 2021). The combination of tactical engagements as well as the integration of technology will continue to create efficient HR processes as long as organizations develop the agile and responsive workforces they expect. This means HR professionals themselves need to commit to continuous upskilling as they learn how to work effectively with new technology and develop supporting systemic reflexive relationships that underpin the developmental cycle of digital competence that exist within the firm (Nankervis & Cameron, 2022). Organizations are undoubtedly taking steps toward a more hybrid future that also signals the importance of digital dexterity - the capability of people and organizations to adopt agility and agency in their work is being used as a foundational enabler of successful HR digitalization. Digital dexterity, its elements and attributes, and the antecedents to and barriers for embodying it must be embraced to enable organizations access to develop and embed agility and resilience in their current HR practice today.

2. DIGITALIZATION OF HR PRACTICES: UNDERSTANDING DIGITAL DEXTERITY

Digital dexterity is the ability to adapt and use technological tools to achieve better business results (Hadlaa AlFedaghi, 2024). Digital dexterity includes digital capabilities, digital proficiency, and digital awareness, that allows organizations to more easily adapt to new digital possibilities (Soule et al., 2016). The key characteristics of digital dexterity includes basic skills such as mobilization, execution, transformation, and agility. A successful organization has a continuing capacity to self-organize and adapt to new digital possibilities (Soule et al., 2016). Digital dexterity entails more than a certain level of technical skill; it entails the ability to adapt, to be creative, and approach the world with a mindset of continuous learning and digital fluency. In the world of HR, digital dexterity is crucial to being able to facilitate digital transformation, as well as follow talent strategies in a technological landscape that is ever-changing. Following are the core dimensions of the digital dexterity.

2.1 Importance of Digital Dexterity

***Organizational Success*:** Digital dexterity means the relevance of employing so as for success within organizations where actual work is done through digital channels, increasing productivity and promoting innovative methods in the process (Ahmed et al., 2020).
***Healthcare Applications*:** Digital dexterity can, in clinical settings, create conducive environments for better assessments and rehabilitation methods, for example, interactive electronic pegboards that can help augment patient outcomes (Chien et al., 2023).

The Competitive Advantage of a Digitally Skilled Workforce

***Enhanced Productivity*:** Digitization of HR practices—using AI-based recruitment tools, e-learning platforms, and data-driven performance management—improves productivity by streamlining workflows and reducing inefficiencies.

Digital skills integrate technology into work; improve workflow and work that avoids inefficiencies through operations (Castellacci et al., 2020). Individuals who have engaged more with digital literacy are more likely to engage upstream training that leads to good performance of roles and productivity gains.

***Innovation and Adaptability*:** HR practices that promote digital upskilling and innovation are crucial for organizations to be adaptable in constantly changing environments. HR flexibility, which includes both the employees' flexibility of skill and behavior, and flexible HR practices, positively influence adaptability culture and organisational innovation (Ben-Roy Do et al, 2016). HR professionals also help make culture agile through HR practices such as educational programs, innovation programmes, and flexible working (Dejan Ječmenica et al, 2024). All these HR practices lead to team agility, innovation and motivate employees.

***Workforce Development*:** Ongoing learning and training programs facilitated by HR departments guarantee that employees are acquiring and maintaining digital skills that are relevant to their industry and the pace of technological change. Digital skills should be assimilated into education policy change to help workers prepare for the requirements of the digital economy (Štofková et al., 2022).

2.2 Key Components of Digital Dexterity

***Technical Skills Vs. Soft Skills in a Digital Context*:** The digital era has marked a paradigm shift in employment requirements and emphasized the need for technical and employability skills in one basket, along with personal skills and digital literacy (Gouda, 2020). Digital learning promotes and fosters the development of soft skills in technical education, thereby creating an enabling environment for innovation and entrepreneurship (Chen, 2023). For organizations to gain from their digital investments, they should make their employees proficient in an array of different skills; and skills such as critical thinking, complex problem-solving, adaptability, resilience, and creativity are non-negotiables in successful digital transformation (Obermayer et al., 2023). It is this interplay between technical and soft skill sets that is most important for career success across the sphere.

Collaboration, Creativity, and Critical Thinking as Essential Traits

Cognition, collaboration, innovation, and critical thinking are the new engines of digital dexterity in modern education. It has become this way because of the way these three not only build a richer individual learning experience but also expose learners to the challenges encountered in the digital world. The table 1 elaborate on the connections made by these attributes and how they synergize with effective digital engagement:

Table 1. Key components of digital dexterity in a digital work environment

Section	Key Concept	Description	Reference
Technical Skills vs. Soft Skills in a Digital Context	Technical Skills	Technical skills are the different knowledge and abilities necessary to perform tasks regarding technology, such as programming and data analysis, and software proficiency. In the IT world, technical skills are viewed as very critical for job promise-respect to general competencies over specific tools or languages. It allows the profession with these technical skills to use digital tools more effectively, which is an innovative and efficient approach to work.	Bailey & Mitchell (2016)
	Soft Skills	Soft skills include interpersonal abilities, emotional, and adaptability-interpersonal skills increasingly recognized as essential in the digital environment. "Research points towards making soft skills mandatory for architects to champion digital construction and include; critical thinking, digital communication, and ethics professionalism. They facilitate collaboration and creativity where teams can venture into trouble by effectively leveraging it.	Shahruddin et al. (2024)
	Interplay of Skills	The combination of technical and soft skills fosters career success and adaptability in rapidly changing digital environments.	Ahmed et al. (2020); Gouda (2020)
Collaboration, Creativity, and Critical Thinking as Essential Traits	Collaboration	Digital instruments frequently enhance collaborative opportunities, build community among students, and help open new lines of communication. Students using digital space that shows participation and peer interaction are among some behavioral indicators for demonstrating good collaborative skills. Effective collaboration in digital environments also entails flexibility and the ability to juggle different perspectives, which might alleviate cognitive.	Oskarita & Arasy (2024); Iannello et al. (2024)
	Creativity	Creativity is a primary ability for solving issues and inventing something new in the digital sphere. It specifies that cognitive flexibility allows one to adapt to fresh data and to bend or transform existing paradigms. Educational systems hyped how creativity is a core competency and encouraged innovation via digital content generation	Wu et al. (2021); Thornhill-Miller et al. (2023)
	Critical Thinking	Critical scrutiny has been wise in allowing one to possess nearly all available material on the internet and have a sense of dividing the source of that material from false information or trifles. However, this critical thinking should be integrated into any educational curriculum because students need to be able to read and think critically about that digital content so they will also develop a finer.	Thornhill-Miller et al. (2023); Iannello et al. (2024)

2.4 Challenges in Achieving Digital Dexterity

Major challenges on the path toward digital dexterity in organizations arise mainly from resistance to change and skill gaps in the workforce. These hindrances constrain the efficient uptake of digital technologies that organizations so desperately need to grow and adapt within a fast-changing digital ecosystem. The following sections discuss these challenges in detail as shown in figure 1.

Figure 1. Challenges on achieving digital dexterity

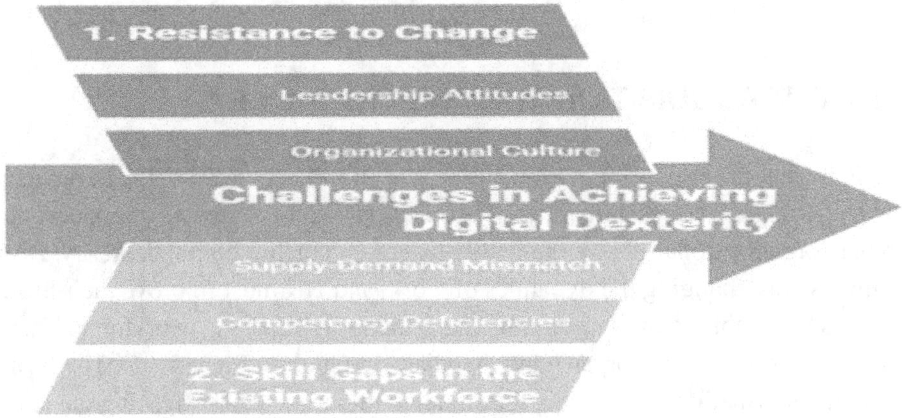

Resistance to Change

***Organizational Culture*:** If a workplace culture is resistant to change, this can be a significant barrier to digital transformation. A lack of trust and openness often will inhibit employees' ability and readiness to adopt and realize new technologies in a meaningful way (Bencsik, 2024).

***Leadership Attitudes*:** Leadership is vital to enabling digital initiatives. When leaders do not facilitate or have ambivalence towards digital change, it can exacerbate resistance and further challenge the transformation (Bencsik, 2024).

Skill Gaps in the Existing Workforce

***Competency Gaps*:** Many employees do not yet have the digital skills required to engage with Industry 4.0, which limits effective implementation. Consequently, a maturity model has been proposed to look at workforce competencies and perform qualifications assessments (Treviño-Elizondo & Garcia-Reyes, 2023).

Supply-Demand Mismatch: There may be an anticipated oversupply of digital talent, such as in Indonesia; however, there is not a match for the supply of specifically required Industry 4.0 skills that are highlighted in many industries, which is a widespread and critical mismatch (Sepúlveda-Ortega, 2022).

Addressing the above barriers not only facilitates digital dexterity but also provides employees for optimal success in a digitally enabled environment. While organizations are committed to bridging the competency gap and softening resistance to change, organizations must re-think how they find and hire talent. This provides a further critical strategic priority in business today.

3. TALENT ACQUISITION FOR THE DIGITAL ERA

HR is integral in developing a workforce with the necessary skills to navigate new technologies successfully. Talent acquisition is now a strategic function that can help organizations achieve the wider goal of enhancing digital dexterity. Digitization is now changing the dynamics of work, and HR must improve their hiring practices to be able to attract, recruit, and build a digital-savvy workforce. Talent acquisition is a "sensory organ" and "mediator" (Gilch & Sieweke, 2021) during digital transformations, signifying the strategic importance of refreshing the talent of the organization. With the utilization of AI and data analytics to support hiring processes, there is a shift in how organizations communicate with candidates, enabling organizations to work faster and accurately in their selection processes (Opada et al., 2024). There are challenges that come with advancements including concerns regarding privacy, algorithmic bias, and transparency. Digital tools influence the entire talent lifecycle from acquisition to retention (Balu, 2024) especially with the rise of remote and hybrid working arrangements. It is important to ensure that their approach to recruitment aligns with their organizational goals and diversity initiatives, but is also in place as a key component to being competitive in the digital age.

3.1 Revamping Recruitment Strategies

Finding Digital Skills: In digitally transforming environments, HR must work to attract employees who possess IT-related skills and qualifications that align with organizational technological goals (Gilch & Sieweke, 2021). It is important to find individuals who can excel in adaptive roles related to the technology that will allow digital readiness to persist over the long term.

***AI and Data in Recruitment*:** AI helps recruitment by allowing tasks to be automated so applications can be processed and analysed, resulting in less human bias in candidate assessments (Sandeep et al., 2025; Pillai & Sivathanu, 2020). For example, machine learning can help assess candidate characteristics or attributes by processing their online presence and activities using data extraction (Chamorro-Premuzic et al., 2017).

3.2 Building a Digital Culture

***Onboarding*:** Creating a functional onboarding strategy requires HR to incorporate an aspect of digital fluency to ensure new personnel are ready to work with incoming technologies that may differ from their previous digital platforms (Rodríguez-Sánchez et al., 2019). Actively engaging resources that expose personnel to digital tools supports new hires transition into their adapted working environment and informs a way of establishing a technologically oriented culture of work.

***Value for Innovation*:** Teaching values that support technology change is needed to regularly attract and retain individuals with digital skill sets. Transformation and innovation must reside at the core of organisations, with digital fluency considered a core competency for a culture that values the support of a workforce dedicated to continual learning and adaption (Rodríguez-Sánchez et al., 2019).

4. SKILL ENHANCEMENT AND DEVELOPMENT

In the era of digital transformation, developing workforce capabilities is a strategic imperative. The rapid pace of technological advancement has intensified the urgency for organizations to invest in upskilling and reskilling programs (Westover, 2024; Sawant et al., 2022; Muchiri, 2022). As part of HR's evolving role, facilitating flexible and targeted learning initiatives is central to building digital dexterity across all organizational levels. Effective programs identify current skills, leverage existing strengths, and deliver learning in adaptable formats such as e-learning and microlearning (Westover, 2024; Iyer, 2020). These approaches support both technical proficiency and essential people skills while fostering a culture of continuous improvement. The global focus on talent development is evident in increasing investments in reskilling strategies aimed at closing critical skills gaps and ensuring long-term competitiveness. For instance, in Kenya, 94.8% of surveyed experts identified skill enhancement as vital for addressing future workforce demands (Muchiri, 2022). This aligns with HR's core responsibility in shaping a workforce ready for the evolving demands of the digital economy.

4.1 Upskilling and Reskilling

From lived experience and insight, organizations that are digitally mature use upskilling and reskilling programs not only to remain relevant amid disruptions, such as Industry 4.0 and the post-COVID-workplace transition, but also to promote lifelong learning and adaptation capabilities. Upskilling and reskilling programs involve more than just technical training. They promote adaptive learning skills and the skill of lifelong learning. Personalised learning vectors, e-learning and microlearning means of content delivery were essential modes of these skilling initiatives, together with talent and learning strategies, where HR frameworks primarily centre around individual career, autonomy, and organizational agility.

Designing Skill Development Programs

***Personalized Models of Training*:** A more personalized training model personalizes content to the role and aspirations of the staff maximising training impact (Wang et al., 2021).
***Strategic Alignment*:** Lifelong learning needs to exist in an organization's strategic vision, and provide equitable and continuous access to reskilling opportunities (Li, L.2022).
***Human-Centric Design*:** By putting people first to develop staff empels organizations to be fair and sustainable growth accelerators (Webb et al., 2022).

The Function of Micro Learning and E-Learning Platforms

Flexibility and accessibility: E-learning platforms allow employees to learn at their own pace and time, making training more equitable across geographies and job roles (Analoui, 1994), and important factors to support in a hybrid and remote work force, which are decentralized, learning systems that are still sufficiently cohesive in nature and practice.
Microlearning: It has become an established form of bite-sized learning to reduce complex content into specific skills and concepts, which result in improved knowledge retention, and improved engagement with the learner, especially beneficial in time-sensitive and challenged learning environments (Li, 2022), Micro learning is also useful for managing just-in-time training, where the learner has relatively immediate access in time and space.

***Data-Driven Recommendations*:** Both e-learning and microlearning are often complemented by data driven LMS's that promote learning by tracking individual performance and offering personalized pathways of learning. Intelligent learning management systems assess employee profiles, identify skill gaps, and recommend specific courses to address gaps in learning, aligning learning outcomes with organizational objectives (Wang et al., 2021).

4.2 Supports Lifelong Learning

Fostering continual learning inside organizations is key to building a workforce that can depopulate itself to accommodate changing technologies and evolving business environments. This takes the form of a desired learning ecosystem and involves developing self-directed, and peer-to-peer learning. These interventions only develop individual capabilities, but also cultivate a culture of continual improvement and increasingly adaptable to change, within organizations.

Ecosystem for Learning

Framework Development: To enable structured and sustainable skill development, organizations need to combine learning strategies with their entrepreneurial ventures. This is consistent with India's National Policy for Skill Development and Entrepreneurship, which emphasizes coordination and systemic support across the national skills development landscape (Shaikh & Ganesh, 2024).

***Multiplatform Learning*:** The Charlas Educativas initiative illustrates how multiple platforms could focus on developing a fast paced learning ecosystem that goes from online to offline interactions (Carpenter et al., 2025).

***Inclusive Practices*:** A human-centered approach to learning must foster educational practices that are inclusive and responsive to the needs of all individuals, thus ensuring equitable access to lifelong learning opportunities, according to the ILO (Webb et al., 2022).

Support for Self-Directed & Peer-to-Peer Learning

***Self-Directed Learning*:** Research shows that enhancing self-directed learning skills would augment the tendency of an individual for lifelong learning and more opportunities in vocational skills upgrading (Mbagwu et al., 2020).

***Employer Support*:** By backing self-directed learning through incorporating MOOCs into the performance appraisal system, employers could increase the internal and external applicability of skills learned and make learning initiatives even more effective (Hamori, 2023).

By proactively enabling self-directed and peer-led learning through personalized and inclusive approaches, organizations are able to develop future-capable, resilient workforces. But for these lifelong learning programs to have concrete deliverables, there is a need to have effective ways of measuring their impact. This brings us to the next area of import—Measuring Skill Development—which enables measurement of progress, detection of gaps, and alignment of learning activities with strategic organizational objectives.

4.3 Measuring Skill Development

The skill development tools and metrics used to measure performance by employees are very important in measuring the progress and effectiveness of work environments. An organized procedure for skill measurement enhances organizational performance and employee development. The table 2 below describe some key aspects of measurement related to skill development:

Table 2. Showing tools and metrics for measuring skill development in employees

Category	Tool/Model	Description	Reference
Performance Measurement Tools	Behavioural Markers	Ensure explicit non-technical skill behavior in software professionals; adopted from aviation and healthcare.	Bender et al., 2014; Lacher et al., 2015
	Remote Working Skills Scale	Measurement of essential remote work skills for the purpose of obtaining cyber-security, problem-solving, time, and communication skills.	Benligiray et al., 2024
Competency and Skill Development Models	Competency Dimensions	It focuses on performance creativity and innovative behavior when assessment of employees of MSMEs is concerned- skills are aligned with job roles.	Kharub et al., 2024
	Industry 4.0 Competency Model	Focuses on developing digital competencies needed for Industry 4.0, with emphasis on talent, organizational culture, and communication.	Treviño-Elizondo & Garcia-Reyes, 2023

continued on following page

Table 2. Continued

Category	Tool/Model	Description	Reference
Visual and Analytical Systems	Workplace Performance Measurement (WPM)	Use digital tools for measuring the duration, frequency, and anomalies in the production process so that the quality of data can be improved along with the improvement of processes.	Nesterak et al., 2024
HR Metrics and Leadership Development	HR Metrics	Descriptive and predictive analytics are used to evaluate the effects of human resource practices on organizational performance and to facilitate strategic decision making.	Pillai & Sivathanu, 2021
	Automated Leadership Assessment	Assessment of leadership capabilities by means of self-reflection and learning analytics, providing insight into the acquisition of skills throughout a career.	Barthakur et al., 2022

5. HR-DRIVEN INNOVATION IN DIGITAL TRAINING

In response to the demands of digital transformation, HR-facilitated innovation in digital training has become a vital vehicle for creating an agile, future-ready workforce. HR-driven innovation in digital training may include technologies, employee-centered design and new models of training that develop impactful learning outcomes and further organizational goals. Follow demonstrate how HR departments are driving the transformation by creating value through technology and personalized employee learning.

5.1 Leveraging Technology in HR Practices

Digital transformation is transforming HR practices, particularly in training and development. Through the use of technologies like artificial intelligence (AI), virtual reality (VR), and gamification, organizations are providing highly personalized and interactive learning experiences that enhance employee engagement and knowledge retention (see Figure 2). These technologies are making possible a transition from fixed training programs to dynamic, employee-driven learning paths focused on self-discovery, autonomy, and continuous improvement (Tran Thi Nhung, 2023). In addition, HR functions are not just making this integration of technology happen, but also becoming

Figure 2. Technology synergy in HR

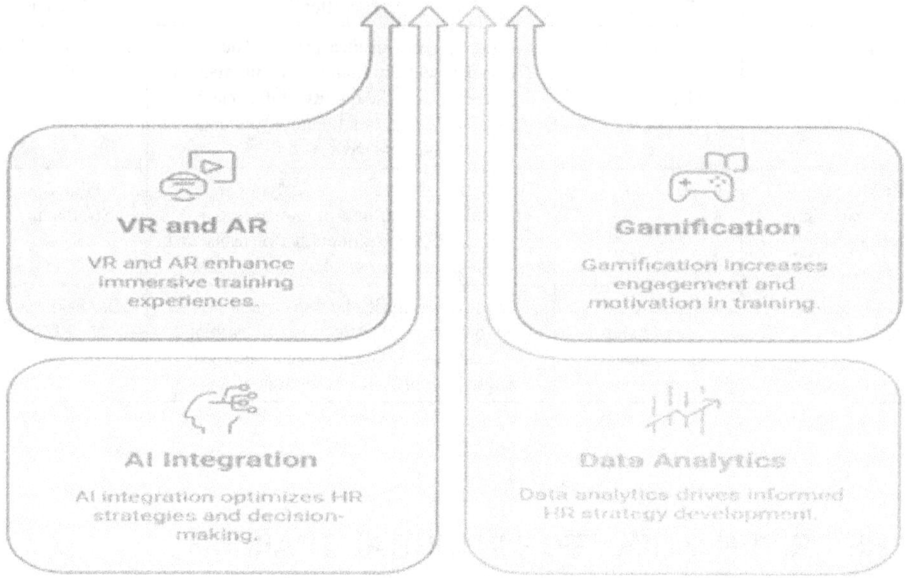

The drivers of larger organizational innovation. Through strategic management of digital tools and building digital competencies, HR fuels the integration of technology and aligns talent development with business innovation (Masdar Ryketeng et al., 2023). According to J. Zhang and Zhisheng Chen (2023), Digital HRM is revolutionizing core functions like selection, appraisal, and learning, in addition to improving the employee experience and building smarter, more responsive digital workplaces. Nevertheless, the introduction of such digital systems also has its challenges. Resistance to change and adverse effects of new digital infrastructures are frequent impediments that HR must handle carefully (Masdar Ryketeng et al., 2023; J. Zhang & Zhisheng Chen, 2023). Regardless of such obstacles, investing in quality digital HR development is crucial for organizations seeking to sustain competitiveness in an ever-changing digital economy.

5.2 Personalized Learning Experiences

A core aspect of HR-led digital training is the shift towards personalized and ongoing learning experiences (discussed in table 3). Digital HRM systems currently enable organizations to step away from generic, one-size-fits-all methods and instead provide adaptive, self-directed learning paths that enable employees to own their development (Tran Thi Nhung, 2023). Personalized models of learning take into account specific contexts, professional aspirations, and current skill levels to bridge gaps through customized learning plans. Such approaches have the backing of various digital media and apps to make training readily available and with work schedules compatible. This adaptive and tailored strategy, commonly referred to as Human Resource Digital Transformation (HRDT), combines digital innovation with organizational and individual capabilities. Effective application of HRDT is not only a function of digital infrastructure and system architecture but also of fostering creativity and individual digital proficiency—especially in times of uncertainty like the COVID-19 pandemic.

Table 3. Key aspects of personalized training and adaptive learning systems

Section	Key Concept	Description	Reference
Tailoring Training Programs to Individual Needs	Personalization	Customization of digital learning environments includes matching the many diverse preferences of learners, increasing access to them and engagement with them.	Chen & Wang (2019)
	Adaptation Criteria	Accurate identification of the significant needs for adaptation is essential for developing relevant learning materials personalized in an effective manner. The study found 13 criteria for adaptation, which govern the personalization process.	Thalmann (2014)
	Workforce Applications	Making relevant and engaging for employees can potentially improve retention levels in workforce training.	Fake & Dabbagh (2020)
Feedback along with Adaptive Learning Systems	Adaptive Learning Systems	Systems with that feature will use algorithms to assess learners' knowledge levels against temps and will then give them tailored resources. The impact of the latter will effectively increase learning efficiency	Xu et al. (2024)
	Feedback Mechanism	Continuous feedback is required for adaptive learning, as this will allow learners to modify their learning strategies based on real-time performance data	Reid (2023)
	Adaptive Learning Modules	Joining adaptive learning modules with recommendation systems into personalized e-learning frameworks ensures that students receive feedback in a timely and relevant way to enhance their overall learning experience.	Murtaza et al. (2022)

Through the use of these technologies and customized approaches, HR makes training relevant, scalable, and strategic in today's digitally disrupted world. While organizations attempt to infuse digital learning into the culture, they need to break down and surmount resistance, skill mismatches, and structural constraints that act as barriers. The following section delves deeper into these obstacles and provides analysis of how to successfully overcome barriers to digital dexterity.

6. OVERCOMING BARRIERS TO DIGITAL DEXTERITY

The digital dexterity of quickly adapting to emerging digital possibilities is an essential organizational skill in the digital age (Soule et al., 2016). However, digital adoption faces several challenges as illustrated in table 4, especially for older adults who contend with technology-related fears and social-cognitive barriers besides physical limitations (Atkinson et al., 2016; Steelman & Wallace, 2017). To counter these challenges, digital champions in governments work using techniques, such as storytelling, building communities, and citizen-centric approaches (Wilson & Mergel, 2022). Organizations can create digital capacity through mindsets, practices, and specific resources (Soule et al., 2016). Intergenerational social-cognitive methods for teaching older adults with younger companions would help them become digitally literate while reducing their anxiety (Atkinson et al., 2016; Steelman & Wallace, 2017). Such approaches stimulate exploration and wayfinding that are critical digital skills and provide students with meaningful experience in helping older adults with technology challenges (Steelman & Wallace, 2017).

Table 4. Overcoming barriers to digital dexterity through cultural, structural, and inclusive strategies

Section	Key Concept	Description	Reference
Cultural and Structural Challenges	Understanding Barriers	The resistance to change, technicalities, and lack of strategy for implementation are issues that can serve as impediments.	Alshibani et al. (2024)
	Leadership Engagement	Visionary Leadership creates a climate conducive to digital transformation, thereby minimizing resistance.	Setiorini et al. (2024)
	User Experience	User experience enhancement is achieved with appropriate digital assistance and seamless communication.	Hwang & Seo (2024)
Building Leadership Buy-In for HR Initiatives	Accountability and Engagement	Leadership provides the necessary impetus for change, instilling ownership of the initiatives, and creating engagement.	Khan et al. (2024)
	Workforce Transformation	HR initiatives have the added responsibility of aligning with digital strategies, with initiatives that promote flexibility and rejuvenation.	Eden et al. (2019)
Diversity and Inclusion	Equity in Access	Enables all employees to be present with equal opportunities, particularly the underrepresented, in accessing digital tools and resources.	Clark (2003)
	Inclusive Policies	Diversity-related hiring and retention strategies and neuro-diversity programs are used to reduce biases in recruitment, which could be otherwise exacerbated by so-called conventional practices.	Walkowiak (2023)

continued on following page

Table 4. Continued

Section	Key Concept	Description	Reference
Bridging the Digital Divide	Service Inclusion Practices	Peer relationships and mentoring can bring a solution to the digital divide from both sides.	Fisk et al. (2022)
	Addressing Vulnerability	The intersection of human capabilities and digital inclusion through role modelling and coaching.	Fisk et al. (2022)

Developing a digitally capable workforce through breaking down digital dexterity barriers not only solves current problems but also places organizations in a strategic position to succeed in the future. As digital change continues transformation accelerates, HR's function will move beyond today's practices to managing and capitalizing on emerging technologies and defining a workforce capable of adapting to the changing nature of work.

In this regard, future trends and opportunities for HR development are all about such innovations as blockchain, AI, and automation that hold the promise of greater transparency, efficiency of operations, and better decision-making. Further, future-proofing the workplace will also call for a greater emphasis on digital skills, intrapreneurial mindset, and continuous learning. HR will have a key role to play in strategic workforce planning, remote working facilitation, and a culture that can evolve and prosper in a digitally dominated world.

7. FUTURE TRENDS AND OPPORTUNITIES

As the digital environment continues to change, organizations need to stay dynamic and futuristic in managing and developing human capital. The incorporation of new technologies in Human Resource Development (HRD) is not merely an operational change but a strategic imperative. The future will be determined by the ability of the HR function to leverage innovation, create digital dexterity, and expect the evolving dynamics of the workforce.

7.1 Emerging Technologies in HR Development

The accelerating rate of technological development is meaningfully remaking the landscape of HR development. Organizations are increasingly integrating new technologies to ease operations, enhance performance metrics, and realize fresh ideas (Banton, 2019). AI and robots, specifically, are remodelling HR by automating mundane duties, improving decision-making, and ushering in flexibility in work arrangements (Parry & Battista, 2019). Virtual HRD (VHRD), encompassing immersive training environments, has become a primary vehicle to facilitate realistic and scalable HRD practices (McWhorter, 2010).

These technologies provide significant advantages of time and cost savings, enhanced data accuracy, and enhanced productivity, all of which contribute to employee satisfaction (Banton, 2019). Nevertheless, they also have disadvantages such as ethical issues, security threats, and heightened demands for new skill sets. HR experts are therefore called upon to enable employee reskilling while promoting the protection of well-being and data integrity (Parry & Battista, 2019).

Major technologies set to shape the future of HRD are blockchain, artificial intelligence (AI), and automation:

Blockchain in HR Development

***Data Security*:** Blockchain does away with the need for a centralized database, enhancing security by minimizing the chance of unauthorized access and fraud in HR transactions (Tyagi et al., 2022; Sharma et al., 2023).

***Process Efficiency*:** It streamlines and automates processes like payroll and credentials verification, thus reducing administrative time and operational expenses (Ramachandran et al., 2022).

***Transparency*:** Blockchain technology provides transparent and tamper-proof records, increasing trust in recruitment and employee management processes (Sharma et al., 2023).

Artificial Intelligence and Automation

***Improved Recruitment*:** AI-based algorithms effectively process large sets of data to pair candidates with positions, thereby enhancing the quality and speed of recruitment (Ekuma, 2023; Sala. D, 2024).

***Employee Engagement*:** Automation increases employee engagement through personalized feedback and development tools. Too much control via digital channels can however cause burnout unless properly managed (Sala. D, 2024).

***Decision Support System*:** AI provides HR groups with fact-based insights to make informed decisions in domains like workforce planning, talent management, and optimization of performance (Ekuma, 2023).

7.2 Digital Dexterity Preparing for the Future of Work

The future of work is being determined by ongoing technological advancements and changing expectations of the contemporary workforce. To stay competitive, organizations need to develop digital dexterity—referring to the ability to adapt to and utilize digital technology efficiently—and actively prepare for future skill needs. This calls for building a culture of learning and developing strategic talent alignment with technological advancements.

Anticipating Tomorrow's Skills

Digital skills: With more automation, skills in digital tools, AI, and data analysis become imperative. In 2025, around 50% of the workforce is anticipated to require reskilling owing to sudden technology shifts (Li, 2022).
***Intrapreneurial Competencies*:** Organisations that are ready for the future will count on workers with the ability to think creatively and perform entrepreneurially in their workplaces to address emerging needs (David et al., 2024).
***Lifelong Learning*:** Institutionalizing ongoing learning as a key organizational strategy guarantees long-term flexibility and prepares the workforce to address changing skill needs (Li, 2022).

Changing Role of HR in Future-Ready Team Building

***Strategic Workforce Planning*:** HR needs to predict future talent demand and lead the building of applicable competencies to match technological growth (Nankervis & Cameron, 2022).
***Remote Work Enablement*:** With remote and hybrid working models becoming here-to-stay, HR would play a key role in defining virtual workflows and training mechanisms in order to preserve team productivity (Johnson, 2020).
***Cultural Transformation*:** Embedding a change-readiness culture and an innovative culture will become critical for HR to align the workforce capabilities with changing organizational aspirations (Nankervis & Cameron, 2022).

As organizations confront the shifting landscape of work—marked by emerging technologies, evolving roles, and a continuous need for reskilling—the strategic function of HR becomes more vital than ever. Beyond just managing talent, HR must champion a culture that embraces innovation, adaptability, and digital fluency. The ability of HR to lead in fostering a workforce that is future-ready will directly impact an organization's success in the digital age.This brings us to a critical juncture: the realization of HR's imperative in building digital dexterity across all levels of the organization. The concluding section delves into HR's pivotal role in shaping digital capabilities and issues a clear call to action—urging HR leaders to step up as transformative agents in driving organizational change.

8. CONCLUSION

Digital dexterity—the capacity to quickly adapt and react to new digital technologies—has emerged as a core driver of success in the digital age (Soule et al., 2016). It involves not just technical competencies but also cognitive and behavioral competencies like personal innovativeness, self-efficacy, agility, and transformational thinking (Ahmed.w. et al., 2020. As more and more organizations rely on such capabilities in order to sustain competitiveness, the task of Human Resource Management (HRM) in developing digital dexterity assumes strategic significance. HR's role is in incorporating digital skills into the very heart of organizational development interventions. This entails planning specialty digital training programs, inducting digital competency frameworks into HR policy, and making sure that the workforce is technologically qualified people. But there are challenges. Most organizations continue to lack proper access to digital technologies, infrastructure, and training support necessary for successful digital transformation. In such a scenario, developing digital dexterity becomes not just an option but an imperative for the long-term, demanding bold leadership from HR to create innovation-led organizational cultures (Soule et al., 2016).

As businesses work in more sophisticated digital environments, HR needs to play a leading role in preparing employees with the skills, attitude, and adaptability to succeed in these environments. This goes beyond upskilling; it requires creating an environment of ongoing learning and change-readiness. The subsequent sections highlight HR's changing roles in this area and call for its role as a driver of organizational change.

8.1 HR's Pivotal Contribution to Building Digital Skills

Successful digital transformation heavily depends on whether HR can see digital skill needs and coordinate talent development in tune with organizational agendas. Zervas and Stiakakis (2024) highlight the significant role HR needs to play to balance employees' expectations with continuously changing digital abilities. HR's function now includes reengineering its fundamental activities—like hiring, induction, training, and engagement—using digital tools and platforms (Shivaraj, 2021). This transformational leadership is necessary not only for building capabilities but also for reorganizing organizational systems to achieve digital agility (Albannai et al., 2024). With strategic interventions, HR can influence a digitally capable workforce that can address challenges in the future.

8.2 Call to Action: HR as a Change Leader

HR, in order to be an effective leader in the digital era, needs to create a strong digital plan that supports the overall organizational mission (Shivaraj, 2021). This requires building a culture of innovation that promotes adaptability, experimentation, and fast response to change. Klus and Müller (2021) underscore the need to create spaces in which workers are enabled to learn, create, and react dynamically to changing digital environments. Focusing on lifelong learning and constant growth will not only fill skill gaps existing today but also prepare companies to stay resilient and competitive against future disruptions.

In summary, HR's work is no longer limited to old-fashioned administrative roles—it needs to become a major force behind digital innovation and cultural transformation. Accepting this challenge will allow HR to guide organizations boldly into a future characterized by technological progress and human-centric resilience.

REFERENCES

Ahmed, W., Hizam, S. M., & Sentosa, I. (2020). Digital Dexterity: Employee As Consumer Approach Towards Organizational Success. *Human Resource Development International*, •••, 1–11. https://Doi.Org/10.1080/13678868.2020.1835107

Alfedaghi, H. S. (2024). Digital Dexterity: Building Capabilities in the Era of AI. DOI: 10.2118/222277-MS

Alshibani, A., Alkhathami, S. M., Hassanain, M. A., Tuffaha, F., Ouis, D., & Mohammed, A. (2024). Hybrid Framework for Investigating Digital Transformation Barriers in The Oil and Gas Sector. *Energies*, *17*(23), 6151. https://Doi.Org/10.3390/En17236151. DOI: 10.3390/en17236151

Analoui, F. (1994). Training And Development. *Journal of Management Development*, *13*(9), 61–72. https://Doi.Org/10.1108/02621719410072107. DOI: 10.1108/02621719410072107

Atkinson, K., Barnes, J., Albee, J., Anttila, P., Haataja, J., Nanavati, K., Steelman, K., & Wallace, C. (2016). Breaking Barriers to Digital Literacy. Iee. https://Doi.Org/10.1145/2982142.2982183

Bailey, J. L., & Mitchell, R. B. (2016). Industry Perceptions of The Competencies Needed by Computer Programmers: Technical, Business, And Soft Skills. *Journal of Computer Information Systems*, *47*, 28–33. https://Doi.Org/10.1080/08874417.2007.11645951

Banton, C. L. (2019). Advancing Technologies in Human Resource Development (HRD). In Emerald Publishing Limited Ebooks (Pp. 25–36). https://Doi.Org/10.1108/978-1-78973-073-920191003

Barthakur, A., Kovanović, V., Joksimović, S., Zhang, Z., Richey, M., & Pardo, A. (2022). Measuring Leadership Development in Workplace Learning Using Automated Assessments: Learning Analytics and Measurement Theory Approach. *British Journal of Educational Technology*, *53*(6), 1842–1863. https://Doi.Org/10.1111/Bjet.13218. DOI: 10.1111/bjet.13218

Bencsik, A. (2024). Challenges Of a Digitalizing World in The Light of An International Survey. RIMCIS : International And Multidisciplinary Journal of Social Sciences, 1–23. https://Doi.Org/10.17583/Rimcis.12502

Bender, L. L., Walia, G. S., Fagerholm, F., Pagels, M., Nygard, K. E., & Münch, J. (2014). Measurement Of the Non-Technical Skills of Software Professionals: An Empirical Investigation. International Conference on Software Engineering, 478–483. http://Ksiresearchorg.Ipage.Com/Seke/Seke14paper/Seke14paper_216.Pdf

Benligiray, S., Güngör, A. Y., & Akbaş, İ. (2024). Measuring Remote Working Skills: Scale Development and Validation Study. *PLoS One*, *19*(4), e0299074. https://Doi.Org/10.1371/Journal.Pone.0299074. DOI: 10.1371/journal.pone.0299074 PMID: 38603683

Carmeli, A., Reiter-Palmon, R., & Ziv, E. (2010). Inclusive leadership and employee involvement in creative tasks in the workplace: The mediating role of psychological safety. *Creativity Research Journal*, *22*(3), 250–260. DOI: 10.1080/10400419.2010.504654

Carpenter, J. P., Mosquera Gende, I., & Marcelo-Martínez, P. (2025). Multiplatform Ecosystems of Professional Learning: The Case of the #Charlaseducativas. *Journal Of New Approaches in Educational Research*, *14*(1), 6. https://Doi.Org/10.1007/S44322-024-00024-7. DOI: 10.1007/s44322-024-00024-7

Castellacci, F., Consoli, D., & Santoalha, A. (2020). The Role Of E-Skills in Technological Diversification in European Regions. *Regional Studies*, *54*(8), 1123–1135. https://Doi.Org/10.1080/00343404.2019.1681585. DOI: 10.1080/00343404.2019.1681585

Chamorro-Premuzic, T., Akhtar, R., Winsborough, D., & Sherman, R. A. (2017). The Datafication of Talent: How Technology Is Advancing the Science of Human Potential at Work. *Current Opinion in Behavioral Sciences*, *18*, 13–16. https://Doi.Org/10.1016/J.COBEHA.2017.04.007. DOI: 10.1016/j.cobeha.2017.04.007

Chen, S. Y., & Wang, J. H. (2019). Human Factors and Personalized Digital Learning: An Editorial. *International Journal of Human-Computer Interaction*, *35*(4-5), 297–298. https://Doi.Org/10.1080/10447318.2018.1542891. DOI: 10.1080/10447318.2018.1542891

Chen, T. (2023). Advancing Technical Education and Fostering Soft Skills Development Through Digital Learning. Advances In Education Humanities and Social Science Research, 7(1), 91. https://Doi.Org/10.56028/Aehssr.7.1.91.2023

Chien, S.-Y., Wu, C.-Y., Chen, C.-K., & Beckman, S. L. (2023). Exploring The Impact of An Interactive Electronic Pegboard on Manual Dexterity and Cognitive Skills of Stroke Patients: A Preliminary Analysis (Preprint). JMIR Rehabilitation and Assistive Technologies. https://Doi.Org/10.2196/55481

Clark, K. (2003). Using Self-Directed Learning Communities to Bridge the Digital Divide. *British Journal of Educational Technology, 34*(5), 663–665. https://Doi.Org/10.1046/J.0007-1013.2003.00358.X. DOI: 10.1046/j.0007-1013.2003.00358.x

David, S., Zinica, D., Bărbuţă-Mişu, N., Savga, L., & Virlanuta, F. O. (2024). Public Administration Managers' and Employees' Perceptions of Adaptability to Change Under "The Future of Work" Paradigm. Technological Forecasting and Social Change. https://Doi.Org/10.1016/J.Techfore.2023.123088

Della Sala, V. (2024). Research Handbook on Human Resource Management and Disruptive Technologies. British Journal of Industrial Relations. https://Doi.Org/10.1111/Bjir.12868

Deshpande, A. (2021). Creating agile learning culture for the workforce. SSRN Electronic Journal. DOI: 10.2139/ssrn.3774225

Do, B., Yeh, P., & Madsen, J. (2016). Exploring the relationship among human resource flexibility, organizational innovation and adaptability culture. *Chinese Management Studies, 10*(4), 657–674. DOI: 10.1108/CMS-01-2016-0022

Doeze Jager-van Vliet, S. (2017). Proactive and adaptive agility among employees: The relationship with personal and situational factors.

Eden, R., Burton-Jones, A., Casey, V., & Draheim, M. (2019). Digital Transformation Requires Workforce Transformation. *MIS Quarterly Executive, 18*(1), 4. https://Doi.Org/10.17705/2MSQE.00005. DOI: 10.17705/2msqe.00005

Ekuma, K. (2023). Artificial Intelligence and Automation in Human Resource Development: A Systematic Review. Human Resource Development Review. https://Doi.Org/10.1177/15344843231224009

Fake, H., & Dabbagh, N. (2020). Personalized Learning Within Online Workforce Learning Environments: Exploring Implementations, Obstacles, Opportunities, And Perspectives of Workforce Leaders. Technology, Knowledge, And Learning, 25(4), 789–809. https://Doi.Org/10.1007/S10758-020-09441-X

Feng, H., Jia, X., Wang, Y., Niu, L., & Xu, Y. (2019). Digital Memory: A New Paradigm for Cultural Heritage. Digital Presentation and Preservation of Cultural and Scientific Heritage. Available From: https://Doi.Org/10.55630/Dipp.2019.9.8

Fisk, R. P., Gallan, A. S., Joubert, A. M., Beekhuyzen, J., Cheung, L., & Russell-Bennett, R. (2022). Healing The Digital Divide with Digital Inclusion: Enabling Human Capabilities. *Journal of Service Research, 109467052211401*, •••. https://Doi.Org/10.1177/10946705221140148

Gilch, P. M., & Sieweke, J. (2020). Recruiting Digital Talent: The Strategic Role of Recruitment in Organizations' Digital Transformation. *German Journal of Human Resource Management Zeitschrift Für Personalforschung*, *35*(1), 53–82. https://Doi.Org/10.1177/2397002220952734

Gouda, H. (2020). Exploring The Relevant Skills Needed for The Digital Age Employees. European Journal of Business and Management. https://Doi.Org/10.7176/Ejbm/12-2-07

Hamori, M. (2023). Self-Directed Learning in Massive Open Online Courses and Its Application at The Workplace: Does Employer Support Matter? *Journal of Business Research*, *157*, 113590. https://Doi.Org/10.1016/J.Jbusres.2022.113590. DOI: 10.1016/j.jbusres.2022.113590

Hilbert, M., & Cairo, O. (2008, July). The Binary Digit to Technological Convergence. In WSEAS International Conference. Proceedings. Mathematics and Computers in Science and Engineering (No. 12). WSEAS.

Hwang, I., & Seo, R. (2024). Organizational Support for Digital Transformation in The Metaverse: A Contingent Pathway from User Experience to Digitalization Resistance. R & D Management. https://Doi.Org/10.1111/Radm.12706

Iannello, P., Cancer, A., Zmigrod, L., Antonietti, A., & Salvi, C. (2024). Creative Minds in A Polarized World. Journal Of Creative Behavior. https://Doi.Org/10.1002/Jocb.1509

Iyer, R. K. (2021). *Upskilling And Reskilling for Workforce of The Future*. Larson & Toubro Company.

Ječmenica, D., Mandić, D., & Stanišić, N. (2024). HR's Role in Fostering Agile Culture and Upskilling IT Talent. In Proceedings of the 11th International Scientific Conference - FINIZ 2024 (pp. 115–120). DOI: 10.15308/finiz-2024-115-120

Johnson, S. S. (2020). The Future of Work. *American Journal of Health Promotion*, *34*, 809–812. https://Doi.Org/10.1177/0890117120943748 PMID: 32921140

Khan, A., Shahzad, K., & Khan, N. A. (2024). Fostering Accountability Through Digital Transformation: Leadership's Role in Enhancing Techno-Work Engagement in Public Sector. *Public Money & Management*, •••, 1–8. https://Doi.Org/10.1080/09540962.2024.2424384. DOI: 10.1080/09540962.2024.2424384

Kharub, M., Mondal, S., Singh, S., & Gupta, H. C. (2024). Evaluation Of Competency Dimensions for Employee Performance Assessment: Evidence from Micro, Small, And Medium Enterprises. International Journal of Productivity and Performance Management. https://Doi.Org/10.1108/Ijppm-07-2023-0379

Khatri, M., Duggal, H. K., Thomas, A., & Varma, A. (2024). Increasing Digitalization of The Workplace: Is the Workforce Ready? Journal Of Asia Business Studies. https://Doi.Org/10.1108/Jabs-03-2024-0144

Kretschmer, T., & Khashabi, P. Digital Transformation and Organization Design: An Integrated Approach. California Management Review (2020) Jul 13;62(4):86–104. Available From: https://Doi.Org/10.1177/0008125620940296

Kumar, S., Narayan, S., Sharma, K., Kaur, R., & Sen, R. (2023). Creating Sustainable High-Performance Human Resource Practice Through Employees Learning Agility. The Transition Adaptive Approach. ABAC Journal. https://Doi.Org/10.59865/Abacj.2023.40

Lacher, L. L., Walia, G. S., Fagerholm, F., Pagels, M., Nygard, K. E., & Münch, J. (2015). A Behavior Marker Tool for Measurement of The Non-Technical Skills of Software Professionals: An Empirical Investigation. International Conference on Software Engineering, 409–414. https://Doi.Org/10.18293/SEKE2015-227

Li, L. (2022). Reskilling And Upskilling the Future-Ready Workforce for Industry 4.0 And beyond. *Information Systems Frontiers*, •••, 1–16. Doi.Org/10.1007/S10796-022-10308-Y PMID: 35855776

Mbagwu, F. O., Chukwuedo, S. O., & Ogbuanya, T. C. (2020). Promoting Lifelong Learning Propensity and Intentions for Vocational Training Among Adult and Vocational Educational Undergraduates. *Vocations and Learning*, *13*(3), 419–437. Doi.Org/10.1007/S12186-020-09245-1. DOI: 10.1007/s12186-020-09245-1

Mcwhorter, R. R. (2010). Exploring The Emergence of Virtual Human Resource Development. *Advances in Developing Human Resources*, *12*(6), 623–631. Doi.Org/10.1177/1523422310395367. DOI: 10.1177/1523422310395367

Mian, S. S., & Mian, M. S. (2017). Impact of high-performance work practices (HPWPs) on the employee agility. In 10th International Conference on Law, Business, Marketing and Education (LBME-17). Pattaya (Thailand) Dec (pp. 27-28).

Milani, R., Sommovigo, V., Ghirotto, L., & Setti, I. (2024). Individual Differences in Learning Agility at Work: A Mixed Methods Study to Develop and Validate a New Scale. Human Resource Development Quarterly. Available From: https://Doi.Org/10.1002/Hrdq.21528

Mirković, V., Lukić, J., Lazarević, S., & Vojinović, Ž. (2019). Key Characteristics of Organizational Structure That Supports Digital Transformation. Available From: https://Doi.Org/10.46541/978-86-7233-380-0_46

Muchiri, D. G. (2022). Skilling, Reskilling, And Upskilling a Workforce: A Perspective from Kenyan Enterprises. Strategic Journal of Business & Change Management, 9(4). https://Doi.Org/10.61426/Sjbcm.V9i4.2368

Muduli, A., & Choudhury, A. (2024). Exploring The Role of Workforce Agility On Digital Transformation: A Systematic Literature Review. Benchmarking: An International Journal. https://Doi.Org/10.1108/Bij-02-2023-0108

Murtaza, M., Ahmed, Y., Shamsi, J. A., Sherwani, F., & Usman, M. (2022). AI-Based Personalized E-Learning Systems: Issues, Challenges, And Solutions. *IEEE Access : Practical Innovations, Open Solutions*, *10*, 81323–81342. https://Doi.Org/10.1109/Access.2022.3193938. DOI: 10.1109/ACCESS.2022.3193938

Nankervis, A., & Cameron, R. (2022). Capabilities And Competencies for Digitized Human Resource Management: Perspectives from Australian HR Professionals. *Asia Pacific Journal of Human Resources*, *61*(1), 232–251. https://Doi.Org/10.1111/1744-7941.12354. DOI: 10.1111/1744-7941.12354

Nesterak, J., Szelągowski, M., & Radziszewski, P. (2024). Workplace Performance Measurement: Digitalization Of Work Observation and Analysis. Journal Of Intelligent Manufacturing. https://Doi.Org/10.1007/S10845-024-02419-X

Nhung, T. T. (2023). How Does Digital HRM Transform Training to Learning in Organizations? *Journal Of Economics Finance and Management Studies*, *06*(08). https://Doi.Org/10.47191/Jefms/V6-I8-66

Obermayer, N., Csizmadia, T., Banász, Z., & Purnhauser, P. (2023). Importance Of Digital and Soft Skills in The Digital Age. European Conference on Knowledge Management, 24(2), 978–987. https://Doi.Org/10.34190/Eckm.24.2.1550

Opada, F. M. M., Ibrahim, M. B. H., Irawan, A., Akbar, M. A., & Rasyid, A. (2024). Talent Acquisition Strategies: A Comprehensive Examination of Recruitment Policies for Organizational Success. Advances In Human Resource Management Research, 2(2). https://Doi.Org/10.60079/Ahrmr.V2i2.185

Oskarita, E., & Nur'afra Arasy, H. (2024). The Role of Digital Tools in Enhancing Collaborative Learning in Secondary Education. International Journal of Educational Research. https://Doi.Org/10.62951/Ijer.V1i1.15

Parry, E., & Battista, V. (2019). The Impact of Emerging Technologies on Work: A Review of The Evidence and Implications for The Human Resource Function. *Emerald Open Research*, *1*(4), 5. https://Doi.Org/10.12688/Emeraldopenres.12907.1. DOI: 10.1108/EOR-04-2023-0001

Pihir, I., Tomičić-Pupek, K., & Furjan, M. T. (2018). Digital Transformation Insights and Trends. In Central European Conference on Information and Intelligent Systems (Pp. 141-149). Faculty Of Organization and Informatics Varazdin.

Pillai, R., & Sivathanu, B. (2020). Adoption Of Artificial Intelligence (AI) For Talent Acquisition In IT/Ites Organizations. *Benchmarking*, *27*(9), 2599–2629. https://Doi.Org/10.1108/BIJ-04-2020-0186. DOI: 10.1108/BIJ-04-2020-0186

Pillai, R., & Sivathanu, B. (2021). Measure What Matters: Descriptive And Predictive Metrics Of HRM-Pathway Toward Organizational Performance. International Journal of Productivity and Performance Management. https://Doi.Org/10.1108/IJPPM-10-2020-0509

Ramachandran, R., Babu, V. R., & Murugesan, V. P. (2022). The Role of Blockchain Technology in The Process of Decision-Making in Human Resource Management: A Review and Future Research Agenda. *Business Process Management Journal*, *29*(1), 116–139. https://Doi.Org/10.1108/Bpmj-07-2022-0351. DOI: 10.1108/BPMJ-07-2022-0351

Reid, J. R. (2023). Precision Education for Personalized Learning. Journal Of the American College of Radiology. https://Doi.Org/10.1016/J.Jacr.2023.05.018

Reis, J., Amorim, M., Melão, N., & Matos, P. (2018). Digital Transformation: A Literature Review and Guidelines for Future Research. Advances In Intelligent Systems and Computing. Available From: https://Doi.Org/10.1007/978-3-319-77703-0_41

Rodríguez-Sánchez, J.-L., Montero-Navarro, A., & Gallego-Losada, R. (2019). The Opportunity Presented by Technological Innovation to Attract Valuable Human Resources. *Sustainability (Basel)*, *11*(20), 5785. https://Doi.Org/10.3390/SU11205785. DOI: 10.3390/su11205785

Ryketeng, M., Syachbrani, W., & Syamsuri, N. (2023). Optimising Human Resources Capacity: Driving Adoption of Latest Technology and Driving Business Innovation Amidst the Dynamics of The Digital Era. [ADMAN]. *Journal Of Contemporary Administration and Management*, *1*(3), 229–236. https://Doi.Org/10.61100/Adman.V1i3.86. DOI: 10.61100/adman.v1i3.86

Sandeep, M., Lavanya, V., & Balakrishnan, J. (2025). Leveraging AI In Recruitment: Enhancing Intellectual Capital Through Resource-Based View and Dynamic Capability Framework. Journal Of Intellectual Capital. https://Doi.Org/10.1108/Jic-05-2024-0155

Sawant, R., Thomas, B., & Kadlag, S. (2022). Reskilling And Upskilling: To Stay Relevant in Today's Industry. Deleted Journal, 7(1). https://Doi.Org/10.56902/Irbe.2022.7.1.4

Sepúlveda-Ortega, A. (2022). The Indonesian Digital Workforce Gaps In 2021–2025. *Sustainability (Basel)*, *15*(1), 754. https://Doi.Org/10.3390/Su15010754. DOI: 10.3390/su15010754

Setiorini, R., Aimah, S., & Fakhruddin, F. (2024). Transformation Of Pesantren Organizational Culture: Strategies for Pesantren to Become Centers of Innovation in The Digital Era. *Leadership*, *6*(1), 1–11. https://Doi.Org/10.32478/Leadership.V6i1.2879. DOI: 10.32478/leadership.v6i1.2879

Shahruddin, S., Sonet, U. N., Azmi, A., & Zainordin, N. (2024). Traversing The Complexity of Digital Construction and Beyond Through Soft Skills: Experiences of Malaysian Architects. Engineering, Construction and Architectural Management. https://Doi.Org/10.1108/Ecam-01-2024-0147

Shaikh, S., & Ganesh, M. (2024). Upskilling India: The National Policy On Skill Development and Entrepreneurship. *F1000 Research*, *13*, 1141. Doi.Org/10.12688/F1000research.154936.1. DOI: 10.12688/f1000research.154936.1

Sharma, D., Pandey, S., Gehlot, A., Sudhanshu, S., & Duggal, A. S. (2023). Automated Intervention of Blockchain in Human Resource Management. International Conference on Database Theory, 609–612. https://Doi.Org/10.1109/ICDT57929.2023.10150995

Shivaraj, G. (2021). A Study on The Digitalized Human Resources (HR) Practices in Digitalized Business Era in India. *Management Science*, *8*(3), 83–89. https://Doi.Org/10.34293/Management.V8I3.3560

Smith P, Beretta M. (2020). The Gordian Knot of Practicing Digital Transformation: Coping with Emergent Paradoxes in Ambidextrous Organizing Structures*. Journal Of Product Innovation Management. (1):166–91. Doi.Org/10.1111/Jpim.12548.

Soule, D., Deora Puram, A., Deora Puram, A., Westerman, G., & Bonnet, D. (2016). Becoming a Digital Organization: The Journey to Digital Dexterity. Social Science Research Network. https://doi.org/DOI: 10.2139/SSRN.2697688

Soule, D. L., Puram, A., Westerman, G. F., & Bonnet, D. (2016). Becoming A Digital Organization: The Journey to Digital Dexterity. SSRN Electronic Journal. https://Doi.Org/10.2139/Ssrn.2697688

Steelman, K., & Wallace, C. (2021). Breaking Barriers, Building Understanding. ACM SIGCAS Computers and Society, 49(1), 23–24. https://Doi.Org/10.1145/3447892.3447901

Štofková, J., Poliaková, A., Repkova Stofkova, K., Malega, P., Krejnus, M., Binasova, V., & Daneshjo, N. (2022). Digital Skills as A Significant Factor of Human Resources Development. *Sustainability (Basel)*, *14*(20), 13117. https://Doi.Org/10.3390/Su142013117. DOI: 10.3390/su142013117

Tahir, A. (2024). Exploring New Paradigms in Auditing: Challenges and Opportunities in The Digital Era. MSJ Majority Science Journal. 2(2):83–90. Available From: https://Doi.Org/10.61942/Msj.V2i2.145

Tang, D. (2021). What Is Digital Transformation? EDPACS. 64 (1):9–13. Available From: https://Doi.Org/10.1080/07366981.2020.1847813

Thalmann, S. (2014). Adaptation Criteria for The Personalized Delivery of Learning Materials: A Multi-Stage Empirical Investigation. *Australasian Journal of Educational Technology*, *30*(1), 45–60. https://Doi.Org/10.14742/AJET.235. DOI: 10.14742/ajet.235

Thornhill-Miller, B., Camarda, A., Mercier, M., Burkhardt, J.-M., Morisseau, T., Bourgeois-Bougrine, S., Vinchon, F., El Hayek, S., Augereau-Landais, M., Mourey, F., Feybesse, C., Sundquist, D., & Lubart, T. (2023). Creativity, Critical Thinking, Communication, And Collaboration: Assessment, Certification, And Promotion Of 21st Century Skills for The Future of Work and Education. *Journal of Intelligence*, *11*(3), 54. https://Doi.Org/10.3390/Jintelligence11030054. DOI: 10.3390/jintelligence11030054 PMID: 36976147

Treviño-Elizondo, B. L., & Garcia-Reyes, H. (2023). An Employee Competency Development Maturity Model for Industry 4.0 Adoption. Sustainability. https://Doi.Org/10.3390/Su151411371

Tyagi, S., Kumar, R., Joshi, K., Rastogi, N., & Hussien, N. M. (2022). Blockchain In HRM: *Application and Future Perspective. International Conference on Communication, Computing & Security*, 1–5. Doi.Org/10.1109/ICCCS55188.2022.10079644

Walkowiak, E. (2023). Digitalization And Inclusiveness of HRM Practices: The Example of Neurodiversity Initiatives. Human Resource Management Journal. https://Doi.Org/10.1111/1748-8583.12499

Wang, C., Zhu, H., Wang, P., Zhu, C., Zhang, X., Chen, E., & Xiong, H. (2021). Personalized And Explainable Employee Training Course Recommendations: A Bayesian Variational Approach. *ACM Transactions on Office Information Systems*, *40*(4), 1–32. https://Doi.Org/10.1145/3490476

Webb, S., Hodge, S., Holford, J., Milana, M., & Waller, R. (2022). Aligning Skills and Lifelong Learning for Human-Centred Sustainable Development. *International Journal of Lifelong Education*, *41*(2), 127–132. Doi.Org/10.1080/02601370.2022.2057167. DOI: 10.1080/02601370.2022.2057167

Westover, J. (2024). Building a Resilient and Adaptive Organization Through Mindset Shifts and Continuous Learning. DOI: 10.70175/hclreview.2020.14.4.1

Westover, J. (2024). Designing A Skills Evolution Program: A Framework for Success. Human Capital Leadership., 12(2). https://Doi.Org/10.70175/Hclreview.2020.12.2.6

Wilson, C., & Mergel, I. (2022). Overcoming Barriers to Digital Government: Mapping the Strategies of Digital Champions. *Government Information Quarterly*, *39*(2), 101681. https://Doi.Org/10.1016/J.Giq.2022.101681. DOI: 10.1016/j.giq.2022.101681

Wu, W.-C. V., Wu, W.-C. V., Manabe, K., Marek, M. W., & Shu, Y. (2021). Enhancing 21st-Century Competencies Via Virtual Reality Digital Content Creation. *Journal of Research on Technology in Education*, •••, 1–22. Doi.Org/10.1080/15391523.2021.1962455

Xiao, H. (2024, November 20). Employee Role Transformation and Adaptation in Digital Transformation: Barriers, Misalignments, And Solutions in Digital Tool Application. *Deleted Journal.*, *13*(1), 33–38. Doi.Org/10.54254/2977-5701/13/2024115. DOI: 10.54254/2977-5701/13/2024115

Xu, R., Zhang, L., & Chollathanrattanapong, J. (2024). A Study of The Adaptability of Adaptive Learning Systems to Individualized Educational Strategies. Applied Mathematics and Nonlinear Sciences, 9(1). https://Doi.Org/10.2478/Amns-2024-2737

Zervas, I., & Stiakakis, E. Economic Sustainable Development Through Digital Skills Acquisition: The Role of Human Resource Leadership. Sustainability 2024 Sep 4;16(17):7664. Available From: https://Doi.Org/10.3390/Su16177664

Zhang, J., & Chen, Z. (2023). Exploring Human Resource Management Digital Transformation in The Digital Age. *Journal of the Knowledge Economy*, *15*(1), 1482–1498. https://Doi.Org/10.1007/S13132-023-01214-Y. DOI: 10.1007/s13132-023-01214-y

Zhang, X., Wang, P., & Peng, L. (2024). Developing A Competency Model for Human Resource Directors (Hrds) In Exponential Organizations Undergoing Digital Transformation. *Sustainability (Basel)*, *16*(23), 10540. https://Doi.Org/10.3390/Su162310540. DOI: 10.3390/su162310540

Chapter 14
Human Resource Development in the Digital Era:
Talent Management and Skill Enhancement

Sakshi Mann
https://orcid.org/0009-0002-8238-5268
School of Business, Indira University, Pune, India

Shikha Mann
School of Business, Indira University, Pune, India

ABSTRACT

Technological advancements have revolutionized Human Resource Development (HRD) and substituted traditional talent management. Organizations are operating in an AI-enabled, automated, big data, and digital learning environment. The chapter discusses digital transformation of HRD with focus on AI-driven hiring, digital learning, and performance tracking. The focus is on lifelong learning, upskilling, and reskilling to align with evolving industry needs. HR professionals must embrace digital enablers like Learning Management Systems (LMS), gamification, and microlearning. Remote work and the gig economy demand agile and inclusive talent solutions. Digitalization is advantageous but poses challenges in data protection, algorithmic bias, and technology resistance. The chapter, with case studies of MNCs and start-ups, provides best practices and ethical concerns in AI adoption. It finally provides strategic suggestions to HR leaders, academia, and business to align technology with people-first leadership to make HRD impactful in the digital era.

DOI: 10.4018/979-8-3373-1290-3.ch014

1. INTRODUCTION

The 21st century has seen a profound reorganization of the nature of work spurred by the extensive spread of information and communication technologies, population shifts, and economic crises. Human Resource Development (HRD), previously occupied with isolated training interventions and official career development, is now increasingly being conceptualized as a dynamic, strategic process supporting organizational learning, adaptability, and competitiveness. Contemporary organizations operate in a VUCA world, where flexibility, innovation, and capability development continuously are no longer an option, but they are a necessity (Bennett & Lemoine, 2014; Swanson, 2022).

Digitalization has also been a disruptor and an enabler. Technologies like Artificial Intelligence (AI), machine learning, robotic process automation, cloud computing, and data analytics are redefining the HR function (Marler & Boudreau, 2017; Tambe, Cappelli, & Yakubovich, 2019). These technologies allow organizations to transition from reactive to predictive talent management, individualized learning journeys, and data-driven decisions along the employee journey. As Arora and Nabi (2022) note in their analysis of the adoption of blockchain in banking systems, technology adoption is not merely about infrastructure but also cultural and ethical rebalancing, an observation also valid in the HRD context.

At the same time, expectations of the workforce have also altered significantly. Millennials and Gen Z, who represent the biggest chunk of the world's workforce today, expect not just career advancement but also flexibility, self-development, and meaningful work experiences (Pandita, 2022). The speed at which remote and hybrid work patterns have grown all over the world following the COVID-19 pandemic has also accelerated the speed to fuel the demand for digital-first HR platforms which can connect, develop, and retain a remote workforce (Carnevale & Hatak, 2020).

The new economies such as India's have a double opportunity and challenge. With its youth and big population, the country must invest now in digital empowerment and skill development to capture its demographic dividend. Programs such as Skill India, Digital India, and the sectoral missions for capacity building reflect a strategic shift towards building a future-ready, knowledge-based workforce.

Against this background, this chapter focuses on the evolving role of HRD in the digitalization era, particularly in talent management, digital learning, and skill development. This chapter attempts to ask and answer the following significant questions:

- How has the role and function of HRD evolved because of digital disruption?
- What paradigms and theoretical models inform the evolution of digitally enabled HRD?

- In what ways are learning, interaction, and growth processes reengineered by digital technology?
- What are the strategic, operational, and ethical issues in the case of e-HRD?
- How can organizations anticipate upskilling and reskilling their employees for long-term growth?

Drawn from a synthesis of theory, evidence, and practice, the chapter offers academics, practitioners, and policymakers an integrated view of the challenges and opportunities of reconceptualizing HRD to meet the demands of a complex, technology-enabled, and rapidly changing world.

2. EVOLUTION AND HISTORY OF HUMAN RESOURCE DEVELOPMENT

2.1 Evolutionary History of HRD

Human Resource Development (HRD) has been primarily focused on employment-related education, training, and coaching and mentoring, in response to industry and business growth needs. Over the 20th century, its focus broadened from skill development to organizational learning, career development, and organizational change. From reactive to proactive development approaches was the paradigm change, linking HRD with business strategy (Garavan, 2007).

The technology era has brought with it a new benchmark. Workers in the current age learn from e-learning websites, microlearning lessons, virtual reality exercises, and AI-suggested materials, a paradigm shift in learning delivery and engagement (Noe, Clarke, & Klein, 2014). The democratization of learning provided by MOOCs and digital credentialing has reduced the differences between the formal and informal learning settings (Yoo & Huang, 2013).

Above all, the change is not just technological but also philosophical. HRD philosophy in contemporary times is focused on empowerment, employee self-management, and continuous capability development are fundamental features in developing flexible and innovation-enabled workforces.

2.2 Core Conceptual Frameworks Directing Digital HRD

2.2.1 Human Capital Theory

It was formulated by Gary Becker in 1964, and Human Capital Theory emphasizes that workers are assets whose value can be cultivated through investments in education, skills, and health. In the age of the digital economy, the theory is becoming increasingly significant as organizations seek to develop not only functional skills but also digital skills, flexibility, and emotional intelligence (Subrahmanyam, 2025).

Corporate instances reinforce the pertinence. Amazon's "Upskilling 2025" program invests more than $700 million in future career development in AI, cloud computing, and cybersecurity. Indian IT majors such as Infosys and TCS also established robust in-house learning systems to connect skill development with changing business requirements (Bartlett & Ghoshal, 2002).

2.2.2 AMO Model (Ability–Motivation–Opportunity)

AMO model proposes three drivers of employee performance: ability (skills and knowledge), motivation (intrinsic motivation), and opportunity (work environment). For the digital world, it proposes personalized learning, gamification, and inclusive culture as the foundation of HRD strategy. Deloitte and Unilever are leveraging AI to create dynamic upskilling paths, involving employees with micro-certifications and assigning talent to critical jobs.

2.2.3 Ulrich's HR Model

Dave Ulrich's initial model places HR's function in four quadrants: Strategic Partner, Administrative Expert, Employee Champion, and Change Agent. Nowadays, these functions are being fulfilled through digital channels; everything from AI-driven recruitment platforms to well-being analytics and workforce planning dashboards (Yahia, Hlel, & Colomo-Palacios, 2021). The model remains a strategic compass for HR leaders in the age of digital transformation.

2.2.4 Learning Organization Theory

Peter Senge's Learning Organization Theory is all about continuous learning as the basis for innovation and responsiveness. Not only is this a wonderful concept in this era of the internet, but it is also a necessity. Google and Unilever, among others, are investing in systems thinking, knowledge sharing, and peer-to-peer learning to create responsive, forward-looking organizations.

3. LITERATURE REVIEW

The nexus between digital transformation and Human Resource Development (HRD) is increasingly being used as a theme of reference in research and practice. Nevertheless, to comprehend how digital tools, talent solutions, and learning spaces are transforming HRD, there is a necessity to scan the path of the literature across core, contemporary, and next-generation themes. This section integrates major developments across five themes: classical models of HRD, digital HR practices, geographical and contextual boundaries, ethical and inclusion issues, and theory blind spots.

3.1 Classical Foundations of HRD and Talent Management

HRD has long been theorized as a formal reaction to organizational requirements for workforce competencies. Formal training, competency building, and learning through performance were the initial concerns highlighted in early literature (Swanson, 2022). The discipline then expanded to organizational learning, leadership development, and change management, in sync with the overall objectives of human capital development (Garavan, 2007).

This strategic shift was reflected in Ruona and Gibson's (2004) alignment of HRM, HRD, and Organizational Development (OD), and calling for HRD to be embedded in the total organizational and talent design system. Swanson and Holton (2001) also stressed the foundational role of adult learning theory, systems thinking, and performance improvement in the design of HRD interventions.

Simultaneously, talent management became a career discipline of HRD. Succession planning was initially linked to the term, and its application was later extended to creating high-potential talent, acquiring, and retaining it (Collings & Mellahi, 2009). Their influential model emphasized finding key positions and channelling resources to individuals holding or about to hold these positions and thus creating disproportionate value. With increasing demands for strategic agility, as Doz (2020) noted, HRD and talent management were no longer back-office operations but organizational responsiveness drivers.

But all those older models presume quite stable work patterns, hierarchical career structures, and linear skill development trajectories as their default assumptions that are increasingly at variance with project-based, technology-enabled, and rapidly evolving work patterns today.

3.2 Digital Disruption in HRD: New Practices and Platforms

The last ten years have seen a radical transformation in the way organizations are addressing HRD, driven primarily by digital technology. Emerging technologies like Artificial Intelligence (AI), machine learning, and cloud computing have transformed learning, engagement, performance, and talent mobility.

Learning and Development (L&D) has been among the most revolutionized areas. Instructor-led training has given way to flexible, self-paced, and personalized e-learning architectures. MOOCs (Massive Open Online Courses), microlearning modules, and AI-driven learning experience platforms (LXPs) have provided scalable, just-in-time learning (Noe, Clarke, & Klein, 2014; Bokhari & Ghaffar, 2024). Indian IT majors like Infosys ("Lex") and TCS ("iON") have made significant investments in in-house learning platforms that facilitate technical upskilling and leadership development (Bartlett & Ghoshal, 2002).

Talent analytics and AI-powered recruitment also revolutionize how organizations recruit, assess, and manage talent. Predictive tools such as LinkedIn Talent Insights, HireVue, and Pymetrics apply behavioural data and machine learning to quantify the fit and potential of candidates. Tambe, Cappelli, and Yakubovich (2019) refer to this as a shift from "gut-based" to "evidence-based" talent management.

Skills-based talent models are increasingly trending globally. These models move away from job functions and move toward capabilities. Gloat, Fuel50, and other in-house marketplaces leverage AI to match employees with stretch tasks and jobs, thus enabling customized career growth (Morandini et al., 2023). This shift aligns with Jesuthasan and Kapilashrami's (2024) "skills-powered organizations" vision of agility and alignment rather than structure.

Despite these advances, digital platform integration remains uneven. Disconnected systems, data silos, and low levels of digital fluency among HR professionals are still barriers to optimal realization of these technologies' potential (Abdali, 2019).

3.3 Contextual Blind Spots: Global South, Informality, and Sectoral Gaps

Its most enduring limitation in HRD literature is its organizational and geographical scope. Most research to date is based on large, multinational companies in the Global North, usually in tech, finance, or consulting industries (Esposito, Akbar, & Campbell, 2025). Although such companies are at the fore of embracing cutting-edge digital tools, their operating context, resilient infrastructure, tech-embracing leadership, and formal labour frameworks is not typical of most global organizations.

Dynamics of these emerging economies, such as India, South Africa, and Brazil, are presented with challenges ranging from unstable digital access, skill imbalances, and informal employment systems. Alternatives such as digital credentialing, vernacular e-learning, and low-tech human resource systems may be more sustainable and effective in these contexts. Nevertheless, these alternatives are not well studied.

Moreover, small and medium-sized enterprises (SMEs), not-for-profits, and the public sector are absent from digital HRD literature. Their absence reinforces a narrow view of how HRD change takes place, ignoring learning in places where constraints are likely to drive innovation.

The gig economy is also an under-explored area. Upwork, Toptal, and corporate gig platforms are reshaping how individuals engage with organizations, but the HRD implications for gig workers learning, career development, well-being are not investigated sufficiently (Stewart & Stanford, 2017).

3.4 Ethics, Inclusion, and the Missing Voice of the Employee

As technology becomes increasingly embedded in HRD, ethics concerns about privacy, autonomy, and fairness arise. Researchers warn that AI, left unregulated, can reinforce bias, erode trust, and push people out of organizations (Scatiggio, 2020; Raghavan, Barocas, Kleinberg, & Levy, 2020). Algorithmic decision-making in promotion and hiring is often black-boxed and untested, and employees are not usually involved in design or governance discussions.

Well-being is also a growing concern. Carnevale and Hatak (2020) recognize how poorly designed digital platforms can create "technostress," engagement, or digital burnout especially in remote or hybrid work environments. Sentiment analysis and well-being tools have the potential, but only if organizations listen to employee input and if employees believe such systems are helpful and not surveillance based.

There is also scant research that reflects the learning experience of workers in digital spaces—what motivates them, what holds them back, and where learning streams cross with inclusion, psychological safety, or personal development. This absence invites more people-centred research beyond efficiency and ROI.

3.5 Fragmented Integration and Theoretical Underutilization

Although interest is increasing, e-HRD research remains scattered. Research is mainly tool or outcome oriented, rarely testing the whole life cycle of HRD interventions or connecting them with broader business strategy. According to Bondarouk and Brewster (2016), HR must evolve from a "technology user" to a "co-creator of technological value" but most models continue to place HRD into an auxiliary rather than transformational position.

The literature is also suffering from under-theorization. While older theories like Human Capital Theory or the AMO model are sometimes used, newer ones like socio-technical systems theory, institutional logics, or behavioural economics are rarely used in the field of HRD. This makes the field unable to account for phenomena like technology adoption, user resistance, or the automation-empathy balancing act.

Moreover, longitudinal and mixed-method studies are scarce. According to Jooss et al. (2024), we have no knowledge of the long-term impacts of skill-based models, online learning platforms, or algorithmic HR tools, particularly regarding outcomes like innovation, flexibility, or organisational resilience.

Garavan and McGuire (2010) demand an "ethical and sustainable HRD," but this demand remains largely an ideal in present-day literature. Practice and theory will need to be reconciled by more interdisciplinary, cross-sectoral, and critical analysis of electronic HRD.

The digital HRD and talent management literature has evolved significantly; yet more important gaps remain. These are: excessive reliance on large, Western companies; superficial alignment of digital strategy and HRD practice; poor examination of ethics and employee perspectives; and inadequate use of contemporary theoretical frameworks. These gaps need to be filled not only to advance research development but also to ensure HRD systems become inclusive, ethical, and robust to continuous disruption.

Overall, the literature of today is transitional, but not transformative. Though many frameworks and technologies are changing, more profound integration of ethical awareness, local difference, and long-term effects is still in the process of being developed. To close these gaps, scholars must go beyond single case studies or technical reviews, and approach matters systematically, at the cutting-edge intersection of people and not platforms.

4. DIGITAL TALENT MANAGEMENT: REINVENTING STRATEGY FOR A NEW ERA

As businesses are faced with relentless disruption like running from marketplace uncertainty to AI adoption, the way they manage talent is being revolutionized. Talent management is no longer a linear process of recruitment, training, and development. Instead, it is evolving into a strategic, responsive system in which technology enables businesses to discover, connect, and grow talent at velocity and scale. Pioneering this revolution is the shift towards digital-first, skills-first, and people-first models of talent strategy.

4.1 The Shift from Job Titles to Skill-Based Models

Fixed positions in a job are being substituted by skill-based design, where employees are valued not for where they fit in a hierarchy but for what they are able to bring in the way of skills to a fluid set of tasks. Jesuthasan and Kapilashrami (2024) describe this as a shift to the "skills-powered organization," where fit and flexibility are valued over tenure and role.

Companies such as Unilever, IBM, and Schneider Electric are at the forefront. Unilever's "Flex Experiences," an internal talent platform, is AI-driven to allocate employees to temporary work on short-term projects by allowing them to be matched with their strengths, interests, and aspirations. Not only does the in-house gig arrangement facilitate career advancement, but it improves project staffing and workforce agility too. IBM, for example, uses AI-driven skills maps to anticipate future needs and recommend personalized learning and job rotation to the employees reskilling becoming business-driven, real-time.

This isn't so much a technology shift; it's a sea change in how organizations do work, build talent, and approach growth.

4.2 Talent Acquisition in the AI Age

Digital adaptation does not begin once you work for the company. The recruitment process is also increasingly being fuelled by algorithmic solutions that sift through CVs, filter cognitive potential, and even analyse video interviews. HireVue and Pymetrics automate the assessment process, and LinkedIn Talent Insights allows recruiters to monitor macro-skills trends and simplify their hiring processes.

While these technologies provide scale and velocity, they also introduce enormous issues of bias and fairness. Tambe, Cappelli, and Yakubovich (2019) observe that while AI could enhance hiring consistency, it can also reinforce historical biases if biased data used to train it are utilized. Raghavan et al. (2020) observe the necessity for algorithmic audits and human monitoring to avoid unfair decision-making. Absent such controls, technology can turn into a black box which is effective but impenetrable.

Therefore, ethical governance is not an extravagance in digital talent management but a necessity that needs to be built into systems at the very beginning.

4.3 Continuous Development through Digital Learning Ecosystems

Once inside an organization, employees expect continuous, tailored, and unbroken learning. Legacy Learning Management Systems (LMS) are being supplanted by Learning Experience Platforms (LXPs) like Degreed, EdCast, and Cornerstone, which collect microlearning units, track skill growth, and integrate external content from providers like Coursera and edX.

Infosys's "Lex" platform is a case in point here in the Indian context. Built to facilitate massive employee upskilling demands, Lex hosts over 1,500 AI-driven courses in areas such as cloud computing, cybersecurity, and data analytics. What lends strength to Lex is not just its content, but also how it aligns with Infosys's internal career framework—employees who get certificated are qualified for internal mobility, promotion, and project assignment (NASSCOM, 2022).

All this is part of a greater movement to link more tightly learning with career, motivation, and organizational strategy.

4.4 From Engagement to Experience: An Integrated Approach

Talent practices no longer merely imply learning or performance. They are all about designing start-to-finish employee experiences and comprehensive journeys that include well-being, belonging, feedback, and safety. This shift recognizes that engagement is every bit as much about feeling that you are understood, supported, and heard as it is about liking what you do.

Modern-day HR technology like SAP SuccessFactors, Microsoft Viva, and Workday possess features like real-time pulse surveys, burnout prevention nudges, and intelligent feedback loops. These help organizations keep track of employees' sentiment, measure cultural fit, and detect disengagement in its early stages.

Although, as Carnevale and Hatak (2020) also warn, technology can be empowering or alienating depending on design and implementation, over-surveillance, black box metrics, or ambiguous feedback mechanisms can destroy trust. A digital-first strategy must then be human-centric to make sure that employees do not feel they are not masters of their own development, data, and career.

4.5 Implementation Challenges: Systems, Equity, and Mindsets

While digital talent solutions are value-saturated, it is challenging to execute them. System fragmentation is one of the major issues and organizations have various standalone tools, which limit data consolidation and user experience. Also, digital maturity lags in most HR teams, and therefore, it is challenging for them to execute the tools.

Equity is another issue. All workers do not gain equally from digitalization. Lower digital competencies or being in non-desk roles can make it more difficult for them to gain access to LXPs or applications of AI. This creates a "participation divide" that reflects other social inequalities—"especially in large, diverse economies such as India and Brazil" (Esposito et al., 2025).

Finally, managerial attitudes take their time to change. Command-and-control talent managers may begrudge democratization of learning or fear becoming obsolete in self-directed learning spaces. Cultural readiness is therefore as critical as technological capability.

4.6 Redesigning Talent Strategy: Integration, Ethics, and Purpose

Digital talent management is not a set of tools; it's a way of thinking. It means organizations must think of talent as dynamic, skills as assets, and learning as a strategic asset. Leaders must integrate systems, build ethical systems, and ensure that technology complements and not substitutes for human judgment.

The most ambitious companies don't initiate digital transformation as a wager to be more efficient. Instead, they use it to build resilient, inclusive, and meaningful workplaces; workplaces where talent is accumulated over several years, experiences are customized, and people are empowered to grow.

This human-centred approach brings capability development into the spotlight; reshaping capability development as a strategic facilitator rather than a back-office function, driving resilience, equity, and innovation.

5. CAPABILITY DEVELOPMENT STRATEGIES IN THE DIGITAL WORKPLACE

As businesses struggle with the pace of technology disruption speeding up, developing capabilities is no longer a back-office activity but a strategic imperative. The speed of obsolescence of skills, combined with shifting business models and talent desires, drives businesses to create flexible, future-ready talent systems. Unlike how training was conducted in the past, developing capabilities now must be embedded in the digital DNA of the business, powered by data, linked to business strategy, and scaled to levels and geographies.

5.1 Transitions from Competency Models to Dynamic Skill Frameworks

Past capability development frameworks were competency model-based that were fixed, structured matrices that defined behavioural and technical competencies for a role. While good for linear career progression, they were not able to cope with dynamic skill demands brought about by automation, digitization, and blended work.

Contemporary organizations are moving toward dynamic skill architectures, prioritizing temporal, market-sensitive skills ahead of static competencies. Solutions such as Eightfold.ai and SkyHive provide AI-powered skill intelligence to assist organizations in mapping existing talent, detecting gaps, and suggesting personalized learning journeys. Jesuthasan and Kapilashrami (2024) advocate for such systems as the drivers of the "skills-powered enterprise" where talent strategy is determined in real time, data-driven versus hierarchy-driven.

This change can be seen in both developed and emerging economies. For instance, in Singapore, the government's "SkillsFuture" program aligns national workforce planning with lifelong learning, with finance and access extended to citizens to upskill in highly sought-after digital skills (World Bank, 2022). Meanwhile, companies like Tata Steel (India) and Siemens (Germany) have set up in-company skill schools that combine technical upskilling with business programs that are enabling contextual, and continuous development.

5.2 Personalized, Digital Learning at Scale

Digital transformation has made capability development go beyond the classroom. Learning Experience Platforms (LXPs), AI-powered microlearning, and real-time feedback loops have enabled organizations to now deliver personalized development journeys at scale.

Infosys's "Lex" and Unilever's "MyLearning Hub" platforms are just an example. They integrate enterprise-wide learning with proficiency-based job design that allows employees to build skills directly applicable to internal mobility and future positions (NASSCOM, 2022). The platforms track usage, recommend next actions based on career aspirations, and link digital credentials to promotion pathways.

It is within the Global North that Siemens leverages EdCast to power its "Future Maker" program, coupling AI-facilitated learning suggestions with tangible application through project-based challenges. In other regions, the UAE Ministry of Human Resources launched a national digital capability-based platform to prepare its citizens for AI-era careers in the government and private sectors; a precursor to the way governments are increasingly taking direct stakes in capability development (UAE Gov, 2023).

The trend is simple: capability building is no longer a matter of content delivery but it's a matter of creating environments that facilitate learning-in-the-flow-of-work, directly connected to performance, engagement, and strategy.

5.3 Leadership for the Digital Age

Digital transformation has reshaped leadership as well. Capability-building is no longer simply technical skill but digital fluency, emotional intelligence, resilience, and change leadership are also joined to the mix.

Firms such as Microsoft, Novartis, and Mahindra Group have redefined leadership development to meet these needs. Novartis's "Unboss" initiative, for example, is intended to create leaders as coaches and change drivers, not managers. They are taught to drive hybrid teams, deal with data-driven intelligence, and generate psychological safety that are essential skills in distributed, digital-first environments.

In India, Infosys Global Leadership Institute (GLI) integrates neuroscience, digital business strategy, and inclusive leadership in its high-potential leader programs. Such cross-functional, integrative learning is proof of growing awareness that capability of the future is not all about technical domains, but it is also about mindsets, values, and flexibility.

5.4 Inclusion, Access, and Equity in Capability Development

A future-proof capacity approach in the strictest sense of the word must also be inclusive. Empirical research has demonstrated that online learning reaches already privileged groups who are digitally literate, urban, and highly skilled while the gig workers, return-to-work women, and non-desk or low-skilled workers are left behind (Esposito et al., 2025; Scatiggio, 2020).

Firms like Unilever and EY have started by developing capability programs that accommodate different learning styles, languages, and time zones. For instance, mobile-first, locally language content has been rolled out to factory workers in Unilever's African and Asian factories. Similarly, Amazon's Career Choice program offers frontline warehouse associates pathways to high-growth careers like IT, health care, and cloud computing.

Government initiatives are also gaining prominence. In Brazil, the Skills and Digital Inclusion Initiative aims to close rural-urban capability gaps using public-private partnerships and mobile technology labs. These strategies highlight the pivotal position of cross-sector partnerships in democratizing access to capability-enabling resources.

5.5 Linking Capability to Organizational Agility

Lastly, capability building will have to go beyond retention or compliance, it will have to become an organizational driver of agility. In today's uncertain markets, the successful companies are those where workers can learn, unlearn, and reskill rapidly, and where systems are able to reconvene talent in response to new needs.

World Economic Forum (2023) highlights "talent mobility and internal agility" as critical pillars to being future-of-work ready. Building capability must thus be modular, agile, and performance-oriented, allowing individuals and teams to react in real-time.

Agile companies inject development into business cycles through peer-to-peer learning, knowledge-sharing systems, and "development sprints." The work of HR is to build the environment in which learning occurs naturally enacted by data, digital systems, and leadership alignment.

Digital capability building is increasingly a driver of growth, a force of innovation and fairness, and a strategic one. As companies transition to develop powerful, high-performing talent pools, they are forced to adopt strategies that are global in scope, inclusive, and proactive. Companies that view learning as culture rather than function are most likely to lead and thrive.

To consolidate the strategic factors outlined in this section, the framework below captures the most vital digitally integrated HRD enablers.

Figure 1. The integrated framework for digital HRD transformation

Source: Developed by the authors (2025).

This conceptual model charts the dynamic interplay between Talent Management, Capability Development, Technology Integration, and Ethical Governance in the interdependent ecosystem of industry, academia, and government. It simplifies to Digital Human Resource Development as the strategic driver to organizational outcomes of agility, inclusion, and growth.

6. DILEMMAS AND ETHICAL CHALLENGES OF E-HRD

Whereas digital transformation is powerful drivers of Human Resource Development (HRD), it is also highly challenging in both operational and moral aspect. When companies adopt AI-based systems, digital learning platforms, as well as people analytics software, new questions of fairness, inclusion, surveillance, autonomy, and accountability are being faced. These cannot be seen as technical challenges; they are manifestations of deeper tensions in the evolving nexus of people, work, and technology.

6.1 Surveillance and Data Privacy

Arguably the most urgent concern in e-HRD is the collection, storage, and utilization of employee data. Learning activity tracking software, behaviour metrics tracking software, or communication pattern analysis software can be useful, but also intrusive.

Surveillance procedures that appear in disguise as productivity or performance management can lead to psychological distress and mistrust. Carnevale and Hatak (2020) warn that poorly implemented digital systems are going to generate "technostress," diminishing instead of improving well-being.

These are not theoretical concerns. In India, call centre staff have protested constant keyboard and screen monitoring. In Europe, due to GDPR regulations necessitating greater control of data, a few companies have been legally contested for the use of facial recognition and biometric clock-in software. The balance between data-based wisdom and employee autonomy is tenuous, especially in remote or hybrid work environments where boundaries between work and personal life are already fragile.

6.2 Algorithmic Bias and Discrimination

But another moral concern is bias in algorithmic decision-making, here in hiring, promotion, and so-called tailored learning. AI algorithms are no more neutral than the data that they are trained on. If previous hiring practices were biased towards groups, so can be programmed and amplified by the algorithm (Raghavan et al., 2020).

That has real-world consequences. Amazon cancelled an AI recruiting tool after it was found to suppress resumes with the word "women" in them, a typical word in a training dataset filled with mostly male candidates. Likewise, in the United States, the Equal Employment Opportunity Commission (EEOC) has opened investigations of hiring software companies whose tools were found to hold back neurodiverse and minority candidates.

In emerging economies, where data may be absent or culturally biased, dangers are compounded. Esposito et al. (2025) observe that enterprises in the Global South must be especially cautious, with AI systems locally contextualized, regularly audited, and transparent in logic.

6.3 Unbalanced Access and Digital Exclusion

Computer HRD tools tend to assume for granted that all employees have access to devices, connectivity, and digital literacy. In practice, such an assumption creates exclusion.

Low-bandwidth workers, frontline workers, or informal workers won't be able to access or gain benefits from digital capacity-development. Rural workers in Brazil were observed to be left behind from national digital upskilling because they had poor mobile data access (World Bank, 2022). In tier-3 cities of India, most organizations are still using paper-based HRD practices because of infrastructure gaps.

Besides, women, older workers, and disabled individuals are disproportionately affected by these limitations. Scatiggio (2020) warns that digital HR technologies might inadvertently widen extant inequalities if they are not created with inclusive intent.

To fight back, organizations need to implement universal design principles, provide alternative learning modes (e.g., audio classes via mobile, local language videos), and onboard digital platforms as primary HRD strategies.

6.4 AI-Driven HR: Transparency and Accountability

HR AI is typically black-boxed i.e., both employees and HR leaders have no complete visibility into decision-making. That "black box" erodes trust and generates a sense of lack of accountability. Who gets the blame when an AI-generated performance rating means a missed promotion? Who inspects the learning algorithm if it systematically suggests fewer leadership courses to women?

Raghavan et al. (2020) and Tambe et al. (2019) highlight algorithmic transparency, regular audits, and cross-functional governance mechanisms. Systemic HRD demands measures where human control is embedded and through which employees can appeal and object to machine-generated decisions.

To counter, certain organizations are adopting Explainable AI (XAI) in HR, systems that provide transparent explanations for each decision rendered. Though still on the rise, the practice is crucial to guaranteeing fairness, transparency, and redress.

6.5 Cultural and Legal Ambiguity

Finally, digital HRD ethical conduct varies significantly across countries and cultures. What is intrusive in one culture is acceptable in the other. In Germany, there are stringent labour laws against digital surveillance, while in the Philippines or Kenya, the same would be acceptable in terms of law but contentious from a cultural perspective.

The absence of worldwide HR technology regulation guarantees that multinational firms often operate with uneven ethics worldwide. Garavan and McGuire (2010) suggest that HRD practitioners must develop ethically adaptive strategies, that are value-driven yet flexible to legal and cultural diversity.

A global ethics also demands HR to address not only compliance by corporations but also to operate based on greater social objectives like digital inclusion, dignity of labour, and human-centred innovation.

Digital HRD is full of promise but it must be guided by values centring on equity, transparency, and trust. Ethical capability-building cannot be an afterthought; it must be built into technologies, codified into systems, and embedded through leadership. As businesses invest in future-proof HRD, they must ask not just what their tools can do, but what they ought to do.

What this ethical contemplation produces is not the rejection of digital technology, but the need for intentionality. The destiny of HRD will depend on how far organizations can balance innovation and responsibility, scale and care, and performance and people-focused values. Ethical agility, the ability to take principles from one situation and apply them to another without compromising core values, can be the most significant competence of HR leaders in the future.

7. BUILDING COLLABORATION: A STRATEGIC IMPERATIVE FOR SCALABLE HRD

As digital transformation redefines Human Resource Development (HRD), it becomes increasingly clear that it will be not possible for any one of the stakeholders; HR, tech, gov, or academics to handle the range of issues around skill development, digital engagement, and sustainable talent management in a siloed fashion. The future of HRD is collaboration: within and across disciplines, sectors, and geographies. Collaborations multiply the reach of intervention as well as inclusivity, cultural sensitivity, and sustainability.

7.1 Cross-Functional Teamwork in Organizations

Within organizations, successful digital HRD requires tight collaboration among HR, IT, learning and development (L&D), data teams, and business leadership. HR experts may not necessarily have technical expertise to deploy AI-powered learning platforms or analytics tools; technologists may not have behavioural know-how to create learner-focused systems.

Forward-looking organizations are establishing cross-functional HR innovation squads. IBM and Google, for example, each have distinct "people analytics" squads made up of behavioural scientists, statisticians, and HR leaders working together. These squads not only track engagement but also use predictive modelling to inform leadership pipelines and capability needs (Tambe et al., 2019).

These models allow firms to treat learning not as an isolated function but as the central component of business transformation ensuring that HRD interventions are evidence-based, scalable, and context-sensitive.

7.2 Industry-Academia-Government Partnerships

Apart from the organizational level, public-private-academic partnership is also a key factor. Governments globally are introducing national mission skill development with employers and universities to fill talent gaps and minimize digital disparity.

The Singapore "SkillsFuture" program, for instance, is a tripartite initiative that brings together government sponsorship, university course design, and employer engagement to provide citizens modular, in-demand upskilling streams (World Bank, 2022).

In India, the National Skill Development Corporation (NSDC) partners with industry bodies like NASSCOM and educational institutions to certify training centres and launch mass-scale vocational learning programs mainly focusing on rural and semi-skilled people.

Likewise, Germany's dual education system is a model for the world in terms of cooperation between industry and education, integrating school-based formal education with on-the-job vocational training to provide a constant supply of workforce-ready graduates.

They encapsulate the key point: effective HRD at scale requires systems thinking and coordination among multiple stakeholders who can each address a distinct layer of the ecosystem; policy, pedagogy, access, and application.

7.3 Technology Provider and Startups Partnership

HR technology start-ups are now key collaborators for digital HRD innovation, offering learning platforms, engagement, talent mobility, and evaluation. Organizations now partner with edtech and HRtech vendors strategically, not only as service providers but also as co-creators.

For instance, Unilever partnered with Degreed to make its "MyLearning Hub" personalized, incorporating content from Coursera, edX, as well as knowledge bases to offer people customized learning experiences to 100,000+ workers. Similarly, Infosys partnered with Coursera to implement certification-based learning on its "Lex" platform, linking digital badges to career progression.

Tech startups also offer localized, mobile-first solutions in the Global South. Indian startups like upGrad and EnglishBolo offer vernacular, mobile-friendly learning content for first-generation learners and gig workers. Such alliances ensure that HRD strategies are inclusive, culturally relevant, and context specific.

The future of capability development will not be driven by large enterprise platforms but by nimble, focused partnerships with innovators who are able to respond rapidly to new needs and communities.

7.4 Enabling Joint Metrics and Governance

One of the biggest barriers to effective collaboration is that there are no shared metrics of success. Universities may be tracking enrolments, employers' retention, and platform engagement, but without coordination, these metrics don't mean much.

More recent ones like the OECD Skills Strategy promote shared measurement frameworks measuring outcomes across institutions; cognitive, digital, and soft skill development. Similarly, large employers are partnering with university researchers to develop longitudinal studies quantifying the long-term impact of learning interventions on performance, equity, and well-being (Jooss et al., 2024).

Collaboration should also have governance structures that set moral standards, data privacy guidelines, and equitable access requirements. The European Union Digital Skills and Jobs Coalition provides a governance structure for cross-sector collaboration, practiced with transparency, inclusivity, and accountability.

In an age of hyper connection, it's not a matter of whether we work together but a matter of strategic necessity. Whether it's cross-functional HR operations, government-industry collaborations, or co-designed learning systems, the future of HRD is an ecosystem, not a silo. Organizations that invest capital in collaborative capability like trust, common purposes, sharing data, and co-innovation will be best positioned to grow capability development in a human-centric, ethical, and globally applicable way.

What distinguished high-impact collaboration is not just shared infrastructure or investment, but shared purpose. In global coalitions or neighbourhood alliances, thriving ecosystems are ones that honour contextual realities but are working towards shared capability goals. As differences between talent development and economic development blur more and more, collaborative HRD will be the prime catalyst for inclusive, resilient, and future-resilient societies.

8. CONCLUSION AND FUTURE DIRECTIONS

This chapter has attempted to explore the ways in which Human Resource Development (HRD) is being reconfigured in the context of accelerating technological change, changing workforce demographics, and changing organizational agendas. Through an interrelated examination of talent management, capability development, ethical considerations, and collaborative approaches, we have attempted to capture both the promise and contradictions of the digital transformation of HRD.

At the heart of this shift is a profound philosophical transformation: from HRD as a transactional support function to HRD as a strategic, systemic, and human-focused facilitator of organizational agility and societal resilience. Whether AI-driven learning platforms, skills-first talent models, or collaborative national skilling projects, the evidence is that organizations are starting to view development as a cost and not an expense.

But this change is not equal or unstructured. As the chapter has argued, attempts to build digital capability tend to reproduce existing inequalities unless designed expressly inclusive. Algorithmic technologies are possible drivers of efficiency but also possible drivers of built in prejudice where not suitably managed. Intersectoral partnership is of immense potential but most often hindered by internally fragmented systems, conflicting incentives, or missing metrics. These issues underpin the need for ethical adaptability, interdisciplinarity, and contextual understanding in the creation of future HR systems.

Going back to the research questions posed in the introduction, the following are the contributions of this chapter:

- **On HRD development:** The profession is shifting away from event-driven, role-based training to dynamic, competency-based development frameworks that are based on time-critical business needs and individual development patterns.
- **On guiding frameworks:** Conceptual models such as Human Capital Theory, AMO Framework, Ulrich's HR roles, and Learning Organization Theory provide a strong foundation for practice even in digital realities. They

were also incorporated in the conceptual model in Section 7, where there was a template for future-proof HRD.

- **For digital talent practices:** Organizations are increasingly leveraging AI-powered platforms, internal talent marketplaces, and predictive analytics to reimagine learning, mobility, and engagement. But their success or failure depends on their ethical design, human governance, and inclusive accessibility.
- **On ethics and challenges:** Data privacy, algorithmic bias, inequities in access, and the transparency of decision-making resources must be addressed right away. Ethical considerations, regulatory harmonization, and employee voice must be incorporated into all digital HRD initiatives.
- **On collaboration:** The future of HRD is founded on the strength of ecosystems rather than silos. Public-academic-private partnership, co-creation with start-ups, and cross-functional integration of HR are the drivers of large-scale, inclusive impact.

8.1 Suggestions for Future Studies

To build on this, subsequent research may address the following issues:

- Longitudinal observation studies of the effects of online HRD on performance, retention, and well-being across industries and geographic regions.
- Intersectional studies of gender, age, class, caste, and disability intersections with digital HRD opportunities access, particularly in developing economies.
- Cross-continental comparison of skill development models (e.g., SkillsFuture, NSDC, EU's Skills Agenda) to determine lessons transferable.
- Develop research in Explainable AI (XAI), ethical learning algorithms, and human-centered digital learning interfaces.
- Measurement systems that go beyond use rates or completion rates to measure actual capability development and involvement.

8.2 Final Reflections

As work continues to change, HRD will not only have to reskill people but transform organizations and societies. Digital transformation in this scenario must be envisioned not as a destination but as a rolling process, it must be supported by foresight, by flexibility, and most importantly, a people commitment.

The thesis of this chapter is straightforward: Digital HRD is not technology, it's developing systems of human growth suitable for a networked, complex, and continuously changing world. Those firms that recognize this imperative, and act upon it with purpose and integrity, will be the success stories, not only financially, but ethically.

REFERENCES

Appelbaum, E. (2000). *Manufacturing advantage: Why high-performance work systems pay off.* Cornell University Press.

Arora, S., & Nabi, T. (2022). Blockchain adoption in banking systems: A boon or bane? In *Applications, challenges, and opportunities of blockchain technology in banking and insurance* (pp. 19–42). IGI Global. DOI: 10.4018/978-1-6684-4133-6.ch002

Asfahani, A. M. (2024). Fusing talent horizons: The transformative role of data integration in modern talent management. *Discover Sustainability*, *5*(1), 25. DOI: 10.1007/s43621-024-00212-7

Bartlett, C. A., & Ghoshal, S. (2002). Building competitive advantage through people. *MIT Sloan Management Review*, *43*(2), 34.

Bennett, N., & Lemoine, J. (2014). What VUCA really means for you. *Harvard Business Review*, *92*(1/2).

Bokhari, S. S. A., & Ghaffar, A. (2024). Emerging Trends In Human Resource Management: Exploring Digital Transformation, Employee Well-Being, And Remote Work Paradigms. *Journal for Business Education and Management*, *4*(2), 1–16. DOI: 10.56596/jbem.v4i2.139

Bondarouk, T., & Brewster, C. (2016). Conceptualising the future of HRM and technology research. *International Journal of Human Resource Management*, *27*(21), 2652–2671. DOI: 10.1080/09585192.2016.1232296

Boudreau, J. W., & Jesuthasan, R. (2011). *Transformative HR: how great companies use evidence-based change for sustainable advantage*. John Wiley & Sons.

Carnevale, J. B., & Hatak, I. (2020). Employee adjustment and well-being in the era of COVID-19: Implications for human resource management. *Journal of Business Research*, *116*, 183–187. DOI: 10.1016/j.jbusres.2020.05.037 PMID: 32501303

Collings, D. G., & Mellahi, K. (2009). Strategic talent management: A review and research agenda. *Human Resource Management Review*, *19*(4), 304–313. DOI: 10.1016/j.hrmr.2009.04.001

Doz, Y. (2020). Fostering strategic agility: How individual executives and human resource practices contribute. *Human Resource Management Review*, *30*(1), 100693. DOI: 10.1016/j.hrmr.2019.100693

Esposito, M., Akbar, Y., & Campbell, F. X. (2025). *Digitalization in Emerging Economies*. Cambridge University Press. DOI: 10.1017/9781009433921

Garavan, T. N. (2007). A strategic perspective on human resource development. *Advances in Developing Human Resources*, *9*(1), 11–30. DOI: 10.1177/1523422306294492

Garavan, T. N., & McGuire, D. (2010). Human resource development and society: Human resource development's role in embedding corporate social responsibility, sustainability, and ethics in organizations. *Advances in Developing Human Resources*, *12*(5), 487–507. DOI: 10.1177/1523422310394757

Garavan, T. N., & McGuire, D. (2010). Human resource development and society: Human resource development's role in embedding corporate social responsibility, sustainability, and ethics in organizations. *Advances in Developing Human Resources*, *12*(5), 487–507. DOI: 10.1177/1523422310394757

Jesuthasan, R., & Kapilashrami, T. (2024). *The Skills-Powered Organization: The Journey to the Next-Generation Enterprise*. MIT Press. DOI: 10.7551/mitpress/15432.001.0001

Jesuthasan, R., & Kapilashrami, T. (2024). *The Skills-Powered Organization: The Journey to the Next-Generation Enterprise*. MIT Press. DOI: 10.7551/mitpress/15432.001.0001

Kareem, M. A. (2019). The impact of human resource development on organizational effectiveness: An empirical study. *Management Dynamics in the Knowledge Economy*, *7*(1), 29–50. DOI: 10.25019/mdke/7.1.02

Kässi, O., & Lehdonvirta, V. (2018). Online labour index: Measuring the online gig economy for policy and research. *Technological Forecasting and Social Change*, *137*, 241–248. DOI: 10.1016/j.techfore.2018.07.056

Marin-Garcia, J. A., & Tomas, J. M. (2016). Deconstructing AMO framework: A systematic review. Intangible capital, 12(4), 1040-1087.

Marler, J. H., & Boudreau, J. W. (2017). An evidence-based review of HR Analytics. *International Journal of Human Resource Management*, *28*(1), 3–26. DOI: 10.1080/09585192.2016.1244699

Morandini, S., Fraboni, F., De Angelis, M., Puzzo, G., Giusino, D., & Pietrantoni, L. (2023). The impact of artificial intelligence on workers' skills: Upskilling and reskilling in organisations. *Informing Science*, *26*, 39–68. DOI: 10.28945/5078

Noe, R. A., Clarke, A. D., & Klein, H. J. (2014). Learning in the twenty-first-century workplace. *Annual Review of Organizational Psychology and Organizational Behavior*, *1*(1), 245–275. DOI: 10.1146/annurev-orgpsych-031413-091321

Pandita, D. (2022). Innovation in talent management practices: Creating an innovative employer branding strategy to attract generation Z. *International Journal of Innovation Science*, *14*(3/4), 556–569. DOI: 10.1108/IJIS-10-2020-0217

Raghavan, M., Barocas, S., Kleinberg, J., & Levy, K. (2020, January). Mitigating bias in algorithmic hiring: Evaluating claims and practices. In *Proceedings of the 2020 conference on fairness, accountability, and transparency* (pp. 469-481). DOI: 10.1145/3351095.3372828

Raghavan, M., Barocas, S., Kleinberg, J., & Levy, K. (2020, January). Mitigating bias in algorithmic hiring: Evaluating claims and practices. In *Proceedings of the 2020 conference on fairness, accountability, and transparency* (pp. 469-481). DOI: 10.1145/3351095.3372828

Ruona, W. E., & Gibson, S. K. (2004). The making of twenty-first-century HR: An analysis of the convergence of HRM, HRD, and OD. Human Resource Management: Published in Cooperation with the School of Business Administration, The University of Michigan and in alliance with the Society of Human Resources Management, 43(1), 49-66.

Scatiggio, V. (2020). Tackling the issue of bias in artificial intelligence to design ai-driven fair and inclusive service systems. How human biases are breaching into ai algorithms, with severe impacts on individuals and societies, and what designers can do to face this phenomenon and change for the better.

Stewart, A., & Stanford, J. (2017). Regulating work in the gig economy: What are the options? *Economic and Labour Relations Review*, *28*(3), 420–437. DOI: 10.1177/1035304617722461

Stewart, A., & Stanford, J. (2017). Regulating work in the gig economy: What are the options? *Economic and Labour Relations Review*, *28*(3), 420–437. DOI: 10.1177/1035304617722461

Subrahmanyam, S. (2025). Employee Skillsets in the Digital Age. In Organizational Sociology in the Digital Age (pp. 369-388). IGI Global Scientific Publishing. DOI: 10.4018/979-8-3693-7398-9.ch018

Swanson, R. A. (2022). *Foundations of human resource development.* Berrett-Koehler Publishers.

Swanson, R. A. (2022). *Foundations of human resource development.* Berrett-Koehler Publishers.

Tambe, P., Cappelli, P., & Yakubovich, V. (2019). Artificial intelligence in human resources management: Challenges and a path forward. *California Management Review, 61*(4), 15–42. DOI: 10.1177/0008125619867910

Torraco, R. J., & Lundgren, H. (2020). What HRD is doing—What HRD should be doing: The case for transforming HRD. *Human Resource Development Review, 19*(1), 39–65. DOI: 10.1177/1534484319877058

Urme, U. N. (2023). The impact of talent management strategies on employee retention. *International Journal of Science and Business, 28*(1), 127–146. DOI: 10.58970/IJSB.2209

Yahia, N. B., Hlel, J., & Colomo-Palacios, R. (2021). From big data to deep data to support people analytics for employee attrition prediction. *IEEE Access : Practical Innovations, Open Solutions, 9*, 60447–60458. DOI: 10.1109/ACCESS.2021.3074559

Yoo, S. J., & Huang, W. D. (2013). Engaging online adult learners in higher education: Motivational factors impacted by gender, age, and prior experiences. *The Journal of Continuing Higher Education, 61*(3), 151–164. DOI: 10.1080/07377363.2013.836823

Chapter 15
HR Evolution in Gig Economy: Strategies for Agility and Efficiency

Tanya Rabban
https://orcid.org/0009-0009-5925-8384
Chandigarh University, India

Rohan Singh
https://orcid.org/0000-0002-3588-4876
Chandigarh University, India

ABSTRACT

The gig economy, revolutionized with the dynamics of the workforce and driven by digital platforms, offers businesses flexibility, while passing the challenges in human resources management. The chapter investigates the evolution in the gig economy and the implications for HR practices which could address the challenges such as agility and workforce differentiation for efficiency. Through the actionable strategies for onboarding, recruitment, performance managed tailored towards gig works. This chapter also highlights the cost efficiency and ethical workforce management approaches. By aligning the practices with agility and efficiency, it offers the road-map to the business for leveraging the gig economy as a competitive advantage.

DOI: 10.4018/979-8-3373-1290-3.ch015

INTRODUCTION

The concept of agility within the gig economy revolves around the ability of the business to swiftly adapt to market demands and changes in the workforce with technological integrations. Unlike the traditional employment models, which require longer-term commitments and hierarchies, the gig economy ensures the business is more responsive and flexible with cost-effectiveness to leverage the on-demand workforce. (Vu & Nguyen, 2024). The key drivers for the agility to move swiftly and with the availability of the on-demand workforce(Fuller et al., 2020). The companies can hire gig workers or freelancers for short-term projects, allowing them to work on the rotations quickly without exceeding the employment contracts. This model ensures that the business can execute projects efficiently while optimizing the allocation of resources based on real-time needs (Lo & Hsieh, 2023). Another aspect is efficiency, which has key advantages through cost optimization and streamlines (Bateyo, 2025). In contrast to the traditional employment models, wherein the focused costs like benefits and office institutions are huge, the gig economy enables businesses to hire workers on a task basis and eliminate any overhead expenses(Fuller et al., 2020: Cika, 2021). This particular approach shall increase the optional sustainability and flexibility. The gig economy emergency is result-oriented, which is the key advantage of this economy focusing on efficiency through time management and streamlined workflows. The pay-per-task structure significantly minimise expenses to better allocate resources where needed. Efficiency in the gig economy is reflected in the ability to save more time. Organizations onboard skilled professionals for the projects without undergoing recruitment or training. Even the gig workers are highly specialized in the fields and have fewer supervisors who could deliver higher quality work within the adhered deadlines(Elayan, 2022). The efficiency allows the buses to meet more fluctuating demands and the project as a department without committing to long-term employment contracts (Cika, 2021). Furthermore, scalability and adaptability play an integral role in enhancing efficiency within the context of the gig economy. The businesses could scale the workforce based on their demands and ensure optimal resource utilization. This dynamic workforce management can prevent unnecessary expenditures during peak periods and maintain seamless operations while demand is high. Effective HR practices enable businesses to scale the workforce without excessive administrative burden, creating a more sustainable model for employers and workers (Bateyo, 2025). In the gig economy, wherein the employment structures are based on projects and decentralized, the balance of agility and efficiency is essential for improving workforce productivity and maintaining compliance with labour regulations.

Understanding Agility and Efficiency within the Gig Economy Context

The gig economy is a dynamic workforce redefining traditional employment by shifting from full-time roles towards task-based and freelancing work models. The shift is primarily driven by the digital platform, which could connect businesses with independent workers, facilitating remote and flexible employment opportunities. Companies like Uber, Zomato, and Upwork have transformed the organization's access and management talent, minimizing the dependency on traditional workforce structures(Elayan, 2022). With a more significant advantage in cloud computing and artificial intelligence, digital platforms have made it much easier for businesses to hire specialized workers from different geographies and foster a globally connected labour market. A shift in human resources is necessitated with the rapid transformation in the working environments, emphasizing agility and efficiency as the critical factors for success. Agility in Human Resources refers to the ability of the organization to adapt quickly to changes in workforce dynamics, which include the evolution of job roles, demands in the market, and emerging technologies(Elayan, 2022). It enables the HR process to remain flexible and responsive while being proactive. Organizations are, therefore, allowed to attract and retain talent in the labour market. On the contrary, Efficiency in Human Resources focuses on maximising productivity to optimize costs and resources. This chapter delves into the evolving role of HR in managing gig work, exploring the key strategies for agility and efficiency(Fuller et al., 2020). It provides actionable insights into the businesses to optimise recruitment, compensation and workforce integration to ensure ethical and suitable employment practices. The aim is to have a comprehensive roadmap enabling the organization to leverage the gig economy as one of the competitive advantages to foster a fair and supportive work environment for the workers.

Another driving force that supports the gig economy is the change in the workforce's preference towards flexibility and autonomy. Many professionals practice project-based engagement, which allows them to maintain a work-life balance rather than being rigid and having full-time roles(Fuller et al., 2020). For the business, there is a shift that offers significant cost advantages by reducing overhead expenses and offering flexibility for scaling the workforce based on fluctuations in demand(Elayan, 2022). With the gig economy pricing benefits, there are challenges related to workforce differentiation, compensational models, and performance management; organisations must develop agile and efficient HR strategies that accommodate gig workers, enhance innovation and be suitable for the longer run. The chapter revolves around the central and sub-research question.

How can the organization develop agile and efficient human resource management strategies for optimizing gig workers and ensuring mutual benefits for workers and platforms?

- What challenges and opportunities do gig workers and freelancers face regarding human resource management?
- How can organizations engage in HR practices to foster sustainable productivity and innovation?
- How can organizations balance flexibility and regulatory compliance while employing gig workers?

Literature Review

Gig workers come from various backgrounds with different skills and employment motivations. Some individuals choose gig work for its flexibility, ensuring they manage their personal and professional lives. On the other hand, others view gig work as a side income source, specifically for those working to operate in highly skilled professions like data analysis and content creation, and others engage themselves in lesser specialized work, which includes food delivery and ride-sharing. The National Council of Applied Economic Research conducted a survey in 2023 titled: Socio-Economic Impact Assessment of Food Delivery Platform Workers," which provided valuable insights into the demographics and characteristics of gig workers in the food delivery sector of India. The survey revealed that most food delivery platforms are aged 35, with an average of 28. This also determines a younger workforce. Regarding education, 90% of the workers have completed 10th grade, and 40% in Tier 2 cities hold college diplomas. It suggests that the gig economy not only attracts less educated individuals but also includes those with higher educational qualifications who are seeking flexibility in employment opportunities.

A study conducted by McKinsey Global Institute found that 30% of the workforce in developed economies are engaged in gig work, with a higher concentration among the younger workers seeking autonomy in their careers (Manyika et al., 2016). The composition of gender in gig work varies in industries. For example, women are more attracted to social media management or tutoring, whereas men dominate the field with the technologically driven gig workers and food delivery workers. Industries rely on gig work in terms of the nature of operations. The ride-hailing and food delivery industry represented by companies such as Zomato, Uber, and Swiggy exemplifies the sector, which depends entirely on the gig workers and the drivers operate towards flexible schedules without having fixed employment contracts. Similarly, delivery services reduce the fixation laborious and ensure on-demand efficiency within the logistic sectors. On the other hand, creative industries have also witnessed the significance of gig workforce integration. Platforms such as Upwork and Freelancer.con also provide business access towards highly skilled freelancers in digital marketing. Recognizing the growing trend for on-demand work, Microsoft has partnered with Upwork, which is leading an online marketplace connecting freelancers and businesses. The collaboration offers enterprises easy access to curated oil from Microsoft Azure certification. The professionals undergo the certifications at expert and associate levels. This ensures the agility and quality in service delivery. (Microsoft, 2022).

Workplace Planning

Strategic workforce planning within the gig economy requires organizations to balance flexibility, workforce engagement and resource optimization to align the gig employment models with organizational goals that are much broader(Fuller et al., 2020). Companies must ensure that workforce planning meets the demands of the operations and addresses the characteristics of gig work arrangements. One of the notable instances of effectiveness in workforce planning is seen in the talent acquisition model of Airbnb, which integrates gig workers across different functions, from customer support to content development. It leveraged the decentralized hiring models wherein professionals across different geographical regions contribute towards the brand bulging on a demand basis. The approach has enabled the company to scale the workforce without increasing the full-time employment costs, ensuring agility in their allocation of resources. Bateyo (2025) in their paper examines the areas for reimagining workforce strategies for improvements in gig workforce management and building more continuous models for feedback within the organization towards gig workers.

Aligning Gig Workforce Models with Organizational Goals

There is an organization that develops clever workforce segmentation strategies that can distinguish gig roles from full-time positions. The growing reliance on gig workers across efficient industries necessitated incorporating workforce segmentation to optimize labour utilization. The emergence of digital platforms has fundamentally reshaped workplace planning strategies. Kathuria et al. (2017) highlight the transformation of potential and online freelancing, focusing towards digital platforms that ensure organisations' access to the distributed workforce at lower costs. The research also underscores the fig world offering the advantages of increased labour market flexibility; it presented the challenges related to worker protection, inconsistent earnings, and job scarcity.

In their paper, Lo and Hsieh (2024) explain the working patterns in which the gig economy is aligned with how companies adopt the hybrid workforce model. Another such case is Google while they are engaging with the gig workers through their "**extended workforce strategy**".The company employs a more significant number of contract and gig workers who are often full-time employees(Fuller et al., 2020). The workers handle different roles, including product testing, IT support and content moderation. By segmenting gig tasks based on the ends of the project, Google ensures that the workforce planning strategy supports efficiency in costs and innovation (Google, 2020). This strategy has allowed Google to ensure that skilled professionals do specialized tasks on a demand basis. Building a scalable hiring model is efficient for workforce planning, and digital talent platforms' role in streamlining recruitment and onboarding processes is significant (Keegan & Meijerink, 2022). Platforms like Upwork and Freelancer offer businesses the aces towards a global talent pool and reduce hiring costs.

Horney (2016) explains that HR leaders must adapt to agile strategies to manage evolving employment models. The rise of gig workers has introduced unprecedented unpredictability into conventional employment models, which is making it necessary to shift towards agile HR practices. This shift is leading towards disruptions as organizations must be able to rapidly adjust their workforce structures with the response towards fluctuation demands. HR planning requires more technology to streamline talent acquisition and workforce segmentation. The conventional HR practices are slower adaptation, which could be detrimental in this fast-paced gig workforce environment. The companies shall leverage the digital talent platforms, which could create more on-demand talent pools and allow them to match the skills with the project's requirements efficiently. This has also been reinforced by Keegan & Meijerink (2022), who have explored the online labour platform ecosystem, blaming the business towards capturing the value of dynamically adjusting the structure of the workforce. Organizations like PwC and Deloitte have also developed compliance frameworks that could allow businesses to navigate the legal complexities to benefit from the flexibility of gig labour (Krishnan & Mishra, 2021).

Master et al. (2024), in the paper, have determined the global popularity within the gig economy, including freelancers and online platform workers. The study for review emphasises the gig economy and explores working for alternative working arrangements. A systematic literature review was conducted based on 258 studies on gig work. (Keegan & Meijerink, 2022) The study used gig work profiles to define the patterns in workforce strategies. The findings show that the gig economy needs to reshape HR practices within digital applications. The recent studies "Uber Happy? Work and Well being in the Gig Economy" (2022) by Berger et al. has shown a popular promise for gig workers but raises concerns about workers' well-being with a lack of HR practices.

Performance and Engagement in the Context of the Gig Economy

Management of performance and Engagement in the gig economy requires a fundamental departure from the conventional HR approaches. Unlike full-time employees, gig workers operate with a higher degree of flexibility and often lack direct supervision or structured work environments. Businesses must implement agility in HR practices, which could ensure having more quality output and enhance the motivation of the workers while also maintaining operational efficiency(Jacob & Shaikh, 2023, p. 62). Given the autonomous and decentralized gig work nature, organizations must adapt to agile HR practices focusing on outcome-based performance metrics and real-time feedback mechanisms with dynamic compensation models to ensure productivity.

Outcome-Based Performance Metrics

Traditional performance evaluations are more centred on longer-term goals and reviews, which are unsuitable for gig workers engaged in short-term tasks. Instead, outcome-based metrics could be implemented to assess the deliverables and client satisfaction more efficiently. For instance, platforms such as Upwork utilise milestones-based evaluations wherein the freelancers are accessed with the completion of the project and the feedback of the clients, which ensures accountability (Hodor, 2020). Traditional performance metrics like attendance tracking are inefficient in gig-based working arrangements. The performance needs to be evaluated using the outcome-based criteria, which could emphasize the deliverables, customer satisfaction and the quality of service. For instance, Uber's driver rating system assesses drivers (Gig workers) based on the complete rates of the rides, customer feedback, and adherence to service guidelines rather than any reviews from managers or logging hours. Similarly, the freelancer platforms employ them based on the rating, which is linked towards the completion of the project. This system helps create transparency with the result-driven performance structures for scoring a higher quality delivery and giving gig workers transparent performance expectations. HR agility plays an integral role in developing and designing these evaluation systems. The company must have real-time data analytics and AI-driven tracking tools that could monitor the production of gig workers continuously; for instance, driver feedback systems should always leverage GPS tracking to provide insights for punctuality and efficiency. By using such tools, the human resources teams could also make more evidence-based decisions and ensure more gig work is aligned with the goals of the businesses. Moreover, companies are investing in the professional growth of gig workers with access to training programs and skill development. The investment is not just advantageous for the gig worker but also improves the quality of work that is being delivered. The report by Deloittte (2024) highlights that the organization is focusing towards upskilling gig workers to gain leverage in this dynamic market.

Real-Time Feedback Mechanism

This decentralized structure also underscores the significance of immediate feedback to facilitate more continuous enhancements. Utilizing digital communication towards AI-driven permanent tracking systems can also provide these gig workers with rapid ingots of their performance(Pine, 2023). For example, companies should adopt performance management processes, which include regular check-in and feedback sessions, with a sense of inclusion and recognition within gig works. The fluidity of the economy demands that HR practices be agile and efficient. Adding technology for streamlined tracking can minimize the overhead and enhance the response times. This could better align the gig worker contribution with the goal of the organization, ensuring a more productive workforce.

Performance-Based Compensation

Based on the real-time needs of the market, the workers can maximize their earnings. Compensation management in the gig economy context requires task-based and demand-driven models. Not having a fixed salary structure, the gig work compensation is based on variables such as market demand and peak working hours. A company like DoorDash uses dynamic pricing models wherein the workers are offered higher compensation for higher-demand tasks or during the operation periods. The agile pricing strategies benefit both the workers and businesses. Considering the financial perspective, performance pay shall provide a cost-effective alternative to traditional structures. Hodor (2022) suggests that firms can reduce labour costs by 22% by leveraging gig workers with pay models like dynamic pricing, especially during surge periods. The findings also recognized that HR practices with compensation models should align with the agility in workforce segmentation, ensuring the companies attract and retain talent. However, with the gig-based incentives, there are burnouts, income instability, and location of demand fluctuations (Kost et al., 2019). In order to mitigate the challenges, firms are suggested to incorporate the supplementary benefits. Dynamic compensation could ensure fair remuneration that is aligned with the variables. Maintaining a transparent model for building more trust and motivation among gig workers is important. There shall be transparent communication with the payment structures, and the potential earnings shall improve satisfaction and management. Even with the transient nature of the gig work, this could foster a sense of belongingness that could significantly influence the Engagement of the work as well as productivity, strategies such as including gig work in the team communication and also providing access towards organization resources which could bridge a significant gap within the gig as well as traditional employees.

Learning and Development

Having continuous skill development is important for the gig workers in order to remain more competitive. Organisations are even adopting e-learning platforms but they shall make it more accessible to the gig workers. These paltoms can be integration with the existing HR systems in order to assess the effectiveness of those training programs. The professional growth of the gig needs to be given attention. Inectim in this platform not just benefits the gig worker though meaning the skills but it also improves the quality of work which is being delivered to the clients. Zhang (2024) in his paper has discussed the training aspect with the gig work, identified the rationales behind the training of workers and highly unaddressed the needs of the training within the digital platforms.

Hara (2014) determines the link between wages and training. In the context of the gig economy, the learning and development initiatives shall be tied towards the financial incentives. The palforms should introduce the reward based training and premium listing. These models could ensure having both the enhancements of the skills and also the economic benefits which could foster long term engagement with the platform. While the gig platforms act as the intermediaries, there is an integration of the corporate partnerships for the upskills that could bridge the gaps in the skills. The formal shall collaborate with the online learning platforms in order to have sponsored training for the high performing gig works. For instance an e-commerce company would hire freelancers through upwork and offer training in creative designing for improving the quality of the project(Keegan & Meijerink, 2023). HR agility is a critical aspect. Unlike conventional employment, the gig needs to have more adaptation towards the HR practices which could cater towards the remote, diverse and fluctuating workforce. The HR professionals shall ensure the learning initiative to be more personalised, scalable and also efficient in order to meet the demands of this emerging market. There is a pressing need for HR teams to anticipate the gaps in skills for pricing the gig workers with the learning resources that are more real time. For instance the industries like content retention, the systems could detect the need for the relevant courses and suggest them to make them more emotive according to the trends in the market. With the analysis of the worker engagement and performance metrics, the HR shall customise the train programs for a more impact and use AI influenced dashboards which could assess the training modules yielding with the results and optimising the offerings of the course accordingly. This might be overwhelming to the gig workers but there must be efficiency in the learning amazement as HR implementation must be more towards targeted learning interventions. Offering a more structured learning can significantly have an impact on the worker's retention and satisfaction. The research indicates that the gig workers receive continuous training. HR can significantly improve the engagement of the gig work though virtual enoking spaces wherein the freelancers would have open platform to share their experiences, and collaborate on the projects while also receiving mentorship from the experts in the industry(Keegan & Meijerink, 2023, p. 167).

Role of Technological in the HR Practices

The dependency on gig workers has been increasing which is driving organsion to invest in the advanced HR technologies for stealing the workforce management, and improvise the worker satisfaction as well as improve collaboration. The conventional HR practices fail to address the decentralised gig work. By adopting the AI driven tools and data analytics, the organisations can create more efficient and productive work movement for the gig workers. One of the key challenges which occurs in the management of the gig workforce is the identification as wella s recruitment of the skilled worker. The AI powered platforms enable the analysis of the gig work profiles, requirements of the past performance data for ensuring the best match within the needs of the employer and the freelancer skill. For instance Linkedin Talent Solutions has been using AI recruitment matching algorithms for connecting the business along with the freelancers who are more relevant with expertise. The tools not just expedite the purpose of charging but he also improvise on the retention by algintin towards the expectation of the projects with the capabilities of the worker (LinkedIn, 2023) moreover the usage for AI driven tools also reduce biases and enhances dicey within the gig workforce.

Automated Performance Tracking and Feedback Systems

Management of the performance of the gig works requires a dynamic system which could handle the fluidity nature of gig engagement.the conventional performance appraisal methods are odeon not adequate, so the organisation turning towards digital performance managements offering real time feedback as well as analytics(Pine, 2023). The system tracks the key performance indicators which provide insights with the gig work efficiency and quality of the work. For instance platforms shall build performance tracking features which would allow the monitor progress and provide immediate feedback to the workforce. These tools would help in maintaining the higher standards but they shall also help in identification of the area wherein gig workers might need additional training or support.

Compensation and Payroll

The diverse and short term nature of gig work and the conventional payroll process. These automated payroll systems are customised for the gig workers which could manage the different payment schedules, comply with the laws of the labor and tax considerations. Thes systems must ensure more timely as well as accurate payments which enhance the satisfaction of the workers and retention. The companies shall implement the automated billing as well as payment system which will allow them to have more efficient transactions and allow the gig workers to emphasise on the task without any delay in the payment and also allow the gig workers to focus towards the task without any concerns related to the delays in the payment. One of the most debated topics in the gig economy is compensation fairness. Unlike traditional employment, gig workers face fluctuating incomes based on demand variability. Barbu and Song (2016) argue that offshoring and digital work platforms have exacerbated income instability for many workers. To address this, organizations must introduce structured compensation models, such as guaranteed minimum earnings during low-demand periods or milestone-based payment frameworks.Leading gig platforms like Uber have introduced dynamic wage protection policies, ensuring minimum earnings per trip, while Amazon Flex provides earnings transparency through upfront pay estimates. Additionally, some governments and organizations advocate for portable benefits systems, where gig workers receive prorated benefits based on their work volume across multiple platforms. This hybrid compensation model offers income stability while preserving the gig economy's inherent flexibility.This could provide more transparency and enable the workers to also track their ranting and understand the fees or deductions. For example, there are platforms such as Jemini (2021) which provide payroll solutions which are particularly developed for the gig economy, the system offers multi currency support and real time payment processing which are necessary for management of such a diversified gig economy workforce. Through these technologies the company could significantly enhance the efficiency and also ensure the compliances with customisation in the geographical regulations. Apart from this there has beena study by Nium (2024) wherein the importance of having accurate payments as discussed for training the top gig talents. The research also determines that the implementation of automated payroll processing solutions can significantly reduce the administrative errors.

Collaboration Tools for Improving HR Efficiency

Effective collaboration within the gig workers as well as traditional employees are necessary for the cohesion and prediction of the organisations. Implementing the right tools Communication platforms and real time communications have an inter-link as this is necessary for integration the gig works within the project times. The platforms such as Microsoft Teams offer the channels wherein the gig workers can interact with a full time traditional employee, and can also stay updated regarding the development of the project. The tools support the voice, video communication and offers towards the interactional needs. The use of the platforms ensures that the gig workers are not at all isolated and shall effectively contribute, which increases the levels of engagement of conventional employees. This particular inclusivity plays a crucial role for maintaining the morale and also snaring the gig workers to be more valued being in the organisation(NITI Aayog, 2023). Coordination within the gig workers and the staff requires solutions from the perception of project management. There are platforms which could offer transparency ensuring the team members to be more aware about their responsibilities as well as timelines of the project. By using such tools,the organisation could manage the workload in an effective manner and prevent any overlaps which could ensure the gig works to be more aligned with the objectives of the company and standards(Fuller et al., 2023). The alignments can then be essential for delivering the consistency in projects for the clients as well as stakeholders Access for the important documents and collaborative editing permissions are a must for the gig workers to operate remotely. Cloud based services such as Google Workspace ensures simultaneous collaborations towards presentations, spreadsheets or documents. The tools ensure that the gig workers shall have resources which they ended up with and can also contribute with the collaborative tasks effectively (Malik et al., 2023, p. 75). Securing the documents also addresses the concerns which shall be related to data privacy but it can be controlled and monitored enabling the snake information to remain protected. Accuracy of tracking the working hours and the quality of projects is significant for the compensation aspect in the project management. There are tools which could allow the gig workers to log and provide more transparency for the performance assessment (Malik et al., 2023, p. 75). These platforms, if used regularly, could help the HR to generate the reports and project managers understand how the time is being calculated, allocated and identify the areas for improvement. Implementing the tools ensures the gig workers are compensated fairly with time and cognition.

HR Practices for Integration

In order to achieve this integration of full time and gig work, the HR leaders must be adaptive towards the talent management packs which could put more significance in the inclusivity as well as equitable engagement. The companies must ensure the gig works to have access towards the essential resources, including the mentorship opportunities and real time feedback mechanisms (Lo & Hsieh, 2023). The usage of AI powered workforce analytics could enable the execution of the workload fluctuations and the resource allocation more efficiently. Establishing more clear expectations and aligning with the contribution of the gig workers along with the organisational goals could prevent the concepts and improve the cohesion. Learning platforms and pricing of skills development opportunities can also cater to both sets of employees for fostering the culture of continuous improvements.

RESEARCH METHODOLOGY

This chapter provides an exploratory research design which is deep rooted towards secondary data analysis. Since the nature of the gig economy is evolving and is multifaceted there is a wave approach which is more usitan;e in order to explore the aspects of the agility and efficiency towards HR practices. The study also follows a conceptual farm in the form of extensive literature review and also case based examples. The approach in the chapter is to aim for synthesising the existing theories, reports in order to propose actionable strategies. The data sources which have been used in the chapter are Peer reviews journals, Government and Policy reports and research surveys. The sources were chosen in accordance with the contribution, relevance and credibility to understand the evolution of HR in the gig economy context.

FINDINGS FROM THE STUDY

The growth of gig work has led to innovation in workforce management strategies, which could balance operational agility, efficiency, and worker engagement. The company leverages the gig workers to develop tailored HR Strategies to ensure job satisfaction and productivity. A crucial example is the food delivery sector, where companies like Zomato and Swiggy have introduced incentive pay structures adjusting based on peak hours and surge demands. The NCAER (2023) Survey of Socio-Economic Assessment of Food Delivery Workers has highlighted fluctuations in income levels, job insecurity and lack of traditional employment benefits.

This policy, which includes a base pay guarantee and health insurance provisions, is recommended for a more suitable gig work environment. This reflects the need for broader and more studied HR policies that can improve gig work retention and well-being. There is limited access towards social security benefits, which highlights the critical area for improvement. Pricing paid leaves, health coverage, and retirement saving options shall be addressed to align the gig worker's isolation with the employment benefits.

Organisations Managing Workforce Flexibility With Efficacy

The gig workforce model for Uber has been straightforward with the improvisation of employment strategies. The company has adopted surge pricing algorithms, which encourage drivers to operate during periods with high demands and ensure customer service availability. The model also exemplifies flexibility, which shall be integrated with performance management (Berger et al., 2018). However, Uber has faced criticisms regarding the clarification policies as there are debates about whether the drivers are employees or independent contractors. Uber uses a real-time performance tracking system, another HR practice that provides drivers with immediate feedback on the quality of items, customer satisfaction, and performance metrics. This aligns with the broader economic patterns wherein the continuous feedback loops replace the traditional annual performance review. However, in India, this aspect of HR practices is still lacking; as stated in the NITI Aayog 2022 report on India's gig economy, there are concerns with the performance and compensation models adaptation in India within the digital platforms, so there is a lack of social security with the income predicativity to the Uber drivers, recommending more worker protections schemes and minimum earning guarantees pays. Uber has revolutionized workforce management by offering flexibility to the workforce, which impacts both consumer demands and the driver's preferences. Understanding the flexibility models of Uber with algorithm workforce management, drivers can leave the platform at their own will, choosing when and how much time to work. According to the ESG report 2023, the platform optimized the allocation of drivers through real-time demand forecasting, using the drivers to earn maximum incomes and balance their schedules. The approach has removed the strictness of having flexible shifts, allowing the driver multiple employments. However, the practice needs to be implemented in India with workforce flexibility. The International Labour Organisation (ILO) 2024 report " Expansion of the Gig and Platform Economy in India" focuses on gig work, which has transformed the conventional traditional employment structures with technology shaping worker's rights, contracts and income security. The report has identified that gig platforms are creating new employment opportunities. HR strategies are needed in the platform-based work to inculcate skill development programs and access the credits. Policymakers are forced to create an equitable gig work environment with minimum wage standards and regulations in the compliance framework(BCG, 2023).

Digital freelancing platforms such as Freelancer.com offer flexibility to work in opportunities across different skill levels. The platforms employ algorithm-driven job marching and neutered efficiency. One key difference in the HR approach here is the incorporation of community engagement as well as learning resources to enhance the workers' products (Fuller et al., 2023).

Fiverr's Pro program, for example, also ensures that high-performing workers have access to exclusive live projects which offer structure and career progressions within the unstructured gig landscapes (Fiverr, 2023). It explores the models facing issues with higher platform fees and the absence of a dispute resolution mechanism. Similarly, a preferred freelancer program investigates progressions through better job visibility and lower commission fees. The models must be developed for HR practices that are equipped with fair governance and structured for gig work. From an HR perspective, the initiatives are inconsistent with regions, highlighting the key issues of income volatility, executive working hours and the lack of social security. This often leads to the exploration of the workers due to the lack of formal labour protections. (NCAER, 2023). Organizations must maintain workforce agility without compromising workers' well-being. Leveraging AI for performance management with data-driven HR practices can ensure worker feedback with optimization. Larger businesses shall leverage the gig platform to meet the demands of optimal cost structures and a predictable return on investment(Batmunkh et al., 2023). There has been a rise in the number of gig workers in Tier 2 and Tier 3 cities, increasing the number of businesses to rise at an unprecedented pace(ILO, 2024). Tech-driven gig platforms scale their operations quickly as they can minimise their set time from month to day, benefiting industries like logistics and e-commerce. Freelancers are bringing more innovative solutions and contributing towards efficiency and creativity. Working with minimal supervision reduces operational delays and ensures fair project turnaround with enhanced outcomes. Hiring the workers and allowing businesses to do so can be a cost-effective workforce alternative and significantly minimise the additional and retention expenses. With the transitions in the business from situational explosion, there is a strike balance between agility and efficiency. With the growing government supporting the economy, it can foster goal-driven refinement of the workplace environment. Embracing the tradition of HR practice is more than the need of the hour, which can strengthen the ever-evolving market.

DISCUSSION

With the expansion of the gig economy, there is a need for the blended work-force force models with focus on the HR practices. The companies shall refine the workforce strategies by leveraging the labor demands and also optimising the work structures. Organizations need to implement more well positioned HR practices to balance agility with efficiency for this dynamic workforce (Lehdonvirta et al., 2023, p. 567). According to a report by the Forbes Human Resources Council (2024) the companies are embracing the blended workforce models which focuses towards the organisation efficiency with clarity in the roles, and integration of technology. Effective workforce planning is required for the initial platforms;s HR departments to refine these job roles and ensure the gig works to have transparent deliveries which shall complement each other and not create conflicts. Another strategy which has been highlighted by Forbes (2024) is the usage of centralised workforce management platforms that could provide more visibility into the allocation of work for both the gig as well as full time employees. These particular platforms could allow the HR teams for tracking performance, addressing the gaps in the workforce engagement. Companies such as Google and IBM have already started theri blended workforce models for their ecosystems (Liu et al, 2024) wherein the freelancers and full time employees are collaborating efficiently. Google hires some amount of freelancers in order to perform the specialised task while also using the integration into the work-flow of the projects. The company leverages the AI driven workforce management systems that could balance the gig and full time work. There is a particular need for digital platforms such as Uber, Zomato to follow.Ensuring more transparency in the payment structure is another aspect that will mitigate the inconsistencies. The dynamics pricing, as well as fair wages, are to be ensured. With the growing gig work, the compass shall design the practices which could promote fairness and work satisfaction in future trends. According to the NITI Aayog Report 2022, the gig workforce will grow by 23.5 million by 2029 -2030 (NITI Aayog, 2022). Therefore, there is a need for more workforce optimization and a platform based on collective bargaining. Integration of gig work with full-time employees facilitating the blended workforce models is necessary for cost reduction agility and knowledge sharing. In order to have workforce satisfaction, there is a need for government-backed regulatory compliances to ensure ethical and suitable gig employment. Looking at the significant transition in the evolution of different industries, the gig economy is contributing 40%, with more than 15 million skilled workers in India today embracing flexibility and making their way for effective business agility and increased productivity. The outcome-based approach ensures that the enterprise shifts from fixed payroll accounts towards result-driven models(Tan et al ., 2021).

Blended Workforce Models

Integration of gig workers with the full time employers for collaboration. A fundamental aspect which includes the agility in human resources with content to the gig economy is the adaptation of AI driven workforce management tools. Banik and Padalkar (2021) highlight the significance of real time data analytics in order to optimise the performance of the gig worker. The platforms such as Uber and DoorDash use AI based algorithms for allocation of tasks, optimising the efficiency of delivery, managing of peak hour pricing and also ensuring a worker as well as customer benefit from this dynamic allocation of workforce. It also includes the integration of feedback mechanisms(Okatta et al., 2023). With many digital platforms there is an incorporation of rating and review systems which shall pride the immediate performance assessments. While these systems could improve the transparency through these algorithms also remain fairer and reduce any business which might negatively impact the opportunities of the gig worker. A hybrid evaluation model could combine the easements on the algorithms which could mitigate the risks and foster a more equitable working environment. The evolution of the workforce might lead to an increase in the integration of the gig works with conventional full time employees which are now identified as the blended workforce model. This particular model is significant in the post pandemic era as the organisations are leveraging the difficulty in the employment structures for optimising the workforce agility as well as efficiency (Mahato et al, 2021). Furthermore, this integration can allow the organisation to maintain flexibility and reduce costs while pressing challenges which are required for cohesion and equitable treatment. While the gig economy is reshaping the businesses, the human resources too need to reshape by inoculation of the on demand talent. This shift is mostly driven through the cost efficiency, and the ability to tap within the specialised expertise and the evolving nature for modern business environments, with the companies adopting the blended workforce, there is a need to address the disparities within it including jobs security, benefits between the full time and the gig work. Another crucial point of the successful blended workforce models is the strategic workplace planning which could align with the gig work and the business functions in order to ensure the contribution of both the employees whether it is full time or gig works efficiently. There are many of the organisations which are developing the bybeid employment strategy which could combine both the permanent roles and the gig roles which could bring innovation as well as adaptability. With the many benefits of blended workforce models, the organisations face some significant challenges in the maintenance of collaboration as well as engagement between the gig as well as full time employees. The traditional employees perceive the gig workers as "outsiders" which puts them in a stage or lack of inclusivity. Additionally, the gig workers are operating in remote environments and towards flexible schedules which sometimes makes it difficult for establishing team dynamics(Masta & Kaushiva, 2023).

In order to counter these issues, the companies shall implement strategies which can encourage more cross functional collaborations. The approach to be follword is the integration of the digital collation tools such as Microsoft Teams or Slack which could enable seamless communication within in-house teams and also the external gig works. Morer, the structure of onboarding programs could help in fostering belongingness and engagement.

Recommendations and Future Trends in Gig Economy HR Practices

The gig economy presents a more complex and transformative landscape for human resources. In order to ensure sustainability in the workforce, organizations must adopt strategies that promote maintenance with agility and efficiency (NITI Aayog, 2022). The actionable strategy for agility and the best practices that could be adopted to maintain the gig workforce effectively are technologically driven workforce management. Agility, being the aspect of the gig economy, hinges towards leveraging technology for more seamless workforce management. The organization shall implement AI-driven HR platforms, which could automate onboarding and tracking performance and compensation aspects. The Integration of real-time analysis is necessary for matching the gig works with their suitable prints and ensuring more optimal workforce utilization. AI-driven workforce satisfaction is required to enhance efficiency and reduce recruitment as well as the cost of training.

Table 1. Human resource strategy matrix: Authors own work derived from literature (2025)

HR Strategy	Agility Focus	Efficiency Focus	Example
Workforce Segmentation	High	Medium	Extended Workforce Strategy by Google
AI driven tools for Recruitment	High	High	Talent Solutions by LinkedIn
Real time Feedback	High	Medium	AI performance tracking (Pine, 2023)
Automated Payroll	Low	High	Jemini
Surge Based Pay Models	Medium	High	Uber - peak hour incentive

Conventional payroll structures are obsolete for gig work, given their transient nature. Dynamic compensation models depend on fluctuating demand and skill levels, ensuring fair pay and wages. Companies use algorithms to determine earnings, enabling the workers to capitalize on peak demand hours (ILO, 2024). However, a regulatory framework must be implemented to prevent worker exploitation, ensuring more equity and wage transparency.

In addition, continuing education in the required skills must be provided. The organization shall provide continuous learning opportunities through the microlearning platform and training modules. Platforms such as LinkedIn Learning offer gig workers access to relevant courses, which could enhance their employability and market presence. According to the NCAER report, the skill-building initiative improves gig workers' retention and long-term earning potential.

Furthermore, the blended workforce models could integrate gig workers while enhancing collaborations through knowledge sharing. Mahato et al. (2023) argued in their paper that creating a mixed-team workforce fosters more inclusivity. The critical concern with the gig economy is the lack of employment benefits and healthcare and retirement plans. The organization shall introduce portable benefits which can move with the works across the different gig platforms. According to the NITI Aayog report, the government must collaborate to design the scheme for social scarcity and tailor it towards gig work, ensuring more financial stability and healthcare coverage.

Effective Practices for HR strategies in the Gig Economy Context

Transparency and ethical employee practices are paramount in ensuring fair work conditions in the gig economy. The International Labour Organization (ILO) focuses on the need for minimum wage policies and contractual transparency. Platforms such as Freelancer and Fiverr have introduced more ethical guidelines to safeguard workers' rights and foster a sustainable gig workforce. Since traditional employment operates traditional performance appraisals, there is a different implementation needed for gig workers on outcome-based performance metrics, which focus on the deliverables and the feedback of the clients. For instance, Upwork evaluates freelancers on milestones-based feedback, enduring more control over quality. HR agility requires predictive analysis for forecasting to predict surges in demand and manage workforce allocation efficiently. A more data-driven approach must be enabled to scale the business's operations dynamically by balancing the cost of labour and the efficiency of the service (Waldrick et al., 2021).

The challenge also becomes for the business to work on flexibility while complying with labour regulations. The business must work closely with policymakers to develop frameworks to support gig workers' rights, which can allow flexibility in operations. Uber, for instance, has faced regulatory scrutiny across different jurisdictions, highlighting the necessity for balancing the interests of the business with worker protections as well(Waldrick et al., 2021) (ILO, 2024). Therefore, building a gig workers community that will improve engagement is necessary. Organizations can create more virtual communities where, in the gig, we could connect and access their career growth opportunities by building network ecosystems fostering professional peer support and networking.

CONCLUSION

The gig economy has transformed the dynamics of this particular workforce by ensuring that the organization can leverage labour flexibility while posing new challenges for human resources. The chapter has explored the emergence and evolution of the gig economy, focusing on the need for agility and efficiency in HR strategies for optimizing workforce engagement and sustainability.

The key finding is that digital platforms facilitate the gig economy by creating highly supervised workforce skills, demographics, and industry-specific segments. The gig workers include freelancers who require a different approach to HR management than conventional employees. Organizations challenges as agents of gig work involve workforce differentiation, compositional structure, and performance management.

Agile HR processes, which could be customized with the gig works, are important for addressing the challenges. The study has identified strategies that could practise the skill of baked herring and screening tools, ensuring organizations onboard the right talent. Performance management within the gig economy, dependent on outcome-based metrics despite the transitional supervision, focuses on the measurable deliverables and adaptive compensation models. Technical advancements play an internal role in facilitating efficiency in HR with automation and digital collation tools to streamline workforce management.

Industry insights have been considered with Uber, Fiverr, and Freelancer, which highlight effective HR practices that could balance workplace flexibility with operational efficiency. Uber's workforce model determines the Integration of agility scheduling and demand-based compensation to ensure workforce agility. Platforms such as Freelancer.com and Fiver could implement rating systems and job-matching algorithms to optimize the engagement of the works. The models identify the significance of technology in scaling the HR strategies for the gig works.

Another significant finding in the exploration is the bleeding workforce model, wherein the organization integrates gig work with full-time employees to enhance cohesion and collaboration. The strategy could create a more positive work environment, such as communication, shared project management systems, and flexible work policies.

Adding to this, organizations navigate the balance between cost efficiency and also ethical workforce management. Ensuring fair compensation provides gig workers access to professional development and adherence to labour laws, which can contribute to a sustainable and beneficial work environment. The chapter determines the business that aligns with HR practices that provide a competitive edge with agility and efficiency while catering towards innovation and productivity.

Looking ahead, the future for Human resources in the gig economy continues to rise with AI advancements and adaptive workforce planning. Organizations actively implement flexibility in their HR frameworks, which can better position them to attract and retain gig talents and improve operational efficiency and compliance.

The chapter provides a roadmap for organizations to seek and optimize HR strategies for gig workers. By integrating such agile methodologies and balancing efficiencies, the business can harness the full potential of the gig economy. Implementing the strategy can benefit the organization and empower the gig workers by providing them with structured opportunities for growth and sustainability.

ACKNOWLEDGEMENT

Declaration of Conflicting Interest:

The authors declare no potential conflicts of interest with respect to the research, authorship and/or publication of this chapter

Funding:

The authors received no financial support for the research, authorship, and/or publication of this chapter.

REFERENCES

Aayog, N. I. T. I. (2022). *Policy brief: India's booming gig and platform economy*. National Institution for Transforming India. https://www.niti.gov.in/sites/default/files/2022-06/Policy_Brief_India%27s_Booming_Gig_and_Platform_Economy_27062022.pdf

Ashford, S. J., Caza, B. B., & Reid, E. M. (2018). From surviving to thriving in the gig economy: A research agenda for individuals in the new world of work. *Research in Organizational Behavior*, *38*, 23–41. DOI: 10.1016/j.riob.2018.11.001

Banik, N., & Padalkar, M. (2021). The spread of the gig economy: Trends and effects. *Foresight*, *15*(1), 19–29. DOI: 10.17323/2500-2597.2021.1.19.29

Barbu, E., & Song, X. (2016). The effects of offshoring on employer-provided training. *The Journal of International Trade & Economic Development*, *25*(4), 479–503. DOI: 10.1080/09638199.2015.1068838

Bateyo, A. (2025). The gig economy: Implications for workforce management. *Research Invention Journal of Current Issues in Arts and Management*, *4*(1), 39–42. DOI: 10.59298/RIJCIAM/2025/413942

Batmunkh, A., Fekete-Farkas, M., & Lakner, Z. (2022). Bibliometric analysis of gig economy. *Administrative Sciences*, *12*(2), 1–15. DOI: 10.3390/admsci12020051

BCG. (2021). Unlocking the potential of the gig economy in India. *Boston Consulting Group*. https://www.bcg.com/en-in/unlocking-gigeconomy-in-india

Berger, T., Frey, C. B., Levin, G., & Danda, S. R. (2019). Is Uber happy? Work and wellbeing in the gig economy. *Economic Policy*, *34*(99), 429–477. https://www.jstor.org/stable/26954821. DOI: 10.1093/epolic/eiz007

Bhandari, B., Das, G. K., Gupta, S., Sahu, A. K., Urs, K. S., Pal, N., & Raj, K. (2023). Socio-economic impact assessment of food delivery platform workers. *August 2023*.

Bush, J. T., & Balven, R. M. (2019). Catering to the crowd: An HRM perspective on crowd worker engagement. *Human Resource Management Review*.

Cheng, B. (2019, August 24). Agility is key for working in India's gig economy. *BusinessWorld*. https://www.businessworld.in/article/agility-is-key-for-working-in-india's-gig-economy-175053

Cheng, B. (2019, August 24). Agility is key for working in India's gig economy. *BusinessWorld*.https://www.businessworld.in/article/agility-is-key-for-working-in-india's-gig-economy-175053

Chitte, S. (2025, January). The gig economy: Navigating complexities in human resource management. *International Journal of Research and Innovation in Social Science*.https://www.researchgate.net/publication/388277619_The_Gig_Economy_Navigating_Complexities_in_Human_Resource_Management

Cika, A. (2021). Developing new skills is the key to boosting productivity and financial services gaining a competitive advantage. *PwC*.https://www.pwc.com/id/en/media-centre/press-release/2021/english/developing-new-skills-is-the-key-to-boosting-productivity-and-financial-services-gaining-a-competitive-advantage.html

Deloitte. (2024). Gig workforce talent management strategy. *Deloitte*.https://www2.deloitte.com/content/dam/Deloitte/in/Documents/human-capital/in-hc-gig-workforce-talent-management-strategy-noexp.pdf

Elayan, M. B. (2022). Transformation of human resources management solutions as a strategic tool for gig workers contracting. In *IGI Global eBooks* (pp. 790–813). https://doi.org/DOI: 10.4018/978-1-6684-4503-7.ch039

Fiverr. (n.d.). Fiverr Pro: High-end professional freelancers for your business. *Fiverr*. https://pro.fiverr.com

Forbes Human Resources Council. (2024, August 9). Organizational efficiency in the age of the blended workforce. *Forbes*. Retrieved from https://www.forbes.com/councils/forbeshumanresourcescouncil/2024/08/09/organizational-efficiency-in-the-age-of-the-blended-workforce

Fuller, J. B., Raman, M., Palano, J., Bailey, A., Vaduganathan, N., Kaufman, E., & Laverdière, R. Sibley Lovett, & Boston Consulting Group. (2020). Building the on-demand workforce. *Harvard Business School and Boston Consulting Group*. https://www.hbs.edu/managing-the-future-of-work/Documents/Building_The_On-Demand_Workforce.pdf

Hara, H. (2014). The impact of firm-provided training on productivity, wages, and transition to regular employment for workers in flexible arrangements. *Journal of the Japanese and International Economies, 34*, 336–359. DOI: 10.1016/j.jjie.2014.10.002

Hodor, M. (2020). Gig workers and performance pay: A dynamic equilibrium analysis of an on-demand industry.

Horney, N. (2016). The gig economy: A disruptor requiring HR agility. *People and Strategy, 39*(3), 20.

Huet, E. (2014, October 8). Uber skimps on driver training, then charges drivers $65 for basic driver skills courses. *Forbes.* Retrieved from www.forbes.com/sites/ellenhuet/2014/10/08/uber-skimps-on-driver-training-then-charges-drivers-65-for-basic-driver-skills-course/

Inside Microsoft's freelance services program. (n.d.). *Business Talent Group.*https://resources.businesstalentgroup.com/btg-insights-on-demand/microsoft-freelance-services-program-podcast

Jacob, B., & Shaikh, M. (2021). Growth and challenges of gig employees in India. *Parikalpana: KIIT Journal of Management, 17*(1), 62–68. https://ksom.ac.in/wp-content/uploads/2021/06/6268Parikalpana-Vol.17I.Pdf?x335

Keegan, A., & Meijerink, J. (2022). HRM practices for value creation and value capture in online labor platform ecosystems: Towards an integrative perspective. In *A Research Agenda for Strategic Human Resource Management* (pp. 167–194). Edward Elgar Publishing., https://www.masi-journal.com/journal/article/view/26 DOI: 10.4337/9781800883802.00017

Kost, D., Fieseler, C., & Wong, S. I. (2019). Boundaryless careers in the gig economy: An oxymoron? *Human Resource Management Journal, 30*(1), 100–113. DOI: 10.1111/1748-8583.12265

Kuhn, K. M., Meijerink, J., & Keegan, A. (2021). Human resource management and the gig economy: Challenges and opportunities at the intersection between organizational HR decision-makers and digital labor platforms. *Research in Personnel and Human Resources Management, 39*, 1–46. DOI: 10.1108/S0742-730120210000039001

Lehdonvirta, V., Kässi, O., Hjorth, I., Barnard, H., & Graham, M. (2019). The global platform economy: A new offshoring institution enabling emerging-economy micro providers. *Journal of Management, 45*(2), 567–599. DOI: 10.1177/0149206318786781 PMID: 30774168

Liu, M., Li, Y., Lin, Z., Zhou, J., & Liu, S. (2024). The cost of 'cost reduction': An integrative review of blended workgroups. *Human Resource Management Review, 101054*. Advance online publication. DOI: 10.1016/j.hrmr.2024.101054

Lo, Y. F., & Hsieh, K. L. (2024). The study of working patterns in the gig economy. *Management Analytics and Social Insights, 1*(1), 70–87.

Mahato, M., Kumar, N., & Jena, L. K. (2021). Re-thinking gig economy in conventional workforce post-COVID-19: A blended approach for upholding fair balance. *Journal of Work-Applied Management, 13*(2), 261–276. DOI: 10.1108/JWAM-05-2021-0037

Manyika, J., Lund, S., Bughin, J., Robinson, K., Mischke, J., & Mahajan, D. (2016). *Independent work: Choice, necessity and the gig economy.* McKinsey Global Institute. https://www.mckinsey.com/featured-insights/employment-and-growth/independent-work-choice-necessity-and-the-gig-economy# Malik

Malik, A., Budhwar, P., & Srikanth, N. R. (2020). Gig economy, 4IR and artificial intelligence: Rethinking strategic HRM. In Human & technological resource management (HTRM): New insights into revolution 4.0 (pp. 75-88). Emerald Publishing Limited.

Masta, R., & Kaushiva, P. (2024). Work in the platform economy: A systematic literature review. *Employee Relations, ahead-of-print*(ahead-of-print). https://doi.org/DOI: 10.1108/ER-12-2023-0638

Meijerink, J., & Keegan, A. (2019). Conceptualizing human resource management in the gig economy: Toward a platform ecosystem perspective. *Journal of Managerial Psychology, 34*(4), 214–232. DOI: 10.1108/JMP 07 2018-0277

Nium. (2024, February 1). *Automating payroll: Attracting top gig economy workers done right.* Nium. https://www.nium.com/blog/automating-payroll-attracting-top-gig-economy-workers-done-right?utm_source=chatgpt.com

Okatta, C. G., Ajayi, F. A., & Olawale, O. (2024). Navigating the future: Integrating AI and machine learning in HR practices for a digital workforce. *Computer Science & IT Research Journal, 5*(4), 1008–1030. DOI: 10.51594/csitrj.v5i4.1085

Pereira, V., Behl, A., Jayawardena, N., Laker, B., Dwivedi, Y. K., & Bhardwaj, S. (2022). The art of gamifying digital gig work: A theoretical assessment of engagement and motivation. *Production Planning and Control*, •••, 1–17. Advance online publication. DOI: 10.1080/09537287.2022.2083524

Pine, R. (n.d.). Beyond 9-to-5: Payroll solutions for the gig economy. *Jemini.*https://www.jemini.com/insights/latest-insights/payroll-solutions-gig-economy-modern-work/?utm_source=chatgpt.com

Rabban, T., & Singh, R. (2025). Talent Management in the Gig Economy: Leveraging Workforce Strategies in the Digital Age. In Doon, R. (Ed.), *Sustainability and Adaptability of Gig Economies in Global Business* (pp. 177–204). IGI Global Scientific Publishing., DOI: 10.4018/979-8-3693-9385-7.ch007

Rahman, S. U., Sultan, M. S., & Tabassam, A. (2024). The impact of the gig economy on traditional employment and the necessity for revised business, HR, and legal strategies. *Pakistan Journal of International Affairs*, *7*(1).

Roy, G., & Shrivastava, A. K. (2020). Future of gig economy: Opportunities and challenges. *IMI Konnect*, *9*(1), 14–27.

Salmah, E., Astuti, E., & Harsono, I. (2024). Employee engagement in the gig economy. *Deleted Journal*, *1*(1), 116–122. DOI: 10.62207/1e5dd842

Suryawanshi, M., & Ponde, P. (2024). Gig economy: Changing the dynamics of the workforce. In *The role of HR in the transforming workplace* (pp. 79–94). Productivity Press.

Tan, Z. M., Aggarwal, N., Cowls, J., Morley, J., Taddeo, M., & Floridi, L. (2021). The ethical debate about the gig economy: A review and critical analysis. *Technology in Society*, *65*, 101594. DOI: 10.1016/j.techsoc.2021.101594

Waldkirch, M., Bucher, E., Schou, P. K., & Grünwald, E. (2021). Controlled by the algorithm, coached by the crowd – How HRM activities take shape on digital work platforms in the gig economy. *International Journal of Human Resource Management*, *32*(12), 2643–2682. DOI: 10.1080/09585192.2021.1914129

Zhang, P. (2024). Training for gig workers: A systematic review and research agenda. *The Learning Organization, ahead-of-print*(ahead-of-print). https://doi.org/DOI: 10.1108/TLO-10-2022-0124

Chapter 16
Human Resource Management in the Gig Economy:
Strategies for Agility and Efficiency

Preeti Umesh Sharma
https://orcid.org/0000-0002-8167-1361
Savitribai Phule Pune University, India

Kirti Dang Longani
https://orcid.org/0009-0002-1990-0634
Akemi Business School, India

ABSTRACT

Gig economy, or temporary, flexible work, has damaged traditional HRM systems. As businesses use more contract, freelance, and platform-based labour, HR managers must adapt to maintain flexibility, effectiveness, and employee engagement. Hiring is challenging since gig workers seek freedom and flexibility. Digital recruitment platforms, social media outreach, and AI-powered technologies that swiftly match people to positions must replace long-term recruitment methods. To satisfy gig workers, HR departments must hire on-demand, project-based. Performance management should prioritise task completion and deliverables over long-term goals. Digital technologies enable remote goal alignment, performance monitoring, and feedback. Independent gig work makes engagement and retention tough. HR should foster community through online networks, growth possibilities, equal compensation, and bonuses to boost motivation and loyalty.

DOI: 10.4018/979-8-3373-1290-3.ch016

1 INTRODUCTION

The gig economy has caused a paradigm shift in how companies handle their employees. It prioritises contract, freelance, and platform-based work above traditional full-time employment and is characterised by transitory and flexible labour arrangements. In order to preserve organisational agility, efficiency, and employee engagement, this shift calls into question established Human Resource Management (HRM) approaches and calls for creative solutions (Bartik et al., 2020; Arora et al., 2023). The influence of the gig economy is best illustrated by the growth of online marketplaces such as Uber, TaskRabbit, and Upwork, which give people the freedom to select jobs that fit their schedules and skill set. Businesses can scale operations up or down in response to market needs thanks to this model's availability to a varied talent pool. But this adaptability has its own set of drawbacks, especially for HRM, which has to modify conventional procedures to satisfy the specialised needs of this workforce (Verma et al., 2024).

Redefining the employer-employee relationship is one of the biggest difficulties facing the gig economy. Gig workers, in contrast to regular employees, are highly independent and may interact with several organisations at once (Bélanger and Crossler, 2011). HRM must create creative strategies for hiring engagement, performance management, and retention in light of this decentralised structure. Because gig labour is dynamic and project-based, traditional approaches that depend on long-term employment models are insufficient. In the gig economy, hiring requires flexibility and the application of cutting-edge technology. Digital platforms, social media, and AI-powered tools are becoming essential for finding and luring gig workers (Boudreau and Lawler, 2017; Arora and Nabi, 2022). With the help of these technologies, HR managers can quickly evaluate candidates' abilities, pair them with suitable tasks, and guarantee a smooth onboarding process. Additionally, the move away from strict recruiting cycles and towards on-demand hiring procedures underscores the need for HR departments to be more responsive and flexible.

Another area where conventional HR procedures need to be updated is performance management. In traditional contexts, long-term performance criteria like hours worked and annual reviews are used to evaluate personnel (Brynjolfsson and McAfee, 2014; Kansra and Gill, 2016). However, the accomplishment of particular tasks or projects is frequently used to gauge success for gig workers. This calls for the implementation of task-oriented evaluation systems that give deliverables and results top priority. Even in a dispersed workforce, digital technologies are essential for enabling real-time performance tracking and feedback and guaranteeing alignment with organisational goals (Cappelli, 2015).

In the gig economy, engagement and retention pose particular difficulties. Because they work individually and are frequently spread out geographically, gig workers might not feel like they belong to the company. HRM needs to promote diversity and a sense of community in order to address this. Top talent can be retained by implementing tactics like establishing online communities, providing chances for professional growth, and paying fairly. Furthermore, offering gig workers advantages like health insurance and retirement plans can increase their dedication and loyalty to the company.

HRM in the gig economy is further complicated by ethical and legal issues. The benefits and protections that full-time employees enjoy, such paid time off and job stability, are usually not available to gig workers. In order to maintain compliance and promote equitable treatment for gig workers, HR professionals must negotiate a complex web of labour rules. Transparency and trust are maintained by well-defined contracts that include employment terms, intellectual property rights, and dispute resolution procedures (Carmeli and Spreitzer, 2009). Effective management of the gig labour requires the integration of digital tools and technologies. From hiring and onboarding to performance management and teamwork, HR departments may expedite procedures with the use of AI-powered platforms, cloud-based systems, and real-time communication tools. In addition to increasing productivity, these technologies offer the scalability required to oversee a dispersed and diverse workforce. To sum up, the gig economy is a revolutionary change in the nature of the workforce that calls for creative solutions and challenges conventional HRM procedures. To tackle the distinct obstacles presented by the gig economy, human resource professionals can embrace flexibility, make use of digital resources, and cultivate an inclusive and engaged culture. This strategy maximises the advantages of having a flexible and dynamic workforce in addition to ensuring organisational agility and efficiency.

2 TALENT ACQUISITION IN THE GIG ECONOMY

Changing personnel acquisition tactics to meet the demands of the gig economy is one of HRM's biggest issues. Gig workers that value flexibility, autonomy, and project-based work are not attracted by traditional recruitment approaches, which concentrate on long-term employment. HR managers need to: Make use of social media, digital recruitment platforms, and AI-powered tools to swiftly find and connect with gig workers. Use flexible, on-demand hiring procedures to effectively connect qualified candidates with suitable tasks. The gig economy offers a distinct combination of opportunities and difficulties for talent acquisition, which forces HR managers to reconsider conventional hiring practices (Choudhury et al., 2020).

Gig workers emphasise project-based engagement, flexibility, and autonomy over traditional long-term employment in this new paradigm. Therefore, HRM needs to use creative strategies to draw in and keep this vibrant talent pool while coordinating with organisational goals.

The gig economy depends on hiring people quickly and accurately. Gig economy hiring necessitates agility, in contrast to traditional recruitment approaches that can entail drawn-out procedures. The adoption of cutting-edge technologies, like AI-powered platforms and digital recruitment tools, is required due to the fast turnaround times for certain capabilities. By using these technologies, HR managers can quickly find, assess, and onboard gig workers, guaranteeing that the right people are working on the right projects. Social media sites have become effective resources for finding gig workers. HR professionals have access to a large pool of possible candidates through platforms such as LinkedIn, Twitter, and specialised forums. HR departments can develop focused recruitment efforts that emphasise the freedom and flexibility of gig labour by utilising these platforms. Additionally, companies can create a powerful employer brand that appeals to gig workers by participating in online communities and professional networks.

2.1 AI Powered

AI-powered hiring solutions are essential for expediting the hiring procedure (Dube and Chattopadhyay, 2021). These technologies can forecast a candidate's likelihood of fitting in with the company, streamline the screening process, and match abilities with project requirements. Machine learning algorithms, for instance, can evaluate applications and portfolios to find applicants who have the necessary skills, greatly cutting down on the time and effort needed for the hiring process. In the gig economy, hiring procedures that are dynamic and on-demand are essential to acquiring talent. On-demand recruiting enables businesses to react swiftly to shifting business requirements, in contrast to typical cycles that have a set schedule. With this strategy, a flexible talent pipeline is established, allowing gig workers to be hired as needed. HR specialists may guarantee that the company is always ready to satisfy project expectations by keeping a database of pre-screened applicants.

Another crucial component of hiring people in the gig economy is retention. In addition to seeking fair salary, opportunities for professional development, and a nice work atmosphere, gig workers often enjoy independence. In order to meet these demands, HRM must provide competitive pay rates, chances for skill improvement, and access to perks like retirement plans and health insurance (Eisenstat and Taylor, 2019). Creating an inclusive and encouraging work environment can increase gig workers' devotion to the company. Additionally, when hiring gig workers, HR managers have to handle the nuances of ethical and regulatory issues. Creating transparent and unambiguous contracts that specify the conditions of engagement, payment schedules, and intellectual property rights is part of this. Maintaining trust with gig workers and preventing disputes need adherence to labour laws and regulations.

Additionally, digital tools let gig workers and businesses collaborate and communicate. Gig workers can be easily included into project teams using cloud-based technologies, which enables them to contribute productively from any place. Slack and Microsoft Teams are examples of real-time communication solutions that guarantee gig workers stay in touch with the company and on the same page about project objectives. Finding talent in the gig economy necessitates a tech-driven, strategic strategy (Friedman, 2014). HR managers may successfully recruit and engage gig workers by utilising digital platforms, AI-powered technologies, and dynamic hiring procedures. Long-term success and retention are also guaranteed when gig workers' needs and preferences are met through competitive pay, chances for professional advancement, and inclusive workplace policies. Adopting these tactics maximises the advantages of a flexible and varied workforce while also improving organisational agility.

2.2 Reimagining Performance Management in the Gig Economy

Traditional performance management methods face a unique problem in the gig economy. Gig workers' success is judged primarily on completing individual tasks or projects, as opposed to full-time employees whose performance is usually measured against long-term objectives. This change calls for a revised performance management strategy that takes into account the adaptable and dynamic character of gig labour (Kaufman, 2019). HR managers must use cutting-edge technologies and techniques to guarantee that gig workers' contributions complement company objectives while creating a stimulating and effective work environment.

2.2.1 Task-Oriented Evaluation Systems

Deliverables and outputs are more important in the gig economy than traditional criteria like tenure or hours spent. Task-oriented assessment systems provide an equitable and useful means of evaluating gig workers by emphasising the calibre and timeliness of project deliverables. By defining quantifiable objectives and performance metrics for every work, these systems establish clear expectations right away. For instance, delivery staff may be judged on timeliness and customer happiness, while creative freelancers may be judged on the calibre of their designs and compliance with client specifications. In addition to making the evaluation process easier, this clarity gives gig workers a clear idea of what is expected of them. By ensuring that assessments are impartial and pertinent to their line of work, this method promotes openness and trust (Kelliher and Anderson, 2010).

2.2.2 Leveraging Digital Tools

In the gig economy, digital technology is essential to efficient performance management. HR managers can keep an eye on performance and progress as activities are finished thanks to real-time tracking technologies. Dashboards showing task statuses, due dates, and employee contributions are offered by platforms like as Trello, Asana, and specialised gig management software. By seeing trends in employee performance, pointing out possible problems, and offering data-driven insights, AI-driven analytics can improve the procedure even more. For example, a gig worker may be flagged for preferential task assignments or recognition programs if they routinely produce excellent outcomes ahead of schedule. Additionally, these tools make feedback and communication more efficient. Gig workers can quickly modify their efforts by receiving real-time information on task requirements or performance evaluations. Despite their autonomous work schedules, gig workers are kept in line with company objectives by regular evaluations carried out through digital platforms (Kuhn and Maleki, 2017).

2.2.3 Providing Constructive Feedback

Feedback is essential for engagement and performance enhancement. Despite the temporary nature of gig work, constructive feedback and acknowledgement are beneficial to gig workers. HR divisions ought to set up systems for giving prompt, useful feedback. For example, a gig worker may receive a quick performance assessment outlining their areas of strength and progress following the completion of a project (Lepak and Snell, 2002). In addition to improving individual performance, this feedback loop fortifies the employee's bond with the company. By showing that they care about their professional development, employers can encourage loyalty and inspire gig workers to uphold high standards.

2.2.4 Setting Clear Expectations

Task requirements that are unclear might result in inefficiency, discontent, and results that are not aligned. HR managers must establish thorough and unambiguous expectations right away in order to lessen this. Project scope, deliverables, timelines, and quality standards should all be covered in thorough project briefs. Gig workers are more likely to produce outcomes that meet or above expectations when they have a solid understanding of the task.

2.2.5 Fostering Collaboration and Community

Even though gig workers work on their own, performance and engagement are improved when they are incorporated into the larger organisational structure. Teamwork can be facilitated via virtual platforms and collaborative tools, which let gig workers communicate with other independent contractors and full-time staff. For instance, using Slack or Microsoft Teams, gig workers participating in a product launch may cooperate with internal marketing teams.

Creating a feeling of belonging among gig workers can also increase their level of participation. Gig workers have a platform to exchange ideas and feel appreciated by the company thanks to online forums, frequent check-ins, and inclusive virtual events.

3 ALIGNING PERFORMANCE WITH ORGANIZATIONAL GOALS

Systems for performance management must close the gap between individual efforts and more general company goals. Gig workers ought to be aware of how their job affects the overall performance of the business. For example, a content creator should know how their work enhances consumer engagement metrics or supports a marketing strategy.

Strategic goal-setting and open communication are two ways to attain alignment. Regular updates on business accomplishments and progress provide gig workers a sense of purpose and help them understand the wider picture (McKinsey & Company, 2016).

4 RECOGNITION AND REWARDS

Even with flexible work arrangements, recognition is still a key motivator. Recognising the efforts of gig workers through public recognition, testimonials, or performance incentives raises spirits and promotes further partnerships. Simple actions can have a big impact, like highlighting top-performing gig workers in newsletters or rewarding them with bonuses for their outstanding work.

5 OVERCOMING CHALLENGES

There are difficulties with performance management in the gig economy. Problems could include cultural differences, communication difficulties, and uneven job quality. A combination of technical tools, efficient communication techniques, and an inclusive approach to employee involvement are necessary to proactively address these issues. For example, giving gig workers access to tools like project management manuals or training modules can improve their skills and match their output with company requirements. In order to rethink performance management in the gig economy, traditional methods must give way to more flexible, task-oriented approaches. HR executives may maximise gig worker contributions while preserving high levels of satisfaction by implementing digital technologies, giving frequent feedback, and encouraging a feeling of community (Parker and Axtell, 2001). When individual performance is in line with organisational objectives, gig workers are guaranteed to be crucial to the success of the business. This innovative strategy unlocks the gig economy's full potential for organisational growth while simultaneously addressing its particular challenges.

5.1 Enhancing Engagement and Retention in the Gig Economy

Engaging and keeping workers in the gig economy is more difficult than it is for full-time employees. A sense of alienation may result from gig workers' frequent independence and lack of direct contact with their employers. Attempts to cultivate long-term loyalty are made more difficult by their project-based commitments and ephemeral character. Despite these challenges, businesses can use creative approaches to improve engagement and retention by attending to the particular requirements and preferences of gig workers.

5.2 Fostering a Sense of Belonging

Retaining gig workers who might otherwise feel alienated from the company depends on creating a feeling of community. Employers can accomplish this by setting up online forums and communities. Interactions between gig workers and full-time employees might be facilitated by online forums or special channels in communication platforms like Slack or Microsoft Teams. Peer support, idea sharing, and a sense of community are all promoted by these platforms. Additionally, frequent online gatherings like town halls, webinars, or casual coffee chats can foster a sense of belonging among gig workers (Pereira and Bisson, 2021). Their importance to the company is further reinforced when milestones, like project completions or individual accomplishments, are celebrated.

5.3 Offering Professional Development Opportunities

Putting money into the professional development of gig workers is one of the best ways to keep them interested. Giving them access to online workshops, training courses, or certifications can help them improve their abilities and stay competitive in the gig economy. Courses on cutting-edge design tools or new trends in the business, for example, could be beneficial for a freelance graphic designer. Programs for professional development not only raise employee performance but also demonstrate the organization's dedication to their advancement. This investment encourages gig workers to prioritise assignments from companies that support their career advancement and cultivates loyalty.

5.4 Ensuring Competitive Compensation and Benefits

One of the most important components of engagement and retention is timely and equitable compensation. Although gig workers frequently appreciate flexibility, they also anticipate receiving competitive compensation for their work. Payment plans that are transparent and performance-based, like bonuses for outstanding work or milestone-based reimbursements, might increase their level of satisfaction. Benefit extensions like as access to wellness initiatives, retirement savings plans, or health insurance can improve retention even more. Although these kinds of benefits are rare in gig agreements, companies who provide them are seen as desirable employers (Scholz, 2016; Stone, 2018). To increase gig workers' sense of security and attachment, a company could, for example, negotiate with insurance companies to develop reasonably priced plans just for them.

5.5 Building a Supportive Work Environment

Retaining gig workers requires fostering an inclusive and encouraging work atmosphere. The varied backgrounds and abilities that gig workers contribute should be recognised and appreciated by employers. Publicly praising their efforts, whether via awards, internal newsletters, or social media shout-outs, raises spirits and shows gratitude. Gig workers' experiences are also improved by creating open lines of communication where they may express issues or ask for advice. As points of contact, committed HR managers or project managers make sure gig workers feel appreciated and supported.

5.6 Balancing Flexibility with Stability

Although flexibility is important to gig workers, providing some stability helps strengthen their loyalty to the company. Businesses might, for instance, create a talent pool of preferred gig workers and give them preference for upcoming projects. This strategy guarantees that the company gains access to a pool of dependable and knowledgeable contributors while giving gig workers a steady flow of chances.

6 LEVERAGING TECHNOLOGY FOR ENGAGEMENT

Digital tools are essential for interacting with gig workers. In addition to streamlining workflow, project management apps like Asana and Trello offer insight into team relationships and advancement. Leaderboards and badges for finishing tasks are examples of gamification elements that can provide enjoyment and motivation. Additionally, survey tools can collect feedback on gig workers' experiences and measure their level of satisfaction. The company's dedication to ongoing development and employee well-being is demonstrated by its consistent implementation of this feedback.

7 TAILORING ENGAGEMENT STRATEGIES

Gig workers come from a wide range of backgrounds, occupations, and experience levels. The success of engagement initiatives is ensured by customising them for particular demographics. For example, a software engineer would place more importance on access to state-of-the-art tools and difficult assignments than a freelance writer, who might value creative autonomy and constructive criticism. HR staff can create customised engagement programs that appeal to various employee profiles by being aware of these subtleties.

8 ADDRESSING CHALLENGES IN RETENTION

Overcoming innate obstacles, like the appeal of competing offers, is necessary for retention in the gig economy. It is essential to build enduring relationships based on openness, respect, and trust. Providing high-performing gig workers with exclusive project possibilities or retention bonuses can encourage them to stay with the company. Additionally, establishing a favourable brand image as an employer that supports gig workers draws and keeps great talent. Businesses with a reputation for providing meaningful employment opportunities and treating gig workers decently will have an advantage in keeping them on board (Sundararajan, 2016).

A diversified strategy catered to the particular traits of gig workers is necessary to improve engagement and retention in the gig economy. Organisations may cultivate loyalty among gig workers by providing professional development opportunities, ensuring competitive compensation, establishing a friendly work environment, and developing a sense of belonging. These initiatives are further strengthened by utilising technology and customising tactics to meet the demands of each individual (Tucker and Varga, 2020). Businesses that put engagement and retention first will be better positioned to prosper in this competitive and dynamic environment as the gig economy grows.

9 ADDRESSING LEGAL AND ETHICAL CONSIDERATIONS IN MANAGING GIG WORKERS

Managing gig workers requires negotiating tricky ethical and legal situations. HR specialists must: Create detailed contracts that include terms of employment, remuneration, intellectual property rights, and dispute resolution procedures because gig workers usually lack the rights of full-time employees. As you promote fair treatment and equal working conditions for gig workers, be sure that labour rules are followed.

9.1 Legal Considerations in Managing Gig Workers

Many individuals are increasingly working under flexible, short-term contracts rather than full-time, permanent jobs as a result of the gig economy's growth. However, because gig workers are classified as independent contractors rather than employees, managing them comes with a number of legal complications. In order to maintain both legal compliance and an equitable workplace, HR practitioners must overcome these obstacles.

9.2 Employment Contracts and Terms of Agreement

Creating precise, comprehensive contracts is one of the main legal obligations in managing gig workers. The terms of employment, such as the salary scale, duties, deadlines, and expected deliverables, should all be spelt out in detail in these contracts. In order to ensure that the contractor's status is accurately stated, it is also crucial to specify the nature of the relationship between the worker and the company. Contracts should also contain provisions addressing intellectual property

(IP) rights in order to avoid disagreements over who owns the work produced during the engagement. Incorporating unambiguous dispute resolution procedures is also necessary to reduce legal obstacles.

9.3 Compliance with Labor Laws

HR specialists must make sure that businesses adhere to relevant labour rules even though gig workers are categorised as independent contractors rather than full-time employees. Depending on the jurisdiction, these laws may include rules pertaining to maximum working hours, minimum wages, and health and safety requirements. Some jurisdictions are giving gig workers more legal protections, including paid time off and perks that are typically provided to full-time workers. To reduce the risk of non-compliance and possible litigation, HR professionals need to be informed on the changing legal landscape.

9.4 Taxation and Benefits

Gig workers must file their own taxes, including income tax and self-employment tax, since they are independent contractors. To guarantee correct reporting, HR departments should make sure gig workers understand their tax responsibilities and supply the required documentation, such as 1099 forms in the US. Additionally, although they are not required, businesses may choose to provide benefits like access to insurance or retirement plans. Careful preparation and attention to local laws are necessary due to legal considerations pertaining to benefits, taxes, and worker categorisation.

9.5 Dispute Resolution and Arbitration

Issues with payment, job requirements, or contract violations can lead to disputes between gig workers and employers. HR specialists should incorporate strong dispute resolution procedures in the gig worker contract to reduce such dangers. These mechanisms, which guarantee that both parties have a defined procedure for resolving disagreements, may include clauses for mediation, arbitration, or litigation. These legal frameworks are essential for preserving equitable and open partnerships, reducing the likelihood of legal action, and making sure that each party is aware of their rights and responsibilities.

10 ETHICAL CONSIDERATIONS IN MANAGING GIG WORKERS

Even though gig workers are not entitled to the same benefits as full-time employees, managing them ethically entails making sure they are treated fairly, are transparent, and have their rights respected. In their interactions with gig workers, HR professionals must respect the values of justice and respect.

10.1 Fair Compensation and Transparent Pay Structures

Making sure gig workers receive appropriate compensation for their labour is a crucial ethical factor in managing them. When compared to full-time employees, gig workers frequently have large pay gaps, and many are not eligible for benefits like paid time off, health insurance, or retirement contributions. Pay rates must be competitive, represent the value of the work done, and adhere to industry norms, according to HR professionals. Pay structure transparency and timely payment are essential ethical measures that uphold confidence and guarantee employees feel appreciated.

10. 2 Access to Benefits and Support

Giving gig workers access to benefits like healthcare, paid time off, or retirement savings programs might enhance their ethical treatment, even though it is not legally mandated. Not every company can afford benefits, so HR managers can think about other ways to help, like flexible work schedules or mental health services. Offering assistance or benefits to gig workers shows that the business cares about their welfare, which raises job satisfaction levels and fosters a healthy work atmosphere.

10.3 Ensuring Equal Treatment and Non-Discrimination

Like other employees, gig workers ought to get fair and equal treatment. HR specialists are responsible for making sure gig workers are not subjected to discrimination on the basis of age, gender, colour, or any other protected trait. Fair access to opportunities, such as training and career development programs, is another aspect of equal treatment. To the greatest extent feasible, giving gig workers the same possibilities as full-time workers promotes a more welcoming and encouraging workplace.

10.4 Respect for Worker Autonomy and Privacy

Compared to full-time employees, gig workers usually have more freedom, including the option to select their tasks and work flexible hours. While juggling the demands of the business, HR professionals must respect this liberty. Because gig workers frequently interact with businesses via digital platforms, protecting workers' privacy and personal information is another ethical consideration. To preserve trust and advance ethical standards, it is essential to make sure that gig workers' personal information is kept safe and utilised solely for the purposes specified in their contracts.

10.5 Open Communication and Transparency

In order to manage gig workers ethically, transparency is essential. HR managers should keep the lines of communication open with gig workers on job requirements, policy changes, and any possible problems that may come up. Employees should be able to voice problems and offer suggestions through regular feedback procedures. This openness promotes productive working relationships and lessens the likelihood of miscommunications or conflicts.

10.6 Streamlining Recruitment and Onboarding Processes

Simplifying the hiring and onboarding procedures, which are essential for attracting gig workers, is one of the biggest advantages of digital tools. Platforms with AI capabilities are being utilised more and more to match applicants with job criteria, automate resume screening, and forecast success based on prior performance and skill sets. HR departments may increase the calibre of hires and cut down on the amount of time spent on human screening by utilising algorithms that evaluate big datasets.

Furthermore, cloud-based technologies facilitate smooth hiring processes, giving HR departments the ability to handle applications, hold virtual interviews, and monitor applicants' progress in real time. By integrating with social media and job boards, these platforms may increase the talent pool and make sure that businesses can locate the most qualified candidates for flexible, short-term positions. Digital tools also enable faster responses and updates for gig workers, who may apply for several positions across various platforms, enhancing the candidate experience.

Digital onboarding solutions can further improve productivity after a gig worker is employed. Cloud-based solutions that enable employees to remotely access pertinent information, watch training videos, and complete required paperwork can automate and customise onboarding procedures. This guarantees uniform onboarding for different employees and projects and does away with the need for time-consuming paperwork. Additionally, real-time tracking of onboarding progress is made possible by digital tools, which facilitates HR professionals' ability to quickly identify and address possible problems

11 LEVERAGING DIGITAL TOOLS FOR HRM EFFICIENCY

Human resource management (HRM) now faces both new opportunities and problems as a result of the gig economy, which forces businesses to swiftly and effectively adjust to a changing workforce. Digital solutions that increase productivity, improve communication, and expedite procedures are gradually replacing or supplementing traditional HRM approaches. HR teams may better manage remote teams and gig workers by utilising technologies like cloud-based platforms and artificial intelligence (AI). In order to increase productivity and make sure that HR procedures meet the demands of a contemporary, adaptable workforce, this integration is essential.

11.1 Facilitating Remote Collaboration and Communication

Since remote work makes up a big portion of the gig economy, efficient communication and teamwork are crucial to its success. HR departments can stay in constant contact with gig workers, no matter where they are, thanks to digital solutions like communication platforms (like Slack and Microsoft departments). These systems make it possible for employees and HR professionals to communicate and stay in touch by facilitating file sharing, video conferencing, and instant messaging

Furthermore, cloud based collaboration platforms like Asana or Google Workspace can support task distribution, progress tracking, and collaboration among geographically dispersed teams. These technologies give gig workers a single point of contact where they can stay up to know on project updates, due dates, and expectations. It makes managing several employees across time zones and regions easier for HR departments, guaranteeing that projects are finished on schedule and to a high standard.

Digital tools also aid in resolving issues like disengagement and loneliness that arise from working remotely. Regular check-ins via video conferencing tools and virtual meetings can help maintain employee motivation and create a feeling of community. These solutions allow HR managers to stay in contact with gig workers, providing assistance, getting feedback, and making sure that remote work environments are productively optimised.

11.2 Monitoring Performance and Managing Distributed Workforces

Due to the variable nature of gig labour and the absence of direct supervision, it can be difficult to manage a scattered workforce and keep an eye on performance in the gig economy. Digital technologies, however, have made it simpler to monitor performance, establish objectives, and provide gig workers feedback. By measuring key performance indicators (KPIs) and offering real-time insights into employee performance, AI-driven technologies can assist with productivity monitoring. AI is capable of analysing data from finished activities, evaluating their quality, and spotting patterns in employee behaviour, for instance (World Economic Forum, 2020). This information can be utilised to pinpoint areas in need of development and to offer tailored comments. HR staff can also remotely conduct performance evaluations, set targets, and track KPIs with performance management platforms like BambooHR or Workday.

HR teams may efficiently manage distributed workforces with the use of cloud-based project management technologies. Large teams of gig workers can be more easily coordinated with the use of these platforms' features, which include task allocation, progress tracking, and deadline management. Without continual supervision, managers may give assignments, track progress, and make sure employees are keeping on course. Because it enables them to manage their workloads and achieve deadlines without direct supervision, this is especially crucial for gig workers who might be working on several projects or clients at once.

These tools can also be utilised to promote a culture of learning and development and offer ongoing feedback. HR specialists can find areas where gig workers might need more assistance or training by utilising data from performance tracking tools. Providing ongoing feedback via digital platforms not only improves output but also raises employee satisfaction by showcasing a dedication to their career development.

HRM procedures must incorporate digital tools in order to meet the demands of the gig economy. Cloud-based platforms and artificial intelligence (AI) offer the infrastructure required to improve communication, manage performance across remote teams, and expedite the hiring process. HR managers may concentrate on key projects and employee engagement by automating time-consuming processes like hiring and onboarding. These tools also make it easier to collaborate and communicate, which keeps gig workers engaged and connected no matter where they are. Lastly, mechanisms for performance management and monitoring enable efficient supervision and ongoing development, guaranteeing that gig workers provide excellent work. HR teams may work more effectively, enhance the employee experience, and manage a varied, remote workforce more effectively by embracing these digital technologies.

12 CONCLUSION

Traditional HRM procedures need to be fundamentally rethought in light of the gig economy. HR managers may overcome the difficulties of overseeing a dispersed and varied staff by adopting cutting-edge approaches in talent acquisition, performance management, engagement, and compliance. Agility and efficiency are further improved by integrating digital tools, which helps organisations prosper in this changing environment. Using these tactics guarantees that the benefits of the gig labour are maximised and that they are in line with changing organisational goals.

Human resources (HR) procedures have undergone a dramatic change as a result of the gig economy's quick transformation of business operations. In order to effectively manage a varied and distributed workforce, human resources professionals must modify their approaches as more employees choose flexible, temporary work over traditional full-time employment. Traditional HRM procedures must be rethought in light of the gig economy, with an emphasis on adaptability, effectiveness, and creativity. Organisations may effectively manage this change and realise the full potential of their gig workforce by adopting innovative approaches in talent acquisition, performance management, engagement, and compliance.

Talent acquisition is one of the main areas where traditional HRM methods need to change. To satisfy changing business demands, the gig economy necessitates a more flexible approach to hiring that can swiftly find and onboard talent. In an environment where employees may only be employed for brief periods of time, traditional recruitment techniques like drawn-out interview procedures and strict hiring procedures are no longer successful. HR professionals may increase the speed and accuracy of candidate selection, automate administrative chores, and expedite the hiring process by utilising cloud-based systems, digital platforms, and AI-driven recruitment solutions. By matching candidates' skills with the particular requirements of short-term employment, these solutions not only save time but also improve the quality of recruits. Organisations can thus swiftly close gaps and continue to adapt to shifting business requirements.

Another crucial area that needs to change in the gig economy is performance management. HR professionals want solutions that enable them to efficiently monitor and manage performance without the conventional control associated with full-time employees, as gig workers frequently operate remotely or on a project-by-project basis. HR teams may monitor key performance indicators (KPIs), give real-time feedback, and evaluate the calibre of work performed by gig workers with the help of cloud-based performance management solutions and AI-powered analytics. By facilitating constant contact between supervisors and employees, these systems guarantee that performance standards are understood and fulfilled. Additionally, the information gathered by these platforms may be utilised to offer gig workers individualised feedback, development opportunities, and targeted training, which will help them advance their careers and perform better over time.

Another issue in the gig economy is engagement. Because they might not feel the same feeling of community or belonging that full-time employees do, gig workers frequently run the risk of becoming isolated. In the absence of effective engagement tactics, gig workers would feel alienated from the company's goals, which would reduce output and increase attrition. Even for geographically scattered employees, HR professionals must promote a feeling of community and connection in order to counteract this. Gig workers may stay engaged, communicate regularly, and stay in line with the company's values and objectives with the use of digital tools like employee engagement applications, virtual meetings, and collaboration platforms. Providing possibilities for professional growth, rewards, and recognition can help raise engagement levels and make gig workers feel valued and appreciated.

One of the biggest challenges in managing gig workers is compliance. Because tax rules and labour laws are complicated, particularly when it comes to independent contractors, HR professionals need to be on the lookout for ways to make sure their companies are in compliance with the law. This involves making certain that gig workers receive just compensation, the right benefits when needed, and accurate classification in accordance with regional labour regulations. HR professionals must keep up with developments in the regulatory environment since compliance is made more difficult by the growing drive for legal reforms that would extend some employee benefits to gig workers. By automating processes like contract administration, tax documentation, and reporting, digital technologies like compliance management software may help businesses remain on top of legal requirements while lowering the risk of non-compliance and legal issues.

Furthermore, agility and efficiency are significantly increased when digital tools are incorporated into HRM procedures. Real-time tracking, management, and communication with gig workers enables businesses to respond swiftly to changes in the market, priorities, and labour demands. Digital tools let teams coordinate more easily, make decisions more quickly, and develop better-informed strategies. HR professionals can improve their organization's capacity to react quickly to opportunities or challenges by utilising AI, data analytics, and cloud-based platforms. This will help the business stay competitive in a dynamic and fast-paced environment.

In addition to maximising the benefits of a gig workforce, using creative HRM methods backed by digital tools also helps to link these initiatives with the larger goals of the company. An organization's capacity to prosper in the contemporary economy is influenced by the flexibility, cost-effectiveness, and access to a worldwide talent pool that a well-managed gig workforce may offer. HR professionals can create a more nimble, inclusive, and efficient work environment that benefits the company and its gig workers by embracing the changes and difficulties of the gig economy. By using a comprehensive strategy, companies may better handle the intricacies of the gig economy, improve performance, optimise talent management procedures, and achieve long-term success.

REFERENCES

Arora, S., & Nabi, T. (2022). Blockchain adoption in banking systems: A boon or bane? In *Applications, challenges, and opportunities of blockchain technology in banking and insurance* (pp. 19–42). IGI Global. DOI: 10.4018/978-1-6684-4133-6.ch002

Arora, S., Nabi, T., & Bhardwaj, M. (2023). Blockchain technology: A double-edged sword when it comes to sustainable food security. *Empirical Economics Letters*, *22*, 67–88.

Bartik, A. W., Cullen, Z. B., Glaeser, E. L., & Luca, M. (2020). The impact of the COVID-19 crisis on small business outcomes and expectations. *Proceedings of the National Academy of Sciences of the United States of America*, *117*(30), 17693–17701. DOI: 10.1073/pnas.2006991117 PMID: 32651281

Bélanger, F., & Crossler, R. E. (2011). Privacy in the digital age: A review of the literature and a new conceptual framework. *Journal of Organizational and End User Computing*, *23*(2), 15–38.

Boudreau, J. W., & Lawler, E. E. (2017). HRM in the age of the gig economy: Implications and practices. *Human Resource Management*, *56*(6), 949–962. DOI: 10.1002/hrm.21856

Brynjolfsson, E., & McAfee, A. (2014). *The second machine age: Work, progress, and prosperity in a time of brilliant technologies*. W. W. Norton & Company.

Cappelli, P. (2015). The gig economy and the future of work. *Harvard Business Review*. https://hbr.org/2015/10/the-gig-economy-and-the-future-of-work

Carmeli, A., & Spreitzer, G. M. (2009). Trust, connectedness, and thriving: Implications for employees' performance and well-being. *The Journal of Applied Behavioral Science*, *45*(3), 306–327.

Choudhury, P., Foroughi, C., & Larson, B. Z. (2020). Work-from-anywhere: The productivity effects of virtual meetings. *Strategic Management Journal*, *41*(9), 1596–1619. DOI: 10.1002/smj.3165

Dube, A., & Chattopadhyay, P. (2021). How digital platforms are reshaping HRM: A framework for managing the gig economy. *Journal of Business Research*, *129*, 710–718.

Eisenstat, R. A., & Taylor, B. (2019). Future of work: Managing the gig economy and remote teams. *MIT Sloan Management Review*. https://sloanreview.mit.edu/article/the-future-of-work-managing-the-gig-economy/

Friedman, G. (2014). Workers without employers: Shadow corporations and the rise of the gig economy. *The Review of Radical Political Economics, 46*(4), 363–378. DOI: 10.1177/0486613414549399

Kansra, P., & Gill, H. S. (2016). Occupational Differences in the Awareness and Perception of Health Insurance of Workers Employed in Urban Informal Sector of Punjab. *Journal of Health Management, 18*(3), 410–423. DOI: 10.1177/0972063416663533

Kaufman, B. E. (2019). *Theoretical perspectives on work and the labor market* (7th ed.). Industrial Relations Research Association.

Kelliher, C., & Anderson, D. (2010). Changing employment relationships in the 21st century: Implications for HRM practices and employee well-being. *Employee Relations, 32*(4), 324–342. DOI: 10.1108/01409171011055766

Kuhn, P., & Maleki, A. (2017). The economics of the gig economy. *IZA World of Labor*. https://wol.iza.org/articles/the-economics-of-the-gig-economy

Lepak, D. P., & Snell, S. A. (2002). Examining the human resource architecture: The relationships among human capital, employment, and human resource configurations. *Journal of Management, 28*(4), 517–543. DOI: 10.1177/014920630202800403

McKinsey & Company. (2016). Independent work: Choice, necessity, and the gig economy. *McKinsey Global Institute*. https://www.mckinsey.com/business-functions/organization/our-insights/independent-work-choice-necessity-and-the-gig-economy

Parker, S. K., & Axtell, C. M. (2001). Seeing another viewpoint: Antecedents and outcomes of employee perspective taking. *Academy of Management Journal, 44*(6), 1054–1071. DOI: 10.2307/3069390

Pereira, V., & Bisson, J. (2021). Gig economy and HRM: Managing remote, flexible, and distributed teams in the digital age. *International Journal of Human Resource Management, 32*(5), 887–903.

Scholz, T. (2016). Platform cooperativism: A new economic model for the gig economy. *The New York Times*.

Stone, R. J. (2018). *Human resource management* (9th ed.). Wiley.

Sundararajan, A. (2016). *The sharing economy: The end of employment and the rise of crowd-based capitalism*. MIT Press.

Sundararajan, A. (2017). The sharing economy: A new era of human and economic progress. In *The Oxford Handbook of the Gig Economy* (pp. 1–28). Oxford University Press.

Tucker, J., & Varga, J. (2020). The role of AI in talent management and HRM practices in the gig economy. *Journal of Business Research, 116*, 345–357. DOI: 10.1016/j.jbusres.2019.12.021

Verma, D., Kansra, P., & Kumar, P. (2024). Role of Industry 5.0 in Bancassurance: A Theoretical Perspective. In *Convergence of Human Resources Technologies and Industry 5.0* (pp. 240–255). IGI Global. DOI: 10.4018/979-8-3693-1343-5.ch013

World Economic Forum. (2020). The future of work in the gig economy. https://www.weforum.org/reports/the-future-of-work-in-the-gig-economy

Compilation of References

Aayog, N. I. T. I. (2022). *Policy brief: India's booming gig and platform economy.* National Institution for Transforming India. https://www.niti.gov.in/sites/default/files/2022-06/Policy_Brief_India%27s_Booming_Gig_and_Platform_Economy_27062022.pdf

Aayog, N. I. T. I. (2022). *India's booming gig and platform economy: Perspectives and recommendations on the future of work.* Government of India.

Abdallah, W., Tfaily, F., & Harraf, A. (2025). The impact of digital financial literacy on financial behavior: Customers' perspective. *Competitiveness Review*, *35*(2), 347–370. DOI: 10.1108/CR-11-2023-0297

Abdelhamid, M., & Hassan, G. (2019, April). Blockchain and smart contracts. In *Proceedings of the 8th International Conference on Software and Information Engineering* (pp. 91-95).

Abdulmalek, S., Nasir, A., Jabbar, W. A., Almuhaya, M. A. M., Bairagi, A. K., Khan, M. A. M., & Kee, S. H. (2022). IoT-Based Healthcare-Monitoring System towards Improving Quality of Life: A Review. *Healthcare (Basel)*, *10*(10), 1993. DOI: 10.3390/healthcare10101993 PMID: 36292441

Abu Mizar, Y. S. M. (2021). Decentralized Project Management for the Gig Economy Using Blockchain to Ensure Trust and Reliable Ranking (Bachelor's thesis). Retrieved from https://opus4.kobv.de/opus4-haw/files/1087/I000992830Thesis.pdf

Adelakun, B. O. (2023). Tax compliance in the gig economy: the need for transparency and accountability. Journal of Knowledge Learning and Science Technology ISSN: 2959-6386 (Online), 1(1), 191-198. DOI: 10.60087/jklst.vol1.n1.p219

Adhikari, M., Ghimire, D. M., & Lama, A. D. (2024). FinTech and Financial Inclusion: Exploring the Mediating Role of Digital Financial Literacy in Enhancing Access to Financial Services. *Journal of Emerging Management Studies*, *1*(2), 117–136. DOI: 10.3126/jems.v1i2.71512

Agarwal, J. D., Agarwal, M., Agarwal, A., & Agarwal, Y. (2021). Economics of cryptocurrencies: Artificial intelligence, blockchain, and digital currency. In *Information for efficient decision making: big data, blockchain and relevance* (pp. 331-430).

Agarwalla, S. K., Barua, S. K., Jacob, J., & Varma, J. R. (2015). Financial literacy among working young in urban India. *World Development*, *67*, 101–109. DOI: 10.1016/j.worlddev.2014.10.004

Aggarwal, S. C. (2023, July). *'Gig' workers in India: An overview* [Preprint]. ResearchGate. DOI: 10.13140/RG.2.2.29650.32964

Aggarwal, V., & Karwasra, N. (2023). A bibliometric analysis on trade openness and economic growth: Current dynamics and future direction. *Competitiveness Review*. Advance online publication. DOI: 10.1108/CR-11-2022-0177

Agrawal, T. K., Kumar, V., Pal, R., Wang, L., & Chen, Y. (2021). Blockchain-based framework for supply chain traceability: A case example of the textile and clothing industry. *Computers & Industrial Engineering*, *154*, 107130. DOI: 10.1016/j.cie.2021.107130

Ahmad, K., Samad, K., Rahman, N., Daud, S., Marmaya, N., Nasution, Y., & Hamzah, R. (2024). Policies improving the well-being of gig workers in Malaysia. *Information Management and Business Review*, *16*(1(I)), 182–189. DOI: 10.22610/imbr.v16i1(I).3698

Ahmad, V., Arora, M., Sayal, A., Kumar, R., & Kumar, P. (2025). Exploring trends in e-business and sustainable finance: An integrated analytical approach. *Frontiers in Sustainable Cities*, *7*, 1549874. DOI: 10.3389/frsc.2025.1549874

Ahmed, W. A., & MacCarthy, B. L. (2023). Blockchain-enabled supply chain traceability–How wide? How deep? *International Journal of Production Economics*, *263*, 108963. DOI: 10.1016/j.ijpe.2023.108963

Ahmed, W., Hizam, S. M., & Sentosa, I. (2020). Digital Dexterity: Employee As Consumer Approach Towards Organizational Success. *Human Resource Development International*, •••, 1–11. https://Doi.Org/10.1080/13678868.2020.1835107

Aizenman, J., Cheung, Y. W., & Ito, H. (2019). The interest rate effect on private saving: Alternative perspectives. *Journal of International Commerce. Economic Policy*, *10*(01), 1950002.

Akir, Z. (2003). Diffusion of innovations. In *Education and Technology: An Encyclopedia* (Vol. 1–2, pp. 205–210). Routledge., DOI: 10.4337/9781800883284.diffusion.of.innovations

Al Kholilah, N., & Iramani, R. (2013). Studi financial management behavior pada masyarakat surabaya. *Journal of Business & Banking*, *3*(1), 69–80. DOI: 10.14414/jbb.v3i1.255

Alam, M. Z., Patwary, M. M., & Rahim, M. A. (2013). Mobile money system: The Bangladesh experience. *International Journal of Scientific and Research Publications*, *3*(10), 1–5.

Alanzi, T. M. (2021). Gig health vs ehealth: Future prospects in saudi arabian health-care system. *Journal of Multidisciplinary Healthcare*, *14*, 1945–1953. DOI: 10.2147/JMDH.S304690 PMID: 34326645

Alareeni, B., & Hamdan, A. (2023). Sustainable Finance, Digitalization and the Role of Technology. In *Proceedings of the International Conference on Business and Technology (ICBT 2021)*. Springer International Publishing. DOI: 10.1007/978-3-031-08084-5

Al-Azawei, A., Serenelli, F., & Lundqvist, K. (2017). Universal design for learning.

Al-Azawei, A., Serenelli, F., & Lundqvist, K. (2017). The effectiveness of adaptive learning technologies for students with learning disabilities: A systematic review. *Computers in Human Behavior*.

Albahri, O. S., Albahri, A. S., Mohammed, K. I., Zaidan, A. A., Zaidan, B. B., Hashim, M., & Salman, O. H. (2018). Systematic Review of Real-time Remote Health Monitoring System in Triage and Priority-Based Sensor Technology: Taxonomy, Open Challenges, Motivation and Recommendations. In *Journal of Medical Systems* (Vol. 42, Issue 5, pp. 1–27). Springer. DOI: 10.1007/s10916-018-0943-4

Albahri, O. S., Zaidan, A. A., Zaidan, B. B., Hashim, M., Albahri, A. S., & Alsalem, M. A. (2018). Real-Time Remote Health-Monitoring Systems in a Medical Centre: A Review of the Provision of Healthcare Services-Based Body Sensor Information, Open Challenges and Methodological Aspects. In *Journal of Medical Systems* (Vol. 42, Issue 9, pp. 1–47). Springer. DOI: 10.1007/s10916-018-1006-6

Alenezi, M. (2023). Digital Learning and Digital Institution in Higher Education. *Education Sciences*, *13*(1), 88. Advance online publication. DOI: 10.3390/educsci13010088

Alfedaghi, H. S. (2024). Digital Dexterity: Building Capabilities in the Era of AI. DOI: 10.2118/222277-MS

Ali, M., Naqi, S. M. A., & Habib, M. (2023). The study "Unravelling the Impact: Assessing the Impacts of Rising Rates of Interest and Inflation on Individual Finances". sjesr, 6(2), 56-62.

Alliance for Financial Inclusion. DFSWG, & CEMCWG. (2021). *Digital financial literacy toolkit*. Alliance for Financial Inclusion. Retrieved from https://www.ssrn.com/abstract=2715350

Allon, G., Cohen, M. C., & Sinchaisri, W. P. (2023). The impact of behavioral and economic drivers on gig economy workers. *Manufacturing & Service Operations Management*, *25*(4), 1376–1393. DOI: 10.1287/msom.2023.1191

Alsharif, A. H., Salleh, N. O. R. Z. M. D., & Baharun, R. O. H. A. I. Z. A. T. (2020). Bibliometric analysis. *Journal of Theoretical and Applied Information Technology*, *98*(15), 2948–2962.

Alshehhi, A., Nobanee, H., & Khare, N. (2018). The Impact of Sustainability Practices on Corporate Financial Performance: Literature Trends and Future Research Potential. *Sustainability (Basel)*, *10*(2), 494–519. DOI: 10.3390/su10020494

Alshibani, A., Alkhathami, S. M., Hassanain, M. A., Tuffaha, F., Ouis, D., & Mohammed, A. (2024). Hybrid Framework for Investigating Digital Transformation Barriers in The Oil and Gas Sector. *Energies*, *17*(23), 6151. https://Doi.Org/10.3390/En17236151. DOI: 10.3390/en17236151

Alves, B., Schumacher, M., Cretton, F., Calvé, A. L., Cherix, G., Werlen, D., . . . Cloux, P. (2014). Fairtrace: applying semantic web tools and techniques to the textile traceability. In *Enterprise Information Systems: 15h International Conference, ICEIS 2013, Angers, France, July 4-7, 2013, Revised Selected Papers 15* (pp. 68-84). Springer International Publishing. DOI: 10.1007/978-3-319-09492-2_5

Amagir, A., Groot, W., Maassen van den Brink, H., & Wilschut, A. (2018). A review of financial-literacy education programs for children and adolescents. *Citizenship. Social and Economics Education*, *17*(1), 56–80.

Ameer, R., & Othman, R. (2012). Sustainability practices and corporate financial performance: A study based on the top global corporations. *Journal of Business Ethics*, *108*(1), 61–79. https://link.springer.com/article/10.1007/s10551-011-1063-y. DOI: 10.1007/s10551-011-1063-y

Amoozad Mahdiraji, H., Govindan, K., Yaftiyan, F., Garza-Reyes, J. A., & Razavi Hajiagha, S. H. (2023). Unveiling coordination contracts' roles considering circular economy and eco-innovation toward pharmaceutical supply chain resiliency: Evidence of an emerging economy. *Journal of Cleaner Production*, *382*, 135135. DOI: 10.1016/j.jclepro.2022.135135

Analoui, F. (1994). Training And Development. *Journal of Management Development, 13*(9), 61–72. https://Doi.Org/10.1108/02621719410072107. DOI: 10.1108/02621719410072107

Anan, K. (2024). The evolution of employment law in the gig economy. *Journal of Modern Law and Policy, 4*(2), 29–41. DOI: 10.47941/jmlp.2160

Anđelković, B., Jakobi, T., Ivanović, V., Kalinić, Z., & Radonjić, Lj. (2024). *Gigmetar Region.* Public Policy Research Center. http://gigmetar.publicpolicy.rs/en/region-en-2024-1

Anwar, M. A., & Graham, M. (2021). Hidden transcripts of the gig economy: Labour agency and the new art of resistance. *Review of International Political Economy, 28*(2), 309–331. DOI: 10.1080/09692290.2020.1737569

Anwar, M. A., Otieno, E., & Stein, M. (2022). Locked in, logged out: Pandemic and ride-hailing in South Africa and Kenya. *The Journal of Modern African Studies, 60*(4), 457–478. DOI: 10.1017/S0022278X22000234

Apouey, B. H., Roulet, A., Solal, I., & Stabile, M. (2020). Gig workers during the covid-19 crisis in France: financial precarity and mental well-being. SSRN Electronic Journal. DOI: 10.2139/ssrn.3688445

Appelbaum, E. (2000). *Manufacturing advantage: Why high-performance work systems pay off.* Cornell University Press.

Arafin Ayon, S. M. M. (2023). Digital dreams, gendered realities: insights from Bangladesh's freelance sector... DOI: 10.31235/osf.io/95tsy

Archana K, Hanis Sultana A, Vishnu Priya V, Prabakaran V, Krishnaveni P, Swarnam S, Senthil Kumar S and Shamini SD. (2023). Blockchain Technology As A Tool For Effective Recruitment: A Design Thinking Approach. 1603-1604.

Arora, R. (2017). Financial inclusion: understanding concept, barriers and measurement. [PDF]

Arora, S., & Nabi, T. (2022). Blockchain adoption in banking systems: A boon or bane.

Arora, S., Nabi, T., & Bhardwaj, M. Blockchain technology: A double-edged sword when it comes to sustainable food security. *Empirical Economics Letters, 22*, 67-88.

Arora, S., Pawar, M., Joshi, M., Pargaien, S., Mer, A., & Misra, A. (2025). Handshake between humans and artificial intelligence: A review. *Challenges in Information, Communication and Computing Technology*, 693-697.

Arora, A. (2016). Assessment of financial literacy among working Indian women. *Business Analyst, 36*(2), 219–237.

Arora, S., & Nabi, T. (2022). Blockchain adoption in banking systems: A boon or bane? In *Applications, challenges, and opportunities of blockchain technology in banking and insurance* (pp. 19–42). IGI Global. DOI: 10.4018/978-1-6684-4133-6.ch002

Arora, S., Nabi, T., & Bhardwaj, M. (2023). Blockchain technology: A double-edged sword when it comes to sustainable food security. *Empirical Economics Letters, 22*, 67–88.

Arora, S., Oberoi, S., Nabi, T., & Verma, B. (2024). How does blockchain impact sustainable food security? Insights from literature review. *International Journal of Information Management Data Insights, 4*(2), 100276. DOI: 10.1016/j.jjimei.2024.100276

Arruda, E., Melatto, R., & Braga da Silva, N. (2021). Circular economy: A brief literature review (2015–2020). *Sustainable Operations and Computers., 2*, 79–86. Advance online publication. DOI: 10.1016/j.susoc.2021.05.001

Arulmurugan, P., Karthikeyan, P., & Devi, N. (2013). Financial Inclusion in India: A Theoretical Assessment. *Indian Journal of Applied Research, 3*(3), 217–222. DOI: 10.15373/2249555X/MAR2013/71

Asfahani, A. M. (2024). Fusing talent horizons: The transformative role of data integration in modern talent management. *Discover Sustainability, 5*(1), 25. DOI: 10.1007/s43621-024-00212-7

Asfahani, A., Alsobahi, G., & Dahlan, D. (2023). Navigating the Saudi gig economy: The role of human resource practices in enhancing job satisfaction and career sustainability. *Sustainability (Basel), 15*(23), 16406. DOI: 10.3390/su152316406

Ashford, S. J., Caza, B. B., & Reid, E. M. (2018). From surviving to thriving in the gig economy: A research agenda for individuals in the new world of work. *Research in Organizational Behavior, 38*, 23–41. DOI: 10.1016/j.riob.2018.11.001

Ashta, A., & Herrmann, H. (2021). Artificial intelligence and fintech: An overview of opportunities and risks for banking, investments, and microfinance. *Strategic Change, 30*(3), 211–222. DOI: 10.1002/jsc.2404

Asyik, N. F., Wahidahwati, W., Laily, N., & Wahidahwati, W. (2022). The role of intellectual capital in intervening financial behavior and financial literacy on financial inclusion. *WSEAS Transactions on Business and Economics, 19*(1), 805–814. DOI: 10.37394/23207.2022.19.70

Atkinson, A., & Messy, F. A. (2012). Measuring financial literacy: Results of the OECD/International Network on Financial Education (INFE) pilot study.

Atkinson, K., Barnes, J., Albee, J., Anttila, P., Haataja, J., Nanavati, K., Steelman, K., & Wallace, C. (2016). Breaking Barriers to Digital Literacy. Iee. https://Doi.Org/10.1145/2982142.2982183

Auguste, D., Roll, S., & Despard, M. (2023). Democratizing the economy or introducing economic risk? gig work during the covid-19 pandemic. *Work and Occupations*, *51*(4), 550–606. DOI: 10.1177/07308884231202032

Avkiran, N. K. (2006). Developing foreign bank efficiency models for DEA grounded in finance theory. *Socio-Economic Planning Sciences*, *40*(4), 275–296. DOI: 10.1016/j.seps.2004.10.006

Awasthi, V., & Kansra, P. (2023). Blockchain in the healthcare industry: process and applications. In *Advanced machine learning algorithms for complex financial applications* (pp. 81–93). IGI Global. DOI: 10.4018/978-1-6684-4483-2.ch006

Ayentimi, D., Abadi, H., & Burgess, J. (2022). Decent gig work in sub-Sahara Africa? *The Journal of Industrial Relations*, *65*(1), 112–125. DOI: 10.1177/00221856221111693

Azeez, N. A., & Akhtar, S. J. (2021). Digital financial literacy and its determinants: An empirical evidences from rural India. *South Asian Journal of Social Studies and Economics*, *11*(2), 8–22. DOI: 10.9734/sajsse/2021/v11i230279

Babalola, A., Manu, P., Cheung, C., Yunusa-Kaltungo, A., & Bartolo, P. (2023). Applications of immersive technologies for occupational safety and health training and education: A systematic review. In *Safety Science* (Vol. 166, p. 106214). Elsevier., DOI: 10.1016/j.ssci.2023.106214

Baddeley, M. (2018). *Behavioural Economics and Finance*. Routledge. DOI: 10.4324/9781315211879

Bailey, J. L., & Mitchell, R. B. (2016). Industry Perceptions of The Competencies Needed by Computer Programmers: Technical, Business, And Soft Skills. *Journal of Computer Information Systems*, *47*, 28–33. https://Doi.Org/10.1080/08874417.2007.11645951

Bajwa, U., Gastaldo, D., Di Ruggiero, E., & Knorr, L. (2018). The health of workers in the global gig economy. In *Globalization and Health* (Vol. 14, Issue 1). BioMed Central Ltd. DOI: 10.1186/s12992-018-0444-8

Baker, R. S., & Siemens, G. (2014). Educational data mining and learning analytics.

Baker, R. S., & Siemens, G. (2022). The role of AI in personalized learning.

Baker, R. S., & Siemens, G. (2014). Educational data mining and learning analytics. In Gilbert, S. J., & O'Brien, T. G. (Eds.), *Learning analytics: From research to practice*. DOI: 10.1007/978-1-4614-3305-7_4

Banik, N., & Padalkar, M. (2021). The spread of gig economy: Trends and effects. *Foresight and STI Governance*, *15*(1), 19–29. DOI: 10.17323/2500-2597.2021.1.19.29

Banker, R. D., Charnes, A., & Cooper, W. W. (1984). Some models for estimating technical and scale inefficiencies in data envelopment analysis. *Management Science*, *30*(9), 1078–1092. DOI: 10.1287/mnsc.30.9.1078

Banna, H., & Alam, M. R. (2021). Impact of digital financial inclusion on ASEAN banking stability: Implications for the post-Covid-19 era. *Studies in Economics and Finance*, *38*(2), 504–523. DOI: 10.1108/SEF-09-2020-0388

Bansal, R., & Singh, R. (2020). The emergence of gig economy in India: A paradigm shift. *Parishodh Journal*, *9*(3), 123–134.

Banton, C. L. (2019). Advancing Technologies in Human Resource Development (HRD). In Emerald Publishing Limited Ebooks (Pp. 25–36). https://Doi.Org/10.1108/978-1-78973-073-920191003

Barbu, E., & Song, X. (2016). The effects of offshoring on employer-provided training. *The Journal of International Trade & Economic Development*, *25*(4), 479–503. DOI: 10.1080/09638199.2015.1068838

Barik, R., & Sharma, P. (2019). Analyzing the progress and prospects of financial inclusion in India. *Journal of Public Affairs*, *19*(4), e1948. DOI: 10.1002/pa.1948

Barney, J. (1991). Firm resources and sustained competitive advantage. *Journal of Management*, *17*(1), 99–120. DOI: 10.1177/014920639101700108

Barrette, C. M. (2015). Usefulness of technology adoption research in introducing an online workbook. *System*, *49*, 133–144. DOI: 10.1016/j.system.2015.01.005

Barthakur, A., Kovanović, V., Joksimović, S., Zhang, Z., Richey, M., & Pardo, A. (2022). Measuring Leadership Development in Workplace Learning Using Automated Assessments: Learning Analytics and Measurement Theory Approach. *British Journal of Educational Technology*, *53*(6), 1842–1863. https://Doi.Org/10.1111/Bjet.13218. DOI: 10.1111/bjet.13218

Bartik, A. W., Cullen, Z. B., Glaeser, E. L., & Luca, M. (2020). The impact of the COVID-19 crisis on small business outcomes and expectations. *Proceedings of the National Academy of Sciences of the United States of America*, *117*(30), 17693–17701. DOI: 10.1073/pnas.2006991117 PMID: 32651281

Bartlett, C. A., & Ghoshal, S. (2002). Building competitive advantage through people. *MIT Sloan Management Review*, *43*(2), 34.

Bashir, I. (2022). Blockchain consensus. In *Blockchain Consensus: An Introduction to Classical, Blockchain, and Quantum Consensus Protocols* (pp. 207–257). Apress. DOI: 10.1007/978-1-4842-8179-6_5

Bass, B. (2021). How Blockchain Could Work for Staffing: Hint, Direct Sourcing and Diversity. Retrieved from https://www.olooptech.com/post/how-blockchain-could-work-for-staffing-hint-direct-sourcing-and-diversity#:~:text=The%20Blockchain%20Direct%20Sourcing%20Process%201%20A%20client,the%20requisition%20once%20it%E2%80%99s%20released.%20...%20More%20items)

Bateyo, A. (2025). The gig economy: Implications for workforce management. *Research Invention Journal of Current Issues in Arts and Management*, *4*(1), 39–42. DOI: 10.59298/RIJCIAM/2025/413942

Batmunkh, A., Fekete-Farkas, M., & Lakner, Z. (2022). Bibliometric analysis of gig economy. *Administrative Sciences*, *12*(2), 51. DOI: 10.3390/admsci12020051

BCG. (2021). Unlocking the potential of the gig economy in India. *Boston Consulting Group*. https://www.bcg.com/en-in/unlocking-gigeconomy-in-india

Beatrice Oyinkansola, A. (2024). The gig economy: challenges for tax system. Journal of Knowledge Learning and Science Technology ISSN: 2959-6386 (Online), 3(3), 1-8. DOI: 10.60087/jklst.vol3.n3.p1-8

Behar, J. A., Liu, C., Kotzen, K., Tsutsui, K., Corino, V. D. A., Singh, J., Pimentel, M. A. F., Warrick, P., Zaunseder, S., Andreotti, F., Sebag, D., Kopanitsa, G., McSharry, P. E., Karlen, W., Karmakar, C., & Clifford, G. D. (2020). Remote health diagnosis and monitoring in the time of COVID-19. In *Physiological Measurement* (Vol. 41, Issue 10, p. 10TR01). IOP Publishing. DOI: 10.1088/1361-6579/abba0a

Bekal, S., Harish, A., Bhandari, K., Sachin, Y., Marda, K., & Bishnoi, Y. (2023). Review of Literature on the Topic of the Gig Economy in India. *International Journal of Innovative Science and Research Technology.*, *8*(4), 1049–1056.

Bélanger, F., & Crossler, R. E. (2011). Privacy in the digital age: A review of the literature and a new conceptual framework. *Journal of Organizational and End User Computing*, *23*(2), 15–38.

Bello, M. I., & Daniel, T. R. (2022). Potentials of Blockchain Technology for Payroll Systems. Potentials of Blockchain Technology for Payroll Systems" (2022). *SAIS 2022 Proceedings*. 20.https://aisel.aisnet.org/sais2022/20

Bencsik, A. (2024). Challenges Of a Digitalizing World in The Light of An International Survey. RIMCIS : International And Multidisciplinary Journal of Social Sciences, 1–23. https://Doi.Org/10.17583/Rimcis.12502

Bender, L. L., Walia, G. S., Fagerholm, F., Pagels, M., Nygard, K. E., & Münch, J. (2014). Measurement Of the Non-Technical Skills of Software Professionals: An Empirical Investigation. International Conference on Software Engineering, 478–483. http://Ksiresearchorg.Ipage.Com/Seke/Seke14paper/Seke14paper_216.Pdf

Benligiray, S., Güngör, A. Y., & Akbaş, İ. (2024). Measuring Remote Working Skills: Scale Development and Validation Study. *PLoS One*, *19*(4), e0299074. https://Doi.Org/10.1371/Journal.Pone.0299074. DOI: 10.1371/journal.pone.0299074 PMID: 38603683

Bennett, N., & Lemoine, J. (2014). What VUCA really means for you. *Harvard Business Review*, *92*(1/2).

Benton, M. C., Radziwill, N. M., Purritano, A. W., & Gerhart, C. J. (2018). Blockchain for Supply Chain: Improving Transparency and Efficiency Simultaneously. *Software Quality Professional, 20*(3).

Berde, É., Mengesha, S. T., Mola, B. A., & Remsei, S. (2024). Massive Open Online Courses (MOOCs) for Ethiopian Educators: Evaluating MOOCs as a global development tool. *Research in Globalization*, *9*, 100263. DOI: 10.1016/j.resglo.2024.100263

Berger, T., Frey, C. B., Levin, G. I., & Danda, S. R. (2019). Uber happy? work and well-being in the 'gig economy'. *Economic Policy*, *34*(99), 429–477. DOI: 10.1093/epolic/eiz007

Berg, J., Furrer, M., Harmon, E., Rani, U., & Silberman, M. S. (2018). Digital labour platforms and the future of work – Towards decent work in the online world. International Labour Organization. https://doi.org/DOI: 10.2139/ssrn.3355364

Berg, J., Furrer, M., Harmon, E., Rani, U., & Silberman, M. S. (2018). *Digital labour platforms and the future of work: Towards decent work in the online world.* International Labour Organization. https://doi.org/DOI: 10.2139/ssrn.3197539

Bhandari, B., Das, G. K., Gupta, S., Sahu, A. K., Urs, K. S., Pal, N., & Raj, K. (2023). Socio-economic impact assessment of food delivery platform workers. *August 2023.*

Bhattacharya, M. (2015). A conceptual framework of RFID adoption in retail using Rogers stage model. *Business Process Management Journal, 21*(3), 517–540. DOI: 10.1108/BPMJ-06-2014-0047

Bhushan, P., & Medury, Y. (2014). An empirical analysis of inter linkages between financial attitudes, financial behaviour and financial knowledge of salaried individuals. *Indian Journal of Commerce and Management Studies*, *5*(3), 58–64.

Bokhari, S. S. A., & Ghaffar, A. (2024). Emerging Trends In Human Resource Management: Exploring Digital Transformation, Employee Well-Being, And Remote Work Paradigms. *Journal for Business Education and Management*, *4*(2), 1–16. DOI: 10.56596/jbem.v4i2.139

Bondarouk, T., & Brewster, C. (2016). Conceptualising the future of HRM and technology research. *International Journal of Human Resource Management*, *27*(21), 2652–2671. DOI: 10.1080/09585192.2016.1232296

Boudreau, J. W., & Jesuthasan, R. (2011). *Transformative HR: how great companies use evidence-based change for sustainable advantage*. John Wiley & Sons.

Boudreau, J. W., & Lawler, E. E. (2017). HRM in the age of the gig economy: Implications and practices. *Human Resource Management*, *56*(6), 949–962. DOI: 10.1002/hrm.21856

Broccardo, L., Truant, E., & Dana, L. P. (2023). The interlink between digitalization, sustainability, and performance: An Italian context. *Journal of Business Research*, *158*, 113621. DOI: 10.1016/j.jbusres.2022.113621

Brown, A., & Green, T. (2021). Digital literacy in the classroom: Bridging the gap..

Brown, P., & Lee, J. (2022). AI-driven personalized learning and its impact on academic success.

Brown, R. (2021). The shift to e-learning: The cost-effectiveness of e-books in the U.S.

Brown, T. (2021). Sustainable learning: The role of cloud-based education in reducing environmental impact.

Brynjolfsson, E., & McAfee, A. (2014). *The second machine age: Work, progress, and prosperity in a time of brilliant technologies*. W. W. Norton & Company.

Bucos, T. (2023). The gig economy – result of the labour market platformization. *Economica*, (2(124)), 25–42. DOI: 10.53486/econ.2023.124.025

Budhi, V. (2022). Advantages And Di. (Behera, B. (2022). Should you start accepting salary in Bitcoin? Retrieved from, https://economictimes.indiatimes.com/markets/cryptocurrency/should-you-start-accepting-a-salary-in-bitcoin/articleshow/90455216.cms

Bulathwela, S., Perez-Ortiz, M., Yaneva, V., & Luckin, R. (2021). Towards an open data ecosystem for education: Addressing challenges of a machine learning pipeline for educational applications.

Bunders, D. J., Arets, M., Frenken, K., & De Moor, T. (2022). The feasibility of platform cooperatives in the gig economy. *Journal of Co-operative Organization and Management, 10*(1), 100167. DOI: 10.1016/j.jcom.2022.100167

Burke, A. E. (2019). *The freelance project and gig economies of the 21st century.* Centre for Research on Self-Employment (CRSE).

Burrell, D. N. (2023). Dynamic Evaluation Approaches to Telehealth Technologies and Artificial Intelligence (AI) Telemedicine Applications in Healthcare and Biotechnology Organizations. *Merits, 3*(4), 700–721. DOI: 10.3390/merits3040042

Bush, J. T., & Balven, R. M. (2019). Catering to the crowd: An HRM perspective on crowd worker engagement. *Human Resource Management Review.*

Business Standard. (2024). *India's gig economy may add 90 million jobs, contribute 1.25% to GDP.*https://www.business-standard.com

Cappelli, P. (2015). The gig economy and the future of work. *Harvard Business Review.* https://hbr.org/2015/10/the-gig-economy-and-the-future-of-work

Carlin, B. I., Olafsson, A., & Pagel, M. (2019, January). FinTech and consumer financial well-being in the information age. In *AFFECT Conference. University of Miami. https://www. fdi c. gov/bank/analytical/fintech/papers/carlin-paper. pdf.*

Carmeli, A., Reiter-Palmon, R., & Ziv, E. (2010). Inclusive leadership and employee involvement in creative tasks in the workplace: The mediating role of psychological safety. *Creativity Research Journal, 22*(3), 250–260. DOI: 10.1080/10400419.2010.504654

Carmeli, A., & Spreitzer, G. M. (2009). Trust, connectedness, and thriving: Implications for employees' performance and well-being. *The Journal of Applied Behavioral Science, 45*(3), 306–327.

Carnevale, J. B., & Hatak, I. (2020). Employee adjustment and well-being in the era of COVID-19: Implications for human resource management. *Journal of Business Research, 116*, 183–187. DOI: 10.1016/j.jbusres.2020.05.037 PMID: 32501303

Carpenter, J. P., Mosquera Gende, I., & Marcelo-Martínez, P. (2025). Multiplatform Ecosystems of Professional Learning: The Case of the #Charlaseducativas. *Journal Of New Approaches in Educational Research, 14*(1), 6. https://Doi.Org/10.1007/S44322-024-00024-7. DOI: 10.1007/s44322-024-00024-7

Casanova, D., Bastos, G., & Antonaci, A. (2024). *Follow-up and analysis of national and EU policy developments on micro-credentials*. Research Report No. 6.1., Zenodo. https://doi.org/DOI: 10.5281/zenodo.13850890

Castellacci, F., Consoli, D., & Santoalha, A. (2020). The Role Of E-Skills in Technological Diversification in European Regions. *Regional Studies, 54*(8), 1123–1135. https://Doi.Org/10.1080/00343404.2019.1681585. DOI: 10.1080/00343404.2019.1681585

Chain. (2023, August 26). Chain Insights — Redefining the Post-Pandemic Freelance Economy with Web3. Retrieved from https://medium.com/@chaininc/chain-insights-redefining-the-post-pandemic-freelance-economy-with-web3-1ea280b27dd1

Chamorro-Premuzic, T., Akhtar, R., Winsborough, D., & Sherman, R. A. (2017). The Datafication of Talent: How Technology Is Advancing the Science of Human Potential at Work. *Current Opinion in Behavioral Sciences, 18*, 13–16. https://Doi.Org/10.1016/J.COBEHA.2017.04.007. DOI: 10.1016/j.cobeha.2017.04.007

Chandana, B. H., Shaik, N., & Chitralingappa, P. (2023). Exploring the Frontiers of User Experience Design: VR, AR, and the Future of Interaction. In *2023 International Conference on Computer Science and Emerging Technologies (CSET)* (pp. 1-6). IEEE. DOI: DOI: 10.1109/CSET58993.2023.10346724

Chang, S. C., Hsu, T. C., Chen, Y. N., & Jong, M. S. (2020). The effects of spherical video-based virtual reality implementation on students' natural science learning effectiveness. *Interactive Learning Environments, 28*(7), 915–929. DOI: 10.1080/10494820.2018.1548490

Chang, S. E., & Chen, Y. (2020). When blockchain meets supply chain: A systematic literature review on current development and potential applications. *IEEE Access : Practical Innovations, Open Solutions, 8*, 62478–62494. DOI: 10.1109/ACCESS.2020.2983601

Chang, S. E., Chen, Y. C., & Lu, M. F. (2019). Supply chain re-engineering using blockchain technology: A case of smart contract-based tracking process. *Technological Forecasting and Social Change, 144*, 1–11. DOI: 10.1016/j.techfore.2019.03.015

Charnes, A., Cooper, W. W., & Rhodes, E. (1978). Measuring the efficiency of decision-making units. European Journal of Operational Research, 2(6), 429–444. https://doi.org/ 90229-7.DOI: 10.1016/0377-2217(79)

Chatterjee, J. M., & Sujatha, R. (2024). *Transforming Healthcare: The Synergy of Telemedicine, Telehealth, and Artificial Intelligence*. Springer., DOI: 10.1007/978-981-97-2938-8_1

Chaturvedi, A., Armstrong, B., & Chaturvedi, R. (2014). Securing the food supply chain: Understanding complex interdependence through agent-based simulation. *Health and Technology*, *4*(2), 159–169. DOI: 10.1007/s12553-014-0086-7 PMID: 32219055

Chaudhary, R., & Mitra, S. (2019, November 22). *Labour practices in the emerging gig economy in India: A case study of Urban Clap* [Conference presentation]. Formalisation, Informalisation and the Labour Process Workshop, CeMIS, Goettingen.

Chauhan, M., & Sahoo, D. R. (2024). Towards a greener tomorrow: Exploring the potential of AI, blockchain, and IoT in sustainable development. *Nature Environment and Pollution Technology*, *23*(2), 1105–1113. DOI: 10.46488/NEPT.2024.v23i02.044

Chen, T. (2023). Advancing Technical Education and Fostering Soft Skills Development Through Digital Learning. Advances In Education Humanities and Social Science Research, 7(1), 91. https://Doi.Org/10.56028/Aehssr.7.1.91.2023

Cheng, B. (2019, August 24). Agility is key for working in India's gig economy. *BusinessWorld*. https://www.businessworld.in/article/agility-is-key-for-working-in-india's-gig-economy-175053

Cheng, B. (2019, August 24). Agility is key for working in India's gig economy. *BusinessWorld*.https://www.businessworld.in/article/agility-is-key-for-working-in-india's-gig-economy-175053

Chen, S. Y., & Wang, J. H. (2019). Human Factors and Personalized Digital Learning: An Editorial. *International Journal of Human-Computer Interaction*, *35*(4-5), 297–298. https://Doi.Org/10.1080/10447318.2018.1542891. DOI: 10.1080/10447318.2018.1542891

Cherry, M. A., & Aloisi, A. (2017). 'Dependent contractors' in the gig economy: A comparative approach. *American University Law Review, 66*, 635. Saint Louis University Legal Studies Research Paper No. 2016-15. https://doi.org/DOI: 10.2139/ssrn.2847869

Chhillar, N., & Arora, S. (2022). Personal financial management behavior using digital platforms and its domains. *Journal of Financial Management. Markets and Institutions*, *10*(02), 2250009. DOI: 10.1142/S2282717X22500098

Chien, S.-Y., Wu, C.-Y., Chen, C.-K., & Beckman, S. L. (2023). Exploring The Impact of An Interactive Electronic Pegboard on Manual Dexterity and Cognitive Skills of Stroke Patients: A Preliminary Analysis (Preprint). JMIR Rehabilitation and Assistive Technologies. https://Doi.Org/10.2196/55481

Chillakuri, B., & Attili, V. P. (2022). Role of blockchain in HR's response to new-normal. *The International Journal of Organizational Analysis*, *30*(6), 1359–1378. DOI: 10.1108/IJOA-08-2020-2363

Chitte, S. (2025, January). The gig economy: Navigating complexities in human resource management. *International Journal of Research and Innovation in Social Science*.https://www.researchgate.net/publication/388277619_The_Gig_Economy_Navigating_Complexities_in_Human_Resource_Management

Chopra, M. A., Collyns, M. C., Hemming, M. R., Parker, M. K. E., Chu, W., & Fratzscher, M. O. (1995). *India: economic reform and growth*. International Monetary Fund.

Choudhury, P., Foroughi, C., & Larson, B. Z. (2020). Work-from-anywhere: The productivity effects of virtual meetings. *Strategic Management Journal*, *41*(9), 1596–1619. DOI: 10.1002/smj.3165

Christensen, C. M., McDonald, R., Altman, E. J., & Palmer, J. E. (2018). Disruptive innovation: An intellectual history and directions for future research. *Journal of Management Studies*, *55*(7), 1043–1078. DOI: 10.1111/joms.12349

Chujan, W., Ngoc, N. L. B., & Faizi, A. S. (2022). Locus of Control on Financial Behavior and Financial Risk Attitude. *Annals of Economics and Finance*, *23*(2).

Churchill, B., & Craig, L. (2019). Gender in the gig economy: Men and women using digital platforms to secure work in Australia. *Journal of Sociology (Melbourne, Vic.)*, *55*(4), 741–761. DOI: 10.1177/1440783319894060

Cika, A. (2021). Developing new skills is the key to boosting productivity and financial services gaining a competitive advantage. *PwC*.https://www.pwc.com/id/en/media-centre/press-release/2021/english/developing-new-skills-is-the-key-to-boosting-productivity-and-financial-services-gaining-a-competitive-advantage.html

CIMEA. (2024). *Micro-credentials for higher education institutions: Approaches developed in the EHEA using peer support*. https://www.cimea.it/Upload/Documenti/Micro-credentials%20in%20HE_1.pdf

Cipresso, P., Giglioli, I. A. C., Raya, M. A., & Riva, G. (2018). The past, present, and future of virtual and augmented reality research: a network and cluster analysis of the literature. Frontiers in psychology, p.2086. https://doi.org/DOI: 10.3389/fpsyg.2018.02086

Clarence, J., & Pertiwi, D. (2023). Financial management behavior among students: The influence of digital financial literacy. [IJFIS]. *International Journal of Financial and Investment Studies*, *4*(1), 9–16. DOI: 10.9744/ijfis.4.1.9-16

Clark, K. (2003). Using Self-Directed Learning Communities to Bridge the Digital Divide. *British Journal of Educational Technology*, *34*(5), 663–665. https://Doi.Org/10.1046/J.0007-1013.2003.00358.X. DOI: 10.1046/j.0007-1013.2003.00358.x

Cloudpay (2021). Three Essential Uses for Blockchain in Payroll and HR. retrieved from, https://www.cloudpay.com/resources/three-essential-uses-for-blockchain-in-payroll-and-hr)

Collings, D. G., & Mellahi, K. (2009). Strategic talent management: A review and research agenda. *Human Resource Management Review*, *19*(4), 304–313. DOI: 10.1016/j.hrmr.2009.04.001

Collomb, A., & Sok, K. (2016). Blockchain/distributed ledger technology (DLT): What impact on the financial sector? *Digiworld Economic Journal*, (103).

Colombage, S. (2023). Financial Technology (Fintech) and Sustainable Financing: A New Paradigm for Risk Management. *Journal of Risk and Financial Management*, *16*(12), 502. DOI: 10.3390/jrfm16120502

Conte de Leon, D., Stalick, A. Q., Jillepalli, A. A., Haney, M. A., & Sheldon, F. T. (2017). Blockchain: Properties and misconceptions. *Asia Pacific Journal of Innovation and Entrepreneurship*, *11*(3), 286–300. DOI: 10.1108/APJIE-12-2017-034

Cook, C., Diamond, R., Hall, J. V., List, J. A., & Oyer, P. (2020). The gender earnings gap in the gig economy: Evidence from over a million rideshare drivers. *The Review of Economic Studies*, *88*(5), 2210–2238. DOI: 10.1093/restud/rdaa081

Cornet, V. P., Toscos, T., Bolchini, D., Ghahari, R. R., Ahmed, R., Daley, C., Mirro, M. J., & Holden, R. J. (2020). Untold stories in user-centered design of mobile health: Practical challenges and strategies learned from the design and evaluation of an app for older adults with heart failure. *JMIR mHealth and uHealth*, *8*(7), e17703. DOI: 10.2196/17703 PMID: 32706745

Cowley, S. (2012). FBI Director: Cybercrime Will Eclipse Terrorism. Available at: https://money.cnn.com/2012/03/02/technology/fbi_cybersecurity/

Cropanzano, R., Keplinger, K., Lambert, B. K., Caza, B., & Ashford, S. J. (2022). The Organizational Psychology of Gig Work: An Integrative Conceptual Review. *The Journal of Applied Psychology*, *108*(3), 492–519. DOI: 10.1037/apl0001029 PMID: 36222635

Croxton, K. L., Garcia-Dastugue, S. J., Lambert, D. M., & Rogers, D. S. (2001). The supply chain management processes. *International Journal of Logistics Management*, *12*(2), 13–36. DOI: 10.1108/09574090110806271

Cude, B. J. (2021). Defining financial literacy. *The Routledge handbook of financial literacy*, 5-17.

Curtis, M. (2020). Toward Understanding Secondary Teachers' Decisions to Adopt Geospatial Technologies: An Examination of Everett Rogers' Diffusion of Innovation Framework. *The Journal of Geography*, *119*(5), 147–158. DOI: 10.1080/00221341.2020.1784252

D'Silva, B., D'Silva, S., & Bhuptani, R. S. (2012). Assessing the financial literacy level among women in India: An empirical study. *Journal of Entrepreneurship and Management*, *1*(1), 46.

Dahiya, S., & Kumar, M. (2020). Linkage between financial inclusion and economic growth: An empirical study of the emerging Indian economy. *Vision (Basel)*, *24*(2), 184–193. DOI: 10.1177/0972262920923891

Daniel, B. (2015). Big Data and analytics in higher education: Opportunities and challenges.

Das, A., & Ghosh, S. (2006). Financial deregulation and efficiency: An empirical analysis of Indian banks during the post-reform period. Review of Financial Economics, 15(3), 193–221. https://doi.org/. rfe.2005.06.002DOI: 10.1016/j

Datta, N., Rong, C., Singh, S., Stinshoff, C., Iacob, N., Nigatu, N. S., Nxumalo, M., & Klimaviciute, L. (2023). *Working without borders: The promise and peril of online gig work.* World Bank. DOI: 10.1596/40066

Davcev, L., Hourvouliades, N., & Komic, J. (2018). Impact of interest rate and inflation on GDP in Bulgaria, Romania and FYROM. *Journal of Balkan & Near Eastern Studies*, *20*(2), 131–147. DOI: 10.1080/19448953.2018.1379746

David, S., Zinica, D., Bărbuţă-Mişu, N., Savga, L., & Virlanuta, F. O. (2024). Public Administration Managers' and Employees' Perceptions of Adaptability to Change Under "The Future of Work" Paradigm. Technological Forecasting and Social Change. https://Doi.Org/10.1016/J.Techfore.2023.123088

Davis, J. (2020). The role of AI in providing academic support to students. *Learning and Individual Differences.*

De Groen, W. P., & Maselli, I. (2016). *The Impact of the Collaborative Economy on the Labour Market.* CEPS.

De Stefano, V. (2016). The rise of the "just-in-time workforce": On-demand work, crowd work, and labor protection in the gig economy. *SSRN, 37*(3), 471–504. DOI: 10.2139/ssrn.2682602

Dean, M., & Spoehr, J. (2018). The fourth industrial revolution and the future of manufacturing work in Australia: Challenges and opportunities. *Labour & Industry, 28*(3), 166–181. DOI: 10.1080/10301763.2018.1502644

Della Sala, V. (2024). Research Handbook on Human Resource Management and Disruptive Technologies. British Journal of Industrial Relations. https://Doi.Org/10.1111/Bjir.12868

Deloitte. (2024). Gig workforce talent management strategy. *Deloitte.*https://www2.deloitte.com/content/dam/Deloitte/in/Documents/human-capital/in-hc-gig-workforce-talent-management-strategy-noexp.pdf

Demirguc-Kunt, A., Klapper, L., Singer, D., Ansar, S., & Hess, J. (2018). *The Global Findex Database 2017: Measuring financial inclusion and the fintech revolution.* World Bank Publications. DOI: 10.1596/978-1-4648-1259-0

Deng, X., Taylor, J., & Moussawi, S. (2020). Introduction to the minitrucks on crowdsourcing and digital workforce in the gig economy. *Proceedings of the Annual Hawaii International Conference on System Sciences.* DOI: 10.24251/HICSS.2020.488

Department for Promotion of Industry and Internal Trade (DPIIT). (2024). *Foreign direct investment statistics.*https://www.dpiit.gov.in

Deshpande, A. (2021). Creating agile learning culture for the workforce. SSRN Electronic Journal. DOI: 10.2139/ssrn.3774225

Deshpande, A., Stewart, K., Lepetit, L., & Gunashekar, S. (2017). Distributed Ledger Technologies/Blockchain: Challenges, opportunities and the prospects for standards. *Overview report The British Standards Institution (BSI), 40*(40), 1-34.

Devagiri, J. S., Paheding, S., Niyaz, Q., Yang, X., & Smith, S. (2022). Augmented Reality and Artificial Intelligence in industry: Trends, tools, and future challenges. In *Expert Systems with Applications* (Vol. 207, p. 118002). Pergamon., DOI: 10.1016/j.eswa.2022.118002

Dev, S. M. (2006). Financial inclusion: Issues and challenges. *Economic and Political Weekly*, •••, 4310–4313.

Dey, P. K., Malesios, C., Chowdhury, S., Saha, K., Budhwar, P., & De, D. (2022). Adoption of circular economy practices in small and medium-sized enterprises: Evidence from Europe. *International Journal of Production Economics*, *248*, 108496. Advance online publication. DOI: 10.1016/j.ijpe.2022.108496

Diener, E., & Seligman, M. E. P. (2004). Beyond Money: Toward an Economy of Well-Being. *Psychological Science in the Public Interest*, *5*(1), 1–31. DOI: 10.1111/j.0963-7214.2004.00501001.x PMID: 26158992

DinarStandard. (2023). *Global Digital Platform Power Index 2023*. https://2feea378-8f71-46c9-9424-36229a900f86.usrfiles.com/ugd/2feea3_b69dbe6fa1ea49548d3768008b168446.pdf

Dinh, A., Tseng, E., Yin, A. L., Estrin, D., Greenwald, P., & Fortenko, A. (2023). Perceptions About Augmented Reality in Remote Medical Care: Interview Study of Emergency Telemedicine Providers. *JMIR Formative Research*, *7*, e45211. DOI: 10.2196/45211 PMID: 36976628

Diploma, B. C. (2023). Blockchain: how do "verifiable credentials" work? Retrieved from https://www.bcdiploma.com/en/blog/blockchain-verifiable-credentials

Diptyana, P., Rokhmania, N., & Herlina, E. (2022). Financial Literacy, Digital Literacy and Financing Preferences Role to Micro and Small Enterprises' Performance. *International Journal of Enterpreneurship and Business Development*, *5*(02), 346–358. DOI: 10.29138/ijebd.v5i2.1785

Do, B., Yeh, P., & Madsen, J. (2016). Exploring the relationship among human resource flexibility, organizational innovation and adaptability culture. *Chinese Management Studies*, *10*(4), 657–674. DOI: 10.1108/CMS-01-2016-0022

Doeze Jager-van Vliet, S. (2017). Proactive and adaptive agility among employees: The relationship with personal and situational factors.

Dolgui, A., Ivanov, D., Potryasaev, S., Sokolov, B., Ivanova, M., & Werner, F. (2020). Blockchain-oriented dynamic modelling of smart contract design and execution in the supply chain. *International Journal of Production Research*, *58*(7), 2184–2199. DOI: 10.1080/00207543.2019.1627439

Dominic, L. M., Sowmiya, S., & Venkateswaran, P. S. (2023). Study on the importance of entrepreneurship skill development programme (ESDP) for sustainable growth of MSMEs in India. *Proceedings on Engineering Sciences*, *05*(3), 553–564. DOI: 10.24874/PES05.03.018

Don't Do It Yourself (DDIY). (2024). *Freelance statistics: Facts, figures, and trends in the gig economy.* Retrieved from https://ddiy.co/freelance-statistics/

Donthu, N., Kumar, S., Mukherjee, D., Pandey, N., & Lim, W. M. (2021). How to conduct a bibliometric analysis: An overview and guidelines. *Journal of Business Research, 133*, 285–296. DOI: 10.1016/j.jbusres.2021.04.070

Doz, Y. (2020). Fostering strategic agility: How individual executives and human resource practices contribute. *Human Resource Management Review, 30*(1), 100693. DOI: 10.1016/j.hrmr.2019.100693

Drake, L., & Hall, M. J. (2003). Efficiency in Japanese banking: An empirical analysis. *Journal of Banking & Finance, 27*(5), 891–917. DOI: 10.1016/S0378-4266(02)00240-6

Drishti, I. A. S. (2024). *Impact of AI and Automation on India's Employment Landscape.*https://www.drishtiias.com

Du Toit, I. (2017). Copyright and Citation Considerations for This Thesis/ Dissertation. In *Ujcontent.Uj.Ac.Za.* https://ujcontent.uj.ac.za/vital/access/manager/Index?site_name=Research Output

Duan, K., Onyeaka, H., & Pang, G. (2024). Leveraging blockchain to tackle food fraud: Innovations and obstacles. *Journal of Agriculture and Food Research, 18*, 101429. DOI: 10.1016/j.jafr.2024.101429

Dube, A., & Chattopadhyay, P. (2021). How digital platforms are reshaping HRM: A framework for managing the gig economy. *Journal of Business Research, 129*, 710–718.

Duggan, J., Sherman, U., Carbery, R., & McDonnell, A. (2019). Algorithmic management and app-work in the gig economy: A research agenda for employment relations and hrm. *Human Resource Management Journal, 30*(1), 114–132. DOI: 10.1111/1748-8583.12258

Dunleavy, M., & Dede, C. (2014). Augmented reality teaching and learning.

Dutta, P., Choi, T. M., Somani, S., & Butala, R. (2020). Blockchain technology in supply chain operations: Applications, challenges and research opportunities. *Transportation research part e: Logistics and transportation review, 142*, 102067.

Dzingirai, M., & Mveku, B. (2023). The role of technology in sustainable finance towards the 5th industrial revolution: A dynamic capability view. *Business, Technology and Finance*, 1.

Eager, B., Maritz, A., & Millemann, J. (2022). The silver economy on wheels: A narrative review of the mature-aged, hypermobile gig worker phenomena. *Small Enterprise Research*, *29*(1), 68–85. DOI: 10.1080/13215906.2022.2032295

Easton-Calabria, E. (2019). *Digital livelihoods for people on the move*. UNDP. https://www.undp.org/content/dam/undp/library/prosperity/economic-recovery-mobility/MASTER%20-%20Migrant%20Union%20-%20Digital%20Livelihoods%20for%20People%20on%20the%20Move.pdf

Eaton, T. V., Grenier, J. H., & Layman, D. (2019). Accounting and Cybersecurity Risk Management. *Current Issues in Auditing*, *13*(2), C1–C9. https://publications.aaahq.org/cia/article/13/2/C1/7123/Accounting-and-Cybersecurity-Risk-Management. DOI: 10.2308/ciia-52419

Economic Policy Institute (EPI). (2022). *National survey of gig workers paints a picture of poor working conditions, low pay*. https://www.epi.org/publication/gig-worker-survey/

Eden, R., Burton-Jones, A., Casey, V., & Draheim, M. (2019). Digital Transformation Requires Workforce Transformation. *MIS Quarterly Executive*, *18*(1), 4. https://Doi.Org/10.17705/2MSQE.00005. DOI: 10.17705/2msqe.00005

edX. (n.d.). *About edX*. https://www.edx.org/about-us

Eisenstat, R. A., & Taylor, B. (2019). Future of work: Managing the gig economy and remote teams. *MIT Sloan Management Review*. https://sloanreview.mit.edu/article/the-future-of-work-managing-the-gig-economy/

Ekuma, K. (2023). Artificial Intelligence and Automation in Human Resource Development: A Systematic Review. Human Resource Development Review. https://Doi.Org/10.1177/15344843231224009

El Bourainy, M., Salah, A., & El Sherif, M. (2021). Assessing the impact of financial inclusion on inflation rate in developing countries. *Open Journal of Social Sciences*, *9*(01), 397–424. DOI: 10.4236/jss.2021.91030

Elayan, M. B. (2022). Transformation of human resources management solutions as a strategic tool for gig workers contracting. In *IGI Global eBooks* (pp. 790–813). https://doi.org/DOI: 10.4018/978-1-6684-4503-7.ch039

Electronic Frontier Foundation (EFF). (2016). *How Safe Is Your Data in the Gig Economy?*https://www.eff.org/press/releases/how-safe-your-data-gig-economy

Eliaçık, E. (2022, August 12). Is HR ready for blockchain? Dataconomy. Retrieved from https://dataconomy.com/2022/06/22/blockchain-in-hr/#:~:text=IBM%20 Garage%20created%20a%20private,employers%20or%20across%20the%20network

Ellegaard, O., & Wallin, J. A. (2015). The bibliometric analysis of scholarly production: How great is the impact? *Scientometrics*, *105*(3), 1809–1831. DOI: 10.1007/s11192-015-1645-z PMID: 26594073

Emmanuel, C. (2023, October 10). Revolutionizing HR and Finance: Chrono.tech's Path to a Seamless Future. Medium. https://medium.com/@clemzyemmanuel/revolutionizing-hr-and-finance-chrono-techs-path-to-a-seamless-future-af972b71eed3

Enyedy, N., & Yoon, S. (2021). Immersive environments: Learning in augmented+ virtual reality. International handbook of computer-supported collaborative learning, pp.389-405. DOI: 10.1007/978-3-030-65291-3_21

Esposito, M., Akbar, Y., & Campbell, F. X. (2025). *Digitalization in Emerging Economies*. Cambridge University Press. DOI: 10.1017/9781009433921

Eu, J., & Houska, D. (2019). Sustainable Finance for a Circular Economy. . Report from Japan/EU Joint Workshop at the G20 Resource Efficiency Dialogue 2019 held on 10 October 2019 in Tokyo (Japan).DOI: 10.2779/171661

Eurofound (2018). *Employment and working conditions of selected types of platform work*. Publications Office of the European Union, Luxembourg. https://www.eurofound.europa.eu/en/publications/2018/employment-and-working-conditions-selected-types-platform-work

Eurofound. (n.d.). *Amsterdam Court of Appeal decision in Uber case*. European Foundation for the Improvement of Living and Working Conditions. Retrieved March 12, 2025, from https://apps.eurofound.europa.eu/platformeconomydb/amsterdam-court-of-appeal-decision-in-uber-case-110150

European Commission. (2021). *Commission proposals to improve the working conditions of people working through digital labour platforms*.https://ec.europa.eu/commission/presscorner/detail/en/ip_21_6605

European Commission. (2025). *Improving the working conditions of platform workers*. https://www.europarl.europa.eu/thinktank/en/document/EPRS_BRI(2022)698923 Office.

Eurostat (2023). *Employment statistics - digital platform workers*. https://ec.europa.eu/eurostat/statistics-explained/index.php?title=Employment_statistics_-_digital_platform_workers

Eveland, T., & MacLennan, H. (2019). A micro-entrepreneur in the gig economy: Case study and implications for higher education. *Journal of Developmental Entrepreneurship, 24*(3), 1950016. DOI: 10.1142/S108494671950016X

Fairwork India. (2022). *Fairwork India ratings 2022: Labour standards in the platform economy.* https://fair.work/en/fw/publications

Fake, H., & Dabbagh, N. (2020). Personalized Learning Within Online Workforce Learning Environments: Exploring Implementations, Obstacles, Opportunities, And Perspectives of Workforce Leaders. Technology, Knowledge, And Learning, 25(4), 789–809. https://Doi.Org/10.1007/S10758-020-09441-X

Far, S. B., Rad, A. I., & Asaar, M. R. (2023). Blockchain and its derived technologies shape the future generation of digital businesses: A focus on decentralized finance and the Metaverse. *Data Science and Management*, *6*(3), 183–197. DOI: 10.1016/j.dsm.2023.06.002

Fatima, A. (2024). Examining the Impact of Gig Economy on employment and poverty reduction in India. *International Journal of Legal Research and Applications*, *2*(7).

Feng, H., Jia, X., Wang, Y., Niu, L., & Xu, Y. (2019). Digital Memory: A New Paradigm for Cultural Heritage. Digital Presentation and Preservation of Cultural and Scientific Heritage. Available From: https://Doi.Org/10.55630/Dipp.2019.9.8

Feng, H., Wang, X., Duan, Y., Zhang, J., & Zhang, X. (2020). Applying blockchain technology to improve agri-food traceability: A review of development methods, benefits and challenges. *Journal of Cleaner Production*, *260*, 121031. DOI: 10.1016/j.jclepro.2020.121031

Fernández-Caramés, T. M., Blanco-Novoa, O., Froiz-Míguez, I., & Fraga-Lamas, P. (2019). Towards an autonomous industry 4.0 warehouse: A UAV and blockchain-based system for inventory and traceability applications in big data-driven supply chain management. *Sensors (Basel)*, *19*(10), 2394. DOI: 10.3390/s19102394 PMID: 31130644

Finck, M. (2021). *Blockchain and the General Data Protection Regulation: Reconciling immutable ledgers with data privacy rights*. Oxford Internet Institute.

Fisk, R. P., Gallan, A. S., Joubert, A. M., Beekhuyzen, J., Cheung, L., & Russell-Bennett, R. (2022). Healing The Digital Divide with Digital Inclusion: Enabling Human Capabilities. *Journal of Service Research*, *109467052211401*, •••. https://Doi.Org/10.1177/10946705221140148

Fiverr. (n.d.). Fiverr Pro: High-end professional freelancers for your business. *Fiverr.* https://pro.fiverr.com

Flanagan, F. (2019). Freedom or precarity? Freelancers and the future of the gig economy. *Work, Employment and Society, 33*(3), 418–426. DOI: 10.1177/0950017018781870

Forbes Human Resources Council. (2024, August 9). Organizational efficiency in the age of the blended workforce. *Forbes.* Retrieved from https://www.forbes.com/councils/forbeshumanresourcescouncil/2024/08/09/organizational-efficiency-in-the-age-of-the-blended-workforce

Forde, C., Stuart, M., Joyce, S., Oliver, L., Valizade, D., Alberti, G., & Hardy, K. (2017). *The social protection of workers in the platform economy.* https://www.europarl.europa.eu/RegData/etudes/STUD/2017/614184/IPOL_STU(2017)614184_EN.pdf

Frankenfield, J. (2023). Distributed Ledger Technology (DLT): Definition and How It Works. *Investopedia.Retrieved*, (February), 26.

Frank, M. L., Grenier, J. H., & Pyzoha, J. S. (2019). How disclosing a prior cyberattack influences the efficacy of cybersecurity risk management reporting and independent assurance. *Journal of Information Systems, 33*(3), 183–200. Advance online publication. DOI: 10.2308/isys-52374

Friedland, J., & Balkin, D. B. (2023). When gig workers become essential: Leveraging customer moral self-awareness beyond COVID-19. *Business Horizons, 66*(2), 181–190. DOI: 10.1016/j.bushor.2022.05.003 PMID: 35601275

Friedman, B. M., & Kuttner, K. N. (2010). Implementation of monetary policy: How do central banks set interest rates? In *Handbook of Monetary Economics* (Vol. 3), 1345-1438.

Friedman, G. (2014). Workers without employers: Shadow corporations and the rise of the gig economy. *Review of Keynesian Economics, 2*(2), 171–188. DOI: 10.4337/roke.2014.02.03

Friedman, G. (2014). Workers without employers: Shadow corporations and the rise of the gig economy. *The Review of Radical Political Economics, 46*(4), 363–378. DOI: 10.1177/0486613414549399

Fuller, J. B., Raman, M., Palano, J., Bailey, A., Vaduganathan, N., Kaufman, E., & Laverdière, R. Sibley Lovett, & Boston Consulting Group. (2020). Building the on-demand workforce. *Harvard Business School and Boston Consulting Group.* https://www.hbs.edu/managing-the-future-of-work/Documents/Building_The_On-Demand_Workforce.pdf

Fusco, F. (2020). Rethinking the allocation criteria of the labour law rights and protections: A risk-based approach. *European Labour Law Journal, 11*(2), 131–141. DOI: 10.1177/2031952520905152

Fu, Y., & Zhu, J. (2019). Big production enterprise supply chain endogenous risk management based on blockchain. *IEEE Access : Practical Innovations, Open Solutions, 7*, 15310–15319. DOI: 10.1109/ACCESS.2019.2895327

Gad, A. G., Mosa, D. T., Abualigah, L., & Abohany, A. A. (2022). Emerging trends in blockchain technology and applications: A review and outlook. *Journal of King Saud University. Computer and Information Sciences, 34*(9), 6719–6742. DOI: 10.1016/j.jksuci.2022.03.007

Ganguly, N. (2024, October 23). *Kirana stores are losing the battle against Zepto, Blinkit and Instamart.* Outlook Business. https://www.outlookbusiness.com/start-up/explainers/kirana-stores-are-losing-the-battle-against-zepto-blinkit-and-instamart

Ganne, E. (2018). *Can Blockchain revolutionize international trade?* World Trade Organization.

Gao, Z., Xu, L., Chen, L., Zhao, X., Lu, Y., & Shi, W. (2018). CoC: A unified distributed ledger based supply chain management system. *Journal of Computer Science and Technology, 33*(2), 237–248. DOI: 10.1007/s11390-018-1816-5

Garai-Fodor, M., Varga, J., & Csiszárik-Kocsir, Á. (2022, March). Generation-specific perceptions of financial literacy and digital solutions. In *2022 IEEE 20th Jubilee World Symposium on Applied Machine Intelligence and Informatics (SAMI)* (pp. 000193-000200). IEEE. DOI: 10.1109/SAMI54271.2022.9780717

Garavan, T. N. (2007). A strategic perspective on human resource development. *Advances in Developing Human Resources, 9*(1), 11–30. DOI: 10.1177/1523422306294492

Garavan, T. N., & McGuire, D. (2010). Human resource development and society: Human resource development's role in embedding corporate social responsibility, sustainability, and ethics in organizations. *Advances in Developing Human Resources, 12*(5), 487–507. DOI: 10.1177/1523422310394757

Garcia, M. J. R. (2013). Financial education and behavioral finance: New insights into the role of information in financial decisions. *Journal of Economic Surveys, 27*(2), 297–315. DOI: 10.1111/j.1467-6419.2011.00705.x

Geng, Y., Chen, L., Li, J., & Iqbal, K. (2023). Higher education and digital Economy: Analysis of their coupling coordination with the Yangtze River economic Belt in China as the example. *Ecological Indicators*, *154*, 110510. DOI: 10.1016/j.ecolind.2023.110510

Gevorkyan, A. V., & Kvangraven, I. H. (2016). Assessing recent determinants of borrowing costs in sub-Saharan Africa. *Review of Development Economics*, *20*(4), 721–738. DOI: 10.1111/rode.12195

Ghadge, A., Duck, A., Er, M., & Caldwell, N. (2021, April). Deceptive counterfeit risk in global supply chains. In *Supply Chain Forum* [). Taylor & Francis.]. *International Journal (Toronto, Ont.)*, *22*(2), 87–99.

Ghazwani, Y., & Smith, S. (2020). Interaction in augmented reality: Challenges to enhance user experience. In *Proceedings of the 2020 4th International Conference on Virtual and Augmented Reality Simulations* (pp. 39- 44). https://doi.org/DOI: 10.1145/3385378.3385384

Gilch, P. M., & Sieweke, J. (2020). Recruiting Digital Talent: The Strategic Role of Recruitment in Organizations' Digital Transformation. *German Journal of Human Resource Management Zeitschrift Für Personalforschung*, *35*(1), 53–82. https://Doi.Org/10.1177/2397002220952734

Gill, A., Dana, L. P., & Obradovich, J. D. (2018). Financial risk management and financial performance of new small business ventures: Evidence from Indian survey data. *Journal for International Business and Entrepreneurship Development*, *11*(2), 75–95. DOI: 10.1504/JIBED.2018.091205

Glickman, C., & Choi, A. (2022). The role of public-private partnerships in bridging the digital divide in education.

Goel, S., & Sharma, R. (2017). Developing a financial inclusion index for India. *Procedia Computer Science*, *122*, 949–956. DOI: 10.1016/j.procs.2017.11.459

Gopalkrishnan, S., Mohanty, S. P., & Jaiwani, M. (2023). Do efficiencies really matter? Analysing the housing finance sector and deriving insights through data envelopment analysis. *Cogent Economics & Finance*, *11*(2), 2285158. DOI: 10.1080/23322039.2023.2285158

Gouda, H. (2020). Exploring The Relevant Skills Needed for The Digital Age Employees. European Journal of Business and Management. https://Doi.Org/10.7176/Ejbm/12-2-07

Gourène, G. A. Z., & Mendy, P. (2017). Financial inclusion and economic growth in WAEMU: A multiscale heterogeneity panel causality approach.

Government of Australia. (2023). *Fair Work Legislation Amendment (Protecting Worker Entitlements) Act 2023.*https://www.fairwork.gov.au

Government of India. (2020). *The Code on Social Security, 2020 (No. 36 of 2020).* Ministry of Law and Justice.

Goyal, N., Chauhan, S. S., Pandey, S., Singh, R., Kumar, A., & Joshi, K. (2023) Financial Services 4.0-Future Perspective based on Mixed Reality. In 2023 IEEE International Conference on Contemporary Computing and Communications (InC4) (Vol. 1, pp. 1-4). IEEE. DOI: DOI: 10.1109/InC457730.2023.10263246

Goyal, K., Kumar, S., & Xiao, J. J. (2021). Antecedents and consequences of Personal Financial Management Behavior: A systematic literature review and future research agenda. *International Journal of Bank Marketing*, *39*(7), 1166–1207. DOI: 10.1108/IJBM-12-2020-0612

Grable, J. E., Park, J. Y., & Joo, S. H. (2009). Explaining financial management behavior for Koreans living in the United States. *The Journal of Consumer Affairs*, *43*(1), 80–107. DOI: 10.1111/j.1745-6606.2008.01128.x

Graham, M., Hjorth, I., & Lehdonvirta, V. (2019). Decent work and the digital gig economy: A developing country perspective. SSRN *Electronic Journal.*https://doi.org/DOI: 10.2139/ssrn.3153436

Graham, C., Danaa, G., Purevsuren, T., Martinez, A., Spricigo, C., Camilotti, B., & Batsukh, T. (2023). Digital Learning Transformation in Higher Education: International Cases of University Efforts to Evaluate and Improve Blended Teaching Readiness. *Education Sciences*, *13*(11), 1143. DOI: 10.3390/educsci13111143

Graham, M., Hjorth, I., & Lehdonvirta, V. (2017). Digital labour and development. Impacts of global digital labour platforms and the gig economy on worker livelihoods. *Transfer: European Review of Labour and Research*, *23*(2), 135–162. DOI: 10.1177/1024258916687250 PMID: 28781494

Grand View Research. (2024). Education technology market size & share report, 2030.

Grant, M., & Startz, M. (2022). *Cutting out the middleman: The structure of chains of intermediation* (No. w30109). National Bureau of Economic Research.

Gulati, R., & Kumar, S. (2017). Analysing banks' intermediation and operating efficiencies using the two-stage network DEA model. *International Journal of Productivity and Performance Management*, *66*(4), 500–516. DOI: 10.1108/IJPPM-03-2016-0055

Guo, B., Geng, Y., Sterr, T., Zhu, Q., & Liu, Y. (2017). Investigating public awareness on circular economy in western China: A case of Urumqi Midong. *Journal of Cleaner Production*, *142*, 2177–2186. https://doi.org/https://doi.org/10.1016/j.jclepro.2016.11.063. DOI: 10.1016/j.jclepro.2016.11.063

Guo, Y., & Liang, C. (2016). Blockchain application and outlook in the banking industry. *Financial Innovation*, *2*(1), 1–12. DOI: 10.1186/s40854-016-0034-9

Guo, Y., Li, P., & Li, A. (2021). Tail risk contagion between international financial markets during COVID-19 pandemic. [HTML]. *International Review of Financial Analysis*, *73*, 101649. DOI: 10.1016/j.irfa.2020.101649

Gupta, A., & Basu, S. (2022). Challenges and opportunities in India's digital education transformation.

Gupta, S. (2023). AI and language learning: Implications for regional education.

Gwalani, H., & Parkhi, S. (2014). Financial Inclusion–Building a success model in the Indian context. *Procedia: Social and Behavioral Sciences*, *133*, 372–378. DOI: 10.1016/j.sbspro.2014.04.203

Hagiu, A., Teh, T.-H., & Wright, J. (2020). Should platforms be allowed to sell on their own marketplaces? *RAND Journal of Economics*. Forthcoming. Available at *SSRN*: https://ssrn.com/abstract=3606055 DOI: 10.2139/ssrn.3606055

Hale, T., & Webster, S. (2020). Oxford COVID-19 government response tracker.

Hale, T., Angrist, N., Goldszmidt, R., Kira, B., Petherick, A., Phillips, T., ... & Webster, S. (2020). Global assessment of COVID-19 school closures.

Halliday, D. (2019). Is there a moral problem with the gig economy? *Uehiro Oxford Institute*.https://podcasts.ox.ac.uk/there-moral-problem-gig-economy

Hamori, M. (2023). Self-Directed Learning in Massive Open Online Courses and Its Application at The Workplace: Does Employer Support Matter? *Journal of Business Research*, *157*, 113590. https://Doi.Org/10.1016/J.Jbusres.2022.113590. DOI: 10.1016/j.jbusres.2022.113590

Hanggoro, D., Windiatmaja, J. H., & Sari, R. F. (2022, July). Blockchain-based Attendance Management and Payroll System using Hyperledger Composer Framework. In *2022 IEEE Region 10 Symposium (TENSYMP)* (pp. 1-6). IEEE. DOI: 10.1109/TENSYMP54529.2022.9864383

Haque, A., & Zulfiqar, M. (2015). Women's economic empowerment through financial literacy, financial attitude and financial wellbeing. *International Journal of Business and Social Science*, *7*(3), 78–88.

Hara, H. (2014). The impact of firm-provided training on productivity, wages, and transition to regular employment for workers in flexible arrangements. *Journal of the Japanese and International Economies*, *34*, 336–359. DOI: 10.1016/j.jjie.2014.10.002

Hardy, T., & McCrystal, S. (2022). The importance of competition and consumer law in regulating gig work and beyond. *The Journal of Industrial Relations*, *64*(5), 785–800. DOI: 10.1177/00221856211068868

Hartono, J. (2022). Teori portofolio dan analisis investasi.

Hasan, M., Le, T., & Hoque, A. (2021). How does financial literacy impact on inclusive finance? *Financial Innovation*, *7*(1), 40. DOI: 10.1186/s40854-021-00259-9

Hasler, A., & Lusardi, A. (2017). The gender gap in financial literacy: A global perspective. *Global Financial Literacy Excellence Center, The George Washington University School of Business*, 2-16.

Hassani, H., Huang, X., & Silva, E. (2018). Banking with blockchain-ed big data. *Journal of Management Analytics*, *5*(4), 256–275. DOI: 10.1080/23270012.2018.1528900

He, J., & Li, Q. (2020). Can online social interaction improve the digital finance participation of rural households? *China Agricultural Economic Review*, *12*(2), 295–313. DOI: 10.1108/CAER-11-2019-0213

Herrmann, A. M. (2023). How the Online Gig Economy Challenges the Education-Income Paradigm. *Entrepreneurship in Focus, 7*. https://www.ifm-bonn.org/fileadmin/data/redaktion/publikationen/policy_brief/dokumente/policybrief-07-23-EN.pdf

Herrmann, A. M., Zaal, P. M., Chappin, M. H., Schemmann, B., & Lühmann, B. (2023). "We don't need no (higher) education" - How the gig economy challenges the education-income paradigm. *Technological Forecasting and Social Change*, *186*, 122136. DOI: 10.1016/j.techfore.2022.122136

Heuberger, B., Kasman, M., & Hammond, R. A. (2018). *Recommendations for improving youth financial literacy education*. Economic Studies At Brookings.

Hewa, T., Ylianttila, M., & Liyanage, M. (2021). Survey on blockchain based smart contracts: Applications, opportunities and challenges. *Journal of Network and Computer Applications*, *177*, 102857. DOI: 10.1016/j.jnca.2020.102857

Hickson, J. (2023). Freedom, domination and the gig economy. *New Political Economy*, *29*(2), 321–336. DOI: 10.1080/13563467.2023.2254712

Higgins, M. (2022, April). Blockchain in Supply Chain. *Forbes*.https://www.forbes.com/councils/forbestechcouncil/2021/11/08/blockchain-in-supply-chain/

Hilbert, M., & Cairo, O. (2008, July). The Binary Digit to Technological Convergence. In WSEAS International Conference. Proceedings. Mathematics and Computers in Science and Engineering (No. 12). WSEAS.

Hodor, M. (2020). Gig workers and performance pay: A dynamic equilibrium analysis of an on-demand industry.

Holland, P., & Brewster, C. (2020). The gig economy: A threat to employment relations? *Human Resource Management Journal*, *30*(1), 90–101. DOI: 10.1111/1748-8583.12220

Holmes, W., Bialik, M., & Fadel, C. (2019). Artificial intelligence in education promises and implications for teaching and learning.

Holon, I. Q. (2020). *Global EdTech market trends and forecasts*. HolonIQ.

Hong, E. (2015, October 23). Making it work: A closer look at the gig economy. *Pacific Standard*. https://psmag.com/economics/making-it-work-a-closer-look-at-the-gig-economy/

Hook, L. (2015, December 29). Year in a word: gig economy. *Financial Times*. https://www.ft.com/content/b5a2b122-a41b-11e5-8218-6b8ff73aae15

Horney, N. (2016). The gig economy: A disruptor requiring HR agility. *People and Strategy*, *39*(3), 20.

Hornik, R. (2004). Some reflections on diffusion theory and the role of everett rogers. In *Journal of Health Communication* (Vol. 9, Issue S1, pp. 143–148). Taylor & Francis Group. DOI: 10.1080/10810730490271610

Horowitz, S. (2011, September 1). The Freelance Surge is the Industrial Revolution of Our Time. *The Atlantic*. https://www.theatlantic.com/business/archive/2011/09/the-freelance-surge-is-the-industrial-revolution-of-our-time/244229/

Hosseini, H. (2023). Platform Economy 2023: U.S. leads; Europe lags. *Platform Economy*. https://www.platformeconomy.io/blog/platform-economy-2023-u-s-leads-europe-lags

Hoyle, R. H. (1995). The structural equation modeling approach: Basic concepts and fundamental issues. In Hoyle, R. H. (Ed.), *Structural equation modeling: Concepts, issues, and applications* (pp. 1–15).

Huang, X., Zou, D., Cheng, G., & Xie, H. (2021). A systematic review of AR and VR enhanced language learning. In *Sustainability (Switzerland)* (Vol. 13, Issue 9, p. 4639). Multidisciplinary Digital Publishing Institute. DOI: 10.3390/su13094639

Huang, H. (2023). Algorithmic management in food-delivery platform economy in China. *New Technology, Work and Employment, 38*(2), 185–205. DOI: 10.1111/ntwe.12228

Huang, K. T., Ball, C., Francis, J., Ratan, R., Boumis, J., & Fordham, J. (2019). Augmented versus virtual reality in education: An exploratory study examining science knowledge retention when using augmented reality/virtual reality mobile applications. *Cyberpsychology, Behavior, and Social Networking, 22*(2), 105–110. DOI: 10.1089/cyber.2018.0150 PMID: 30657334

Huđek, I., & Širec, K. (2023). Unveiling the impact of the gig economy on sustainable development. In V. Bevanda (Ed.), *ERAZ Conference – Knowledge-based sustainable development: Vol. 9. Selected papers* (pp. 125–133). Association of Economists and Managers of the Balkans. https://doi.org/DOI: 10.31410/ERAZ.S.P.2023.125

Huet, E. (2014, October 8). Uber skimps on driver training, then charges drivers $65 for basic driver skills courses. *Forbes.* Retrieved from www.forbes.com/sites/ellenhuet/2014/10/08/uber-skimps-on-driver-training-then-charges-drivers-65-for-basic-driver-skills-course/

Huston, S. J. (2010). Measuring financial literacy. *The Journal of Consumer Affairs, 44*(2), 296–316. DOI: 10.1111/j.1745-6606.2010.01170.x

Huynh-The, T., Gadekallu, T. R., Wang, W., Yenduri, G., Ranaweera, P., Pham, Q.-V., da Costa, D. B., & Liyanage, M. (2023). Blockchain for the metaverse: A review. *Future Generation Computer Systems, 143*, 401–419. DOI: 10.1016/j.future.2023.02.008

Hwang, I., & Seo, R. (2024). Organizational Support for Digital Transformation in The Metaverse: A Contingent Pathway from User Experience to Digitalization Resistance. R & D Management. https://Doi.Org/10.1111/Radm.12706

Hwang, J. (2024). The gig economy and its effects on the labor market. *International Journal of Science and Research Archive, 13*(1), 3394–3404. DOI: 10.30574/ijsra.2024.13.1.1231

Hwang, J. (2024). The gig economy and its implications for labor laws and worker protections. *International Journal of Science and Research Archive, 13*(1), 3405–3416. DOI: 10.30574/ijsra.2024.13.1.1714

Iannello, P., Cancer, A., Zmigrod, L., Antonietti, A., & Salvi, C. (2024). Creative Minds in A Polarized World. Journal Of Creative Behavior. https://Doi.Org/10.1002/Jocb.1509

IBM. (2021). *IBM-AT&T blockchain talent platform: A case study*. IBM Reports.

IBM. (n.d.). What are Smart Contracts? *IBM*. https://www.ibm.com/topics/smart-contracts

Ibrahim, M. E., & Alqaydi, F. R. (2013). Financial literacy, personal financial attitude, and forms of personal debt among residents of the UAE. *International Journal of Economics and Finance*, *5*(7), 126–138. DOI: 10.5539/ijef.v5n7p126

Ida, I. D. A., & Dwinta, C. Y. (2010). Pengaruh Locus Of Control, financial knowledge, income terhadap financial management behavior. *Jurnal Bisnis dan Akuntansi, 12*(3), 131-144.

Ilyas, A. M., & Rajasekaran, S. (2019). An empirical investigation of efficiency and productivity in the Indian non-life insurance market. *Benchmarking*, *26*(7), 2343–2371. DOI: 10.1108/BIJ-01-2019-0039

IMF. (2022). *Fintech and Financial Inclusion: Opportunities and Challenges*. International Monetary Fund.

Inc42. (2024, March 11). *Swiggy extends financial aid package worth INR 63 Cr to its restaurant partners*. Inc42. https://inc42.com/buzz/swiggy-extends-financial-aid-package-worth-inr-63-cr

Indian Council for Research on International Economic Relations (ICRIER). (n.d.). *Regulation of gig workers.* Retrieved from https://icrier.org/policy_bank/regulation-of-gig-worker/

Information Systems Research. Journal of Information Systems. Volume XX, Number XX, pp.1-46. https://publications.aaahq.org/jis/article/doi/10.2308/ISYS-2023-061/13339/Neuroaccounting-Integrating-Neurophysiological

Inside Microsoft's freelance services program. (n.d.). *Business Talent Group.*https://resources.businesstalentgroup.com/btg-insights-on-demand/microsoft-freelance-services-program-podcast

International Labour Organization (ILO). (2022). *The gender gap in employment: What's holding women back?*https://webapps.ilo.org/infostories/en-GB/Stories/Employment/barriers-women

Islam, M. D. (2023). A survey on the use of blockchains to achieve supply chain security. *Information Systems*, *117*, 102232. DOI: 10.1016/j.is.2023.102232

Ivanov, D., Dolgui, A., & Sokolov, B. (2019). The impact of digital technology and Industry 4.0 on the ripple effect and supply chain risk analytics. *International Journal of Production Research*, *57*(3), 829–846. DOI: 10.1080/00207543.2018.1488086

IYER, M. (2018). Nature of Relationship Between Inflation and Savings: Evidence from India. *NMIMS Journal of Economics and Public Policy*, 46-60.

Iyer, R. K. (2021). *Upskilling And Reskilling for Workforce of The Future*. Larson & Toubro Company.

Jabagi, N., Croteau, A. M., Audebrand, L. K., & Marsan, J. (2019). Gig-workers' motivation: Thinking beyond carrots and sticks. *Journal of Managerial Psychology*, *34*(4), 192–213. DOI: 10.1108/JMP-06-2018-0255

Jacob, B., & Shaikh, M. (2021). Growth and challenges of gig employees in India. *Parikalpana: KIIT Journal of Management, 17*(1), 62–68. https://ksom.ac.in/wp-content/uploads/2021/06/6268Parikalpana-Vol.17I.Pdf?x335

Jain, K. A. V. I. T. A. (2022). Measuring Financial Literacy and understanding its impact on enhancing usage of Digital Financial Services by Indian consumers. *Int J Bus Manage Res*, *12*(1).

Janasz, S. C., Kim, S. W., Schneer, J. A., Beutell, N. J., & Wong, C. M. (2020). Work-family integration and segmentation in the gig economy: Airbnb hosts' challenges and strategies. *Proceedings - Academy of Management*, *2020*(1), 20130. DOI: 10.5465/AMBPP.2020.20130abstract

Javaid, M., Haleem, A., Singh, R. P., Khan, S., & Suman, R. (2021). Blockchain technology applications for Industry 4.0: A literature-based review. *Blockchain: Research and Applications*, *2*(4), 100027.

Javaid, M., Haleem, A., Singh, R. P., Suman, R., & Khan, S. (2022). A review of Blockchain Technology applications for financial services. *BenchCouncil Transactions on Benchmarks. Standards and Evaluations*, *2*(3), 100073.

Ječmenica, D., Mandić, D., & Stanišić, N. (2024). HR's Role in Fostering Agile Culture and Upskilling IT Talent. In Proceedings of the 11th International Scientific Conference - FINIZ 2024 (pp. 115–120). DOI: 10.15308/finiz-2024-115-120

Jesuthasan, R., & Kapilashrami, T. (2024). *The Skills-Powered Organization: The Journey to the Next-Generation Enterprise*. MIT Press. DOI: 10.7551/mitpress/15432.001.0001

Jha, S., Mehta, P., & Gupta, P. (2021). Millennials and the gig economy: Understanding the changing workplace preferences. *Journal of Management Research*, *21*(2), 122–138.

Johnson, R., & Lee, M. (2023). E-books and sustainability: Evaluating environmental benefits of digital learning. Journal of Educational Technology.

Johnson, S. S. (2020). The Future of Work. *American Journal of Health Promotion*, *34*, 809–812. https://Doi.Org/10.1177/0890117120943748 PMID: 32921140

Jones, R. (2023). The Future of Payroll Powered by Blockchain Technology. Retrieved from, https://chainbulletin.com/the-future-of-payroll-powered-by-blockchain-technology

Joo, B. A. and Shawl, S. (2021). Covid-19 pandemic and the rising gig economy: an emerging perspective. Global Economics Science, 16-23. DOI: 10.37256/ges.232021917

Joof, F., & Jallow, O. (2020). The impact of interest rate and inflation on the exchange rate of the Gambia. *International Journal of Economics, Commerce and Management,, 8.*

Joshi, A. (2022). The expansion of EdTech in rural India: AI-powered solutions.

Joshi, A., Jain, S., & Gupta, P. K. (2024). Challenges and impact of the gig economy. *Sustainable Economies*, *2*(2), 96. DOI: 10.62617/se.v2i2.96

Kadolkar, I., Kepes, S., & Subramony, M. (2024). Algorithmic management in the gig economy: A systematic review and research integration. *Journal of Organizational Behavior*, job.2831. Advance online publication. DOI: 10.1002/job.2831

Kaine, S., & Josserand, E. (2019). The organization and experience of work in the gig economy. *The Journal of Industrial Relations*, *61*(4), 479–501. DOI: 10.1177/0022185619865480

Kalbalia, P., & Koushik, K. (2025). Regulating the gig economy: Addressing worker rights in India's quick commerce sector. In *Sustainability and Adaptability of Gig Economies in Global Business* (pp. 85–105). IGI Global., DOI: 10.4018/979-8-3693-9385-7.ch004

Kalbalia, P., Nath, N. J., & Haneefa, K. V. (2024). Utilisation and Accessibility of Healthcare Services Among Gig Workers: A Systematic Review. *Population. Environmental Disease*, •••, 77–95. DOI: 10.1007/978-3-031-67624-6_5

Kalekye, P., & Memba, F. (2015). The role of financial literacy on the profitability of women owned enterprises in Kitui town, Kitui County, Kenya. *International Journal of Scientific Research*, *4*(6), 2360–2365.

Kang, G. L., Park, C. W., & Jang, S. H. (2024). A Study on the impact of financial literacy and digital capabilities on entrepreneurial intention: Mediating effect of entrepreneurship. *Behavioral Sciences (Basel, Switzerland)*, *14*(2), 121. DOI: 10.3390/bs14020121 PMID: 38392474

Kansra, P., Kumar, P., & Paul, P. J. D. (2025). Sustainable Digitalisation: A Review of Literature and Indian Initiatives. *Digital Transformation for Business Sustainability and Growth in Emerging Markets*, 275-292.

Kansra, P., & Gill, H. S. (2016). Occupational Differences in the Awareness and Perception of Health Insurance of Workers Employed in Urban Informal Sector of Punjab. *Journal of Health Management*, *18*(3), 410–423. DOI: 10.1177/0972063416663533

Kansra, P., & Gill, H. S. (2017). Role of perceptions in health insurance buying behaviour of workers employed in informal sector of India. *Global Business Review*, *18*(1), 250–266. DOI: 10.1177/0972150916666992

Kansra, P., Oberoi, S., Gupta, S. L., & Singh, N. (2024). Factors limiting the application of consumer neuroscience: A systematic review. *Journal of Consumer Behaviour*, *23*(1), 31–42. DOI: 10.1002/cb.2131

Kansra, P., Oberoi, S., Singh, N., & Choi, H. (2024). Role of Innovation, Policy, Social Media, and Environmental Munificence for Sustainable Ecotourism Development in Punjab, India. *Sustainability (Basel)*, *16*(21), 9359. DOI: 10.3390/su16219359

Kansra, P., Singh, N., Verma, R., Gupta, S. L., & Bali, V. (2024). Guest editorial: Applications of blockchain technology for performance and reliability of business operations. *International Journal of Quality & Reliability Management*, *41*(8), 2001–2003. DOI: 10.1108/IJQRM-09-2024-456

Karam, A. A. (2023). Central Bank Digital Currency (CBDC) and blockchain enable the future of payments. *Retrieved*, (September), 13.

Kareem, M. A. (2019). The impact of human resource development on organizational effectiveness: An empirical study. *Management Dynamics in the Knowledge Economy*, *7*(1), 29–50. DOI: 10.25019/mdke/7.1.02

Kashif, M., Pinglu, C., Ullah, S., & Zaman, M. (2024). Evaluating the influence of financial technology (FinTech) on sustainable finance: A comprehensive global analysis. *Financial Markets and Portfolio Management*, *38*(1), 123–155. DOI: 10.1007/s11408-023-00439-w

Kasliwal, R. (2020, May). *Gender and the gig economy: A qualitative study of gig platforms for women workers* (ORF Issue Brief No. 359). Observer Research Foundation. https://www.orfonline.org/research/gender-and-the-gig-economy-65974/

Kass-Hanna, J., Lyons, A. C., & Liu, F. (2022). Building financial resilience through financial and digital literacy in South Asia and Sub-Saharan Africa. *Emerging Markets Review*, *51*, 100846. DOI: 10.1016/j.ememar.2021.100846

Kässi, O., & Lehdonvirta, V. (2018). Online labour index: Measuring the online gig economy for policy and research. *Technological Forecasting and Social Change, 137*, 241–248. DOI: 10.1016/j.techfore.2018.07.056

Katnic, I., Katnic, M., Orlandic, M., Radunovic, M., & Mugosa, I. (2024). Understanding the Role of Financial Literacy in Enhancing Economic Stability and Resilience in Montenegro: A Data-Driven Approach. *Sustainability (Basel), 16*(24), 11065. DOI: 10.3390/su162411065

Katsnelson, L., & Oberholzer-Gee, F. (2021). *Being the Boss: Gig Workers' Value of Flexible Work*. Harvard Business School.

Kaufman, B. E. (2019). *Theoretical perspectives on work and the labor market* (7th ed.). Industrial Relations Research Association.

Kaur, S., & Gupta, P. K. (2015). Productive efficiency mapping of the Indian banking system using data envelopment analysis. *Procedia Economics and Finance, 25*, 227–238. DOI: 10.1016/S2212-5671(15)00733-9

Kaushik, A. (2024). Comprehensive impact of on-demand platforms: Examining the gig economy\'s influence on specialized professionals, work-life balance, and gig workers\' perspectives. *International Journal for Research in Applied Science and Engineering Technology, 12*(1), 552–559. DOI: 10.22214/ijraset.2024.58005

Keegan, A., & Meijerink, J. (2022). HRM practices for value creation and value capture in online labor platform ecosystems: Towards an integrative perspective. In *A Research Agenda for Strategic Human Resource Management* (pp. 167–194). Edward Elgar Publishing., https://www.masi-journal.com/journal/article/view/26 DOI: 10.4337/9781800883802.00017

Kelliher, C., & Anderson, D. (2010). Changing employment relationships in the 21st century: Implications for HRM practices and employee well-being. *Employee Relations, 32*(4), 324–342. DOI: 10.1108/01409171011055766

Keswani, S., Cavaliere, L. P. L., Venkateswaran, P. S., Muda, I., Raj, K. B., & Khanna, R. (2022). Economic practices and financial performances of pharmaceutical companies in rural areas. *Journal of Positive School Psychology, 6*(3), 4091–4110. DOI: 10.1080/2168009X.2022.2123342

Keynes, J. M. (1936). *The general theory of employment, interest, and money*. Macmillan. Retrieved from https://www.files.ethz.ch/isn/125515/1366_keynestheoryof employment.pdf

Khan, F., & Mer, A. (2023). Embracing Artificial Intelligence Technology: Legal Implications with Special Reference to European Union Initiatives of Data Protection. In *Digital Transformation, Strategic Resilience, Cyber Security and Risk Management* (pp. 119-141). Emerald Publishing Limited.

Khan, A., Shahzad, K., & Khan, N. A. (2024). Fostering Accountability Through Digital Transformation: Leadership's Role in Enhancing Techno-Work Engagement in Public Sector. *Public Money & Management*, •••, 1–8. https://Doi.Org/10.1080/09540962.2024.2424384. DOI: 10.1080/09540962.2024.2424384

Khanal, S., & Khanal, M. (2024). Regulating gig economy in Nepal: How can Nepal benefitted from the gig platform? *J. Musikot Campus*, *2*(1), 173–192. DOI: 10.3126/jmc.v2i1.70844

Khan, F., Khati, K., Pargaien, S., Mer, A., Arora, S., & Gangola, S. (2024). Harnessing Artificial Intelligence and Blockchain: Advancing Cybersecurity and Identity Protection. *Available atSSRN* 5091178.

Khan, L. (2017). Amazon's antitrust paradox. *The Yale Law Journal*, *126*(3). https://www.yalelawjournal.org/note/amazons-antitrust-paradox

Khan, M. I. K., Meher, M. A. K. M., & Syed, S. M. K. (2013). Impact of inflation on dividend policy: Synchronization of capital gain and interest rate. *Pensee Journal*, *75*, 389–393.

Khan, S. N., Loukil, F., Ghedira-Guegan, C., Benkhelifa, E., & Bani-Hani, A. (2021). Blockchain smart contracts: Applications, challenges, and future trends. *Peer-to-Peer Networking and Applications*, *14*(5), 2901–2925. DOI: 10.1007/s12083-021-01127-0 PMID: 33897937

Khan, T. H., MacEachen, E., Hopwood, P., & Goyal, J. (2021). Self-employment, work and health: A critical narrative review. *Work (Reading, Mass.)*, *70*(3), 945–957. DOI: 10.3233/WOR-213614 PMID: 34744041

Kharub, M., Mondal, S., Singh, S., & Gupta, H. C. (2024). Evaluation Of Competency Dimensions for Employee Performance Assessment: Evidence from Micro, Small, And Medium Enterprises. International Journal of Productivity and Performance Management. https://Doi.Org/10.1108/Ijppm-07-2023-0379

Khatri, M., Duggal, H. K., Thomas, A., & Varma, A. (2024). Increasing Digitalization of The Workplace: Is the Workforce Ready? Journal Of Asia Business Studies. https://Doi.Org/10.1108/Jabs-03-2024-0144

Khosrowshahi, D. (2020, August 10). *I am the C.E.O. of Uber. Gig workers deserve better.* The New York Times. https://www.nytimes.com/2020/08/10/opinion/uber-ceo-dara-khosrowshahi-gig-workers-deserve-better.html

Kişi, N. (2022). Exploratory research on the use of blockchain technology in recruitment. *Sustainability (Basel), 14*(16), 10098. DOI: 10.3390/su141610098

Kitaria, D., & Mwadulo, M. (2022). Adoption of Augmented Reality (AR) and Virtual Reality (VR) in healthcare systems. African Journal of Science, Technology. *Innovation and Sustainability, 1*(1). Advance online publication. DOI: 10.58506/ajstss.v1i1.70

Klapper, L., & Singer, D. (2019). *The Impact of Digital Financial Services on Poverty Reduction.* World Bank.

Klontz, B., Britt, S. L., Mentzer, J., & Klontz, T. (2011). Money beliefs and financial behaviors: Development of the Klontz Money Script Inventory. *Journal of Financial Therapy, 2*(1), 1. DOI: 10.4148/jft.v2i1.451

Kolmar, C. (2023). 25 gig economy statistics [2023]: Facts, trends, and impacts. Zippia Research. Retrieved from https://www.zippia.com/advice/gig-economy-statistics/

Komalavalli, C., Saxena, D., & Laroiya, C. (2020). Overview of blockchain technology concepts. In *Handbook of research on blockchain technology* (pp. 349–371). Academic Press. DOI: 10.1016/B978-0-12-819816-2.00014-9

Koohang, A., Nord, J. H., Ooi, K.-B., Tan, G. W.-H., Al-Emran, M., Aw, E. C.-X., Baabdullah, A. M., Buhalis, D., Cham, T.-H., Dennis, C., Dutot, V., Dwivedi, Y. K., Hughes, L., Mogaji, E., Pandey, N., Phau, I., Raman, R., Sharma, A., Sigala, M., & Wong, L.-W. (2023). Shaping the Metaverse into Reality: A Holistic Multidisciplinary Understanding of Opportunities, Challenges, and Avenues for Future Investigation. *Journal of Computer Information Systems, 63*(3), 735–765. DOI: 10.1080/08874417.2023.2165197

Koskelainen, T., Kalmi, P., Scornavacca, E., & Vartiainen, T. (2023). Financial literacy in the digital age—A research agenda. *The Journal of Consumer Affairs, 57*(1), 507–528. DOI: 10.1111/joca.12510

Kost, D., Fieseler, C., & Wong, S. I. (2019). Boundaryless careers in the gig economy: An oxymoron? *Human Resource Management Journal, 30*(1), 100–113. DOI: 10.1111/1748-8583.12265

Kovács, M., Muity, G., Szapáry, Á., Nemeskéri, Z., Váradi, I., Kapus, K., Tibold, A., Zalayné, N. M., Horvath, L., & Fehér, G. (2023). The prevalence and risk factors of burnout and its association with mental issues and quality of life among hungarian postal workers: A cross-sectional study. *BMC Public Health*, *23*(1), 75. Advance online publication. DOI: 10.1186/s12889-023-15002-5 PMID: 36627594

KPMG. (2023). EdTech market trends and future projections. https://www.kpmg.com

Kretschmer, T., & Khashabi, P. Digital Transformation and Organization Design: An Integrated Approach. California Management Review (2020) Jul 13;62(4):86–104. Available From: https://Doi.Org/10.1177/0008125620940296

Krishnakumar, R., & Vijayakumar, L. (2013). The effectiveness of the financial inclusion products. IRACST–International Journal of Commerce, Business and Management (IJCBM), ISSN, 2319-2828.

Krstić, B., Stanišić, T., & Radivojević, V. (2016). The impact of innovativeness' factors on the EU countries competitiveness. *Industrija*, *44*(2), 101–116. DOI: 10.5937/industrija44-10674

Krstić, M., & Radivojević, V. (2022). Regional competitiveness: Theoretical and empirical aspects. In Akkuk, U. (Ed.), *Disruptive technologies and eco-innovation for sustainable development* (pp. 150–170). IGI Global. DOI: 10.4018/978-1-7998-8900-7.ch009

Kshetri, N. (2017). Blockchain's roles in strengthening cybersecurity and protecting privacy. *Telecommunications Policy*, *41*(10), 1027–1038. DOI: 10.1016/j.telpol.2017.09.003

Kuhn, P., & Maleki, A. (2017). The economics of the gig economy. *IZA World of Labor*. https://wol.iza.org/articles/the-economics-of-the-gig-economy

Kuhn, K. M., Meijerink, J., & Keegan, A. (2021). Human resource management and the gig economy: Challenges and opportunities at the intersection between organizational HR decision-makers and digital labor platforms. *Research in Personnel and Human Resources Management*, *39*, 1–46. DOI: 10.1108/S0742-730120210000039001

Kulik, J. A., & Kulik, C.-L. C. (1991). Effectiveness of computer-based instruction: An updated analysis. *Computers in Human Behavior*, *7*(1-2), 75–94. DOI: 10.1016/0747-5632(91)90030-5

Kumar, P. (2023). *Gig Workers in Chhattisgarh: Emerging Opportunities in the New Economy*. http://www.centralasianstudies.org

Kumar, P., & Bhardwaj, M. (2023). Comparative analysis of e-books and physical books in Indian education.

Kumar, S. (2023). Bridging the digital divide in Indian education: The role of regional language content.

Kumar, S. (2023). Digital inclusion through regional languages: The next frontier in Education 4.0.

Kumar, S., Narayan, S., Sharma, K., Kaur, R., & Sen, R. (2023). Creating Sustainable High-Performance Human Resource Practice Through Employees Learning Agility. The Transition Adaptive Approach. ABAC Journal. https://Doi.Org/10.59865/Abacj.2023.40

Kumar, N. (2013). Financial inclusion and its determinants: Evidence from India. *Journal of Financial Economic Policy*, *5*(1), 4–19. DOI: 10.1108/17576381311317754

Kumar, N., Sharma, S., & Vyas, M. (2019). Impact of digital banking on financial inclusion: An investigation on youngsters in Rupnagar city, Punjab. *International Journal of Management. IT and Engineering*, *9*(5), 365–374.

Kumar, S., & Gulati, R. (2008). An examination of technical, pure technical, and scale efficiencies in Indian public sector banks using data envelopment analysis. *Eurasian Journal of Business and Economics*, *1*(2), 33–69.

Kumar, V., Hallqvist, C., & Ekwall, D. (2017). Developing a framework for traceability implementation in the textile supply chain. *Systems*, *5*(2), 33. DOI: 10.3390/systems5020033

Kurian, J. S., & Bindu Madhavi, N. (2024). Navigating the gig economy: Exploring challenges and motivations for the wellbeing of Gen Y and Gen Z gig workers. *Cogent Psychology*, *11*(1), 2357458. Advance online publication. DOI: 10.1080/23311908.2024.2357458

Lacher, L. L., Walia, G. S., Fagerholm, F., Pagels, M., Nygard, K. E., & Münch, J. (2015). A Behavior Marker Tool for Measurement of The Non-Technical Skills of Software Professionals: An Empirical Investigation. International Conference on Software Engineering, 409–414. https://Doi.Org/10.18293/SEKE2015-227

Laha, A. (2015). Association between financial inclusion and human development in South Asia: A cross-country analysis with special reference to India. *Journal of Economic Policy and Research*, *10*(2), 69.

Lai, H. K., & Hsieh, S. F. (2024). Evaluating the Impact of Robotic Process Automation on Earnings Management. *Journal of Information Systems*, *XX*(XX), 1–31. https://publications.aaahq.org/jis/article/doi/10.2 08/ISYS-2024-032/13273/Evaluating-the-Impact-of-Robotic-Process

Lamb, K. (2018). Blockchain and Smart Contracts: What the AEC sector needs to know.

Larrier, J. H. (2021). A brief history of blockchain. *Transforming Scholarly Publishing With Blockchain Technologies and AI*, 85-100.

Lashkari, B., & Musilek, P. (2021). A comprehensive review of blockchain consensus mechanisms. *IEEE Access : Practical Innovations, Open Solutions*, *9*, 43620–43652. DOI: 10.1109/ACCESS.2021.3065880

Lee, A. T., Ramasamy, R. K., & Subbarao, A. (2025). Understanding Psychosocial Barriers to Healthcare Technology Adoption: A Review of TAM Technology Acceptance Model and Unified Theory of Acceptance and Use of Technology and UTAUT Frameworks. In *Healthcare (Switzerland)* (Vol. 13, Issue 3, p. 250). Multidisciplinary Digital Publishing Institute. DOI: 10.3390/healthcare13030250

Lee, J., Kim, H., & Park, S. (2023). VR and AR in education: AI-enhanced immersive learning.

Lee, C. H., Wu, K. J., & Tseng, M. L. (2018). Resource management practice through eco-innovation toward sustainable development using qualitative information and quantitative data. *Journal of Cleaner Production*, *202*, 120–129. DOI: 10.1016/j.jclepro.2018.08.058

Lehdonvirta, V., Kässi, O., Hjorth, I., Barnard, H., & Graham, M. (2019). The global platform economy: A new offshoring institution enabling emerging-economy micro providers. *Journal of Management*, *45*(2), 567–599. DOI: 10.1177/0149206318786781 PMID: 30774168

Lenka, S. K., & Sharma, R. (2017). Does financial inclusion spur economic growth in India? *Journal of Developing Areas*, *51*(3), 215–228. DOI: 10.1353/jda.2017.0069

Lepak, D. P., & Snell, S. A. (2002). Examining the human resource architecture: The relationships among human capital, employment, and human resource configurations. *Journal of Management*, *28*(4), 517–543. DOI: 10.1177/014920630202800403

Lepanjuuri, K., Wishart, R., & Cornick, P. (2018). *The characteristics of those in the gig economy: Final report*. Department for Business, Energy & Industrial Strategy (BEIS).

Lester, G. V., Brock Baskin, M. E., & Clinton, M. S. (2021). Employer-Sponsored Benefits in the United States: The Past, Present, and Future. *Compensation and Benefits Review*, *53*(1), 24–42. DOI: 10.1177/0886368720947609 PMID: 34955602

Le, T. T. (2022). Linking big data, sustainable supply chain management and corporate performance: The moderating role of circular economy thinking. *International Journal of Logistics Management*, *34*(3), 744–771. Advance online publication. DOI: 10.1108/IJLM-01-2022-0011

Le, T. T., Ferraris, A., & Dhar, B. K. (2023). The contribution of circular economy practices on the resilience of production systems: Eco-innovation and cleaner production's mediation role for sustainable development. *Journal of Cleaner Production*, *424*, 138806. https://doi.org/https://doi.org/10.1016/j.jclepro.2023.138806. DOI: 10.1016/j.jclepro.2023.138806

Le, T. T., Vo, X. V., & Venkatesh, V. G. (2022). Role of green innovation and supply chain management in driving sustainable corporate performance. *Journal of Cleaner Production*, *374*, 133875. https://doi.org/https://doi.org/10.1016/j.jclepro.2022.133875. DOI: 10.1016/j.jclepro.2022.133875

Levis, D., Fontana, F., & Ughetto, E. (2021). A look into the future of blockchain technology. *PLoS One*, *16*(11), e0258995. DOI: 10.1371/journal.pone.0258995 PMID: 34788307

Levy, K. E. (2017). Book-smart, not street-smart: Blockchain-based smart contracts and the social workings of law. *Engaging Science, Technology, and Society*, *3*, 1–15. DOI: 10.17351/ests2017.107

Lewis, W. A. (1954). Economic development with unlimited supplies of labor. *Manchester School*, *22*(2), 139–191. DOI: 10.1111/j.1467-9957.1954.tb00021.x

Liao, Z., & Cheung, M. T. (2002). Internet-based e-banking and consumer attitudes: An empirical study. *Information & Management*, *39*(4), 283–295. DOI: 10.1016/S0378-7206(01)00097-0

Libby, R., & Witz, P. D. (2024). Artificial Intelligence in Auditing: How Auditor AI Use Can Mitigate Legal Liability. *Current Issues in Auditing*, *XX*(XX), 1–11. https://www.researchgate.net/publication/378512804_Can_artificial_intelligence_reduce_the_effect_of_independence_conflicts_on_audit_firm_liability. DOI: 10.2308/CIIA-2024-029

Libby, R., & Witz, P. D. (2024). Can artificial intelligence reduce the effect of independence conflicts on audit firm liability? *Contemporary Accounting Research*, *41*(2), 1346–1375. DOI: 10.1111/1911-3846.12941

Li, L. (2022). Reskilling And Upskilling the Future-Ready Workforce for Industry 4.0 And beyond. *Information Systems Frontiers*, •••, 1–16. Doi.Org/10.1007/S10796-022-10308-Y PMID: 35855776

Ling, E. C., Tussyadiah, I., Tuomi, A., Stienmetz, J., & Ioannou, A. (2021). Factors influencing users' adoption and use of conversational agents: A systematic review. *Psychology and Marketing*, *38*(7), 1031–1051. DOI: 10.1002/mar.21491

Li, S. (2023). The gig economy and labour market dynamics. Advances in Economics. *Management and Political Sciences*, *61*(1), 275–281. DOI: 10.54254/2754-1169/61/20231285

Liu, M., Li, Y., Lin, Z., Zhou, J., & Liu, S. (2024). The cost of 'cost reduction': An integrative review of blended workgroups. *Human Resource Management Review*, *101054*. Advance online publication. DOI: 10.1016/j.hrmr.2024.101054

Liu, M., Wu, K., & Xu, J. (2019). How Will Blockchain Technology Impact Auditing and Accounting: Permission less Versus Permissioned Blockchain. *Current Issues in Auditing*, *13*(2), A19–A29. https://publications.aaahq.org/cia/article/13/2/A19/7134/How-Will-Blockchain-Technology-Impact-Auditing-and. DOI: 10.2308/ciia-52540

Li, X., Jiang, P., Chen, T., Luo, X., & Wen, Q. (2020). A Survey on the Security of Blockchain Systems. *Future Generation Computer Systems*, *107*, 841–853. DOI: 10.1016/j.future.2017.08.020

Li, Y. (2023). Gig economy growth rate outpaces traditional employment: A comparative statistical analysis. *Labour Economics Review*, *28*(1), 44–57.

López Barreda, R., Robertson-Preidler, J., & Bedregal García, P. (2019). Health assessment and the capability approach. *Global Bioethics = Problemi di Bioetica*, *30*(1), 19–27. DOI: 10.1080/11287462.2019.1673028 PMID: 31632214

Lo, Y. F., & Hsieh, K. L. (2024). The study of working patterns in the gig economy. *Management Analytics and Social Insights*, *1*(1), 70–87.

Luchkin, A. G., Lukasheva, O. L., Novikova, N. E., Melnikov, V. A., Zyatkova, A. V., & Yarotskaya, E. V. (2020, August). Cryptocurrencies in the global financial system: problems and ways to overcome them. In *Russian Conference on Digital Economy and Knowledge Management (RuDEcK 2020)* (pp. 423-430). Atlantis Press. DOI: 10.2991/aebmr.k.200730.077

Luckin, R., & Holmes, W. (2016). Intelligence unleashed: An argument for AI in education.

Luo, D., Luo, M., & Lv, J. (2022). Can digital finance contribute to the promotion of financial sustainability? A financial efficiency perspective. *Sustainability (Basel)*, *14*(7), 3979. DOI: 10.3390/su14073979

Luo, J., Pan, Z., & Zhang, S. (2024). Greening the economy: Techniques and regulations to promote natural resource efficiency. *Resources Policy*, *90*, 104686. https://doi.org/https://doi.org/10.1016/j.resourpol.2024.104686. DOI: 10.1016/j.resourpol.2024.104686

Lusardi, A., & Mitchell, O. S. (2007). Financial literacy and retirement planning: New evidence from the Rand American Life Panel. Michigan Retirement Research Centre Research Paper No. WP 2007-157.

Lusardi, A., & Mitchell, O. S. (2007). Baby boomer retirement security: The roles of planning, financial literacy, and housing wealth. *Journal of Monetary Economics*, *54*(1), 205–224. DOI: 10.1016/j.jmoneco.2006.12.001

Lyons, A. C., & Kass-Hanna, J. (2021). A methodological overview to defining and measuring "digital" financial literacy. *Financial Planning Review*, *4*(2), e1113. DOI: 10.1002/cfp2.1113

Lyons, A., Kass-Hanna, J., & Greenlee, A. (2020). Impacts of financial and digital inclusion on poverty in South Asia and Sub-Saharan Africa. *Available atSSRN* 3684265. DOI: 10.2139/ssrn.3684265

Macrinici, D., Cartofeanu, C., & Gao, S. (2018). Smart contract applications within blockchain technology: A systematic mapping study. *Telematics and Informatics*, *35*(8), 2337–2354. DOI: 10.1016/j.tele.2018.10.004

Magid, A. A., Hussainey, K., De Andrés, J., & Lorca, P. (2024). Powering the Future of Sustainable Finance: FinTech, Big Data Analytics, and the Evolving Investment Landscape in the Post-COVID-19 Era. In *Business Sustainability with Artificial Intelligence (AI): Challenges and Opportunities* (Vol. 1, pp. 215–225). Springer Nature Switzerland.

Maglio, Monica(2022). Visions of cities beyond the Green Deal: From imagination to reality, *Journal of Urban Regeneration & Renewal*, Volume 15 / Number 2 / Winter 2022, pp. 176-192(17).

Mahadeva, M. (2008). Financial growth in India: Whither financial inclusion Margin. *Margin*, *2*(2), 177–197. DOI: 10.1177/097380100800200202

Mahato, M., Kumar, N., & Jena, L. K. (2021). Re-thinking gig economy in conventional workforce post-COVID-19: A blended approach for upholding fair balance. *Journal of Work-Applied Management*, *13*(2), 261–276. DOI: 10.1108/JWAM-05-2021-0037

Malaysia, P., Uchiyama, Y., Nasrudin, M., & Akhir, M. (2022). Gig workers, social protection and labour market inequality: Lessons from Malaysia. *Jurnal Ekonomi Malaysia, 56*(3). Advance online publication. DOI: 10.17576/JEM-2022-5603-09

Malik, A., Budhwar, P., & Srikanth, N. R. (2020). Gig economy, 4IR and artificial intelligence: Rethinking strategic HRM. In Human & technological resource management (HTRM): New insights into revolution 4.0 (pp. 75-88). Emerald Publishing Limited.

Malik, H. R., Nawaz, N. A., & Al-Zghoul, M. B. (2020). Impact of Augmented Reality and Virtual Reality in the Transformation of Virtual Customer Relationship Management Sector. In 2020 IEEE 7th International Conference on Engineering Technologies and Applied Sciences (ICETAS) (pp. 1-5). IEEE. DOI: DOI: 10.1109/ICETAS51660.2020.9484306

Malik, R., Visvizi, A., & Skrzek-Lubasińska, M. (2021). The gig economy: Current issues, the debate, and the new avenues of research. *Sustainability (Basel), 13*(9), 5023. DOI: 10.3390/su13095023

Manasseh, C. O., Abada, F. C., Ogbuabor, J. E., Onwumere, J. U. J., Urama, C. E., & Okoro, O. E. (2018). The effects of interest and inflation rates on consumption expenditure: Application of consumer spending model. *International Journal of Economics and Financial Issues*, *8*(4), 32–38.

Mandolla, C., Petruzzelli, A. M., Percoco, G., & Urbinati, A. (2019). Building a digital twin for additive manufacturing through the exploitation of blockchain: A case analysis of the aircraft industry. *Computers in Industry*, *109*, 134–152. DOI: 10.1016/j.compind.2019.04.011

Mann, S., Potdar, V., Gajavilli, R. S., & Chandan, A. (2018, December). Blockchain technology for supply chain traceability, transparency and data provenance. In *Proceedings of the 2018 international conference on blockchain technology and application* (pp. 22-26). DOI: 10.1145/3301403.3301408

Manta, O. (2022). Digital financial technologies and green finance, support tools for the sustainable development of the economy. In *Creşterea economică în condiţiile globalizării* (pp. 23-42). DOI: 10.36004/nier.cecg.III.2022.16.2

Manyika, J., Lund, S., Bughin, J., Robinson, K., Mischke, J., & Mahajan, D. (2016). *Independent work: Choice, necessity and the gig economy*. McKinsey Global Institute. https://www.mckinsey.com/featured-insights/employment-and-growth/independent-work-choice-necessity-and-the-gig-economy# Malik

Marin-Garcia, J. A., & Tomas, J. M. (2016). Deconstructing AMO framework: A systematic review. Intangible capital, 12(4), 1040-1087.

Marler, J. H., & Boudreau, J. W. (2017). An evidence-based review of HR Analytics. *International Journal of Human Resource Management*, *28*(1), 3–26. DOI: 10.1080/09585192.2016.1244699

Marr, B. (2023). The 5 Biggest Problems With Blockchain Technology Everyone Must Know About. Retrieved from https://www.forbes.com/sites/bernardmarr/2023/04/14/the-5-biggest-problems-with-blockchain-technology-everyone-must-know-about/?sh=78079bf855d2

Masta, R., & Kaushiva, P. (2024). Work in the platform economy: A systematic literature review. *Employee Relations, ahead-of-print*(ahead-of-print). https://doi.org/DOI: 10.1108/ER-12-2023-0638

Mathew, J., Mer, A. & Khan, F. (2025). 5 Blockchain Smart. *Digital HR: Technologies for HR Transformation and Performance Improvement*, 64.

Mbagwu, F. O., Chukwuedo, S. O., & Ogbuanya, T. C. (2020). Promoting Lifelong Learning Propensity and Intentions for Vocational Training Among Adult and Vocational Educational Undergraduates. *Vocations and Learning*, *13*(3), 419–437. Doi .Org/10.1007/S12186-020-09245-1. DOI: 10.1007/s12186-020-09245-1

Mc Kinsey & Company. (2023). *What is the gig economy?*https://www.mckinsey.com/featured-insights/mckinsey-explainers/what-is-the-gig-economy

McDonnell, A., Carbery, R., Burgess, J., & Sherman, U. (2021). Technologically mediated human resource management in the gig economy. *International Journal of Human Resource Management*, *32*(19), 3995–4015. DOI: 10.1080/09585192.2021.1986109

Mcgrath, C., & Zell, D. (2001). The Future of Innovation Diffusion Research and its Implications for Management: A Conversation with Everett Rogers. *Journal of Management Inquiry*, *10*(4), 386–391. DOI: 10.1177/1056492601104012

McKinsey & Company. (2016). *Independent work: Choice, necessity, and the gig economy*.https://www.mckinsey.com

McKinsey & Company. (2016). Independent work: Choice, necessity, and the gig economy. *McKinsey Global Institute*. https://www.mckinsey.com/business-functions/organization/our-insights/independent-work-choice-necessity-and-the-gig-economy

McLean, G., & Wilson, A. (2019). Shopping in the digital world: Examining customer engagement through augmented reality mobile applications. *Computers in Human Behavior*, *101*, 210–224. DOI: 10.1016/j.chb.2019.07.002

Mcwhorter, R. R. (2010). Exploring The Emergence of Virtual Human Resource Development. *Advances in Developing Human Resources*, *12*(6), 623–631. Doi.Org/ 10.1177/1523422310395367. DOI: 10.1177/1523422310395367

Meena, R. (2023). The Impact of Financial technology on Financial Services: A Comprehensive Analysis. *Research Review International Journal of Multidisciplinary*, *8*(3), 185–192. DOI: 10.31305/rrijm.2023.v08.n03.022

Mehta, A. (2022). Analyse The Challenges Faced By Gig Workers During The Covid Pandemic In India-Case Study Of OLA Drivers. *Public Policy and Research International.*

Meijerink, J., & Keegan, A. (2019). Conceptualizing human resource management in the gig economy: Toward a platform ecosystem perspective. *Journal of Managerial Psychology*, *34*(4), 214–232. DOI: 10.1108/JMP-07-2018-0277

Mekpor, E. S. (2019). Anti-money laundering and combating the financing of terrorism compliance: Are FATF member states just scratching the surface? *Journal of Money Laundering Control*, *22*(3), 451–471. DOI: 10.1108/JMLC-09-2018-0057

Memon, M., Bajwa, U. A., Ikhlas, A., Memon, Y., Memon, S., & Malani, M. (2018, November). Blockchain beyond Bitcoin: block maturity level consensus protocol. In *2018 IEEE 5th International Conference on Engineering Technologies and Applied Sciences (ICETAS)* (pp. 1-5). IEEE. DOI: 10.1109/ICETAS.2018.8629232

Meoli, M., Rossi, A., & Vismara, S. (2022). Financial literacy and security-based crowdfunding. *Corporate Governance*, *30*(1), 27–54. DOI: 10.1111/corg.12355

Mer, A., & Srivastava, A. (2023). Employee engagement in the new normal: Artificial intelligence as a buzzword or a game changer? In *The adoption and effect of artificial intelligence on human resources management, Part A* (pp. 15-46). Emerald Publishing Limited.

Mer, A., & Virdi, A. S. (2023). Navigating the paradigm shift in HRM practices through the lens of artificial intelligence: A post-pandemic perspective. *The Adoption and Effect of Artificial Intelligence on Human Resources Management, Part A*, 123-154.

Mer, A., Mathew, J., & Arora, S. (2024). Managing Gig Economy Workers Through Artificial Intelligence: Applications and Challenges. *Fostering Industry-Academia Partnerships for Innovation-Driven Trade*, 17-30.

Mer, A., & Virdi, A. S. (2022). Artificial intelligence disruption on the brink of revolutionizing HR and marketing functions. In *Impact of artificial intelligence on organizational transformation* (pp. 1–19). Wiley. DOI: 10.1002/9781119710301.ch1

MERRILL, R. K., SCHILLEBEECKX, S. J., & BLAKSTAD, S. (2019). Sustainable digital finance in Asia: Creating environmental impact through bank transformation.

Mhlanga, D., & Shao, D. (2025). Blockchain Technology and Sustainable Supply Chain Finance: A Pathway to Environmental Responsibility and Profitability. In *Financial Inclusion and Sustainable Development in Sub-Saharan Africa* (pp. 215-230). Routledge.

Mian, S. S., & Mian, M. S. (2017). Impact of high-performance work practices (HPWPs) on the employee agility. In 10th International Conference on Law, Business, Marketing and Education (LBME-17). Pattaya (Thailand) Dec (pp. 27-28).

Milana, C. & Ashta, A. (2021). Artificial intelligence techniques in finance and financial markets: a survey of the literature. Strategic Change. researchgate.net

Milani, R., Sommovigo, V., Ghirotto, L., & Setti, I. (2024). Individual Differences in Learning Agility at Work: A Mixed Methods Study to Develop and Validate a New Scale. Human Resource Development Quarterly. Available From: https://Doi .Org/10.1002/Hrdq.21528

Miller, T., & Johnson, K. (2023). AI-enhanced gamification in education.

Miller, J., & Lee, P. (2021). AI in education: Managing administration and instructional efficiency. *Journal of Educational Technology & Society*.

Min, H. (2019). Blockchain technology for enhancing supply chain resilience. *Business Horizons*, *62*(1), 35–45. DOI: 10.1016/j.bushor.2018.08.012

Ministry of Finance. (2023). *Jan Dhan accounts update: Financial inclusion progress*. Government of India.

Ministry of Finance. (2024). Economic Survey 2023–24: Volume I & II. Department of Economic Affairs, Government of India. https://www.indiabudget.gov.in/economicsurvey/

Ministry of Finance. (2024). *Pradhan Mantri Jan Dhan Yojana progress report*. Government of India.

Ministry of Social Justice and Empowerment. India. (2021). National Policy on Persons with Disabilities. https://socialjustice.nic.in

Minter, K. (2017). Negotiating labour standards in the gig economy: Airtasker and Unions New South Wales. *Economic and Labour Relations Review*, *28*(3), 438–454. DOI: 10.1177/1035304617724305

Mirković, V., Lukić, J., Lazarević, S., & Vojinović, Ž. (2019). Key Characteristics of Organizational Structure That Supports Digital Transformation. Available From: https://Doi.Org/10.46541/978-86-7233-380-0_46

Mishra, S., Reddy, N., & Sharma, V. (2021). Mental Health and Online Learning: Addressing the Issues in EdTech.

Mishra, H., & Venkatesan, M. (2021). Blockchain in human resource management of organizations: An empirical assessment to gauge HR and non-HR perspective. *Journal of Organizational Change Management*, *34*(2), 525–542. DOI: 10.1108/JOCM-08-2020-0261

MIT. (n.d.). *MITx MicroMasters Programs*. https://micromasters.mit.edu/

Mohamed, S., & Mat, N. H. N. (2023). Gig work in post pandemic times: Does it an agile work structure? *Journal of Entrepreneurship and Business*, *11*(2), 56–68. DOI: 10.17687/jeb.v11i2.1014

Mohanty, S. P., Gopalkrishnan, S., & Mahendra, A. (2021). The intertwined relationship of shadow banking and commercial banks' deposit growth: Evidence from India. *International Journal of Innovation Science*, *14*(3/4), 570–587. DOI: 10.1108/IJIS-01-2021-0022

Mondal, S. (2015). Financial inclusion: A step towards eradicates poverty. *American Journal of Theoretical and Applied Business*, *1*(1), 21–26.

Montgomery, T., & Baglioni, S. (2020). Defining the gig economy: Platform capitalism and the reinvention of precarious work. *The International Journal of Sociology and Social Policy*, *41*(9/10), 1012–1025. DOI: 10.1108/IJSSP-08-2020-0400

Morandini, S., Fraboni, F., De Angelis, M., Puzzo, G., Giusino, D., & Pietrantoni, L. (2023). The impact of artificial intelligence on workers' skills: Upskilling and reskilling in organisations. *Informing Science*, *26*, 39–68. DOI: 10.28945/5078

Morgan, P. J., & Long, T. Q. (2019). *Fintech and financial literacy in the Lao PDR* (No. 933). ADBI Working Paper Series.

Morgan, P., Huang, B., & Trinh, L. Q. (2020). Minding the gaps in digital financial education strategies. *G20 Insights, 24*.

Moşteanu, N. R. (2019, December). Green sustainable regional development and digital era. In *Green buildings and renewable energy: Med green forum 2019-part of world renewable energy congress and network* (pp. 181–197). Springer International Publishing.

Mouazen, A., & Hernández-Lara, A. (2023). Entrepreneurial ecosystem, gig economy practices and women's entrepreneurship: The case of Lebanon. *International Journal of Gender and Entrepreneurship*, *15*(3), 249–274. DOI: 10.1108/IJGE-07-2022-0116

Moyo, O. M. (2018). The nexus between financial inclusion and financial development in Zimbabwe (2009-2015).

Muchiri, D. G. (2022). Skilling, Reskilling, And Upskilling a Workforce: A Perspective from Kenyan Enterprises. Strategic Journal of Business & Change Management, 9(4). https://Doi.Org/10.61426/Sjbcm.V9i4.2368

Muduli, A., & Choudhury, A. (2024). Exploring The Role of Workforce Agility On Digital Transformation: A Systematic Literature Review. Benchmarking: An International Journal. https://Doi.Org/10.1108/Bij-02-2023-0108

Munari, S. A. L. H., & Susanti, S. (2021). The effect of ease of transaction, Digital Literacy, and Financial Literacy on the Use of E-Banking. *Economic Education Analysis Journal*, *10*(2), 298–309.

Murtaza, M., Ahmed, Y., Shamsi, J. A., Sherwani, F., & Usman, M. (2022). AI-Based Personalized E-Learning Systems: Issues, Challenges, And Solutions. *IEEE Access : Practical Innovations, Open Solutions*, *10*, 81323–81342. https://Doi.Org/10.1109/Access.2022.3193938. DOI: 10.1109/ACCESS.2022.3193938

Myhill, K., Richards, J., & Sang, K. (2021). Job quality, fair work and gig work: The lived experience of gig workers. *International Journal of Human Resource Management*, *32*(19), 4110–4135. DOI: 10.1080/09585192.2020.1867612

Nagrjuna, B., Gawande, N. M., Bhandari, D., Roy, M. S., & Adhav, S. (2012). Marketing Effectiveness and Business Performance of Housing Finance Institutions.

Nair, A. J., Manohar, S., Mittal, A., & Chaudhry, R. (2024). Unleashing Digital Frontiers: Bridging Realities of Augmented Reality, Virtual Reality, and the Metaverse. *The Metaverse Dilemma: Challenges and Opportunities for Business and Society*, 85–112. DOI: 10.1108/978-1-83797-524-220241006

Nair, M. R., Kumar, S. S., Babu, S. S., Chandru, B. A., Kunjumon, K. S., Divya, C. S., & Varma, R. P. (2023). Health inequities around gender, disability and internal migration: Are local governments doing enough? *Public Health Action*, *13*(1), 6–11. DOI: 10.5588/pha.22.0032 PMID: 36949745

Nankervis, A., & Cameron, R. (2022). Capabilities And Competencies for Digitized Human Resource Management: Perspectives from Australian HR Professionals. *Asia Pacific Journal of Human Resources*, *61*(1), 232–251. https://Doi.Org/10.1111/1744-7941.12354. DOI: 10.1111/1744-7941.12354

National Payments Corporation of India (NPCI). (2023). *UPI transaction trends and digital payment adoption in India.*

National Payments Corporation of India (NPCI). (2024). *UPI transaction statistics.* https://www.npci.org.in

Nesterak, J., Szelągowski, M., & Radziszewski, P. (2024). Workplace Performance Measurement: Digitalization Of Work Observation and Analysis. Journal Of Intelligent Manufacturing. https://Doi.Org/10.1007/S10845-024-02419-X

Netto, A. J., & Tello-Gamarra, J. (2020). The gig economy and human capital development: Empirical perspectives. *Global Journal of Human Resource Management, 8*(1), 12–25.

Nhung, T. T. (2023). How Does Digital HRM Transform Training to Learning in Organizations? *Journal Of Economics Finance and Management Studies, 06*(08). https://Doi.Org/10.47191/Jefms/V6-I8-66

Nie, P., Zhong, J., Ren, Z., & Huang, J. (2024). Sustainable financing solutions for the growth of resource-driven economies in the digital economy age. *Resources Policy, 98*, 105350. DOI: 10.1016/j.resourpol.2024.105350

Nimmagadda, B., Vangaveti, Y., Aaluri, S., Mallikarjuna Rao, C., & Singh, B. (2024). An analytical study on navigating sustainability challenges and opportunities in the era of ai and the gig economy. MATEC Web of Conferences, 392, 01044. DOI: 10.1051/matecconf/202439201044

Ningsih, R. U., & Rita, M. R. (2010). Financial Attitudes dan Komunikasi Keluarga Tentang Pengeluaran Uang Saku: Ditinjau dari Perbedaan Gender. *Informatics & Business Institute Darmajaya, 8*(2), 206–219.

Nium. (2024, February 1). *Automating payroll: Attracting top gig economy workers done right.* Nium. https://www.nium.com/blog/automating-payroll-attracting-top-gig-economy-workers-done-right?utm_source=chatgpt.com

Nnamonu, O., Hammoudeh, M., & Dargahi, T. (2023). Metaverse Cybersecurity Threats and Risks Analysis: The case of Virtual Reality Towards Security Testing and Guidance Framework. In *2023 IEEE International Conference on Metaverse Computing, Networking and Applications (MetaCom)* (pp. 94-98). IEEE. DOI: DOI: 10.1109/MetaCom57706.2023.00028

Nobanee, H., & Ellili, N. O. (2016). Corporate Sustainability Disclosure in Annual Reports: Evidence from UAE Banks: Islamic versus Conventional. *Renewable & Sustainable Energy Reviews, 55*(March), 1336–1341. DOI: 10.1016/j.rser.2015.07.084

Noe, R. A., Clarke, A. D., & Klein, H. J. (2014). Learning in the twenty-first-century workplace. *Annual Review of Organizational Psychology and Organizational Behavior, 1*(1), 245–275. DOI: 10.1146/annurev-orgpsych-031413-091321

NPCI. (2023). Uttar Pradesh Payments Corporation.

Nunn, J. (2019). Bitcoin's Emerging Gig Economy. Retrieved from https://www.forbes.com/sites/jeffersonnunn/2019/02/19/bitcoins-emerging-gig-economy/

Nwariaku, H., Fadojutimi, B., Lawson, L. G. L., Agbelusi, J., Adigun, O. A., Udom, J. A., & Olajide, T. D. (2024). Blockchain technology as an enabler of transparency and efficiency in sustainable supply chains. *International Journal of Science and Research Archive, 12*(2), 1779–1789. DOI: 10.30574/ijsra.2024.12.2.1454

Obermayer, N., Csizmadia, T., Banász, Z., & Purnhauser, P. (2023). Importance Of Digital and Soft Skills in The Digital Age. European Conference on Knowledge Management, 24(2), 978–987. https://Doi.Org/10.34190/Eckm.24.2.1550

Oberoi, S., & Kansra, P. (2021). Motivating antecedents and consequences of blockchain technology in the insurance industry.

Oberoi, S., & Kansra, P. (2022). Blockchain technology in the insurance industry.

Oberoi, S., Arora, S., Verma, B., & Roy, K. K. (2024). What do we know about artificial intelligence and blockchain technology integration in the healthcare industry.

Oberoi, S., Arora, S., Verma, B., & Roy, K. K. (2024). What do we know about artificial intelligence and blockchain technology integration in the healthcare industry? In *Driving decentralization and disruption with digital technologies* (pp. 124–138). IGI Global Scientific Publishing. DOI: 10.4018/979-8-3693-3253-5.ch009

Oberoi, S., & Kansra, P. (2021). Motivating antecedents and consequences of blockchain technology in the insurance industry. In *Blockchain technology and applications for digital marketing* (pp. 276–285). IGI Global. DOI: 10.4018/978-1-7998-8081-3.ch017

OECD. (2023). *Platform cooperatives and employment: An alternative for platform work.* OECD Local Economic and Employment Development (LEED). *Papers, 2023*(16). Advance online publication. DOI: 10.1787/20794797

OECD/INFE. (2013, June). *Financial literacy and inclusion: Results of OECD/INFE survey across countries and by gender.* Financial Literacy & Education in Russia.

Oggero, N., Rossi, M. C., & Ughetto, E. (2020). Entrepreneurial spirits in women and men. The role of financial literacy and digital skills. *Small Business Economics, 55*(2), 313–327. DOI: 10.1007/s11187-019-00299-7

Okatta, C. G., Ajayi, F. A., & Olawale, O. (2024). Navigating the future: Integrating AI and machine learning in HR practices for a digital workforce. *Computer Science & IT Research Journal*, *5*(4), 1008–1030. DOI: 10.51594/csitrj.v5i4.1085

Oladele, O. K. (2024). Internet of Things (IoT) in Logistics: Transforming Supply Chains with Connected Devices and Data Analytics.

Opada, F. M. M., Ibrahim, M. B. H., Irawan, A., Akbar, M. A., & Rasyid, A. (2024). Talent Acquisition Strategies: A Comprehensive Examination of Recruitment Policies for Organizational Success. Advances In Human Resource Management Research, 2(2). https://Doi.Org/10.60079/Ahrmr.V2i2.185

OPS. (2025). How Blockchain Technology is Transforming Payroll. Retrirved from https://ops.ae/how-blockchain-technology-is-transforming-payroll/

Oskarita, E., & Nur'afra Arasy, H. (2024). The Role of Digital Tools in Enhancing Collaborative Learning in Secondary Education. International Journal of Educational Research. https://Doi.Org/10.62951/Ijer.V1i1.15

Oyer, P. (2020). The gig economy. *IZA World of Labor: Evidence-Based Policy Making*. Advance online publication. DOI: 10.15185/izawol.471

Oyewole, A. T., Adeoye, O. B., Addy, W. A., Okoye, C. C., Ofodile, O. C., & Ugochukwu, C. E.Adedoyin Tolulope OyewoleOmotayo Bukola AdeoyeWilhelmina Afua AddyChinwe Chinazo OkoyeOnyeka Chrisanctus OfodileChinonye Esther Ugochukwu. (2024). Augmented and virtual reality in financial services: A review of emerging applications. *World Journal of Advanced Research and Reviews.*, *21*(03), 551–567. DOI: 10.30574/wjarr.2024.21.3.0623

Ozili, P. K. (2021). Financial inclusion: a strong critique. In *New challenges for future sustainability and wellbeing* (pp. 1–16). Emerald Publishing Limited. DOI: 10.1108/978-1-80043-968-920211002

Pal, A., & Kant, K. (2019). Using blockchain for provenance and traceability in internet of things-integrated food logistics. *Computer*, *52*(12), 94–98. DOI: 10.1109/MC.2019.2942111

Pal, B., & Varanasi, S. (2021). Rising popularity in gig economy: A case study from india. *International Journal of Religious and Cultural Studies*, *3*(2). Advance online publication. DOI: 10.34199/ijracs.2021.09.08

Palhad, S., Onwubu, S., Singh, R., Thakur, R., Thakur, S., & Mkhize, G. (2023). The benefits and challenges of the gig economy: perspective of gig workers and small medium and micro enterprises (SMMES) in South Africa. African Journal of Inter/Multidisciplinary Studies, 5(1), 1-12. DOI: 10.51415/ajims.v5i1.1051

Pan, C., Sun, T., Mirza, N., & Huang, Y. (2022). The pricing of low emission transitions: Evidence from stock returns of natural resource firms in the GCC. *Resources Policy*, *79*, 102986. https://doi.org/https://doi.org/10.1016/j.resourpol.2022.102986. DOI: 10.1016/j.resourpol.2022.102986

Pandita, D. (2022). Innovation in talent management practices: Creating an innovative employer branding strategy to attract generation Z. *International Journal of Innovation Science*, *14*(3/4), 556–569. DOI: 10.1108/IJIS-10-2020-0217

Pangrazio, L., Bishop, C., & Lee, F. (2021). Old media, new gigs: The discursive construction of the gig economy in Australian news media. *Work, Employment and Society*, *37*(3), 606–624. DOI: 10.1177/09500170211034663

Panos, G. A., & Wilson, J. O. (2020). Financial literacy and responsible finance in the FinTech era: Capabilities and challenges. *European Journal of Finance*, *26*(4-5), 297–301. DOI: 10.1080/1351847X.2020.1717569

Panwar, A., & Bhatnagar, V. (2020, February). Distributed ledger technology (DLT): The beginning of a technological revolution for blockchain. In the 2nd *International Conference on Data, Engineering and Applications (IDEA)* (pp. 1-5). IEEE.

Papadopoulos, G. (2019). Blockchain and the law: Resolving data protection conflicts across jurisdictions. *Computer Law & Security Review*, *35*(4), 105344.

Papanastasiou, G. P., Drigas, A., Skianis, C., Lytras, M. D., & Papanastasiou, E. (2018). Virtual and augmented reality effects on K-12, higher and tertiary education students' twenty-first century skills. *Virtual Reality (Waltham Cross)*, *23*(4), 425–436. DOI: 10.1007/s10055-018-0363-2

Pardo, A., Han, F., & Kloos, C. D. (2019). Student engagement in personalized learning environments: The role of technology. *Computers in Human Behavior*.

Parker, S. K., & Axtell, C. M. (2001). Seeing another viewpoint: Antecedents and outcomes of employee perspective taking. *Academy of Management Journal*, *44*(6), 1054–1071. DOI: 10.2307/3069390

Parry, E., & Battista, V. (2019). The Impact of Emerging Technologies on Work: A Review of The Evidence and Implications for The Human Resource Function. *Emerald Open Research*, *1*(4), 5. https://Doi.Org/10.12688/Emeraldopenres.12907.1. DOI: 10.1108/EOR-04-2023-0001

Patel, A., & Singh, M. (2021). The role of NLP and AI in regional language inclusion in Indian EdTech.

Patel, A., & Singh, N. (2022). AI-driven localization in e-learning: Challenges and opportunities.

Patel, R. (2022). AI in blended learning environments.

Patel, S., & Kumar, R. (2021). E-learning in India: Trends and challenges in digital education. Indian Journal of Education and Technology.

Patel, V. (2020). Big tech's strategies in EdTech: A review of global trends.

Patel, S., & Singh, R. (2022). *AI-based translation for localizing digital education content*. Computers in Educatio.

Păun, T., & Pinzaru, F. (2021). Advancing strategic management through sustainable finance. *Management Dynamics in the Knowledge Economy*, *9*(2), 279–291. DOI: 10.2478/mdke-2021-0019

Pereira, L., Santos, P., & Costa, D. (2021). Digital education programs in Latin America: Overcoming barriers to equity.

Pereira, V., Behl, A., Jayawardena, N., Laker, B., Dwivedi, Y. K., & Bhardwaj, S. (2022). The art of gamifying digital gig workers: A theoretical assessment of evaluating engagement and motivation. *Production Planning and Control*. Advance online publication. DOI: 10.1080/09537287.2022.2083524

Pereira, V., & Bisson, J. (2021). Gig economy and HRM: Managing remote, flexible, and distributed teams in the digital age. *International Journal of Human Resource Management*, *32*(5), 887–903.

Perry, V. G., & Morris, M. D. (2005). Who is in control? The role of self-perception, knowledge, and income in explaining consumer financial behavior. *The Journal of Consumer Affairs*, *39*(2), 299–313. DOI: 10.1111/j.1745-6606.2005.00016.x

PFRDA. (2018, October 09). About page. Retrieved from Pension Fund Regulatory and Development Authority Website: http://www.pfrda.org.in/

Philipp, R., Prause, G., & Gerlitz, L. (2019). Blockchain and smart contracts for entrepreneurial collaboration in maritime supply chains. *Transport and Telecommunication Journal*, *20*(4), 365–378. DOI: 10.2478/ttj-2019-0030

Piasna, A., Zwysen, W., & Drahokoupil, J. (2022). The platform economy in Europe: Results from the second ETUI Internet and Platform Work Survey. ETUI. https://www.etui.org/sites/default/files/2022-02/The%20platform%20economy%20in%20Europe_2022.pdf

Pihir, I., Tomičić-Pupek, K., & Furjan, M. T. (2018). Digital Transformation Insights and Trends. In Central European Conference on Information and Intelligent Systems (Pp. 141-149). Faculty Of Organization and Informatics Varazdin.

Pilatti, G. R., Pinheiro, F. L., & Montini, A. A. (2024). Systematic Literature Review on Gig Economy: Power Dynamics, Worker Autonomy, and the Role of Social Networks. *Administrative Sciences*, *14*(10), 267. DOI: 10.3390/admsci14100267

Pillai, R., & Sivathanu, B. (2021). Measure What Matters: Descriptive And Predictive Metrics Of HRM-Pathway Toward Organizational Performance. International Journal of Productivity and Performance Management. https://Doi.Org/10.1108/IJPPM-10-2020-0509

Pillai, R., & Sivathanu, B. (2020). Adoption Of Artificial Intelligence (AI) For Talent Acquisition In IT/Ites Organizations. *Benchmarking*, *27*(9), 2599–2629. https://Doi.Org/10.1108/BIJ-04-2020-0186. DOI: 10.1108/BIJ-04-2020-0186

Pine, R. (n.d.). Beyond 9-to-5: Payroll solutions for the gig economy. *Jemini.*https://www.jemini.com/insights/latest-insights/payroll-solutions-gig-economy-modern-work/?utm_source=chatgpt.com

Polkowska, D. (2020). Platform work during the covid-19 pandemic: a case study of glove couriers in Poland. European Societies, 23(sup1), S321-S331. DOI: 10.1080/14616696.2020.1826554

Poole, W. (1972). The role of interest rates and inflation in the consumption function. *Brookings Papers on Economic Activity*, *1972*(1), 211–220. DOI: 10.2307/2534122

Popovski, L., Soussou, G., & Webb, P. B. (2018). A brief history of blockchain. *Legaltech news, 2018*, 3.

Popper, N. (2015). *Digital gold: The untold story of Bitcoin.* Penguin UK.

Pradeep, A. S. E., Yiu, T. W., Zou, Y., & Amor, R. (2021). Blockchain-aided information exchange records for design liability control and improved security. *Automation in Construction*, *126*, 103667. DOI: 10.1016/j.autcon.2021.103667

Prasad, H., Meghwal, D., & Dayama, V. (2018). Digital financial literacy: A study of households of Udaipur. *Journal of Business and Management*, *5*, 23–32. DOI: 10.3126/jbm.v5i0.27385

Queiroz, M. M., Telles, R., & Bonilla, S. H. (2020). Blockchain and supply chain management integration: A systematic review of the literature. *Supply Chain Management*, *25*(2), 241–254. DOI: 10.1108/SCM-03-2018-0143

Radhakrishnan, A., & Singha Roy, N. (2023). Gig economy workers' livelihood: A qualitative study of ride-hailing platforms in Bangalore City, India. *Artha Vijnana, 65*(2). Advance online publication. DOI: 10.21648/OPST6018

Radivojević, V., Kahrović, E., & Krstić, M. (2019). Population skills as an indicator of European countries competitiveness in the modern economy. *Vojno delo, 71*(5), 105-116. https://doi.org/DOI: 10.5937/vojdelo1905105R

Radu, I. (2014). Augmented reality in education: A meta-review and cross-media analysis. *Personal and Ubiquitous Computing, 18*(6), 1533–1543. DOI: 10.1007/s00779-013-0747-y

Raghavan, M., Barocas, S., Kleinberg, J., & Levy, K. (2020, January). Mitigating bias in algorithmic hiring: Evaluating claims and practices. In *Proceedings of the 2020 conference on fairness, accountability, and transparency* (pp. 469-481). DOI: 10.1145/3351095.3372828

Rahimi, R. A., & Oh, G. S. (2024). Beyond theory: a systematic review of strengths and limitations in technology acceptance models through an entrepreneurial lens. *Journal of Marketing Analytics*, 1–24. DOI: 10.1057/s41270-024-00318-x

Rahimi, M., Kumar, P., Moazzamigodarzi, M., & Mishra, A. R. (2022). Digital transformation challenges in sustainable financial service systems using novel interval-valued Pythagorean fuzzy double normalization-based multiple aggregation approach. *Environment, Development and Sustainability*, •••, 1–33. DOI: 10.1007/s10668-022-02719-3 PMID: 36373028

Rahman, M., Isa, C. R., Masud, M. M., Sarker, M., & Chowdhury, N. T. (2021). The role of financial behaviour, financial literacy, and financial stress in explaining the financial well-being of B40 group in Malaysia. *Future Business Journal, 7*(1), 1–18. DOI: 10.1186/s43093-021-00099-0

Rahman, S. U., Sultan, M. S., & Tabassam, A. (2024). The impact of the gig economy on traditional employment and the necessity for revised business, HR, and legal strategies. *Pakistan Journal of International Affairs, 7*(1).

Raja Santhi, A., & Muthuswamy, P. (2022). Influence of blockchain technology in manufacturing supply chain and logistics. *Logistics (Basel), 6*(1), 15. DOI: 10.3390/logistics6010015

Rajna, A., Ezat, W. S., Al Junid, S., & Moshiri, H. (2011). Financial management attitude and practice among the medical practitioners in public and private medical service in Malaysia. *International Journal of Business and Management, 6*(8), 105.

Ramachandran, R., Babu, V. R., & Murugesan, V. P. (2022). The Role of Blockchain Technology in The Process of Decision-Making in Human Resource Management: A Review and Future Research Agenda. *Business Process Management Journal, 29*(1), 116–139. https://Doi.Org/10.1108/Bpmj-07-2022-0351. DOI: 10.1108/BPMJ-07-2022-0351

Randolph, S. A. (2019). Gig Workers. *Workplace Health & Safety, 67*(8), 439–440. DOI: 10.1177/2165079919860545 PMID: 31313647

Rane, N. (2023). Enhancing customer loyalty through Artificial Intelligence (AI), Internet of Things (IoT), and Big Data technologies: improving customer satisfaction, engagement, relationship, and experience. Internet of Things (IoT), and Big Data Technologies: Improving Customer Satisfaction, Engagement, Relationship, and Experience. http://dx.doi.org/DOI: 10.2139/ssrn.4616051

Ranjan, V., & Bose, S. (2022). Overcoming linguistic barriers in digital education: Policy interventions and future strategies.

Rao, M., & Swaminathan, K. (2022). Regional languages in digital learning: Impacts on student engagement and economic mobility.

Rao, P., & Gupta, M. (2021). Data privacy challenges in EdTech: The way forward.

Rao, P., & Swaminathan, S. (2022). Localized e-learning solutions: The role of AI in multilingual education. Indian Journal of Educational Technology.

Rao, R. (2019). Did gig economy change ways of work? evidence from American time use survey. *Proceedings of the International Academic Conference on Management and Economics*. DOI: 10.33422/conferenceme.2019.11.654

Rashid, A., & Khalid, S. (2020). Exploring the impacts of inflation, interest rates, and their uncertainty on deposits and advances of conventional and Islamic Banks of Pakistan. *Journal of Economic Cooperation & Development, 41*(3), 117–150.

Raut, R., Deshpande, A., Arora, S., Mittal, A., & Alandikar, R. (2022). An examination of the pricing of IPOs: The Indian perspective.

Raut, R., Deshpande, A., Arora, S., Mittal, A., & Alandikar, R. (2022, December). An examination of the pricing of IPOs: The Indian perspective. In 2022 5th International Conference on Contemporary Computing and Informatics (IC3I) (pp. 155-159). IEEE.

Ravenelle, A. J. (2017). Sharing economy workers: Selling, not sharing. *Cambridge Journal of Regions, Economy and Society, 10*(2), 281–295. DOI: 10.1093/cjres/rsw043

Ravenelle, A. J., Kowalski, K. C., & Janko, E. (2021). The Side Hustle Safety Net: Precarious Workers and Gig Work during COVID-19. *Sociological Perspectives*, *64*(5), 898–919. DOI: 10.1177/07311214211005489

Ravikumar, T., Suresha, B., Prakash, N., Vazirani, K., & Krishna, T. A. (2022). Digital financial literacy among adults in India: Measurement and validation. *Cogent Economics & Finance*, *10*(1), 2132631. DOI: 10.1080/23322039.2022.2132631

RBI. (2023). Annual Report on Financial Inclusion in India.

Reddit user. (2024, March). *What are some side income jobs/gigs that can make decent money in India?* [Online forum post]. Reddit. https://www.reddit.com/r/personalfinanceindia/comments/1hjwj9c/what_are_some_side_income_jobsgigs_that_can_make/

Reid, J. R. (2023). Precision Education for Personalized Learning. Journal Of the American College of Radiology. https://Doi.Org/10.1016/J.Jacr.2023.05.018

Reis, J., Amorim, M., Melão, N., & Matos, P. (2018). Digital Transformation: A Literature Review and Guidelines for Future Research. Advances In Intelligent Systems and Computing. Available From: https://Doi.Org/10.1007/978-3-319-77703-0_41

Remund, D. L. (2010). Financial literacy explicated: The case for a clearer definition in an increasingly complex economy. *The Journal of Consumer Affairs*, *44*(2), 276–295. DOI: 10.1111/j.1745-6606.2010.01169.x

Renz, A., Krishnaraja, S., & Schildhauer, T. (2020, June). A new dynamic for EdTech in the age of pandemics.

Report, P. W. C. (2017). *How will blockchain technology impact HR and the world of work.*, Retrieved from https://www.pwc.co.uk/issues/futuretax/assets/blockchain-can%20impact-hr.pdf

Reserve Bank of India - Reports. rbi.org.in

Reserve Bank of India (RBI). (2024). *Handbook of statistics on Indian economy.* https://www.rbi.org.in

Respati, D. K., Widyastuti, U., Nuryati, T., Musyaffi, A. M., Handayani, B. D., & Ali, N. R. (2023). How do students' digital financial literacy and financial confidence influence their financial behavior and financial well-being? *Nurture*, *17*(2), 40–50. DOI: 10.55951/nurture.v17i2.154

Ricciardi, V., & Simon, H. K. (2000). What is behavioral finance? *Business. Education & Technology Journal*, *2*(2), 1–9.

Risman, A. (2024). The Behavioral Finance of MSME: Digital Finance, Managerial Biases, Financial Literacy. Dinasti International Journal of Economics, Finance & Accounting (DIJEFA), 5(2).

Robinson, L., Schulz, J., Dunn, H. S., Casilli, A. A., Tubaro, P., Carvath, R., Chen, W., Wiest, J. B., Dodel, M., Stern, M. J., Ball, C., Huang, K.-T., Blank, G., Ragnedda, M., Ono, H., Hogan, B., Mesch, G. S., Cotten, S. R., Kretchmer, S. B., & Khilnani, A. (2020). Digital inequalities 3.0: Emergent inequalities in the information age. *First Monday*. Advance online publication. DOI: 10.5210/fm.v25i7.10844

Rodrigo-González, A., Grau-Grau, A., & Bel-Oms, I. (2021). Circular Economy and Value Creation: Sustainable Finance with a Real Options Approach. *Sustainability (Basel)*, *13*(14), 7973. DOI: 10.3390/su13147973

Rodriguez, P. (2022). AI and lifelong learning: Upskilling for the future.

Rodríguez-Sánchez, J.-L., Montero-Navarro, A., & Gallego-Losada, R. (2019). The Opportunity Presented by Technological Innovation to Attract Valuable Human Resources. *Sustainability (Basel)*, *11*(20), 5785. https://Doi.Org/10.3390/SU11205785. DOI: 10.3390/su11205785

Rodriguez-Segura, D. (2022). EdTech in developing countries: A review of the evidence.

Rotaru, K., Rose, J. M., Ganbold, O., Anna, M. R., Loveridge, J., & Stamatelatos, A. (2024). Neuroaccounting. *Integrating Neurophysiological Techniques into Accounting and Accounting*, *13*(3), 21582440231190821. DOI: 10.1177/21582440231190821

Roy, G., & Shrivastava, A. K. (2020). Future of gig economy: Opportunities and challenges. *IMI Konnect*, *9*(1), 14–27.

Ruckelshaus, C. (2008). Labor's wage war. *The Fordham Urban Law Journal*, *35*(2), 373.

Ruhland, T. (2015), 5 Common Problems With Payroll Management. Retrieved from, https://blog.accuchex.com/5-common-problems-with-payroll-management

Ruona, W. E., & Gibson, S. K. (2004). The making of twenty-first-century HR: An analysis of the convergence of HRM, HRD, and OD. Human Resource Management: Published in Cooperation with the School of Business Administration, The University of Michigan and in alliance with the Society of Human Resources Management, 43(1), 49-66.

Ryketeng, M., Syachbrani, W., & Syamsuri, N. (2023). Optimising Human Resources Capacity: Driving Adoption of Latest Technology and Driving Business Innovation Amidst the Dynamics of The Digital Era. [ADMAN]. *Journal Of Contemporary Administration and Management, 1*(3), 229–236. https://Doi.Org/10.61100/Adman.V1i3.86. DOI: 10.61100/adman.v1i3.86

Salmah, E., Astuti, E., & Harsono, I. (2024). Employee engagement in the gig economy. [PRODUCTIVITY]. *Management Studies and Business Journal, 1*(1), 116–122. DOI: 10.62207/1e5dd842

Sandeep, M., Lavanya, V., & Balakrishnan, J. (2025). Leveraging AI In Recruitment: Enhancing Intellectual Capital Through Resource-Based View and Dynamic Capability Framework. Journal Of Intellectual Capital. https://Doi.Org/10.1108/Jic-05-2024-0155

Sanderson, A. (2015). *Importance of financial literacy. Bankers Association of Zimbabwe (BAZ).* Newsletter.

Sandner, P. (2022). Three Ways How Blockchain Technology Is Already Changing The Lives Of Thousands Of Workers In Emerging Countries. Retrieved by, https://www.forbes.com/sites/philippsandner/2022/08/31/three-ways-how-blockchain-technology-is-already-changing-the-lives-of-thousands-of-workers-in-emerging-countries/?sh=5af53afb4f3f

Saraji, S. (2023). Introduction to Blockchain. In *Sustainable Oil and Gas Using Blockchain* (pp. 57–74). Springer International Publishing. DOI: 10.1007/978-3-031-30697-6_3

Saraswathi, C. (2023). The role and challenges of gig work platforms in Indian economic development. *International Journal of Research and Analytical Reviews, 10*(2), 92–97.

Saraswathi, S., Suresh, J., & Gandhi, D. M. (2024). Combating Counterfeit Products with Blockchain Technology to Enhance Trust and Authenticity in Consumer Markets. *Indian Journal of Science and Technology, 17*(34), 3512–3521. DOI: 10.17485/IJST/v17i34.1449

Sarma, M. (2008). Index of financial inclusion (No. 215). DOI: 10.1007/978-81-322-1650-6_28

Sarmah, S. S. (2018). Understanding blockchain technology. *Computing in Science & Engineering, 8*(2), 23–29.

Sarma, M., & Pais, J. (2011). Financial inclusion and development. *Journal of International Development, 23*(5), 613–628. DOI: 10.1002/jid.1698

Sarma, M., & Pais, J. (2019). Financial Inclusion and Socioeconomic Disparities. *Economics and Politics*.

Sarra, Janis. (2020). Sustainable Finance and the Move to a Circular Economy. .DOI: 10.1093/oso/9780198852308.003.0008

Saudagar, A. K. J., Kumar, A., & Khan, M. B. (2023). MediverseBeyond Boundaries: A Comprehensive Analysis of AR and VR Integration in Medical Education for Diverse Abilities. *Journal of Digital Research.*, *3*(1), 20230066. DOI: 10.57197/JDR-2023-0066

Sawant, R., Thomas, B., & Kadlag, S. (2022). Reskilling And Upskilling: To Stay Relevant in Today's Industry. Deleted Journal, 7(1). https://Doi.Org/10.56902/Irbe.2022.7.1.4

Scatiggio, V. (2020). Tackling the issue of bias in artificial intelligence to design ai-driven fair and inclusive service systems. How human biases are breaching into ai algorithms, with severe impacts on individuals and societies, and what designers can do to face this phenomenon and change for the better.

Schneider, H. (2017). *Creative destruction and the sharing economy – Uber as disruptive innovation*. Edward Elgar Publishing., DOI: 10.4337/9781786433435

Scholkmann, A., Olsen, D., & Wollscheid, S. (2024). Perspectives on disruptive change in higher education. A critical review of digital transformation during COVID-19. *Higher Education Research & Development*, *43*(6), 1355–1369. DOI: 10.1080/07294360.2024.2325140

Scholz, T. (2016). *Platform Cooperativism Challenging the Corporate Sharing Economy*. Rosa Luxemburg Stiftung – New York Office. Retrieved from https://rosalux.nyc/wp-content/uploads/2020/11/RLS-NYC_platformcoop.pdf

Scholz, T. (2016). Platform cooperativism: A new economic model for the gig economy. *The New York Times*.

Scholz, T. (2017). *Uberworked and underpaid: How workers are disrupting the digital economy*. Polity Press.

Schor, J. B., & Attwood-Charles, W. (2017). The "sharing" economy: Labor, inequality, and social connection on for-profit platforms. *Sociology Compass*, *11*(8), e12493. DOI: 10.1111/soc4.12493

Schumpeter, J. (1942). *Capitalism, socialism, and democracy*. Harper & Bros.

Seldal, M. N., & Nyhus, E. K. (2022). Financial vulnerability, financial literacy, and the use of digital payment technologies. *Journal of Consumer Policy*, *45*(2), 281–306. DOI: 10.1007/s10603-022-09512-9 PMID: 35283545

Seligman, L. (2006). Sensemaking throughout adoption and the innovation-decision process. *European Journal of Innovation Management*, *9*(1), 108–120. DOI: 10.1108/14601060610640050

Selwyn, N. (2021). *Education and technology: Key issues and debates.* Bloomsbury Publishing.

Sengupta, S. (2009). *Speeding Financial Inclusion Through BCBF Model: Issues.* Challenge & Oppurtunities.

Sepetis, A., Pierrakos, G., & Schallmo, D. (2022). Sustainable Finance and the Digital Transformation in the Healthcare system. In *ISPIM Conference Proceedings* (pp. 1-21). The International Society for Professional Innovation Management (ISPIM).

Sepúlveda-Ortega, A. (2022). The Indonesian Digital Workforce Gaps In 2021–2025. *Sustainability (Basel)*, *15*(1), 754. https://Doi.Org/10.3390/Su15010754. DOI: 10.3390/su15010754

Seth, H. (2023). Blockchain-based identity verification: A solution to the growing problem of job candidate fraud. Retrieved from https://www.financialexpress.com/business/blockchain-blockchain-based-identity-verification-a-solution-to-the-growing-problem-of-job-candidate-fraud-3084923/

Sethaput, V., & Innet, S. (2023). Blockchain application for central bank digital currencies (CBDC). *Cluster Computing*, *26*(4), 2183–2197. DOI: 10.1007/s10586-022-03962-z PMID: 36686339

Setiawan, M., Effendi, N., Santoso, T., Dewi, V. I., & Sapulette, M. S. (2022). Digital financial literacy, current behavior of saving and spending and its future foresight. *Economics of Innovation and New Technology*, *31*(4), 320–338. DOI: 10.1080/10438599.2020.1799142

Setiorini, R., Aimah, S., & Fakhruddin, F. (2024). Transformation Of Pesantren Organizational Culture: Strategies for Pesantren to Become Centers of Innovation in The Digital Era. *Leadership*, *6*(1), 1–11. https://Doi.Org/10.32478/Leadership.V6i1.2879. DOI: 10.32478/leadership.v6i1.2879

Setyowati, A., Harmadi, H., & Sunarjanto, S. (2018). Islamic financial literacy and personal financial planning: A socio-demographic study. *Jurnal Keuangan dan Perbankan, 22*(1), 63-72.

Seuring, S., Sarkis, J., Müller, M., & Rao, P. (2008). Sustainability and supply chain management–an introduction to the special issue. *Journal of Cleaner Production, 16*(15), 1545–1551. DOI: 10.1016/j.jclepro.2008.02.002

Shahruddin, S., Sonet, U. N., Azmi, A., & Zainordin, N. (2024). Traversing The Complexity of Digital Construction and Beyond Through Soft Skills: Experiences of Malaysian Architects. Engineering, Construction and Architectural Management. https://Doi.Org/10.1108/Ecam-01-2024-0147

Shaikh, S., & Ganesh, M. (2024). Upskilling India: The National Policy On Skill Development and Entrepreneurship. *F1000 Research, 13*, 1141. Doi.Org/10.12688/F1000research.154936.1. DOI: 10.12688/f1000research.154936.1

Sharma, D. (2016). Nexus between financial inclusion and economic growth: Evidence from the emerging Indian economy. Journal of financial economic policy, 8(1), 13-36.

Sharma, D., Pandey, S., Gehlot, A., Sudhanshu, S., & Duggal, A. S. (2023). Automated Intervention of Blockchain in Human Resource Management. International Conference on Database Theory, 609–612. https://Doi.Org/10.1109/ICDT57929.2023.10150995

Sharma, N. (2023). AI and digital education in India: Expanding reach and impact.

Sharma, R. (2023). AI-powered translation tools in e-learning: Enhancing accessibility and efficiency.

Sharma, R. (2023). Economic implications of digital education resources in emerging economies.

Sharma, S. (2023). Unleashing the Potential of Blockchain-Based Background Verification. Retrieved from https://www.forbes.com/sites/forbeshumanresourcescouncil/2023/05/12/unleashing-the-potential-of-blockchain-based-background-verification/?sh=2fbdac065a9c)

Sharma, V., & Reddy, S. (2023). Barriers to regional language integration in Indian EdTech platforms.

Sharma, P. (2023). *The impact of e-books on sustainable education in India*. Environmental Studies in Education.

Shaya, N., Abukhait, R., Madani, R., & Ahmed, V. (2025). Conceptualizing blended learning models as a sustainable and inclusive educational approach: An organizational dynamics perspective. *International Journal of Sustainability in Higher Education, 26*(9), 90–111. DOI: 10.1108/IJSHE-03-2024-0167

Sheel, A., & Nath, V. (2019). Effect of blockchain technology adoption on supply chain adaptability, agility, alignment and performance. *Management Research Review*, *42*(12), 1353–1374. DOI: 10.1108/MRR-12-2018-0490

Sheldon, R. (2021). A timeline and history of blockchain technology. *URL:*https:// www. techtarget. com/whatis/feature/A-timeline-and-history-of-blockchain-technology

Sheldon, M. D. (2018). Using Blockchain to Aggregate and Share Misconduct Issues across the Accounting Profession. *Current Issues in Auditing*, *12*(2), A27–A35. https://publications.aaahq.org/cia/article/12/2/A27/6992/Using-Blockchain-to-Aggregate-and-Share-Misconduct. DOI: 10.2308/ciia-52184

Shen, Y., Hu, W., & Hueng, C. J. (2018). The effects of financial literacy, digital financial product usage and internet usage on financial inclusion in China. In *MATEC Web of Conferences* (Vol. 228, p. 05012). EDP Sciences. DOI: 10.1051/matecconf/201822805012

Shen, Y., Hueng, C. J., & Hu, W. (2020). Using digital technology to improve financial inclusion in China. *Applied Economics Letters*, *27*(1), 30–34. DOI: 10.1080/13504851.2019.1606401

Shivaraj, G. (2021). A Study on The Digitalized Human Resources (HR) Practices in Digitalized Business Era in India. *Management Science*, *8*(3), 83–89. https://Doi.Org/10.34293/Management.V8I3.3560

Shobande, O. A., & Lanre, I. R. (2018). Do financial inclusion drive boom-bust cycles in Africa? *Journal of Economics Bibliography*, *5*(3), 159–174.

Shute, V. J. (2008). Focus on formative feedback. *Review of Educational Research*, *78*(1), 153–189. DOI: 10.3102/0034654307313795

Siddiqui, N. (2022). Adaptive learning technologies: Opportunities for innovation in EdTech start-ups.

Siemens, G. (2013). Learning analytics: The emergence of a discipline. *International Review of Research in Open and Distance Learning*.

Sik Lanyi, C., & Withers, J. D. A.SikLanyi. (2020). Striving for a Safer and More Ergonomic Workplace: Acceptability and Human Factors Related to the Adoption of AR/VR Glasses in Industry 4.0. *Smart Cities*, *3*(2), 289–307. DOI: 10.3390/smartcities3020016

Silva, M. F., & Moreira, A. C. (2022). The gig economy: A critical review of the literature and implications for human resource management. *International Journal of Human Resource Studies*, *12*(1), 123–145. DOI: 10.5296/ijhrs.v12i1.19665

Sine, R. (2018). How The Blockchain Will Change Recruiting. Retrieved from, https://www.forbes.com/sites/adp/2018/03/21/how-the-blockchain-will-change-recruiting/?sh=152778a45f32)

Singh, A. (2024, November 27). *Uber introduces new safety measures primarily focusing on female users*. Business Standard. Retrieved March 12, 2025, from https://www.business-standard.com/companies/news/uber-introduces-new-safety-measures-primarily-focusing-on-female-users-124112701083_1.html

Singh, R., & Verma, S. (2021). Affordable EdTech solutions for inclusive education: An Indian perspective.

Singh, N., Kansra, P., & Gupta, S. L. (Eds.). (2024). *Digital influence on consumer habits: marketing challenges and opportunities*. Emerald Publishing Limited. DOI: 10.1108/9781804553428

Sisodia, A., & Maheshwari, G. C. (2023). Exploring Sustainable Finance: A Review and Future Research Agenda. *Vision (Basel)*, *0*(0), 09722629231209177. Advance online publication. DOI: 10.1177/09722629231209177

Smith P, Beretta M. (2020). The Gordian Knot of Practicing Digital Transformation: Coping with Emergent Paradoxes in Ambidextrous Organizing Structures*. Journal Of Product Innovation Management. (1):166–91. Doi.Org/10.1111/Jpim.12548.

Smith, A. (2021). Personalized learning and AI: Trends and impact..

Smith, J., Clark, P., & Lee, R. (2024). Adapting to the Future of Work in EdTech.

Smith, J., Green, L., & Carter, A. (2022). Digital textbooks and environmental sustainability: A comparative study.

Soccini, A. M. (2016). Virtual and Augmented Reality in the Art of Lucio Fontana. In *EVA'16 Proceedings of the conference on Electronic Visualisation and the Arts* (pp. 144-149). British Computer Society. http://dx.doi.org/DOI: 10.14236/ewic/EVA2016.30

Sodhi, T. (2021, August 14). *'We are slaves to them': Zomato, Swiggy delivery workers speak up against unfair practices*. Newslaundry. https://www.newslaundry.com/2021/08/14/we-are-slaves-to-them-zomato-swiggy-delivery-workers-speak-up-against-unfair-practices

Soni, S., Yadav, U., & Soni, A. (2022). Virtual Reality & Augmented Reality: A way to Digital Transformation of Customer Engagement. In *2022 International Conference on Machine Learning, Big Data, Cloud and Parallel Computing (COM-IT-CON)* (Vol. 1, pp. 573-577). IEEE. DOI: DOI: 10.1109/COM-IT-CON54601.2022.9850954

Sood, A., & Singh, R. (2023). The new emerging world of work: Growth story of India's gig economy. *International Journal of Management and Economics Invention*, *09*(10). Advance online publication. DOI: 10.47191/ijmei/v9i10.03

Soule, D. L., Puram, A., Westerman, G. F., & Bonnet, D. (2016). Becoming A Digital Organization: The Journey to Digital Dexterity. SSRN Electronic Journal. https://Doi.Org/10.2139/Ssrn.2697688

Soule, D., Deora Puram, A., Deora Puram, A., Westerman, G., & Bonnet, D. (2016). Becoming a Digital Organization: The Journey to Digital Dexterity. Social Science Research Network. https://doi.org/DOI: 10.2139/SSRN.2697688

Spirina, Y., Gorbunova, N., & Samoilova, I. (2024). Using MOOCs to organise problem-based learning in the professional training of IT students. *Obrazovanie i Nauka-Education and Science*, *26*(10), 166–189. DOI: 10.17853/1994-5639-2024-10-166-189

Spreitzer, G. M., Cameron, L., & Garrett, L. (2017). Alternative work arrangements: Two images of the new world of work. *Annual Review of Organizational Psychology and Organizational Behavior*, *4*(1), 473–499. DOI: 10.1146/annurev-orgpsych-032516-113332

Srihita, H. S., Goli, G., Rajyalaxmi, M., & Gobinath, R. (2025). Transformative dynamics of the gig economy: Technological impacts, worker well-being and global research trends. *International Journal of Engineering Business Management*, *17*, 18479790241310362. Advance online publication. DOI: 10.1177/18479790241310362

Srijanani, D. (2012). Financial inclusion: Taking banking services to the common man. International journal of Management and Business studies, 2(3), 54-58.

Srnicek, N. (2017). The challenges of platform capitalism: Understanding the logic of a new business model. *Juncture*, *23*(4), 254–257. DOI: 10.1111/newe.12023

Staffing Industry Analysts. (2024). *India's gig economy projected to create 90 million jobs.*https://www.staffingindustry.com/news/global-daily-news/indias-gig-economy-projected-to-create-90-million-jobs

Stanford online (n.d.). *Stanford Credentials.* https://online.stanford.edu/stanford-credentials

Statista (2024). *Number of freelancers in the United States from 2017 to 2028*. https://www.statista.com/statistics/921593/gig-economy-number-of-freelancers-us/

Statista. (2024). Indian EdTech market projections: Growth from $7.5B to $29B by 2030.

Steelman, K., & Wallace, C. (2021). Breaking Barriers, Building Understanding. ACM SIGCAS Computers and Society, 49(1), 23–24. https://Doi.Org/10.1145/3447892.3447901

Stefano, V. D. (2019). The gig economy and labour regulation: an international and comparative approach. Revista Direito Das Relações Sociais E Trabalhistas, 4(2), 68-79. DOI: 10.26843/mestradodireito.v4i2.158

Stephen, G. (2022). Digital financial literacy skills among library and information science professionals in northeast India. A study. *Library Philosophy and Practice*, *6709*, 1–12.

Stewart, A., & Stanford, J. (2017). Regulating work in the gig economy: What are the options? *Economic and Labour Relations Review*, *28*(3), 420–437. DOI: 10.1177/1035304617722461

Štofková, J., Poliaková, A., Repkova Stofkova, K., Malega, P., Krejnus, M., Binasova, V., & Daneshjo, N. (2022). Digital Skills as A Significant Factor of Human Resources Development. *Sustainability (Basel)*, *14*(20), 13117. https://Doi.Org/10.3390/Su142013117. DOI: 10.3390/su142013117

Stone, R. J. (2018). *Human resource management* (9th ed.). Wiley.

Strauss, J., & Frost, R. (2014). *E-marketing*. Pearson.

Subrahmanyam, S. (2025). Employee Skillsets in the Digital Age. In Organizational Sociology in the Digital Age (pp. 369-388). IGI Global Scientific Publishing. DOI: 10.4018/979-8-3693-7398-9.ch018

Sufian, F. (2008). Revenue shift and the non-bank institutions' productivity: Empirical evidence from Malaysia. *Studies in Economics and Finance*, *25*(2), 75–92. DOI: 10.1108/10867370810879410

Sufian, F. (2011). Benchmarking the efficiency of the Korean banking sector: A DEA approach. *Benchmarking*, *18*(1), 107–127. DOI: 10.1108/14635771111109841

Suhasti, W., Muhamad, M., Penggalih, R., Handayani, L. F., & Nugroho, A. P. (2022). The Influence of Islamic Financial Literacy on The Use of Digital Financial Services in Yogyakarta. *KnE Social Sciences*, 50-55.

Sundararajan, A. (2016). *The sharing economy: The end of employment and the rise of crowd-based capitalism*. MIT Press.

Sundararajan, A. (2017). The sharing economy: A new era of human and economic progress. In *The Oxford Handbook of the Gig Economy* (pp. 1–28). Oxford University Press.

Sun, L. (2020, September). Service Chaining Security Based on Blockchain. [). IOP Publishing.]. *Journal of Physics: Conference Series*, *1634*(1), 012031. DOI: 10.1088/1742-6596/1634/1/012031

Sunny, J., Undralla, N., & Pillai, V. M. (2020). Supply chain transparency through blockchain-based traceability: An overview with demonstration. *Computers & Industrial Engineering*, *150*, 106895. DOI: 10.1016/j.cie.2020.106895

Sun, T. (2024). Role of Inclusive Finance on oil Resource production targets: How Fiscal Pressures influence natural resources policy and green recovery in Gulf countries? *Resources Policy*, *88*, 104337. https://doi.org/https://doi.org/10.1016/j.resourpol.2023.104337. DOI: 10.1016/j.resourpol.2023.104337

Suryawanshi, M., & Ponde, P. (2024). Gig economy: Changing the dynamics of the workforce. In *The role of HR in the transforming workplace* (pp. 79–94). Productivity Press.

Sutherland, W., & Jarrahi, M. H. (2018). The sharing economy and digital platforms: A review and research agenda. *International Journal of Information Management*, *43*, 328–341. DOI: 10.1016/j.ijinfomgt.2018.07.004

Sutherland, W., Jarrahi, M. H., Dunn, M., & Nelson, S. (2019). Work precarity and gig literacies in online freelancing. *Work, Employment and Society*, *34*(3), 457–475. DOI: 10.1177/0950017019886511

Swan, M. (2015). Blockchain: Blueprint for a new economy. O'Reilly Media, Inc. Tapscott, D., & Tapscott, A. (2017). How blockchain will change organizations. *MIT Sloan Management Review*, *58*(2), 10–13.

Swanson, R. A. (2022). *Foundations of human resource development*. Berrett-Koehler Publishers.

Taghizadeh-Hesary, F., & Hyun, S. (Eds.). (2022). *Green digital finance and sustainable development goals*. Springer. DOI: 10.1007/978-981-19-2662-4

Taherdoost, H. (2023). Smart contracts in blockchain technology: A critical review. *Information (Basel)*, *14*(2), 117. DOI: 10.3390/info14020117

Tahir, A. (2024). Exploring New Paradigms in Auditing: Challenges and Opportunities in The Digital Era. MSJ Majority Science Journal. 2(2):83–90. Available From: https://Doi.Org/10.61942/Msj.V2i2.145

Tallat, R., Hawbani, A., Wang, X., Al-Dubai, A., Zhao, L., Liu, Z., Min, G., Zomaya, A. Y., & Hamood Alsamhi, S. (2024). Navigating Industry 5.0: A Survey of Key Enabling Technologies, Trends, Challenges, and Opportunities. *IEEE Communications Surveys and Tutorials*, *26*(2), 1080–1126. DOI: 10.1109/COMST.2023.3329472

Tambe, P., Cappelli, P., & Yakubovich, V. (2019). Artificial intelligence in human resources management: Challenges and a path forward. *California Management Review*, *61*(4), 15–42. DOI: 10.1177/0008125619867910

Tanchangya, T., Islam, N., Naher, K., Mia, M. R., Chowdhury, S., Sarker, S. R., & Rashid, F. (2025). Financial technology-enabled sustainable finance for small-and medium-sized enterprises. *Environment. Innovation and Management*, *1*, 2550006.

Tandon, N., Basu, P., Krishnan, O., & Bhavani, R. V. (2022). Emerging work trends in Urban India: COVID-19 and beyond. *Emerging Work Trends in Urban India: COVID-19 and Beyond*, 1–208. DOI: 10.4324/9781003264194

Tang, D. (2021). What Is Digital Transformation? EDPACS. 64 (1):9–13. Available From: https://Doi.Org/10.1080/07366981.2020.1847813

Tan, Y., Xu, W., Li, S., & Chen, K. (2022). Augmented and Virtual Reality (AR/VR) for Education and Training in the AEC Industry: A Systematic Review of Research and Applications. *Buildings (Basel, Switzerland)*, *12*(10), 1529. DOI: 10.3390/buildings12101529

Tan, Z. M., Aggarwal, N., Cowls, J., Morley, J., Taddeo, M., & Floridi, L. (2021). The ethical debate about the gig economy: A review and critical analysis. *Technology in Society*, *65*, 101594. DOI: 10.1016/j.techsoc.2021.101594

Taylor, M. (2018). Good work: The Taylor review of modern working practices. HM Government. Retrieved from https://www.gov.uk/government/publications/good-work-the-taylor-review-of-modern-working-practices

Taylor, C., & Noë, A. (2021). *The explanation of behaviour*. Routledge. DOI: 10.4324/9781003146742

Technavio. (2024). Edtech market growth analysis - size and forecast 2025-2029.

Thalmann, S. (2014). Adaptation Criteria for The Personalized Delivery of Learning Materials: A Multi-Stage Empirical Investigation. *Australasian Journal of Educational Technology*, *30*(1), 45–60. https://Doi.Org/10.14742/AJET.235. DOI: 10.14742/ajet.235

The Rockefeller Foundation. (2013). *Digital jobs in Africa: Catalyzing inclusive opportunities for youth.* https://www.rockefellerfoundation.org/report/digital-jobs-in-africa-catalyzing-inclusive-opportunities-for-youth/

Thomas, A., & Gupta, V. (2021). Social capital theory, social exchange theory, social cognitive theory, financial literacy, and the role of knowledge sharing as a moderator in enhancing financial well-being: From bibliometric analysis to a conceptual framework model. *Frontiers in Psychology*, *12*, 664638. DOI: 10.3389/fpsyg.2021.664638 PMID: 34093360

Thornhill-Miller, B., Camarda, A., Mercier, M., Burkhardt, J.-M., Morisseau, T., Bourgeois-Bougrine, S., Vinchon, F., El Hayek, S., Augereau-Landais, M., Mourey, F., Feybesse, C., Sundquist, D., & Lubart, T. (2023). Creativity, Critical Thinking, Communication, And Collaboration: Assessment, Certification, And Promotion Of 21st Century Skills for The Future of Work and Education. *Journal of Intelligence*, *11*(3), 54. https://Doi.Org/10.3390/Jintelligence11030054. DOI: 10.3390/jintelligence11030054 PMID: 36976147

Tian, G. (2022). Influence of digital finance on household leverage ratio from the perspective of consumption effect and income effect. *Sustainability (Basel)*, *14*(23), 16271. DOI: 10.3390/su142316271

Tiwari, C. K., Gopalkrishnan, S., Kaur, D., & Pal, A. (2020). Promoting Financial Literacy through Digital Platforms: A Systematic Review of Literature and Future Research Agenda. *Journal of General Management Research*, *7*(2).

Top Universities. (n.d.). *MOOCs: The future of higher education.* https://www.topuniversities.com/student-info/distance-learning/moocs-future-higher-education

Torraco, R. J., & Lundgren, H. (2020). What HRD is doing—What HRD should be doing: The case for transforming HRD. *Human Resource Development Review*, *19*(1), 39–65. DOI: 10.1177/1534484319877058

Treviño-Elizondo, B. L., & Garcia-Reyes, H. (2023). An Employee Competency Development Maturity Model for Industry 4.0 Adoption. Sustainability. https://Doi.Org/10.3390/Su151411371

Tripathi, G., Ahad, M. A., & Casalino, G. (2023). A comprehensive review of blockchain technology: Underlying principles and historical background with future challenges. *Decision Analytics Journal*, 100344.

Trivedi, P., Ravisankar, A., Kumar, G. P., Krishnamoorthy, V., Shukla, S., & Boopathi, S. (2024). Finance and Technology-Integrated Digital Economy: Circular Age of a Sustainable Digital Revolution. In *Navigating the Circular Age of a Sustainable Digital Revolution* (pp. 91-120). IGI Global.

Tseng, M-L, Bui, T-D, Lim, M, Tsai, FM & Tan, RR (2021), 'Comparing world regional sustainable supply chain finance using big data analytics: A bibliometric analysis', *Industrial Management and Data Systems,* vol. (In-Press), pp. (In-Press). https://dx.doi.org/DOI: 10.1108/IMDS-09-2020-0521

Tucker, J., & Varga, J. (2020). The role of AI in talent management and HRM practices in the gig economy. *Journal of Business Research, 116*, 345–357. DOI: 10.1016/j.jbusres.2019.12.021

Turczynski, B. (2023). Lying on a Resume (2022 Study). Retrieved from https://resumelab.com/resume/lying#:~:text=When%20we%20broke%20down%20the%20data%20by%20industry%2C,lying%20on%20a%20resume%20based%20on%20education%20level.

Turek, J., Ocicka, B., Rogowski, W., & Jefmański, B. (2023). The role of Industry 4.0 technologies in driving the financial importance of sustainability risk management. *Equilibrium.Quarterly Journal of Economics and Economic Policy, 18*(4), 1009–1044.

Tyagi, S., Kumar, R., Joshi, K., Rastogi, N., & Hussien, N. M. (2022). Blockchain In HRM: *Application and Future Perspective. International Conference on Communication, Computing & Security*, 1–5. Doi.Org/10.1109/ICCCS55188.2022.10079644

Udanoh, M. U., & Zouria, A. (2023). Impact of investment in EdTech: Government and entrepreneurial partnership venture in education in North and West Africa.

Uddin, M. A., Stranieri, A., Gondal, I., & Balasubramanian, V. (2021). A survey on the adoption of blockchain in iot: Challenges and solutions. *Blockchain: Research and Applications*, *2*(2), 100006.

Ullah, N., & Asghar, U. (2023). The effect of an increase in the interest rate and inflation on personal finances in Islamic Republic of Pakistan. Al-Qamar, 81-94.

UNESCO Institute of Statistics. (2020). UIS Statistics. https://data.uis.unesco.org/#

UNESCO. (2021). The importance of multilingual education in the digital era. https://unesdoc.unesco.org

UNICEF. (2021). Inclusive education for children with disabilities: A guide to digital tools. https://www.unicef.org

United Kingdom Supreme Court. (2021). *R (on the application of KBR, Inc) v Director of the Serious Fraud Office* (UKSC 5). British and Irish Legal Information Institute. Retrieved March 12, 2025, from https://www.bailii.org/uk/cases/UKSC/2021/5.html

University of Texas System. (2022). *UT System and Google announce Google Career Certificates for up to 10,000 Texas university students*. https://www.utsystem.edu/news/2022/12/09/ut-system-and-google-announce-google-career-certificates-10000-texas-university-students

Unnikrishnan, P., & Baral, R. (2023). Reimagining hr practices to attract and engage gig talent: An organizational perspective. *NHRD Network Journal*, *16*(3), 248–257. DOI: 10.1177/26314541231170433

Urme, U. N. (2023). The impact of talent management strategies on employee retention. *International Journal of Science and Business*, *28*(1), 127–146. DOI: 10.58970/IJSB.2209

Utkarsh, P., Pandey, A., Ashta, A., Spiegelman, E., & Sutan, A. (2020). Catch them young: Impact of financial socialization, financial literacy and attitude towards money on financial well-being of young adults. *International Journal of Consumer Studies*, *44*(6), 531–541. DOI: 10.1111/ijcs.12583

Vadavi, S., & Sharmiladevi, J. C. (2024). Analysing the evolution and patterns of the gig economy: A bibliometric examination of growth and trends. *Cogent Business & Management*, *11*(1), 2424480. Advance online publication. DOI: 10.1080/23311975.2024.2424480

van Dijck, J. (2018). The platform society : public values in a connective world / José van Dijck, Thomas Poell, Martijn de Waal. In *Platform Society*. https://books.google.co.in/books?hl=en&lr=&id=xLhwDwAAQBAJ&oi=fnd&pg=PT8&dq=Existing+research+suggests+that+knowledge+diffusion+in+gig+work+settings+is+largely+mediated+by+platform-driven+exposure,+peer+networks,+and+targeted+training+initiatives&ots=AUv1

Van Doorn, N. (2017). Platform labor: On the gendered and racialized exploitation of low-income workers in the on-demand economy. *Information Communication and Society*, *20*(6), 898–914. DOI: 10.1080/1369118X.2017.1294194

Van Doorn, N., Ferrari, F., & Graham, M. (2022). Migration and digital labour: A relational perspective on platform work. Environment and Planning A. *Economy and Space*, *54*(3), 491–510. DOI: 10.1177/0308518X211044853

Vázquez, D., & García, M. (2020). Innovating education through technology: Policies and practices in the digital age.

Velenturf, A., & Purnell, P. (2021). Principles for a Sustainable Circular Economy. *Sustainable Production and Consumption*, *27*, 1437–1457. DOI: 10.1016/j.spc.2021.02.018

Venkateswaran, P. S., Arun, B., Byloppilly, R., Rameshkkumar, S. R., & Reddy, M. S. (2025). *A Study on Evaluating Brand Reputation by Measuring Sentiment and Response Rates in the Digital Age. E-Commerce, Marketing, and Consumer Behavior in the AI Era*. IGI Global Publications.

Venkateswaran, P. S., Sabarirajan, A., Rajest, S. S., & Regin, R. (2019). The theory of postmodernism in consumerism, mass culture, and globalization. *Journal of Research on the Lepidoptera*, *50*(4), 97–113. DOI: 10.36872/LEPI/V50I4/201075

Venkateswaran, P. S., & Sriramkumar, M. (2025). *Predictive Analytics: Utilizing Machine Learning and Big Data for Forecasting Future Trends in Business and Consumer Behavior. Strategic Brand Management in the Age of AI and Disruption*. IGI Global Publications., DOI: 10.4018/979-8-3693-9461-8.ch019

Venkateswaran, P. S., Sriramkumar, M., Vaddy, R. K., Kotagiri, A., Rajest, S. S., & Regin, R. (2024). Applications of artificial intelligence and robots in service industries. In *Advancing intelligent networks through distributed optimization* (pp. 61–80). IGI Global Publications., DOI: 10.4018/979-8-3693-3739-4.ch004

Verma, B., Bhardwaj, M., Arora, S., & Oberoi, S. (2025). Unveiling the impact of remittances on productive efficiencies: Investigating productivity growth of prominent remittance-receiving developing nations. *International Journal of Productivity and Performance Management*, *74*(4), 1101–1124. DOI: 10.1108/IJPPM-05-2023-0213

Verma, D., Kansra, P., & Kumar, P. (2024). Role of Industry 5.0 in Bancassurance: A Theoretical Perspective. In *Convergence of Human Resources Technologies and Industry 5.0* (pp. 240–255). IGI Global. DOI: 10.4018/979-8-3693-1343-5.ch013

Vincent, N. E., & Wilkins, A. M. (2020). Challenges when Auditing Cryptocurrencies. *Current Issues in Auditing*, *14*(1), A46–A58. https://publications.aaahq.org/cia/article/14/1/A46/7049/Challenges-when-Auditing-Cryptocurrencies. DOI: 10.2308/ciia-52675

Visciano, P., & Schirone, M. (2021). Food frauds: Global incidents and misleading situations. *Trends in Food Science & Technology*, *114*, 424–442. DOI: 10.1016/j.tifs.2021.06.010

Waldkirch, M., Bucher, E., Schou, P. K., & Grünwald, E. (2021). Controlled by the algorithm, coached by the crowd – How HRM activities take shape on digital work platforms in the gig economy. *International Journal of Human Resource Management*, *32*(12), 2643–2682. DOI: 10.1080/09585192.2021.1914129

Walkowiak, E. (2023). Digitalization And Inclusiveness of HRM Practices: The Example of Neurodiversity Initiatives. Human Resource Management Journal. https://Doi.Org/10.1111/1748-8583.12499

Wang, C., Zhu, H., Wang, P., Zhu, C., Zhang, X., Chen, E., & Xiong, H. (2021). Personalized And Explainable Employee Training Course Recommendations: A Bayesian Variational Approach. *ACM Transactions on Office Information Systems*, *40*(4), 1–32. https://Doi.Org/10.1145/3490476

Wang, Y., Lucey, B. M., Vigne, S. A., & Yarovaya, L. (2022). The effects of central bank digital currencies news on financial markets. [sciencedirect.com]. *Technological Forecasting and Social Change*, *180*, 121715. DOI: 10.1016/j.techfore.2022.121715

Wang, Y., Singgih, M., Wang, J., & Rit, M. (2019). Making sense of blockchain technology: How will it transform supply chains? *International Journal of Production Economics*, *211*, 221–236. DOI: 10.1016/j.ijpe.2019.02.002

Watson, W. R., & Watson, S. L. (2007). An argument for clarity: What are learning management systems, what are they not, and what should they become?

Webb, S., Hodge, S., Holford, J., Milana, M., & Waller, R. (2022). Aligning Skills and Lifelong Learning for Human-Centred Sustainable Development. *International Journal of Lifelong Education*, *41*(2), 127–132. Doi.Org/10.1080/02601370.2022.2057167. DOI: 10.1080/02601370.2022.2057167

Webcom Systems Pvt Ltd. (2023, July 20). Smart Contracts: Revolutionizing Transactions through Impeccable Automation. LinkedIn. https://www.linkedin.com/pulse/smart-contracts-revolutionizing-transactions-through/

Were, M., & Wambua, J. (2013). Assessing the determinants of interest rate spread of commercial banks in Kenya: An empirical investigation (No. 4). KBA Centre for Research on Financial Markets and Policy Working Paper Series.

Westover, J. (2024). Building a Resilient and Adaptive Organization Through Mindset Shifts and Continuous Learning. DOI: 10.70175/hclreview.2020.14.4.1

Westover, J. (2024). Designing A Skills Evolution Program: A Framework for Success. Human Capital Leadership., 12(2). https://Doi.Org/10.70175/Hclreview.2020.12.2.6

Wheelahan, L., & Moodie, G. (2022). Gig qualifications for the gig economy: Micro-credentials and the 'hungry mile'. *Higher Education*, *83*(6), 1279–1295. DOI: 10.1007/s10734-021-00742-3 PMID: 34366441

Whitehead, L., Talevski, J., Fatehi, F., & Beauchamp, A. (2023). Barriers to and Facilitators of Digital Health Among Culturally and Linguistically Diverse Populations: Qualitative Systematic Review. In *Journal of Medical Internet Research* (Vol. 25, Issue 1, p. e42719). JMIR Publications Inc. DOI: 10.2196/42719

Wilson, C., & Mergel, I. (2022). Overcoming Barriers to Digital Government: Mapping the Strategies of Digital Champions. *Government Information Quarterly*, *39*(2), 101681. https://Doi.Org/10.1016/J.Giq.2022.101681. DOI: 10.1016/j.giq.2022.101681

Wood, A. J., Graham, M., Lehdonvirta, V., & Hjorth, I. (2018). Good gig, bad gig: Autonomy and algorithmic control in the global gig economy. *Work, Employment and Society*, *33*(1), 56–75. DOI: 10.1177/0950017018785616 PMID: 30886460

Woolf, B. P. (2010). Building intelligent interactive tutors: Student-centered strategies for revolutionizing e-learning.

Workcred & The University of Texas System. (2023). *Integrating Microcredentials into Undergraduate Experiences*. https://share.ansi.org/wc/Shared%20Documents/Workcred-Reports/Integrating-Microcredentials-into-Undergraduate-Experiences.pdf

World Bank Group. (2018). *Developing and Operationalizing a National Financial Inclusion Strategy*. World Bank Group.

World Bank. (2015). *Jobs without borders*. https://www.worldbank.org/en/news/feature/2015/06/02/jobs-without-borders

World Bank. (2023). Global Findex Database.

World Bank. (2023). *The gig economy in Latin America: Trends and challenges*. https://www.worldbank.org

World Bank. (2024). *Working Without Borders: The Promise and Peril of Online Gig Work*. https://www.worldbank.org/en/topic/jobsanddevelopment/publication/online-gig-work-enabled-by-digital-platforms

World Economic Forum. (2020). Reskilling Revolution. Initiatives.weforum.org. https://initiatives.weforum.org/reskilling-revolution/home

World Economic Forum. (2020). The future of jobs report. WEF.

World Economic Forum. (2020). The future of work in the gig economy. https://www.weforum.org/reports/the-future-of-work-in-the-gig-economy

World Economic Forum. (2021). Education technologies are making learning more accessible.

Wu, H. (2023). The future of work: A comprehensive study of the gig economy beyond low labor-value added jobs. Advances in Economics. *Management and Political Sciences*, *64*(1), 112–120. DOI: 10.54254/2754-1169/64/20231511

Wu, K. J., Tseng, M. L., Yang, W. H., Ali, M. H., & Chen, X. (2023). Re-shaping sustainable value chain model under post pandemic disruptions: A fast fashion supply chain analysis. *International Journal of Production Economics*, *255*, 108704. Advance online publication. DOI: 10.1016/j.ijpe.2022.108704

Wu, W.-C. V., Wu, W.-C. V., Manabe, K., Marek, M. W., & Shu, Y. (2021). Enhancing 21st-Century Competencies Via Virtual Reality Digital Content Creation. *Journal of Research on Technology in Education*, •••, 1–22. Doi.Org/10.1080/15391523.2021.1962455

Xiao, H. (2024, November 20). Employee Role Transformation and Adaptation in Digital Transformation: Barriers, Misalignments, And Solutions in Digital Tool Application. *Deleted Journal.*, *13*(1), 33–38. Doi.Org/10.54254/2977-5701/13/2024115. DOI: 10.54254/2977-5701/13/2024115

Xiao, J. J., & Tao, C. (2021). Consumer finance/household finance: The definition and scope. *China Finance Review International*, *11*(1), 1–25. DOI: 10.1108/CFRI-04-2020-0032

Xiao, Z., Duritan, M. J. M., & Jia, R. (2024). Resourceful futures: Integrating responsible mining and green education for sustainable development in developing and emerging economies. *Resources Policy*, *88*, 104377. https://doi.org/https://doi.org/10.1016/j.resourpol.2023.104377. DOI: 10.1016/j.resourpol.2023.104377

Xu, R., Zhang, L., & Chollathanrattanapong, J. (2024). A Study of The Adaptability of Adaptive Learning Systems to Individualized Educational Strategies. Applied Mathematics and Nonlinear Sciences, 9(1). https://Doi.Org/10.2478/Amns-2024-2737

Xu, P., Lee, J., Barth, J. R., & Richey, R. G. (2021). Blockchain as supply chain technology: Considering transparency and security. *International Journal of Physical Distribution & Logistics Management*, *51*(3), 305–324. DOI: 10.1108/IJPDLM-08-2019-0234

Xu, T., Yang, G., & Chen, T. (2024). The role of green finance and digital inclusive finance in promoting economic sustainable development: A perspective from new quality productivity. *Journal of Environmental Management, 370*, 122892. DOI: 10.1016/j.jenvman.2024.122892 PMID: 39447370

Yadav, M., & Banerji, P. (2023). A bibliometric analysis of digital financial literacy. *American Journal of Business, 38*(3), 91–111. DOI: 10.1108/AJB-11-2022-0186

Yadav, M., & Banerji, P. (2024). Digital financial literacy, saving and investment behaviour in India. *Journal of Social and Economic Development*, •••, 1–19. DOI: 10.1007/s40847-024-00367-z

Yadav, M., & Banerji, P. (2024). Systematic literature review on Digital Financial Literacy. *SN Business & Economics, 4*(11), 142. DOI: 10.1007/s43546-024-00738-y

Yahia, N. B., Hlel, J., & Colomo-Palacios, R. (2021). From big data to deep data to support people analytics for employee attrition prediction. *IEEE Access : Practical Innovations, Open Solutions, 9*, 60447–60458. DOI: 10.1109/ACCESS.2021.3074559

Yang, J., Wu, Y., & Huang, B. (2020). *Digital finance and financial literacy: An empirical investigation of Chinese households* (No. 1209). ADBI Working Paper Series.

Yang, C., & Masron, T. A. (2022). Impact of digital finance on energy efficiency in the context of green sustainable development. *Sustainability (Basel), 14*(18), 11250. DOI: 10.3390/su141811250

Yazdanparast, A., & Alhenawi, Y. (2022). Impact of COVID-19 pandemic on household financial decisions: A consumer vulnerability perspective. *Journal of Consumer Behaviour, 21*(4), 806–827. DOI: 10.1002/cb.2038 PMID: 37519436

Yi, Z., Yu, M., & Cheung, K. L. (2022). Impacts of counterfeiting on a global supply chain. *Manufacturing & Service Operations Management, 24*(1), 159–178. DOI: 10.1287/msom.2020.0912

Yoganandham, G., & Varalakshmi, D. (2024). The gig economy in India: The rise of start-ups, infrastructure, and the organization of the informal workforce. *GIS Science Journal, 11*(2), 16–26.

Yoo, M., & Won, Y. (2018). A study on the transparent price tracing system in supply chain management based on blockchain. *Sustainability (Basel), 10*(11), 4037. DOI: 10.3390/su10114037

Yoo, S. J., & Huang, W. D. (2013). Engaging online adult learners in higher education: Motivational factors impacted by gender, age, and prior experiences. *The Journal of Continuing Higher Education, 61*(3), 151–164. DOI: 10.1080/07377363.2013.836823

Yunus, M. (2021). Microfinance for Socioeconomic Development. *Microfinance Review*.

Zaman, U., Nawaz, S., Javed, A., & Rasul, T. (2020). Having a whale of a time: Linking self-determination theory (SDT), job characteristics model (JCM) and motivation to the joy of gig work. Cogent Business &Amp. *Cogent Business & Management, 7*(1), 1807707. DOI: 10.1080/23311975.2020.1807707

Zarrin, J., Wen Phang, H., Babu Saheer, L., & Zarrin, B. (2021). Blockchain for decentralization of the internet: Prospects, trends, and challenges. *Cluster Computing, 24*(4), 2841–2866. DOI: 10.1007/s10586-021-03301-8 PMID: 34025209

Zeid, R., Alrayess, D., Ajwad, M. I., Soytas, M. A., & Rivera, N. (n.d.). *The gig economy and the future of work: Global trends and policy directions for non-standard forms of employment.*

Zelbst, P. J., Green, K. W., Sower, V. E., & Bond, P. L. (2020). The impact of RFID, IIoT, and Blockchain technologies on supply chain transparency. *Journal of Manufacturing Technology Management, 31*(3), 441–457. DOI: 10.1108/JMTM-03-2019-0118

Zervas, I., & Stiakakis, E. Economic Sustainable Development Through Digital Skills Acquisition: The Role of Human Resource Leadership. Sustainability 2024 Sep 4;16(17):7664. Available From: https://Doi.Org/10.3390/Su16177664

Zhang, P. (2024). Training for gig workers: A systematic review and research agenda. *The Learning Organization, ahead-of-print*(ahead-of-print). https://doi.org/DOI: 10.1108/TLO-10-2022-0124

Zhang, P., Zhang, M., Zhou, Q., & Anees Haider Zaidi, S. (2022). The Relationship Among Financial Inclusion, Non-Performing Loans, and Economic Growth: Insights From OECD Countries. ncbi.nlm.nih.gov

Zhang, C., Wu, C., & Wang, X. (2020, May). Overview of blockchain consensus mechanism. In *Proceedings of the 2020 2nd International Conference on Big Data Engineering* (pp. 7-12).

Zhang, J., & Chen, Z. (2023). Exploring Human Resource Management Digital Transformation in The Digital Age. *Journal of the Knowledge Economy, 15*(1), 1482–1498. https://Doi.Org/10.1007/S13132-023-01214-Y. DOI: 10.1007/s13132-023-01214-y

Zhang, X., Wang, P., & Peng, L. (2024). Developing A Competency Model for Human Resource Directors (Hrds) In Exponential Organizations Undergoing Digital Transformation. *Sustainability (Basel), 16*(23), 10540. https://Doi.Org/10.3390/Su162310540. DOI: 10.3390/su162310540

Zhang, Y. (2021, July). The design of a Mobile app to promote young people's digital financial literacy. In *International Conference on Human-Computer Interaction* (pp. 118-136). Cham: Springer International Publishing. DOI: 10.1007/978-3-030-78227-6_10

Zhang, Y.-D., & Liu, M.-J. (2020). Analysis of the Influencing Factors of Enterprise Management on Employee Loyalty in Gig Economy. In *2020 International Conference on Wireless Communications and Smart Grid (ICWCSG)*, Qingdao, China (pp. 331-334). DOI: 10.1109/ICWCSG50807.2020.00076

Zhang, Y., Lee, E. W. J., & Teo, W. P. (2023). Health-Seeking Behavior and Its Associated Technology Use: Interview Study among Community-Dwelling Older Adults. *JMIR Aging, 6*, e43709. Advance online publication. DOI: 10.2196/43709 PMID: 36996003

Zhao, X., Ren, Y. and Cheah, K.S. (2023). Leading Virtual Reality (VR) and Augmented Reality (AR) in Education: Bibliometric and Content Analysis from the Web of Science (2018–2022). SAGE Open

Zhao, Q., Tsai, P. H., & Wang, J. L. (2019). Improving financial service innovation strategies for enhancing china's banking industry competitive advantage during the fintech revolution: A Hybrid MCDM model. *Sustainability (Basel), 11*(5), 1419. DOI: 10.3390/su11051419

Zheng, Z., Xie, S., Dai, H. N., Chen, W., Chen, X., Weng, J., & Imran, M. (2020). An overview on smart contracts: Challenges, advances and platforms. *Future Generation Computer Systems, 105*, 475–491. DOI: 10.1016/j.future.2019.12.019

Zhihong, L., Yuxiang, H., Zechun, C., Tiancheng, L., & Yuehua, W. (2019). Creativity in trusted data: Research on application of blockchain in supply chain. *International Journal of Performability Engineering, 15*(2), 526.

Zhu, G., Huang, J., Lu, J., Luo, Y., & Zhu, T. (2024). Gig to the left, algorithms to the right: A case study of the dark sides in the gig economy. *Technological Forecasting and Social Change, 199*, 123018. DOI: 10.1016/j.techfore.2023.123018

Ziegler, A., Fischer, J., & Mertens, A. (2020). Psychosocial impacts of gig work: Stress, job satisfaction, and work-life balance. *Journal of Business Ethics, 167*(2), 225–240. DOI: 10.1007/s10551-019-04183-4

Zielinski, D. (2021). How Blockchain Benefits Recruiters, Job Candidates. Retrieved from, https://workplacetechcommunity.shrm.org/s/articles/a2D1T000005sbksUAA/how-blockchain-benefits-recruiters-job-candidates)

Zulaihati, S., Susanti, S., & Widyastuti, U. (2020). Teachers' financial literacy: Does it impact on financial behaviour. *Management Science Letters*, *10*(3), 653–658. DOI: 10.5267/j.msl.2019.9.014

About the Contributors

Anna Masłoń-Oracz is a business-oriented researcher who analyzed how clusters influence regional development competitiveness from a smart specialisation perspective. She is involved in international projects in Rwanda, Kenya, and Zambia concerning regional innovation systems to enhance the role and importance of regional innovation systems (RIS) in economic development and growth, attracting considerable attention in recent years. She's been a senior manager for over 12 years, with extensive experience in global organisations, managing various areas of business operations in the Poland/CEE/Africa region and partnering with business stakeholders on all people-related initiatives. She's vice-president of the Polish European Community Study Association (belonging to an international network of ECSA-World) and a member of the International Women's Forum. Completed postgraduate studies in Human Resources Management (University of Warsaw) and Project Management (Warsaw School of Economics), with a master's degree in the field of International Relations (University of Warsaw). Former Chairman of the Supervisory Board of Centrum Edukacji S.A. and a President of the Management Board of Technology and Industrial Park S.A. (with its majority of shares owned by the PKN ORLEN SA, the biggest petroleum company in Europe). She has experience in launching and managing entrepreneurial education programs within an academic institution such as the Warsaw School of Economics (Warsaw School of Economics Rector's 1st-degree award for involvement in the EUINTEGRATO project within the 7th Framework Programme) as well as experience in grant funding management or technology investment in a university or accelerator environment.

Pooja Kansra is presently working as an Associate Professor of Economics at Mittal School of Business, Lovely Professional University, Phagwara (India). She has teaching experience of fourteen plus years. Her research areas include health economics, labour economics, gender economics, insurance and the informal sector. She is a lifetime member of the Indian Economic Association. She is an avid researcher and has presented papers at national and international conferences. She has to her credit various research papers published in Scopus Indexed Journals, including Economic and Political Weekly (EPW) and the Journal of Health Management (Sage Publications). Global Business Review (Sage Publications), International Journal of Diabetes in Developing Countries (Springer Publications), Health and Population: Perspectives and Issues (MOHFW), etc. She has published several books on the various aspects of health economics and COVID-19. She was granted three copyrights by the Government of India. She is an editorial board member/reviewer in several national and international journals.

Sugandh Arora is currently working as an Assistant Professor at the Symbiosis School of Economics, Symbiosis International University, Pune, India. She has received his Ph.D. degree from Mittal School of Business, ACBSP USA, Accredited, Lovely Professional University, Punjab. Her areas of interest are the effectiveness of household food security, systematic literature review, vulnerability, maternal health, blockchain, and the National Food Security Act and Reforms. She published research articles in international and national journals. Her recent publications are in the Indian Economic Journal (Sage), Empirical Economic Letters, and Int. J. Economic Policy in Emerging Economies (Inderscience); Emerging Trends in Business Economics, International Journal of Research and Analytical Reviews and Management in Practice Challenges and Strategies and also a reviewer for various international journals such as International Journal of Quality & Reliability Management (Emerald), Journal of Public Affairs (Wiley), and Cogent Food and Agriculture (Taylor and Francis). She won the best paper award at Christ University and delivered a lecture on constructing a scale at the University of Human Sciences and Economics, Poland. She has also received two copyrights from the Govt. of India on the Conceptual Framework for Effectiveness of Household Food Security and the Functional Grid of the National Food Security Mission through Activity Mapping.

Sumit Oberoi is a Post-Doctoral Fellow at the Indian Institute of Management Bangalore (IIMB), India. He is an avid researcher with a demonstrated history of working in academia and industry. His areas of interest include Public Health & Policy, Health Costing, Tourism, Microeconomic Theory, Systematic Literature Review, Bibliometric Analysis, International Trade, and Blockchain Technology. He has managed to publish research articles in highly indexed journals and is also a reviewer for various international journals such as Int. J. Diabetes in Dev. Countries, Current Issues in Tourism (T&F), International Economics (Elsevier), etc. Sumit has won several best paper awards and is a principal investigator/member of the research project granted by NABARD/SIU. He has received a copyright from Govt.

of India on developing the "Framework for Healthcare Utilization and Economic Enquiry of Diabetes".

***

R.S. Balasenthil is an Associate Professor with an MBA, M.Phil (Entrepreneurship), and Ph.D., having 27.5 years of experience at KLN College of Engineering, Sivagangai District, Tamilnadu, India in the Department of Master of Business Administration. He has published 16 research papers (9 international, 7 national) and authored 4 books. His contributions include 18 resource person roles, 21 paper presentations, and participation in 6 conferences and 30 seminars. He has received 8 awards, delivered 3 expert talks, and holds 2 patents. His academic involvement spans workshops, FDPs, short-term courses, consultancy work, and training programs. He is actively engaged in research, teaching, and knowledge dissemination in business and management.

Shyam Sunder Agrawal, working as Assistant Professor, Mittal School of Business, Lovely Professional University, Phagwara, Punjab, India. He has been associated with the education industry since 2015. He has presented papers at various reputed IIM conferences and published several research papers in UGC CARE, SCOPUS, and ABDC Journals. He has earned his Ph.D. in management from Devi Ahilya Vishwavidyalaya, Indore. His fields of interest are Behavioral finance, Sustainable Finance, Capital Market, Banking, and Insurance. He has published and granted 2 patents from Govt of India. He received the International Case Study Award in 2022. He is a reviewer of Emerald, Springer, and peer-reviewed journals. He is also a financial advisor in Life Insurance Corporation of India.

Anjaly B is working as an Assistant Professor at SGI Food and Agri Business School (FABS), Hyderabad, Telangana. Her area of expertise is in International Finance and Monetary Policy. She has published papers in Scopus and ABDC-indexed journals.

Swati Bhatia is presently working as Professor and Head Research & Development Cell with Asian Business School under the aegis of Asian Education Group, Noida. With assignments in areas of Administration, Human Resource Management, Liaison Coordination, Team Management, Training & Development, Swati has a noteworthy cross-functional experience of over 22 years in Strategic & Tactical Planning, Problem Resolution, Connexion, Performance Management and Onboarding. An out-of-the-box thinker with a flair education while identifying & adopting emerging trends and addressing industry requirements to achieve objectives bearing adherence to norms, her insightful experience in technical activities including scoping, planning, outlook finalization, resource administration & quality management. She has to her credit notable Books, Book Chapters, Research papers in several National and International Publications.

Yash Bidhuri is pursuing a four-year BA Economics (Hons.) Research course at Amity University, Noida. His academic interests include macroeconomic policies, sustainable development, and digital economics. He has explored emerging economic trends, AI-driven innovations, and their impact on global markets. Yash aspires to contribute to research in economic policy and technological advancements shaping the future economy.

Poppy Febriana is an Assistant Professor in the Communication Studies program at the Faculty of Business, Law, and Social Sciences at Muhammadiyah University of Sidoarjo. She specializes in new media, branding, and gender studies, bringing a contemporary lens to these dynamic fields. Beyond her teaching responsibilities, Poppy is deeply involved in various academic associations related to communication and business economics, enhancing her engagement with the academic community. She actively contributes as a reviewer for several prestigious journals, ensuring the advancement of scholarly standards within her expertise. Additionally, Poppy extends her impact beyond national borders by serving as a visiting lecturer at numerous universities across Southeast Asia, including Indonesia, Malaysia, Thailand, and Singapore. Her work influences her students and fosters cross-cultural academic exchanges, enriching the global dialogue on communication and business practices.

Oindrilla Ghosh is a Research Scholar hailing from the School of Law at Christ (Deemed to be University) Bangalore, India, who focuses her research on the health of tribal communities. Her work includes Neuroscience on Organizational Behavior publications at IGI Global and Environmental Disasters, indexed in SCOPUS and Web of Sciences conference proceedings. She completed her early education at Loreto Day School, Bowbazar, and achieved distinction in her undergraduate (B.A/ LL.B) and postgraduate (LL.M) studies at Calcutta University. Having served as an Assistant Professor of Law at Kingston Law College, Barasat, Kolkata, Ghosh has actively participated in numerous National Conferences, International Conferences, UN Global Summits, webinars, and seminars organized by prestigious academic institutions. Her expertise lies in health perspectives, environmental studies, human behavior, and related areas. Additionally, she has conducted various workshops and lectures in educational institutions, and is engaged with NGO's to help the needy

Santosh Gopalkrishnan is a Professor at Symbiosis International University, Dubai, with 18+ years of experience in academia and the corporate sector. He holds a Ph.D. in Finance, an MBA, and is a SEBI-certified Financial Education Resource Person. Previously, he was Deputy Head – Corporate Relations at Symbiosis Institute of Business Management, Pune. He has worked with IBM, HDFC Bank, and top universities, and has conducted corporate training for leading organizations like Tata Motors, Vodafone Idea, Capgemini, and Mahindra & Mahindra. His expertise includes Banking, Credit Risk, FinTech, and Personal Finance.

Aarti Gupta, Assistant Professor working with Asian Business School is a distinguished & dynamic academic and research professional with over 15 years of rich experience in teaching and research. Being a Kurukshetra University alumnus while achieving first division from high school through post-graduation, she also qualified UGC-NET with JRF (2007) in Commerce and is a recipient of the prestigious Young Researcher Award (2016) conferred by Indian Accounting Association (IAA). She holds a Ph.D. in the field of commerce from MLSU, Udaipur (2018), with the research area on "Application of Neural Network in Financial Statement Fraud Detection" which is a blend of accounting, finance, data mining and artificial intelligence. As a lifetime member of the Indian Accounting Association (IAA), Dr. Gupta has consistently achieved Best research paper award (2015) by UOR, Jaipur and doctoral research fellowship (2014) by ICSSR, New Delhi during the tenure of perusing Ph.D. She is dedicated to advancing the field of commerce through her extensive experience and dedication to education. Renowned for her excellence in teaching, Dr. Gupta has a robust track record of motivating students to achieve significant academic and professional success.

Khushi Jain is an MBA post graduate at Balaji Institute of Management and Human Resource development(BIMHRD), Sri Balaji University, Pune. Her area of expertise is in Finance and Fixed income securities. She has experience in relevant fields as well.

Vishal Jain is presently working as Professor at the Department of Computer Science and Engineering, School of Engineering and Technology, Sharda University, Greater Noida, India. Before that, he worked for several years as an Associate Professor at Bharati Vidyapeeth's Institute of Computer Applications and Management (BVICAM), New Delhi. He has more than 18 years of experience in the academics. He has earned degrees: Ph.D (CSE), M.Tech (CSE), MBA (HR), MCA, MCP, and CCNA. He has more than 2200 research citations with Google Scholar (h-index score 24 and i-10 index 55) and has authored more than 150 research papers in professional journals and conferences. He has authored and edited more than 60 books (most of them are indexed at the Scopus) with various reputed publishers, including Elsevier, Springer, IET, Apple Academic Press, CRC, Taylor and Francis Group, Scrivener, Wiley, Emerald, NOVA Science, River Publishers, IGI-Global and Bentham Science. He has more than 200 Scopus publications. His research areas include machine learning, information retrieval, semantic web, ontology engineering, data mining, ad hoc networks, sensor networks and network security.

Akanksha Kathuria is a dynamic and accomplished Assistant Professor of Marketing with over 15 years of academic experience. Currently associated with KR Mangalam University, Gurugram, she brings deep expertise in Digital Marketing and Marketing, along with a strong commitment to academic excellence and holistic education. A certified POSH (Prevention of Sexual Harassment) Trainer, Ms. Kathuria regularly conducts impactful training sessions on gender sensitization and POSH compliance across institutions. Her work in this area reflects her commitment to creating safe and inclusive educational environments. She has been honored with several accolades, including Employee of the Year (2024) and the Best Yoga Trainer Award—twice—recognizing her multifaceted contributions in both education and wellness. An accomplished researcher, she has authored a book on Research Methodology, holds two patents, and has published extensively in reputed ABDC, Scopus, and UGC Care journals. Ms. Kathuria is an editorial board member of the Samvakti Journals Journal of Research in Business Management. She has successfully organized over 100 academic and co-curricular events, headed international conferences, and mentored students with passion and purpose throughout her career. Beyond the classroom, she is deeply involved in community service. She serves as the District Coordinator for the Youth Wing of Patanjali Yog Samiti in Faridabad and is recognized as a Health & Wellness Influencer with Womennovator, showcasing her dedication to societal wellbeing and youth empowerment.

Nikhat Khalid is an economist with a Ph.D. in Economics from Jamia Millia Islamia, New Delhi. Her doctoral research focuses on international trade, technological change in manufacturing, and regional economic integration. With a strong academic foundation from Panjab University, where she earned both her Bachelor's and Master's degrees in Economics (Honours), she has been a consistent rank holder. Dr. Khalid has published extensively in reputed national and international journals, including Scopus- and Web of Science-indexed outlets, and has presented her work at various academic conferences. She has also authored a book and contributes as a peer reviewer to multiple journals. Presently, she is working at the Bharti Institute of Public Policy, Indian School of Business as a Research Fellow and is engaged in research on public policy and development issues in South Asia. s

Shalu Kotwani is a Ph.D. in Management, M.B.A in Finance and Marketing, M.A. English Literature. She has done numerous certifications from NISM, NCFM, NPTEL in the field of finance. She is currently associated with PIMR as an Assistant Professor. She is having 11 years of teaching experience in academia. During this tenure, she coordinated and handled various academic and administrative responsibilities. She has presented and published more than 20 research papers and 2 case studies in various National, International and IIM conferences, and case study workshops.

Binod Kumar is a graduate student known for his academic excellence, with his scholarly works indexed in Scopus database. Hailing from Ranchi, Jharkhand in India, Binod is currently pursuing a Master of Laws (LL.M) at the prestigious Radha Govind University. His passion for technology and innovation along with climate changes is evident through his high academic performance and numerous projects. Binod has a keen interest in artificial intelligence, machine learning, neuropsychology, climate changes and disaster management, fields in which he has undertaken several research projects. He is particularly fascinated by the potential of AI to solve real-world problems and is dedicated to learning and applying new techniques in these areas. He volunteers at local NGOs, teaching underprivileged children basic computer skills. With a strong foundation in law and a commitment to making a positive impact, Binod Kumar is poised to become a future leader in the legal industry.

Firdous Ahmad Malik was born in India and is currently employed by the University of People as an Assistant Professor of Economics (instructor), Department of Management. Currently he is perceiving Post Doctoral research at Amity Dubai University. Before that, he was a research fellow at the National Institute of Public Finance and Policy (NIPFP) in Delhi, India. Prior to this, he was a senior research associate at the O.P. Jindal Global University in Sonipat, Haryana's Jindal Center for the Global South. From Babasaheb Bhimrao Ambedkar University in Lucknow, India, he received his Ph.D. He has a Master's in Economics from the University of Kashmir and an MPhil in Economics from Babasaheb Bhimrao Ambedkar University Lucknow. Microfinance, financial inclusion, and financial literacy are his main areas of study interest. He has articles in journals that are Scopus-indexed from Springer, Elsevier, Taylor Francis, and others. Moreover, he has published more than seven books.

Sakshi Mann is an Assistant Professor of Human Resource Management at Indira Institute of Management, Pune. With a Ph.D. in HR and over 11 years of combined industry and academic experience, she brings a practical edge to her teaching. Her expertise spans Organizational Behavior, Recruitment & Selection, Employee Engagement, and Leadership. Having managed HR operations across various organizations, she seamlessly integrates real-world insights into academia. Passionate about research, she explores contemporary HR challenges to contribute valuable insights to the field. Committed to bridging academia and industry, Dr. Mann fosters critical thinking and practical application, equipping students for the evolving HR landscape.

Shikha Mann is an academician, Certified MBTI Coach, internationally certified TIFF Provider, Enneagram Coach, Certified SII coach, Motivational Speaker, Leadership Coach, Organizational Culture Consultant and Corporate Trainer. She is associated with Indira School of Business Studies PGDM, Pune as Deputy Director. She completed her Ph.D. from Symbiosis International (Deemed University) in Organizational Behaviour. She is an academician, trainer and a consultant. She was conferred upon the award of "40under40 education leaders by Business World Education in 2024" and "Best Faculty on Human Resource" in Pune Education Leadership Awards 2019. She has been involved as Assessor in Development centre and Assessment centres for various renowned MNCs. She has set up HR processes for start-ups. She has done succession planning for many organizations in Pharmaceuticals and manufacturing domain. She has worked with senior management of various organizations and has been involved in developing leadership. She regularly provides trainings on areas such as Team Building, Business Communication, Presentation Skills, Stress management, Leadership, Motivation and Body Language. She has conducted various workshops for many MNCs and B Schools on topics such as Employability Skills, Personality Development, Be the Best version of Yourself, Know your Potential, Explore the "real you". She has been invited as a guest speaker in many national and state level conferences. She has teaching experience of 9 years, she has written many research papers in national and international journals. Her subject expertise include Organizational Behaviour, HRM, Psychometric Tests, Compensation & Benefits, Performance Management System, SHRM, Industrial Relations, Learning & Development, Talent Management and OD

Akansha Mer is an Assistant Professor in the Department of Commerce and Management, Banasthali Vidyapith, Rajasthan, India.She has earned her doctorate on Work Engagement in NPOs from Banasthali Vidyapith. She has 2.5 years of corporate and about a decade of academic work experience. Her research interests include work engagement, adoption of technology by consumers, mindfulness, workplace spirituality, working pattern of non-profit organizations and Artificial Intelligence in HRM and marketing. She has published research papers and book chapters with leading publishers like Taylor and Francis (Routledge), Sage, Wiley & Scrivener, Inderscience, etc.

Ananya Pandey is a Research Scholar in School of Law at Christ University, Bangalore. She has her research interests in the field of Constitutional Law, Environment Law, Human Rights, Food Security, Intellectual Property Law and Jurisprudence.

Shiba Prasad Mohanty is working as an Assistant Professor at Symbiosis School of Banking and Finance (SSBF) of Symbiosis International (Deemed University) Pune. He has completed his Ph.D. in the area of Banking and finance. Inter alia, his interest lies in the field of financial astrology, financial economics, corporate governance and asset quality. He has published research papers in several SCOPUS, ABDC and ABS listed peer-reviewed journals. Apart from the academics he had also an international experience of course designer at Middlesex University, London (UK) in the area of cost and management accounting. He worked with premier institutions like IIM-Nagpur, IIM-Ahmedabad, IIM-Bangalore and NISM in the profile of academic as well as in research on accounting and finance.

Dhruv Relan is the founder of Agilityo Executive School (AES Paris), where he serves as Professor of Strategic Leadership. With over 15 years of international experience spanning Europe, India, and Australia, he has led large-scale transformations in product operations, agile delivery, and digital strategy across major global organizations including Danone, Citi, and Aleia. His expertise lies in bridging executive leadership with operational execution, particularly in complex, multicultural environments. Dhruv holds an MBA from IPAG Business School in Paris and a Bachelor of Business Administration (Honours) from the University of South Australia. He is certified in Project Management (PMP), SAFe Agile, and Product Management, and is recognized for his ability to integrate cutting-edge methodologies such as Design Thinking, OKRs, and agile frameworks into both corporate and academic settings. At AES Paris, he brings a visionary approach to higher education, focused on cultivating strategic thinkers and adaptive leaders. His current research and teaching interests include leadership in the digital age, organizational agility, and the intersection of business innovation and education reform.

Neeru Sidana is working as Associate Professor in Amity School of Economics (ASE), Amity University, Noida. Her areas of interest & research are: Applied Economics, Econometrics, Capital Market and gradings. Her doctorate degree is in "Financial Inclusion in India" from Department of Economics, MDU- Rohtak -Haryana, India. She has taught postgraduate & undergraduate students for the last 14 years and involved in research since 2012. She also worked as Associate Professor in Lovely Professional University, Jalandhar, Punjab, India and also served as Sr. Lecturer in Kurukshetra University affiliated college namely Shri Siddhivinayak Educational Trust's Group of Institutions, Haryana. She is life time member of professional bodies such as Indian Commerce Association (ICA), All India Management Association (AIMA). She has published 25+ research articles and research papers in various international and national repute journals. She is recognized as editor and reviewer for various referred and peer-reviewed national and international journals. She is recognized as Research Supervisor and supervised two Ph. D Scholars and three are pursuing under her guidance.

Mehek Singh is a final-year Economics (Hons.) student at Amity University, Noida. She has a keen interest in technology-driven economic transformations, labor economics, and the EdTech sector. She has conducted research on AI in education, workforce agility, and regional economic development and interned at a venture capital firm, analyzing trends in EdTech and AI-driven learning. She aims to contribute to research in digital economics, labor markets, and sustainable development.

Rohan Singh currently holds the Associate Professor in Management position at Chandigarh University, Punjab. His primary focus in research lies within the domains of Human Resource Management, delving into the complex dynamics shaping HR strategies and their adaptation in the era of AI, gig workers, and hybrid work practices and also exploring the relation between HRM and various performance metrics. Additionally, he engages in various academic activities, including serving as a guest faculty, keynote speaker, session chair, acting as a resource person for FDP sessions and participating as an external examiner (Master's and Research Scholars), among others. He has showcased his research prowess by publishing in esteemed international journals and conferences, accumulating an impressive citation count of over 500. In addition to his academic role, Dr. Singh boasts over 14 years of comprehensive experience in the field of Overall Project Management at the Sponsored Research & Industrial Consultancy Cell of the esteemed Indian Institute of Technology Kharagpur. He has extensive experience in evaluating scholarly manuscripts. Over the years, he has contributed to the peer-review process for numerous prestigious journals, ensuring the integrity and quality of published research as Associate Editor, Editorial Review Board Member, Advisory Board Member, Reviewer Board Member, Advisory-cum-Reviewers' Board Member and National Member.

Jyoti Tyagi is an Assistant Professor in the Department of management at IAMR Group of Institution, Ghaziabad. Her research interests include Financial technology, Digital Payments, and operation Management, AI. She has contributed to academic publications and actively engages in interdisciplinary research that bridges theory and practice in Finance.

P.S. Venkateswaran is currently working as a Professor in the Department of Management Studies, PSNA College of Engineering & Technology, Dindigul affiliated to Anna University, Chennai where he teaches courses in Advertising, marketing and Research Methods. He has served in various faculty positions from Assistant Professor to Professor in leading Arts & Colleges such as Cherran Arts and Science College, Kangeyam and Sree Saraswathi Thyagaraja College, Pollachi. He received MSc in Physics, an M.B.A., from Bharathiar University and MPhil from Alagappa University Karaikudi. He received his Ph.D in Business Administration from Madurai Kamaraj University, Madurai. He is having twenty two years of teaching and nine years of research & consultancy experience. His research activities include on Branding, Advertising and Digital marketing He conducted more than 90 Entrepreneurship Awareness Camps and trained around 8000 Engineering, Arts and Science College students and motivated them towards entrepreneurship. He also conducted 10 Faculty Development programmes, 10 EDP/WEDP programmes and 7 TEDP programmes. He trained more the 200 women entrepreneurs in Dindigul District.

Mansi Yadav is a dedicated Assistant Professor at K.R. Mangalam University, specializing in Business Analytics, Econometrics, and Finance. With a strong foundation in quantitative research and data-driven decision-making, her expertise lies in predictive modeling, financial behavior analysis, and digital financial literacy. Her research has been published in Scopus, ABDC, and Web of Science-indexed journals, focusing on the impact of Digital Financial Literacy on Retirement Planning. She is passionate about teaching and equipping students with industry-relevant skills in statistical modeling, data visualization, and business intelligence, bridging the gap between academic concepts and real-world applications. Her key areas of expertise include business analytics, predictive modeling, machine learning, econometrics, digital financial literacy, visualization techniques. She has conducted extensive research on financial decision-making, savings behavior, and retirement planning, using methodologies such as ANOVA, t-tests, Structural Equation Modeling (SEM), Confirmatory Factor Analysis (CFA), and Exploratory Factor Analysis (EFA). As an educator, she teaches Business Analytics, Predictive Modeling, Econometrics, and Finance covering tools such as Python), Excel (Advanced Functions, Solver, Macros, Dashboards), Power BI, Tableau, and

SmartPLS 4.0. She also conducts Management Development Programs (MDPs) and workshops on Business Analytics using Excel & Python, Statistical Analysis for Decision-Making, Predictive Modeling, Financial Analytics, and Digital Financial Literacy. Her industry applications span financial data analysis, behavioral finance, marketing analytics, HR analytics.

Index

F

G

H

S

T

U

W

www.ingramcontent.com/pod-product-compliance
Lightning Source LLC
LaVergne TN
LVHW080353011026
849161LV00009B/2288